JAPANESE AND ENGLISH IDIOMS

日本語慣用句・英語イディオム

Nobuo Akiyama
Professorial Lecturer, Japanese Language
The Paul H. Nitze
School of Advanced International Studies
Johns Hopkins University

and

Carol Akiyama
Language Training Consultant
Washington, D.C.

BARRON'S

D0181862

All inquiries should be addressed to:
Barron's Educational Series, Inc.
250 Wireless Boulevard
Hauppauge, New York 11788

International Standard Book Number 0-8120-9433-6
Library of Congress Catalog Card Number 96-83957

PRINTED IN THE UNITED STATES OF AMERICA

98765

目次

CONTENTS

INTRODUCTION

This book is for speakers of English or of Japanese who want to understand and use the idioms of each other's language and who also want to express their own idioms in the new language. To help achieve these two goals, the book is divided into two parts: JAPANESE-ENGLISH, and ENGLISH-JAPANESE. Each part contains more than 2,000 idioms that students of either language will find useful. Each entry is written in English, Romaji, and Japanese characters. For each part, a preface in each language introduces the concept and the organization.

The authors wish to thank Dimitry Popow, Languages Editor at Barron's, for his unfailing support of this project, and Keiko Kamei, former staff member, National Diet Library, Tokyo, for her invaluable reading of and suggestions for Part II.

まえがき

　英語及び日本語を母国語とする人々が、相手国の国語の慣用句を理解し使用する、また自国語の慣用句を相手国の国語の中で表現する。本書は、このような望みを抱く人々を対象に書かれている。

　以上の二つの目的を達成するため、本書は日本語慣用句、英語イディオムの2部に分けられている。各部とも、それぞれの言葉を学ぶ人々に役立つであろう2000を越す慣用句、或いはイディオムが含まれている。慣用句もイディオムも各項目は、英語、ロ－マ字、日本語から成り立っている。第1部、第2部とも、英語及び日本語の序文で、その部の概念及び構成が紹介してある。

　この本の執筆にあたっては、バロンズ・エジュケ－ショナル・シリ－ズ社言語担当編集員のディミトリ・ポポウ氏の惜しみない支援に、また第2部においては元国会図書館勤務の亀井慶子氏の掛け替え無い助言に深く感謝する次第である。

第1部
日本語慣用句篇

PART I
JAPANESE-ENGLISH

日本人読者への序文

慣用句とは何か

　慣用句を、ことわざや、単なる複合語と混同している著書がなきにしもあらず。しかし定義としては、二つ以上の単語を組み合わせ、全体として別の意味を表すものと見なすべきであろう。日本語の慣用句も、英語のイディオムも、その点では共通といえる。ただしことわざとの違いは、人生の知恵や教訓のような特別の意味合いがないことだ。本書はこの観点に基づき、日本語の慣用句を扱っている。

　慣用句もイディオムも、その国の文化、国民の発想法を如実に反映し、日常生活と密接な関係を持っている。その場その場にふさわしい考え、感情、ユーモアなどを込め、言いたいことに味を添える。このような背景や機能があるだけに、慣用句はその言葉が母国語の人々が好んで使う表現。だが同時に、文字通り解釈しても分からないのが難点。外国語を学ぶ人にとっては、やっかいなことになる。

日本人としての慣用句の用途

　日本人も、英語で苦労する点では、その例に漏れない。本書は、日本語を学ぶ欧米人を意図してはいる。しかし日本人を除外するどころか、この本を積極的に利用できるようにも構成してある。日常会話の日本語を、つまり、言いたいことを同じようなニュアンスの英語で伝えたい。そんな考えがある人ならば、本書を大いに活用できることは疑いない。

　英語を学ぶ日本人が、言葉に詰まってしまうことがしばしばある。その理由には、言いたい日本語の慣用句が英語で出てこなかったり、それをどう言えばいいか頭をひねりすぎてしまうことだ。

　日本語の慣用句の入ったセンテンスを英語で話そうとする。その時、文字通りに訳してしまうと、意味をなさなくなるのは当然のこと。だがその危険を知ってはいても、ではどうすればいいのか。そのような場合に本書を使い、英語らしい表現をすることが可能になる。つまり、日本人は、この本を日本語イディオムの和英辞典として手引きにできる。

　ここには、ことわざもある程度含まれてはいるが、主として２０００を越す純粋な日本語の慣用句が選ばれている。慣用句の基礎概念になる見出し語をアルファベット順に載せ、見出し語の下に、関連した慣用句が、これもアルファベット順に載せてある。

　紙面の制限上、選択を強いられたが、本書の掲載分で、普段使う日本語を英語で話し書くためには、これでまず十分といえる。慣用句を含めた日本語のニュアンスを自然な英語で伝えられるようになれば、コミュニケーションの度合いも一段と深まるだろう。

体裁と使い方

第1篇は、次のようにアレンジされている。

　先ず見出し語が、ローマ字と日本語と英語の順に載せてある。その後は、見出し語に関連するイディオムの例が、日本語、ローマ字、英語の順で書かれている。

　[lit. ...]は、ほぼ純粋な直訳を用い、語源に基づき、日本人の考え方の発展を外国人に知ってもらうのが目的。日本人でも語学に興味のある人は、日本語を再考する上でも、注意を払うといいだろう。理屈はともかく、日本語の考えを英語で伝えられればそれでいい。そう思う人は、これを無視して何のさしさわりもない。

　用例のセンテンスに関しては、ローマ字は明らかに日本語を学ぶ外国人を助けるために含まれている。これが目障りならば、これを全く無視してかまわない。ただし漢字の読みを確かめるためには、辞書を引くより、最初にここにあるローマ字を読んでみる方が効率的かもしれない。

最後に

　日本語の慣用句には、先ずそれに相当する英語のイディオムがあればそれを、無ければ、それに近い口語的表現を用いるようにしている。これによって、現代アメリカ英語を理解する上での一助となることはまず間違いない。日米両国の言語と意思流通の架け橋として、いくぶんでも貢献できれば幸いである。

Preface to Part I

For the language learner, idioms are a dimension beyond grammar, pronunciation, and vocabulary. They add color, spice, and humor. They provide insights into the culture. If you know the idioms, you can understand expressions that cannot be translated by just their constituent parts. A speaker of English who hears the phrase "a fly on the wall" knows that it means "an eavesdropper," or that "to get someone's goat" means "to annoy someone." If you are learning Japanese, or if you have already achieved some proficiency and want to enrich your knowledge, you will find it invaluable to develop similar awarenesses in your new language. This book will help you achieve your goal.

You can look up idioms as you hear or read them. Or you can browse through the more than 2,000 entries at your leisure to see how the idioms reveal Japanese views on life, love, respect, duty, honor, shame, work, relationships, nature, deities, and much more.

Idioms are entered by key Japanese words, usually nouns, listed alphabetically in Romaji. Thus if you hear the Japanese word for "bean paste" in an expression you don't know, you look it up under the key word *miso*. Under this heading appear the most common idioms containing the word. Each entry contains the idiom in both Romaji and Japanese characters, the English meaning, the literal translation, and finally, a Japanese sentence to illustrate the usage with the English translation. Look up *miso o tsukeru* this way, and you'll find it means "to make a mess of something," literally, "to spread bean paste on something." Or if you hear an unfamiliar expression containing the Japanese for "cat," look it up under the key word *neko*, then the expression, *neko no hitai*, which means "a very small area," literally, "a cat's forehead." This is the only size piece of land the average person in Japan can afford!

Because each entry is based on the Japanese idiom and the Japanese illustrative sentence, there are certain implications for the English. For the literal translations, the language conveys the Japanese words as closely as possible. For the English meanings and the illustrative sentences, every attempt is made to use language that is as natural as possible under the circumstances. But since the two languages and cultures are so different, some translations may leave you shaking your head. For example, the idiom that means "a bride's changing clothes during the wedding reception," and the illustrative sentence "How often did the bride change her clothes during the wedding reception?" may strike the English speaker as odd. But to the Japanese, it's quite normal.

As you use the book, you'll enjoy seeing how the literal meanings of the idioms relate to the actual usage. And you'll continue enriching your knowledge of the unique ways in which the Japanese express things in their daily lives.

abura — 油 — *oil*
abura ga kireru — 油が切れる — *to be exhausted*
[lit. Oil runs out.]
油が切れそうなので、バカンスが必要です。Abura ga kiresō nanode,
bakansu ga hitsuyō desu.   *I need a vacation because I'm just about
exhausted.*

abura o shiboru — 油をしぼる — *to take someone to task*
[lit. to squeeze oil]
顧客に連絡するのを忘れて、課長に油をしぼられました。Kokyaku
ni renraku suru no o wasurete, kachō ni abura o shiboraremashita.
*Because I forgot to get in touch with the client, I was taken to task by the
section chief.*

abura o sosogu — 油を注ぐ — *to fuel, to inflame*
[lit. to pour oil]
その新聞の記事は、彼の怒りに油を注ぎました。Sono shinbun no kiji
wa, kare no ikari ni abura o sosogimashita.   *That newspaper article
fueled his anger.*

abura o uru — 油を売る — *to goof off, to loaf*
[lit. to sell oil]
あの人は仕事をするより、油を売るのが得意です。Ano hito wa
shigoto o suru yori, abura o uru no ga tokui desu.   *He's better at
goofing off than working.*

---

abura — 脂 — *fat*
abura ga noru — 脂がのる — *to be in one's prime*
[lit. to increase in fat content]
あの歌手は、最近脂がのってきました。Ano kashu wa, saikin abura ga
notte kimashita.   That singer has recently come into her prime.

---

ago — 顎 — *chin, jaw*
ago de tsukau — 顎で使う — *to order someone around*
[lit. to use someone with one's chin]
彼は人を顎で使うので、彼が好きな人はあまりいません。Kare wa

hito o ago de tsukau node, kare ga suki na hito wa amari imasen.
Because he orders everyone around, not many people like him.

ago ga hazureru — 顎が外れる — *to die laughing*
[lit. One's jaw gets dislocated.]
彼女の話があまり面白いので、顎が外れるほど笑いました。Kanojo
no hanashi ga amari omoshiroi node, ago ga hazureru hodo
waraimashita.   *Her story was so funny that I almost died laughing.*

ago ga hiagaru — 顎が干上がる — *to suffer from loss of income*
[lit. One's jaw dries up.]
遊んでばかりいると、そのうち顎が干上がってしまいますよ。
Asonde bakari iru to, sono uchi ago ga hiagatte shimaimasu yo.   *If you
keep playing around, you won't be able to pay your bills.*

ago o dasu — 顎を出す — *to get exhausted*
[lit. to stick one's chin out]
久しぶりに運動したので、すぐに顎を出してしまいました。
Hisashiburi ni undō shita node, sugu ni ago o dashite shimaimashita.
Because I exercised for the first time in ages, I got exhausted fast.

ago o naderu — 顎をなでる — *to pride oneself on something*
[lit. to stroke one's own chin]
彼はテニスの試合に勝って、顎をなでていました。Kare wa tenisu no
shiai ni katte, ago o nadete imashita.   *He prided himself on winning the
tennis match.*

---

ai — 愛 — *love*

ai no kesshō — 愛の結晶 — *child(ren)*
[lit. the crystallization of love]
あの夫婦に、先月愛の結晶が生まれました。Ano fūfu ni, sengetsu ai
no kesshō ga umaremashita.   *That couple had a baby last month.*

ai no su — 愛の巣 — *the home of a newlywed couple*
[lit. a love nest]
新婚の太郎と花子は、京都に愛の巣を構えました。Shinkon no Tarō
to Hanako wa, Kyōto ni ai no su o kamaemashita.   *The newlyweds
Taro and Hanako set up their new home in Kyoto.*

---

aji — 味 — *taste*

aji mo sokke mo nai — 味も素気もない — *curt*
[lit. no taste, no warmth]

親切に聞いてあげたのに、その女性は味も素気もない返事をしました。Shinsetsu ni kiite ageta noni, sono josei wa aji mo sokke mo nai henji o shimashita. *I offered to help her, but she gave me a curt reply.*

aji na koto o yaru — 味なことをやる — *to act smart*
[lit. to do something of taste]
パーティーでギターを弾くなんて、彼もなかなか味なことをやるね。Pātī de gitā o hiku nante, kare mo nakanaka aji na koto o yaru ne. *How smart of him to play the guitar during the party!*

aji o shimeru — 味を占める — *to get a taste of something*
[lit. to occupy taste]
一度の成功に味を占めて、彼は相変わらず同じ事をしています。Ichido no seikō ni aji o shimete, kare wa aikawarazu onaji koto o shite imasu. *After tasting success once, he's still doing the same old thing.*

aji o shiru — 味を知る — *to experience something*
[lit. to get to know the taste]
一度贅沢の味を知ると、元に戻るのは容易ではありません。Ichido zeitaku no aji o shiru to, moto ni modoru no wa yōi dewa arimasen. *When you experience luxury once, it's not easy to go back to your old lifestyle.*

---

aka — 赤 — *red*

aka no tanin — 赤の他人 — *total stranger*
[lit. a red stranger]
赤の他人に、そんな話をしてはいけません。Aka no tanin ni, sonna hanashi o shitewa ikemasen. *Don't tell such a story to a total stranger.*

akahaji — 赤恥 — *utter shame, total disgrace*
[lit. red shame]
この間は会議に出ることを忘れて、赤恥をかきました。Kono aida wa kaigi ni deru koto o wasurete, akahaji o kakimashita. *The other day, I totally disgraced myself by forgetting to attend the meeting.*

akashingō ga tsuku — 赤信号が付く — *to become precarious*
[lit. A red light comes on.]
社長が病気になって、会社の運営に赤信号が付きました。Shachō ga byōki ni natte, kaisha no un-ei ni akashingō ga tsukimashita. *With the president's illness, the management of the company has become precarious.*

---

aka — 垢 — grime

akanuke shinai — 垢抜けしない — unpolished, crude
[lit. grime not coming off]
あの人は都会に来て十年たつのに、まだ垢抜けしていません。Ano
hito wa tokai ni kite jū nen tatsu noni, mada akanuke shite imasen.
Although it's been 10 years since he came to the city, he's still not
urbane.

akanuke shita — 垢抜けした — polished, refined
[lit. grime off]
彼女は、いつも垢抜けした服装をしています。Kanojo wa, itsumo
akanuke shita fukusō o shite imasu.   She always wears sophisticated
clothes.

akashi — 証し — proof

mi no akashi o tateru — 身の証しを立てる — to prove one's innocence
[lit. to make proof stand up]
汚職をマスコミに非難された政治家は、身の証しを立てるために弁護
士を雇いました。Oshoku o masukomi ni hinan sareta seijika wa, mi
no akashi o tateru tame ni bengoshi o yatoimashita.   When the media
accused him of corruption, the politician hired a lawyer to prove his
innocence.

aki — 秋 — autumn

aki no sora — 秋の空 — to be fickle (love)
[lit. autumn sky]
彼は、彼女の秋の空のような心に悩みました。Kare wa, kanojo no aki
no sora no yō na kokoro ni nayamimashita.   He was hurt by her
fickleness.

akikaze ga tatsu — 秋風が立つ — to cool mutually (love)
[lit. Autumn breeze begins to blow.]
半年もたたない内に、二人の間に秋風が立ち始めました。Hantoshi
mo tatanai uchi ni, futari no aida ni akikaze ga tachihajimemashita.
Their love began to cool in less than a half year.

ama — 天 — **heaven**

amakudari — 天下り — senior government official landing a high
position in the private sector
[lit. to descend from heaven]

彼は政府を定年退職した後、天下りで銀行の社長になりました。
Kare wa seifu o teinen taishoku shita ato, amakudari de ginkō no shachō
ni narimashita. *He landed a position as a bank president after retiring
from the government.*

amanojaku — 天の邪鬼 — *perverse person*
[lit. a devil in heaven]
彼は天の邪鬼だから、人の助言に従いません。Kare wa amanojaku
dakara, hito no jogen ni shitagaimasen. *He is perverse and doesn't
follow other people's advice.*

---

amai — 甘い — *sweet*
amai kotoba ni noru — 甘い言葉に乗る — *to believe sweet talk*
[lit. to ride on sweet words]
彼女は彼の甘い言葉に乗って、結婚してしまいました。Kanojo wa
kare no amai kotoba ni notte, kekkon shite shimaimashita.
Unfortunately, she married him believing his sweet talk.

amai shiru o suu — 甘い汁を吸う — *to benefit oneself by exploiting
others*
[lit. to suck sweet juice]
あの人は周りの人から甘い汁を吸って、金持ちになりました。Ano
hito wa mawari no hito kara amai shiru o sutte, kanemochi ni
narimashita. *He became rich by exploiting people around him.*

amaku kangaeru — 甘く考える — *to take things too easy*
[lit. to consider things sweetly]
物理の試験は甘く考えていたために、成績はあまり良くありません
でした。Butsuri no shiken wa amaku kangaete ita tame ni, seiseki wa
amari yoku arimasen deshita. *Since I didn't take the physics exam
seriously, my grade wasn't that good.*

amaku miru — 甘く見る — *to take someone lightly*
[lit. to view a person sweetly]
相手を甘く見たため、交渉はうまくいきませんでした。Aite o
amaku mita tame, kōshō wa umaku ikimasen deshita. *The negotiations
failed because I took my counterpart too lightly.*

amatō — 甘党 — *to have a sweet tooth*
[lit. a partisan of something sweet]
彼は甘党で、特にチョコレートに目がありません。Kare wa amatō

de, toku ni chokorēto ni me ga arimasen.   *He has a sweet tooth, especially for chocolate.*

---

ame — 雨 — *rain*

ame ga furō ga yari ga furō ga — 雨が降ろうが槍が降ろうが — *no matter what*
[lit. even if it rains or spears shower down]
雨が降ろうが槍が降ろうが、計画は実行します。Ame ga furō ga yari ga furō ga, keikaku wa jikkō shimasu.   *No matter what happens, I'll carry out the plan.*

ame onna/ame otoko — 雨女／雨男 — *woman/man who brings rain wherever she/he goes*
[lit. a rain woman/ a rain man]
彼女は雨女なので、誘うと危ないです。Kanojo wa ame onna nanode, sasou to abunai desu.   *It's risky to invite her, because she brings rain wherever she goes.*

ame tsuyu o shinogu seikatsu — 雨露をしのぐ生活 — *poverty*
[lit. living by sheltering oneself from the rain and dew]
あの作家は成功する前、雨露をしのぐ生活を経験しました。Ano sakka wa seikō suru mae, ame tsuyu o shinogu seikatsu o keiken shimashita.   *That novelist experienced poverty before he became successful.*

---

ami — 網 — *net*

ami no me o kuguru — 網の目をくぐる — *to evade the law*
[lit. to pass through the mesh of a net]
彼は、網の目をくぐって象牙を輸入しました。Kare wa, ami no me o kugutte zōge o yunyū shimashita.   *He evaded the law and imported ivory.*

ami o haru — 網を張る — *to set up a dragnet*
[lit. to stretch a net]
警察は誘拐の容疑者を捕らえようと、全国に網を張りました。Keisatsu wa yūkai no yōgisha o toraeyō to, zenkoku ni ami o harimashita. *The police set up a nationwide dragnet for the kidnapping suspect.*

---

ana — 穴 — *hole*

ana ga attara hairitai — 穴があったら入りたい — *to be ashamed, to be humiliated*

[lit. to want to crawl into a hole if there is one]

みんなの前で大失敗して、穴があったら入りたい気持ちでした。
Minna no mae de daishippai shite, ana ga attara hairitai kimochi deshita.
When I made a mistake in front of everybody, I was so ashamed.

ana no aku hodo mitsumeru — 穴のあくほど見つめる — to stare at someone or something
[lit. to look at something to the extent that a hole will open up]

その絵のあまりの見事さに、穴のあくほど見つめずにはいられませんでした。Sono e no amari no migotosa ni, ana no aku hodo mitsumezu niwa iraremasen deshita.   The painting was so fantastic that I couldn't stop staring at it.

ana o akeru — 穴をあける — to cause a deficit
[lit. to dig a hole]

今月は買い物をしすぎて、家計に穴をあけてしまいました。
Kongetsu wa kaimono o shisugite, kakei ni ana o akete shimaimashita.
I made a hole in the family budget this month because I shopped too much.

anaba — 穴場 — great secret spot
[lit. a place with a hole]

あそこに釣りに行くなら、穴場を教えてあげましょう。Asoko ni tsuri ni iku nara, anaba o oshiete agemashō.   If you go fishing there, I'll tell you a great secret spot.

anaume o suru — 穴埋めをする — to make up a loss
[lit. to fill in a hole]

政府は財政赤字の穴埋めをするために、増税しなければなりませんでした。Seifu wa zaisei akaji no anaume o suru tame ni, zōzei shinakereba narimasen deshita.   To make up the financial deficit, the government had to raise taxes.

---

anbai — 塩梅 — condition

ii anbai ni — いい塩梅に — fortunately
[lit. with good salt and plums]

雨が降ってきたら、いい塩梅にタクシーが来ました。Ame ga futte kitara, ii anbai ni takushī ga kimashita.   Fortunately, a taxi came by when it started to rain.

---

anraku — 安楽 — *comfort*
anraku shi — 安楽死 — *euthanasia*
[lit. death for comfort]
その患者は苦しみに耐えかねて、安楽死を求めました。Sono kanja
wa kurushimi ni taekanete, anraku shi o motomemashita. *The patient
couldn't bear the pain and asked for euthanasia.*

---

anshō — 暗礁 — *submerged reef*
anshō ni noriageru — 暗礁に乗り上げる — *to hit a snag*
[lit. to run aground on a submerged reef]
その計画が暗礁に乗り上げることは、最初から分かっていました。
Sono keikaku ga anshō ni noriageru koto wa, saisho kara wakatte
imashita. *I knew all along that the plan would hit a snag.*

---

ao — 青 — *blue, green*
aoiki toiki — 青息吐息 — *to be suffering*
[lit. sighing with blue breath]
不景気のため、どの店も青息吐息です。Fukeiki no tame, dono mise
mo aoiki toiki desu. *All the stores are suffering because of the
recession.*

aojashin — 青写真 — *blueprint*
[lit. a blue photograph]
今度のプロジェクトのための青写真を作りました。Kondo no
purojekuto no tame no aojashin o tsukurimashita. *I made a blueprint
for the upcoming project.*

aokusai — 青臭い — *inexperienced*
[lit. green-smelling]
あんな青臭い人に、この企画は任せられません。Anna aokusai hito
ni, kono kikaku wa makaseraremasen. *We can't trust someone so
inexperienced with this project.*

aonisai — 青二才 — *greenhorn*
[lit. a green two-year-old]
あの男は青二才のくせに、ずいぶん生意気なことをいいます。Ano
otoko wa aonisai no kuse ni, zuibun namaiki na koto o iimasu.
Although he's just a greenhorn, he says such arrogant things.

aosuji o tateru — 青筋を立てる — *to become enraged*
[lit. to show blue veins]

そんなつまらないことに青筋を立てるなよ。Sonna tsumaranai koto
ni, aosuji o tateruna yo. *Don't become enraged over something so
trivial.*

aotagai — 青田買い — *to contract to employ college students
prematurely*
[lit. to buy green rice-fields]
青田買いは禁じられていますが、それはなかなか無くなりません。
Aotagai wa kinjirarete imasu ga, sore wa nakanaka nakunarimasen.
*Although the premature hiring of college students is forbidden, it doesn't
go away easily.*

---

arau — 洗う — *to wash*
arainaosu — 洗い直す — *to reexamine*
[lit. to wash again]
その計画は洗い直すべきです。Sono keikaku wa arainaosu beki desu.
We should reexamine the project.

araitateru — 洗い立てる — *to expose*
[lit. to wash incessantly]
新聞は、その政治家の過去を洗い立てました。Shinbun wa, sono
seijika no kako o araitatemashita. *The newspaper exposed the
politician's past.*

araizarai — 洗いざらい — *everything*
[lit. to wash and carry off]
殺人の容疑者は、犯した罪を洗いざらい白状しました。Satsujin no
yōgisha wa, okashita tsumi o araizarai hakujō shimashita. *The murder
suspect confessed to every crime he committed.*

---

ari — 蟻 — *ant*
ari no haideru sukima mo nai — 蟻の這い出る隙間もない — *to guard
closely*
[lit. no gap for even ants to crawl from]
警察は、首相官邸を蟻の這い出る隙間もないほど警戒しました。
Keisatsu wa, shushō kantei o ari no haideru sukima mo nai hodo keikai
shimashita. *The police closely guarded the prime minister's official
residence.*

---

asa — 朝 — *morning*
asameshi mae — 朝飯前 — *easy, a piece of cake*

9

[lit. before breakfast]

そんな仕事は朝飯前です。Sonna shigoto wa asameshi mae desu.
That's a cinch.

---

ase — 汗 — *sweat*

ase no kesshō — 汗の結晶 — *result of one's hard work*
[lit. a crystal of sweat]

この小説は、あの作家の汗の結晶です。Kono shōsetsu wa, ano sakka
no ase no kesshō desu.   *This is the result of that writer's hard work.*

asemizu tarasu — 汗水垂らす — *to toil*
[lit. to drip sweat]

彼は大家族を養うため、汗水垂らして働いています。Kare wa dai
kazoku o yashinau tame, asemizu tarashite hataraite imasu.   *He has
been toiling to support his big family.*

te ni ase o nigiru — 手に汗を握る — *breathtaking*
[lit. to hold sweat in one's palm]

その試合は、手に汗を握る大接戦でした。Sono shiai wa, te ni ase o
nigiru daisessen deshita.   *The game was breathtakingly close.*

---

ashi — 足 — *leg, foot*

ageashi o toru — 揚げ足を取る — *to carp, to nitpick*
[lit. to grab someone's raised leg]

彼には、いつも人の揚げ足を取る悪い癖があります。Kare niwa,
itsumo hito no ageashi o toru warui kuse ga arimasu.   *He has a bad
habit of always nitpicking.*

ashi ga bō ni naru — 足が棒になる — *One's legs become stiff.*
[lit. The legs become sticks.]

彼女は、足が棒になるまで歩き続けました。Kanojo wa, ashi ga bō ni
naru made arukitsuzukemashita.   *She kept walking till her legs got very
stiff.*

ashi ga chi ni tsukanai — 足が地に着かない — *to be restless and
excited*
[lit. One's legs don't touch the ground.]

結婚式が近付いて、彼女は足が地に着きません。Kekkon shiki ga
chikazuite, kanojo wa ashi ga chi ni tsukimasen.   *With her wedding
approaching, she's restless and excited.*

ashi ga deru — 足が出る — *to exceed one's budget or income*
[lit. Legs stick out.]

新年会では、予算よりかなり足が出てしまいました。Shinnen kai dewa, yosan yori kanari ashi ga dete shimaimashita. *We spent considerably more than our budget for the New Year's party.*

ashi ga muku — 足が向く — *to head somewhere spontaneously*
[lit. One's legs turn toward somewhere.]
夏の暑い日には、仕事の後よくビヤホールに足が向いてしまいます。
Natsu no atsui hi niwa, shigoto no ato yoku biyahōru ni ashi ga muite shimaimasu. *On hot summer days, I often find myself heading toward a beer hall after work.*

ashi ga niburu — 足が鈍る — *to be less eager to go*
[lit. One's legs become dull.]
フランスに行きたいけれど、言葉のことを考えると足が鈍ります。
Furansu ni ikitai keredo, kotoba no koto o kangaeru to ashi ga niburimasu. *I want to go to France, but when I think about the language, I become less eager.*

ashi ga omoi — 足が重い — *to be reluctant to go*
[lit. One's legs are heavy.]
試験は出来なかったのが分かっているので、結果を見に行くのは足が重いです。Shiken wa dekinakatta no ga wakatte iru node, kekka o mini iku no wa ashi ga omoi desu. *Since I know I didn't do well, I'm reluctant to go see the results of the exam.*

ashi ga tōnoku — 足が遠のく — *to come and go less frequently than before, to come and go at longer intervals*
[lit. One's legs become distant.]
最近、銀座のバーから足が遠のいています。Saikin, Ginza no bā kara ashi ga tōnoite imasu. *These days, I've been going to bars in Ginza less frequently.*

ashi ga tsuku — 足が付く — *identity to be learned*
[lit. One's legs are connected.]
現場に残した指紋から、犯人の足が付きました。Genba ni nokoshita shimon kara, hannin no ashi ga tsukimashita. *The criminal's identity was learned from his fingerprints at the scene of the crime.*

ashi o arau — 足を洗う — *to wash one's hands of something*
[lit. to wash one's feet]
彼女は芸能界から足を洗って、結婚しました。Kanojo wa geinō kai kara ashi o aratte, kekkon shimashita. *She washed her hands of show business and got married.*

ashi o fumiireru — 足を踏み入れる — *to get involved in something*
[lit. to put one's legs in something]

彼が政治に足を踏み入れてから、二十年たちます。Kare ga seiji ni
ashi o fumiirete kara, nijū nen tachimasu.   *It's been 20 years since he
got involved in politics.*

ashi o hakobu — 足を運ぶ — *to go to visit*
[lit. to carry one's legs]

野球のチームに入りたくて、監督の家に何度も足を運びました。
Yakyū no chīmu ni hairitakute, kantoku no ie ni nando mo ashi o
hakobimashita.   *Since I wanted to join the baseball team, I often went
to visit the manager's home.*

ashi o hipparu — 足を引っ張る — *to drag someone down*
[lit. to drag someone's legs]

同僚は彼女の成功を妬んで、足を引っ張ろうとしました。Dōryō wa
kanojo no seikō o netande, ashi o hipparō to shimashita.   *Her
colleagues were jealous of her success and tried to drag her down.*

ashi o ireru — 足を入れる — *to set foot in*
[lit. to put one's feet in]

夫は、飲屋街には決して足を入れません。Otto wa, nomiya gai niwa
kesshite ashi o iremasen.   *My husband never sets foot in a bar district.*

ashi o nobasu — 足を延ばす — *to extend a trip*
[lit. to stretch a leg]

アメリカへ行ったとき、メキシコまで足を延ばしました。Amerika e
itta toki, Mekishiko made ashi o nobashimashita.   *When I went to the
United States, I extended the trip to include Mexico.*

ashi o sukuu — 足をすくう — *to trip someone up*
[lit. to scoop up someone's legs]

彼女を信用して、足をすくわれた人が沢山います。Kanojo o shin-yō
shite, ashi o sukuwareta hito ga takusan imasu.   *There are many people
who were tripped up by her while they trusted her.*

ashi o torareru — 足を取られる — *to lose one's footing*
[lit. to get one's feet taken away]

階段で足を取られて、下まで転げ落ちてしまいました。Kaidan de
ashi o torarete, shita made korogeochite shimaimashita.   *I lost my
footing and tumbled to the bottom of the stairs.*

ashi o ubawareru — 足を奪われる — *to be deprived of transportation*
[lit. to get one's legs stolen]
地下鉄のストで足を奪われて、会社に行けませんでした。Chikatetsu
no suto de ashi o ubawarete, kaisha ni ikemasen deshita. *I couldn't go
to work because the subway was on strike.*

ashiba o katameru — 足場を固める — *to secure a foothold*
[lit. to set up scaffolding]
彼は、その町で立候補するための足場を固めています。Kare wa,
sono machi de rikkōho suru tame no ashiba o katamete imasu. *He's
securing a foothold to run for election in that town.*

ashibumi suru — 足踏みする — *to be at a standstill*
[lit. to step on a spot]
いくら勉強しても、成績は足踏みを続けています。Ikura benkyō
shitemo, seiseki wa ashibumi o tsuzukete imasu. *No matter how much
I study, my grades stay the same.*

ashidai — 足代 — *transportation costs*
[lit. leg price]
そこへ行く足代は、会社が払ってくれました。Soko e iku ashidai wa,
kaisha ga haratte kuremashita. *The company paid my transportation
costs to get there.*

ashidome — 足止め — *restrictions on travel*
[lit. to stop one's legs]
政府は、災害地域への足止めを解きました。Seifu wa, saigai chiiki e

no ashidome o tokimashita.   *The government lifted the restrictions on travel to the disaster area.*

ashigatame — 足固め — *preparations for the future*
[lit. to fix one's legs]
もうそろそろ、結婚のために足固めをして置いた方がいいですよ。
Mō sorosoro, kekkon no tame ni ashigatame o shite oita hō ga ii desu yo.
It's about time that you start preparing yourself for marriage.

ashige ni suru — 足蹴にする — *to treat someone horribly*
[lit. to kick someone]
彼は人を足蹴にしても、自分の利益を得ようとします。Kare wa hito o ashige ni shite mo, jibun no rieki o eyō to shimasu.   *He tries to profit even if he has to treat other people horribly.*

ashikase ni naru — 足枷になる — *to become a hindrance*
[lit. to become shackles]
足枷になりませんから、作業班に入れて下さい。Ashikase ni narimasen kara, sagyō han ni irete kudasai.   *I won't be a hindrance, so please let me join the task force.*

ashimoto e tsukekomu — 足下へつけ込む — *to take unfair advantage of someone's weakness*
[lit. to enter close to someone's feet]
あの人は、友達の足下につけ込んで借金しました。Ano hito wa, tomodachi no ashimoto ni tsukekonde shakkin shimashita.   *He borrowed money from his friend by taking advantage of her weakness.*

ashimoto ni hi ga tsuku — 足下に火が付く — *Danger is imminent.*
[lit. Fire ignites at one's foot.]
信頼不足で、現政権の足下に火が付いています。Shinrai busoku de, gen seiken no ashimoto ni hi ga tsuite imasu.   *The current administration is in imminent danger because of lack of confidence.*

ashimoto nimo oyobanai — 足下にも及ばない — *to be no match for someone*
[lit. to be unable to reach someone's feet]
柔道では、あの人の足下にも及びません。Jūdō dewa, ano hito no ashimoto nimo oyobimasen.   *Where judo is concerned, I'm no match for him.*

ashimoto nimo yoritsukenai — 足下にも寄りつけない — *to be unable to touch someone*
[lit. to be unable to come close even to someone's feet]

雄弁さでは、誰も彼の足下にも寄りつけません。Yūbensa dewa, daremo kare no ashimoto nimo yoritsukemasen. *With respect to eloquence, nobody can touch him.*

ashimoto o miru — 足下を見る — *to take unfair advantage of someone's weakness*
[lit. to look at someone's feet]
値段の交渉をするときには、足下を見られないように気を付けなさい。Nedan no kōshō o suru toki niwa, ashimoto o mirarenai yō ni ki o tsukenasai. *When you try to negotiate a price, be careful not to be taken advantage of.*

ashinami ga midareru — 足並みが乱れる — *to fall apart*
[lit. The pace gets disturbed.]
政府と民間の景気回復協力の足並みが乱れ始めました。Seifu to minkan no keiki kaifuku kyoryoku no ashinami ga midarehajimemashita. *The collaboration between the government and the private sector on economic recovery has started to fall apart.*

ashinami ga sorou — 足並みが揃う — *to fall into line*
[lit. The pace is in harmony.]
やっとの事で、参加者全員の足並みが揃いました。Yatto no koto de, sankasha zen-in no ashinami ga soroimashita. *Finally, all the participants have fallen into line.*

ashite matoi — 足手まとい — *to be a drag*
[lit. to cling to one's legs and hands]
あの人は、何をするにもいつも足手まといになります。Ano hito wa, nani o suru ni mo itsumo ashite matoi ni narimasu. *No matter what we do, he's always a drag.*

ni no ashi o fumu — 二の足を踏む — *to hesitate*
[lit. to step on the same spot with the second foot]
彼女は結婚について二の足を踏んでいます。Kanojo wa kekkon ni tsuite ni no ashi o funde imasu. *She's hesitating about getting married.*

ukiashidatsu — 浮き足立つ — *to begin to waver*
[lit. Legs start floating.]
指導者が辞めて、抗議中の学生は浮き足立ってしまいました。Shidōsha ga yamete, kōgi chū no gakusei wa ukiashidatte shimaimashita. *When their leader quit, the protesting students began to waver.*

atama — 頭 — *head*

atama ga agaranai — 頭が上がらない — *to feel deep indebtedness or respect*
[lit. One's head does not go up.]
あの人にはいつも助けてもらっているので、頭が上がりません。
Ano hito niwa itsumo tasukete moratte iru node, atama ga agarimasen.
Because I have been getting help from him constantly, I feel deeply indebted.

atama ga itai — 頭が痛い — *It's a pain.*
[lit. One's head hurts.]
借金のことを考えると、頭が痛いです。Shakkin no koto o kangaeru to, atama ga itai desu. *It's a pain to think about my debts.*

atama ga furui — 頭が古い — *to be old-fashioned*
[lit. One's head is old.]
彼女のお父さんは、頭が古いです。Kanojo no otōsan wa, atama ga furui desu. *Her father is an old fogy.*

atama ga hikui — 頭が低い — *to be humble*
[lit. One's head is low.]
彼女は、有名になっても頭が低いです。Kanojo wa, yūmei ni nattemo atama ga hikui desu. *Even though she has become famous, she's still humble.*

atama ga ippai — 頭が一杯 — *to be preoccupied*
[lit. One's head is full.]
試験のことで頭が一杯で、あまりご飯が食べられません。Shiken no koto de atama ga ippai de, amari gohan ga taberaremasen. *Since I'm preoccupied with the exam, I can't eat much.*

atama ga katai — 頭が固い — *to be inflexible*
[lit. One's head is hard.]
彼は頭が固くて、違う意見を聞き入れません。Kare wa atama ga katakute, chigau iken o kikiiremasen. *Because he's inflexible, he doesn't listen to opinions different from his.*

atama ga sagaru — 頭が下がる — *to take off one's hat to someone or something*
[lit. One's head goes lower.]
彼女の努力には、頭が下がります。Kanojo no doryoku niwa, atama ga sagarimasu. *I take off my hat to her efforts.*

atama ni ireru — 頭に入れる — *to learn something by heart*
[lit. to put something in one's head]

日本に行く前に、大切な語句を頭に入れておきました。Nihon ni iku mae ni, taisetsu na goku o atama ni irete okimashita. *Before going to Japan, I learned some useful phrases by heart.*

atama ni kuru — 頭に来る — *to get mad*
[lit. to go to one's head]
家族の前で馬鹿にされて、頭に来ました。Kazoku no mae de baka ni sarete, atama ni kimashita. *I got mad at being slighted in front of my family.*

atama no kaiten ga hayai — 頭の回転が速い — *sharp*
[lit. The spin of one's head is fast.]
彼女は、頭の回転がとても速いです。Kanojo wa, atama no kaiten ga totemo hayai desu. *She's a very sharp person.*

atama no kaiten ga osoi — 頭の回転が遅い — *slow*
[lit. The spin of one's head is slow.]
あの学生は、やや頭の回転が遅いです。Ano gakusei wa, yaya atama no kaiten ga osoi desu. *That student is somewhat slow.*

atama o haneru — 頭をはねる — *to pocket a percentage of money*
[lit. to cut off a head]
あの仕事の仲介者は、日雇い賃金の三割も頭をはねています。Ano shigoto no chūkaisha wa, hiyatoi chingin no san wari mo atama o hanete imasu. *That middleman is pocketing as much as 30 percent of the day laborers' wages.*

atama o hineru — 頭をひねる — *to rack one's brains*
[lit. to incline one's head]
新事業計画の発案に、頭をひねりました。Shin jigyō keikaku no
hatsuan ni, atama o hinerimashita.   *I racked my brains to come up with*
a new business plan.

atama o hiyasu — 頭を冷やす — *to calm down*
[lit. to cool one's head]
喧嘩をやめて、頭を冷やしなさい。Kenka o yamete, atama o
hiyashinasai.   *Stop fighting and take it easy.*

atama o itameru — 頭を痛める — *to be concerned about someone or*
something
[lit. to make one's head hurt]
彼は、引退後の暮らしについて頭を痛めています。Kare wa, intai go
no kurashi ni tsuite atama o itamete imasu.   *He's concerned about his*
life after he retires.

atama o kakaeru — 頭を抱える — *at one's wit's end*
[lit. to hold one's head]
彼は、難問に頭を抱えています。Kare wa, nanmon ni atama o kakaete
imasu.   *He's at his wit's end facing a very difficult problem.*

atama o marumeru — 頭を丸める — *to become a Buddhist monk*
[lit. to shave one's head]
彼は、最近頭を丸める決心をしました。Kare wa, saikin atama o
marumeru kesshin o shimashita.   *Recently, he decided to become a*
Buddhist monk.

atama o motageru — 頭をもたげる — *to come to the fore, to emerge*
[lit. to hold up one's head]
彼女は、最近一流の歌手として頭をもたげてきました。Kanojo wa,
saikin ichiryū no kashu to shite atama o motagete kimashita.   *Recently,*
she has emerged as a top-class singer.

atama o nayamasu — 頭を悩ます — *to rack one's brains*
[lit. to bother one's head]
彼女は、子供の教育のことで頭を悩ましています。Kanojo wa,
kodomo no kyōiku no koto de atama o nayamashite imasu.   *She's*
racking her brains over her children's education.

atama o osaeru — 頭を抑える — *to keep someone under control*
[lit. to hold someone's head down]
映画監督はスターの頭を抑えるのに苦労しました。Eiga kantoku wa

18

sutā no atama o osaeru noni kurō shimashita.   *The movie director had a difficult time keeping the star under control.*

atama o sageru — 頭を下げる — *to knuckle under*
[lit. to lower one's head]
チームワークのために、先輩に頭を下げなければなりませんでした。
Chīmuwāku no tame ni, senpai ni atama o sagenakereba narimasen deshita.   *For the sake of teamwork, we had to knuckle under to the senior members.*

atama o shiboru — 頭を絞る — *to rack one's brains*
[lit. to squeeze one's head]
いくら頭を絞っても、良い考えが浮かびませんでした。Ikura atama o shibottemo, ii kangae ga ukabimasen deshita.   *No matter how much I racked my brains, I couldn't come up with a good idea.*

atamakabu — 頭株 — *key figure*
[lit. a head stump]
暴動の頭株が逮捕されました。Bōdō no atamakabu ga taiho saremashita.   *The key figure in the riot was arrested.*

atamakazu — 頭数 — *head count*
[lit. the number of heads]
頭数が揃わなくて、野球が出来ませんでした。Atamakazu ga sorowanakute, yakyū ga dekimasen deshita.   *We couldn't play baseball because we didn't have enough people.*

atamakin — 頭金 — *down payment*
[lit. head money]
家を買う頭金のために、貯金しています。Ie o kau atamakin no tame ni, chokin shite imasu.   *I'm saving money for a down payment to buy a house.*

atamauchi — 頭打ち — *lagging*
[lit. hitting one's head]
あの俳優の人気は、最近頭打ちです。Ano haiyū no ninki wa, saikin atamauchi desu.   *Recently, the popularity of that actor has been lagging.*

atamawari — 頭割り — *Dutch treat, to pay an equal share*
[lit. to divide a bill by the head count]
宴会の費用は、頭割りで払いましょう。Enkai no hiyō wa, atamawari de haraimashō.   *Let's go Dutch for the party expenses.*

ato — 後 — *back, rear, consequences, after, later*

ato no matsuri — 後の祭り — *too late*
[lit. the day after a festival]
今一生懸命勉強を始めても、後の祭りですよ。Ima isshōkenmei
　benkyō o hajimetemo, ato no matsuri desu yo.　*Even if you start*
　studying hard now, it's too late.

ato o hiku — 後を引く — *It's hard to quit something after starting.*
[lit. to drag the consequences]
一度甘い物を食べ出すと、後を引くので困ります。Ichido amai mono
　o tabedasu to, ato o hiku node komarimasu.　*Once I start eating sweets,*
　I'm in trouble because it's hard to stop.

atoaji ga warui — 後味が悪い — *to leave a bad taste in one's mouth*
[lit. The aftertaste is bad.]
友達と口論した後は、後味が悪かつたです。Tomodachi to kōron shita
　ato wa, atoaji ga warukatta desu.　*The quarrel with my friend left me*
　with a bad taste in my mouth.

atobō o katsugu — 後棒を担ぐ — *to be a party to something*
[lit. to shoulder the back end of a stick]
あの人は、社長失脚の陰謀の後棒を担ぎました。Ano hito wa, shachō
　shikkyaku no inbō no atobō o katsugimashita.　*He was a party to the*
　conspiracy for the president's downfall.

atogama ni suwaru — 後がまに座る — *to step into another's shoes*
[lit. to sit as a replacement pot]
社長が死んだ後、奥さんが後がまに座りました。Shachō ga shinda
　ato, okusan ga atogama ni suwarimashita.　*After the president of the*
　company died, his wife stepped into his shoes.

atogusare — 後腐れ — *trouble later*
[lit. future rot]
後腐れを避けるために、問題があれば今解決しておきなさい。
　Atogusare o sakeru tame ni, mondai ga areba ima kaiketsu shite okinasai.
　If there's a problem, you should solve it now to avoid trouble later.

atooshi — 後押し — *to back someone*
[lit. to push someone's back]
この間の選挙では、大勢の人が彼を後押ししました。Kono aida no
　senkyo dewa, ōzei no hito ga kare o atooshi shimashita.　*A lot of people*
　backed him in the recent election.

atosaki kamawazu — 後先構わず — *without thinking*
[lit. not caring if it's front or rear]

彼は、後先構わず家を飛び出しました。Kare wa, atosaki kamawazu ie o tobidashimashita. *Without thinking, he rushed out of his house.*

ato — 跡 — *mark, trace*

ato o ou — 跡を追う — *to die following the death of someone close*
[lit. to chase a trace]
彼は奥さんの死の一年後に跡を追いました。Kare wa okusan no shi no ichi nen go ni ato o oimashita. *He died one year after his wife's death.*

ato o tatanai — 跡を絶たない — *no end to something*
[lit. not to cut off traces]
就職希望者が、跡を絶ちませんでした。Shūshoku kibōsha ga, ato o tachimasen deshita. *The job applicants kept coming.*

ato o tatsu — 跡を絶つ — *to disappear without a trace*
[lit. to cut off traces]
あの人が後を絶ってから、三年になります。Ano hito ga ato o tatte kara, san nen ni narimasu. *It's been three years since he disappeared without a trace.*

ato o tsukeru — 跡をつける — *to tail, to shadow*
[lit. to follow a mark]
刑事は、一日中容疑者の跡をつけました。keiji wa, ichi nichi jū yōgisha no ato o tsukemashita. *The police detective tailed the suspect all day long.*

atome o tsugu — 跡目を継ぐ — *to succeed the head of a group*
[lit. to sew the mesh of a trace]
彼は、茶道の流派の家元としてお父さんの跡目を継ぎました。Kare wa, sadō no ryūha no iemoto to shite otōsan no atome o tsugimashita. *He succeeded his father as headmaster of the tea ceremony school.*

atotori — 跡取り — *heir, heiress*
[lit. picking up a trace]
彼の跡取りは、ビジネスの感覚が欠けています。Kare no atotori wa, bijinesu no kankaku ga kakete imasu. *His heir is lacking in business sense.*

awa — 泡 — *bubble, foam, froth*

awa o fukaseru — 泡を吹かせる — *to defeat someone to the point of humiliation*
[lit. to let someone blow bubbles]

彼女は討論で相手に勝って泡を吹かせました。Kanojo wa tōron de
aite ni katte awa o fukasemashita. *While winning the debate, she
humiliated her opponent.*

awa o kuu — 泡を食う — *to be taken aback*
[lit. to eat foam]
試験の難しさに泡を食いました。Shiken no muzukashisa ni awa o
kuimashita. *I was taken aback by the difficulty of the exam.*

mizu no awa to naru — 水の泡となる — *to come to nothing*
[lit. to become a water bubble]
私の調停の努力は水の泡となりました。Watakushi no chōtei no
doryoku wa mizu no awa to narimashita. *My efforts at mediation came
to nothing.*

B

ba — 馬 — *horse*

bakyaku o arawasu — 馬脚を現す — *to show one's true colors*
[lit. to reveal the legs of a horse]
彼は慎ましい振りをしていましたが、じきに馬脚を現しました。
Kare wa tsutsumashii furi o shite imashita ga, jiki ni bakyaku o
arawashimashita. *He was pretending to be modest, but he soon showed
his true colors.*

bariki ga aru — 馬力がある — *to have stamina*
[lit. to have horsepower]
あのマラソンの選手は、非常に馬力があります。Ano marason no
senshu wa, hijō ni bariki ga arimasu. *That marathon runner has great
stamina.*

bariki o kakeru — 馬力をかける — *to work one's fingers to the bone*
[lit. to apply horsepower]
渡辺さんは、卒業試験のために馬力をかけて勉強しています。
Watanabe san wa, sotsugyō shiken no tame ni bariki o kakete benkyō
shite imasu. *Miss Watanabe is working her fingers to the bone to pass
the graduation exam.*

---

ba — 場 — *place, spot*
bachigai — 場違い — *inappropriate*
[lit. The place is wrong.]
ここでそんなことをするのは、場違いです。Koko de sonna koto o
suru no wa, bachigai desu.   *It's inappropriate to do such things.*
bakazu o fumu — 場数を踏む — *to be experienced*
[lit. to step on a number of spots]
この仕事には、場数を踏んだ人が必要です。Kono shigoto niwa,
bakazu o funda hito ga hitsuyo desu.   *We need an old hand for this job.*
baokure suru — 場遅れする — *to get nervous*
[lit. to come late to a place]
歌を歌おうとしましたが、大勢の人がいるので場遅れしてしまいま
した。Uta o utaō to shimashita ga, ōzei no hito ga iru node baokure
shite shimaimashita.   *I tried to sing a song, but I got nervous because
there were so many people.*

---

baka — 馬鹿 — *fool, idiot, absurdity*
baka na mane o suru — 馬鹿なまねをする — *to act silly*
[lit. to pretend to be a fool]
人前で馬鹿なまねをするんじゃありません。Hitomae de baka na
mane o surunja arimasen.   *Don't act silly in front of the other people.*
baka ni naranai — 馬鹿にならない — *substantial, nothing to sneeze at*
[lit. to not become absurdity]
彼女の地域社会への貢献は馬鹿になりません。Kanojo no chiiki
shakai e no kōken wa baka ni narimasen.   *Her contribution to local
society is substantial.*
baka ni suru — 馬鹿にする — *to slight, to insult, to make fun of*
[lit. to make a fool of someone]
学生たちは、あの先生を馬鹿にしています。Gakusei tachi wa, ano
sensei o baka ni shite imasu.   *The students are making fun of that
teacher.*
baka o miru — 馬鹿を見る — *to make a fool of oneself*
[lit. to see a fool]
安物を買って馬鹿を見ました。Yasumono o katte baka o mimashita.
I made a fool of myself buying that junk.
bakaatari — 馬鹿当たり — *smash hit*
[lit. a crazy hit]

あのショ－は、馬鹿当たりしています。Ano shō wa, bakaatari shite imasu. *That show is a smash hit.*

bakabakashii — 馬鹿馬鹿しい — *absurd, ridiculous*
[lit. fool-like]
あの人は、馬鹿馬鹿しい将来の夢を持っています。Ano hito wa, bakabakashii shōrai no yume o motte imasu. *He has an absurd dream for his future.*

bakabanashi — 馬鹿話 — *foolish talk*
[lit. a fool's talk]
仕事中に、馬鹿話はやめて下さい。Shigoto chū ni, bakabanashi wa yamete kudasai. *Please stop the foolish conversation during work.*

bakajikara — 馬鹿力 — *great physical strength*
[lit. a fool's power]
彼は引っ越しの時、馬鹿力を発揮しました。Kare wa hikkoshi no toki, bakajikara o hakki shimashita. *He showed great physical strength during the move.*

bakakusai — 馬鹿臭い — *foolish, absurd*
[lit. smelling like a fool]
そんなことにお金を使うのは、馬鹿臭いです。Sonna koto ni okane o tsukau no wa bakakusai desu. *It's absurd to spend money for such a thing.*

bakasawagi — 馬鹿騒ぎ — *racket*
[lit. a fool's commotion]
馬鹿騒ぎをやめなさい。Bakasawagi o yamenasai. *Stop making such a racket.*

bakashōjiki — 馬鹿正直 — *excessively honest*
[lit. a fool's honesty]
彼は馬鹿正直なので、気分を損ねる人が大勢います。Kare wa bakashōjiki nanode, kibun o sokoneru hito ga ōzei imasu. *There are many people who get upset at him because he's too honest.*

bakateinei — 馬鹿丁寧 — *excessively polite*
[lit. a fool's politeness]
丁寧なのは大切ですが、あまり馬鹿丁寧にならないように気をつけなさい。Teinei nano wa taisetsu desu ga, amari bakateinei ni naranai yō ni ki o tsukenasai. *It's important to be polite, but be careful not to be too polite.*

bakawarai — 馬鹿笑い — *to laugh like an idiot*
[lit. an idiot's laugh]
みっともないから、馬鹿笑いはやめなさい。Mittomonai kara,
bakawarai wa yamenasai. *Stop laughing like an idiot; it's unseemly.*

ban — 万 — *10,000, everything, all things*
banji kyūsu — 万事休す — *It's all over. It's finished.*
[lit. Ten thousand things rest.]
旅行の途中で財布をなくして、万事休すになりました。Ryokō no
tochū de saifu o nakushite, banji kyūsu ni narimashita. *I lost my wallet
in the middle of the trip, and it was all over.*

bannan o haishite — 万難を排して — *at all costs*
[lit. by eliminating 10,000 difficulties]
ご招待、有り難うございます。パーティーには、万難を排して伺い
ます。Goshōtai, arigatō gozaimasu. Pātī niwa, bannan o haishite
ukagaimasu. *Thank you very much for the invitation. I'll come to your
party at all costs.*

bansaku tsukiru — 万策尽きる — *to be at the end of one's rope*
[lit. Ten thousand schemes end.]
彼女は万策尽きて、留学をあきらめました。Kanojo wa bansaku
tsukite, ryūgaku o akiramemashita. *She was at the end of her rope and
gave up studying abroad.*

batsu — ばつ — *circumstances, convenience*
batsu ga warui — ばつが悪い — *to feel awkward, to be embarrassed*
[lit. The circumstances are bad.]
ばつが悪いけれど、友達のお父さんに仕事を頼みに行きました。
Batsu ga warui keredo, tomodachi no otōsan ni shigoto o tanomini
ikimashita. *Although I felt awkward, I went to see my friend's father
to ask for a job.*

batsu o awaseru — ばつを合わせる — *to make one's story sound
plausible*
[lit. to fit the circumstances]
私の言い訳に、彼がばつを合わせてくれました。Watakushi no
iiwake ni, kare ga batsu o awasete kuremashita. *He was kind enough to
make my excuse sound plausible.*

Benkei — 弁慶 — *Benkei (a historical figure known for his strength)*
Benkei no nakidokoro — 弁慶の泣き所 — *Achilles heel*
[lit. a spot so sensitive that even Benkei cries when it's hit]
彼は素晴らしい野球の選手ですが、バッターとしてはカーブが
弁慶の泣き所です。Kare wa subarashii yakyū no senshu desu ga, battā
toshite wa kābu ga Benkei no nakidokoro desu.   *He's a great baseball*
player, but as a batter, curve balls are his Achilles heel.

---

benkyō — 勉強 — *study*
benkyō ni naru — 勉強になる — *to gain good experience*
[lit. to become useful for study]
初めて中国へ行って、良い勉強になりました。Hajimete Chūgoku e
itte, ii benkyō ni narimashita.   *When I first went to visit China, I gained*
some good experience.

benkyōka — 勉強家 — *hard worker*
[lit. a study expert]
彼女は勉強家だから、新しいことでもすぐ覚えます。Kanojo wa
benkyōka dakara, atarashii koto demo sugu oboemasu.   *Since she is a*
hard worker, she learns even new things quickly.

nedan o benkyō suru — 値段を勉強する — *to lower a price*
[lit. to study a price]
これを買っても良いけれど、値段をもう少し勉強してもらえませんか。
Kore o kattemo ii keredo, nedan o mō sukoshi benkyō shite moraemasen
ka.   *I may buy it, but would you lower the price a little?*

---

benri — 便利 — *convenience*
benriya — 便利屋 — *handyman*
[lit. a person of convenience]
彼は便利屋で、何でも直せます。Kare wa benriya de, nandemo naosemasu.
He's such a good handyman that he can fix anything for you.

---

benzetsu — 弁舌 — *speech*

benzetsu no tatsu — 弁舌の立つ — *eloquent*
[lit. the tongue standing up for a speech]
あの評論家は、弁舌の立つ人としても知られています。Ano
hyōronka wa, benzetsu no tatsu hito to shite mo shirarete imasu.   *That*
critic is also known as an eloquent speaker.

benzetsu o furuu — 弁舌を振るう — *to speak eloquently*
[lit. to shake the tongue for a speech]
部長は、会議で弁舌を振るいました。Buchō wa, kaigi de benzetsu o
furuimashita.   *The department chief spoke eloquently at the meeting.*

---

binbō — 貧乏 — *poverty*

binbōkuji o hiku — 貧乏くじを引く — *to be the least lucky of all*
[lit. to draw a poor lottery ticket]
貧乏くじを引いてしまい、みんなのためにお使いをしなければなり
ませんでした。Binbōkuji o hiite shimai, minna no tame ni otsukai o
shinakereba narimasen deshita.   *Because I was the least lucky of all, I*
had to do errands for everybody.

binbōkusai — 貧乏臭い — *shabby*
[lit. smelling like a poor person]
彼は金持ちなのに、いつも貧乏くさい服を着ています。Kare wa
kanemochi nanoni, itsumo binbōkusai fuku o kite imasu.   *Although he's*
rich, he's always wearing shabby clothes.

bō — 棒 — *stick, pole*

bō ni furu — 棒に振る — *to waste, to ruin*
[lit. to swing something like a stick]
あの人は、麻薬で人生を棒に振りました。Ano hito wa, mayaku de jinsei o bō ni furimashita. *He ruined his life with drugs.*

bō o furu — 棒を振る — *to conduct (music)*
[lit. to swing a stick]
一度でも、オ－ケストラで棒を振ってみたいです。Ichido demo, ōkesutora de bō o futte mitai desu. *I would love to conduct an orchestra even once.*

bōanki — 棒暗記 — *memorizing without understanding, straight memorization*
[lit. stick memorization]
試験では、答えの棒暗記はしないように。Shiken dewa, kotae no bōanki wa shinai yō ni. *Don't memorize answers for an exam without understanding the meaning.*

bōbiki — 棒引き — *to write off, to cancel*
[lit. to draw a stick]
あなたの借金を、棒引きしてあげましょう。Anata no shakkin o, bōbiki shite agemashō. *I'll write off your debt.*

bōdachisuru — 棒立ちする — *to stand stiffly*
[lit. to stand like a stick]
彼女はあまりの恐さに、棒立ちしてしまいました。Kanojo wa amari no kowasa ni, bōdachishite shimaimashita. *Fearful, she stood stiffly.*

bōyomisuru — 棒読みする — *to read in a monotone*
[lit. to read like a stick]
詩を棒読みしても、感情が伝わりません。Shi o bōyomishitemo, kanjō ga tsutawarimasen. *If you read poetry in a monotone, you can't convey feelings.*

katabō o katsugu — 片棒を担ぐ — *to take part in something*
[lit. to carry one end of a stick]
彼は、社内の陰謀の片棒を担いで出世した男です。Kare wa, shanai no inbō no katabō o katsuide shusse shita otoko desu. *He is the man who made it by taking part in a company conspiracy.*

---

bōzu — 坊主 — *Buddhist priest*
mikkabōzu — 三日坊主 — *quitter*

[lit. a Buddhist priest for three days]

あの人は三日坊主で、何をやっても長続きしません。Ano hito wa mikkabōzu de, nani o yattemo nagatsuzuki shimasen. *Because she's a quitter, she can't last long at anything she does.*

bu — 分 — *rate, percentage*

bu ga aru — 分が有る — *to be at an advantage*
[lit. There is a percentage.]

明日の試合は、こちら側に分があります。Ashita no shiai wa, kochiragawa ni bu ga arimasu. *We have an advantage in the game tomorrow.*

bu ga warui — 分が悪い — *to be at a disadvantage*
[lit. The percentage is bad.]

わが社の分が悪い市場で、競争しなければなりません。Waga sha no bu ga warui shijō de, kyōsō shinakereba narimasen. *Our company has to compete in a market where we're at a disadvantage.*

cha — 茶 — *tea, green tea*

chaban — 茶番 — *farce, sham*
[lit. a facetious Noh drama]

彼女は泣いて謝っているけれど、また茶番です。Kanojo wa naite ayamatte iru keredo, mata chaban desu. *Although she's crying and apologizing, once again it's a farce.*

chacha o ireru — 茶々を入れる — *to interrupt with banter*
[lit. to make tea after tea]

彼女は、私が話すといつも茶々を入れます。Kanojo wa, watakushi ga hanasu to itsumo chacha o iremasu. *She interrupts me with banter whenever I talk.*

ocha o nigosu — お茶を濁す — *to pussyfoot*
[lit. to make tea cloudy]

政府は環境問題について、お茶を濁しています。Seifu wa kankyō mondai ni tsuite, ocha o nigoshite imasu. *The government is pussyfooting on environmental issues.*

ochame — お茶目 — *playful, mischievous (a child)*
[lit. an eye of tea]
あの子は、お茶目なことが大好きです。Ano ko wa, ochame na koto ga daisuki desu. *That child loves to play pranks.*

---

chi — 血 — *blood*

chi de chi o arau arasoi — 血で血を洗う争い — *intense internal strife*
[lit. to wash blood with blood]
今党では次の党首を選ぶために、血で血を洗う争いが起こっています。Ima tō dewa tsugi no tōshu o erabu tame ni, chi de chi o arau arasoi ga okotte imasu. *The party is experiencing intense internal strife over the choice of their next president.*

chi ga hiku omoi — 血が引く思い — *to be horrified, to make one's flesh crawl*
[lit. One's blood recedes.]
交通事故の現場を見て、血が引く思いをしました。Kōtsū jiko no genba o mite, chi ga hiku omoi o shimashita. *The scene of the traffic accident made my flesh crawl.*

chi ga kayotta — 血が通った — *warm, humane, thoughtful*
[lit. blood flowing]
政府は、血が通った政策を約束しています。Seifu wa, chi ga kayotta seisaku o yakusokushite imasu. *The government promises people-oriented policies.*

chi ga kayotte iru — 血が通っている — *alive*
[lit. One's blood flows.]
血が通っている間は、働き続けるつもりです。Chi ga kayotte iru aida wa, hataraki tsuzukeru tsumori desu. *I intend to keep working as long as I'm alive.*

chi ga noboru — 血が上る — *to fly off the handle*
[lit. One's blood rushes up.]
彼があまりにも無礼なので、頭に血が上りました。Kare ga amari nimo burei nanode, atama ni chi ga noborimashita. *His rudeness made me fly off the handle.*

chi ga sawagu — 血が騒ぐ — *to get excited*
[lit. One's blood makes noises.]
明日の旅行のことを考えると、血が騒ぎます。Ashita no ryokō no

koto o kangaeru to, chi ga sawagimasu. *I get excited when I think about tomorrow's trip.*

chi ga tsunagaru — 血がつながる — *to be a blood relative*
[lit. One's blood is connected.]
叔父は血がつながっているのに、私にとても冷淡です。Oji wa chi ga tsunagatte iru noni, watakushi ni totemo reitan desu. *My uncle is very cold to me although he is a blood relative.*

chi ga waku — 血が沸く — *stirring, thrilling*
[lit. One's blood boils.]
昨日私たちのチ-ムが勝って、血が沸きました。Kinō watakushitachi no chīmu ga katte, chi ga wakimashita. *Our team's victory yesterday was thrilling.*

chi mo namida mo nai — 血も涙もない — *cold-blooded*
[lit. having no blood and no tears]
社員は、会社の血も涙もない仕打ちに憤慨しています。Shain wa, kaisha no chi mo namida mo nai shiuchi ni fungai shite imasu. *The employees are enraged at their cold-blooded treatment by the company.*

chi no ame — 血の雨 — *bloodshed*
[lit. rain of blood]
今の状態が続くと、血の雨を降らせる恐れがあります。Ima no jōtai ga tsuzuku to, chi no ame o furaseru osore ga arimasu. *If the current situation continues, there is great danger of bloodshed.*

chi no deru yō na — 血の出るような — *extremely hard*
[lit. like bleeding]
彼女は、血の出るような努力をしてお金を貯めました。Kanojo wa, chi no deru yō na doryoku o shite okane o tamemashita. *She saved money by working extremely hard.*

chi no ke no ōi — 血の気の多い — *hotheaded*
[lit. much indication of blood]
あの人は血の気が多くてすぐ怒るので、気をつけなさい。Ano hito wa chi no ke ga ōkute sugu okoru node, ki o tsukenasai. *You should be careful of him becuase he's hotheaded and gets angry easily.*

chi no meguri no warui — 血の巡りの悪い — *stupid*
[lit. poor blood circulation]
彼は血の巡りが悪いから、よく失敗します。Kare wa chi no meguri ga warui kara, yoku shippai shimasu. *Because he's stupid, he makes mistakes often.*

chi no namida — 血の涙 — *tears of anguish*
[lit. tears of blood]
両親に突然死なれて、彼女は血の涙を流しました。Ryōshin ni
totsuzen shinarete, kanojo wa chi no namida o nagashimashita.   *She
shed tears of anguish over the sudden deaths of her parents.*

chi o haku omoi — 血を吐く思い — *determination*
[lit. a feeling of vomiting blood]
彼は大学に行くために、血を吐く思いで勉強しました。Kare wa
daigaku ni iku tame ni, chi o haku omoi de benkyō shimashita.
Because of his determination to go to college, he studied hard.

chi o hiku — 血を引く — *to inherit a trait or talent*
[lit. to draw blood]
あの子はお母さんの音楽の才能の血を引いています。Ano ko wa
okāsan no ongaku no sainō no chi o hiite imasu.   *That child inherited
her mother's talent for music.*

chi o miru — 血を見る — *to cause casualties*
[lit. to see blood]
デモ隊が機動隊と衝突して、血を見ることになりました。Demotai
ga kidōtai to shōtotsu shite, chi o miru koto ni narimashita.   *When the
demonstrators clashed with the mobile police units, there were
casualties.*

chi o wakeru — 血を分ける — *to be blood relatives*
[lit. to share the same blood]
兄と私は血を分けた仲でも、考え方がまるで違います。Ani to
watakushi wa chi o waketa naka demo, kangaekata ga marude
chigaimasu.   *Although we're blood relatives, my brother and I have
totally different ways of thinking.*

chi to ase no kesshō — 血と汗の結晶 — *fruit of someone's blood,
sweat, and tears*
[lit. a crystal of blood and sweat]
彼女の博士号は、血と汗の結晶です。Kanojo no hakasegō wa, chi to ase
no kesshō desu.   *Her Ph.D. is the fruit of her blood, sweat, and tears.*

chi to nari niku to naru — 血となり肉となる — *to be a key*
[lit. to become blood and muscles]
若いときの経験が、今の成功の血となり肉となっています。Wakai
toki no keiken ga, ima no seikō no chi to nari niku to natte imasu.   *An
experience in my youth was the key to my current success.*

chi wa arasoenai — 血は争えない — *in the blood*
[lit. The blood can't compete.]

あの医者の子供はみんな医者になりました。血は争えないものです。
Ano isha no kodomo wa minna isha ni narimashita. Chi wa arasoenai
mono desu. *That doctor's children all became doctors. It's indeed in
the blood.*

chimanako ni naru — 血眼になる — *to become frantic*
[lit. to get bloodshot eyes]

落とした財布を、血眼になって探しました。Otoshita saifu o,
chimanako ni natte sagashimashita. *I looked frantically for my lost
wallet.*

chimatsuri ni ageru — 血祭りに上げる — *to make someone a scapegoat*
[lit. to hoist someone for a blood festival]

チームのオーナーは、監督を血祭りに上げて首を切りました。
Chīmu no ōnā wa, kantoku o chimatsuri ni agete kubi o kirimashita.
The team owner made a scapegoat of the head coach and fired him.

chimayou — 血迷う — *to lose one's mind*
[lit. One's blood is at a loss.]

その学生は、血迷って先生を殴りつけました。Sono gakusei wa,
chimayotte sensei o naguritsukemashita. *The student lost his mind and
punched his teacher.*

chimichi o ageru — 血道を上げる — *to be infatuated with someone*
[lit. to raise blood vessels]

彼は、赤坂の芸者に血道を上げています。Kare wa, Akasaka no
geisha ni chimichi o agete imasu. *He's infatuated with a geisha in
Akasaka.*

chisuji — 血筋 — *lineage, ancestry*
[lit. a line of blood]

彼は、貴族の血筋を引いています。Kare wa, kizoku no chisuji o hiite
imasu *He's from a family of noble ancestry.*

---

chi — 地 — *ground, soil*

chi ni mamireru — 地にまみれる — *to be defeated*
[lit. to be covered with mud]

あの政治家は、この前の選挙で地にまみれました。Ano seijika wa,
kono mae no senkyo de chi ni mamiremashita. *That politician lost the
last election.*

chi ni ochiru — 地に落ちる — *to decline, to drop*
[lit. to fall to the ground]
あの学者の名声は、急激に地に落ちました。Ano gakusha no meisei
wa, kyūgeki ni chi ni ochimashita.   *The fame of that scholar rapidly
declined.*

chiho o katameru — 地歩を固める — *to secure a foothold*
[lit. to occupy the ground for one's own steps]
彼は、将来重役になるための地歩を固めました。Kare wa, shōrai
jūyaku ni naru tame no chiho o katamemashita.   *He secured a foothold
to become a senior executive in the future.*

---

chichi — 乳 — *milk*

chichikusai — 乳臭い — *green, immature*
[lit. smelling of milk]
あの人は大学生なのに、まだ乳臭いです。Ano hito wa daigakusei
nanoni, mada chichikusai desu.   *He's a college student, but he's still
immature.*

---

chie — 知恵 — *wisdom, intelligence*

chie ga asai — 知恵が浅い — *slow, dull-witted*
[lit. One's wisdom is shallow.]
彼は知恵が浅いから、大切な仕事は頼めません。Kare wa chie ga asai
kara, taisetsu na shigoto wa tanomemasen.   *We can't ask him to do
anything important because he's slow.*

chie ga mawaru — 知恵が回る — *to be resourceful*
[lit. One's wisdom spins.]
彼女は知恵が回るので、旅行中は頼りになります。Kanojo wa chie
ga mawaru node, ryokō chū wa tayori ni narimasu.   *During a trip, you
can rely on her because she's resourceful.*

chie o kariru — 知恵を借りる — *to ask for advice*
[lit. to borrow wisdom]
留学について、先生に知恵を借りました。Ryūgaku ni tsuite, sensei ni
chie o karimashita.   *I asked my teacher's advice about my studying
abroad.*

chie o kasu — 知恵を貸す — *to give advice*
[lit. to lend wisdom]

会計士は、投資についていとこに知恵を貸しました。Kaikeishi wa,
tōshi ni tsuite itoko ni chie o kashimashita.   *The accountant gave advice
about investments to my cousin.*

chie o shiboru — 知恵を絞る — *to exert one's wits*
[lit. to squeeze wisdom]
新しい事業計画を提出するために、知恵を絞りました。Atarashii
jigyō keikaku o teishutsusuru tame ni, chie o shiborimashita.   *I exerted
my wits to submit a new business plan.*

chie o tsukeru — 知恵を付ける — *to instigate, to incite*
[lit. to fasten wisdom to someone]
彼は同僚にストライキを起こすように知恵を付けました。Kare wa
dōryō ni sutoraiki o okosu yō ni chie o tsukemashita.   *He instigated his
colleagues to strike.*

---

chikai — 誓い — *oath, vow*
chikai o tateru — 誓いを立てる — *to make a vow*
[lit. to erect a vow]
彼は、毎日運動する誓いを立てました。Kare wa, mainichi undō suru
chikai o tatemashita.   *He made a vow to exercise every day.*

---

chikara — 力 — *power, force*
chikara ni amaru — 力に余る — *beyond one's ability*
[lit. more than one's power]
その要求は、私の力に余りました。Sono yōkyū wa, watakushi no
chikara ni amarimashita.   *The request was beyond my capability.*

chikara ni naru — 力になる — *to help*
[lit. to become power]
彼女が困っているので、力になってあげました。Kanojo ga komatte
iru node, chikara ni natte agemashita.   *I helped her because she was
having trouble.*

chikara no aru — 力のある — *convincing*
[lit. There is power.]
彼は力のある話し方で、理由を説明しました。Kare wa chikara no aru
hanashikata de, riyū o setsumei shimashita.   *He explained the reasons
in a convincing speech.*

chikara o furuu — 力を振るう — *to be influential*
[lit. to brandish power]

あの教授は、経済理論の分野で力を振るっています。Ano kyōju wa, keizai riron no bun-ya de chikara o furutte imasu. *That professor is influential in the field of economic theory.*

chikara o ireru — 力を入れる — *to take great interest in someone or something*
[lit. to put power in]
あの政党は、環境問題に力を入れています。Ano seitō wa, kankyō mondai ni chikara o irete imasu. *That political party is taking great interest in environmental issues.*

chikara o kariru — 力を借りる — *to enlist the help of someone*
[lit. to borrow power]
難問を解決するために、弁護士の力を借りました。Nanmon o kaiketsu suru tame ni, bengoshi no chikara o karimashita. *We enlisted the help of a lawyer to solve some difficult problems.*

chikara o kasu — 力を貸す — *to help*
[lit. to lend power]
友達が自分の会社を作るとき、力を貸しました。Tomodachi ga jibun no kaisha o tsukuru toki, chikara o kashimashita. *I helped my friend when she set up her own company.*

chikara o otosu — 力を落とす — *to be dejected*
[lit. to drop power]
彼は彼女が婚約を解消して以来、力を落としています。Kare wa kanojo ga kon-yaku o kaishō shite irai, chikara o otoshite imasu. *He's been dejected since she broke off their engagement.*

chikarakobu o ireru — 力瘤を入れる — *to help actively, to make efforts*
[lit. to make one's biceps swell]
彼女は、政治改革の草の根運動に力瘤を入れています。Kanojo wa, seiji kaikaku no kusa no ne undō ni chikarakobu o irete imasu. *She's actively helping the grass-roots movement for political reform.*

chikarazoe — 力添え — *help*
[lit. to accompany power]
友達のお父さんの力添えで、いい仕事を見つけることが出来ました。Tomodachi no otōsan no chikarazoe de, ii shigoto o mitsukeru koto ga dekimashita. *I was able to find a good job with the help of my friend's father.*

chikarazukeru — 力付ける — *to encourage, to reassure*
[lit. to attach power]

彼がインタビュ－を心配していたので、力付けてあげました。Kare ga intabyū o shinpai shite ita node, chikarazukete agemashita. *Because he was worried about his interview, I reassured him.*

chikarazuku de — 力ずくで — *by sheer force*
[lit. for the sake of force]
彼は、力ずくで今の地位を築きました。Kare wa, chikarazuku de ima no chii o kizukimashita. *He established his current status by sheer force.*

---

chiri — 塵 — *dust*
chiri hodo mo — 塵ほども — *not a bit*
[lit. (not) even a speck of dust]
彼女は約束を破っても、すまないとは塵ほども思いませんでした。Kanojo wa yakusoku o yabuttemo, sumanai to wa chiri hodo mo omoimasen deshita. *Although she broke her promise, she didn't feel a bit sorry.*

chiri ni mamireru — 塵にまみれる — *to be defeated; to lose*
[lit. to be covered with dust]
彼は市長選に出馬しましたが、塵にまみれました。Kare wa shichō sen ni shutsuba shimashita ga, chiri ni mamiremashita. *He ran for mayor, but he lost.*

---

chōchin — 提灯 — *lantern*
chōchin o motsu — 提灯を持つ — *to flatter*
[lit. to hold a lantern]
彼女は、社長の提灯を持つ機会を見逃しません。Kanojo wa, shachō no chōhin o motsu kikai o minogashimasen. *She never misses a chance to flatter the president.*

---

chōshi — 調子 — *tune*
chōshi ga ii — 調子がいい — *fawning, obsequious*
[lit. The tune is good.]
彼は調子がいいから、あまり信用できません。Kare wa chōshi ga ii kara, amari shin-yō dekimasen. *Because he's obsequious, I can't trust him much.*

chōshi ni noru — 調子に乗る — *to be on a roll*
[lit. to ride on a tune]
私たちは仕事がやっと調子に乗って、締め切りに間に合います。
Watakushitachi wa shigoto ga yatto chōshi ni notte, shimekiri ni
maniaimasu.   *Now that we're on a roll, we can meet the deadline.*

chōshi ni noru — 調子に乗る — *to get a swelled head*
[lit. to ride on a tune]
あの人は、誉められるとすぐ調子に乗ります。Ano hito wa,
homerareru to sugu chōshi ni norimasu.   *She easily gets a swelled head*
when she's praised.

chōshi o awaseru — 調子を合わせる — *to play along with someone*
[lit. to fit a tune]
彼は、上司が言うことには何でも調子を合わせます。Kare wa, jōshi
ga iu koto niwa nandemo chōshi o awasemasu.   *He plays along with*
whatever his boss says.

chōshi o nomikomu — 調子を飲み込む — *to get the hang of something*
[lit. to swallow a tune]
先月コンピュータを買いましたが、やっと調子を飲み込むことが
出来ました。Sengetsu konpyūta o kaimashita ga, yatto chōshi o
nomikomu koto ga dekimashita.   *I bought a computer last month, and*
I've finally gotten the hang of it.

chōshi o otosu — 調子を落とす — *to slow down, to be in a slump*
[lit. to drop a tune]
あの選手は、初夏以来調子を落としています。Ano senshu wa, shoka

irai chōshi o otoshite imasu. *That player has been in a slump since the beginning of summer.*

chōshi o yawarageru — 調子を和らげる — *to tone down*
[lit. to soften a tune]
マスコミは政府攻撃の調子を和らげました。Masukomi wa seifu kōgeki no chōshi o yawaragemashita. *The mass media toned down their attack on the government.*

---

chū — 宙 — *space, air*

chū de yomu — 宙で読む — *to recite from memory*
[lit. to read in space]
あの女優は、詩を宙で読むことが得意です。Ano joyū wa, shi o chū de yomu koto ga tokui desu. *That actress is good at reciting poems from memory.*

chū ni mayou — 宙に迷う — *to remain unsettled*
[lit. to get lost in space]
交渉は、意見の衝突で宙に迷っています。Kōshō wa, iken no shōtotsu de chū ni mayotte imasu. *The negotiations remain unsettled because of the clash of opinions.*

chū ni uku — 宙に浮く — *to be suspended, to be up in the air*
[lit. to float in the air]
建築計画は、住民の反対で宙に浮いています。Kenchiku keikaku wa, jūmin no hantai de chū ni uite imasu. *The construction project is up in the air because of opposition by the residents.*

---

chūmon — 注文 — *order*

chūmon no urusai — 注文のうるさい — *fussy*
[lit. An order is noisy.]
彼は、礼儀については注文がうるさい人です。Kare wa, reigi ni tsuite
wa chūmon ga urusai hito desu. *He's fussy about etiquette.*

chūmon o tsukeru — 注文を付ける — *to attach conditions*
[lit. to attach an order]
母はもっと勉強する注文を付けて、コンピュータを買ってくれました。
Haha wa motto benkyō suru chūmon o tsukete, konpyūta o katte kuremashita.
My mother bought me a computer on the condition that I study harder.

daiji — 大事 — *important, valuable*

daiji ni itaru — 大事にいたる — *to get out of control, to reach a serious
level*
[lit. to reach an important thing]
犯罪が大事にいたる前に、予防策を作るべきです。Hanzai ga daiji ni
itaru mae ni, yobō saku o tsukuru beki desu. *We should establish
prevention measures before crime gets out of control.*

daiji o toru — 大事をとる — *to be cautious, to play it safe*
[lit. to pick up an important thing]
風邪だと思いますが、大事をとって明日医者に行きます。Kaze da to
omoimasu ga, daiji o totte ashita isha ni ikimasu. *I think it's a cold, but
to play it safe, I'm going to see a doctor tomorrow.*

daku — 抱く — *to embrace*

dakikomu — 抱き込む — *to win someone over*
[lit. to hold someone to one's chest]
彼は、彼女を策略に抱き込みました。Kare wa, kanojo o sakuryaku ni
dakikomimashita. *He won her over to his plot.*

dakyō — 妥協 — *compromise*

dakyōan o neru — 妥協案を練る — *to work out a compromise*
[lit. to knead a compromise plan]

急いで決着するために、妥協案を練っています。Isoide ketchaku suru tame ni, dakyōan o nette imasu.   *To settle quickly, we're working out a compromise.*

---

dame — 駄目 — *useless, no use*

dame o dasu — 駄目を出す — *to reject, to not accept*
[lit. to issue uselessness]
学校は、学生の要求に駄目を出しました。Gakkō wa, gakusei no yōkyū ni dame o dashimashita.   *The school rejected the students' demands.*

dame o osu — 駄目を押す — *to make sure*
[lit. to press uselessness]
医者は、患者が薬を規則的に飲むように駄目を押しました。Isha wa, kanja ga kusuri o kisokuteki ni nomu yō ni dame o oshimashita.
The doctor made sure his patient would take the medicine regularly.

---

dashi — だし — *stock, broth*

dashi ni tsukau — だしに使う — *to use someone, to exploit someone*
[lit. to use someone for stock]
彼女は、パートナーをだしに使って目的を遂げました。Kanojo wa, pātonā o dashi ni tsukatte mokuteki o togemashita.   *She achieved her goal by exploiting her partner.*

---

da — 蛇 — *snake*

dasoku — 蛇足 — *excessive, superfluous*

[lit. snake legs]

その説明の、最後の言葉は蛇足です。Sono setsumei no, saigo no kotoba wa dasoku desu. *The last part of the explanation is superfluous.*

debana — 出鼻 — *extruding nose*

debana o kujiku — 出鼻を挫く — *to squelch someone's initial enthusiasm*
[lit. to break someone's nose]

教授は講義の出鼻を挫かれて、後を続けられませんでした。Kyōju wa kōgi no debana o kujikarete, ato o tsuzukeraremasen deshita. *The professor's enthusiasm was squelched at the beginning of his lecture and he couldn't go on.*

do — 度 — *degree, time(s)*

do o sugosu — 度を過ごす — *to go too far, to be overbearing*
[lit. to exceed a degree]

監督の度を過ごした態度に、選手は憤っています。Kantoku no do o sugoshita taido ni, senshu wa ikidootte imasu. *The players resent the manager's overbearing attitude.*

do o ushinau — 度を失う — *to lose one's composure*
[lit. to lose a degree]

彼女は突然演説を頼まれて、度を失いました。Kanojo wa totsuzen enzetsu o tanomarete, do o ushinaimashita. *She lost her composure at the sudden request for her to give a speech.*

dogimo — 度肝 — *liver*

dogimo o nukareru — 度肝を抜かれる — *to be dumbfounded*
[lit. One's liver is extracted.]

娘に婚約を告げられて、度肝を抜かれました。Musume ni kon-yaku o tsugerarete, dogimo o nukaremashita. *I was dumbfounded by my daughter's announcing her engagement.*

doko — どこ — *where*

doko fuku kaze — どこ吹く風 — *complete indifference*
[lit. Where is the wind blowing?]

彼は何度注意されても、どこ吹く風といった様子です。Kare wa nando chūi saretemo, doko fuku kaze to itta yōsu desu. *No matter how many times he is warned, he seems completely indifferent.*

doku — 毒 — *poison*

dokudokushii — 毒々しい — *venomous, spiteful*
[lit. poison-like]
あの人は、毒々しい話し方で反論しました。Ano hito wa,
   dokudokushii hanashikata de hanron shimashita.   *He argued back using*
   spiteful language.

dokuke ni aterareru — 毒気に当てられる — *to be stunned*
[lit. to be exposed to the poisonous air]
私は、図々しく好意を要求する彼女の毒気に当てられてしまいました。
   Watakushi wa, zūzūshiku kōi o yōkyū suru kanojo no dokuke ni
   aterarete shimaimashita.   *I was stunned by her brazen demands for*
   favors.

dokuke o nukareru — 毒気を抜かれる — *to be deflated (feelings)*
[lit. the poisonous air to be drawn out]
抗議するつもりだったら謝られて、毒気を抜かれてしまいました。
   Kōgi suru tsumori dattara ayamararete, dokuke o nukarete
   shimaimashita.   *I intended to protest, but when they apologized, my*
   anger subsided.

dokyō — 度胸 — *courage, pluck*

dokyō ga ii — 度胸が良い — *bold*
[lit. One's courage is good.]
彼女は度胸が良いから、質問をためらうことはありません。Kanojo
   wa dokyō ga ii kara, shitsumon o tamerau koto wa arimasen.   *She's*
   bold and never hesitates to ask questions.

dokyō ga suwaru — 度胸が据わる — *to have nerves of steel*
[lit. One's courage is in position.]
彼は、度胸が据わっています。Kare wa, dokyō ga suwatte imasu.   *He*
   has nerves of steel.

dokyō o sueru — 度胸を据える — *to pluck up one's courage*
[lit. to set one's courage]
度胸を据えて、社長に昇給を頼みに行きました。Dokyō o suete,
   shachō ni shōkyū o tanomini ikimashita.   *After plucking up my*
   courage, I went to the president to ask for a raise.

doro — 泥 — *mud*

doro o haku — 泥を吐く — *to confess to one's crime*

[lit. to vomit mud]

容疑者は、逮捕されるとすぐに泥を吐きました。Yōgisha wa, taiho sareru to sugu ni doro o hakimashita.   The suspect confessed to the crime right after his arrest.

doro o kaburu — 泥をかぶる — to assume someone else's responsibility
[lit. to pour mud upon oneself]
課長は部下の失敗の泥をかぶって、辞職しました。Kachō wa buka no shippai no doro o kabutte, jishoku shimashita.   The section chief assumed responsibility for his subordinate's mistake by resigning.

dorojiai — 泥仕合 — mudslinging
[lit. a mud bout]
この選挙戦では、候補者が泥仕合を繰り広げています。Kono senkyo sen dewa, kōhosha ga dorojiai o kurihirogete imasu.   In this election campaign, the candidates are engaging in mudslinging.

dorokusai — 泥臭い — unrefined, sloppy
[lit. smelling like mud]
彼は、いつも泥臭い服装をしています。Kare wa, itsumo dorokusai fukusō o shite imasu.   He's always wearing sloppy clothes.

doronawashiki — 泥縄式 — after the fact
[lit. a method of making a rope after seeing a thief]
政府の災害予防対策は、泥縄式でした。Seifu no saigai yobō taisaku wa, doronawashiki deshita.   The government took disaster-prevention measures after the fact.

doronuma ni hamaru — 泥沼にはまる — to be bogged down
[lit. to fall into a muddy marsh]
友達は賭事の泥沼にはまっています。Tomodachi wa kakegoto no doronuma ni hamatte imasu.   My friend is bogged down in gambling.

kao ni doro o nuru — 顔に泥を塗る — to disgrace someone
[lit. to apply mud to someone's face]
あの人は、親の顔に泥を塗っても平気です。Ano hito wa, oya no kao ni doro o nuttemo heiki desu.   She doesn't care even if she disgraces her parents.

---

dosu — どす — dagger

dosu no kiita — どすの利いた — intimidating
[lit. A dagger is effective.]
やくざは、どすの利いた声でキャバレーの客にすごみました。

Yakuza wa, dosu no kiita koe de kyabarē no kyaku ni sugomimashita.
The gangster threatened the cabaret patrons in an intimidating voice.

eiki — 英気 — *spirit*
  eiki o yashinau — 英気を養う — *to renew one's spirits*
  [lit. to nourish one's spirit]
  英気を養うために、休暇を取りました。Eiki o yashinau tame ni,
  kyūka o torimashita. *I took a vacation to renew my spirits.*

eimin — 永眠 — *eternal rest*
  eiminsuru — 永眠する — *to pass away*
  [lit. to sleep forever]
  彼は、長い病気の末永眠しました。Kare wa, nagai byōki no sue eimin
  shimashita. *He passed away after a long illness.*

eiri — 営利 — *profit*
  eiri o musaboru — 営利を貪る — *to make undue profits*
  [lit. to devour profit]
  彼は営利を貪るので、悪名が高いです。Kare wa eiri o musaboru node,
  akumei ga takai desu. *He is notorious for making undue profits.*

eiten — 栄転 — *job transfer on promotion*
  eitensuru — 栄転する — *to be transferred on promotion*
  [lit. an honorable switchover]
  彼は、パリの支店長に栄転しました。Kare wa, Pari no shitenchō ni
  eiten shimashita. *He was transferred to head the Paris branch office.*

ejiki — 餌食 — *prey*
  ejiki ni naru — 餌食になる — *to fall victim to someone or something*
  [lit. to become prey]
  彼女は、詐欺の餌食になりました。Kanojo wa, sagi no ejiki ni
  narimashita. *She fell victim to a fraud.*

en — 縁 — *blood relation, connection*

en ga nai — 縁が無い — *to have no connection to something*
[lit. no relation]

私は、お金とは縁がありません。Watakushi wa, okane to wa en ga
arimasen.   *I have no luck with money.*

en mo yukari mo nai hito — 縁もゆかりもない人 — *perfect stranger*
[lit. a person to whom one has no relation]

あの人とは、縁もゆかりもありません。Ano hito to wa, en mo yukari
mo arimasen.   *He's a perfect stranger to me.*

en o kiru — 縁を切る — *to break off with someone, to sever a relationship*
[lit. to sever a relationship]

彼女は、ボーイフレンドと縁を切りたがっています。Kanojo wa,
bōifurendo to en o kiritagatte imasu.   *She wants to break off with her
boyfriend.*

en o musubu — 縁を結ぶ — *to tie the knot*
[lit. to conclude a relationship]

大学の級友は長年の交際の後、縁を結びました。Daigaku no kyūyū
wa naganen no kōsai no ato, en o musubimashita.   *The college
classmates tied the knot after dating for many years.*

---

en — 縁 — *veranda*

en no shita no chikaramochi — 縁の下の力持ち — *to work in the
background*
[lit. a strong man under a veranda]

彼は政策決定で、縁の下の力持ちの役を果たしています。Kare wa
seisaku kettei de, en no shita no chikaramochi no yaku o hatashite imasu.
He's functioning as the brains behind the scenes for policy formulation.

---

engi — 縁起 — *omen, luck*

engi demo nai — 縁起でもない — *ominous*
[lit. no luck]

結婚の日に、縁起でもない話はやめて下さい。Kekkon no hi ni, engi
demo nai hanashi wa yamete kudasai.   *Please stop talking about
ominous things on the wedding day.*

engi o katsugu — 縁起を担ぐ — *to be superstitious*
[lit. to carry an omen]

あの野球の選手は縁起を担いで、試合の日には髭を剃りません。Ano

yakyū no senshu wa engi o katsuide, shiai no hi ni wa hige o sorimasen.
That baseball player is superstitious and doesn't shave on game day.

---

eri — 襟 — *collar*

eri o tadasu — 襟を正す — *to be awestruck*
[lit. to straighten one's own collar]
その人の過去を知って、襟を正しました。Sono hito no kako o shitte, eri o tadashimashita. *I was awestruck when I learned of his past.*

---

etsu — 悦 — *joy*

etsu ni iru — 悦に入る — *to gloat*
[lit. to enter into joy]
彼はゴルフで勝って、悦に入っています。Kare wa gorufu de katte, etsu ni itte imasu. *He's gloating over his win in the golf tournament.*

---

fu — 腑 — *bowels*

fu ni ochinai — 腑に落ちない — *to be hard to swallow*
[lit. not going down to the bowels]
その説明は、腑に落ちません。Sono setsumei wa, fu ni ochimasen.
That explanation is hard to swallow.

fu no nuketa yō na — 腑の抜けたような — *to be numb*
[lit. like the bowels being removed]
彼は離婚してから、腑の抜けたような顔をしています。Kare wa rikon shite kara, fu no nuketa yō na kao o shite imasu. *He's been looking numb since his divorce.*

---

fuda — 札 — *card, ticket*

fudadome — 札止め — *sellout*
[lit. stopping the sale of tickets]
相撲は、毎日札止めの人気です。Sumō wa, mainichi fudadome no ninki desu. *The sumo tournament is so popular that every day is a sellout.*

fudatsuki no — 札付きの — *notorious*
[lit. card-bearing]
彼女は、札付きのうそつきです。Kanojo wa, fudatsuki no usotsuki
desu.   *She's a notorious liar.*

---

fude — 筆 — *writing brush*
fude ga suberu — 筆が滑る — *slip of the pen*
[lit. A writing brush glides.]
筆が滑って、報告書に間違いを書いてしまいました。Fude ga
subette, hōkokusho ni machigai o kaite shimaimashita.   *With a slip of
the pen, I made a mistake in the report.*

fude ga tatsu — 筆が立つ — *to have a gift for literature*
[lit. A writing brush stands out.]
彼女は筆が立つから、大作家になるでしょう。Kanojo wa fude ga
tatsu kara, dai sakka ni naru deshō.   *With her gift for literature, she'll
become a great novelist.*

fude no ayamari — 筆の誤り — *slip of the pen*
[lit. a mistake by a writing brush]
手紙を書くときには、筆の誤りに気をつけなさい。Tegami o kaku
toki niwa, fude no ayamari ni ki o tsukenasai.   *When you write a letter,
be careful not to make any slips of the pen.*

fude o hashiraseru — 筆を走らせる — *to write fast*
[lit. to let a writing brush run]
素晴らしいニュースを急いでお知らせしようと、筆を走らせました。
Subarashii nyūsu o isoide oshirase shiyō to, fude o hashirasemashita.
I wrote quickly to let you know the wonderful news.

fude o ireru — 筆を入れる — *to edit, to correct (writing)*
[lit. to insert a writing brush]
先生は、私の作文にたくさん筆を入れました。Sensei wa, watakushi
no sakubun ni takusan fude o iremashita.   *My teacher made a lot of
corrections in my composition.*

fude o kuwaeru — 筆を加える — *to edit, to refine (writing)*
[lit. to add a writing brush]
報告書を提出する前に、もう一度筆を加えました。Hōkokusho o
teishutsu suru mae ni, mō ichido fude o kuwaemashita.   *Before
submitting the report, I edited it once more.*

fude o oku — 筆を置く — *to stop writing*

[lit. to put down a writing brush]

長い手紙になりましたので、この辺で筆を置きます。Nagai tegami ni narimashita node, kono hen de fude o okimasu. *Since the letter has gotten very long, I'll stop here.*

fude o oru — 筆を折る — *to end one's literary career*
[lit. to break a writing brush]

あの作家は、健康が理由で筆を折りました。Ano sakka wa, kenkō ga riyū de fude o orimashita. *That novelist ended his literary career for reasons of health.*

fude o someru — 筆を染める — *to start writing*
[lit. to dye a writing brush]

良い考えが浮かばないので、まだ筆を染めていません。Ii kangae ga ukabanai node, mada fude o somete imasen. *I can't come up with great ideas, so I haven't started writing yet.*

fude o toru — 筆を執る — *to write*
[lit. to pick up a writing brush]

お願いすることがあって、筆を執りました。Onegai suru koto ga atte, fude o torimashita. *I'm writing to you to ask a favor.*

fudebushō — 筆無精 — *lazy writer*
[lit. lazy with a writing brush]

彼女は筆無精で、旅先からご主人に手紙を書いたことがありません。Kanojo wa fudebushō de, tabisaki kara goshujin ni tegami o kaita koto ga arimasen. *Because she's a lazy writer, she's never written a letter to her husband when she's been away.*

fudemame — 筆まめ — *diligent writer*
[lit. hardworking with a writing brush]

彼女は筆まめで、毎週お母さんに手紙を書きます。Kanojo wa fudemame de, maishū okāsan ni tegami o kakimasu. *She's a diligent writer and writes a letter to her mother every week.*

---

fui — 不意 — *sudden and unexpected*

fui o kuu — 不意を食う — *to be taken by surprise*
[lit. to eat unexpectedness]

突然のお客に不意を食いました。Totsuzen no okyaku ni fui o kuimashita. *I was taken by surprise by a sudden guest.*

fui o tsuku — 不意をつく — *to take someone by surprise*
[lit. to charge at unexpectedness]

競争相手の不意をついて、ビジネスに成功しました。Kyōsō aite no
fui o tsuite, bijinesu ni seikō shimashita. *We succeeded in business by
taking our competitors by surprise.*

fui o utsu — 不意を打つ — *to take someone by surprise*
[lit. to hit unexpectedness]
討論会では他の参加者の不意を打って、勝つことが出来ました。
Tōronkai dewa hoka no sankasha no fui o utte, katsu koto ga dekimashita.
I won the debate by taking the other participants by surprise.

fuiuchi o kuu — 不意打ちを食う — *to be taken by surprise*
[lit. to eat a surprise attack]
彼女は選挙に勝つべきでしたが、不意打ちを食って負けました。
Kanojo wa senkyo ni katsu beki deshita ga, fuiuchi o kutte makemashita.
*She should have won the election but lost because she was taken by
surprise.*

fuku — 腹 — *abdomen, belly*
fukuan — 腹案 — *rough idea*
[lit. a belly idea]
腹案はありますが、本格的な計画はまだです。Fukuan wa arimasu ga,
honkakuteki na keikaku wa mada desu. *I have a rough idea but not a
full-scale plan yet.*

fukushin — 腹心 — *one's confidante*
[lit. a belly and a soul]
彼女は私の腹心で、何でも打ち明けることが出来ます。Kanojo wa
watakushi no fukushin de, nandemo uchiakeru koto ga dekimasu. *She
is my confidante, and I can tell her anything.*

fukuzō no nai — 腹蔵のない — *frank*
[lit. without storing anything in one's belly]
何でも、腹蔵無くお話下さい。Nandemo, fukuzō naku ohanashi
kudasai. *Please say whatever is on your mind.*

fune — 船 — *ship*
norikakatta fune — 乗りかかった船 — *having obligated oneself*
[lit. a ship one is about to board]
乗りかかった船だから、ずっと手伝ってあげましょう。Norikakatta
fune dakara, zutto tetsudatte agemashō. *Since I've obligated myself,
I'll help you see it through.*

ōbune ni notta yō — 大船に乗ったよう — *to be at ease*
[lit. like boarding a big ship]
仕事は彼が手伝ってくれるので、大船に乗ったような気持ちです。
Shigoto wa kare ga tetsudatte kureru node, ōbune ni notta yō na kimochi
desu. *I'm at ease because he's going to help me.*

watari ni fune — 渡りに船 — *chance, opportunity*
[lit. a ship at a ferry landing]
彼女はその申し出に、渡りに船と飛びつきました。Kanojo wa sono
mōshide ni, watari ni fune to tobitsukimashita. *She jumped at the offer
as a great opportunity.*

furoshiki — 風呂敷 — *wrapping cloth*

ōburoshiki o hirogeru — 大風呂敷を広げる — *to brag*
[lit. to spread a big wrapping cloth]
彼はいつも大風呂敷を広げるので、彼の話は信用できません。Kare
wa itsumo ōburoshiki o hirogeru node, kare no hanashi wa shin-yō
dekimasen. *Since he brags all the time, I can't trust his stories.*

fushin — 不審 — *doubt, suspicion*

fushin o idaku — 不審を抱く — *to have a suspicion, to be suspicious*
[lit. to embrace a suspicion]
国民は、政府の動きに不審を抱いています。Kokumin wa, seifu no
ugoki ni fushin o idaite imasu. *The people were suspicious of the move
by the government.*

fushin o kau — 不審を買う — *to incur suspicion*
[lit. to buy suspicion]
あの政治家はインタビューで失言して、不審を買ってしまいました。
Ano seijika wa intabyū de shitsugen shite, fushin o katte shimaimashita.
*That politician incurred suspicion by making a slip of the tongue in an
interview.*

futa — 蓋 — *lid*

futa o akeru — 蓋を開ける — *to start, to open*
[lit. to lift a lid]
野球のシーズンが蓋を開けました。Yakyū no shīzun ga futa o
akemashita. *Baseball season has started.*

futatsu — 二つ — *two*

futatsu ni hitotsu — 二つに一つ — *one way or another*
[lit. one out of two]

行くのかどうか、彼らは二つに一つの返事を迫りました。Iku no ka
dō ka, karera wa futatsu ni hitotsu no henji o semarimashita.   *They
pressed me to give them an answer one way or another about going.*

futatsuhenji — 二つ返事 — *enthusiastic consent*
[lit. two answers]

彼女の招待に、二つ返事で承諾しました。Kanojo no shōtai ni,
futatsuhenji de shōdaku shimashita.   *I readily accepted her
invitation.*

---

futoi — 太い — *thick*

futoi koto — 太いこと — *shameless thing*
[lit. a thick thing]

あの人は太いことを平気でします。Ano hito wa futoi koto o heiki de
shimasu.   *He does shameless things without any concern for the
consequences.*

futoi yatsu — 太い奴 — *shameless fellow*
[lit. a thick fellow]

あれは借りた金を返さない太い奴です。Are wa karita kane o kaesanai
futoi yatsu desu.   *A shameless fellow, he doesn't pay back money he
borrows.*

---

futokoro — 懐 — *pocket, breast*

futokoro ga atatakai — 懐が暖かい — *to have a lot of money*
[lit. One's pocket is warm.]

今日は懐が暖かいから、晩御飯をご馳走してあげましょう。Kyō wa
futokoro ga atatakai kara, bangohan o gochisō shite agemashō.   *I have a
lot of money today, so I'll take you out for dinner.*

futokoro ga fukai — 懐が深い — *to be big-hearted*
[lit. One's breast is deep.]

彼は懐が深いので、何でも話しやすいです。Kare wa futokoro ga
fukai node, nandemo hanashiyasui desu.   *Because he's big-hearted, it's
easy to talk to him about anything.*

futokoro ga itamu — 懐が痛む — *financially burdensome*
[lit. One's pocket hurts.]

先月は思わぬ出費があって、懐が痛みました。Sengetsu wa omowanu shuppi ga atte, futokoro ga itamimashita. *Because of an unexpected expense last month, things were tough financially.*

futokoro ga sabishii — 懐が寂しい — *to be short of money*
[lit. One's pocket is lonely.]
懐が寂しいので、映画を見に行けません。Futokoro ga sabishii node, eiga o mini ikemasen. *I can't go to a movie because I'm short of money.*

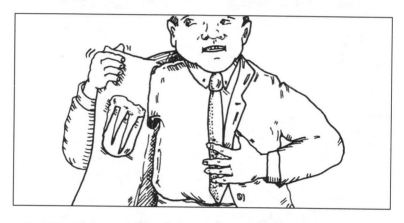

futokoro ga samui — 懐が寒い — *to be short of money*
[lit. One's pocket is cold.]
無駄遣いばかりしていると、すぐに懐が寒くなりますよ。
Mudazukai bakari shite iru to, sugu ni futokoro ga samuku narimasu yo.
If you keep wasting it, you'll be short of money soon.

futokoro o itameru — 懐を痛める — *to suffer financially*
[lit. to hurt one's pocket]
懐を痛めても、子供はぜんぶ大学にやるつもりです。Futokoro o itametemo, kodomo wa zenbu daigaku ni yaru tsumori desu. *Even if I suffer financially, I'll send all my children to college.*

futokoro o koyasu — 懐を肥やす — *to feather one's nest*
[lit. to fatten one's pocket]
彼女は周りの人を犠牲にして、自分の懐を肥やしました。Kanojo wa mawari no hito o gisei ni shite, jibun no futokoro o koyashimashita. *She feathered her nest at the expense of those around her.*

futokorogatana — 懐刀 — one's right-hand man
[lit. a dagger in a pocket]
息子は、有力な政治家の懐刀です。Musuko wa, yūryoku na seijika no
futokorogatana desu.　My son is the right-hand man of an influential
politician.

futokoroguai — 懐具合 — one's financial position
[lit. the state of one's pocket]
やっと、懐具合がよくなってきました。Yatto, futokoroguai ga yoku
natte kimashita.　Finally, my financial position is getting better.

ga — 我 — ego, self
　ga ga tsuyoi — 我が強い — egoistic
　[lit. One's ego is strong.]
　彼女は我が強くて、つき合いづらいです。Kanojo wa ga ga tsuyokute,
　tsukiaizurai desu.　She is egoistic, and it's difficult to be around her.

　ga o haru — 我を張る — to assert oneself
　[lit. to put up one's ego]
　彼は我を張って、誰の意見にも従いませんでした。Kare wa ga o
　hatte, dare no iken nimo shitagaimasen deshita.　He asserted himself
　and followed nobody else's opinions.

　ga o oru — 我を折る — to yield to someone's will
　[lit. to break one's own ego]
　彼女は我を折って、お母さんの意見に従いました。Kanojo wa ga o otte,
　okāsan no iken ni shitagaimashita.　She yielded to her mother's opinion.

　ga o seisuru — 我を制する — to control oneself
　[lit. to limit one's ego]
　理由がないのに非難されて、我を制するのに苦労しました。Riyū ga
　nai noni hinan sarete, ga o seisuru noni kurō shimashita.　Because I
　was criticized for no reason, I had a tough time controlling myself.

　ga o tōsu — 我を通す — to have one's own way
　[lit. to put through one's ego]
　彼は、つまらないことまで我を通そうとします。Kare wa, tsumaranai

koto made ga o tōsō to shimasu.   *He tries to have his own way even for insignificant things.*

---

gara — 柄 — *character, nature*

gara no ii — 柄のいい — *genteel, elegant*
[lit. One's character is fine.]
あの柄のいい女性は、友達のお婆さんです。Ano gara no ii josei wa, tomodachi no obāsan desu.   *That elegant woman is my friend's grandmother.*

gara no warui — 柄の悪い — *vulgar*
[lit. One's character is bad.]
柄の悪い人とは、つき合わない方がいいですよ。Gara no warui hito to wa, tsukiawanai hō ga ii desu yo.   *You'd better not socialize with vulgar people.*

---

gei — 芸 — *performance*

gei ga komakai — 芸が細かい — *to be mindful of details*
[lit. A performance is detailed.]
彼は、何をするにも芸が細かいです。Kare wa, nani o suru nimo gei ga komakai desu.   *He's mindful of details in anything he does.*

gei ga nai — 芸がない — *to lack creativity*
[lit. There is no performance.]
あの人は芸がないから、いつも同じ事ばかりしています。Ano hito wa gei ga nai kara, itsumo onaji koto bakari shite imasu.   *Since he lacks creativity, he does the same things repeatedly.*

---

geijutsu — 芸術 — *art*

geijutsuhada — 芸術肌 — *artistic nature*
[lit. artistic skin]
彼女には、芸術肌の所があります。Kanojo niwa, geijutsu hada no tokoro ga arimasu.   *She has something of an artistic nature.*

---

genkin — 現金 — *cash*

genkin na — 現金な — *calculating*
[lit. cash-like]
あの人は、現金な人です。Ano hito wa, genkin na hito desu.   *He's eager to promote his own interests.*

---

geta — 下駄 — *wooden clogs*

  geta o azukeru — 下駄を預ける — *to leave everything up to someone*
[lit. to check one's wooden clogs in]

最終決定は、彼に下駄を預けました。Saishū kettei wa, kare ni geta o azukemashita. *We left the final decision to him.*

  geta o hakaseru — 下駄を履かせる — *to inflate figures*
[lit. to let someone put wooden clogs on]

まじめな学生の試験の結果には、少し下駄を履かせました。Majime na gakusei no shiken no kekka niwa, sukoshi geta o hakasemashita. *I padded the test scores of the good students a little.*

---

gō — 業 — *someone's action*

  gō o niyasu — 業を煮やす — *to become irritated*
[lit. to boil someone's action]

会議ではつまらないことを討議し続けるので、業を煮やしました。
Kaigi dewa tsumaranai koto o tōgi shitsuzukeru node, gō o niyashimashita. *In the meeting, I became irritated by the long debate over trivial matters.*

---

goma — 胡麻 — *sesame*

  goma o suru — 胡麻を擂る — *to toady, to flatter*
[lit. to grind sesame]

彼は、いつも上役に胡麻を擂っています。Kare wa, itsumo uwayaku ni goma o sutte imasu. *He's constantly flattering his boss.*

  gomashio atama — 胡麻塩頭 — *salt-and-pepper hair*
[lit. sesame-and-salt head]

父はまだ若いのに、もう胡麻塩頭になっています。Chichi wa mada wakai noni, mō gomashio atama ni natte imasu. *Although my father is still young, he already has salt-and-pepper hair.*

  gomasuri — 胡麻擂り — *apple polisher*
[lit. a sesame grinder]

彼女は会社で、胡麻擂りとして知られています。Kanojo wa, kaisha de gomasuri toshite shirarete imasu. *She's known as an apple polisher in the company.*

---

gu — 愚 — *folly*

  gu nimo tsukanai — 愚にもつかない — *absurd*
[lit. to not even reach the level of absurdity]

愚にもつかない言い訳はやめなさい。Gu nimo tsukanai iiwake wa yamenasai.   *Stop making absurd excuses.*

gu no kotchō — 愚の骨頂 — *the height of folly*
[lit. the high point of a bone regarding absurdity]
そんなことをするのは、愚の骨頂ですよ。Sonna koto o suru no wa, gu no kotchō desu yo.   *If you do such a thing, it'll be the height of folly.*

---

gun — 群 — *crowd*
gun o nuku — 群を抜く — *to excel*
[lit. to surpass the crowd]
彼女は、英語にかけては群を抜いています。Kanojo wa, eigo ni kakete wa gun o nuite imasu.   *She excels in English.*

---

gyū — 牛 — *ox*
gyūho — 牛歩 — *snail's pace*
[lit. an ox's walk]
審議は、牛歩で進みました。Shingi wa, gyūho de susumimashita.   *The deliberations progressed at a snail's pace.*

gyūji o toru — 牛耳を執る — *to have a firm grip on something*
[lit. to hold an ox's ear]
あの政治家は、党の防衛政策の牛耳を執っています。Ano seijika wa, tō no bōei seisaku no gyūji o totte imasu.   *That politician has a firm grip on the defense policy of his party.*

gyūjiru — 牛耳る — *to control*
[lit. to grab an ox's ear]
極端な意見を持つ人が、クラブを牛耳っています。Kyokutan na iken o motsu hito ga, kurabu o gyūjitte imasu.   *Those with the most extreme opinions are controlling our club.*

---

ha — 歯 — *tooth, teeth*
ha ga tatanai — 歯が立たない — *to be no match for, not able to handle something*

[lit. to be unable to sink one's teeth into something]

テニスでは、彼に歯が立ちません。 Tenisu dewa, kare ni ha ga tachimasen. *As far as tennis is concerned, I'm no match for him.*

ha ga uku — 歯が浮く — *nauseating*
[lit. to loosen one's teeth]

あの人の話を聞くと、いつも歯が浮きます。 Ano hito no hanashi o kiku to, itsumo ha ga ukimasu. *His talk is always nauseating.*

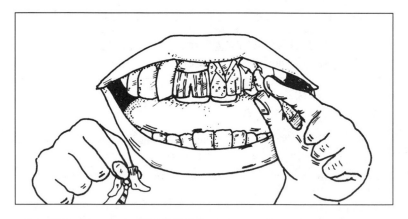

ha ni kinu kisenu — 歯に衣着せぬ — *to not mince words*
[lit. to not put clothes on one's teeth]

彼は誰に対しても、歯に衣を着せません。 Kare wa dare ni taishite mo, ha ni kinu o kisemasen. *He doesn't mince words with anybody.*

ha no nuketayō — 歯の抜けたよう — *deserted*
[lit. as if some teeth are missing]

地元のチームが負けてばかりいるので、球場は歯が抜けたようです。 Jimoto no chīmu ga makete bakari iru node, kyūjō wa ha ga nuketa yō desu. *Since the local team has been losing, the ball park has a lot of empty seats.*

hagayui — 歯痒い — *to feel impatient*
[lit. One's teeth itch.]

彼の仕事があまり遅いので、見ていると歯痒くなります。 Kare no shigoto ga amari osoi node, mite iru to hagayuku narimasu. *Because he works so slowly, watching him makes me feel impatient.*

hagishiri suru — 歯ぎしりする — *to be mortified at something*
[lit. to grind one's teeth]
勝てるはずの試合に負けて、歯ぎしりしてしまいました。Kateru
hazu no shiai ni makete, hagishiri shite shimaimashita.   *I was mortified
at losing the game we should have won.*

hagotae ga aru — 歯ごたえがある — *tough*
[lit. There is resistance to one's teeth.]
もっと歯ごたえがある仕事がしてみたいです。Motto hagotae ga aru
shigoto ga shitemitai desu.   *I'd like to try tougher work.*

hagotae ga nai — 歯ごたえがない — *too easy*
[lit. There is no resistance to one's teeth.]
歯ごたえがない仕事は、したくありません。 Hagotae ga nai shigoto
wa, shitaku arimasen.   *I don't want to do work that's too easy.*

---

haba — 幅 — *width, range*

haba ga kiku — 幅が利く — *to be influential*
[lit. One's range is effective.]
あの学者は、保守的な政治家の間で幅が利いています。Ano gakusha
wa, hoshuteki na seijika no aida de haba ga kiite imasu.   *That scholar is
influential among the conservative politicians.*

haba o kikaseru — 幅を利かせる — *to carry a lot of weight, to be powerful*
[lit. to make one's range effective]
あのビジネスマンは、そこの地方政治で幅を利かせています。Ano
bijinesuman wa, soko no chihō seiji de haba o kikasete imasu.   *That
businessman carries a lot of weight in local politics there.*

---

haburi — 羽振り — *flapping of wings*

haburi ga ii — 羽振りがいい — *to be popular, to have money or power*
[lit. The flapping of wings is great.]
あの歌手は、中年の男性の間で羽振りがいいです。Ano kashu wa,
chūnen no dansei no aida de haburi ga ii desu.   *That singer is popular
among middle-aged men.*

haburi o kikaseru — 羽振りを利かせる — *to exercise one's influence*
[lit. to apply the flapping of wings]
この町で、何事にも羽振りを利かせているのがあの人です。Kono
machi de, nanigoto nimo haburi o kikasete iru no ga ano hito desu.   *He
is the man who exercises his influence over everything in this town.*

hada — 肌 — *skin*

hada de kanjiru — 肌で感じる — *to have first-hand experience*
[lit. to feel it with one's own skin]

コンピュータは役に立つ道具であることを肌で感じました。

Konpyūta wa yaku ni tatsu dōgu dearu koto o hada de kanjimashita.

I have first-hand experience that the computer is a useful tool.

hada ga au — 肌が合う — *to get along well*
[lit. The skin matches.]

彼は彼女と肌が合います。Kare wa kanojo to hada ga aimasu. 　*He gets along well with her.*

hada ga awanai — 肌が合わない — *to not get along well*
[lit. The skin does not match.]

彼女とは、全然肌が合いません。Kanojo to wa, zenzen hada ga aimasen. 　*I can't get along well with her at all.*

hitohada nugu — 一肌脱ぐ — *to help*
[lit. to take off one's skin]

親友が契約を取るために、一肌脱ぎました。Shin-yū ga keiyaku o toru tame ni, hitohada nugimashita. 　*I helped my best friend to win the contract.*

---

hadaka — 裸 — *naked body*

hadaka ikkan de — 裸一貫で — *starting from scratch*
[lit. thoroughly naked]

彼は巨額の富を、裸一貫から築き上げました。Kare wa kyogaku no tomi o, hadaka ikkan kara kizukiagemashita. 　*He built an enormous fortune starting from scratch.*

hadaka ni naru — 裸になる — *to go broke*
[lit. to become naked]

彼は賭事に夢中になって、すっかり裸になってしまいました。Kare wa kakegoto ni muchū ni natte, sukkari hadaka ni natte shimaimashita. *He went crazy gambling and went totally broke.*

---

haji — 恥 — *shame, humiliation, disgrace, dishonor*

haji no uwanuri — 恥の上塗り — *to incur further disgrace*
[lit. to apply a second coat of disgrace over the first one]

自分の失敗なのに人を非難するなんて、恥の上塗りです。Jibun no shippai nanoni hito o hinan suru nante, haji no uwanuri desu. 　*It's a further disgrace to blame others for your own mistakes.*

haji o kakaseru — 恥をかかせる — *to humiliate someone*
[lit. to make someone's shame surface]
傲慢な奴に人前で恥をかかせて、いい気持ちがしました。Gōman na
yatsu ni hitomae de haji o kakasete, ii kimochi ga shimashita.   *It felt
good to humiliate the arrogant scoundrel in front of everyone.*

haji o kaku — 恥をかく — *to disgrace oneself*
[lit. to make one's own shame surface]
社長を掃除夫と間違えて、恥をかきました。Shachō o sōjifu to
machigaete, haji o kakimashita.   *I disgraced myself by mistaking the
president for a janitor.*

haji o sarasu — 恥をさらす — *to make a spectacle of oneself*
[lit. to expose one's own shame]
彼は友達の結婚披露宴で酔っぱらって、恥をさらしました。Kare
wa tomodachi no kekkon hirōen de yopparatte, haji o sarashimashita.
*He made a spectacle of himself by getting drunk at his friend's wedding
reception.*

haji o shinobu — 恥を忍ぶ — *to suppress one's shame*
[lit. to endure one's own shame]
恥を忍んで、友達の親からお金を借りました。Haji o shinonde,
tomodachi no oya kara okane o karimashita.   *Suppressing my shame, I
borrowed money from my friend's parents.*

haji o shiranai — 恥を知らない — *shameless*
[lit. to not know shame]
あの人は恥を知らずに、いつも人の悪口ばかり言っています。Ano
hito wa haji o shirazuni, itsumo hito no warukuchi bakari itte imasu.
She's always badmouthing other people shamelessly.

haji o shiru hito — 恥を知る人 — *honorable person*
[lit. a person who knows what shame is]
彼女は恥を知る人だから、信頼できます。Kanojo wa haji o shiru hito
dakara, shinrai dekimasu.   *We can trust her because she is an
honorable person.*

haji o sosogu — 恥をそそぐ — *to clear one's name*
[lit. to wash one's own shame]
非難が間違っていることを証明して、恥をそそぎました。Hinan ga
machigatte iru koto o shōmei shite, haji o sosogimashita.   *By proving
that the charges against me were wrong, I cleared my name.*

hajisarashi — 恥さらし — *disgrace*
[lit. exposing one's own shame]
そんなことをすると家族の恥さらしになるからやめなさい。Sonna
koto o suru to kazoku no hajisarashi ni naru kara yamenasai.   *Stop
doing such things, or you'll disgrace your family.*

hajishirazu — 恥知らず — *shameless person*
[lit. someone who is not aware of his or her own shame]
あの人は、自分の家族の面倒を見ない恥知らずです。Ano hito wa,
jibun no kazoku no mendō o minai hajishirazu desu.   *He is a shameless
person who doesn't take care of his own family.*

haku — 箔 — *foil, leaf, tinsel*
haku ga ochiru — 箔が落ちる — *to lose some prestige*
[lit. The tinsel falls.]
首相は公約が果たせなくて、箔が落ちてしまいました。Shushō wa
kōyaku ga hatasenakute, haku ga ochite shimaimashita.   *The prime
minister lost some prestige when he couldn't keep his public pledge.*

haku ga tsuku — 箔がつく — *to gain prestige*
[lit. The tinsel is put on someone.]
先生は博士号を取って、箔がつきました。Sensei wa hakasegō o totte,
haku ga tsukimashita.   *My teacher gained prestige by getting a Ph.D.*

hakuhyō — 薄氷 — *thin ice*
hakuhyō o fumu — 薄氷を踏む — *to be on thin ice*
[lit. to step on thin ice]
上司に昇給を頼みに行くのに、薄氷を踏む思いをしました。Jōshi ni
shōkyū o tanomini iku noni, hakuhyō o fumu omoi o shimashita.   *I felt
as if I were on thin ice when I went to see my boss to ask for a raise.*

hakusha — 拍車 — *spur*
hakusha o kakeru — 拍車を掛ける — *to give impetus to something*
[lit. to spur]
相次ぐスキャンダルが、政治改革運動に拍車をかけています。
Aitsugu sukyandaru ga, seiji kaikaku undō ni hakusha o kakete imasu.
A series of scandals is giving impetus to a political reform movement.

hakushi — 白紙 — *blank paper*

hakushi ni modosu — 白紙に戻す — *to go back to the drawing board*
[lit. to put something back on a blank paper]

計画は条件が変わったため、白紙に戻すことにしました。Keikaku
wa jōken ga kawatta tame, hakushi ni modosu koto ni shimashita.
*Because conditions changed, we decided to go back to the drawing
board.*

hame — 羽目 — *paneling*

hame o hazusu — 羽目を外す — *to make a racket*
[lit. to detach paneling]

パーティーを開くのはいいけれど、羽目を外さないようにしなさい。
Pātī o hiraku no wa ii keredo, hame o hazusanai yō ni shinasai. *It's all
right to have a party, but don't make a racket.*

hamon — 波紋 — *ripple*

hamon o tōjiru — 波紋を投じる — *to create a stir*
[lit. to cast a ripple]

大蔵省の声明が、財界に波紋を投じました。Ōkurashō no seimei ga,
zaikai ni hamon o tōjimashita. *The statement by the Finance Ministry
created a stir in the financial world.*

han — 判 — *seal, stamp*

han de oshita yō ni — 判で押したように — *like clockwork*
[lit. just like affixing a seal]

彼女は毎朝、判で押したように七時に家を出ます。Kanojo wa
maiasa, han de oshita yō ni shichiji ni ie o demasu. *Like clockwork,
she leaves her home every morning at seven.*

hana — 花 — *flower*

hana ga saku — 花が咲く — *to grow, to develop, to thrive*
[lit. A flower blooms.]

彼との友情に花が咲きました。Kare to no yūjō ni hana ga sakimashita.
My friendship with him grew.

hana mo mi mo aru — 花も実もある — *warmhearted*
[lit. There are both flowers and fruit.]

彼は花も実もある人として尊敬されています。Kare wa hana mo mi

mo aru hito toshite sonkei sarete imasu.   *He's respected for being warmhearted.*

hana o chirasu — 花を散らす — *to die young*
[lit. to let a flower go]
友達は二十二歳で花を散らしました。Tomodachi wa nijūni sai de hana o chirashimashita.   *My friend died when she was 22 years old.*

hana o motaseru — 花を持たせる — *to give someone the credit for something*
[lit. to let someone have flowers]
事業の成功について、社長は奥さんに花を持たせました。Jigyō no seikō ni tsuite, shachō wa okusan ni hana o motasemashita.   *The president gave his wife the credit for his successful business.*

hana o sakaseru — 花を咲かせる — *to attain success*
[lit. to let a flower bloom]
彼女は十五歳の時、音楽界ですでに花を咲かせました。Kanojo wa jūgo sai no toki, ongaku kai de sude ni hana o sakasemashita.   *When she was 15 years old, she had already attained success in the music world.*

hanamichi o kazaru — 花道を飾る — *to make a graceful exit (retirement)*
[lit. to decorate a runway]
あの選手は最後の試合でホームランを打って、花道を飾りました。Ano senshu wa saigo no shiai de hōmuran o utte, hanamichi o kazarimashita.   *That player made a graceful exit by hitting a home run in his last game.*

hanashi ni hana ga saku — 話に花が咲く — *to have a lively conversation*
[lit. Flowers bloom in a conversation.]
友達との話に花が咲きました。Tomodachi tono hanashi ni hana ga sakimashita.   *I had a lively conversation with my friends.*

iwanu ga hana — 言わぬが花 — *It's better left unsaid.*
[lit. Saying nothing is the flower.]
それを彼女に言いたいかも知れないけれど、言わぬが花ですよ。Sore o kanojo ni iitai kamoshirenai keredo, iwanu ga hana desu yo.   *You may want to tell her that, but it's better left unsaid.*

ryōte ni hana — 両手に花 — *to be doubly blessed*
[lit. to have a flower in each hand]
彼は素晴らしい奥さんといい仕事を持って、両手に花です。Kare

wa subarashii okusan to ii shigoto o motte, ryōte ni hana desu. *He's doubly blessed because he has a wonderful wife and a great job.*

takane no hana — 高嶺の花 — *beyond one's reach*
[lit. a flower on a high mountain]
彼女は良家の出身で、私にとっては高嶺の花です。Kanojo wa ryōke no shusshin de, watakushi ni totte wa takane no hana desu. *Because she's from an upper-class family, she's beyond my reach.*

---

hana — 鼻 — *nose*
hana de ashirau — 鼻であしらう — *to turn up one's nose at something*
[lit. to treat someone with one's nose]
夫は妻の願いを鼻であしらいました。Otto wa tsuma no negai o hana de ashiraimashita. *The husband turned up his nose at his wife's wishes.*

hana de warau — 鼻で笑う — *to snicker*
[lit. to laugh with one's nose]
聴衆は、政治家の言い訳を鼻で笑いました。Chōshū wa, seijika no iiwake o hana de waraimashita. *The audience snickered at the politician's excuses.*

hana ga takai — 鼻が高い — *to be proud*
[lit. One's nose is high.]
お嬢さんが医者になって、鼻が高いでしょう。Ojōsan ga isha ni natte, hana ga takai deshō. *You must be proud that your daughter has become a doctor!*

hana ni kakeru — 鼻に掛ける — *to be vain*
[lit. to hang something on one's nose]
彼は家族が金持ちなのを鼻にかけています。Kare wa kazoku ga kanemochi nano o hana ni kakete imasu. *He's vain about his family's wealth.*

hana ni tsuku — 鼻につく — *to be disgusting, to stink*
[lit. to assail one's nose]
彼女の図々しさは鼻につきます。Kanojo no zūzūshisa wa hana ni tsukimasu. *Her pushiness is disgusting.*

hana no sa de — 鼻の差で — *by a nose*
[lit. with the difference of a nose]
この前の選挙では、運良く鼻の差で勝ちました。Kono mae no senkyo dewa, un yoku hana no sa de kachimashita. *In the last election, luckily, I won by a nose.*

hana no saki — 鼻の先 — *very close*
[lit. the tip of a nose]
その店は、すぐ鼻の先です。Sono mise wa, sugu hana no saki desu.
That shop is very close to here.

hana no shita ga nagai — 鼻の下が長い — *to be lewd toward women*
[lit. The space below a nose is long.]
彼は、鼻の下が長いのが大欠点です。Kare wa, hana no shita ga nagai
no ga dai ketten desu.   *His big shortcoming is lewdness toward women.*

hana o akasu — 鼻を明かす — *to succeed despite others' low
expectations*
[lit. to make someone's nose open]
一流の会社に入って、回りの鼻を明かしました。Ichiryū no kaisha ni
haitte, mawari no hana o akashimashita.   *I surprised everyone when I
was hired by a top company.*

hana o narasu — 鼻を鳴らす — *to sweet-talk someone*
[lit. to speak through the nose]
ガールフレンドは、鼻を鳴らして指輪をねだりました。Gārufurendo
wa, hana o narashite yubiwa o nedarimashita.   *My girlfriend tried to
sweet-talk me into buying her a ring.*

hana o oru — 鼻を折る — *to mortify, to take someone down a peg*
[lit. to break someone's nose]
あの高慢な男の鼻を折る機会をうかがっています。Ano kōman na
otoko no hana o oru kikai o ukagatte imasu.   *I'm looking for an
opportunity to take the guy down a peg or two.*

hana o takakusuru — 鼻を高くする — *to brag, to boast*
[lit. to make one's own nose taller]
彼は大した成功ではないのに、鼻を高くしています。Kare wa
taishita seikō dewa nai noni, hana o takaku shite imasu.   *He's bragging
over nothing.*

hana o tsukiawaseru — 鼻を突き合わせる — *to be face to face*
[lit. to bring one's nose against someone's]
彼と鼻を突き合わせて相談しました。Kare to hana o tsukiawasete
sōdan shimashita.   *I consulted with him face to face.*

hanamochi naranai — 鼻持ちならない — *appalling*
[lit. to stink even when holding one's nose]
彼女の無神経さは鼻持ちなりません。Kanojo no mushinkeisa wa
hanamochi narimasen.   *Her insensitivity is appalling.*

hanatsumami — 鼻摘まみ — *a nuisance*
[lit. someone for whom one holds one's nose]
彼は会社で鼻摘まみになっています。Kare wa kaisha de hanatsumami
ni natte imasu. *He is a nuisance in our company.*

hana — はな — *nasal mucus*
　hana mo hikkakenai — はなも引っかけない — *to ignore someone or
　something*
　[lit. to not even dash nasal mucus on someone]
　彼女はお金のない人には、はなも引っかけません。Kanojo wa okane no
　nai hito niwa, hana mo hikkakemasen. *She ignores men who aren't rich.*

hanabashira — 鼻柱 — *bridge of a nose*
　hanabashira ga tsuyoi — 鼻柱が強い — *obstinate*
　[lit. The bridge of a nose is strong.]
　彼は新入社員なのに、鼻柱が強いです。Kare wa shinnyū shain
　nanoni, hanabashira ga tsuyoi desu. *Although he's a new employee,
　he's obstinate.*

　hanabashira o oru — 鼻柱を折る — *to humiliate someone*
　[lit. to break the bridge of someone's nose]
　討論で高慢な男の鼻柱を折って、すっきりしました。Tōron de
　kōman na otoko no hanabashira o otte, sukkiri shimashita. *It felt good
　to humiliate the arrogant guy in the debate.*

hanage — 鼻毛 — *hair of the nostrils*
　hanage o nuku — 鼻毛を抜く — *to dupe someone*
　[lit. to pull the hair out of someone's nostrils]
　彼は人の鼻毛を抜きかねない男だから、気をつけなさい。
　Kare wa hito no hanage o nukikanenai otoko dakara, ki o
　tsukenasai. *Be careful of him; he can dupe anyone.*

hanagusuri — 鼻薬 — *nose medicine*
　hanagusuri o kikaseru — 鼻薬を効かせる — *to grease someone's palm*
　[lit. to make nose medicine effective]
　彼は政治家に鼻薬を効かせて、建築許可をもらいました。Kare wa
　seijika ni hanagusuri o kikasete, kenchiku kyoka o moraimashita. *He
　obtained the building permit by greasing a politician's palm.*

hanaiki — 鼻息 — *breathing through the nose*
hanaiki ga arai — 鼻息が荒い — *to be keyed up*
[lit. One's breathing through the nose is heavy.]
友達は明日の試合に勝つのだと、鼻息が荒いです。Tomodachi wa
ashita no shiai ni katsu no da to, hanaiki ga arai desu.   *My friend is all
keyed up to win the game tomorrow.*

hanaiki o ukagau — 鼻息をうかがう — *to curry favor with someone*
[lit. to look out for someone's breathing through the nose]
彼はいつも上役の鼻息をうかがっています。Kare wa itsumo uwayaku
no hanaiki o ukagatte imasu.   *He's always currying favor with his boss.*

---

hanashi — 話 — *talk*
hanashi ga au — 話が合う — *to find each other's company enjoyable*
[lit. The talk fits.]
彼女と私は話がよく合います。Kanojo to watakushi wa hanashi ga
yoku aimasu.   *She and I find each other's company enjoyable.*

hanashi ga hayai — 話が早い — *easy to get to the point*
[lit. The talk is fast.]
あなたも同じ考えなら、話が早いです。Anata mo onaji kangae nara,
hanashi ga hayai desu.   *If your idea is the same as mine, it'll be easy to
get to the point.*

hanashi ga hazumu — 話が弾む — *The conversation becomes lively.*
[lit. The talk bounces.]
久しぶりに友達にあって、話が弾みました。Hisashiburi ni tomodachi
ni atte, hanashi ga hazumimashita.   *I met my friend after a long time,
and the conversation got lively.*

hanashi ga kamiawanai — 話がかみ合わない — *to not go anywhere*
[lit. The talk doesn't engage one.]
いくら交渉しても、話がかみ合いませんでした。Ikura kōshō
shitemo, hanashi ga kamiaimasen deshita.   *No matter how much we
negotiated, it didn't go anywhere.*

hanashi ga ochiru — 話が落ちる — *The talk becomes lewd.*
[lit. The talk falls.]
話が落ちてきたので、席を外しました。Hanashi ga ochite kita node,
seki o hazushimashita.   *Because the talk became lewd, I left the table.*

hanashi ga tsuku — 話がつく — *to come to an agreement*
[lit. The talk arrives.]

交渉は簡単に話がつきました。Kōshō wa kantan ni hanashi ga tsukimashita. *We easily came to an agreement in the negotiations.*

hanashi ga wakaru — 話が分かる — *sensible*
[lit. to understand the talk]

彼女は話が分かるから、何でも相談できます。Kanojo wa hanashi ga wakaru kara, nandemo sōdan dekimasu. *Since she is sensible, you can consult with her about anything.*

hanashi ni mi ga hairu — 話に実が入る — *to be engrossed in a story*
[lit. A fruit enters the talk.]

友達との話に実が入って、家に帰るのが遅くなりました。
Tomodachi to no hanashi ni mi ga haitte, ie ni kaeru no ga osoku narimashita. *Because I was engrossed in conversation with my friend, I was late going back home.*

hanashi ni naranai — 話にならない — *to be out of the question*
[lit. to not become talk]

車を買いたくても、それだけのお金では話になりません。Kuruma o kaitakutemo, sore dake no okane dewa hanashi ni narimasen. *You may want to buy a car, but with that little money, it's out of the question.*

hanashi ni noru — 話に乗る — *to counsel*
[lit. to ride the talk]

仕事のことで話に乗ってもらえますか。Shigoto no koto de hanashi ni notte moraemasu ka. *Would you counsel me about a job?*

hanashi no tane — 話の種 — *topic of conversation*
[lit. the seed of a talk]

それはここでの話の種として、相応しくありません。Sore wa koko de no hanashi no tane to shite, fusawashiku arimasen. *That isn't suitable as a topic of a conversation here.*

hanashi o tsukeru — 話をつける — *to settle something*
[lit. to fix the talk]

話をつけるために、妥協しました。Hanashi o tsukeru tame ni, dakyo shimashita. *To settle the matter, I compromised.*

hanashihanbun — 話半分 — *to take something with a grain of salt*
[lit. half of the talk]

彼は彼女の説明を話半分で聞きました。Kare wa kanojo no setsumei o hanashihanbun de kikimashita. *He listened to her explanation with a grain of salt.*

hayai hanashi ga — 早い話が — *to make a long story short*
[lit. A fast story is . . . .]
早い話が、結果は良かったという事です。Hayai hanashi ga, kekka wa
yokatta to iu koto desu.   *To make a long story short, it turned out to be
fine.*

hane — 羽 — *feather, wing*
hane ga haeta yō ni — 羽が生えたように — *like hot cakes*
[lit. as if wings spring up]
この本は、羽が生えたように売れています。Kono hon wa, hane ga
haeta yō ni urete imasu.   *This book is selling like hot cakes.*

hane o nobasu — 羽を伸ばす — *to kick up one's heels*
[lit. to spread one's wings]
父がいないので、羽を伸ばしています。Chichi ga inai node, hane o
nobashite imasu.   *With my father away, I'm kicking up my heels.*

hanjō — 半畳 — *half a tatami mat*
hanjō o ireru — 半畳を入れる — *to interrupt*
[lit. to throw in half a tatami mat]
人が深刻な話をしているとき、半畳を入れてはなりません。Hito ga
shinkoku na hanashi o shite iru toki, hanjō o irete wa narimasen.   *Don't
interrupt when others are talking about serious matters.*

hanki — 反旗 — *standard of revolt*
hanki o hirugaesu — 反旗を翻す — *to rise in revolt*
[lit. to unfurl the standard of revolt]
学生は厳しい学校の規則に反旗を翻しました。Gakusei wa kibishii
gakkō no kisoku ni hanki o hirugaeshimashita.   *The students rose in
revolt against the rigid school regulations.*

happa — 発破 — *blasting*
happa o kakeru — 発破をかける — *to urge someone on*
[lit. to set dynamite]
先生はもっと勉強するように、生徒に発破をかけました。Sensei wa
motto benkyō suru yō ni, seito ni happa o kakemashita.   *The teacher
urged the pupils on to study harder.*

happō — 八方 — all directions

happōbijin — 八方美人 — a sycophant
[lit. a beauty to all eight directions]
彼は八方美人だから、本音が分かりません。 Kare wa happōbijin
dakara, honne ga wakarimasen.　　Since he is a sycophant, you don't
know his true intentions.

happōfusagari — 八方塞がり — in a fix
[lit. all directions being closed]
借金がたまって、八方塞がりの状態です。 Shakkin ga tamatte,
happōfusagari no jōtai desu.　　Since I've accumulated so much debt,
now I'm in a fix.

---

hara — 腹 — abdomen, belly, stomach

hara ga dekiru — 腹ができる — to be resolved
[lit. One's belly is ready.]
やっと、大学院へ行く腹ができました。 Yatto, daigakuin e iku hara ga
dekimashita.　　Finally, I'm resolved to go to graduate school.

hara ga fukureru — 腹が膨れる — to get frustrated (from keeping quiet)
[lit. One's belly balloons.]
言いたい意見が言えないで、腹が膨れました。 Iitai iken ga ienai de,
hara ga fukuremashita.　　Because I couldn't say what I wanted to, I got
frustrated.

hara ga futoi — 腹が太い — big-hearted
[lit. One's belly is thick.]
彼は腹が太いから、人が失敗しても咎めません。 Kare wa hara ga
futoi kara, hito ga shippai shitemo togamemasen.　　Since he's big-
hearted, he doesn't blame people even if they make mistakes.

hara ga ieru — 腹がいえる — anger to subside
[lit. One's belly gets cured.]
彼女に対して腹がいえるのに、一ヶ月かかりました。 Kanojo ni
taishite hara ga ieru no ni, ikkagetsu kakarimashita.　　It took an entire
month for my anger toward her to subside.

hara ga kudaru — 腹が下る — to have diarrhea
[lit. One's stomach comes down.]
キャンプで腹が下ったのは、水のせいでした。 Kyanpu de hara ga
kudatta no wa, mizu no sei deshita.　　The water was the cause of
diarrhea on the camping trip.

hara ga kuroi — 腹が黒い — *deceitful*
[lit. One's belly is black.]
あの人は親切そうでも、実は腹がとても黒いです。Ano hito wa
shinsetsu sō demo, jitsu wa hara ga totemo kuroi desu.   *She looks kind,
but she's actually quite deceitful.*

hara ga kusatta — 腹が腐った — *despicable*
[lit. One's belly is rotten.]
彼は、金儲けしか興味のない腹が腐った人間です。Kare wa, kane
mōke shika kyōmi no nai hara ga kusatta ningen desu.   *He is a
despicable person who doesn't care about anything but making money.*

hara ga miesuku — 腹が見え透く — *One's true intentions are obvious.*
[lit. One's belly is transparent.]
どんなにお世辞を言っても、彼の腹は見え透いています。Donna ni
oseji o ittemo, kare no hara wa miesuite imasu.   *No matter how much
he flatters me, his true intentions are obvious.*

hara ga niekurikaeru — 腹が煮えくり返る — *to be furious*
[lit. One's belly boils over.]
汚職の疑いをかけられて、腹が煮えくり返っています。Oshoku no
utagai o kakerarete, hara ga niekurikaette imasu.   *I'm furious that I was
suspected of corruption.*

hara ga ōkii — 腹が大きい — *generous*
[lit. One's belly is big.]
彼は腹が大きい人で、頼み事はいつでも聞いてくれます。Kare wa

hara ga ōkii hito de, tanomigoto wa itsudemo kiite kuremasu.   *He is a generous person, and he always agrees to my requests.*

hara ga osamaru — 腹が収まる — *to calm down*
[lit. One's stomach is restored.]
彼に憤慨していましたが、謝ったので腹が収まりました。Kare ni fungai shite imashita ga, ayamatta node hara ga osamarimashita.   *I was very angry with him, but I calmed down when he apologized.*

hara ga suwaru — 腹が据わる — *to become bolder*
[lit. One's stomach is set.]
一度それをやる決心をしたら、腹が据わりました。Ichido sore o yaru kesshin o shitara, hara ga suwarimashita.   *Once I decided to do it, I became bolder.*

hara ga tatsu — 腹が立つ — *to be angry*
[lit. One's belly stands up.]
彼の嘘には、本当に腹が立ちます。Kare no uso niwa, hontō ni hara ga tachimasu.   *I'm really angry about his lie.*

hara ni ichimotsu aru — 腹に一物有る — *to have an ulterior motive*
[lit. There's something in someone's belly.]
あの男には、腹に一物ありそうです。Ano otoko niwa, hara ni ichimotsu arisō desu.   *He seems to have an ulterior motive.*

hara ni suekaneru — 腹に据えかねる — *hard to take*
[lit. to be unable to set something in one's belly]
息子の怠け癖は、腹に据えかねます。Musuko no namakeguse wa, hara ni suekanemasu.   *It's hard to take my son's laziness.*

hara no kawa ga yojireru — 腹の皮がよじれる — *to nearly die laughing*
[lit. One's stomach skin is distorted.]
彼女の滑稽な話に、腹の皮がよじれました。Kanojo no kokkei na hanashi ni, hara no kawa ga yojiremashita.   *I nearly died laughing at her hilarious story.*

hara no mushi ga osamaranai — 腹の虫が治まらない — *One's anger doesn't subside.*
[lit. Worms in one's belly don't calm down.]
理由もなく非難されて、腹の虫が治まりません。 Riyū mo naku hinan sarete, hara no mushi ga osamarimasen.   *Since I was wrongly accused, my anger won't go away.*

hara o awaseru — 腹を合わせる — *to conspire*

[lit. to put one's belly with someone's]

あの二人は腹を合わせて、社長を失脚させました。Ano futari wa hara o awasete, shachō o shikkyaku sasemashita.   *Those two conspired for the president's downfall.*

hara o eguru — 腹をえぐる — *penetrating, piercing*
[lit. to gouge someone's belly]

腹をえぐる質問に、ちょっと答えが詰まりました。Hara o eguru shitsumon ni, chotto kotae ga tsumarimashita.   *I was momentarily at a loss for an answer to a penetrating question.*

hara o itameta ko — 腹を痛めた子 — *one's own child*
[lit. a child who pained one's own abdomen]

腹を痛めた子なのに、ちっとも親に似ていません。Hara o itameta ko nanoni, chittomo oya ni nite imasen.   *Although she's my own child, she doesn't bear any resemblance to me.*

hara o iyasu — 腹をいやす — *to get revenge*
[lit. to cure one's belly]

この前負けたチ－ムに今度は大勝して、腹をいやしました。Kono mae maketa chīmu ni kondo wa taishō shite, hara o iyashimashita.   *By winning big, we got our revenge against the team that had defeated us before.*

hara o kakaeru — 腹を抱える — *to laugh one's head off*
[lit. to embrace one's own belly]

とてもおかしくて、腹を抱えずにはいられませんでした。Totemo okashikute, hara o kakaezu niwa iraremasen deshita.   *It was so funny that I laughed my head off.*

hara o katameru — 腹を固める — *to set one's mind*
[lit. to tighten one's belly]

アメリカに行って、英語を勉強する腹を固めました。Amerika ni itte, eigo o benkyō suru hara o katamemashita.   *I set my mind to go to the United States and study English.*

hara o kimeru — 腹を決める — *to be resolved*
[lit. to decide on something in one's belly]

彼女は離婚する腹を決めました。Kanojo wa rikon suru hara o kimemashita.   *She was resolved to divorce her husband.*

hara o kiru — 腹を切る — *to take responsibility and resign*
[lit. to cut one's belly]

会社の業績が低下したら、腹を切るつもりです。Kaisha no gyōseki ga teika shitara, hara o kiru tsumori desu.   If the company's performance declines, I'll take responsibility and resign.

hara o koshiraeru — 腹をこしらえる — to eat
[lit. to build one's stomach]
仕事を始める前に、腹をこしらえましょう。Shigoto o hajimeru mae ni, hara o koshiraemashō.   Let's eat before starting to work.

hara o koyasu — 腹を肥やす — to feather one's own nest
[lit. to make one's belly fat]
彼は慈善事業を運営する振りをしながら、腹を肥やしました。Kare wa jizenjigyō o un-ei suru furi o shinagara, hara o koyashimashita.   He feathered his own nest while pretending to run a charitable organization.

hara o kukuru — 腹をくくる — to be determined
[lit. to fasten one's belly]
その仕事は、腹をくくってやらないと出来ませんよ。Sono shigoto wa, hara o kukutte yaranai to dekimasen yo.   You can't complete the work unless you show some determination.

hara o minuku — 腹を見抜く — to see through someone's scheme
[lit. to see through someone's belly]
彼の滑らかな言葉にかかわらず、腹を見抜くことが出来ました。Kare no nameraka na kotoba ni kakawarazu, hara o minuku koto ga dekimashita.   In spite of his smooth talk, I could see through his scheme.

hara o mirareru — 腹を見られる — to have one's thoughts found out
[lit. one's belly being seen]
宴会で、早く帰りたい腹を見られてしまいました。Enkai de, hayaku kaeritai hara o mirarete shimaimashita.   At the party, it was detected that I wanted to leave early.

hara o misukasu — 腹を見透かす — to read someone's mind
[lit. to see through someone's belly]
彼は複雑な人で、腹を見透かすのは容易ではありません。Kare wa fukuzatsu na hito de, hara o misukasu nowa yōi dewa arimasen.   Since he's quite complex, it isn't easy to read his mind.

hara o saguru — 腹を探る — to feel someone out
[lit. to search someone's belly]

交渉では、双方とも相手の腹を探ろうとしました。Kōshō dewa,
sōhō tomo aite no hara o sagurō to shimashita.   *In the negotiations,*
both sides tried to feel each other out.

hara o sueru — 腹を据える — *to be prepared*
[lit. to set one's belly]
この一年は、一生懸命勉強する腹を据えました。Kono ichinen wa,
isshōkenmei benkyō suru hara o suemashita.   *I'm prepared to study*
hard for one year.

hara o tateru — 腹を立てる — *to get mad*
[lit. to make one's belly stand up]
彼は彼女がまた約束を破ったので、腹を立てました。Kare wa kanojo
ga mata yakusoku o yabutta node, hara o tatemashita.   *He got mad at*
her because she broke her promise again.

hara o watte — 腹を割って — *frankly*
[lit. by cutting one's belly open]
私たちは、腹を割って話し合いました。Watakushitachi wa, hara o
watte hanashiaimashita.   *We talked frankly to each other.*

hara o yomu — 腹を読む — *to read someone's mind*
[lit. to read someone's belly]
あの人の腹を読むのは、容易ではありません。Ano hito no hara o
yomu no wa, yōi dewa arimasen.   *It's not easy to read his mind.*

harachigai no — 腹違いの — *half-siblings with different mothers*
[lit. by a different belly]

これが、私の腹違いの妹です。Kore ga, watakushi no harachigai no imōto desu. *This is my half-sister.*

haradachimagire ni — 腹立ち紛れに — *in a fit of anger*
[lit. in the chaos of a belly standing up]
腹立ち紛れに、言うべきでないことを言ってしまいました。
Haradachimagire ni, iu beki de nai koto o itte shimaimashita. *In a fit of anger, I said what I shouldn't have.*

haragei — 腹芸 — *maneuvering skills*
[lit. a belly act]
彼は腹芸で、論争を解決しました。Kare wa haragei de, ronsō o kaiketsu shimashita. *He solved the dispute by applying his maneuvering skills.*

haraguroi — 腹黒い — *wicked*
[lit. black-bellied]
あの人は腹黒いから気をつけなさい。Ano hito wa haraguroi kara ki o tsukenasai. *Be careful of him; he's wicked.*

haraise — 腹いせ — *to vent one's anger*
[lit. to press one's belly]
彼女がデートを断ったので、彼は悪口を言って腹いせをしています。
Kanojo ga dēto o kotowatta node, kare wa warukuchi o itte haraise o shite imasu. *Since she turned him down for a date, he's venting his anger by badmouthing her.*

haratsuzumi o utsu — 腹鼓を打つ — *to eat to one's heart's content*
[lit. to beat a belly drum]
イタリアに行ったとき、毎日毎日腹鼓を打ちました。Itaria ni itta toki, mainichi mainichi haratsuzumi o uchimashita. *When I visited Italy, I ate to my heart's content every day.*

katahara itai — 片腹痛い — *ridiculous*
[lit. The side of one's stomach hurts.]
彼が勤勉を説くなんて片腹痛いです。Kare ga kinben o toku nante katahara itai desu. *It's ridiculous for him to preach hard work.*

mukappara o tateru — 向かっ腹を立てる — *to lose one's temper*
[lit. to make a confrontational belly stand up]
あの人はすぐに向かっ腹を立てます。Ano hito wa sugu ni mukappara o tatemasu. *He loses his temper easily.*

harawata — 腸 — *intestines*
  harawata ga chigireru — 腸がちぎれる — *heartbroken*
  [lit. One's intestines are torn.]
  子供に死なれて、実に腸がちぎれる思いです。Kodomo ni shinarete,
  jitsu ni harawata ga chigireru omoi desu.   *Since my child died, I've
  been completely heartbroken.*
  harawata ga kakimushirareru — 腸がかきむしられる — *heartrending*
  [lit. to get one's intestines scratched]
  腸がかきむしられる知らせを、友達から聞きました。Harawata ga
  kakimushirareru shirase o, tomodachi kara kikimashita.   *I heard the
  heartrending news from my friend.*
  harawata ga kusaru — 腸が腐る — *morally corrupt*
  [lit. One's intestines are rotten.]
  彼は女性をだまして平気な、腸が腐った男です。Kare wa josei o
  damashite heiki na, harawata ga kusatta otoko desu.   *He's a morally
  corrupt scoundrel who deceives women without any concern.*
  harawata ga miesuku — 腸が見え透く — *Someone's motive is obvious.*
  [lit. to see through someone's intestines]
  彼女は親切な振りをしていても、腸が見え透いています。Kanojo
  wa shinsetsu na furi o shite itemo, harawata ga miesuite imasu.   *She's
  pretending to be kind, but her motive is obvious.*
  harawata ga niekurikaeru — 腸が煮えくり返る — *to become infuriated*
  [lit. One's intestines boil over.]
  汚職の疑いをかけられて、腸が煮えくり返りました。Oshoku no
  utagai o kakerarete, harawata ga niekurikaerimashita.   *I became
  infuriated because I was suspected of corruption.*
  harawata o tatsu — 腸を断つ — *to break one's heart*
  [lit. to sever one's intestines]
  そのニュースを聞いて、腸を断つ思いでした。Sono nyūsu o kiite,
  harawata o tatsu omoi deshita.   *I felt like my heart was breaking after
  hearing that news.*

hare — 晴れ — *fine weather*
  hare no — 晴れの — *best, formal*
  [lit. fine weather]
  晴れの場に、晴れ着を着て行きました。Hare no ba ni, haregi o kite
  ikimashita.   *I wore my best dress for a formal occasion.*

harebaresuru — 晴れ晴れする — *to feel relieved*
[lit. to become clear]
期末試験が終わって、晴れ晴れした気持ちです。Kimatsu shiken ga
owatte, harebare shita kimochi desu. *I feel relieved at finishing the
final exams.*

haregamashii — 晴れがましい — *radiant*
[lit. feeling like fine weather]
娘の結婚式で、両親は晴れがましそうでした。Musume no
kekkonshiki de, ryōshin wa haregamashisō deshita. *The parents looked
radiant at their daughter's wedding.*

haregi — 晴れ着 — *one's best clothes*
[lit. fine-weather clothes]
招待状によると、そのパーティーには晴れ着を着る必要がありそう
です。Shōtaijō ni yoru to, sono pātī niwa haregi o kiru hitsuyō ga arisō
desu. *According to the invitation, I may need to wear my best clothes
to the party.*

hareru — 晴れる — *to dissipate, to clear up*
[lit. The weather becomes fine.]
説明を聞いて、彼女に対する疑いが晴れました。Setsumei o kiite,
kanojo ni taisuru utagai ga haremashita. *As I listened to her
explanation, my suspicions about her dissipated.*

hareyaka na — 晴れやかな — *bright, cheerful*
[lit. like fine weather]
部屋は、晴れやかな雰囲気にあふれていました。Heya wa, hareyaka
na fun-iki ni afurete imashita. *The room was filled with a cheerful
atmosphere.*

---

haremono — 腫れ物 — *swelling*

haremono ni fureru yō ni — 腫れ物に触るように — *gingerly*
[lit. like touching a swelling]
社長は非常に気短なので、腫れ物に触れるように接しています。
Shachō wa hijō ni kimijika nanode, haremono ni fureru yō ni sesshite
imasu. *Since the president is short-tempered, we're dealing with him
gingerly.*

---

hari — 針 — *needle*

hari no aru — 針のある — *accusatory, harsh*

[lit. There is a needle.]

妻は夫を針のある目つきで見つめました。Tsuma wa otto o hari no aru
metsuki de mitsumemashita.   *The wife stared at her husband with*
accusatory eyes.

hari no mushiro ni suwaru omoi — 針の筵に座る思い — *to be painful*
(emotionally)
[lit. feeling like sitting on a mat made of needles]

全て自分の責任だと思うと、針の筵に座る思いです。Subete jibun no
sekinin da to omou to, hari no mushiro ni suwaru omoi desu.   *When I*
think of how it was all my fault, it's painful.

hari o fukunda kotoba — 針を含んだ言葉 — *nasty tone*
[lit. words containing needles]

彼の機嫌が悪いのは、針を含んだ言葉から明らかでした。Kare no
kigen ga warui no wa, hari o fukunda kotoba kara akiraka deshita.   *It*
was obvious from his nasty tone that he was upset.

---

hashi — 箸 — *chopsticks*

hashi ga susumu — 箸が進む — *to eat a lot*
[lit. chopsticks to proceed]

素晴らしいご馳走で、箸が進みました。Subarashii gochisō de, hashi
ga susumimashita.   *Since it was a wonderful meal, I ate a lot.*

hashi nimo bō nimo kakaranai — 箸にも棒にもかからない — *no*
good, dubious
[lit. not making contact with even chopsticks or a stick]

彼は、箸にも棒にもかからない人です。Kare wa, hashi nimo bō nimo
kakaranai hito desu.   *He's no good.*

hashi no ageoroshi — 箸の上げ下ろし — *trivial matters*
[lit. the picking up and putting down of chopsticks]

彼女は、箸の上げ下ろしにも口うるさい人です。Kanojo wa hashi no
ageoroshi nimo kuchiurusai hito desu.   *She criticizes everyone, even for*
trivial matters.

hashi o toru — 箸を取る — *to start eating*
[lit. to pick up chopsticks]

どうぞ、箸をお取り下さい。Dōzo, hashi o otori kudasai.   *Please*
begin.

hashi o tsukeru — 箸をつける — *to eat*
[lit. to touch food with chopsticks]

あの外国人は、刺身に箸をつけませんでした。Ano gaikokujin wa, sashimi ni hashi o tsukemasen deshita. *The foreigner didn't eat raw fish.*

---

hashi — 橋 — *bridge*
abunai hashi o wataru — 危ない橋を渡る — *to take risks*
[lit. to cross a dangerous bridge]
金儲けのためには、危ない橋も渡りました。Kane mōke no tame niwa, abunai hashi mo watarimashita. *I took risks to make big bucks.*

hashiwatashi — 橋渡し — *mediation*
[lit. construction of a bridge]
経営者と組合の間には、橋渡しが必要でした。Keieisha to kumiai no aida niwa, hashiwatashi ga hitsuyō deshita. *Mediation between management and the labor union was necessary.*

---

hashigo — 梯子 — *ladder*
hashigo suru — 梯子する — *to go bar-hopping*
[lit. to try a ladder]
夫は今晩もまた梯子をしているようです。Otto wa konban mo mata hashigo o shite iru yō desu. *My husband may be out bar-hopping again tonight.*

---

hata — 旗 — *flag*
hata o ageru — 旗を揚げる — *to start a business*
[lit. to hoist a flag]
彼は旗を揚げる準備をしています。Kare wa hata o ageru junbi o shite imasu. *He's preparing to start a business.*

hata o furu — 旗を振る — *to lead*
[lit. to wave a flag]
彼女は消費者団体の旗を振っています。Kanojo wa shōhisha dantai no hata o futte imasu. *She's leading a consumer group.*

hata o maku — 旗を巻く — *to withdraw, to close down*
[lit. to furl a flag]
シカゴに支店を出しましたが、三年で旗を巻きました。Shikago ni shiten o dashimashita ga, san nen de hata o makimashita. *We opened a branch office in Chicago but closed it down after three years.*

hataage — 旗揚げ — *inauguration, beginning*
[lit. raising of a flag]

あの政治家は、新政党の旗揚げを目指しています。Ano seijika wa, shin seitō no hataage o mezashite imasu. *That politician is aiming at the inauguration of a new political party.*

hatafuri — 旗振り — *leader*
[lit. a flagman]
彼は政治改革の旗振りです。Kare wa seiji kaikaku no hatafuri desu.
He is a leader for political reform.

hitohata ageru — 一旗揚げる — *to try one's fortune, to make it*
[lit. to hoist a flag]
彼は一旗揚げるために東京に来ました。Kare wa hitohata ageru tame ni Tōkyō ni kimashita. *He came to Tokyo to try his fortune.*

---

hatairo — 旗色 — *situation*
hatairo ga ii — 旗色がいい — *The odds of winning are favorable.*
[lit. The color of the banner is good.]
この選挙では、保守的な候補者の旗色がいいです。Kono senkyo dewa, hoshuteki na kōhosha no hatairo ga ii desu. *In this election, the odds of winning are in the conservative candidate's favor.*

hatairo ga warui — 旗色が悪い — *The odds of winning are unfavorable.*
[lit. The color of the banner is bad.]
販売競争では、わが社の旗色が悪いです。Hanbai kyōsō dewa, waga sha no hatairo ga warui desu. *In the sales competition, the chances of our company's winning are slim.*

hatairo o miru — 旗色を見る — *to sit on the fence*
[lit. to observe the color of the banner]
どちらの候補者を支持するか決める前、しばらく旗色を見ましょう。
Dochira no kōhosha o shiji suru ka kimeru mae, shibaraku hatairo o mimashō. *Let's sit on the fence awhile before deciding which candidate to support.*

---

hatake — 畑 — *farm*
hatake ga chigau — 畑が違う — *outside one's specialty*
[lit. A farm is different.]
その企画は、畑が違うので苦労しました。Sono kikaku wa, hatake ga chigau node kurō shimashita. *I had a tough time with the project because it was outside my specialty.*

he — 屁 — *fart (vulgar)*

he demo nai — 屁でもない — *nothing, so easy*
[lit. not even a fart]
そんなことするのは、屁でもない。Sonna koto suru nowa, he demo
nai. *That's so easy for me to do.*

he no kappa — 屁の河童 — *cinch*
[lit. a river imp's fart]
マラソンなんて屁の河童だ。Marason nante he no kappa da. *Running
a marathon is a cinch.*

he tomo omowanai — 屁とも思わない — *to think nothing of something*
[lit. to not even think it's a fart]
あの生徒は、遅刻しても屁とも思いません。Ano seito wa, chikoku
shitemo he tomo omoimasen. *That pupil thinks nothing of being late
for school.*

herikutsu o koneru — 屁理屈をこねる — *to quibble*
[lit. to knead fart-like logic]
彼は屁理屈をこねるので、誰も彼と話したがりません。Kare wa
herikutsu o koneru node, daremo kare to hanashitagarimasen. *Since he
quibbles, nobody wants to talk to him.*

---

hedate — 隔て — *partition*

hedate no aru — 隔てのある — *cold, distant*
[lit. There is a partition.]
彼女は隔てのある態度で、彼に応対しました。Kanojo wa hedate no
aru taido de, kare ni ōtai shimashita. *She received him coldly.*

hedate o tsukeru — 隔てをつける — *to discriminate*
[lit. to set up a partition]
着ている物によって、人に隔てをつけてはなりません。Kiteiru
mono ni yotte, hito ni hedate o tsuketewa narimasen. *You shouldn't
discriminate against people because of what they're wearing.*

---

heikō sen — 平行線 — *parallel lines*

heikō sen o tadoru — 平行線をたどる — *There is no progress.*
[lit. to follow parallel lines]
交渉は平行線をたどりました。Kōshō wa heikō sen o tadorimashita.
There was no progress in the negotiations.

---

henji — 返事 — *answer, reply*

futatsu henji de — 二つ返事で — *eagerly, readily*
[lit. with two answers]

その申し出を、二つ返事で引き受けました。Sono mōshide o, futatsu henji de hikiukemashita.   *I eagerly accepted the offer.*

nama henji — 生返事 — *lukewarm reply*
[lit. an uncooked answer]

彼女を映画に誘いましたが、生返事しかしませんでした。Kanojo o eiga ni sasoimashita ga, nama henji shika shimasen deshita.   *I invited her to a movie, but she gave me a lukewarm reply.*

henrin — 片鱗 — *part, glimpse*

henrin o nozokaseru — 片鱗をのぞかせる — *to show a glimpse of something*
[lit. to show a bit of dragon scale]

この子は、音楽の才能の片鱗をのぞかせています。Kono ko wa, ongaku no sainō no henrin o nozokasete imasu.   *This child is showing a glimpse of her musical talent.*

herazuguchi — 減らず口 — *bad loser's retort*

herazuguchi o tataku — 減らず口をたたく — *to retort defensively*
[lit. to drum a never-ending mouth]

減らず口をたたかないで、奥さんが正しいことを認めなさい。
Herazuguchi o tatakanai de, okusan ga tadashii koto o mitomenasai. *Rather than retorting defensively, you should admit that your wife is right.*

heso — 臍 — *navel*

heso ga cha o wakasu — 臍が茶を沸かす — *laughable*
[lit. One's navel boils tea.]

彼が映画俳優になりたいなんて、臍が茶を沸かします。Kare ga eiga haiyū ni naritai nante, heso ga cha o wakashimasu. *His wanting to become a movie actor is laughable.*

heso o mageru — へそを曲げる — *to sulk*
[lit. to twist one's navel]

彼女は演じたかった役を人に取られて、臍を曲げています。Kanojo wa enjitakatta yaku o hito ni torarete, heso o magete imasu. *She's sulking because somebody got the role she wanted.*

hesokuri — 臍繰り — *secret savings*
[lit. to reckon with one's own navel]

彼の奥さんはこの五年、臍繰りをしています。Kare no okusan wa kono go nen, hesokuri o shite imasu. *His wife has been secretly saving money for the last five years.*

hesomagari — へそ曲がり — *someone perverse*
[lit. a twisted navel]

彼はへそ曲がりだから、まともに話せません。Kare wa hesomagari dakara, matomo ni hanasemasen. *Since he's so perverse, I can't be straightforward with him.*

hi — 日 — *sun*

hi no ataru basho — 日の当たる場所 — *charmed position*
[lit. a sunny spot]
彼は、日の当たる場所から日の当たる場所へ渡ってきました。Kare wa, hi no ataru basho kara hi no ataru basho e watatte kimashita. *He's been moving from one charmed position to another.*

hi no me o miru — 日の目を見る — *to gain public recognition*
[lit. to see the eyes of the sun]
あの歌手は、やっと日の目を見ることが出来ました。Ano kashu wa, yatto hi no me o miru koto ga dekimashita. *That singer was finally able to gain public recognition.*

hinode no ikioi — 日の出の勢い — *One's star is ascending.*
[lit. the vigor of the rising sun]
あの政治家は、近頃日の出の勢いです。Ano seijika wa, chikagoro hinode no ikioi desu. *Recently, that politician's star has been ascending.*

---

hi — 火 — *fire*

hi ga tsuku — 火がつく — *to catch fire (figuratively)*
[lit. A fire starts.]
地震の後、政府の対応について論争に火がつきました。Jishin no ato, seifu no taiō ni tsuite ronsō ni hi ga tsukimashita. *After the earthquake, the debate over the government's response caught fire.*

hi ni abura o sosogu — 火に油を注ぐ — *to make things worse*
[lit. to pour oil over fire]
お父さんが怒っているから、火に油を注がないように黙っていなさい。Otōsan ga okotte iru kara, hi ni abura o sosoganai yō ni damatte inasai. *Since your father is angry, keep your mouth shut and don't make things worse.*

hi no deru yō na — 火の出るような — *intense*
[lit. as if flames will come out]
二人は、火の出るような恋の末に結婚しました。Futari wa, hi no deru yō na koi no sue ni kekkon shimashita. *After an intense love affair, they got married.*

hi no kieta yō — 火の消えたよう — *to be deserted, to stand still*
[lit. as if fire went out]
このビジネス街は、週末には火の消えたようになります。Kono

bijinesu gai wa, shūmatsu niwa hi no kieta yō ni narimasu.   *This business district becomes deserted on the weekend.*

hi no tsuita yō — 火の付いたよう — *frantic*
[lit. like catching fire]
年度末を控えて、経理部は今、火のついたような状態です。Nendo matsu o hikaete, keiribu wa ima, hi no tsuita yō na jōtai desu.   *With the end of the fiscal year approaching, the accounting office is frantic.*

hi o fuku — 火を噴く — *to erupt*
[lit. to spew fire]
製造業者の価格操作に、消費者の怒りが火を噴きました。Seizō gyōsha no kakaku sōsa ni, shōhisha no ikari ga hi o fukimashita.   *The consumers' anger at the manufacturers' price manipulation erupted.*

hi o miru yorimo akiraka — 火を見るよりも明らか — *as plain as day*
[lit. clearer than seeing fire]
彼のビジネスが失敗することは、火を見るよりも明らかでした。
Kare no bijinesu ga shippai suru koto wa, hi o miru yorimo akiraka deshita.   *It was as plain as day that his business would fail.*

hi o tōsu — 火を通す — *to heat food thoroughly*
[lit. to let heat go through]
その残り物は、火を通した方がおいしいです。Sono nokorimono wa, hi o tōshita hō ga oishii desu.   *If you heat the leftovers thoroughly, they'll taste better.*

hi o tsukeru — 火をつける — *to trigger something*
[lit. to set fire]
彼の頑固な意見が、口論の火をつけました。Kare no ganko na iken ga, kōron no hi o tsukemashita.   *His headstrong opinion triggered the argument.*

hinokuruma — 火の車 — *to be in financial straits*
[lit. a wheel of fire]
わが家は、毎月火の車です。Wagaya wa, maitsuki hinokuruma desu.
Our family is in financial straits every month.

hinote ga agaru — 火の手が上がる — *to spark*
[lit. to burst into flame]
マスコミの無責任さに、批判の火の手が上がりました。Masukomi no musekininsa ni, hihan no hinote ga agarimashita.   *The media's irresponsibility has sparked criticism.*

hibana — 火花 — *spark*
  hibana o chirasu — 火花を散らす — *to fight tooth and nail*
  [lit. to scatter sparks]
  この前の選挙では、候補者は互いに火花を散らしました。Kono mae
  no senkyo dewa, kōhosha wa tagai ni hibana o chirashimashita. *In the*
  last election, the candidates fought among themselves tooth and nail.

hibi — ひび — *crack*
  hibi ga hairu — ひびが入る — *to go sour*
  [lit. A crack appears.]
  つまらないことが原因で、長年の友情にひびが入ってしまいました。
  Tsumaranai koto ga gen-in de, naganen no yūjō ni hibi ga haitte
  shimaimashita. *Our long-term friendship went sour over something*
  insignificant.

hibuta — 火蓋 — *lid of a musket pan*
  hibuta o kiru — 火蓋を切る — *to launch*
  [lit. to open the lid of a musket pan]
  政党が、増税についての論争の火蓋を切りました。Seitō ga, zōzei ni
  tsuite no ronsō no hibuta o kirimashita. *The political parties launched*
  a discussion about the tax increase.

hidari — 左 — *left*
  hidarikiki — 左利き — *a drinker*
  [lit. good with the left hand]
  彼は左利きだから、ココアよりビールの方がいいでしょう。Kare
  wa hidarikiki dakara, kokoa yori bīru no hō ga ii deshō. *Since he likes*
  to drink, beer would be better than hot chocolate.

  hidarimae — 左前 — *financial difficulty*
  [lit. left side front]
  あの店は左前で、今にも潰れそうです。Ano mise wa hidarimae de,
  ima nimo tsuburesō desu. *That store is losing money, and it looks like*
  it'll go under anytime.

  hidarimaki — 左巻き — *nut, crackpot*
  [lit. counterclockwise]
  あの左巻きの言うことなんか、聞く必要ありません。Ano hidarimaki
  no iu koto nanka, kiku hitsuyō arimasen. *You don't need to listen to*
  what that crackpot says.

hidariuchiwa — 左うちわ — easy life with no work
[lit. a fan in one's left hand]
彼は親の金に頼って、左うちわで暮らしています。Kare wa oya no
kane ni tayotte, hidariuchiwa de kurashite imasu.   He's living an easy
life relying on his parents' money.

hiji — 肘 — elbow
hijideppō o kuwasu — 肘鉄砲を食わす — to rebuff, to snub
[lit. to hit someone with a weapon-like elbow]
彼は彼女にデートを申し込んで、肘鉄砲を食わされました。Kare
wa kanojo ni dēto o mōshikonde, hijideppō o kuwasaremashita.   He
was rebuffed when he asked her for a date.

hikage — 日陰 — shade
hikage no mi — 日陰の — someone in obscurity, social outcast
[lit. someone in shade]
今は日陰の身でも、努力すれば成功します。Ima wa hikage no mi
demo, doryoku sureba seikō shimasu.   You may not be known now, but
if you work at it you can be successful.
彼は汚職の疑いで辞職してから、日陰の身です。Kare wa oshoku no
utagai de jishoku shite kara, hikage no mi desu.   He's been a social
outcast since resigning from his job under suspicion of corruption.

hikari — 光 — light
oya no hikari — 親の光 — the influential position of a parent
[lit. the light of a parent]
彼女は親の光ではなく、自分で成功しました。Kanojo wa oya no
hikari dewa naku, jibun de seikō shimashita.   She made it by herself,
not as the daughter of an influential parent.

hike — 引け — defeat, closing
hike o toranai — 引けを取らない — to compare favorably with someone
[lit. not to get behind]
日本の歴史にかけては、誰にも引けを取りません。Nihon no rekishi
ni kakete wa, dare nimo hike o torimasen.   My knowledge of Japanese
history compares favorably with anyone's.

hike o toru — 引けを取る — to be beaten
[lit. to pick up a defeat]

橋の建設の入札では、競争相手に引けを取ってしまいました。Hashi
no kensetsu no nyūsatsu dewa, kyōsō aite ni hike o totte shimaimashita.
We were beaten by our competitor in the bidding on the bridge
construction.

hikedoki — 引け時 — *quitting time*
[lit. the time for closing]
引け時までに、今の仕事を終えて下さい。Hikedoki made ni, ima no
shigoto o oete kudasai.   *Please finish your work by quitting time.*

hikeme — 引け目 — *inferiority*
[lit. the experience of a defeat]
他の出席者に比べて、自分の経験に引け目を感じました。Hoka no
shussekisha ni kurabete, jibun no keiken ni hikeme o kanjimashita.   *I*
felt inferior about my experience compared to that of the other participants.

---

hikeshi — 火消し — *fire fighter*
hikeshiyaku — 火消し役 — *troubleshooter*
[lit. the role of a fire fighter]
火消し役が要るなら、彼に頼みなさい。Hikeshiyaku ga iru nara, kare
ni tanominasai.   *If you need a troubleshooter, ask him.*

---

hiki — 引き — *pull*
hikimokirazu — 引きも切らず — *immediately*
[lit. without interrupting a pull]
出張から帰って、引きも切らずに新しい企画に手を付けました。
Shutchō kara kaette, hikimokirazu ni atarashii kikaku ni te o
tsukemashita.   *Back from the business trip, I immediately undertook a*
new project.

---

hiku — 引く — *to pull, to retreat*
hiku ni hikenai — 引くに引けない — *no choice but to stay put*
[lit. not able to retreat]
私がその案の提案者なので、今さら引くに引けません。Watakushi
ga sono an no teiansha nanode, imasara hiku ni hikemasen.   *Since I'm*
the one who proposed the plan, I have no choice but to stay put.

hikute amata — 引く手あまた — *many suitors*
[lit. a lot of pulling hands]
彼は引く手あまたで、どの仕事を選ぶか迷っています。Kare wa

hikute amata de, dono shigoto o erabuka mayotte imasu. *With many suitors after him with job offers, he's having trouble choosing one.*

---

hima — 暇 — *time*

hima ni akasete — 暇に飽かせて — *using all one's free time*
[lit. using time to the extent that one gets weary]
暇に飽かせて、小説をたくさん読んでいます。Hima ni akasete, shōsetsu o takusan yonde imasu. *I've been using all my free time to read novels.*

hima o dasu — 暇を出す — *to fire*
[lit. to give time]
あの店員は欠勤が多すぎるので、暇を出しました。Ano ten-in wa kekkin ga ōsugiru node, hima o dashimashita. *Because that salesclerk was absent too often, I fired him.*

hima o nusumu — 暇を盗む — *to make good use of one's free time*
[lit. to steal time]
暇を盗んで、コンピュータの勉強をしています。Hima o nusunde, konpyūta no benkyō o shite imasu. *To make good use of my free time, I'm studying computers.*

hima o saku — 暇を割く — *to find time*
[lit. to cut time out]
忙しかったけれど、暇を割いて彼女の話を聞いてあげました。Isogashikatta keredo, hima o saite kanojo no hanashi o kiite agemashita. *Although I was busy, I found time to listen to her story.*

hima o tsubusu — 暇をつぶす — *to kill time*
[lit. to squash time]
暇を潰すために、映画を見に行きました。Hima o tsubusu tame ni, eiga o mini ikimashita. *To kill time, I went to see a movie.*

himadoru — 暇取る — *to take much time*
[lit. to take up time]
報告書は、調査に思ったより暇取りました。Hōkokusho wa, chōsa ni omotta yori himadorimashita. *The research for the report took much more time than I expected.*

---

hipparu   引っ張る   *to pull*

hipparidako — 引っ張りだこ — *to be much sought after*
[lit. a kite being pulled]

あの弁護士は決して負けないので、ビジネス界で引っ張りだこです。
Ano bengoshi wa kesshite makenai node, bijinesu kai de hipparidako
desu. *Because that lawyer never loses a lawsuit, he's much sought
after in the business world.*

---

hirou — 拾う — *to pick up*
  hiroimono — 拾い物 — *a lucky find*
  [lit. a found article]
  この間のみの市で買った絵は、本当に拾い物でした。Kono aida
  nominoichi de katta e wa, hontō ni hiroimono deshita. *The painting I
  bought at the flea market was truly a lucky find.*

  hiroiyomi — 拾い読み — *to skim through a book*
  [lit. to pick up and read here and there]
  面白い本でしたが、時間がないので拾い読みしました。Omoshiroi
  hon deshita ga, jikan ga nai node hiroiyomi shimashita. *Although the
  book was interesting, I didn't have much time, so I skimmed through it.*

---

hitai — 額 — *forehead*
  hitai ni ase shite hataraku — 額に汗して働く — *to work hard*
  [lit. to work with the sweat on one's forehead]
  彼は車を買うために、額に汗して働きました。Kare wa kuruma o kau
  tame ni, hitai ni ase shite hatarakimashita. *He worked hard to buy a car.*

  hitai o atsumeru — 額を集める — *to huddle together, to put heads
  together*
  [lit. to put people's foreheads together]
  問題を急いで解決するために、額を集めて相談しました。Mondai o
  isoide kaiketsu suru tame ni, hitai o atsumete sōdan shimashita. *We put
  our heads together and conferred to solve the problem quickly.*

---

hito — 人 — *person*
  hito no ii — 人の良い — *good-natured*
  [lit. Someone is good.]
  彼は人の良さから、みんなに好かれています。Kare wa hito no yosa
  kara, minna ni sukarete imasu. *Everybody likes him for his good
  nature.*

  hito no warui — 人の悪い — *bad-natured, unpleasant*
  [lit. Someone is bad.]

彼女は人の悪さで知られています。Kanojo wa hito no warusa de
shirarete imasu.   *She is known for her unpleasant personality.*

hito o kutta — 人を食った — *contemptuous*
[lit. to have eaten a man]
彼の人を食った態度に、みんなが怒りました。Kare no hito o kutta
taido ni, minna ga okorimashita.   *Everyone got angry at his
contemptuous attitude.*

hito o miru mei — 人を見る明 — *good judge of character*
[lit. the wisdom to look at someone]
彼には人を見る明がないので、いつも苦労しています。Kare niwa
hito o miru mei ga nai node, itsumo kurō shite imasu.   *Because he's not
a good judge of character, he's always in trouble.*

hitoatari — 人当たり — *mannered*
[lit. touching someone]
彼は、人当たりがとても穏やかです。Kare wa, hitoatari ga totemo
odayaka desu.   *He is very gentle mannered.*

hitodenashi — 人で無し — *brute*
[lit. not human]
彼は人で無しで、欲しい物を手に入れるには何事もためらいません。
Kare wa hitodenashi de, hoshii mono o te ni ireru niwa nanigoto mo
tameraimasen.   *He's such a brute that he'll stop at nothing to get what
he wants.*

hitogaki — 人垣 — *a throng*
[lit. a fence of people]

交通事故の現場には、すぐに人垣が出来ました。Kōtsū jiko no genba niwa, sugu ni hitogaki ga dekimashita. *A throng immediately gathered at the site of the traffic accident.*

hitoichibai — 人一倍 — *much more than others*
[lit. twice as much as others]
彼は人一倍食べます。Kare wa hitoichibai tabemasu. *He eats much more than other people do.*

hitojichi — 人質 — *hostage*
[lit. a human pawn]
新聞の一面に、人質事件の記事が出ていました。Shinbun no ichi men ni, hitojichi jiken no kiji ga dete imashita. *The front page of the newspaper had an article about the hostage incident.*

hitome ni amaru — 人目に余る — *excessive*
[lit. too much for one's eyes]
彼の最近の振る舞いは、人目に余ります。Kare no saikin no furumai wa, hitome ni amarimasu. *His recent behavior is excessive.*

hitome ni tsuku — 人目に付く — *to attract attention*
[lit. to attach to people's eyes]
彼女の服装は、どこでも人目に付きます。Kanojo no fukusō wa, doko demo hitome ni tsukimasu. *Her clothes attract attention wherever she goes.*

hitome o habakaru — 人目をはばかる — *shady*
[lit. to be afraid of people's eyes]
彼は、人目をはばかる商売をしているそうです。Kare wa, hitome o habakaru shōbai o shite iru sō desu. *I hear that he's in a shady business.*

hitome o nusunde — 人目を盗んで — *covertly*
[lit. by stealing people's eyes]
人目を盗んで質屋へ行きました。Hitome o nusunde shichiya e ikimashita. *I went to a pawnshop covertly.*

hitome o shinonde — 人目を忍んで — *secretly*
[lit. to avoid people's eyes]
彼女と、人目を忍んでつき合っています。Kanojo to, hitome o shinonde tsukiatte imasu. *I've been going out with her secretly.*

hitonami hazureta — 人並み外れた — *unusual*
[lit. beyond average people]

彼は、人並み外れた食欲を持っています。Kare wa, hitonami hazureta shokuyoku o motte imasu. *He has an unusually large appetite.*

hitonami sugureta — 人並み優れた — *extraordinary*
[lit. surpassing average people]
彼は数学では、人並み優れた才能を持っています。Kare wa sūgaku dewa, hitonami sugureta sainō o motte imasu. *He has an extraordinary talent for mathematics.*

hitosawagase o suru — 人騒がせをする — *to trigger a false alarm*
[lit. to disturb people]
先日は人騒がせをして、まことに申し訳ありませんでした。Senjitsu wa hitosawagase o shite, makoto ni mōshiwake arimasen deshita. *I'm truly sorry for causing a false alarm the other day.*

hitozute ni — 人伝に — *indirectly*
[lit. through someone]
人伝に、彼が離婚したのを知りました。Hitozute ni, kare ga rikon shita no o shirimashita. *I heard indirectly that he was divorced.*

hito — 一 — *one*
hitoashi osaki ni — 一足お先に — *before someone*
[lit. one leg ahead]
一足お先に失礼します。Hitoashi osaki ni shitsurei shimasu. *Excuse me for leaving before you.*

hitoawa fukaseru — 一泡吹かせる — *to get someone rattled*
[lit. to let someone foam at the mouth]
討論で、彼に一泡吹かせました。Tōron de, kare ni hitoawa fukasemashita. *I got him rattled in the debate.*

hitohada nugu — 一肌脱ぐ — *to give someone some help*
[lit. to take off one's own skin]
彼が事業を始めるために、一肌脱いであげました。Kare ga jigyō o hajimeru tame ni, hitohada nuide agemashita. *I gave him some help starting his own business.*

hitohana sakaseru — 一花咲かせる — *to attain success*
[lit. to let a flower bloom]
彼は不動産への投機で、一花咲かせました。Kare wa fudōsan e no tōki de, hitohana sakasemashita. *He attained success by speculating in real estate.*

hitohata ageru — 一旗揚げる — *to make it, to try one's fortune*
[lit. to raise a flag]
彼女はファッションの世界で一旗揚げるため、パリに行きました。
Kanojo wa fasshon no sekai de hitohata ageru tame, Pari ni ikimashita.
She went to Paris to make it in the fashion industry.

hitohone oru — 一骨折る — *to make a special effort for someone*
[lit. to break a bone]
息子の就職のために、友達が一骨折ってくれました。Musuko no
shūshoku no tame ni, tomodachi ga hitohone otte kuremashita.
My friend made a special effort to help my son find a job.

hitoiki ireru — 一息入れる — *to take a short rest*
[lit. to let a breath in]
ここで一息入れましょうか。Koko de hitoiki iremashō ka.   *Shall we
take a short rest now?*

hitoiki tsuku — 一息つく — *to have breathing space*
[lit. to take a breath]
中間試験が終わったので、ちょっと一息ついています。Chūkan
shiken ga owatta node, chotto hitoiki tsuite imasu.   *With midterm
exams over, I'm having a little breathing space.*

hitokuchi noru — 一口乗る — *to join in something*
[lit. to take a mouthful]
この企画に、一口乗っていただきたいのですが。Kono kikaku ni,
hitokuchi notte itadakitai no desu ga.   *We would like you to join in this
project.*

hitokuse arisō na — 一癖有りそうな — *sinister-looking*
[lit. to appear to have a vice]
彼は一癖ありそうですが、実は親切で正直です。Kare wa hitokuse
arisō desu ga, jitsu wa shinsetsu de shōjiki desu.   *He seems like a
sinister person, but in reality, he's kind and honest.*

hitomebore — 一目惚れ — *love at first sight*
[lit. love at a glance]
彼は、彼女に一目惚れしてしまいました。
Kare wa, kanojo ni hitomebore shite shimaimashita.
He fell in love with her at first sight.

hitoshibai utsu — 一芝居打つ — *to conspire*
[lit. to run a play]
彼は会議に混乱を起こそうと一芝居打ちましたが、失敗しました。

Kare wa kaigi ni konran o okosō to hitoshibai uchimashita ga, shippai shimashita.   *He conspired to create chaos in the meeting but failed.*

hitosujinawa dewa ikanai — 一筋縄ではいかない — *to be tough to deal with*
[lit. to be unable to handle with a piece of rope]
あの政治家は、一筋縄ではいかないという評判があります。Ano seijika wa, hitosujinawa dewa ikanai to iu hyōban ga arimasu.   *That politician has a reputation for being tough to deal with.*

hitotamari mo naku — 一たまりもなく — *immediately*
[lit. without any holding]
大きいスーパーが出来ると、近くの小さい店は たまりもなく潰れてしまいました。ōkii sūpā ga dekiru to, chikaku no chiisai mise wa hitotamari mo naku tsuburete shimaimashita.   *When the big supermarket opened, the small shops nearby immediately went bankrupt.*

hitotsubudane — 一粒種 — *only child*
[lit. a grain of seed]
隣の家では、息子を一粒種として甘やかしています。Tonari no ie dewa, musuko o hitotsubudane toshite amayakashite imasu.   *Our next door neighbors are indulging their son, an only child.*

hitoyaku kau — 一役買う — *to offer one's service*
[lit. to buy a role]
隣近所の組織化に、一役買いました。Tonarikinjo no soshikika ni, hitoyaku kaimashita.   *I volunteered to take part in organizing our neighborhood.*

hitoyama ateru — 一山当てる — *to strike it rich*
[lit. to guess a mountain]
彼女は、株で一山当てました。Kanojo wa, kabu de hitoyama atemashita.   *She struck it rich in the stock market.*

hitoyama kosu — 一山越す — *to pull through something difficult*
[lit. to go over a mountain]
論文を三つ提出して、今学期も一山越しました。Ronbun o mittsu teishutsu shite, kongakki mo hitoyama koshimashita.   *By submitting three term papers, I pulled through this semester.*

hitomi — 瞳 — *pupil (eye)*
  hitomi o korashite — 瞳を凝らして — *intently*
  [lit. by applying one's pupils]

彼女は芝居を瞳を凝らして見守りました。Kanojo wa shibai o hitomi o korashite mimamorimashita. *She watched the play intently.*

---

hitori — 独り — *one person*

hitoriaruki — 独り歩き — *independence*
[lit. a solitary walk]
彼は大学を出ましたが、まだ財政的に独り歩きできません。Kare wa daigaku o demashita ga, mada zaiseiteki ni hitoriaruki dekimasen. *Although he graduated from college, he isn't financially independent yet.*

hitoributai — 独り舞台 — *unchallenged position*
[lit. alone on a stage]
外交政策の分野は、彼の独り舞台です。Gaikō seisaku no bun-ya wa, kare no hitoributai desu. *He holds an unchallenged position in the field of foreign policy.*

hitorigaten — 独り合点 — *to take something for granted*
[lit. to agree with oneself]
彼女は自分もパーティーに呼ばれたと独り合点しています。Kanojo wa jibun mo pātī ni yobareta to hitorigaten shite imasu. *She took it for granted that she was also invited to the party.*

hitorijime suru — 独り占めする — *to monopolize someone or something*
[lit. to occupy by oneself]
彼は会社の車を独り占めしています。Kare wa kaisha no kuruma o hitorijime shite imasu. *He's monopolizing a company car.*

hitoriyogari — 独り善がり — *self-complacency*
[lit. to make oneself good]
彼女は独り善がりで、人の気持ちなど決して考えません。Kanojo wa hitoriyogari de, hito no kimochi nado kesshite kangaemasen. *She's self-complacent and never thinks about other people's feelings.*

hitorizumō — 独り相撲 — *to tilt at windmills*
[lit. to wrestle alone]
抗議運動は支持が殆ど無く、独り相撲に終わりました。Kōgi undō wa shiji ga hotondo naku, hitorizumō ni owarimashita. *With little support, the protest movement ended up tilting at windmills.*

---

hiyameshi — 冷や飯 — *cold rice*

hiyameshi o kuu — 冷や飯を食う — *to be in the doghouse*
[lit. to eat cold rice]

会社の方針に反対したため、一年冷や飯を食ってしまいました。
Kaisha no hōshin ni hantai shita tame, ichi nen hiyameshi o kutte
shimaimashita.   *I was in the doghouse for a year for opposing company
policies.*

---

hiyori — 日和 — *weather conditions*
hiyori o miru — 日和を見る — *to see how the wind blows*
[lit. to check the weather]

彼はどの政党を支持するか、日和を見ています。Kare wa dono seitō
o shiji suru ka, hiyori o mite imasu.   *He's waiting to see how the wind
blows before deciding which party to support.*

---

hiza — 膝 — *knee*
hiza o kussuru — 膝を屈する — *to yield*
[lit. to bend one's knees]

政府は、国民の反対に膝を屈しました。Seifu wa, kokumin no hantai
ni hiza o kusshimashita.   *The government yielded to the objections of
the people.*

hiza o majieru — 膝を交える — *to have an intimate talk*
[lit. to mingle each other's knees]

母と娘は、膝を交えて話し合いました。Haha to musume wa, hiza o

majiete hanashiaimashita.   *The mother and daughter had an intimate talk.*

hiza o noridasu — 膝を乗り出す — *to show great interest*
[lit. to make one's knees go forward]
彼女の話に、全員が膝を乗り出して聞きました。Kanojo no hanashi ni, zen-in ga hiza o noridashite kikimashita.   *Everybody listened to her story with great interest.*

hiza o tadasu — 膝を正す — *to sit upright*
[lit. to straighten one's knees]
先生の話を、膝を正して聞きました。Sensei no hanashi o, hiza o tadashite kikimashita.   *We listened attentively to the talk by our teacher.*

hiza o tataku — 膝を叩く — *to agree, to be impressed*
[lit. to hit one's knees]
彼の提案に、出席者はみんな膝を叩きました。Kare no teian ni, shussekisha wa minna hiza o tatakimashita.   *All the attendees agreed to his proposal.*

hiza o tsukiawaseru — 膝を突き合わせる — *to have a heart-to-heart talk*
[lit. to get knee to knee]
私たちは、夜遅くまで膝を突き合わせて話し合いました。Watakushitachi wa, yoru osoku made hiza o tsukiawasete hanashiaimashita.   *We had a heart-to-heart talk till late at night.*

hiza o utsu — 膝を打つ — *to agree, to be impressed*
[lit. to hit one's knees]
彼女の名案に膝を打ちました。Kanojo no meian ni hiza o uchimashita.   *I was impressed with her wonderful idea.*

hizazume danpan — 膝詰め談判 — *to press demands for something*
[lit. parley knee to knee]
組合は会社と、賃上げについて膝詰め談判しました。Kumiai wa kaisha to, chin-age ni tsuite hizazume danpan shimashita.   *The labor union pressed demands for a wage increase with the company.*

---

hochō — 歩調 — *pace, step*
  hochō ga au — 歩調が合う — *to get along well with someone*
  [lit. One's steps fit with another's.]
  彼女と私は、いつも歩調が合います。Kanojo to watakushi wa, itsumo hochō ga aimasu.   *She and I always get along well.*

hochō o awaseru — 歩調を合わせる — *to join forces*
[lit. to adjust one's steps]
野党各党は、政府に反対するために歩調を合わせました。Yatō
kakutō wa, seifu ni hantai suru tame ni hochō o awasemashita.
The minority parties joined forces to confront the government.

hogo — ほご — *waste paper*
hogo ni suru — ほごにする   *to scrap, to discard*
[lit. to throw waste paper away]
彼女は約束をほごにしました。Kanojo wa yakusoku o hogo ni
shimashita.   *She broke her promise.*

hoko — 矛 — *halberd*
hoko o osameru — 矛を収める — *to stop fighting*
[lit. to sheathe the halberd]
矛を収めて、長年の訴訟の和解をしました。Hoko o osamete, naganen
no soshō no wakai o shimashita.   *I stopped fighting and settled the
longstanding lawsuit out of court.*

hokosaki ga niburu — 矛先が鈍る — *to lose momentum, to be deflated*
[lit. The tip of a halberd becomes dull.]
彼がすぐ謝ったので、怒りの矛先が鈍ってしまいました。Kare ga
sugu ayamatta node, ikari no hokosaki ga nibutte shimaimashita.   *Since
he apologized immediately, my anger was deflated.*

hokosaki o tenjiru — 矛先を転じる — *to change the focus of attack*
[lit. to turn the tip of a halberd]
彼は不満の矛先を、小売店から製造会社に転じました。Kare wa fuman
no hokosaki o, kouriten kara seizō gaisha ni tenjimashita.   *He switched
the focus of his dissatisfaction from the retailer to the manufacturer.*

hon — 本 — *real, exact, true*
hongoshi o ireru — 本腰を入れる — *to get down to serious business*
[lit. to apply one's hip fully]
大学の入試が近付いて、勉強に本腰を入れています。Daigaku no
nyūshi ga chikazuite, benkyō ni hongoshi o irete imasu.   *With entrance
exams starting soon, I've gotten down to serious studying.*

honne o haku — 本音を吐く — *to reveal one's true intentions*
[lit. to vomit one's true tune]

相次ぐ質問に答えながら、彼はとうとう本音を吐いてしまいました。
Aitsugu shitsumon ni kotaenagara, kare wa tōtō honne o haite
shimaimashita.　*Answering successive questions, he finally revealed*
what he really wanted.

hone — 骨 — *bone*

hone ga aru — 骨がある — *to have strong convictions*
[lit. to have bones]
彼は骨があるので、意見もしっかりしています。Kare wa hone ga aru
node, iken mo shikkari shite imasu.　*Since he's a man of strong*
convictions, his opinion is unshakable.

hone ga oreru — 骨が折れる — *to be tough*
[lit. One's bones break.]
この仕事は、思ったより骨が折れます。Kono shigoto wa, omotta yori
hone ga oremasu.　*This job is tougher than you think.*

hone made shaburu — 骨までしゃぶる — *to exploit someone totally*
[lit. to even suck someone's bones]
彼は彼女の骨までしゃぶった後、別の女性と結婚しました。Kare
wa kanojo no hone made shabutta ato, betsu no josei to kekkon
shimashita.　*After totally exploiting her, he married another woman.*

hone ni kizande — 骨に刻んで — *absolutely*
[lit. by etching something on one's bone]
私の警告を、骨に刻んで覚えておきなさい。Watakushi no keikoku o,
hone ni kizande oboete okinasai.　*You should absolutely heed my warning.*

hone no zui made — 骨の髄まで — *profoundly*
[lit. deep into one's bone marrow]
この間の苦い経験は、骨の髄まで染み込んでいます。Kono aida no
nigai keiken wa, hone no zui made shimikonde imasu.　*The bitter*
experience I had the other day affected me profoundly.

hone o oru — 骨を折る — *to make an extra effort*
[lit. to break one's bones]
交渉を決着させるために、骨を折りました。Kōshō o ketchaku saseru
tame ni, hone o orimashita.　*I made an extra effort to conclude the*
negotiations.

hone o uzumeru — 骨を埋める — *to make a place one's last home*
[lit. to bury one's own bones]
彼はそこに骨を埋めるつもりで、フランスに行きました。Kare wa

soko ni hone o uzumeru tsumori de, Furansu ni ikimashita. *He went to France intending to make it his last home.*

honenashi — 骨無し — *spineless*
[lit. having no bones]
彼は骨無しで、いざというときには役に立ちません。Kare wa honenashi de, iza to iu toki niwa yaku ni tachimasen. *Since he's spineless, he isn't effective in a crisis.*

honenuki ni suru — 骨抜きにする — *to water something down*
[lit. to debone]
私の提案は、すっかり骨抜きにされてしまいました。Watakushi no teian wa, sukkari honenuki ni sarete shimaimashita. *It's regrettable that my proposal was totally watered down.*

honeorizon — 骨折り損 — *wasting one's time and energy*
[lit. no return for breaking one's own bones]
彼女を助けてあげようとしましたが、骨折り損に終わりました。Kanojo o tasukete ageyō to shimashita ga, honeorizon ni owarimashita. *Although I tried to help her, I ended up wasting my time and energy.*

honeoshimi — 骨惜しみ — *unwilling*
[lit. stingy with one's bones]
彼の骨惜しみする態度は、理解できません。Kare no honeoshimi suru taido wa, rikai dekimasen. *I don't understand his unwilling attitude.*

honeppoi — 骨っぽい — *to have firm convictions*
[lit. bony]
彼は骨っぽい男です。Kare wa honeppoi otoko desu. *He's a man of strong convictions.*

honeyasume — 骨休め — *rest*
[lit. letting one's bones rest]
最近は働き過ぎで、骨休めが必要です。Saikin wa hatarakisugi de, honeyasume ga hitsuyō desu. *I need a rest because I've been working too much.*

---

honemi — 骨身 — *flesh and bones*
honemi ni kotaeru — 骨身にこたえる — *to affect someone deeply*
[lit. to affect one's flesh and bones]
彼女の助言は、骨身にこたえずにはいられませんでした。Kanojo no jogen wa, honemi ni kotaezu niwa iraremasen deshita. *Her advice affected me deeply.*

honemi ni shimite — 骨身にしみて — *deeply*
[lit. to penetrate one's bones]
あの人の忠告は、今でも骨身にしみて感じています。Ano hito no
chūkoku wa, ima demo honemi ni shimite kanjite imasu. *Even now,*
his advice affects me deeply.

honemi o kezuru — 骨身を削る — *to go through tremendous hardships*
[lit. to plane one's own flesh and bones]
若いときには、骨身を削る苦労も気にかけませんでした。Wakai
toki niwa, honemi o kezuru kurō mo ki ni kakemasen deshita. *When I*
was young, I didn't mind going through tremendous hardships.

honemi o oshimazuni — 骨身を惜しまずに — *diligently*
[lit. without sparing one's flesh and bones]
彼のためなら、骨身を惜しまず働きます。Kare no tame nara, honemi
o oshimazu hatarakimasu. *If it's for him, I'll work extremely hard.*

hoo — 頬 — *cheek*

hoo ga yurumu — 頬がゆるむ — *to smile*
[lit. One's cheeks get loose.]
素晴らしい知らせを聞いて、頬がゆるまずにはいられませんでした。
Subarashii shirase o kiite, hoo ga yurumazu niwa iraremasen deshita. *I*
couldn't stop smiling at hearing the wonderful news.

hoo o fukuramaseru — 頬を膨らませる — *to sulk*
[lit. to puff one's cheeks]
子供はお母さんがおもちゃを買ってくれないので、頬を膨らませて
います。Kodomo wa okāsan ga omocha o katte kurenai node, hoo o
fukuramasete imasu. *The child is sulking because his mother won't*
buy him a toy.

hoo o tsuneru — 頬をつねる — *to make sure that one's good luck is real*
[lit. to pinch one's cheek]
宝くじに当たって、頬をつねりました。Takarakuji ni atatte, hoo o
tsunerimashita. *When I won the lottery, I pinched myself to make sure*
it was real.

hookaburi o suru — 頬被りをする — *to feign ignorance*
[lit. to cover one's cheeks with a towel]
隣の家の両親は、子供の悪戯に頬被りをしています。Tonari no ie no
ryōshin wa, kodomo no itazura ni hookaburi o shite imasu. *The parents*
next door are feigning ignorance of their child's mischief.

hoshi — 星 — *star*

hoshi ga wareru — 星が割れる — *to find out who the culprit is*
[lit. A star cracks.]
先月の銀行強盗の星が割れました。Sengetsu no ginkō gōtō no hoshi ga waremashita. *The police found out who the culprit was in last month's bank robbery.*

hoshi o ageru — 星を挙げる — *to arrest a criminal*
[lit. to catch a star]
殺人現場のすぐ近くで、警官は星を挙げました。Satsujin genba no sugu chikaku de, keikan wa hoshi o agemashita. *The police arrested the criminal right near the murder scene.*

hoshi o kasegu — 星を稼ぐ — *to win, to gain favor*
[lit. to earn a star]
私のひいきの力士は、今場所は毎日星を稼いでいます。Watakushi no hiiki no rikishi wa, konbasho wa mainichi hoshi o kaseide imasu. *My favorite sumo wrestler has been winning every day in this tournament.*

hoshimawari — 星回り — *luck, fortune*
[lit. a cycle of one's star]
今年は星回りがよくて、いい事が次々に起こっています。Kotoshi wa hoshimawari ga yokute, ii koto ga tsugitsugi ni okotte imasu. *It's a lucky year for me, and good things are happening one after the other.*

---

hotoke — 仏 — *Buddha*

hotoke ni naru — 仏になる — *to die*
[lit. to become a Buddha]
あの人は、去年仏になったそうです。Ano hito wa, kyonen hotoke ni natta sō desu. *I hear that he died last year.*

hotoke no kao mo sando — 仏の顔も三度 — *limits to one's patience*
[lit. the Buddha's face for three times but no more]
また締め切りに間に合わなかったね。仏の顔も三度だよ。Mata shimekiri ni ma ni awanakatta ne. Hotoke no kao mo sando da yo. *You missed the deadline again. I'm running out of patience.*

hotokegokoro — 仏心 — *mercy*
[lit. the Buddha's mind]
彼は、仏心で部下の失策をかばってあげました。Kare wa, hotokegokoro de buka no shissaku o kabatte agemashita. *He mercifully defended his subordinate's mistake.*

hotokekusai — 仏臭い — *preachy*
[lit. smelling like the Buddha]
彼の意見は、いつも仏臭いです。Kare no iken wa, itsumo hotokekusai desu. *His opinions always sound preachy.*

---

hozo — 臍 — *navel*
hozo o kamu — 臍を噛む — *to regret deeply*
[lit. to gnaw one's own navel]
住宅ローンを拒否されて、もっと貯金しなかったことに臍を噛みました。Jūtaku rōn o kyohi sarete, motto chokin shinakatta koto ni hozo o kamimashita. *When my mortgage application was rejected, I deeply regretted that I hadn't saved more.*

hozo o katameru — 臍を固める — *to resolve*
[lit. to harden one's own navel]
会社を辞めて独立する臍を固めました。Kaisha o yamete dokuritsu suru hozo o katamemashita. *I resolved to quit the company and become self-employed.*

---

hyaku — 百 — *one hundred*
hyaku mo shōchi — 百も承知 — *to be fully aware*
[lit. to know even a hundred]
それに危険が伴うことは、百も承知です。Sore ni kiken ga tomonau koto wa, hyaku mo shōchi desu. *I'm fully aware that it involves some danger.*

hyakusen renma no shi — 百戦錬磨の士 — *veteran*
[lit. a skilled soldier through a hundred wars]
市場開拓では、彼は百戦錬磨の士です。Shijō kaitaku dewa, kare wa hyakusen renma no shi desu. *He's a battle-hardened veteran in market development.*

---

hyōzan — 氷山 — *iceberg*
hyōzan no ikkaku — 氷山の一角 — *the tip of the iceberg*
[lit. the tip of the iceberg]
統計の麻薬使用者の数は、氷山の一角に過ぎません。Tōkei no mayaku shiyōsha no kazu wa, hyōzan no ikkaku ni sugimasen. *The number of drug users in the statistics is merely the tip of the iceberg.*

I

i — 意 — *mind, will*

i ni kaisanai — 意に介さない — *to not mind*
[lit. to not put one's mind in between]
彼女はどんな用事を頼まれても、意に介しません。Kanojo wa donna yōji o tanomaretemo, i ni kaishimasen. *She doesn't mind being asked to run any errand.*

i ni mitanai — 意に満たない — *unsatisfactory*
[lit. to not fill someone's will]
そんな言い訳では意に満ちません。Sonna iiwake dewa i ni michimasen. *Such an excuse is unsatisfactory.*

i o kumu — 意を汲む — *to read someone's mind*
[lit. to scoop up someone's mind]
彼女の意を汲んで、それをしてあげました。Kanojo no i o kunde, sore o shite agemashita. *I did it for her by reading her mind.*

---

ibara — 茨 — *thorn*

ibara no michi o tadoru — 茨の道をたどる — *to have a tough life*
[lit. to follow a thorny road]
彼は今は茨の道をたどっています。Kare wa ima wa ibara no michi o tadotte imasu. *He's having a tough life right now.*

---

ichi — 一 — *one*

ichi ka bachi ka yattemiru — 一か八かやってみる — *to put all one's eggs in one basket*
[lit. to try, whether it's one or eight]
一か八か、ジャンクボンドに投資してみました。Ichi ka bachi ka, janku bondo ni tōshi shite mimashita. *I put all my eggs in one basket and invested in junk bonds.*

ichi kara jū made — 一から十まで — *thoroughly*
[lit. from one to ten]
彼には一から十まで説明したのに、まだ分かりませんでした。Kare niwa ichi kara jū made setsumei shita noni, mada wakarimasen deshita. *Although I explained it to him thoroughly, he still didn't understand it.*

ichi mo ni mo naku — 一も二もなく — *readily*
[lit. without one or two]

彼女は、私の意見に一も二もなく賛成しました。Kanojo wa,
watakushi no iken ni ichi mo ni mo naku sansei shimashita.   *She readily
agreed with my opinion.*

ichijitsu no chō — 一日の長 — *to be better and more experienced*
[lit. the merit of one day]

市場分析にかけては、彼女は彼より一日の長があります。Shijō
bunseki ni kakete wa, kanojo wa kare yori ichijitsu no chō ga arimasu.
For market analysis, she's better and more experienced than he is.

ichimai kamu — 一枚噛む — *to take part in something*
[lit. to bite a sheet of paper]

この企画には、私も一枚噛んでいます。Kono kikaku niwa, watakushi
mo ichimai kande imasu.   *I'm taking part in this project.*

ichimoku oku — 一目置く — *to take one's hat off to someone*
[lit. to place one's own *go* stone first]

彼女の親孝行には、一目置いています。Kanojo no oya kōkō niwa,
ichimoku oite imasu.   *I take my hat off to her for her devotion to her
parents.*

ichimyaku tsūjiru — 一脈通じる — *to have something in common*
[lit. to understand someone's heartbeat]

政治については、私と彼には一脈通じるものがあります。Seiji ni
tsuite wa, watakushi to kare niwa ichimyaku tsūjiru mono ga arimasu.
He and I have something in common as far as politics is concerned.

ichiyoku o ninau — 一翼を担う — *to assume an important role*
[lit. to carry one wing on one's shoulder]
彼は政治改革運動で一翼を担って忙しいです。Kare wa seiji kaikaku
undō de ichiyoku o ninatte isogashii desu. *He's busy assuming an
important role in the political reform movement.*

ikka o nasu — 一家を成す — *to establish oneself as an authority*
[lit. to form a family]
彼は物理の分野で一家を成しています。Kare wa butsuri no bun-ya de
ikka o nashite imasu. *He's an acknowledged authority in the field of
physics.*

ikkan no owari — 一巻の終わり — *end*
[lit. the end of the volume of a story]
彼の人生の夢は、事業の失敗で一巻の終わりとなりました。Kare no
jinsei no yume wa, jigyō no shippai de ikkan no owari to narimashita.
His lifelong dream ended with the failure of his business.

ippai kuwasu — 一杯食わす — *to fool someone, to pull a fast one*
[lit. to make someone eat a bowl of food]
彼に一杯食わされて、返ってくる当てがないお金を貸してしまいま
した。Kare ni ippai kuwasarete, kaette kuru ate ga nai okane o kashite
shimaimashita. *I was fooled and lent him money I would never get
back.*

ippon toru — 一本取る — *to score a point*
[lit. to pick up a piece]
国会の審議で、野党は政府から一本取りました。 Kokkai no shingi

de, yatō wa seifu kara ippon torimashita. *In the Diet session, the minority parties scored a point over the government.*

ippondachi — 一本立ち — *self-supporting*
[lit. standing alone]
大学は卒業したけれど、まだ一本立ちできません。Daigaku wa sotsugyō shita keredo, mada ippondachi dekimasen. *Although I graduated from a university, I can't support myself yet.*

ipponjōshi — 一本調子 — *monotonous*
[lit. the same tune]
一本調子の生活に飽き飽きしています。Ipponjōshi no seikatsu ni akiaki shite imasu. *I'm bored with my monotonous life.*

ipponyari — 一本槍 — *nothing but . . .*
[lit. one spear]
最近は勉強一本槍の毎日です。Saikin wa benkyō ipponyari no mainichi desu. *Recently it's been nothing but study, day in and day out.*

issatsu ireru — 一札入れる — *to give someone a signed document*
[lit. to bring in a sheet of paper]
お金は貸して上げるけど、一札入れて下さい。Okane wa kashite ageru kedo, issatsu irete kudasai. *I'll lend you money, but give me a signed document.*

isseki mōkeru — 一席設ける — *to arrange a party*
[lit. to set up a seat]
大切な顧客のために、一席設けました。Taisetsu na kokyaku no tame ni, isseki mōkemashita. *I arranged a party for our important clients.*

isseki o tōjiru — 一石を投じる — *to create a stir*
[lit. to throw a stone]
彼の発言は、学会に一石を投じました。Kare no hatsugen wa, gakkai ni isseki o tōjimashita. *His speech created a stir in academic circles.*

issen o kakusuru — 一線を画する — *to be on opposite sides*
[lit. to draw a line]
環境問題については、彼の意見と一線を画しています。Kankyō mondai ni tsuite wa, kare no iken to issen o kakushite imasu. *On environmental issues, he and I are on opposite sides.*

isshi midarezu — 一糸乱れず — *in unison*
[lit. not even a piece of thread out of place]
野党は一糸乱れずに団結して、政府と対立しました。Yatō wa isshi

midarezu ni danketsu shite, seifu to tairitsu shimashita. *In unison the minority parties confronted the government.*

isshi o mukuiru — 一矢を報いる — *to retaliate*
[lit. to return an arrow]
いつも負けているチ－ムに勝って、一矢を報いました。Itsumo makete iru chīmu ni katte, isshi o mukuimashita. *We retaliated by defeating the team which had been beating us.*

---

ido — 井戸 — *well*
idobata kaigi — 井戸端会議 — *gossiping (by a group of women)*
[lit. a well-side conference]
彼女たちは、毎日昼休みに井戸端会議を開いています。Kanojotachi wa, mainichi hiruyasumi ni idobata kaigi o hiraite imasu. *These women are gossiping during lunch break every day.*

---

ii — いい — *good, fine, nice*
ii kao — いい顔 — *big shot*
[lit. a good face]
彼は地元ではいい顔です。Kare wa jimoto dewa ii kao desu. *He's a big shot in his hometown.*

ii ko ni naru — いい子になる — *to gain credit at others' expense*
[lit. to become a good child]
彼はいつも上役の前では、いい子になろうとします。Kare wa itsumo uwayaku no mae dewa, ii ko ni narō to shimasu. *He always tries to gain credit at other's expense in front of the boss.*

ii tsura no kawa — いい面の皮 — *Serves (one) right!*
[lit. good facial skin]
彼は汚職で首になったそうですね。いい面の皮ですよ。Kare wa oshoku de kubi ni natta sō desu ne. Ii tsura no kawa desu yo. *I hear he was fired for corruption. Serves him right!*

---

ikari — 怒り — *anger*
ikari o kau — 怒りを買う — *to make someone angry*
[lit. to buy someone's anger]
毎晩帰宅が非常に遅くなって、妻の怒りを買ってしまいました。
Maiban kitaku ga hijō ni osokunatte, tsuma no ikari o katte shimaimashita. *I regret that I made my wife angry by returning very late every night.*

ikari o maneku — 怒りを招く — *to trigger someone's anger*
[lit. to invite someone's anger]
政府の無能が、国民の怒りを招いています。Seifu no munō ga,
kokumin no ikari o maneite imasu.   *The government's incompetency
has triggered the people's anger.*

---

iki — 息 — *breathing*
  iki ga au — 息が合う — *to be in perfect tune with each other*
  [lit. Each other's breathing is in harmony.]
  彼女と私は、何をやっても息が合います。Kanojo to watakushi wa,
  nani o yattemo iki ga aimasu.   *Whatever we do, she and I are in perfect
  tune with each other.*

  iki ga kakaru — 息がかかる — *under the patronage of someone*
  [lit. Someone's breathing covers you.]
  彼には、社長の息がかかっているそうです。 Kare niwa, shachō no iki
  ga kakatte iru sō desu.   *I hear he's under the patronage of the president.*

  iki ga kireru — 息が切れる — *to run out of steam, to ebb*
  [lit. to be out of breath]
  彼の指導力は、一年たつと息が切れてきました。Kare no shidōryoku
  wa, ichi nen tatsu to iki ga kirete kimashita.   *His leadership began to
  run out of steam after one year.*

  iki ga nagai — 息が長い — *long-lasting*
  [lit. Breathing is deep.]
  彼女の作家活動は息が長く、ベストセラーを何冊も書きました。
  Kanojo no sakka katsudō wa iki ga nagaku, besuto serā o nansatsu mo
  kakimashita.   *She's had a long career as a writer, and she's written
  many bestsellers.*

  iki ga tsumaru — 息が詰まる — *nervous, to not be able to relax*
  [lit. hard to breathe]
  パーティーには先生も来ていたので、息が詰まりました。Pātī niwa
  sensei mo kite ita node, iki ga tsumarimashita.   *I couldn't relax at the
  party because my teacher was there too.*

  iki mo tsukasezu — 息もつかせず — *rapidly*
  [lit. without letting someone breathe]
  教授は息もつかせず学生に質問を投げかけました。Kyōju wa iki mo
  tsukasezu gakusei ni shitsumon o nagekakemashita.   *The professor
  rapidly hurled questions at her students.*

iki o fukikaesu — 息を吹き返す — *to revive*
[lit. to breathe again]
あの会社は、新しい経営陣を入れて息を吹き返しました。Ano
kaisha wa, atarashii keieijin o irete iki o fukikaeshimashita.   *With the
introduction of the new management team, that company revived.*

iki o hikitoru — 息を引き取る — *to die*
[lit. to withdraw one's breathing]
彼は長い病気の末、息を引き取りました。Kare wa nagai byōki no sue
iki o hikitorimashita.   *He died after a long illness.*

iki o korashite — 息を凝らして — *intently*
[lit. by concentrating one's own breath]
私たちは息を凝らして、彼女の話を聞きました。Watakushitachi wa
iki o korashite, kanojo no hanashi o kikimashita.   *We listened to her
story intently.*

iki o koroshite — 息を殺して — *expectantly*
[lit. by killing one's own breath]
その村の人全員が、息を殺して首相の到着を待ちました。Sono
mura no hito zen-in ga, iki o koroshite shushō no tōchaku o
machimashita.   *All the villagers waited expectantly for the arrival of the
prime minister.*

iki o nomu — 息を呑む — *to be astonished*
[lit. to swallow one's own breath]
景色のあまりの美しさに息を呑みました。Keshiki no amari no
utsukushisa ni iki o nomimashita.   *I was astonished at the extreme
beauty of the scenery.*

iki o nuku — 息を抜く — *to relax*
[lit. to draw a breath]
仕事が忙しくて、息を抜く暇もありません。Shigoto ga isogashikute,
iki o nuku hima mo arimasen.   *I have no time to relax because I'm busy
with work.*

iki o tsuku — 息をつく — *to breathe a sigh of relief*
[lit. to take a breath]
大切な試験が終わって、息をつきました。Taisetsu na shiken ga
owatte, iki o tsukimashita.   *With the big exam over, I breathed a sigh of
relief.*

iki o tsumete — 息を詰めて — *attentively*
[lit. by holding one's breath]

学生は、試験の結果を息を詰めて聞きました。　Gakusei wa,
shiken no kekka o iki o tsumete kikimashita.　*The students listened
attentively to the results of the exam.*

ikinuki o suru — 息抜きをする — *to take a breather*
[lit. to draw a breath]
仕事の息抜きをするために、妻と旅行しました。Shigoto no ikinuki o
suru tame ni, tsuma to ryokō shimashita.　*I went on a trip with my wife
to take a breather from work.*

ikizumaru yō na — 息詰まるような — *thrilling*
[lit. like choking]
今日見た映画には、息詰まるような場面がいくつもありました。
Kyō mita eiga niwa, ikizumaru yō na bamen ga ikutsu mo arimashita.
There were many thrilling scenes in the movie I saw today.

---

imo — 芋 — *potato*
imo o arau yō — 芋を洗うよう — *to be very crowded*
[lit. like washing potaoes]
昨日は祭日で、デパートは芋を洗うようでした。Kinō wa saijitsu de,
depāto wa imo o arau yō deshita.　*Yesterday was a holiday, and the
department store was very crowded.*

---

in — 陰 — *behind, back*
in ni komoru — 陰にこもる — *to be pent up*
[lit. to keep it in the back]
彼には不満が陰にこもっているようです。Kare niwa fuman ga in ni
komotte iru yō desu.　*He seems to have some pent-up discontent.*

---

inga — 因果 — *cause and effect*
inga o fukumeru — 因果を含める — *to persuade someone to accept his
or her fate*
[lit. to include cause and effect]
嫌がる友達に因果を含めて、奥さんに謝らせました。Iyagaru tomodachi
ni inga o fukumete, okusan ni ayamarasemashita.　*I persuaded my
reluctant friend to accept his fate and apologize to his wife.*

---

inochi — 命 — *life*
inochi no oya — 命の親 — *savior*
[lit. the parent of someone's life]

失業中の私に仕事をくれた彼は、命の親です。Shitsugyō chū no watakushi ni shigoto o kureta kare wa inochi no oya desu. *He is my savior because he gave me a job when I was unemployed.*

inochi no sentaku — 命の洗濯 — *diversion*
[lit. laundering of life]
命の洗濯として、一週間温泉に行きました。Inochi no sentaku to shite, isshūkan onsen ni ikimashita. *As a diversion, I went to a hot springs resort for a week.*

inochi no tsuna — 命の綱 — *lifeblood*
[lit. a rope for life]
輸出産業は、日本にとって命の綱です。Yushutsu sangyō wa, Nihon ni totte inochi no tsuna desu. *The export industries are Japan's lifeblood.*

inochishirazu — 命知らず — *reckless*
[lit. not knowing one's own life]
彼は命知らずに車を運転します。Kare wa inochishirazu ni kuruma o unten shimasu. *He drives a car recklessly.*

inu — 犬 — dog

inu mo kuwanai — 犬も食わない — *Nobody takes it seriously.*
[lit. Even a dog won't eat.]
君たちはつまらないことで口論しているけれど、犬も食わないよ。Kimitachi wa tsumaranai koto de kōron shite iru keredo, inu mo kuwanai yo. *You're arguing over something trivial, so nobody will take it seriously.*

inu to saru — 犬と猿 — *to be on bad terms*
[lit. a dog and a monkey]
彼らは犬と猿で、会うといつも口げんかになります。Karera wa inu to saru de, au to itsumo kuchigenka ni narimasu. *They're on bad terms, and they quarrel whenever they meet.*

inujinisuru — 犬死にする — *to die in vain*
[lit. to die like a dog]
彼の死は、全くの犬死にでした。Kare no shi wa, mattaku no inujini deshita. *He died in vain.*

iro — 色 — color

iro ga aseru — 色があせる — *to lose attractiveness*
[lit. The color fades.]

あの政治家の人気は、二年で色があせてしまいました。Ano seijika no ninki wa, ninen de iro ga asete shimaimashita.   *Within two years, the politician lost popularity.*

iro o nasu — 色をなす — *to turn red with anger*
[lit. to turn color]
友達の親切な助言なのに、彼はそれを聞いて色をなしました。
Tomodachi no shinsetsu na jogen nanoni, kare wa sore o kiite iro o nashimashita.   *His friend's advice was meant well, but hearing it, he turned red with anger.*

iro o tsukeru — 色を付ける — *to throw in something extra*
[lit. to color something]
もう少し色を付けてくれたら、それを買ってもいいです。Mō sukoshi iro o tsukete kuretara, sore o kattemo ii desu.   *If you throw in something extra, I'll buy it.*

iro o ushinau — 色を失う — *to lose one's composure*
[lit. to lose color]
突然の悲しい知らせに、色を失ってしまいました。Totsuzen no kanashii shirase ni, iro o ushinatte shimaimashita.   *Hearing the sudden sad news, I lost my composure.*

irojikake — 色仕掛け — *pretense of love*
[lit. a trick of color]
彼は色仕掛けで、彼女から借金することに成功しました。Kare wa irojikake de, kanojo kara shakkin suru koto ni seikō shimashita.   *Under the pretense of love, he succeeded in borrowing money from her.*

iromegane de miru — 色眼鏡で見る — *to have biased opinions*
[lit. to see things through tinted eyeglasses]
彼女には、何事も色眼鏡で見る傾向があります。Kanojo niwa, nanigoto mo iromegane de miru keikō ga arimasu.   *She tends to have biased opinions.*

iromeku — 色めく — *to get excited*
[lit. to become colorful]
町の人はみんな、今お祭りで色めいています。Machi no hito wa minna, ima omatsuri de iromeite imasu.   *All the townspeople are excited about the festival taking place now.*

ironaoshi — 色直し — *bride's changing clothes during the wedding reception*
[lit. a change of color]

花嫁は、披露宴で何度色直しをしましたか。Hanayome wa, hirōen de
nando ironaoshi o shimashita ka.　*How often did the bride change her*
clothes during the wedding reception?

irowake — 色分け — *classification*
[lit. a separation of color]
応募者を、まず特技によって色分けしました。Ōbosha o, mazu tokugi
ni yotte irowake shimashita　*First we classified the applicants*
according to their special skills.

---

isha — 医者 — *doctor*
　yabuisha — 薮医者 — *incompetent doctor*
　[lit. a doctor in the bushes]
　あの病院は、薮医者が多いという噂があります。Ano byōin wa,
　yabuisha ga ōi to iu uwasa ga arimasu.　*There's a rumor that the*
　hospital has many incompetent doctors.

---

ishi — 石 — *stone*
　ishi ni kajiritsuitemo — 石にかじりついても — *no matter what*
　[lit. even biting into a stone]
　石にかじりついても、願いを遂げるつもりです。Ishi ni
　kajiritsuitemo, negai o togeru tsumori desu.　*I intend to make my wish*
　come true no matter what.

　ishiatama — 石頭 — *someone inflexible*
　[lit. a stone head]
　彼は石頭だから、それをいくら説明しても無駄です。Kare wa
　ishiatama dakara, sore o ikura setsumei shitemo muda desu.　*Because*
　he's inflexible, it doesn't matter how much you explain it to him.

---

ita — 板 — *board*
　ita ni tsuku — 板につく — *to get used to something*
　[lit. to belong to a board]
　二番目の子供が産まれて、彼の父親ぶりも板につきました。
　Nibanme no kodomo ga umarete, kare no chichioya buri mo ita ni
　tsukimashita.　*With his second child, he's gotten used to being a father.*

　itabasami — 板挟み — *in a fix, torn*
　[lit. to be squeezed between boards]
　彼は、義理と人情の板挟みになっています。Kare wa, giri to ninjō no

itabasami ni natte imasu. *He's torn between his sympathy and his sense of duty.*

tateita ni mizu — 立て板に水 — *glibly*
[lit. like water running on a standing board]
彼は立て板に水のように話します。Kare wa tateita ni mizu no yō ni hanashimasu. *He's a glib talker.*

---

itachi — 鼬 — *weasel*
itachigokko — 鼬ごっこ — *to be in a vicious circle*
[lit. weasels' play]
物価と賃金の上昇の鼬ごっこが起こっています。Bukka to chingin no jōshō no itachigokko ga okotte imasu. *The vicious circle between the increase in prices and in wages has begun.*

---

itai — 痛い — *painful*
itai me ni au — 痛い目にあう — *to have a bitter experience*
[lit. to encounter a painful eye]
彼女を信用したために、痛い目にあいました。Kanojo o shin-yō shita tame ni, itai me ni aimashita. *Because I trusted her, I had a bitter experience.*

itakumo kayukumo nai — 痛くも痒くもない — *to not affect one at all*
[lit. neither painful nor itchy]
彼が私をいくら批判しても、痛くも痒くもありません。Kare ga watakushi o ikura hihan shitemo, itakumo kayukumo arimasen. *Even if he criticizes me a lot, it doesn't affect me at all.*

itashi kayushi — 痛し痒し — *in a quandary*
[lit. painful and itchy at the same time]
昇進はしたけれど、出張が増えて痛し痒しです。Shōshin wa shita keredo, shutchō ga fuete itashi kayushi desu. *Although I was promoted, I'm in a quandary because I have to make more business trips.*

---

ito — 糸 — *thread*
ito o hiku — 糸を引く — *to manipulate*
[lit. to pull thread]
この抗議運動は、ある政党が糸を引いているそうです。Kono kōgi undō wa, aru seitō ga ito o hiite iru sō desu. *It's said that a certain political party is manipulating this protest movement.*

itoguchi — 糸口 — *clue, first step*
[lit. the end of thread]

それが、問題解決の糸口になりました。Sore ga, mondai kaiketsu no itoguchi ni narimashita. *That turned out to be the first step toward solving the problem.*

iya — 否、嫌 — no

iya demo ō demo — 否でも応でも — *like it or not*
[lit. if it's yes or no]

否でも応でも、会議には出席しなければなりません。Iya demo ō demo, kaigi niwa shusseki shinakereba narimasen. *Like it or not, you must attend the meeting.*

iya to iu hodo — 嫌というほど — *enough*
[lit. to the extent that one says no]

昨日の晩は、嫌というほど鮨を食べました。Kinō no ban wa, iya to iu hodo sushi o tabemashita. *Last night I ate enough sushi.*

ja — 蛇 — *snake*

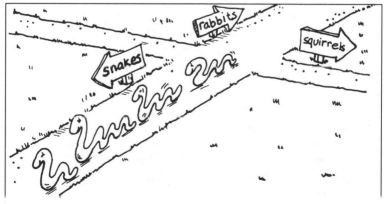

ja no michi wa hebi — 蛇の道は蛇 — *It takes one to know one.*

[lit. Snakes know snakes' paths.]

蛇の道は蛇だから、彼が何をたくらんでいるか分かります。Ja no michi wa hebi dakara, kare ga nani o takurande iru ka wakarimasu. *Because it takes one to know one, I understand what he's plotting.*

---

ji — 時 — *hour*

jikan o kasegu — 時間を稼ぐ — *to buy time, to get an extension of time*
[lit. to earn time]
病気を理由に、締め切りまでの時間を稼ぎました。Byōki o riyū ni, shimekiri made no jikan o kasegimashita. *By pleading illness, I got the deadline extended.*

jiryū ni noru — 時流に乗る — *to be trendy*
[lit. to ride on the flow of the times]
あの店は時流に乗って、若い人たちの間で人気があります。Ano mise wa jiryū ni notte, wakai hitotachi no aida de ninki ga arimasu. *Because that shop is trendy, it's popular among young people.*

---

ji — 地 — *ground*

ji de iku — 地でいく — *to behave naturally*
[lit. to go with the ground]
どんな集まりか知りませんが、私は地でいくつもりです。Donna atsumari ka shirimasen ga, watakushi wa ji de iku tsumori desu. *I don't know what kind of gathering it's going to be, but I'll just behave naturally.*

jidanda o fumu — 地団駄を踏む — *to be mortified*
[lit. to stamp on the ground]
彼は自分の提案が採用されなくて、地団駄を踏みました。Kare wa jibun no teian ga saiyō sarenakute, jidanda o fumimashita. *He was mortified that his suggestion wasn't adopted.*

---

ji — 自 — *self*

ji ta tomo ni yurusu — 自他ともに許す — *acknowledged*
[lit. to be accepted by both oneself and others]
彼女は自他ともに許す、社会問題の権威です。Kanojo wa ji ta tomo ni yurusu, shakai mondai no ken-i desu. *She's the acknowledged authority on social issues.*

jibara o kiru — 自腹を切る — *to pay out of one's own pocket*
[lit. to cut one's own belly]

出張で、洗濯代は自腹を切りました。Shutchō de, sentaku dai wa jibara o kirimashita. *On the business trip, I paid my laundry costs out of my own pocket.*

jigajisan suru — 自画自賛する — *to praise one's own achievement*
[lit. to praise one's own painting]
彼女は自分の報告書を自画自賛しています。Kanojo wa jibun no hōkokusho o jigajisan shite imasu. *She's praising her own report.*

---

jigane — 地金 — *core metal*
jigane o dasu — 地金を出す — *to reveal one's true colors*
[lit. to show core metal]
彼女は話している内に、地金を出してしまいました。Kanojo wa hanashite iru uchi ni, jigane o dashite shimaimashita. *While talking, she unintentionally revealed her true colors.*

---

jigoku — 地獄 — *hell*
jigoku de hotoke — 地獄で仏 — *A friend in need (is a friend indeed).*
[lit. meeting the Buddha in hell]
私の車が故障したそのときにフレッドが車で通りかかって、正に地獄で仏でした。Watakushi no kuruma ga koshō shita sono toki ni Fureddo ga kuruma de tōri kakatte, masa ni jigoku de hotoke deshita. *Fred was truly "a friend in need" when he drove by just as my car broke down.*

jigokumimi — 地獄耳 — *to have a nose for news*
[lit. hellish ears]
彼は地獄耳だから、気をつけなさい。Kare wa jigokumimi dakara, ki o tsukenasai. *Be careful around him: he has a nose for news.*

---

jo — 序 — *order*
jo no kuchi — 序の口 — *beginning, start*
[lit. the lowest class in the sumo tournament]
このくらいの湿気はまだ序の口で、これからもっと高くなります。Kono kurai no shikke wa mada jo no kuchi de, kore kara motto takaku narimasu. *This humidity is just the beginning; it will get much higher from now on.*

---

jō   情   *feeling*
jō ga fukai — 情が深い — *warm-hearted*

[lit. One's feeling is deep.]

彼女は情が深いので、誰からも好かれます。Kanojo wa jō ga fukai node, dare kara mo sukaremasu. *Because she's warm-hearted, she's well liked.*

jō ga usui — 情が薄い — *cold-hearted*
[lit. One's feeling is thin.]

彼は情が薄くて、人の気持ちを理解しようとしません。Kare wa jō ga usukute, hito no kimochi o rikai shiyō to shimasen. *He's cold-hearted and doesn't try to understand other people's feelings.*

jō ga utsuru — 情が移る — *to become attached to someone or to an animal*
[lit. One's feeling shifts.]

友達の猫を一週間預かっていたら、情が移ってしまいました。Tomodachi no neko o isshūkan azukatte itara, jō ga utsutte shimaimashita. *While I was keeping my friend's cat for a week, I got attached to it.*

jō ni moroi — 情にもろい — *soft-hearted*
[lit. sensitive to someone's feelings.]

彼は情にもろいので、借金に来る人がたくさんいます。Kare wa jō ni moroi node, shakkin ni kuru hito ga takusan imasu. *Since he's soft-hearted, many people come to him to borrow money.*

---

jūbako — 重箱 — *stack of lacquer boxes*
jūbako no sumi o hojikuru — 重箱の隅をほじくる — *to be very fussy*
[lit. to pick a corner of a lacquer box]

彼は、重箱の隅をほじくるような男です。Kare wa, jūbako no sumi o hojikuru yō na otoko desu. *He' a very fussy guy.*

---

jūhachi — 十八 — *eighteen*
jūhachiban — 十八番 — *one's forte*
[lit. the eighteenth]

ピアノ演奏が、彼女の十八番です。Piano ensō ga, kanojo no jūhachiban desu. *Playing the piano is her forte.*

---

jūnin — 十人 — *ten people*
jūnin toiro — 十人十色 — *It takes all kinds.*
[lit. ten people with ten different colors]

会議では違った意見がたくさんありましたが、それも十人十色だか

らです。Kaigi dewa chigatta iken ga takusan arimashita ga, sore mo jūnin toiro dakara desu. *There were so many different opinions in the meeting; but as they say, "It takes all kinds."*

jūninnami — 十人並み — *average, ordinary*
[lit. just like ten other people]
彼には、十人並みの才能しかありません。Kare niwa, jūninnami no sainō shika arimasen. *He has only average talent.*

jutsu — 術 — *tactic*
jutchū ni ochiiru — 術中に陥る — *to fall into a trap*
[lit. to fall into a tactic]
上司の術中に陥り、土曜出勤の約束をしてしまいました。Jōshi no jutchū ni ochiiri, doyō shukkin no yakusoku o shite shimaimashita.
I fell into my boss's trap and promised to come to work on Saturday.

ka — 蚊 — *mosquito*
ka ga naku yō na koe de — 蚊が鳴くような声で — *in a whisper*
[lit. with a voice like a mosquito's buzzing]
彼は蚊が鳴くような声で、秘密を打ち明けました。Kare wa ka ga naku yō na koe de, himitsu o uchiakemashita. *He confided his secret to me in a whisper.*

kaban — 鞄 — *bag, briefcase*
kabanmochi — 鞄持ち — *assistant, secretary*
[lit. someone carrying a briefcase]
彼は顧問のように振る舞っているけれど、実は鞄持ちに過ぎません。
Kare wa komon no yō ni furumatte iru keredo, jitsu wa kabanmochi ni sugimasen. *He's pretending to be an advisor, but actually he's only an assistant.*

kabe — 壁 — *wall*
kabe ni tsukiataru — 壁に突き当たる — *to hit a snag, to be bogged down*
[lit. to run into a wall]

貿易交渉は、壁に突き当たっています。Bōeki kōshō wa, kabe ni
tsukiatatte imasu.   The trade negotiations are bogged down.

---

kabi — 黴 — mold
kabi ga haeru — 黴が生える — to become antiquated
[lit. Mold grows.]
彼の考えは、黴が生えています。Kare no kangae wa, kabi ga haete
imasu.   His ideas have become antiquated.

---

kabu — 株 — stock
kabu ga agaru — 株が上がる — to gain respect
[lit. One's stock goes up.]
大切な契約をいくつも取って、社内での株が上がりました。Taisetsu
na keiyaku o ikutsu mo totte, shanai de no kabu ga agarimashita.
I gained respect in the company by winning many important contracts.

okabu o ubawareru — お株を奪われる — to be outdone by someone
[lit. One's stock is robbed.]
彼は歌が得意ですが、昨日は同僚にお株を奪われてしまいました。
Kare wa uta ga tokui desu ga, kinō wa dōryō ni okabu o ubawarete
shimaimashita.   He sings well, but he was outdone by his colleague
yesterday.

---

kabuto — 兜 — helmet
kabuto o nugu — 兜を脱ぐ — to admit defeat
[lit. to take a helmet off]
市場調査の分野で、競争会社に兜を脱ぎました。Shijō chōsa no bun-
ya de, kyōsō gaisha ni kabuto o nugimashita.   We admitted defeat to
our competitor in the field of market research.

---

kachi — 勝ち — victory
kachi ni jōjiru — 勝ちに乗じる — to follow up a victory
[lit. to ride on a victory]
共和党は選挙での勝ちに乗じて、法案を次々に提出しました。
Kyōwatō wa senkyo de no kachi ni jōjite, hōan o tsugitsugi ni teishutsu
shimashita.   To follow up their election victory, the Republicans
introduced successive bills.

---

kado — 角 — *corner, angle*

kado ga tasu — 角が立つ — *to aggravate*
[lit. Angles stand up.]

角が立たないように、言葉遣いに気をつけなさい。Kado ga tatanai yō ni, kotobazukai ni ki o tsukenasai.   *Pay attention to what you say, and don't aggravate anyone.*

kado ga toreru — 角が取れる — *to mellow*
[lit. Angles come off.]

社長も角が取れて、話しやすくなりました。Shachō mo kado ga torete, hanashiyasuku narimashita.   *The president has mellowed, and it has become easier to talk to him.*

kadoban ni tatsu — 角番に立つ — *to face a critical phase*
[lit. to stand at the corner of a board]

彼は大学を卒業できるかできないか、角番に立っています。Kare wa daigaku o sotsugyō dekiru ka dekinai ka, kadoban ni tatte imasu. *He's facing a critical phase: whether or not he can graduate from college.*

me ni kado o tatete — 目に角を立てて — *with eyes glaring*
[lit. by making one's eyes angled]

彼女は目に角を立てて、私を見つめました。Kanojo wa me ni kado o tatete, watakushi o mitsumemashita.   *She stared at me with eyes glaring.*

---

kage — 陰 — *shade*

kage de ito o hiku — 陰で糸を引く — *to control behind the scenes*
[lit. to pull a string in the shade]

あの政治派閥は、彼が陰で糸を引いています。Ano seiji habatsu wa, kare ga kage de ito o hiite imasu.   *He is controlling the political faction behind the scenes.*

kage ni nari hinata ni nari — 陰になり日向になり — *both openly and discreetly*
[lit. both in the shade and the sun]

彼女は陰になり日向になり、私の経歴を助けてくれました。Kanojo wa kage ni nari hinata ni nari, watakushi no keireki o tasukete kuremashita.   *She supported my career both openly and discreetly.*

kageguchi o tataku — 陰口をたたく — *to stab someone in the back*
[lit. to drum up backbites]

彼がいくら陰口をたたいても、私の信用は落ちません。Kare ga

ikura kageguchi o tataitemo, watakushi no shin-yō wa ochimasen.   *No matter how much he stabs me in the back, my reputation won't suffer.*

kagehinata ga aru — 陰日向がある — *to be two-faced*
[lit. to have both the shady and the sunny spot]
彼女には何事にも陰日向があるので、信用できません。Kanojo niwa nanigoto nimo kagehinata ga aru node, shin-yō dekimasen.   *I can't trust her; she's two-faced about everything.*

---

kage — 影 — *shadow, silhouette*
kage ga sasu — 影が差す — *to go wrong*
[lit. A shadow covers something.]
二人の関係に影が差し始めたのは、誰の目にも明らかでした。
Futari no kankei ni kage ga sashihajimeta nowa, dare no me ni mo akiraka deshita.   *It was clear that the couple's relationship began to sour.*

kage ga usui — 影が薄い — *to take a back seat*
[lit. One's shadow is light.]
新しい技術が導入されて、熟練工の影が薄くなりました。Atarashii gijutsu ga dōnyū sarete, jukurenkō no kage ga usuku narimashita.   *With the introduction of new technology, the skilled workers took back seats.*

kage mo katachi mo nai — 影も形もない — *to be nonexistent*
[lit. There is no shape or shadow.]
去年すごく流行った歌手は、今年は陰も形もありません。Kyonen sugoku hayatta kashu wa, kotoshi wa kage mo katachi mo arimasen.
This year we haven't heard a thing about the singer who was extremely popular last year.

kage o hisomeru — 影を潜める — *to lie low*
[lit. to conceal one's shadow]
あの政治家は落選して以来、影を潜めています。Ano seijika wa rakusen shite irai, kage o hisomete imasu.   *That politician has been lying low since losing the election.*

miru kage mo nai — 見る影もない — *to be down and out*
[lit. There isn't even a shadow to look at.]
彼は大金持ちでしたが、今は見る影もありません。Kare wa ōganemochi deshita ga, ima wa miru kage mo arimasen.   *He was an extremely wealthy man, but now he's down and out.*

---

kaji — 舵 — *helm*
kaji o toru — 舵をとる — *to be at the helm*
[lit. to steer]
この会社では、社長の代わりに息子が舵を取っています。Kono
kaisha dewa, shachō no kawari ni musuko ga kaji o totte imasu.
Instead of the president, his son is at the helm of this company.

---

kakeru — 駆ける — *to run*
kakedashi — 駆け出し — *greenhorn*
[lit. someone who is starting to run]
彼女は弁護士としては、まだ駆け出しです。Kanojo wa bengoshi
toshite wa, mada kakedashi desu. *As a lawyer, she's still a greenhorn.*

kakeochisuru — 駆け落ちする — *to elope*
[lit. to run and drop out]
親が結婚に反対したので、彼女とボーイフレンドは駆け落ちしました。
Oya ga kekkon ni hantai shita node, kanojo to bōifurendo wa kakeochi
shimashita. *Since her parents opposed the marriage, she and her
boyfriend eloped.*

---

kama — 鎌 — *sickle*
kama o kakeru — 鎌をかける — *to ask leading questions*
[lit. to apply a sickle]
彼女は人の秘密を聞き出すため、鎌をかけるのが上手です。
Kanojo wa hito no himitsu o kikidasu tame, kama o kakeru no ga jōzu
desu. *She's good at asking leading questions to find out other people's
secrets.*

---

kami — 紙 — *paper*
kami hitoe no sa — 紙一重の差 — *slight difference, paper-thin margin*
[lit. the difference of the thickness of a sheet of paper]
私が支持する候補者は、紙一重の差で勝てて幸運でした。
Watakushi ga shiji suru kōhosha wa, kami hitoe no sa de katete kōun
deshita. *The candidate I supported was lucky to win by a paper-thin
margin.*

---

kami — 神 — *god*
kamiwaza — 神業 — *superhuman feat*
[lit. the work of a god]

彼の発明は、まさに神業でした。Kare no hatsumei wa, masa ni kamiwaza deshita.   *His invention was truly a superhuman feat.*

kaminari — 雷 — *thunder*
kaminari o otosu — 雷を落とす — *to explode at someone*
[lit. to drop thunder]
弟がテレビばかり見ているので、父が雷を落としました。Otōto ga terebi bakari mite iru node, chichi ga kaminari o otoshimashita.   *My father exploded at my younger brother because he does nothing but watch TV.*

kaminari oyaji — 雷親父 — *snarling old man*
[lit. a thundering old man]
彼はよく怒るので、みんなは陰で雷親父と呼んでいます。Kare wa yoku okoru node, minna wa kage de kaminari oyaji to yonde imasu.   *Since he easily gets angry, everyone calls him a snarling old man behind his back.*

kamo — 鴨 — *duck*
ii kamo — いい鴨 — *sucker*
[lit. a good duck]
値切り方を知らなかつたため、海外旅行でいい鴨になつてしまいました。Negirikata o shiranakatta tame, Kaigai ryokō de ii kamo ni natte shimaimashita.   *I was a sucker for merchants on my trip abroad since I didn't know how to haggle.*

kamo ni suru — 鴨にする — *to victimize someone*
[lit. to make a duck of someone]
彼は消費者を鴨にして、安物を高額で売りつけました。Kare wa shōhisha o kamo ni shite, yasumono o kōgaku de uritsukemashita.   *He victimized consumers, selling them cheap products at high prices.*

kamu — 噛む — *to bite, chew*
kande fukumeru yō ni — 噛んで含めるように — *carefully and repeatedly*
[lit. like chewing something and holding it in one's mouth]
先生は、それを生徒に噛んで含めるように説明しました。Sensei wa, sore o seito ni kande fukumeru yō ni setsumei shimashita.   *The teacher explained it to the pupils carefully and repeatedly.*

kande hakidasu yō ni — 噛んで吐き出すように — disgustedly
[lit. like biting something and then spitting it out]
彼女は噛んで吐き出すように、自分の誤りを認めました。Kanojo
wa kande hakidasu yō ni, jibun no ayamari o mitomemashita.
Disgustedly, she admitted her mistake.

kan — 間 — space
kan ippatsu de — 間一髪で — narrowly
[lit. with the breadth of a hair]
締め切りは、間一髪で間に合いました。Shimekiri wa, kan ippatsu de
maniaimashita.   I narrowly met the deadline.

kanban — 看板 — signboard

kanban ga naku — 看板が泣く — to be shameful to one's reputation
[lit. A signboard cries.]
そんな品質が悪いものを売ると、看板が泣きますよ。Sonna
hinshitsu ga warui mono o uru to, kanban ga nakimasu yo.   It's
shameful for the store's good name to sell such poor-quality products.

kanban o nurikaeru — 看板を塗り替える — to change occupation
[lit. to repaint a signboard]
彼女は医者の看板を塗り替えて、小説家になりました。Kanojo wa
isha no kanban o nurikaete, shosetsuka ni narimashita.   She changed
her occupation from doctor to novelist.

kanban o orosu — 看板を下ろす — *to close a shop*
[lit. to take a signboard down]

近くにスーパーができて、駅前の肉屋は看板を下ろしました。
Chikaku ni sūpā ga dekite, ekimae no nikuya wa kanban o
oroshimashita.   *The butcher near the station closed his shop after a*
supermarket had opened nearby.

kanbandaore — 看板倒れ — *showy but little substance*
[lit. falling of a signboard]

政府の実行計画は看板倒れでした。Seifu no jikkō keikaku wa
kanbandaore deshita.   *The action plan by the government was showy,*
but it had little substance.

---

kane — 金 — *money*

kane ga mono o iu — 金が物を言う — *Money talks.*
[lit. Money talks.]

選挙運動では、金がものを言うと言われています。Senkyo undō
dewa, kane ga mono o iu to iwarete imasu.   *They say money talks in*
election campaigns.

kane ga unaru — 金がうなる — *to have lots of money*
[lit. Money is humming.]

彼女の家には、金がうなっています。Kanojo no ie niwa, kane ga
unatte imasu.   *Her family has lots of money.*

kane ni akasu — 金に飽かす — *to pour in unlimited amounts of money*
[lit. to make someone bored with money]

彼は金に飽かせて、土地を買いまくりました。Kare wa kane ni
akasete, tochi o kaimakurimashita.   *He kept buying pieces of land by*
pouring in unlimited amounts of money.

kane ni itome o tsukenai — 金に糸目をつけない — *Money is no object.*
[lit. to not attach strings to money]

彼は絵画収集のためには、金に糸目をつけません。Kare wa kaiga
shūshū no tame niwa, kane ni itome o tsukemasen.   *When he collects*
paintings, money is no object.

kane no naru ki — 金のなる木 — *source of unlimited money*
[lit. a tree that bears money]

彼女にとって、お母さんは金のなる木です。Kanojo ni totte, okāsan
wa kane no nari ki desu.   *For her, her mother is a source of unlimited*
money.

kane o nekasu — 金を寝かす — *to let money sit idle*
[lit. to make money sleep]
金を寝かして置くよりも、株に長期投資した方がいいですよ。Kane
o nekashite oku yori mo, kabu ni chōki tōshi shita hō ga ii desu yo. *It's
better to invest in stocks for a long term rather than letting money sit idle.*

kane o nigiraseru — 金を握らせる — *to grease someone's palm*
[lit. to let someone grasp money]
彼は医者に金を握らせて、病院の個室をもらいました。Kare wa isha
ni kane o nigirasete, byōin no koshitsu o moraimashita. *He got a
private room in the hospital by greasing the palm of a doctor.*

kanezuku de — 金ずくで — *by sheer force of money*
[lit. totally by money]
彼女は金ずくで、その会社を買い取りました。Kanojo wa kanezuku
de sono kaisha o kaitorimashita. *She purchased the company by sheer
force of money.*

---

kane — 鉦 — *bell*
kane ya taiko de sagasu — 鉦や太鼓で探す — *to search for someone or
something actively*
[lit. to search for someone or something with a bell and a drum]
新しくできた野球のチ－ムは、監督を鉦や太鼓で探しています。
Atarashiku dekita yakyū no chīmu wa, kantoku o kane ya taiko de
sagashite imasu. *The newly organized baseball team is actively
searching for a manager.*

---

kankei — 関係 — *relation*
sankaku kankei — 三角関係 — *love triangle*
[lit. a triangular relation]
彼は今、三角関係で悩んでいます。Kare wa ima, sankaku kankei de
nayande imasu. *He's suffering in a love triangle now.*

---

kanmuri — 冠 — *crown*
kanmuri o mageru — 冠を曲げる — *to get upset*
[lit. to tilt a crown]
私が結婚記念日を忘れたので、妻は冠を曲げました。Watakushi ga
kekkon kinenbi o wasureta node, tsuma wa kanmuri o magemashita.
My wife got upset when I forgot our wedding anniversary.

---

kanshin — 歓心 — *favor*

kanshin o kau — 歓心を買う — *to curry favor with someone*
[lit. to buy someone's favor]

得意先をゴルフに招待して、歓心を買いました。Tokuisaki o gorufu
ni shōtai shite, kanshin o kaimashita.   *I curried favor with the clients by
inviting them to play golf.*

---

kantan — 肝胆 — *liver and gall*

kantan aiterasu — 肝胆相照らす — *to be close friends*
[lit. to compare each other's liver and gall]

彼とは肝胆相照らす仲なので、何でも打ち明けられます。Kare to
wa kantan aiterasu naka nanode, nandemo uchiakeraremasu.   *Because
we're close friends, I can confide in him about anything.*

kantan o hiraku — 肝胆を開く — *to unburden one's heart to someone*
[lit. to open up one's liver and gall]

彼女には悩みがあるけれど、肝胆を開く相手がいません。Kanojo
niwa nayami ga aru keredo, kantan o hiraku aite ga imasen.   *Although
she has major problems, she doesn't have anyone to whom she can
unburden her heart.*

---

kao — 顔 — *face*

kao ga au — 顔が合う — *to come across someone*
[lit. Faces meet.]

彼女と、思いがけないところで顔が合いました。Kanojo to,
omoigakenai tokoro de kao ga aimashita.   *I came across her in an
unexpected place.*

kao ga hiroi — 顔が広い — *to know many people*
[lit. One's face is wide.]

彼は顔が広いので、仕事探しの相談に行きました。Kare wa kao ga
hiroi node, shigoto sagashi no sōdan ni ikimashita.   *Since he knows
many people, I went to confer with him before job hunting.*

kao ga kiku — 顔が利く — *to be influential*
[lit. One's face is effective.]

彼は財界で顔が利きます。Kare wa zaikai de kao ga kikimasu.   *He's
influential in business circles.*

kao ga sorou — 顔が揃う — *to have everybody present*
[lit. All faces gather.]

顔が揃ったので、会議を始めましょう。Kao ga sorotta node, kaigi o hajimemashō. *We have everybody here, so let's start the meeting.*

kao ga tatsu — 顔が立つ — *to save one's honor*
[lit. One's face stands up.]
約束を無事に果たせて、顔が立ちました。Yakusoku o buji ni hatasete, kao ga tachimashita. *I saved my reputation when I fulfilled my promise without any problems.*

kao ga tsubureru — 顔が潰れる — *to lose face*
[lit. One's face falls to pieces.]
担当した企画の結果が思わしくなくて、顔が潰れました。Tantō shita kikaku no kekka ga omowashiku nakute, kao ga tsuburemashita. *I lost face when the project I took charge of didn't turn out well.*

kao ga ureru — 顔が売れる — *to be widely known*
[lit. One's face is selling.]
彼女は新進の作家として、顔が売れています。Kanojo wa shinshin no sakka to shite, kao ga urete imasu. *She has become widely known as a rising novelist.*

kao kara hi ga deru — 顔から火が出る — *to blush*
[lit. Flame comes out of one's face.]
宿題を持ってくるのを忘れて、顔から火が出ました。Shukudai o motte kuru no o wasurete, kao kara hi ga demashita. *I blushed because I forgot to bring my homework with me.*

kao ni doro o nuru — 顔に泥を塗る — *to disgrace oneself*
[lit. to put mud on one's face]
その政治家はインタビューで失言して、自らの顔に泥を塗りました。Sono seijika wa intabyū de shitsugen shite, mizukara no kao ni doro o nurimashita. *The politician disgraced himself by making a gaffe during an interview.*

kao o awaseru — 顔を合わせる — *to meet*
[lit. to put faces together]
あのチームとは、最終戦でまた顔を合わせることになりそうです。Ano chīmu to wa, saishū sen de mata kao o awaseru koto ni narisō desu. *It seems as if we'll meet that team again in the final game.*

kao o dasu — 顔を出す — *to show up*
[lit. to stick one's face out]
その集まりには行きたくなくても、顔を出すべきです。Sono

atsumari ni wa ikitaku nakutemo, kao o dasu beki desu. *Even if you may not want to go to the gathering, you ought to show up.*

kao o kasu — 顔を貸す — *to give time*
[lit. to lend one's face]
ちょっと話したいことがあるので、顔を貸してくれませんか。
Chotto hanashishitai koto ga aru node, kao o kashite kuremasen ka.
Can you spare a moment? I have something I want to talk to you about.

kao o kumoraseru — 顔を曇らせる — *to look glum*
[lit. to make one's face cloudy]
父は景気後退の長続きに、顔を曇らせています。Chichi wa keiki
kōtai no nagatsuzuki ni, kao o kumorasete imasu. *My father is looking glum because of the long recession.*

kao o miseru — 顔を見せる — *to visit*
[lit. to show one's face]
叔母は、最近顔を見せていません。Oba wa, saikin kao o misete
imasen. *My aunt hasn't visited us recently.*

kao o tateru — 顔を立てる — *to let someone save face*
[lit. to make someone's face stand]
彼女の顔を立てて、彼女ではなく私が謝りました。Kanojo no kao o
tatete, kanojo dewa naku watakushi ga ayamarimashita. *To let her save face, I apologized rather than letting her do it.*

kao o tsunagu — 顔をつなぐ — *to keep one's presence known*
[lit. to connect one's face]
顔をつなぐために、一週間に一度同じバーで飲んでいます。Kao o
tsunagu tame ni, isshūkan ni ichido onaji bā de nonde imasu. *I drink once a week at the same bar to keep on as a regular customer.*

kaobure — 顔触れ — *cast, lineup*
[lit. faces coming in contact with each other]
今度の内閣の顔触れは素晴らしいです。Kondo no naikaku no kaobure
wa subarashii desu. *The lineup of the new cabinet is wonderful.*

kaodashi — 顔出し — *token appearance*
[lit. sticking out of one's face]
顔出しだけで結構ですから、是非パーティーに来て下さい。
Kaodashi dake de kekkō desu kara, zehi pātī ni kite kudasai.
Please come to the party; even if it's a token appearance, it's quite all right.

kaoiro o ukagau — 顔色をうかがう — *to study someone's mood*
[lit. to observe the color of someone's face]
彼女は何かする前、いつも上司の顔色をうかがいます。Kanojo wa nanika suru mae, itsumo jōshi no kaoiro o ukagaimasu. *She always studies the boss's mood before doing anything.*

kaomake suru — 顔負けする — *to be shocked at something*
[lit. to lose one's face]
彼の図々しさには顔負けです。Kare no zūzūshisa niwa kaomake desu. *I'm shocked at his impertinent manner.*

kaomise — 顔見せ — *debut*
[lit. showing one's face]
このコンサートで、彼女は芸能界に顔見せしました。Kono konsāto de, kanojo wa geinō kai ni kaomise shimashita. *The concert was her debut in the entertainment business.*

kaomuke dekinai — 顔向け出来ない — *to be too ashamed to see someone*
[lit. to be unable to turn a face to someone]
大学の入学試験に落ちてしまって、家族に顔向けできません。Daigaku no nyūgaku shiken ni ochite shimatte, kazoku ni kaomuke dekimasen. *I'm too ashamed to face my family because I failed my college entrance exams.*

kaoyaku — 顔役 — *man of influence*
[lit. the role of a face]
彼がこの村の顔役です。Kare ga kono mura no kaoyaku desu. *He's the man of influence in this village.*

ōkina kao o suru — 大きな顔をする — *to act like a big deal*
[lit. to make a big face]
彼は大きな顔をしているけれど、実は課長に過ぎません。Kare wa ōkina kao o shite iru keredo, jitsu wa kachō ni sugimasen. *He's acting like a big deal, but he is, in fact, just a section chief.*

shoppai kao — しょっぱい顔 — *sullen face*
[lit. a salty face]
父はしょっぱい顔をしながら、兄に車を貸しました。Chichi wa shoppai kao o shinagara, ani ni kuruma o kashimashita. *With a sullen face, my father lent his car to my older brother.*

suzushii kao o suru — 涼しい顔をする — *to look nonchalant*
[lit. to make a cool face]
彼女はみんなに心配をかけながら、全く涼しい顔をしています。

Kanojo wa minna ni shinpai o kakenagara, mattaku suzushii kao o shite imasu. *Although she caused everybody to worry, she looks totally nonchalant.*

wagamonogao — 我が物顔 — *to be egoistic*
[lit. to behave as if it's one's own]
共同作業なのに、彼女は我が物顔に振る舞っています。Kyōdō sagyō nanomi, kanojo wa wagamonogao ni furumatte imasu. *Although it's a joint operation, she is lording it over everyone.*

kara — 殻 — *shell*
kara ni tojikomoru — 殻に閉じこもる — *to withdraw into oneself*
[lit. to keep oneself in shells]
彼は引退して以来、殻に閉じこもっています。Kare wa intai shite irai, kara ni tojikomotte imasu. *He has withdrawn into himself since his retirement.*

kara — 空 — *empty*
karaibari — 空威張り — *bluff*
[lit. an empty boast]
あれは空威張りだから、気にしなくていいですよ。Are wa karaibari dakara, ki ni shinakute ii desu yo. *That's a bluff, so you shouldn't pay any attention to it.*

karasawagi — 空騒ぎ — *much ado about nothing*
[lit. an empty fuss]
大したこと無いのに、みんなが空騒ぎしています。Taishita koto nai noni, minna ga karasawagi shite imasu. *Although it's not a big deal, everybody is making much ado about nothing.*

karada — 体 — *body*
karada ga aku — 体が空く — *to have free time*
[lit. One's body is free.]
今は忙しいけれど、来週体が空きます。Ima wa isogashii keredo, raishū karada ga akimasu. *I'm busy right now, but I'll have free time next week.*

karada ga iu koto o kikanai — 体が言うことを聞かない — *to be physically impossible*
[lit. One's body does not listen to what it is told to do.]

富士山に登りたくても、体が言うことを聞きません。Fujisan ni
noboritakutemo, karada ga iu koto o kikimasen.   Although I want to
climb Mt. Fuji, it's physically impossible for me.

karada ga tsuzuku — 体が続く — to be in good health
[lit. One's body continues.]
体が続く限り、引退するつもりはありません。Karada ga tsuzuku
kagiri, intai suru tsumori wa arimasen.   I have no intention of retiring
as long as I'm in good health.

karada o haru — 体を張る — to devote one's life to something
[lit. to spread one's own body]
彼は体を張って、新しい事業を始めました。Kare wa karada o hatte,
atarashii jigyō o hajimemashita.   He started a new business, devoting
his life to it.

karada o ko ni suru — 体を粉にする — to work very hard
[lit. to turn one's body into powder]
彼は体を粉にして働いて、自分の家を手に入れました。Kare wa
karada o ko ni shite hataraite, jibun no ie o te ni iremashita.   He
bought his own house by working very hard.

karada o kowasu — 体を壊す — to ruin one's health
[lit. to destroy one's body]
彼女は働きすぎて、体を壊してしまいました。Kanojo wa
hatarakisugite, karada o kowashite shimaimashita.   She ruined her
health by working too hard.

---

karai — 辛い — hot, pungent
  karatō — 辛党 — drinker
  [lit. a partisan of things hot]
彼は辛党で、特にビールが好きです。Kare wa karatō de, toku ni bīru
ga suki desu.   He is a drinker and especially likes beer.

---

kasa — 笠 — bamboo hat
  kasa ni kiru — 笠に着る — to exploit someone's influence
  [lit. to wear something like a bamboo hat]
彼女はお父さんが社長なのを笠に着て、態度が大きいです。Kanojo
wa otōsan ga shachō nano o kasa ni kite, taido ga ōkii desu.   Exploiting
her father's influence, the company president's daughter is arrogant.

---

kasa — 嵩 — bulk

kasa ni kakaru — 嵩にかかる — to be arrogant
[lit. to put bulk on something]
彼は嵩にかかって、自分の意見を主張しました。Kare wa kasa ni kakatte, jibun no iken o shuchō shimashita. He pushed his own opinions arrogantly.

kata — 肩 — shoulder

kata de iki o suru — 肩で息する — to gasp for breath
[lit. to breathe through one's shoulder]
テニスをした後、肩で息をしなければなりませんでした。Tenisu o shita ato, kata de iki o shinakereba narimasen deshita. After playing tennis, I had to gasp for breath.

kata de kaze o kiru — 肩で風を切る — to swagger around
[lit. to cut wind with shoulders]
彼は課長になって以来、肩で風を切っています。Kare wa kachō ni natte irai, kata de kaze o kitte imasu. He has been swaggering around since he advanced to section chief.

kata ga haru — 肩が張る — to be tense
[lit. One's shoulders get stiff.]
出張は社長と一緒だったため、肩が張りました。Shutchō wa shachō to issho datta tame, kata ga harimashita. I was tense because the business trip was with the president.

kata ga karukunaru — 肩が軽くなる — to feel relieved
[lit. One's shoulders become light.]
子供たちが大学を卒業して、肩が軽くなりました。Kodomotachi ga daigaku o sotsugyō shite, kata ga karuku narimashita. I feel relieved that all my children graduated from college.

kata ga koru — 肩が凝る — to get a stiff neck
[lit. One's shoulders get stiff.]
締め切り続きで、肩が凝りました。Shimekiri tsuzuki de, kata ga korimashita. With the deadlines coming one after another, I got a stiff neck.

kata no ni ga oriru — 肩の荷がおりる — to feel relieved
[lit. A load of packages on one's shoulders comes down.]
約束を果たして、肩の荷がおりました。Yakusoku o hatashite, kata no ni ga orimashita. I felt relieved at fulfilling my promise.

kata o hogusu — 肩をほぐす — *to relax*
[lit. to loosen one's shoulders]
彼女はご主人が無事なことを聞いて、肩をほぐしました。Kanojo
wa goshujin ga buji na koto o kiite, kata o hogushimashita.   *She relaxed
on hearing that her husband was safe.*

kata o ikaraseru — 肩を怒らせる — *to get angry*
[lit. to make one's own shoulders stiffen]
彼は肩を怒らせて、息子を非難しました。Kare wa kata o ikarasete,
musuko o hinan shimashita.   *He angrily accused his son.*

kata o ireru — 肩を入れる — *to back someone or something*
[lit. to put one's shoulders in]
彼女は長いこと、女性問題に肩を入れています。Kanojo wa nagai
koto josei mondai ni kata o irete imasu.   *She has been backing women's
issues for a long time.*

kata o motsu — 肩を持つ — *to take sides with someone*
[lit. to hold someone's shoulders]
昨日父と母が口論したとき、母の肩を持ちました。
Kinō chichi to haha ga kōron shita toki, haha no kata o mochimashita.
*I took sides with Mother when she and Father had an argument
yesterday.*

kata o naraberu — 肩を並べる — *to equal, to rival*
[lit. to put shoulders side by side]
スキーが上手になって、指導員と肩を並べるようになりました。
Sukī ga jōzu ni natte, shidōin to kata o naraberu yō ni narimashita.
My skiing has become good enough to rival that of any instructor.

kata o otosu — 肩を落とす — *to feel dejected*
[lit. to drop one's shoulders]
彼は結婚の申し込みを断られて、肩を落としています。
Kare wa kekkon no mōshikomi o kotowararete, kata o otoshite imasu.
He's feeling dejected because his marriage proposal was rejected.

kata o sobiyakasu — 肩をそびやかす — *to swell with pride*
[lit. to perk up one's shoulders]
彼は課長になって、肩をそびやかしています。Kare wa kachō ni
natte, kata o sobiyakashite imasu.   *He is swelling with pride at
becoming a section chief.*

katagaki — 肩書き — *title*
[lit. writing on a shoulder]

彼の会社での肩書きは何ですか。Kare no kaisha deno katagaki wa nan
desu ka.   *What is his title in his company?*

katagawari — 肩代わり — *to assume someone else's responsibilities*
[lit. switching one's shoulders with someone else's]
私はいま妹の肩代わりで、借金を支払っています。Watakushi wa
ima imōto no katagawari de, shakkin o shiharatte imasu.   *I'm now
assuming my younger sister's responsibilities by paying her debts.*

katami ga hiroi — 肩身が広い — *to be proud of someone or something*
[lit. One's body and shoulders are wide.]
娘が医者になって、肩身が広い思いです。Musume ga isha ni natte,
katami ga hiroi omoi desu.   *I am proud of my daughter's becoming a
medical doctor.*

katami ga semai — 肩身が狭い — *to be ashamed to face someone*
[lit. One's body and shoulders are narrow.]
約束を破って、友達に対して肩身が狭いです。Yakusoku o yabutte,
tomodachi ni taishite katami ga semai desu.   *I'm ashamed to face my
friends, because I broke my promise to them.*

katasukashi o kuwaseru — 肩すかしを食わせる — *to parry*
[lit. to pull one's shoulder away from someone]
彼女の質問に肩すかしを食わせました。Kanojo no shitsumon ni
katasukashi o kuwasemashita.   *I parried her question.*

---

kata — 片 — *one side*

katabō o katsugu — 片棒を担ぐ — *to take part in something (bad)*
[lit. to carry one end of a pole]
彼は、その会社の乗っ取りの片棒を担ぎました。Kare wa, sono
kaisha no nottori no katabō o katsugimashita.   *He took part in the
hostile takeover of that company.*

katahada nugu — 片肌脱ぐ — *to help someone in particular*
[lit. to bare one shoulder]
あなたのためなら、片肌脱ぎましょう。Anata no tame nara, katahada
nugimashō.   *I'll help only because it's you.*

katahara itai — 片腹痛い — *ridiculous, absurd*
[lit. One side of one's abdomen hurts.]
嘘つきの彼女が私を嘘つきと呼ぶなんて、片腹痛いです。Usotsuki
no kanojo ga watakushi o usotsuki to yobu nante, katahara itai desu.
It's ridiculous for her to call me a liar when she's the liar.

kataiji o haru — 片意地を張る — to be obstinate
[lit. to stick with a one-sided will]

彼は意見の間違いを認める代わりに、まだ片意地を張っています。
Kare wa iken no machigai o mitomeru kawari ni, mada kataiji o hatte imasu.   Instead of admitting that his opinion was wrong, he's still obstinate.

kataomoi — 片思い — unrequited love
[lit. one-sided thinking]

彼は片思いで悩んでいます。Kare wa kataomoi de nayande imasu.
He is agonizing over his unrequited love.

katateochi — 片手落ち — unfair, partial
[lit. one hand dropping]

交渉の分裂で、こちら側だけを非難するのは片手落ちです。
Kōshō no bunretsu de, kochiragawa dake o hinan suru no wa katateochi desu.   It's unfair to blame only this side for the breakdown of the negotiations.

kataude — 片腕 — right-hand man
[lit. one arm]

彼は私の片腕です。Kare wa watakushi no kataude desu.   He is my right-hand man.

---

kata — 型、形 — form, shape, mold

kata ni hamatta — 型にはまつた — conventional
[lit. to fit into a mold]

彼の演説は型にはまっていて、面白くありませんでした。Kare no enzetsu wa kata ni hamatte ite, omoshiroku arimasen deshita.   His speech wasn't interesting because it was too conventional.

kata ni torawareru — 型にとらわれる — conventional
[lit. to be captured by a form]

彼の絵は型にとらわれすぎていて、面白くありません。Kare no e wa kata ni torawaresugite ite, omoshiroku arimasen.   Because her paintings are too conventional, they're not interesting.

katanashi — 形無し — disgrace
[lit. no shape]

テニスが自慢の彼も、息子に負けて形無しでした。Tenisu ga jiman no kare mo, musuko ni makete katanashi deshita.   He was proud of his tennis, but he lost face by losing the game to his son.

katayaburi no — 型破りの — *unconventional*
[lit. of breaking a form]
彼女は、型破りの政治家です。 Kanojo wa, katayaburi no seijika desu.
She is an unconventional politician.

---

katazu — 固唾 — *saliva*
katazu o nomu — 固唾を呑む — *to hold one's breath, breathtakingly*
[lit. to swallow one's saliva]
その庭は、固唾を呑むほどの美しさでした。 Sono niwa wa, katazu o
nomu hodo no utsukushisa deshita. *That garden was breathtakingly
beautiful.*

---

katsu — 活 — *life*
  katsu o ireru — 活を入れる — *to cheer someone up*
[lit. to put life back in]
彼は最近元気がないので、活を入れました。 Kare wa saikin genki ga
nai node, katsu o iremashita. *Since he seemed to have lost heart
recently, I cheered him up.*

---

kayui — 痒い — *itchy*
  kayui tokoro ni te ga todoku — 痒いところに手が届く — *to be very
    attentive*
[lit. Someone's hand reaches one's itchy spot.]
今度の旅行先では、痒いところに手が届く待遇を受けました。
  Kondo no ryokō saki dewa, kayui tokoro ni te ga todoku taigū o
ukemashita. *Where we went on the last trip, we received very attentive
treatment.*

---

kaze — 風 — *wind*
  kazamuki ga warui — 風向きが悪い — *to be in bad mood*
[lit. The wind direction is bad.]
今晩は、父の風向きが悪いです。 Konban wa, chichi no kazamuki ga
warui desu. *My father is in a bad mood tonight.*

  kaze no fukimawashi — 風の吹き回し — *for some reason or other*
[lit. swirling of wind]
どうした風の吹き回しか、突然叔母が訪ねてきました。Dō shita
kaze no fukimawashi ka, totsuzen oba ga tazunete kimashita. *For some
reason or other, my aunt unexpectedly came to visit us.*

kaze no tayori — 風の便り — *rumor*
[lit. a message by wind]
風の便りに聞くと、彼女は去年離婚したそうです。Kaze no tayori ni
kiku to, kanojo wa kyonen rikon shita sō desu. *Rumor has it that she
was divorced last year.*

kazeatari ga tsuyoi — 風当たりが強い — *strong criticism to mount*
[lit. The wind strongly blows onto someone or something.]
政府の経済政策に対する風当たりが強まっています。Seifu no keizai
seisaku ni taisuru kazeatari ga tsuyomatte imasu. *Strong criticism of
the government's economic policy is mounting.*

---

ke — 毛 — *hair, fur*

ke no haeta yō na — 毛の生えたような — *to be not much better than
someone or something*
[lit. like hair coming out]
彼は、素人に毛の生えたような歌手にすぎません。Kare wa, shirōto
ni ke no haeta yō na kashu ni sugimasen. *Simply put, he's not much
better than an amateur singer.*

keiro no kawatta — 毛色の変わった — *strange, unusual*
[lit. The hair color is different.]
彼女の経歴は、毛色が変わっています。Kanojo no keireki wa, keiro
ga kawatte imasu. *Her background is unusual.*

kenami no ii — 毛並みのいい — *to be from a good family*
[lit. The coat of hair is good.]
彼の毛並みがいい事は、会ってすぐに分かりました。Kare no
kenami ga ii koto wa, atte sugu ni wakarimashita. *When we met, I
knew immediately that he was from a good family.*

---

kechi — けち — *bad luck*

kechi o tsukeru — けちを付ける — *to find fault with something*
[lit. to attach bad luck]
彼は、みんなが賛成した計画にけちを付けました。Kare wa, minna
ga sansei shita keikaku ni kechi o tsukemashita. *He found fault with
the plan everybody else agreed on.*

---

keijū — 軽重 — *weight*

keijū o hakaru — 軽重を計る — *to consider something carefully*
[lit. to measure weight]

契約は、その軽重を計ってから合意するべきです。Keiyaku wa, sono keijū o hakatte kara gōi suru beki desu. *You should agree to the contract only after considering it carefully.*

keisan — 計算 — *calculation*
keisan ni ireru — 計算に入れる — *to take something into account*
[lit. to include something in the calculations]
ある程度の遅れは、予定の計算に入れてあります。Aru teido no okure wa, yotei no keisan ni irete arimasu. *When planning the schedule, we've taken into account a certain amount of delay.*

kejime — けじめ — *difference*
kejime o tsukeru — けじめをつける — *to distinguish*
[lit. to attach a difference]
仕事と遊びのけじめをつけなさい。Shigoto to asobi no kejime o tsukenasai. *You should distinguish between work and play.*

kekki — 血気 — *vigor*
kekki ni hayaru — 血気にはやる — *to be rash*
[lit. to be eager with vigor]
彼らは血気にはやって行動したため、戦略に欠けていました。
Karera wa kekki ni hayatte kōdō shita tame, senryaku ni kakete imashita. *Because they acted rashly, they were short on strategy.*

kekkizakari — 血気盛り — *young and vigorous*
[lit. to be at the peak of vigor]
彼は血気盛りだけに、妥協の価値を知りません。Kare wa kekkizakari dake ni, dakyō no kachi o shirimasen. *Since he's still young and vigorous, he doesn't know the value of compromise.*

kemu, kemuri — 煙 — *smoke*
kemu ni maku — 煙に巻く — *to be evasive*
[lit. to wrap something in smoke]
彼はどんな質問をされても、相手を煙に巻くのが上手です。Kare wa donna shitsumon o saretemo, aite o kemu ni maku no ga jōzu desu. *No matter what kind of questions they ask, he's skilled at being evasive.*

kemuri ni naru — 煙になる — *to waste, to dissipate*
[lit. to become smoke]

努力しましたが、結果は煙になってしまいました。Doryoku
shimashita ga, kekka wa kemuri ni natte shimaimashita. *I tried hard,
but my efforts were wasted.*

kemutagaru — 煙たがる — *to keep someone at a distance*
[lit. to be sensitive to smoke]
彼は議論好きなので、みんなが煙たがっています。
Kare wa gironzuki nanode, minna ga kemutagatte imasu.
Because he's argumentative, everybody keeps him at a distance.

---

ken — 犬 — *dog*
ken-en no naka — 犬猿の仲 — *to be on bad terms*
[lit. relations between a dog and a monkey]
彼と彼女は犬猿の仲です。Kare to kanojo wa ken-en no naka desu.
He and she are on bad terms.

---

keta — 桁 — *unit, figure*
keta ga chigau — 桁が違う — *to be no match*
[lit. The unit is different.]
彼のお金の使い方は、普通の人とは桁が違います。
Kare no okane no tsukaikata wa, futsū no hito towa keta ga chigaimasu.
The way he spends money is no match for ordinary people.

ketachigai no — 桁違いの — *extraordinary*
[lit. a different unit]
彼女は桁違いの金持ちです。Kanojo wa ketachigai no kanemochi desu.
She is extraordinarily rich.

ketahazure no — 桁はずれの — *unusual*
[lit. off the units]
彼女は、桁はずれの才能を持ったピアニストです。Kanojo wa, ketahazure
no sainō o motta pianisuto desu. *She is an unusually talented pianist.*

---

ki — 気 — *mind, feeling, intention, mood, attention, sensation*
ki ga aru — 気がある — *to be interested in someone or something*
[lit. There are feelings.]
彼女は私に気があるようです。Kanojo wa watakushi ni ki ga aru yō
desu. *She seems to be interested in me.*

ki ga chiru — 気が散る — *to be distracted*
[lit. One's mind scatters.]

テレビの音に気が散って、仕事に集中できません。Terebi no oto ni ki ga chitte, shigoto ni shūchū dekimasen.　I can't concentrate on my work because I'm distracted by the noise of the TV.

ki ga hareru — 気が晴れる — to feel relieved
[lit. One's feelings are cleared.]
試験期間が終わって、気が晴れました。Shiken kikan ga owatte, ki ga haremashita.　I felt relieved because the exam period was over.

ki ga haritsumeru — 気が張りつめる — to be fully alert
[lit. One's attention stretches to the full extent.]
気が張りつめていたので、全然疲れを覚えませんでした。Ki ga haritsumete ita node, zenzen tsukare o oboemasen deshita.　Since I was fully alert, I didn't feel tired at all.

ki ga hayai — 気が早い — to be hasty
[lit. One's feelings are fast.]
彼は気が早すぎるので、結論には信用が置けません。Kare wa ki ga hayasugiru node, ketsuron niwa shin-yō ga okemasen.　Since he's too hasty, we can't really trust his conclusions.

ki ga hikeru — 気が引ける — to feel ashamed
[lit. One's feeling is pulling oneself backward.]
私の意見でそうなったために、気が引けます。Watakushi no iken de sō natta tame ni, ki ga hikemasu.　I feel ashamed because my opinion led to that result.

ki ga ki de nai — 気が気でない — to be anxious
[lit. One's feeling is not materializing.]
試験の結果に、気が気ではありません。Shiken no kekka ni, ki ga ki dewa arimasen.　I'm very anxious about the results of the exam.

ki ga kiku — 気が利く — to be sensible
[lit. One's sensitivity is effective.]
彼女は気が利くので、何を頼んでも安心です。Kanojo wa ki ga kiku node, nani o tanondemo anshin desu.　Since she's sensible, you can count on her when you ask her to do something.

ki ga magireru — 気が紛れる — to be distracted
[lit. One's intention is indistinguishable.]
気が紛れて、発表の準備を忘れました。Ki ga magirete, happyō no junbi o wasuremashita.　Because I was distracted, I forgot to prepare for my oral report.

ki ga meiru — 気が滅入る — *to get depressed*
[lit. One's feelings go down.]
将来のことを考えると、気が滅入ります。Shōrai no koto o kangaeru
to, ki ga meirimasu. *If I think about the future, I get depressed.*

ki ga momeru — 気がもめる — *to be anxious*
[lit. The feeling is rubbed.]
息子の将来については、気がもめます。Musuko no shōrai ni tsuite wa,
ki ga momemasu. *I feel anxious about my son's future.*

ki ga nai — 気がない — *to be not interested in someone or something*
[lit. One's feelings don't exist.]
山登りには、あまり気がありません。Yamanobori niwa, amari ki ga
arimasen. *I'm not much interested in mountain climbing.*

ki ga okenai — 気が置けない — *to feel very close to someone*
[lit. no way to keep distance between persons' feelings]
彼とは、気が置けない仲です。Kare to wa, ki ga okenai naka desu.
He and I are very close.

ki ga ōkii — 気が大きい — *to be generous*
[lit. One's heart is big.]
彼は気が大きいから、何を頼んでも引き受けてくれます。Kare wa
ki ga ōkii kara, nani o tanondemo hikiukete kuremasu. *Since he's
generous, he'll do whatever you ask.*

ki ga omoi — 気が重い — *to be depressing*
[lit. One's heart is heavy.]
この週末は働かなければならないので、気が重いです。Kono
shūmatsu wa hatarakanakereba naranai node, ki ga omoi desu. *It's
depressing to have to work during the weekend.*

ki ga sasu — 気が差す — *to feel guilty*
[lit. One's feeling fills.]
約束を守れなくて、気が差します。Yakusoku o mamorenakute, ki ga
sashimasu. *I feel guilty because I couldn't keep my promise.*

ki ga seku — 気が急く — *to be too anxious*
[lit. One's feelings are in a hurry.]
気が急いて、試験はあまり出来ませんでした。Ki ga seite, shiken wa
amari dekimasen deshita. *I was too anxious, so I didn't do well on the
exam.*

ki ga sumu — 気が済む — *to feel justified*
[lit. One's feelings end.]

私が正しいことを証明するまでは、気が済みません。 Watakushi ga tadashii koto o shōmei suru made wa, ki ga sumimasen. *I won't feel justified until I prove that I'm right.*

ki ga susumanai — 気が進まない — *to be not in the mood*
[lit. One's feeling doesn't proceed.]
パーティーに誘われましたが、気が進みません。 Pātī ni sasowaremashita ga, ki ga susumimasen. *I was invited to a party, but I'm not in the mood.*

ki ga tatte iru — 気が立っている — *to be on edge*
[lit. One's feelings are standing.]
彼は仕事がはかどらないので、気が立っています。 Kare wa shigoto ga hakadoranai node, ki ga tatte imasu. *He's on edge because his work isn't progressing much.*

ki ga togameru — 気が咎める — *to feel guilty*
[lit. One's feelings accuse oneself.]
昨日は妻の誕生日を忘れてしまい、気が咎めました。 Kinō wa tsuma no tanjōbi o wasurete shimai, ki ga togamemashita. *I felt guilty because I forgot my wife's birthday yesterday.*

ki ga tōkunaru yō — 気が遠くなるよう — *to feel overwhelmed*
[lit. like fainting]
明日しなければならないことを考えると、気が遠くなるようです。 Ashita shinakereba naranai koto o kangaeru to, ki ga tōkunaru yō desu. *When I think about everything I have to do tomorrow, I feel overwhelmed.*

ki ga tsuku — 気がつく — *to be attentive*
[lit. to become aware of something]
新しい秘書は、よく気がつきます。 Atarashii hisho wa, yoku ki ga tsukimasu. *The new secretary is very attentive.*

ki ni iru — 気に入る — *to be pleased with someone or something*
[lit. to enter into one's mind]
昨日行ったレストランがとても気に入りました。 Kinō itta resutoran ga totemo ki ni irimashita. *I was very pleased with the restaurant we went to yesterday.*

ki ni kakaru — 気にかかる — *to be anxious about someone or something*
[lit. Something hangs in one's mind.]
旅行中、残してきた子供のことが気にかかりました。 Ryokō chū, nokoshite kita kodomo no koto ga ki ni kakarimashita. *During the trip,*

we were anxious about our children at home.

ki ni kuwanai — 気に食わない — *to detest*
[lit. to not suit one's feelings]
私は、彼女の人生に対する態度が気に食いません。Watakushi wa,
kanojo no jinsei ni taisuru taido ga ki ni kuimasen. *I detest her attitude
toward life.*

ki ni naru — 気になる — *to feel uneasy*
[lit. to come to one's feelings]
先週受けた就職の面接の結果が気になります。Senshū uketa shūshoku
no mensetsu no kekka ga ki ni narimasu. *I feel uneasy about the results
of the job interview I had last week.*

ki ni sawaru — 気に障る — *to offend*
[lit. to interfere with someone's feelings]
彼女は人の気に障ることを平気でよく言います。Kanojo wa hito no
ki ni sawaru koto o heiki de yoku iimasu. *Without any hesitation, she
often says things that offend others.*

ki ni suru — 気にする — *to be anxious about someone or something*
[lit. to be mindful]
最初のデートの後、彼は彼女がどう思ったか気にしています。
Saisho no dēto no ato, kare wa kanojo ga dō omottaka ki ni shite imasu.
Since their first date, he has been anxious about how she felt about him.

ki ni yamu — 気に病む — *to be worried*
[lit. to be sick to one's heart]
彼は娘の将来をひどく気に病んでいます。Kare wa musume no shōrai
o hidoku ki ni yande imasu. *He is extremely worried about his
daughter's future.*

ki o haku — 気を吐く — *to be elated*
[lit. to spew one's sensation out]
彼は株で大儲けして気を吐いています。Kare wa kabu de ōmōke shite ki
o haite imasu. *He's elated at making a large profit on the stock market.*

ki o hiku — 気を引く — *to attract*
[lit. to pull someone's attention]
彼女の気を引くことに成功しました。Kanojo no ki o hiku koto ni
seikō shimashita. *I succeeded in attracting her.*

ki o ireru — 気を入れる — *to pour one's energy*
[lit. to put one's feelings into something]

遊びより、勉強にもっと気を入れなさい。Asobi yori, benkyō ni motto ki o irenasai. *You should pour more energy into studying than playing.*

ki o kikasu — 気を利かす — *to be considerate*
[lit. to make one's mind work]
母に気を利かせて、お使いをしてあげました。Haha ni ki o kikasete, otsukai o shite agemashita. *To be considerate of my mother, I did errands for her.*

ki o kubaru — 気を配る — *to be attentive to someone or something*
[lit. to deliver one's attention]
彼女は子供の教育に、非常に気を配つています。Kanojo wa kodomo no kyōiku ni, hijō ni ki o kubatte imasu. *She is extremely attentive to her children's education.*

ki o kusarasu — 気を腐らす — *to be depressed*
[lit. to let one's feelings rot]
彼は計画が思い通りにいかなくて、気を腐らせています。Kare wa keikaku ga omoidōri ni ikanakute, ki o kusarasete imasu. *He has been depressed because the plan didn't go as he expected.*

ki o mawashisugiru — 気を回しすぎる — *to be overly concerned*
[lit. to spin one's mind too much]
彼女は街の犯罪について、気を回しすぎます。Kanojo wa machi no hanzai ni tsuite, ki o mawashisugimasu. *She is overly concerned about street crime.*

ki o momu — 気を揉む — *to be anxious*
[lit. to rub one's feelings]
試験の結果については、気を揉む必要はありません。Shiken no kekka ni tsuite wa, ki o momu hitsuyō wa arimasen. *You don't need to be anxious about the results of the exam.*

ki o motaseru — 気を持たせる — *to raise someone's hopes*
[lit. to let someone have one's feelings]
お金を貸す件では、彼に気を持たせるつもりはありませんでした。Okane o kasu ken dewa, kare ni ki o motaseru tsumori wa arimasen deshita. *I didn't have any intention of raising his hopes that I would lend him money.*

ki o nomareru — 気を呑まれる — *to be overwhelmed*
[lit. to get one's mind swallowed]
交渉で、相手側の頑固さに気を呑まれました。Kōshō de, aitegawa no

gankosa ni ki o nomaremashita. *We were overwhelmed by the stubbornness of our counterpart in the negotiations.*

ki o otosu — 気を落とす — *to be disappointed*
[lit. to drop one's mood]
ボーナスが期待していたより少なくて、気を落としました。Bōnasu ga kitai shite ita yori sukunakute, ki o otoshimashita. *I was disappointed because the bonus was less than I had expected.*

ki o torareru — 気を取られる — *to be distracted by someone or something*
[lit. to have one's attention taken away]
締め切りに気を取られて、映画を楽しめませんでした。Shimekiri ni ki o torarete, eiga o tanoshimemasen deshita. *I couldn't enjoy the movie because I was distracted by the deadline.*

ki o torinaosu — 気を取り直す — *to pull oneself together*
[lit. to take one's own feelings up again]
火事で全てを失いましたが、気を取り直してまた働き始めました。Kaji de subete o ushinaimashita ga, ki o torinaoshite mata hatarakihajimemashita. *I lost everything in a fire but pulled myself together and started over again.*

ki o tsukau — 気を遣う — *to worry*
[lit. to spend one's own mind]
彼女は何事にも気を遣いすぎます。Kanojo wa nanigoto nimo ki o tsukaisugimasu. *She worries too much about everything.*

ki o waruku suru — 気を悪くする — *to take offense*
[lit. to make one's own feelings bad]
彼は私が冗談で言ったことに、気を悪くしました。Kare wa watakushi ga jōdan de itta koto ni, ki o waruku shimashita. *He took offense at what I meant as a joke.*

ki o yokusuru — 気をよくする — *to feel good*
[lit. to make one's own feelings good]
彼は息子が有名大学に入学するので、気をよくしています。Kare wa musuko ga yūmei daigaku ni nyūgaku suru node, ki o yoku shite imasu. *He's feeling good because his son is going to a famous university.*

ki o yurusu — 気を許す — *to let one's guard down*
[lit. to let one's mind trust]

彼女に気を許したため、苦い経験をしました。Kanojo ni ki o
yurushita tame, nigai keiken o shimashita.   *I had a bitter experience
because I let my guard down with her.*

kibarashi — 気晴らし — *for a change of pace*
[lit. clearing one's mind]
先週は忙しかったので、週末に気晴らしにテニスをしました。
Senshū wa isogashikatta node, shūmatsu ni kibarashi ni tenisu o
shimashita.   *Since last week was busy, for a change of pace I played
tennis on the weekend.*

kibaru — 気張る — *to exert oneself*
[lit. to stretch one's intention]
彼は大学入試のため、気張って勉強しています。Kare wa daigaku
nyūshi no tame, kibatte benkyō shite imasu.   *He's exerting himself to
study for the college entrance exams.*

kiokure suru — 気後れする — *to feel timid*
[lit. One's mind gets behind.]
今日は大勢の前で演説しなければならず、気後れしました。Kyō wa
ōzei no mae de enzetsu shinakereba narazu, kiokure shimashita.   *Today
I felt timid because I had to give a speech in front of a lot of people.*

kiyasui — 気安い — *to be willing, to be friendly*
[lit. One's mind is easy.]
彼は気安く何でもやってくれます。Kare wa kiyasuku nandemo yatte
kuremasu.   *He does anything for you willingly.*

---

ki — 機 — *chance*
ki ga jukusu — 機が熟す — *The opportunity has come.*
[lit. A chance ripens.]
会社を辞めて独立する機が熟しました。Kaisha o yamete dokuritsu
suru ki ga jukushimashita.   *The opportunity has come to quit the
company and start my own business.*

ki ni jōjiru — 機に乗じる — *to take advantage of an opportunity*
[lit. to ride on a chance]
円高の機に乗じて、家族を連れて海外旅行に行きました。En daka
no ki ni jōjite, kazoku o tsurete kaigai ryokō ni ikimashita.   *Taking
advantage of the strong yen, I traveled abroad with my family.*

---

ki — 木 — *tree*

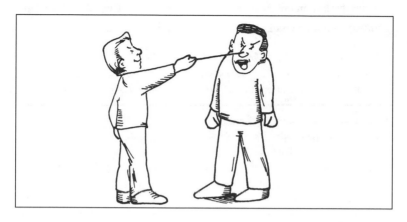

ki de hana o kukuru yō na — 木で鼻をくくるような — *curt*
[lit. like rubbing a nose with a piece of wood]
彼に借金を申し込みましたが、木で鼻をくくるような返事でした。
Kare ni shakkin o mōshikomimashita ga, ki de hana o kukuru yō na henji
deshita.　*I asked him for a loan, but he gave me a curt response.*

ki ni take o tsugu — 木に竹を接ぐ — *to not mix, to not be natural*
[lit. to graft a bamboo to a tree]
その政治連合は、最初から木に竹を接ぐようなものでした。Sono
seiji rengō wa, saisho kara ki ni take o tsugu yō na mono deshita.　*That
political coalition was not natural to begin with.*

kiai — 気合い — *spirit*
kiai o ireru — 気合いを入れる — *to reprimand someone*
[lit. to put spirit into someone]
息子は最近あまり勉強しないので、気合いを入れました。Musuko
wa saikin amari benkyō shinai node, kiai o iremashita.　*I reprimanded
my son for not studying much recently.*

kibisu — きびす — *heel*
kibisu o kaesu — きびすを返す — *to turn back*
[lit. to turn one's heels]
その件については、今更きびすを返すわけにはいきません。Sono

ken ni tsuite wa, imasara kibisu o kaesu wake niwa ikimaen.　I can't
turn back from my position on that subject at such a late date.

kibisu o sessuru yō ni — きびすを接するように — one after another
[lit. by touching one heel with another]
日本各地で、地震がきびすを接するように起こっています。Nihon
kakuchi de, jishin ga kibisu o sessuru yō ni okotte imasu.　There are
earthquakes one after another all over Japan.

---

kibone — 気骨 — mental strain
kibone ga oreru — 気骨が折れる — to be stressful
[lit. One's mind and bones break.]
義母が来ているので、多少気骨が折れます。Gibo ga kite iru node,
tashō kibone ga oremasu.　Because my mother-in-law is staying with
us, it's somewhat stressful.

---

kidō — 軌道 — orbit
kidō ni noru — 軌道に乗る — to get on track
[lit. to get on an orbit]
長期計画が、やっと軌道に乗り始めました。Chōki keikaku ga, yatto kidō
ni norihajimemashita.　The long-term plan finally started to get on track.

---

kigen — 機嫌 — mood
gokigen ga naname — ご機嫌が斜め — to be in a bad temper
[lit. Someone's mood is oblique.]
妻はご機嫌が斜めなので、うっかり口を利くと危ないです。Tsuma
wa gokigen ga naname nanode, ukkari kuchi o kiku to abunai desu.
Because my wife is in a bad temper, it's dangerous if I say something
casually.

gokigentori — ご機嫌取り — flattering
[lit. making someone's mood good]
彼はいつも部長のご機嫌取りをしています。Kare wa itsumo buchō no
gokigentori o shite imasu.　He's always flattering the department chief.

---

kiiroi — 黄色い — yellow
kiiroi koe — 黄色い声 — screeching voice
[lit. a yellow voice]
人気の歌手が出てくると、ファンは黄色い声を上げました。Ninki

no kashu ga dete kuru to, fan wa kiiroi koe o agemashita.   When the popular singer appeared, his fans started screeching.

kikotsu — 気骨 — spirit
kikotsu ga aru — 気骨がある — to be gutsy
[lit. to have a mind and bones]
彼は静かだけれど、とても気骨があります。Kare wa shizuka da keredo, totemo kikotsu ga arimasu.   He is quiet but very gutsy.

kiku — 聞く — to hear, to listen
kikimimi o tateru — 聞き耳を立てる — to be all ears
[lit. to make listening ears stand up]
彼女は娘のボーイフレンドとの電話に、聞き耳を立てました。
Kanojo wa musume no boifurendo to no denwa ni, kikimimi o tatemashita.   She was all ears during her daughter's phone conversation with her boyfriend.

kikishi ni masaru — 聞きしに勝る — to exceed one's expectations
[lit. to surpass what one has heard]
彼の歌は、聞きしに勝るすばらしさでした。Kare no uta wa, kikishi ni masaru subarashisa deshita.   His singing exceeded my expectations.

kikoeyogashi ni — 聞こえよがしに — saying something negative intentionally within someone's earshot
[lit. as if wishing for something to be heard]
彼女は聞こえよがしに、私の悪口を言っています。Kanojo wa kikoeyogashi ni, watakushi no warukuchi o itte imasu.   She's intentionally badmouthing me within my earshot.

kiku — 利く — to be effective
kiita fū na — 利いた風な — presumptuous
[lit. as if effective]
彼はこの会社で新しいのに、利いた風な口を利いています。Kare wa kono kaisha de atarashii noni, kiita fū na kuchi o kiite imasu.   Although he's new in the company, he's making presumptuous statements.

kime — 肌理 — texture
kime no komakai — 肌理の細かい — detailed
[lit. finely textured]
彼は、肌理の細かい企画が得意ではありません。Kare wa kime no

komakai kikaku ga tokui dewa arimasen. *He is not good at detailed planning.*

---

kimo — 肝 — *liver*

dogimo o nukareru — 度肝を抜かれる — *to be dumbfounded*
[lit. One's liver gets extracted.]
息子に突然結婚すると言われ、度肝を抜かれました。Musuko ni totsuzen kekkon suru to iware, dogimo o nukaremashita. *I was dumbfounded by my son's sudden announcement that he was getting married.*

kimo ga futoi — 肝が太い — *bold, plucky*
[lit. One's liver is thick.]
彼は肝が太いので、いざというときに頼りになります。Kare wa kimo ga futoi node, iza to iu toki ni tayori ni narimasu. *Because he's plucky, you can rely on him during an emergency.*

kimo ga suwaru — 肝が据わる — *to have nerves of iron*
[lit. One's liver settles firmly.]
彼はあらゆる経験を積んできただけに、肝が据わっています。Kare wa arayuru keiken o tsunde kita dake ni, kimo ga suwatte imasu. *Because he's had all sorts of experience, he has nerves of iron.*

kimo ni meijiru — 肝に銘じる — *to take something to heart*
[lit. to chisel something into one's liver]
その助言を肝に銘じて、同じ間違いをしないことを誓います。Sono jogen o kimo ni meijite, onaji machigai o shinai koto o chikaimasu. *I promise that I'll take your advice to heart and won't make the same mistake again.*

kimo o hiyasu — 肝を冷やす — *to be scared*
[lit. to chill one's liver]
大切な面会の約束に遅れそうになって、肝を冷やしました。Taisetsu na menkai no yakusoku ni okureso ni natte, kimo o hiyashimashita. *I was scared that I would be late for an important appointment.*

kimo o sueru — 肝を据える — *to be resolved*
[lit. to set one's liver firmly]
どんな結果でもそれを受け入れようと肝を据えました。Donna kekka demo sore o ukeireyō to kimo o suemashita. *I was resolved to accept whatever the outcome would be.*

kimo o tsubusu — 肝を潰す — *to be flabbergasted*
[lit. to smash one's own liver]
彼女のあまりにも図々しい態度に、肝を潰しました。Kanojo no
amari nimo zūzūshii taido ni, kimo o tsubushimashita. *I was
flabbergasted by her extremely cheeky attitude.*

kimoiri — 肝煎り — *good offices, sponsorship*
[lit. roasting of a liver]
地元の政治家の肝煎りで、東京で仕事を見つけることが出来ました。
Jimoto no seijika no kimoiri de, Tōkyō de shigoto o mitsukeru koto ga
dekimashita. *Because of the good offices of the local politician, I was
able to find a job in Tokyo.*

---

kimochi — 気持ち — *feeling, frame of mind*
kimochi o kumu — 気持ちを汲む — *to sense someone's feelings*
[lit. to scoop up someone's feelings]
彼女の罪の意識を汲んで、今度の失敗は大目に見てあげました。
Kanojo no tsumi no ishiki o kunde, kondo no shippai wa ōme ni mite
agemashita. *Sensing her feelings of guilt, I overlooked her mistake this
time.*

---

kimyaku — 気脈 — *blood vessel*
kimyaku o tsūjiru — 気脈を通じる — *to conspire with someone/others*
[lit. to connect one's blood vessels with others']
あの組合の幹部は、会社側と気脈を通じているそうです。Ano
kumiai no kanbu wa, kaishagawa to kimyaku o tsūjite iru sō desu. *That
senior labor union official is said to be conspiring with management.*

---

kinsen — 琴線 — *koto (Japanese harp) strings*
kinsen ni fureru — 琴線に触れる — *to tug at one's heartstrings*
[lit. to touch *koto* strings]
彼女の優しい言葉が、私の心の琴線に触れました。Kanojo no
yasashii kotoba ga, watakushi no kokoro no kinsen ni furemashita. *Her
gentle words tugged at my heartstrings.*

---

kinteki — 金的 — *golden bull's-eye*
kinteki o itomeru — 金的を射止める — *to hit the jackpot*
[lit. to hit the golden bull's-eye]
彼は社長の娘と結婚して、金的を射止めました。Kare wa shachō no

musume to kekkon shite, kinteki o itomemashita.   *He hit the jackpot by marrying the company president's daughter.*

kirin — 麒麟 — *giraffe*

kirinji — 麒麟児 — *prodigy*
[lit. a giraffe child]
あの女の子は、麒麟児のピアニストです。 Ano onna no ko wa, kirinji no pianisuto desu.   *That girl is a prodigy as a pianist.*

kiru — 切る — *to cut*
kiremono — 切れ者 — *capable person*
[lit. someone who can cut things]
彼は切れ者だから、大切な仕事も任せられます。 Kare wa kiremono dakara, taisetsu na shigoto mo makaseraremasu.   *Since he's capable, you can trust him with important work.*

kittemo kirenai — 切っても切れない — *to be closely bound to someone*
[lit. to be not able to cut even if someone tries]
彼らは、切っても切れない仲です。 Karera wa kittemo kirenai naka desu.   *They are closely bound to each other.*

kisei — 気勢 — *spirit, vigor*
kisei o ageru — 気勢を上げる — *to be elated*
[lit. to raise spirits]
わが社の売り上げが競争相手のを抜いたので、気勢を上げました。

Waga sha no uriage ga kyōsō aite no o nuita node, kisei o agemashita.
We were elated because our sales surpassed our competitor's.

kitsune — 狐 — *fox*
kitsune ni tsumamareta yō — 狐につままれたよう — *to be puzzled*
[lit. like being fooled by a fox]
駄目だと思った試験に受かって、狐につままれたような気がしました。
Dame da to omotta shiken ni ukatte, kitsune ni tsumamareta yō na ki ga
shimashita.   *I was puzzled when I passed the exam which I thought I
had failed.*

kitsune no yomeiri — 狐の嫁入り — *rain while the sun is shining*
[lit. a fox's wedding]
ピクニックに行こうとしたら、狐の嫁入りでした。Pikunikku ni ikō
to shitara, kitsune no yomeiri deshita.   *Just as we were about to go on a
picnic, it started raining while the sun was shining.*

kitsune to tanuki no bakashiai — 狐と狸の化かし合い — *to try to
outfox each other*
[lit. A fox and a raccoon dog are trying to bewitch each other.]
あの二人は昇進を争って、狐と狸の化かし合いをしています。Ano
futari wa shōshin o arasotte, kitsune to tanuki no bakashiai o shite imasu.
*Those two are competing for a promotion and trying to outfox each
other.*

kō — 紅 — *red*
kō itten — 紅一点 — *only one woman among men*
[lit. one red spot]
討論会の出席者としては、彼女が紅一点でした。Tōronkai no
shussekisha to shite wa, kanojo ga kō itten deshita.   *As for the
participants in the debate, she was the only woman among the men.*

kobana — 小鼻 — *wings of a nose*
kobana o ugomekasu — 小鼻をうごめかす — *to have a swelled head*
[lit. to move the wings of one's nose incessantly]
彼は高級車を買って、小鼻をうごめかしています。Kare wa
kōkyūsha o katte, kobana o ugomekashite imasu.   *He bought an
expensive car, and he has a swelled head.*

koe — 声 — *voice*

koe ga kakaru — 声が掛かる — *to be asked*
[lit. Someone's voice approaches.]

友達から、映画に行かないかと声が掛かりました。Tomodachi kara, eiga ni ikanaika to koe ga kakarimashita. *I was asked by my friend if I would like to go to a movie with him.*

koe o furishiboru — 声を振り絞る — *to strain one's voice*
[lit. to wring out one's voice]

候補者は声を振り絞つて、街頭の人々に投票を頼みました。Kōhosha wa koe o furishibotte, gaitō no hitobito ni tōhyō o tanomimashita. *Straining his voice, the candidate asked people in the street to vote for him.*

koe o hazumasete — 声を弾ませて — *in a lively tone of voice*
[lit. by making one's voice bounce]

彼女は新婚旅行について、声を弾ませて話しました。Kanojo wa shinkon ryokō ni tsuite, koe o hazumasete hanashimashita. *She talked about her honeymoon in a lively tone of voice.*

koe o hisomeru — 声を潜める — *to lower one's voice*
[lit. to hide one's voice]

医者は患者の奥さんに、声を潜めて診断の結果を告げました。Isha wa kanja no okusan ni, koe o hisomete shindan no kekka o tsugemashita. *Lowering her voice, the doctor told the patient's wife the diagnosis.*

koe o korosu — 声を殺す — *to whisper*
[lit. to kill one's own voice]

彼は声を殺して秘密を打ち明けました。Kare wa koe o koroshite himitsu o uchiakemashita. *In a whisper, he revealed a secret to me.*

koe o kumoraseru — 声を曇らせる — *to murmur sadly*
[lit. to make one's voice cloudy]

父は叔母の病気を聞いて、声を曇らせました。Chichi wa oba no byōki o kiite, koe o kumorasemashita. *On hearing about my aunt's illness, my father murmured sadly.*

koe o nomu — 声を呑む — *to become speechless*
[lit. to swallow one's own voice]

地震の結果のあまりのひどさに声を呑みました。Jishin no kekka no amari no hidosa ni koe o nomimashita. *I became speechless at the terrible results of the earthquake.*

koe o otosu — 声を落とす — *to lower one's voice*
[lit. to drop one's voice]
彼は声を落として、故人の思い出を語りました。Kare wa koe o
otoshite, kojin no omoide o katarimashita.   *He lowered his voice and
talked about his memories of the deceased.*

koe o tateru — 声を立てる — *to raise one's voice*
[lit. to let one's voice stand up]
先生は声を立てて、学生に警告しました。Sensei wa koe o tatete
gakusei ni keikoku shimashita.   *Raising his voice, the teacher warned
the students.*

okoegakari de — お声掛かりで — *at someone's command*
[lit. with the request of an honorable voice]
社長のお声掛かりで、新事業計画に着手しました。 Shachō no
okoegakari de, shin jigyō keikaku ni chakushu shimashita.   *At the
president's command, we embarked on the new business plan.*

ubugoe o ageru — 産声を上げる — *to be born*
[lit. A newborn baby cries at birth.]
ハイテクの分野で、沢山の会社が毎日産声を上げています。Haiteku
no bun-ya de, takusan no kaisha ga mainichi ubugoe o agete imasu.
*Many companies are being born every day in the field of advanced
technology.*

---

kōjin — 後塵 — *dust kicked up backward*
kōjin o haisuru — 後塵を拝する — *to play second fiddle*
[lit. to get covered with dust kicked up backward by someone]
顧客の開拓では、彼の後塵を拝しています。Kokyaku no kaitaku
dewa, kare no kōjin o haishite imasu.   *I'm playing second fiddle to him
in client development.*

---

kokoro — 心 — *mind, heart, feeling, intention, will*
kokoro ga kayou — 心が通う — *to understand each other perfectly*
[lit. Feelings circulate between persons.]
彼女と私は、心が通っています。Kanojo to watakushi wa, kokoro ga
kayotte imasu.   *She and I understand each other perfectly.*

kokoro ga komoru — 心がこもる — *to be considerate, to be thoughtful*
[lit. One's heart is put into something.]
彼の助言には、とても心がこもっていました。Kare no jogen niwa,

totemo kokoro ga komotte imashita. *His advice to me was very thoughtful.*

kokoro ga odoru — 心が躍る — *to get excited*
[lit. One's heart jumps.]
来週の旅行のことを考えると、心が躍ります。Raishū no ryokō no koto o kangaeru to, kokoro ga odorimasu. *I get exited when I think about the trip next week.*

kokoro ga sawagu — 心が騒ぐ — *to feel uneasy*
[lit. One's heart gets agitated.]
父に何度電話しても通じないので、心が騒ぎました。Chichi ni nando denwa shitemo tsūjinai node, kokoro ga sawagimashita. *Since there was no answer no matter how many times I called my father, I felt uneasy.*

kokoro ga ugoku — 心が動く — *to be tempted*
[lit. One's heart moves.]
ゴルフに誘われると、忙しくても心が動きます。Gorufu ni sasowareru to, isogashikutemo kokoro ga ugokimasu. *If I'm asked to play golf, I'm tempted to go even if I'm busy.*

kokoro ni egaku — 心に描く — *to imagine, to picture*
[lit. to paint a picture in one's mind]
将来の成功を心に描いて、一生懸命働きました。Shōrai no seikō o kokoro ni egaite, isshōkenmei hatarakimashita. *Picturing my future success, I worked very hard.*

kokoro ni kanau — 心にかなう — *to suit one's taste*
[lit. to fit one's feelings]
家は買いたいけれど、心にかなうのを見つけるのに苦労しています。Ie wa kaitai keredo, kokoro ni kanau no o mitsukeru noni kurō shite imasu. *I'd like to buy a house, but I'm having trouble finding one that suits my taste.*

kokoro ni kizamu — 心に刻む — *to remember*
[lit. to engrave something on one's heart]
私の言ったことを、よく心に刻んでおきなさい。Watakushi no itta koto o yoku kokoro ni kizande okinasai. *You should remember what I said.*

kokoro ni tomeru — 心に留める — *to keep something in mind*
[lit. to make something remain in one's mind]

子供の教育については、いつも心に留めています。Kodomo no
kyōiku ni tsuite wa, itsumo kokoro ni tomete imasu.　*I'm always
keeping my children's education in mind.*

kokoro o awaseru — 心を合わせる — *to cooperate, to unite*
[lit. to put people's minds together]
意見の違いはありましたが、心を合わせて目的を遂げました。Iken
no chigai wa arimashita ga, kokoro o awasete mokuteki o togemashita.
*We had differences of opinion, but we cooperated and achieved our
goal.*

kokoro o irekaeru — 心を入れ替える — *to change one's habits*
[lit. to replace one's mind]
大学へ行きたかったら、心を入れ替えてもっと勉強しなさい。
Daigaku e ikitakattara, kokoro o irekaete motto benkyō shinasai.　*If you
want to go to college, you should change your habits and study harder.*

kokoro o itameru — 心を痛める — *to worry*
[lit. to make one's heart hurt]
彼女は子供の将来について、心を痛めています。Kanojo wa kodomo
no shōrai ni tsuite, kokoro o itamete imasu.　*She's worrying about her
child's future.*

kokoro o kubaru — 心を配る — *to be attentive*
[lit. to arrange one's mind]
あの店の店員は、客によく心を配ります。Ano mise no ten-in wa,
kyaku ni yoku kokoro o kubarimasu.　*The clerks at that shop are quite
attentive to the customers.*

kokoro o kudaku — 心を砕く — *to rack one's brains*
[lit. to grind one's mind]
契約を成立させるために、心を砕いています。Keiyaku o seiritsu
saseru tame ni, kokoro o kudaite imasu.　*I'm racking my brains to
conclude the contract.*

kokoro o kumu — 心を汲む — *to sense*
[lit. to scoop up someone's feelings]
彼の孤独な心を汲んで、夕食に誘いました。Kare no kodoku na
kokoro o kunde, yūshoku ni sasoimashita.　*Sensing his loneliness, I
invited him for dinner.*

kokoro o oni ni suru — 心を鬼にする — *to steel oneself*
[lit. to make one's mind a devil]

心を鬼にして、社員に一時解雇を伝えました。Kokoro o oni ni shite,
shain ni ichiji kaiko o tsutaemashita.　Steeling myself, I told the
employees about the temporary layoff.

kokoro o ubawareru — 心を奪われる — to be captivated
[lit. to get one's heart stolen]
彼の話に、すっかり心を奪われました。Kare no hanashi ni, sukkari
kokoro o ubawaremashita.　I was totally captivated by his story.

kokoro o utsu — 心を打つ — to touch someone's heart
[lit. to hit someone's heart]
彼女の親への献身は、人々の心を打ちました。Kanojo no oya e no
kenshin wa, hitobito no kokoro o uchimashita.　Her devotion to her
parents touched everyone's heart.

kokoro o yoseru — 心を寄せる — to be interested in someone
[lit. to draw one's heart up to someone]
彼は、彼女に心を寄せているようです。Kare wa, kanojo ni kokoro o
yosete iru yō desu.　He seems to be interested in her.

kokoro o yurusu — 心を許す — to trust
[lit. to set one's mind free]
彼女とは長いつき合いで、すっかり心を許しています。
Kanojo to wa nagai tsukiai de, sukkari kokoro o yurushite imasu.
I have been friendly with her for a long time, and I trust her totally.

kokoroatari — 心当たり — clue, hint
[lit. a guess by one's mind]
彼がどこに行ったか、全く心当たりがありません。Kare ga doko ni
ittaka, mattaku kokoroatari ga arimasen.　I don't have a clue as to
where he went.

kokorobosoi — 心細い — to feel uneasy
[lit. One's heart is thin.]
その問題に一人で取り組むのは、ちょっと心細いです。
Sono mondai ni hitori de torikumu no wa, chotto kokorobosoi desu.
I feel a bit uneasy tackling the problem alone.

kokoroegao de — 心得顔で — knowingly
[lit. with the face of knowledge]
彼女は心得顔で、私を見つめました。
Kanojo wa kokoroegao de watakushi o mitsumemashita.
She looked at me knowingly.

kokorogamae — 心構え — *being prepared for something*
[lit. a mental frame]
いつでも責任を取って辞める心構えです。Itsu demo sekinin o totte
yameru kokorogamae desu.   *I'm prepared to bear the responsibility
and quit anytime.*

kokorogurushii — 心苦しい — *to feel sorry for something*
[lit. One's heart is painful.]
彼女につらい思いをさせて、心苦しいです。Kanojo ni tsurai omoi o
sasete kokorogurushii desu.   *I feel sorry for tormenting her.*

kokoronarazumo — 心ならずも — *against one's will*
[lit. with one's heart not proving something]
店員の滑らかな話に、心ならずもそれを買ってしまいました。
Ten-in no nameraka na hanashi ni, kokoronarazumo sore o katte
shimaimashita.   *Because of the clerk's smooth talk, I ended up buying
it against my will.*

kokoronokori — 心残り — *regret*
[lit. One's heart remains.]
学生の時にもっと勉強しなかったのが、いま心残りです。Gakusei
no toki ni motto benkyō shinakatta no ga, ima kokoronokori desu.
I now regret that I didn't study harder when I was a student.

kokorookinaku — 心置きなく — *without hesitation*
[lit. without leaving one's heart]
言いたいことは、どうぞ心置きなくおっしゃって下さい。Iitai koto
wa, dōzo kokorookinaku osshatte kudasai.   *Please say whatever you'd
like to say without hesitation.*

kokoroyukumade — 心ゆくまで — *to one's heart's content*
[lit. as far as one's heart goes]
昨日の晩は、友達と心ゆくまで話し合いました。Kinō no ban wa,
tomodachi to kokoroyukumade hanashiaimashita.   *Last night, I talked
with my friends to my heart's content.*

kokorozukushi — 心尽くし — *kind, thoughtful*
[lit. exerting one's heart]
お母さんの心尽くしの助言も、彼には効き目がありませんでした。
Okāsan no kokorozukushi no jogen mo, kare niwa kikime ga arimasen
deshita.   *Even his mother's kind advice didn't have any effect on him.*

tegokoro o kuwaeru — 手心を加える — *to go easy on someone*
[lit. to hand one's feelings to someone]

彼は大失敗をしたけれど、初めてだったので手心を加えました。
Kare wa daishippai o shita keredo, hajimete datta node tegokoro o
kuwaemashita. *Although he made a big mistake, since it was his first
one, I went easy on him.*

komimi — 小耳 — *inside an ear*
komimi ni hasamu — 小耳にはさむ — *to happen to hear*
[lit. to put something into an ear]
彼女がこの夏結婚することを、小耳にはさみました。Kanojo ga
kono natsu kekkon suru koto o, komimi ni hasamimashita. *I happened
to hear that she would get married this summer.*

kon — 根 — *root, stamina*
kon ga tsukiru — 根が尽きる — *to have no more patience for something*
[lit. A root comes to an end.]
娘の不精な生活には、根が尽きました。Musume no bushō na seikatsu
niwa, kon ga tsukimashita. *I have no more patience for my daughter's
life of laziness.*

kon o tsumeru — 根を詰める — *to concentrate one's energy*
[lit. to pack stamina]
来週の試験のために、根を詰めて勉強しています。Raishū no shiken
no tame ni, kon o tsumete benkyō shite imasu. *I'm concentrating my
energy and studying hard for the exam next week.*

konkurabe — 根比べ — *a waiting game*
[lit. competition for stamina]
彼らは妥協を拒否して、根比べをしています。Karera wa dakyō o
kyohi shite, konkurabe o shite imasu. *By rejecting a compromise,
they're playing a waiting game.*

kōnō — 効能 — *effectiveness*
kōnōgaki o naraberu — 効能書きを並べる — *to sing the praises of
something*
[lit. to display a statement of effectiveness]
政府はしきりに、新政策の効能書きを並べています。Seifu wa
shikirini, shin seisaku no kōnōgaki o narabete imasu. *The government
is eagerly singing the praises of the new policy.*

koshi — 腰 — *hip, waist*
koshi ga hikui — 腰が低い — *modest, humble, courteous*
[lit. One's waist is low.]
彼は、誰に対しても腰が低いです。Kare wa, dare ni taishite mo koshi
ga hikui desu.   *He is courteous to everyone.*

koshi ga omoi — 腰が重い — *to be slow getting started*
[lit. One's waist is heavy.]
彼は有能ですが、欠点は何事にも腰が重いことです。Kare wa yūnō
desu ga, ketten wa nanigoto nimo koshi ga omoi koto desu.   *He's a
capable person, but his shortcoming is that he's slow getting started.*

koshi ga tsuyoi — 腰が強い — *to be strong-willed*
[lit. One's waist is strong.]
彼女は腰が強いから、この困難も克服できるでしょう。Kanojo wa
koshi ga tsuyoi kara, kono konnan mo kokufuku dekiru deshō.   *Since
she's strong-willed, she'll overcome her current difficulties.*

koshi ga yowai — 腰が弱い — *to be weak-kneed*
[lit. One's waist is weak.]
彼は腰が弱いので、交渉に関わるのは不向きです。Kare wa koshi ga
yowai node, kōshō ni kakawaru no wa fumuki desu.   *Because he's
weak-kneed, he's not suitable for engaging in negotiations.*

koshi o ageru — 腰を上げる — *to take action*
[lit. to pick up one's hips]
女性問題について、政府がやっと腰を上げました。Josei mondai ni
tsuite, seifu ga yatto koshi o agemashita.   *The government finally took
action on the women's issues.*

koshi o nukasu — 腰を抜かす — *to be scared stiff*
[lit. to leave out one's hips]
彼女は蛇を見て、腰を抜かしました。Kanojo wa hebi o mite, koshi o
nukashimashita.   *She was scared stiff at seeing a snake.*

koshi o ochitsukeru — 腰を落ち着ける — *to settle down*
[lit. to make one's hips stay]
彼は結婚して以来、腰を落ち着けました。Kare wa kekkon shite irai,
koshi o ochitsukemashita.   *He's settled down since his marriage.*

koshi o oru — 腰を折る — *to interrupt, to spoil a story*
[lit. to break someone's hips]
彼女はよく人の話の腰を折るので、友達が出来ません。Kanojo wa
yoku hito no hanashi no koshi o oru node, tomodachi ga dekimasen.

Because she often interrupts other people's conversation, she can't make friends.

koshi o sueru — 腰を据える — *to buckle down*
[lit. to steady one's hips]
来月から腰を据えて、論文を書き始めます。 Raigetsu kara koshi o suete, ronbun o kakihajimemasu. *I'll buckle down and start writing my thesis starting next month.*

hongoshi o ireru — 本腰を入れる — *to apply oneself diligently*
[lit. to apply one's hips fully]
仕事に本腰を入れないと、首になりますよ。Shigoto ni hongoshi o irenai to, kubi ni narimasu yo. *If you don't apply yourself more diligently to your work, you'll be fired.*

koshikudake ni naru — 腰砕けになる — *to fall through in the middle of something*
[lit. One's hips break.]
彼の計画は、準備の途中で腰砕けになってしまいました。Kare no keikaku wa, junbi no tochū de koshikudake ni natte shimaimashita. *His plan fell through in the middle of the preparations.*

koshinuke — 腰抜け — *coward*
[lit. One's hips are gone.]
彼は、上司の言うことなら何でも賛成してしまう腰抜けです。Kare wa, jōshi no iu koto nara nandemo sansei shite shimau koshinuke desu. *He's a coward who agrees with everything the boss says.*

nigegoshi ni naru — 逃げ腰になる — *to get ready to back out*
[lit. to fall into fleeing hips]
彼は、約束した仕事から逃げ腰になっています。Kare wa, yakusoku shita shigoto kara nigegoshi ni natte imasu. *He's getting ready to back out of the work he promised to do.*

yowagoshi — 弱腰 — *timid*
[lit. weak hips]
そんな弱腰の態度では、厳しい相手と交渉できませんよ。Sonna yowagoshi no taido dewa, kibishii aite to kōshō dekimasen yo. *If you have such a timid attitude, you can't negotiate with a tough counterpart.*

koshikake — 腰掛け — *chair, stool*
koshikake shigoto — 腰掛け仕事 — *transient work*
[lit. short-term work while sitting on a chair]

腰掛け仕事のつもりなら、採用できません。 Koshikake shigoto no tsumori nara, saiyō dekimasen. *If you're intending this to be transient work, we can't hire you.*

---

koto — 事 — *thing, something, matter, affair, fact, event, accident*
koto ga koto dakara — 事が事だから — *under the circumstances*
[lit. as something matters]
事が事だから、この際あなたの頼みを引き受けましょう。 Koto ga koto dakara, kono sai anata no tanomi o hikiukemashō. *Under the circumstances, I'll grant your request.*

koto o aradateru — 事を荒立てる — *to worsen something*
[lit. to make something rough]
そんなささいなことで、事を荒立てないようにしましょう。Sonna sasai na koto de, koto o aradatenai yō ni shimashō. *Let's not worsen the situation because of such trivial things.*

koto o kamaeru — 事を構える — *to create controversy*
[lit. to set something up]
彼は機会を見つけては、事を構えたがります。Kare wa kikai o mitsukete wa, koto o kamaetagarimasu. *He looks for opportunities to create controversy.*

koto o konomu hito — 事を好む人 — *troublemaker*
[lit. to prefer an incident]
事を好む人たちが待っているから、あそこに着いたら気をつけなさい。 Koto o konomu hitotachi ga matte iru kara, asoko ni tsuitara ki o tsukenasai. *Since those troublemakers are waiting for you, be careful once you get there.*

kotomonage ni — 事も無げに — *casually*
[lit. as if there isn't anything]
彼女は事も無げに彼との約束を破りました。Kanojo wa kotomonage ni kare to no yakusoku o yaburimashita. *She casually broke her promise to him.*

kotokireru — 事切れる — *to pass away*
[lit. Something expires.]
父は家族全員が見守る中で事切れました。 Chichi wa kazoku zen-in ga mimamoru naka de kotokiremashita. *My father died with the entire family looking on.*

kotonaki o eru — 事なきを得る — to save the day
[lit. to have no accident]
子守がいるとき母が来てくれて、事なきを得ました。Komori ga iru
toki haha ga kite kurete, kotonaki o emashita.   When we needed a baby
sitter, my mother saved the day by coming over to our house.

kotoniyoru to — 事によると — might
[lit. depending on something]
事によると、雨が降るかも知れません。Kotoniyoru to, ame ga furu
kamo shiremasen.   It might rain.

kotoyosete — 事寄せて — under pretense of something
[lit. by putting something closer]
彼は仕事に事寄せて、一日に何度も彼女に会いに行きます。Kare
wa shigoto ni kotoyosete, ichinichi ni nando mo kanojo ni ai ni ikimasu.
Under pretense of work, he goes to see her many times a day.

ōgoto — 大事 — serious matter
[lit. a big thing]
それがそんなに大事とは知りませんでした。Sore ga sonna ni ōgoto
towa shirimasen deshita.   I didn't know it was such a serious matter.

tadagoto dewa nai — 只事ではない — out of the ordinary, serious
[lit. It's not something free.]
彼の声から、事態はただ事では無いことが分かりました。Kare no
koe kara, jitai wa tadagoto dewa nai koto ga wakarimashita.   From his
voice, I understood that the situation was out of the ordinary.

---

kotoba — 言葉 — language, speech, term, word
kotoba ni amaeru — 言葉に甘える — to accept someone's kind offer
[lit. to presume upon someone's words]
お言葉に甘えて、ご馳走になります。Okotoba ni amaete, gochisō ni
narimasu.   I'll accept your kind offer of a meal.

kotoba ni amaru — 言葉に余る — beyond description
[lit. too much for words]
その庭の美しさは言葉に余りました。Sono niwa no utsukushisa wa
kotoba ni amarimashita.   The beauty of the garden was beyond
description.

kotoba ni kado ga aru — 言葉に角がある — to speak harshly
[lit. There are angles in speech.]
彼の顔は平静でしたが、言葉に角がありました。 Kare no kao wa

heisei deshita ga, kotoba ni kado ga arimashita.   *His face was calm, but he spoke harshly.*

kotoba no aya — 言葉の綾 — *figure of speech*
[lit. the twill of speech]

彼が言ったことは言葉の綾で、あなたを非難したわけではありません。

Kare ga itta koto wa kotoba no aya de, anata o hinan shita wake dewa arimasen.   *What he said was a figure of speech, and he didn't mean to criticize you.*

kotoba o kaesu — 言葉を返す — *to talk back*
[lit. to return words]

彼は自分の過ちを認める代わりに、いつも言葉を返します。Kare wa jibun no ayamachi o mitomeru kawari ni, itsumo kotoba o kaeshimasu.   *Instead of admitting his mistakes, he always talks back.*

kotoba o kazaru — 言葉を飾る — *to use flowery language*
[lit. to decorate one's words]

彼女は言葉を飾るのは上手でも、話の内容はまあまあです。Kanojo wa kotoba o kazaru no wa jōzu demo, hanashi no naiyō wa māmā desu. *Although she's good at using flowery language, the content of her talk is mediocre.*

kotoba o nigosu — 言葉を濁す — *to speak vaguely*
[lit. to make one's words muddy]

彼は過去について聞かれて、言葉を濁しました。Kare wa kako ni tsuite kikarete, kotoba o nigoshimashita.   *When he was asked about his past, he spoke vaguely.*

kotoba o tsukushite — 言葉を尽くして — *at length*
[lit. by exhausting one's words]
彼は言葉を尽くして、彼女の許しを乞いました。Kare wa kotoba o
tsukushite, kanojo no yurushi o koimashita.   *He begged her forgiveness
at length.*

kotobajiri o toraeru — 言葉尻をとらえる — *to pick apart someone's
words*
[lit. to catch the buttocks of someone's words]
彼は人の言葉尻をとらえて、議論を始める癖があります。Kare wa
hito no kotobajiri o toraete, giron o hajimeru kuse ga arimasu.   *He has
the habit of starting arguments by picking apart other people's words.*

toge no aru kotoba — 刺のある言葉 — *harsh language*
[lit. words with thorns]
刺のある言葉から、彼女の機嫌が悪いことが分かりました。Toge no
aru kotoba kara, kanojo no kigen ga warui koto ga wakarimashita.
I knew from her harsh language that she was upset.

urikotoba ni kaikotoba — 売り言葉に買い言葉 — *exchanging verbal
insults*
[lit. buying words for selling words]
売り言葉に買い言葉から、喧嘩が始まりました。Urikotoba ni
kaikotoba kara, kenka ga hajimarimashita.   *After exchanging verbal
insults, they started fighting.*

kotsu — 骨 — *bone*
kotsuniku no arasoi — 骨肉の争い — *domestic strife*
[lit. the fight between bones and flesh]
あの家族は、遺産相続をめぐって骨肉の争いを繰り広げています。
Ano kazoku wa, isan sōzoku o megutte kotsuniku no arasoi o
kurihirogete imasu.   *That family is engaged in domestic strife over the
inheritance.*

ku — 苦 — *suffering*
kuhai o nameru — 苦杯をなめる — *to be beaten*
[lit. to lick a bitter cup]
公共事業契約の入札で、苦杯をなめました。Kōkyō jigyō keiyaku no
nyūsatsu de, kuhai o namemashita.   *We were beaten in our bid for the
public works contract.*

kū — 空 — emptiness
  kū ni kisuru — 空に帰する — to come to nothing
  [lit. to return to emptiness]
  司法試験に落ちて、彼の努力は空に帰してしまいました。Shihō
  shiken ni ochite, kare no doryoku wa kū ni kishite shimaimashita.   His
  efforts came to nothing when he failed the bar exam.

kubi — 首 — neck, head
  kubi ga abunai — 首が危ない — to face dismissal
  [lit. Someone's neck is in danger.]
  社内に、彼の首が危ないという噂があります。Shanai ni, kare no kubi
  ga abunai to iu uwasa ga arimasu.   There's a rumor in the company that
  he's facing dismissal.

  kubi ga tobu — 首が飛ぶ — to be fired
  [lit. A head flies.]
  汚職事件で、幹部官僚の首がたくさん飛びました。
  Oshoku jiken de, kanbu kanryō no kubi ga takusan tobimashita.
  With the corruption incident, many senior government officials were
  fired.

  kubi ga mawaranai — 首が回らない — to be up to one's ears in debt
  [lit. A neck doesn't turn.]
  借金で首が回りません。Shakkin de kubi ga mawarimasen.   I'm up to
  my ears in debt.

  kubi ga tsunagaru — 首がつながる — to hold on to one's job
  [lit. A neck is intact.]
  支店長の計らいで、首がつながりました。Shitenchō no hakarai de,
  kubi ga tsunagarimashita.   Thanks to the branch manager's discretion,
  I held on to my job.

  kubi ni naru — 首になる — to be fired
  [lit. to be reduced to a neck]
  彼は上司と言い争って、首になりました。Kare wa jōshi to iiarasotte,
  kubi ni narimashita.   He was fired after quarreling with his boss.

  kubi ni suru — 首にする — to fire someone
  [lit. to result in the loss of a neck]
  彼女は全く働く気がないので、首にしました。Kanojo wa mattaku
  hataraku ki ga nai node, kubi ni shimashita.   Because she wasn't willing
  to work at all, I fired her.

kubi o hineru — 首をひねる — to wonder
[lit. to let one's head lean to one side]
彼女は娘の将来について首をひねっています。Kanojo wa musume no shōrai ni tsuite kubi o hinette imasu.　She's wondering about her daughter's future.

kubi o kashigeru — 首を傾げる — to be skeptical
[lit. to cock one's head]
みんなは彼の話に首を傾げました。Minna wa kare no hanashi ni kubi o kashigemashita.　Everybody was skeptical of his story.

kubi o kiru — 首を切る — to fire someone
[lit. to cut someone's head off]
不景気でも、社員の首は切りたくありません。Fukeiki demo, shain no kubi wa kiritaku arimasen.　In spite of the recession, I don't want to fire any employees.

kubi o nagaku shite matsu — 首を長くして待つ — to look forward to something
[lit. to wait for something by stretching one's neck]
母は父が出張から帰るのを、首を長くして待っています。Haha wa chichi ga shutchō kara kaeru no o, kubi o nagaku shite matte imasu. My mother is looking forward to my father's return from the business trip.

kubi o soroeru — 首を揃える — to gather
[lit. to put heads in order]
参加者全員が首を揃えるまで、待ちましょう。Sankasha zen-in ga kubi o soroeru made, machimashō.　Let's wait till all the participants gather.

kubi o sugekaeru — 首をすげ替える — to replace someone
[lit. to change a head]
重役会は社長の首をすげ替えました。Jūyakukai wa shachō no kubi o sugekaemashita.　The board of directors replaced the president.

kubi o tate ni furu — 首を縦に振る — to say yes
[lit. to shake one's head vertically]
先生は、学生の要望にやっと首を縦に振りました。Sensei wa, gakusei no yōbō ni yatto kubi o tate ni furimashita.　The teacher finally said yes to the students' request.

kubi o tsukkomu — 首を突っ込む — to stick one's nose into something
[lit. to thrust one's neck into something]

彼は何にでも首を突っ込みたがります。Kare wa nani ni demo kubi o tsukkomitagarimasu. *He wants to stick his nose into everything.*

kubi o yoko ni furu — 首を横に振る — *to say no*
[lit. to shake one's head horizontally]
彼女は結婚の申し込みに、首を横に振りました。Kanojo wa kekkon no mōshikomi ni, kubi o yoko ni furimashita. *She said no to the marriage proposal.*

kubippiki de — 首っ引きで — *with the constant help of something*
[lit. by pulling one's neck to something]
手引き書と首っ引きで、オートバイを組み立てています。Tebikisho to kubippiki de, ōtobai o kumitatete imasu. *I'm assembling a motorcycle with the constant help of the manual.*

kubittake   首っ丈   *to be head over heels in love*
[lit. one's entire head]
彼は彼女に首っ丈です。Kare wa kanojo ni kubittake desu. *He's head over heels in love with her.*

nekubi o kaku — 寝首を掻く — *to stab someone in the back*
[lit. to cut a sleeping head off]
彼は出世のためなら、人の寝首を掻くのもためらいません。Kare wa shusse no tame nara, hito no nekubi o kaku no mo tameraimasen. *He doesn't hesitate to stab people in the back to promote his own success.*

kuchi — 口 — *mouth, job, word, lips*

kuchi ga hiagaru — 口が干上がる — *to fall on hard times financially*
[lit. One's mouth dries up.]
失業して、口が干上がってしまいました。Shitsugyō shite, kuchi ga hiagatte shimaimashita. *When I lost my job, I fell on hard times financially.*

kuchi ga heranai — 口が減らない — *to be never at loss for words*
[lit. One's words never diminish.]
それがどんな状況でも、彼女は口が減りません。Sore ga donna jōkyō demo, kanojo wa kuchi ga herimasen. *Under any circumstances, she's never at loss for words.*

kuchi ga hogureru — 口がほぐれる — *to loosen up and start to talk*
[lit. One's mouth gets loose.]
彼女の口がやっとほぐれました。Kanojo no kuchi ga yatto hoguremashita. *Finally, she loosened up and started to talk.*

kuchi ga kakaru — 口が掛かる — *to be offered a position*
[lit. A job is dangled.]
夫に、大学から教授の口が掛かりました。Otto ni, daigaku kara kyōju
no kuchi ga kakarimashita.   *My husband was offered a professorship by
a university.*

kuchi ga karui hito — 口が軽い人 — *blabbermouth*
[lit. A mouth is light.]
彼は口が軽いから、個人的なことは話せません。Kare wa kuchi ga
karui kara, kojinteki na koto wa hanasemasen.   *Since he's a
blabbermouth, I don't tell him anything personal.*

kuchi ga katai — 口が堅い — *tight-lipped*
[lit. A mouth is hard.]
彼女は口が堅いから、秘密を話しても安心です。Kanojo wa kuchi ga
katai kara, himitsu o hanashitemo anshin desu.   *Because she's tight-
lipped, I feel comfortable telling her a secret.*

kuchi ga koeru — 口が肥える — *to be a gourmet*
[lit. A mouth gets enriched.]
彼は口が肥えているので、素晴らしいレストランをたくさん知って
います。Kare wa kuchi ga koete iru node, subarashii resutoran o
takusan shitte imasu.   *Since he's a gourmet, he knows many great
restaurants.*

kuchi ga kusattemo — 口が腐っても — *no matter what*
[lit. even if one's mouth rots]
口が腐っても、人の悪口は言いません。Kuchi ga kusattemo, hito no
warukuchi wa iimasen.   *No matter what, I won't badmouth other
people.*

kuchi ga omoi — 口が重い — *man of few words*
[lit. A mouth is heavy.]
あの作家は口が重いので、インタビューするのが大変です。Ano
sakka wa kuchi ga omoi node, intabyū suru no ga taihen desu.   *Because
that novelist is a man of few words, it's difficult to interview him.*

kuchi ga saketemo — 口が裂けても — *no matter what*
[lit. even if one's mouth is torn]
口が裂けても、その秘密は守ります。Kuchi ga saketemo, sono himitsu
wa mamorimasu.   *No matter what, I'll keep the secret.*

kuchi ga suberu — 口が滑る — *to make a slip of the tongue*
[lit. A mouth slips.]

口が滑って、彼女に余計なことを言ってしまいました。

Kuchi ga subette, kanojo ni yokei na koto o itte shimaimashita.

I regret that I made a slip of the tongue and said too much to her.

kuchi ga sugiru — 口が過ぎる — *to say things one is not supposed to say to someone*
[lit. Words are excessive.]

父と口論したとき、口が過ぎてしまいました。

Chichi to kōron shita toki, kuchi ga sugite shimaimashita.

During the quarrel with my father, I said things one isn't supposed to say to one's father.

kuchi ga suppakunaru hodo — 口が酸っぱくなるほど — *repeatedly*
[lit. to the extent that one's mouth gets sour]

彼には口が酸っぱくなるほど説明したのに、まだ分かっていません。

Kare niwa kuchi ga suppakunaru hodo setsumei shita noni, mada wakatte imasen. *Although I explained it to him repeatedly, he still doesn't understand.*

kuchi ga umai — 口がうまい — *smooth-talking*
[lit. A mouth is skillful.]

彼女は口がうまいから、気をつけなさい。Kanojo wa kuchi ga umai kara, ki o tsukenasai. *Be careful, because she's a smooth talker.*

kuchi ga urusai — 口がうるさい — *to be particular about something*
[lit. A mouth is noisy.]

彼は何事にも口がうるさいので、みんなが敬遠します。

Kare wa nanigoto nimo kuchi ga urusai node, minna ga keien shimasu.

Because he's particular about everything, everybody avoids him.

kuchi ga warui — 口が悪い — *to have a sharp tongue*
[lit. A mouth is bad.]

彼は口が悪いかも知れないけれど、悪気はありません。

Kare wa kuchi ga warui kamo shirenai keredo, warugi wa arimasen.

He may have a sharp tongue, but he doesn't have malicious intentions.

kuchi kara saki ni umareru — 口から先に生まれる — *to not know when to shut up*
[lit. to be born mouth-first]

彼は口から先に生まれたような人で、話がいつも長引きます。Kare wa kuchi kara saki ni umareta yō na hito de, hanashi ga itsumo nagabikimasu. *Since he doesn't know when to shut up, his conversation always drags on.*

kuchi ni au — 口に合う — to suit one's taste
[lit. to fit someone's mouth]
おいしそうな料理でしたが、口に合いませんでした。Oishisō na
ryōri deshita ga, kuchi ni aimasen deshita.　　It looked like a delicious
dish, but it didn't suit my taste.

kuchi ni dasu — 口に出す — to utter
[lit. to let something out of one's mouth]
彼女の秘密を口に出してしまいました。Kanojo no himitsu o kuchi ni
dashite shimaimashita.　　Accidentally, I uttered her secret.

kuchi ni noboru — 口に上る — to be mentioned
[lit. to come up to one's mouth]
候補者として、彼の名前が最近よく口に上っています。Kōhosha to
shite, kare no namae ga saikin yoku kuchi ni nobotte imasu.　　His name
has been mentioned often as a candidate recently.

kuchi ni suru — 口にする — to speak of something
[lit. to make something into words]
彼は自分の過去について、決して口にしません。Kare wa jibun no
kako nitsuite, kesshite kuchi ni shimasen.　　He never speaks of his past.

kuchi o dasu — 口を出す — to meddle with something
[lit. to put words out]
そのことには、口を出さないで下さい。Sono koto niwa, kuchi o
dasanai de kudasai.　　Please don't meddle with that.

kuchi o hasamu — 口を挟む — to interrupt while others are talking
[lit. to insert one's words]
彼女は、人の話に口を挟む癖があります。Kanojo wa, hito no hanshi
ni kuchi o hasamu kuse ga arimasu.　　She has a habit of interrupting
while other people are talking.

kuchi o hiraku — 口を開く — to start talking
[lit. to open one's mouth]
彼はやっと口を開きました。Kare wa yatto kuchi o hirakimashita.
He finally started talking.

kuchi o kiku — 口をきく — to speak to someone
[lit. to make one's words effective]
息子とは、この一ヶ月口をきいていません。Musuko to wa, kono
ikkagetsu kuchi o kiite imasen.　　I haven't spoken to my son for a
month.

kuchi o kiru — 口を切る — *to be the first one to speak*
[lit. to cut one's words out]
家族の集まりでは、祖父がまず口を切りました。Kazoku no atsumari
dewa, sofu ga mazu kuchi o kirimashita. *The grandfather was the first
one to speak at the family gathering.*

kuchi o kiwamete — 口を極めて — *outspokenly*
[lit. by making one's words extreme]
彼は口を極めて政府を批判しました。Kare wa kuchi o kiwamete seifu
o hihan shimashita. *He criticized the government outspokenly.*

kuchi o nuguu — 口を拭う — *to pretend not to know something*
[lit. to wipe one's mouth]
彼女は友達がカンニングしたことについて、口を拭っています。
Kanojo wa tomodachi ga kanningu shita koto nitsuite, kuchi o nugutte
imasu. *She's pretending not to know that her friend cheated on the
exam.*

kuchi o soroete — 口を揃えて — *unanimously*
[lit. by putting mouths in order]
母の考えに、家族全員が口を揃えて賛成しました。Haha no kangae
ni, kazoku zen-in ga kuchi o soroete sansei shimashita. *All of us in the
family unanimously agreed with our mother's idea.*

kuchi o suppaku shite — 口を酸っぱくして — *repeatedly*
[lit. by making one's mouth sour]
彼女に口を酸っぱくして警告しましたが、効き目がありませんでした。
Kanojo ni kuchi o suppaku shite keikoku shimashita ga, kikime ga
arimasen deshita. *Although I repeatedly warned her, it had no effect on
her.*

kuchi o togarasu — 口を尖らす — *to get upset*
[lit. to purse one's lips]
彼女はすぐ口を尖らします。Kanojo wa sugu kuchi o togarashimasu.
She gets upset easily.

kuchi o waru — 口を割る — *to confess*
[lit. to split one's mouth open]
容疑者は、逮捕されるとすぐに口を割りました。Yōgisha wa, taiho
sareru to sugu ni kuchi o warimashita. *The suspect confessed
immediately when he was arrested.*

kuchibashiru — 口走る — *to blurt out*
[lit. to run one's mouth]

あの候補者は、競争相手について事実無根のことを口走っています。
Ano kōhosha wa, kyōsō aite ni tsuite jijitsumukon no koto o
kuchibashitte imasu.   *That candidate is blurting out something
unfounded about his opponent.*

kuchidome suru — 口止めする — *to hush someone up*
[lit. to stop someone's mouth]
彼女を口止めするため、高い贈り物を上げねばなりませんでした。
Kanojo o kuchidome suru tame, takai okurimono o ageneba narimasen
deshita.   *I had to give her an expensive gift to hush her up.*

kuchigitanai — 口汚い — *foul-mouthed*
[lit. One's mouth is dirty.]
彼は口汚いので、両親に紹介できません。Kare wa kuchigitanai node,
ryōshin ni shōkai dekimasen.   *Because he's foul-mouthed, I can't
introduce him to my parents.*

kuchigomoru — 口ごもる — *to hem and haw*
[lit. to let words stay in one's mouth]
彼女は彼の求婚に口ごもりました。Kanojo wa kare no kyūkon ni
kuchigomorimashita.   *She hemmed and hawed at his marriage proposal.*

kuchigotae suru — 口答えする — *to talk back*
[lit. to answer with one's words]
彼は人からの助言に、必ず口答えします。Kare wa hito kara no jogen
ni, kanarazu kuchigotae shimasu.   *He habitually talks back to people
who give him advice.*

kuchiguruma ni noseru — 口車に乗せる — *to cajole someone into
doing something*
[lit. to give someone a ride on the wheels of words]
彼女を口車に乗せて、私の宿題をやらせました。 Kanojo o
kuchiguruma ni nosete, watakushi no shukudai o yarasemashita.
I cajoled her into doing my homework.

kuchihabattai — 口幅ったい — *impertinent*
[lit. one's mouth being too wide]
口幅ったいかも知れませんが、もっと丁寧に話すべきです。
Kuchihabattai kamoshiremasen ga, motto teinei ni hanasu beki desu.
This may sound impertinent, but you should speak more politely.

kuchihatchō tehatchō — 口八丁手八丁 — *to be eloquent and talented on
the surface*
[lit. eight mouths and eight hands]

彼は口八丁手八丁だけれど、いい大統領になるかどうか
分かりません。Kare wa kuchihatchō tehatchō da keredo,
ii daitōryō ni naru ka dō ka wakarimasen.
He's eloquent and talented on the surface, but I don't know if he'd be a
good president.

kuchikomi — 口コミ — *word-of-mouth*
[lit. communication by mouths]
彼女の東京での成功は、口コミで故郷の町中に広がりました。
Kanojo no Tōkyō de no seikō wa, kuchikomi de kokyō no machijū ni
hirogarimashita. *Her success in Tokyo spread by word-of-mouth all*
over her hometown.

kuchisaki dake no — 口先だけの — *empty*
[lit. only with the tip of a mouth]
口先だけの約束なら、しない方がましです。Kuchisaki dake no
yakusoku nara, shinai hō ga mashi desu. *If it's an empty promise, it's*
better not to make it.

kuchisaki no umai — 口先のうまい — *smooth-talking*
[lit. being good at the tip of a mouth]
母親は娘に、口先のうまい男には気をつけなさいと言いました。
Hahaoya wa musume ni, kuchisaki no umai otoko niwa ki o tsukenasai
to iimashita. *The mother told her daughter to be careful of smooth-*
talking men.

kuchiura o awaseru — 口裏を合わせる — *to prearrange a story so as*
not to contradict each other later
[lit. to adjust the lining of the words]
彼と彼女は結婚の危機を否定するときに矛盾しないように、口裏を
合わせました。Kare to kanojo wa kekkon no kiki o hitei suru toki ni
mujun shinai yō ni, kuchiura o awasemashita. *He and she prearranged*
a story so as not to contradict each other when denying their marriage
was in crisis.

kuchiyakamashii — 口やかましい — *nagging*
[lit. One's mouth is noisy.]
父は口やかましいので、そばにいるとくつろげません。Chichi wa
kuchiyakamashii node, soba ni iru to kutsurogemasen. *Because my*
father is a nag, I can't relax around him.

kuchiyakusoku — 口約束 — *verbal commitment*
[lit. a word of promise]

彼女の口約束は信用できません。Kanojo no kuchiyakusoku wa shin-yō
dekimasen.　*I can't trust her verbal commitment.*

kuchiyogoshi — 口汚し — *just a morsel (food)*
[lit. something to dirty someone's food]
ほんの口汚しですが、どうぞ召し上がってください。Honno
kuchiyogoshi desu ga, dōzo meshiagatte kudasai.　*It's only a morsel,*
but please eat it.

kuchizoe — 口添え — *recommendation*
[lit. to lend one's words to someone]
叔父の口添えで、クラブの会員になれました。Oji no kuchizoe de,
kurabu no kaiin ni naremashita.　*I was able to become a member of the*
club because of my uncle's recommendation.

mudaguchi o tataku — 無駄口を叩く — *to chatter idly*
[lit. to drum up wasteful words]
友達と電話で無駄口を叩いているより、本を読みなさい。
Tomodachi to denwa de mudaguchi o tataite iru yori, hon o yominasai.
Read books rather than chattering idly on the phone with your friends.

nikumareguchi o tataku — 憎まれ口を叩く — *to say nasty things*
[lit. to drum up the words that will cause hatred]
彼は、誰にも憎まれ口を叩くので知られています。Kare wa, dare
nimo nikumareguchi o tataku node shirarete imasu.　*He's known to say*
nasty things to everyone.

ōguchi o tataku — 大口を叩く — *to talk big*
[lit. to drum up one's own words]
彼は、将来首相になると大口を叩いています。Kare wa, shōrai shushō
ni naru to ōguchi o tataite imasu.　*He's talking big, saying that he'll*
become prime minister in the future.

---

kuchibashi — 嘴 — *beak*

kuchibashi ga kiiroi — 嘴が黄色い — *to be a greenhorn*
[lit. One's beak is yellow.]
彼女は嘴が黄色いのに、自分では専門家だと思っています。
Kanojo wa kuchibashi ga kiiroi noni, jibun dewa senmonka da to omotte
imasu.　*Although she's a greenhorn, she thinks of herself as an expert.*

kuchibashi o ireru — 嘴を入れる — *to poke one's nose into others' affairs*
[lit. to insert one's beak into something]
人のことに嘴を入れたがるのが、彼の欠点です。

Hito no koto ni kuchibashi o iretagaru no ga, kare no ketten desu.
His eagerness to poke his nose into others' affairs is his weakness.

---

kuchibi — 口火 — *fuse*
  kuchibi o kiru — 口火を切る — *to be the first to do something*
  [lit. to ignite a fuse]
  この環境問題で口火を切ったのが彼女です。
  Kono kankyō mondai de kuchibi o kitta no ga kanojo desu.
  She's the one who started this environmental issue.

---

kuchibiru — 唇 — *lip*
  kuchibiru o kamu — 唇を噛む — *to endure*
  [lit. to bite one's own lips]
  不当な批判に、唇を噛みました。Futō na hinan ni, kuchibiru o
  kamimashita. *I endured the unjust accusation.*

---

kuda — 管 — *tube*
  kuda o maku — 管を巻く — *to blather about someone or something*
  over drinks
  [lit. to wind a tube around something]
  友達は、彼の上役について管を巻きました。
  Tomodachi wa kare no uwayaku ni tsuite kuda o makimashita.
  My friend blathered about his boss over drinks.

---

kugi — 釘 — *nail*
  kugi o sasu — 釘をさす — *to remind someone of something*
  [lit. to drive a nail]
  来週必ず論文を提出するように、学生に釘をさしました。
  Raishū kanarazu ronbun o teishutsu suru yō ni, gakusei ni kugi o
  sashimashita.   *I reminded the students to submit their papers without*
  exception next week.

---

kujū — 苦汁 — *bitter juice*
  kujū o nameru — 苦汁を嘗める — *to have a bitter experience*
  [lit. to lick bitter juice]
  去年は失業の苦汁を嘗めました。Kyonen wa shitsugyō no kujū o
  namemashita. *Last year I had the bitter experience of being unemployed.*

kumo — 雲 — *cloud*

kumo o tsukamu yō na — 雲をつかむような — *vague*
[lit. like grasping a cloud]

彼女は、彼の雲をつかむような計画に大金を投資しました。Kanojo
wa, kare no kumo o tsukamu yō na keikaku ni taikin o tōshi shimashita.
She invested a large sum of money in his vague plan.

kumogakuresuru — 雲隠れする — *to drop out of sight*
[lit. to hide behind the clouds]

彼はマスコミの追求を避けて、雲隠れしています。Kare wa
masukomi no tsuikyū o sakete, kumogakure shite imasu. *He's dropped
out of sight to avoid inquiries by the media.*

kumoyuki o miru — 雲行きを見る — *to be still deciding*
[lit. to see the movement of clouds]

彼女は立候補するかどうか、雲行きを見ています。Kanojo wa
rikkōho suru ka dō ka, kumoyuki o mite imasu. *She's still deciding
whether to run for election or not.*

kumo — 蜘蛛 — *spider*

kumo no ko o chirasu yō ni — 蜘蛛の子を散らすように — *in all
directions*
[lit. like scattering baby spiders]

夕立が始まって、人々は蜘蛛の子を散らすように走り出しました。
Yūdachi ga hajimatte, hitobito wa kumo no ko o chirasu yō ni
hashiridashimashita. *When the shower started, people started running
in all directions.*

kusa — 草 — *grass*

kusa no ne o wakete sagasu — 草の根を分けて探す — *to search
thoroughly*
[lit. to look for something even by separating roots of grass]

彼女はいなくなった猫を、草の根を分けて探しました。Kanojo wa
inakunatta neko o, kusa no ne o wakete sagashimashita. *She searched
thoroughly for her missing cat.*

kusaba no kage de naku — 草葉の陰で泣く — *to turn over in one's
grave*
[lit. to cry in the shade of grass and leaves]

そんなことをすると、お父さんが草葉の陰で泣きますよ。Sonna

koto o suru to, otōsan ga kusaba no kage de nakimasu yo.   *If you do that, your father will turn over in his grave.*

---

kusai — 臭い — *bad-smelling*
kusai meshi o kuu — 臭い飯を食う — *to be behind bars, to be in jail*
[lit. to eat bad-smelling rice]
彼はいま、臭い飯を食っています。Kare wa ima kusai meshi o kutte imasu.   *He's behind bars now.*

kusai mono ni futa o suru — 臭い物に蓋をする — *to cover things up*
[lit. to put a lid on a smelly thing]
国民は、政府の臭いものに蓋をするような態度を批判しています。
Kokumin wa, seifu no kusai mono ni futa o suru yō na taido o hihan shite imasu.   *The people are criticizing the government's propensity to cover things up.*

---

kusaru — 腐る — *to rot*
kusaru hodo — 腐るほど — *great number of something*
[lit. to the extent that things will rot]
彼女は、ドレスを腐るほど持っています。Kanojo wa, doresu o kusaru hodo motte imasu.   *She has a great number of dresses.*

---

kutabireru — くたびれる — *to get tired*
kutabiremōke — くたびれ儲け — *to come up empty-handed*
[lit. to earn tiredness]
仕事を探しに行きましたが、くたびれ儲けでした。Shigoto o sagashini ikimashita ga, kutabiremōke deshita.   *Although I went to look for a job, I came up empty-handed.*

---

kuu — 食う — *to eat*
kuitarinai — 食い足りない — *to be dissatisfied with something*
[lit. to not have eaten enough]
彼女の説明は、食い足りませんでした。Kanojo no setsumei wa, kuitarimasen deshita.   *I was dissatisfied with her explanation.*

kutte kakaru — 食って掛かる — *to challenge*
[lit. to set about eating]
彼は駐車違反の券を渡されて、警官に食って掛かりました。Kare wa chūsha ihan no ken o watasarete, keikan ni kutte kakarimashita.

When he was handed a ticket for a parking violation, he challenged the policeman.

kuuka kuwareruka — 食うか食われるか — *life-or-death*
[lit. to eat or be eaten]

与党と野党は、食うか食われるかの闘争を繰り広げています。Yotō to yatō wa, kuuka kuwareruka no tōsō o kurihirogete imasu. *The majority and minority parties are engaged in a life-or-death struggle.*

kuwasemono — 食わせ物 — *fake*
[lit. something to make someone eat]

彼女は食わせ物だから、気をつけなさい。Kanojo wa kuwasemono dakara, ki o tsukenasai. *Be careful of her because she's a fake.*

ippai kuwaseru — 一杯食わせる — *to play a trick on someone*
[lit. to make someone eat whatever is offered]

競争相手に一杯食わせることに成功しました。Kyōsō aite ni ippai kuwaseru koto ni seikō shimashita. *We succeeded in playing a trick on our competitor.*

---

kuzu — 屑 — *waste*
ningen no kuzu — 人間の屑 — *good-for-nothing*
[lit. a waste of a human being]

彼女は人間の屑です。Kanojo wa ningen no kuzu desu. *She is a good-for-nothing.*

---

kyo — 虚 — *void*
kyo ni jōjiru — 虚に乗じる — *to catch someone off guard*
[lit. to ride on someone's void]

今度の入札は、相手の虚に乗じて勝つことが出来ました。Kondo no nyūsatsu wa, aite no kyo ni jōjite katsu koto ga dekimashita. *We won the bidding by catching our competitor off guard.*

---

kyō — 恐 — *to be scared*
kyōsaika — 恐妻家 — *a henpecked husband*
[lit. a husband who is scared of his wife]

彼は恐妻家です。Kare wa kyōsaika desu. *He's a henpecked husband.*

---

ma — 間 — space, time, timing

ma ga warui — 間が悪い — to be embarrassed
[lit. The timing is bad.]

授業中の居眠りを先生に見られて、間が悪い思いをしました。
Jugyō chū no inemuri o sensei ni mirarete, ma ga warui omoi o
shimashita.   I felt embarrassed because the teacher saw me dozing
during class.

ma ga motenai — 間が持てない — to be unable to fill the silences
[lit. to be unable to hold space]

初めてのデートで、間が持てなくて困りました。Hajimete no dēto de
ma ga motenakute komarimashita.   I had a tough time on the first date
because I couldn't fill the silence.

manuke — 間抜け — blockhead
[lit. someone with no sense of timing]

彼女は間抜けだから、何かするといつも失敗があります。
Kanojo wa manuke dakara, nanika suru to itsumo shippai ga arimasu.
Since she's a blockhead, whenever she does something, there's a
mistake.

---

ma — 魔 — devil

ma gasasu — 魔がさす — The devil made (one) do it.
[lit. to be dictated by a devil]

魔がさして、言うべきでないことを言ってしまってすみません。Ma
ga sashite, iu beki de nai koto o itte shimatte sumimasen.   I shouldn't
have said that; the devil made me do it.

---

ma — 真 — truth

ma ni ukeru — 真に受ける — to accept something as true
[lit. to receive something as being true]

彼女の話を真に受けて、同情してしまいました。Kanojo no hanashi o
ma ni ukete, dōjō shite shimaimashita.   I regret that I sympathized with
her by believing her story.

---

magaru — 曲がる — *to curve*
magarinari ni mo — 曲がりなりにも — *at least*
[lit. even with a curve]
曲がりなりにも、コンピュータは使うことが出来ます。Magarinari
ni mo, konpyūta wa tsukau koto ga dekimasu.   *At least I can use a
computer.*

maikyo — 枚挙 — *enumeration*
maikyo ni itoma ga nai — 枚挙にいとまがない — *to be too numerous
to mention*
[lit. to be too busy to count something one by one]
彼は、枚挙にいとまがないほどの沢山の賞を受けています。
Kare wa, maikyo ni itoma ga nai hodo no takusan no shō o ukete imasu.
He received so many awards they were too numerous to mention.

makka — 真っ赤 — *deep red*
makka na uso — 真っ赤な嘘 — *outright lie*
[lit. a deep red lie]
彼女のいいわけは、真っ赤な嘘であることがすぐ分かりました。
Kanojo no iiwake wa, makka na uso dearu koto ga sugu wakarimashita.
I immediately knew that her excuse was an outright lie.

makkō — 抹香 — *incense*
makkō kusai — 抹香臭い — *preachy*
[lit. smelling like incense]
彼の話はいつも抹香臭いので、みんなが彼を避けています。Kare no
hanashi wa itsumo makkō kusai node, minna ga kare o sakete imasu.
Because he's always preachy, everybody avoids him.

maku — 巻く — *to wrap something*
makizoe o kuu   巻き添えを食う   *to get mixed up in trouble*
[lit. to be wrapped and thrown into something]
会社の権力争いの巻き添えを食って、首になってしまいました。
Kaisha no kenryoku arasoi no makizoe o kutte, kubi ni natte
shimaimashita.   *I got fired after getting mixed up in the power struggle
in the company.*

makura — 枕 — *pillow*

makura o takaku shite nemuru — 枕を高くして眠る — *to sleep peacefully*
[lit. to sleep by making one's pillow higher]
借金を払い終わったので、枕を高くして眠れます。
Shakkin o haraiowatta node, makura o takaku shite nemuremasu.
Because I finished repaying the debt, I can start sleeping peacefully.

manaita — まな板 — *cutting board*

manaita ni noseru — まな板に載せる — *to take up something for discussion*
[lit. to put something on a cutting board]
次の会議では、来年の計画をまな板に載せるつもりです。Tsugi no kaigi dewa, rainen no keikaku o manaita ni noseru tsumori desu. *In the next meeting, we'll take up the plans for next year.*

marui — 丸い — *round*

maruku osameru — 丸く収める — *to settle something amicably*
[lit. to finish roundly]
彼女との口論を、丸く収めることが出来ました。Kanojo to no kōron o, maruku osameru koto ga dekimashita. *I was able to settle the quarrel with her amicably.*

masseki — 末席 — *lowest seat*

masseki o kegasu — 末席を汚す — *to have the honor of being present at something*
[lit. to dirty the lowest seat]
今日は、委員会の会議の末席を汚させていただきます。Kyō wa, iinkai no kaigi no masseki o kegasasete itadakimasu. *I'm honored to be present at the committee meeting today.*

mata — 股 — *thigh*

futamata kakeru — 二股かける — *to get involved in two things at the same time*
[lit. to put each thigh on a different thing]
彼女はクラブ活動では、テニスと水泳に二股かけています。Kanojo wa kurabu katsudō dewa, tenisu to suiei ni futamata kakete imasu. *In extracurricular activities, she's involved in both tennis and swimming.*

mato — 的 — *target*
mato o shiboru — 的を絞る — *to focus*
[lit. to squeeze a target]
会議の話題として、新製品開発に的を絞りました。Kaigi no wadai
toshite, shin seihin kaihatsu ni mato o shiborimashita.　*For the subject
of the meeting, we focused on the development of a new product.*

matohazure — 的外れ — *irrelevant*
[lit. off-target]
彼女の質問は、全く的外れでした。Kanojo no shitsumon wa, mattaku
matohazure deshita.　*Her question was totally irrelevant.*

matsu — 待つ — *to wait*
mattanashi — 待った無し — *now or never*
[lit. without a wait]
わが社は今、待った無しの状態に直面しています。Waga sha wa ima,
mattanashi no jōtai ni chokumen shite imasu.　*Our company is facing a
"now or never" situation.*

mawaru — 回る — *to go around*
mawarikudoi — 回りくどい — *to beat around the bush*
[lit. to go around tediously]
彼の話し方は回りくどいので、聞いているといらいらします。Kare no
hanashikata wa mawarikudoi node, kiite iru to iraira shimasu.　*Because
he always beats around the bush, it's irritating to listen to him.*

mawashimono — 回し者 — *spy*
[lit. someone who goes around]
あの店員は、競争相手の店の回し者という噂があります。Ano ten-in
wa kyōsō aite no mise no mawashimono to iu uwasa ga arimasu.
*There's a rumor that the salesclerk over there is a spy for a competing
store.*

mayu — 眉 — *eyebrows*
mayu ni tsuba o nuru — 眉に唾を塗る — *to take something with a
grain of salt*
[lit. to put saliva on one's eyebrows]
彼女の話は、眉に唾を塗って聞かねばなりません。Kanojo no
hanashi wa, mayu ni tsuba o nutte kikaneba narimasen.　*You should
take her story with a grain of salt.*

mayu o hisomeru — 眉をひそめる — *to frown on something*
[lit. to knit one's eyebrows]
彼は、妹の人生に対する態度に眉をひそめました。Kare wa, imōto
no jinsei ni taisuru taido ni mayu o hisomemashita.   *He frowned on his*
younger sister's attitude toward life.

mayu o kumoraseru — 眉を曇らせる — *to be concerned*
[lit. to make one's eyebrows cloudy]
彼女の話を聞いて、眉を曇らせました。Kanojo no hanashi o kiite,
mayu o kumorasemashita.   *After hearing her story, I was concerned*
about it.

mayutsubamono — 眉唾物 — *fake*
[lit. something which causes one to put saliva on one's eyebrows]
彼女の話は、全くの眉唾物です。Kanojo no hanashi wa, mattaku no
mayutsubamono desu.   *Her story is a total fake.*

---

me — 芽 — *bud*

me ga deru — 芽が出る — *to begin to prosper*
[lit. A bud begins to come out.]
彼女の商売は、やっと芽が出始めました。Kanojo no shōbai wa, yatto
me ga dehajimemashita.   *Her business has finally begun to prosper.*

mebaeru — 芽生える — *to emerge*
[lit. to start a bud]
彼に学者になりたい気持ちが芽生えたのは、昔のことです。Kare ni
gakusha ni naritai kimochi ga mebaeta no wa, mukashi no koto desu.
It was long ago that his desire to become a scholar emerged.

---

me — 目 — *eye*

me ga kiku — 目が利く — *to have a critical eye for something*
[lit. One's eye is effective.]
彼女は中国の骨董品に目が利きます。Kanojo wa Chūgoku no kottōhin
ni me ga kikimasu.   *She has a critical eye for Chinese antiques.*

me ga koeru — 目が肥える — *to be a good judge of someone or*
something
[lit. One's eyes grow fertile.]
彼は、新入社員を見る目が肥えています。Kare wa shinnyū shain o
miru me ga koete imasu.   *He's a good judge of new employees in the*
company.

me ga kuramu — 目がくらむ — *to be dazzled by something*
[lit. One's eyes grow dizzy.]

彼は金に目がくらんで、会社の秘密を漏らしてしまいました。Kare wa kane ni me ga kurande, kaisha no himitsu o morashite shimaimashita. *Dazzled by money, he leaked the company secrets.*

me ga nai — 目がない — *to be extremely fond of something*
[lit. no eyes]

彼はゴルフに目がありません。Kare wa gorufu ni me ga arimasen. *He's extremely fond of playing golf.*

me ga mawaru yō ni isogashii — 目が回るように忙しい — *to be as busy as a bee*
[lit. to be so busy as to feel dizzy]

今は会計年度末なので、目が回るように忙しいです。Ima wa kaikei nendo matsu nanode, me ga mawaru yō ni isogashii desu. *Because it's the end of the fiscal year now, we're as busy as bees.*

me ga saeru — 目が冴える — *to be wide awake*
[lit. One's eyes are clear.]

夕べは目が冴えて、午前二時まで眠れませんでした。Yūbe wa me ga saete, gozen niji made nemuremasen deshita. *I was wide awake last night and couldn't fall asleep till two in the morning.*

me ga sameru — 目が覚める — *to come to one's senses*
[lit. to become awake]

彼はやっと目が覚めて、悪い仲間との縁を切りました。Kare wa yatto me ga samete, warui nakama to no en o kirimashita. *He finally came to his senses and severed relations with his no-good friends.*

me ga takai — 目が高い — *to have an expert eye for something*
[lit. One's eyes are high.]

彼女は、美術に対する目が高いです。Kanojo wa, bijutsu ni taisuru me ga takai desu. *She has an expert eye for art.*

me ga tobideru — 目が飛び出る — *to be shocked at an exorbitant price*
[lit. One's eyes pop out.]

そのレストランの勘定があまりにも高かったので、目が飛び出ました。Sono resutoran no kanjō ga amari nimo takakatta node, me ga tobidemashita. *I was shocked at the exorbitant check at the restaurant.*

me ga todoku — 目が届く — *to be attentive to someone*
[lit. One's eyes reach someone.]

あの店では、客一人一人に対する目が届いています。Ano mise

dewa, kyaku hitorihitori ni taisuru me ga todoite imasu. *In that store, they're attentive to each customer.*

me kara hana ni nukeru yō na — 目から鼻に抜けるような — *sharp, intelligent*
[lit. like something passing through one's eyes to the nose]
彼は、目から鼻に抜けるような人です。Kare wa, me kara hana ni nukeru yō na hito desu. *He's very sharp.*

me kara hi ga deru — 目から火が出る — *to see stars*
[lit. Sparks come out of one's eyes.]
ドアに頭をぶつけて、目から火が出ました。Doa ni atama o butsukete, me kara hi ga demashita. *I saw stars when I hit my head against a door.*

me kara uroko ga ochiru — 目から鱗が落ちる — *to see the light*
[lit. The scales drop from one's eyes.]
彼は間違っていると思っていたけれど、話してみて、目から鱗が落ちました。Kare wa machigatte iru to omotte ita keredo, hanashite mite, me kara uroko ga ochimashita. *Although I had thought he was wrong, after talking with him, I saw the light.*

me mo aterarenai — 目も当てられない — *too terrible to look at*
[lit. to be unable to even cast one's eyes]
交通事故の現場は、目も当てられないほどのひどさでした。Kōtsū jiko no genba wa, me mo aterarenai hodo no hidosa deshita. *The scene of the traffic accident was too terrible to look at.*

me mo kurenai — 目もくれない — *to ignore someone or something*
[lit. not even to cast one's eyes]
彼女は、親の忠告には目もくれません。Kanojo wa, oya no chūkoku niwa me mo kuremasen. *She ignores her parents' advice.*

me ni amaru — 目に余る — *to be intolerable*
[lit. to be excessive to one's eyes]
彼の最近の言動は目に余ります。Kare no saikin no gendō wa me ni amarimasu. *His recent speech and conduct are intolerable.*

me ni hairu — 目に入る — *to come across someone or something*
[lit. to enter into one's eyes]
ギフトの買い物をしていると、きれいなセーターが目に入りました。Gifuto no kaimono o shite iru to, kirei na sētā ga me ni hairimashita. *While gift shopping, I came across a beautiful sweater.*

me ni fureru — 目に触れる — *to attract one's attention*
[lit. to touch one's eyes]

デパートでは、外国製品があちこちで目に触れました。Depāto dewa, gaikoku seihin ga achi kochi de me ni furemashita. *Foreign products attracted my attention here and there in the department store.*

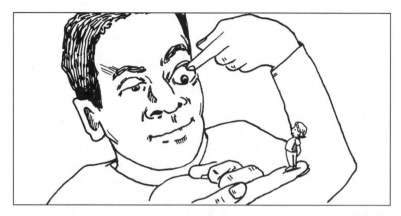

me ni iretemo itakunai — 目に入れても痛くない — *to be the apple of one's eye*
[lit. Even if one puts a child in one's eye, it does't hurt.]

初孫は、目に入れても痛くありません。Hatsumago wa, me ni iretemo itaku arimasen. *My first grandchild is the apple of my eye.*

me ni kado o tateru — 目に角を立てる — *to get angry*
[lit. to make one's eyes angular]

彼はつまらないことなのに、目に角を立てました。Kare wa tsumaranai koto nanoni, me ni kado o tatemashita. *Although it was such a trivial matter, he got angry.*

me ni mieru — 目に見える — *to be obvious*
[lit. to be able to see something with one's own eyes]

選挙は、すでに結果が目に見えています。Senkyo wa, sude ni kekka ga me ni miete imasu. *The election results are already obvious.*

me ni miete — 目に見えて — *visibly*
[lit. being visible in one's eyes]

近頃彼女は、目に見えて幸せそうです。Chikagoro kanojo wa, me ni miete shiawase sō desu. *Nowadays, she looks visibly happy.*

me ni mieteiru — 目に見えている — *to be a foregone conclusion*
[lit. to have been visible]
彼が首になることは、目に見えていました。Kare ga kubi ni naru koto
wa, me ni miete imashita.　*It was a foregone conclusion that he would
be fired.*

me ni mono iwaseru — 目に物言わせる — *to give someone a look*
[lit. to let one's eyes speak]
父は目に物言わせて、兄の態度を戒めました。Chichi wa me ni mono
iwasete, ani no taido o imashimemashita.　*Giving him a look, my father
chided my older brother for his attitude.*

me ni mono miseru — 目に物見せる — *to teach someone a lesson*
[lit. to show someone's eyes something]
この前の仕返しに、彼に目に物を見せてやりました。Kono mae no
shikaeshi ni, kare ni me ni mono o misete yarimashita.　*I taught him a
lesson to retaliate for what he did to me last time.*

me ni suru — 目にする — *to notice*
[lit. to make one's eyes see]
最近は、ここでも外国の高級車をよく目にしています。Saikin wa,
koko demo gaikoku no kōkyūsha o yoku me ni shite imasu.　*Recently,
I've been noticing many expensive foreign cars here.*

me ni tomaru — 目に留まる — *to catch someone's eye*
[lit. to stay with one's eyes]
彼女の素晴らしい才能が、私の目に留まりました。Kanojo no
subarashii sainō ga, watakushi no me ni tomarimashita.　*Her great
talent caught my eye.*

me ni tsuku — 目に付く — *to be noticeable*
[lit. to attach to someone's eyes]
会議での彼の影響力は、全く目に付きませんでした。Kaigi de no
kare no eikyōryoku wa, mattaku me ni tsukimasen deshita.　*His
influence was not at all noticeable at the conference.*

me ni ukabu — 目に浮かぶ — *to flash in front of one's eyes*
[lit. something to float in one's eyes]
母と話しているとき、古里のことが目に浮かびました。
Haha to hanashite iru toki, furusato no koto ga me ni ukabimashita.
*When I was talking to my mother, my hometown flashed in front of my
eyes.*

me no doku — 目の毒 — *to be too much of a temptation*
[lit. poison for one's eyes]
ダイエット中なので、甘い物は目の毒です。Daietto chū nanode, amai
mono wa me no doku desu.　*Since I'm on diet, sweets are too much of a
temptation.*

me no iro o kaeru — 目の色を変える — *to have a serious look, to look
serious*
[lit. to change one's eye color]
彼女は目の色を変えて、一生懸命働いています。Kanojo wa me no
iro o kaete, isshōkenmei hataraite imasu.　*She's working hard with a
serious look on her face.*

me no hoyō — 目の保養 — *feast for one's eyes*
[lit. recreation for one's eyes]
素晴らしい美術品を見て、目の保養になりました。Subarashii
bijutsuhin o mite, me no hoyō ni narimashita.　*It was a feast for my eyes
to see the great art objects.*

me no kataki ni suru — 目の敵にする — *to always show animosity
toward someone*
[lit. to make someone an enemy of one's eyes]
なぜ彼が私を目の敵にするのか、分かりません。Naze kare ga
watakushi o me no kataki ni suru no ka, wakarimasen.　*I don't know
why he always shows animosity toward me.*

me no kuroi uchi — 目の黒いうち — *while alive*
[lit. while one's eyes are still black]
彼女は目の黒い内に、孫の顔を見たがっています。Kanojo wa me no
kuroi uchi ni, mago no kao o mitagatte imasu.　*She wants to see the
face of a grandchild while she's still alive.*

me no mae ga kurakunaru — 目の前が暗くなる — *to feel depressed*
[lit. The front of one's eyes gets dark.]
夫が失業して、目の前が暗くなりました。Otto ga shitsugyō shite, me
no mae ga kurakunarimashita.　*I felt depressed because my husband
lost his job.*

me no ue no tankobu — 目の上のたんこぶ — *constant hindrance*
[lit. a swelling above one's eye]
彼は私の昇進にとって、目の上のたんこぶです。Kare wa watakushi
no shōshin ni totte, me no ue no tankobu desu.　*He's a constant
hindrance to my promotion.*

me o hanasu — 目を離す — *to take one's eyes off someone or something*
[lit. to let one's eyes go]

空港でちょっと目を離した際に、荷物を盗まれてしまいました。
Kūkō de chotto me o hanashita suki ni, nimotsu o nusumarete shimaimashita. *The moment I took my eyes off my luggage at the airport, it was stolen.*

me o hikarasu — 目を光らす — *to keep a sharp eye on something*
[lit. to shine one's eyes]

マスコミは、政治汚職に目を光らせています。 Masukomi wa, seiji oshoku ni me o hikarasete imasu. *The media is keeping a sharp eye on political corruption.*

me o hiku — 目を引く — *to draw someone's attention*
[lit. to pull someone's eyes toward something]

彼女の演説は、ひときわ出席者の目を引きました。Kanojo no enzetsu wa, hitokiwa shussekisha no me o hikimashita. *Her speech particularly drew the participants' attention.*

me o hiraku —- 目を開く — *to realize*
[lit. to open one's eyes]

彼は、辛抱の大切さにやっと目を開きました。Kare wa, shinbō no taisetsusa ni yatto me o hirakimashita. *He finally realized the importance of patience.*

me o hosomeru — 目を細める — *One's eyes light up.*
[lit. to make one's eyes narrow]

彼女はボーイフレンドからプレゼントをもらって、目を細めました。
Kanojo wa bōifurendo kara purezento o moratte, me o hosomemashita. *Her eyes lit up when she received a gift from her boyfriend.*

me o kakeru — 目をかける — *to be partial to someone*
[lit. to set one's eyes on someone]

彼はまじめでよく働くので、目をかけています。Kare wa majime de yoku hataraku node, me o kakete imasu. *I'm partial to him because he's serious and works hard.*

me o korasu — 目を凝らす — *to strain one's eyes*
[lit. to apply one's eyes to something]

彼女は目を凝らして、息子のバイオリン演奏を見守りました。Kanojo wa me o korashite, musuko no baiorin ensō o mimamorimashita. *Straining her eyes, she watched her son play the violin.*

me o kubaru — 目を配る — *to watch carefully*
[lit. to distribute one's eyes]
先生は試験中、不正がないように目を配りました。Sensei wa shiken
chū, fusei ga nai yō ni me o kubarimashita.   *During the exam, the
teacher watched carefully so that there would be no cheating.*

me o maruku suru — 目を丸くする — *to stare in wonder*
[lit. to make one's eyes round]
彼の豪華な家に、友達はみんな目を丸くしました。Kare no gōka na
ie ni, tomodachi wa minna me o marukushimashita.   *All his friends
stared in wonder at his gorgeous house.*

me o mawasu — 目を回す — *to be stunned*
[lit. to faint]
彼女のけち加減には、目を回しました。Kanojo no kechi kagen niwa,
me o mawashimashita.   *I was stunned by the degree of her stinginess.*

me o miharu — 目を見張る — *to be amazed*
[lit. to stretch one's eyes open]
彼の習字の見事さに目を見張りました。Kare no shūji no migotosa ni
me o miharimashita.   *We were amazed at his great calligraphy.*

me o muite — 目をむいて — *with eyes glaring*
[lit. by peeling one's eyes]
彼は、目をむいて同僚を非難しました。Kare wa, me o muite dōryō o
hinan shimashita.   *With eyes glaring, he accused his colleagues.*

me o nusunde — 目を盗んで — *behind someone's back*
[lit. by stealing someone's eyes]
彼は仕事中、ボスの目を盗んでコンピュ－タゲームをしています。
Kare wa shigoto chū, bosu no me o nusunde konpyūta gēmu o shite
imasu.   *He's playing computer games on the job behind the boss's back.*

me o otosu — 目を落とす — *to cast one's eyes down*
[lit. to drop one's eyes]
彼女は試験の結果にがっかりして、目を落としました。Kanojo wa
shiken no kekka ni gakkari shite, me o otoshimashita.   *Disappointed at
the test results, she cast her eyes down.*

me o sankaku ni suru — 目を三角にする — *to look angrily at someone*
[lit. to make one's eyes triangular]
父は目を三角にして、姉をしかりました。Chichi wa me o sankaku ni
shite, ane o shikarimashita.   *Looking angrily at my older sister, my
father scolded her.*

me o sara no yō ni shite — 目を皿のようにして — *with saucer eyes, with one's eyes peeled*
[lit. by making one's eyes like saucers]
落とした財布を目を皿のようにして探したけれど、見つかりませんでした。Otoshita saifu o me o sara no yō ni shite sagashita keredo, mitsukarimasen deshita.   *I kept my eyes peeled for my lost wallet, but I couldn't find it.*

me o shirokuro saseru — 目を白黒させる — *to roll one's eyes in bewilderment*
[lit. to make one's eyes black and white]
彼女はそれを聞いて、目を白黒させました。Kanojo wa sore o kiite, me o shirokuro sasemashita.   *When she heard the story, she rolled her eyes in bewilderment.*

me o sosogu — 目を注ぐ — *to look at something carefully*
[lit. to pour one's eyes over something]
父はテレビでの首相の演説に、目を注いでいました。Chichi wa terebi de no shushō no enzetsu ni, me o sosoide imashita.   *My father was watching the prime minister's speech on TV carefully.*

me o tōsu — 目を通す — *to look through something*
[lit. to let one's eyes go through something]
毎朝、三つの新聞に目を通します。Maiasa, mittsu no shinbun ni me o tōshimasu.   *I look through three newspapers every morning.*

me o tsuburu — 目をつぶる — *to wink at someone's fault or mistake*
[lit. to close one's eyes]
事情が分かるので、今度の彼の失敗に目をつぶることにしました。Jijō ga wakaru node, kondo no kare no shippai ni me o tsuburu koto ni shimashita.   *Because I understood the circumstances, I decided to wink at his mistake this time.*

me o tsukeru — 目をつける — *to focus on someone or something*
[lit. to attach one's eyes to someone or something]
会社は雇用のため、志願者の誠実な人柄に目を付けています。Kaisha wa koyō no tame, shigansha no seijitsu na hitogara ni me o tsukete imasu.   *For hiring, our company is focusing on candidates who show sincerity.*

me o ubawareru — 目を奪われる — *to be dazzled*
[lit. to get one's eyes stolen]
その景色の美しさに、目を奪われました。Sono keshiki no

utsukushisa ni, me o ubawaremashita.   *I was dazzled by the beauty of the scenery.*

meboshi o tsukeru — 目星をつける — *to make an educated guess*
[lit. to attach an estimate]
それを誰がしたか、目星はついています。Sore o dare ga shita ka, meboshi wa tsuite imasu.   *I've already made an educated guess about who did it.*

medama shōhin — 目玉商品 — *loss leader*
[lit. eyeball goods]
あのスーパーの今週の目玉商品はステーキです。Ano sūpā no konshū no medama shōhin wa sutēki desu.   *This week the loss leader at that supermarket is steak.*

megao de shiraseru — 目顔で知らせる — *to give someone a meaningful look*
[lit. to let someone know something through the expression in one's eyes]
彼女は私に同意していることを、目顔で知らせてくれました。Kanojo wa watakushi ni dōi shite iru koto o, megao de shirasete kuremashita. *She gave me a meaningful look that signaled she agreed with me.*

megashira ga atsukunaru — 目頭が熱くなる — *One's eyes fill with tears.*
[lit. The inside corners of one's eyes get hot.]
感動的な話を聞いて、彼は目頭が熱くなりました。Kandōteki na hanashi o kiite, kare wa megashira ga atsuku narimashita.   *When he heard the moving story, his eyes filled with tears.*

mehana ga tsuku — 目鼻がつく — *to be almost complete*
[lit. Eyes and a nose are attached.]
目標達成の目鼻がつきました。Mokuhyō tassei no mehana ga tsukimashita.   *Achieving our goal is almost complete.*

mejiri o sageru — 目尻を下げる — *to be pleased with something*
[lit. to lower the outside corners of one's eyes]
彼はレポートを先生に誉められて、目尻を下げました。Kare wa repōto o sensei ni homerarete, mejiri o sagemashita.   *He was pleased with his teacher's praising his report.*

mekujira o tateru — めくじらを立てる — *to nitpick*
[lit. to make the outside corners of one's eyes stand up]
彼女はいつも何でもめくじらを立てるので、つき合いにくいです。Kanojo wa itsumo nandemo mekujira o tateru node, tsukiainikui desu.

Because she always nitpicks, it's difficult to be friendly with her.

mekuso hanakuso o warau — 目糞鼻糞を笑う — *the pot calling the kettle black*
[lit. Eye mucus laughs at nose snot.]
彼は彼女を批判しているけれど、それは「目糞鼻糞を笑う」ような ものです。Kare wa kanojo o hihan shite iru keredo, sore wa "mekuso hanakuso o warau" yō na mono desu.　*He's criticizing her, but it's like the pot calling the kettle black.*

mesaki ga kiku — 目先が利く — *to have foresight*
[lit. to have an effect on something before one's eyes]
彼女は目先が利くので、変化への対応も上手です。Kanojo wa mesaki ga kiku node, henka e no taiō mo jōzu desu.　*Since she has foresight, she's good at dealing with change.*

mesaki o kaeru — 目先を変える — *to do something for a change*
[lit. to change something before one's eyes]
今回は目先を変えて、顧客をカントリークラブで接待しました。 Konkai wa mesaki o kaete, kokyaku o kantorī kurabu de settai shimashita.　*This time, for a change, we entertained our clients at the country club.*

meyasu ga tsuku — 目安がつく — *to get a general idea*
[lit. to attain a measurement]
やっと、問題解決の目安がつきました。Yatto, mondai kaiketsu no meyasu ga tsukimashita.　*Finally, we got a general idea of how to solve the problem.*

ōme ni miru — 大目に見る — *to give someone a break*
[lit. to look at someone or something with big eyes]
彼の間違いは初めてなので、大目に見てあげることにしました。 Kare no machigai wa hajimete nanode, ōme ni mite ageru koto ni shimashita.　*Since it was his first mistake, I decided to give him a break.*

ōmedama o kuu — 大目玉を食う — *to be scolded severely*
[lit. to eat a big eyeball]
彼女はまた宿題をしなかったので、先生に大目玉を食いました。
Kanojo wa mata shukudai o shinakatta node, sensei ni ōmedama o
kuimashita.   *Because she didn't do her homework again, she was
scolded severely by the teacher.*

shirime ni kakeru — 尻目にかける — *to disregard someone or something*
[lit. to catch someone or something with the bottom of one's eye]
彼女は親の願いを尻目にかけて、彼とデートしています。Kanojo
wa oya no negai o shirime ni kakete, kare to dēto shite imasu.   *She's
dating him disregarding her parents' wishes.*

shiroi me de miru — 白い目で見る — *to look at someone disdainfully*
[lit. to look at someone with white eyes]
彼は自分の利益しか考えないので、みんなが白い目で見ています。
Kare wa jibun no rieki shika kangaenai node, minna ga shiroi me de mite
imasu.   *Because he thinks only of his own interests, everyone looks at
him disdainfully.*

---

megane — 眼鏡 — *eyeglasses*
megane ni kanau — 眼鏡にかなう — *to pass a test*
[lit. to suit someone's eyeglasses]
彼女は、彼が両親の眼鏡にかなって喜んでいます。Kanojo wa, kare
ga ryōshin no megane ni kanatte yorokonde imasu.   *She's delighted that
he passed her parents' test.*

---

meian — 明暗 — *light and darkness*
  meian o wakeru — 明暗を分ける — *to determine the outcome of
  something*
  [lit. to divide light and darkness]
  選手のサイズが、試合の結果の明暗を分けました。Senshu no saizu
  ga, shiai no kekka no meian o wakemashita. *The size of the players
  determined the outcome of the game.*

mekki — めっき — *plating, gilding*
  mekki ga hageru — めっきがはげる — *to reveal one's true colors*
  [lit. The plating comes off.]
  彼は進歩派を装っていましたが、彼の投票からメッキがはげてしま
  いました。Kare wa shinpoha o yosootte imashita ga, kare no tōhyō
  kara mekki ga hagete shimaimashita. *Although he was pretending to be
  a liberal, his vote revealed his true colors.*

men — 面 — *face*
  men to mukatte — 面と向かって — *to someone's face*
  [lit. by facing someone's face]
  彼女は彼に面と向かって、嘘つきだと非難しました。 Kanojo
  wa kare ni men to mukatte, usotsuki da to hinan shimashita. *She
  accused him to his face of being a liar.*

menboku — 面目 — *honor, appearance*
  menboku o hodokosu — 面目を施す — *to maintain one's honor*
  [lit. to perform one's honor]
  企画の成功で、彼は担当者としての面目を施しました。Kikaku no
  seikō de, kare wa tantōsha to shite no menboku o hodokoshimashita.
  *With the success of the project, he maintained his honor as the person in
  charge.*

  menboku o isshin suru — 面目を一新する — *to undergo a complete
  change*
  [lit. to make an appearance totally new]
  我が社はリストラをして、面目を一新しました。Waga sha wa
  risutora o shite, menboku o isshin shimashita. *Our company underwent
  a complete change by restructuring.*

  menboku o ushinau — 面目を失う — *to lose face*
  [lit. to lose one's honor]

約束を果たせなくて、面目を失ってしまいました。Yakusoku o hatasenakute, menboku o ushinatte shimaimashita. *Because I couldn't fulfill my promise, I lost face.*

menbokunai — 面目ない — *to be ashamed of oneself*
[lit. no honor]
大切な会議に遅れて、面目ありませんでした。Taisetsu na kaigi ni okurete, menboku arimasen deshita. *I was ashamed of myself for being late to such an important meeting.*

---

mesu — メス — *surgical knife*
mesu o ireru — メスを入れる — *to take drastic measures (for a cure)*
[lit. to insert a surgical knife into something]
警察は、組織犯罪にメスを入れるべきです。Keisatsu wa, soshiki hanzai ni mesu o ireru beki desu. *The police should take drastic measures against organized crime.*

---

mētoru — メートル — *meter*
mētoru o ageru — メートルを上げる — *to become high-spirited over drinks*
[lit. to run the meter]
昨日の晩、彼は友達とバ－でメートルを上げました。Kinō no ban, kare wa tomodachi to bā de mētoru o agemashita. *Last night, he and his friends became high-spirited over drinks at a bar.*

---

mi — 実 — *fruit*
mi o musubu — 実を結ぶ — *to pay off*
[lit. to bear fruit]
長年の努力が、やっと実を結びました。Naganen no doryoku ga, yatto mi o musubimashita. *All my efforts for many years finally paid off.*

---

mi — 身 — *body, oneself, container*
mi ga hairu — 身が入る — *to accomplish something*
[lit. One's body is into something.]
今日は、仕事にとても身が入りました。Kyō wa, shigoto ni totemo mi ga hairimashita. *I accomplished a lot of work today.*

mi ga motanai — 身が持たない — *to be unable to maintain one's health*
[lit. One's body can't last.]
仕事の圧力がこれ以上続くと、身が持たなくなります。Shigoto no

atsuryoku ga kore ijō tsuzuku to, mi ga motanaku narimasu. *If the pressure on the job continues, I can't maintain my health.*

mi mo futa mo nai — 身も蓋もない — *to be brutally frank* [lit. There's neither a container nor a lid.]
彼の意見は、身も蓋もありませんでした。Kare no iken wa, mi mo futa mo arimasen deshita. *His opinion was brutally frank.*

mi ni amaru — 身に余る — *undeserved* [lit. excessive to one's body]
わが身に余る光栄を感謝いたします。Waga mi ni amaru kōei o kansha itashimasu. *I'd like to thank you for the undeserved honor bestowed upon me.*

mi ni oboe ga nai — 身に覚えがない — *to have nothing to do with something* [lit. no memory for oneself]
私がしたと言われていますが、身に覚えがありません。Watakushi ga shita to iwarete imasu ga, mi ni oboe ga arimasen. *Although they say I did it, I had nothing to do with it.*

mi ni shimiru — 身に染みる — *to feel deeply* [lit. to penetrate one's body]
彼女の親切が身に染みました。Kanojo no shinsetsu ga mi ni shimimashita. *I felt her kindness deeply.*

mi ni tsukeru — 身につける — *to master, to acquire* [lit. to add something to one's body]
一年で、スペイン語を身につけました。Ichi nen de, Supeingo o mi ni tsukemashita. *I mastered Spanish in one year.*

mi ni tsumasareru — 身につまされる — *to deeply sympathize with someone* [lit. to affect one's body]
彼の苦労が身につまされます。Kare no kurō ga mi ni tsumasaremasu. *I deeply sympathize with him over his hardship.*

mi o hiku — 身を引く — *to leave something, to get out of something* [lit. to pull one's own body]
彼女は芸能界から身を引きました。Kanojo wa geinō kai kara mi o hikimashita. *She left the entertainment world.*

mi o katameru — 身を固める — *to get married* [lit. to solidify one's body]
彼は、高校の級友と身を固める決心をしました。Kare wa, kōkō no

kyūyū to mi o katameru kesshin o shimashita.   *He decided to get married to his high-school classmate.*

mi o kirareru omoi — 身を切られる思い — *to feel great pain*
[lit. to feel as if one's body is slashed]
彼は妻に先立たれて、身を切られる思いをしました。Kare wa tsuma ni sakidatarete, mi o kirareru omoi o shimashita.   *When his wife died, he felt great pain.*

mi o kogasu — 身を焦がす — *to be consumed with love for someone*
[lit. to scorch one's own body]
彼女は妻子ある男性との恋に、身を焦がしています。Kanojo wa saishi aru dansei to no koi ni, mi o kogashite imasu.   *She's consumed with love for a man who has a wife and children.*

mi o ko ni suru — 身を粉にする — *to work one's fingers to the bone*
[lit. to make one's own body into powder]
彼は新車を買うため、身を粉にして働いています。Kare wa shinsha o kau tame, mi o ko ni shite hataraite imasu.   *He's working his fingers to the bone to buy a new car.*

mi o mochikuzusu — 身を持ち崩す — *to ruin one's life by indulging in something*
[lit. to worsen one's own body]
彼は酒と女で身を持ち崩しました。Kare wa sake to onna de mi o mochikuzushimashita.   *He ruined his life by indulging in women and liquor.*

mi o tateru — 身を立てる — *to make a career*
[lit. to make one's own body stand up]
彼女は、女優として身を立てる決心をしました。Kanojo wa, joyū toshite mi o tateru kesshin o shimashita.   *She decided to make a career as an actress.*

mi o tōjiru — 身を投じる — *to enter something*
[lit. to throw one's own body into something]
彼は実業界から政治に身を投じました。Kare wa jitsugyōkai kara seiji ni mi o tōjimashita.   *He entered politics from the business world.*

mi o yoseru — 身を寄せる — *to go to live with someone*
[lit. to bring oneself close to someone]
失業中は、兄の所へ身を寄せていました。Shitsugyō chū wa, ani no tokoro e mi o yosete imashita.   *While I was unemployed, I went to live with my older brother.*

minohodo shirazu — 身の程知らず — *conceited*
[lit. to not know the degree of oneself]
彼は身の程知らずで、呼ばれない会議に出てきて意見を述べました。
Kare wa minohodo shirazu de, yobarenai kaigi ni dete kite iken o
nobemashita. *He's so conceited that he came to the meeting uninvited
and gave his opinions.*

minoke ga yodatsu — 身の毛がよだつ — *hair-raising*
[lit. One's body hair stands up.]
身の毛がよだつ怪談をテレビで見ました。Minoke ga yodatsu
kaidan o terebi de mimashita. *We watched a hair-raising ghost story
on TV.*

---

michi — 道 — *way, road, course*

michi ga hirakeru — 道が開ける — *the prospect for something to
  become possible*
[lit. A road opens.]
社長の命令で、妥協の道が開けました。Shachō no meirei de, dakyō
no michi ga hirakemashita. *The prospect for a compromise became
possible with the president's order.*

michi o ayamaru — 道を誤る — *to take a wrong turn*
[lit. to take a wrong road]
彼はいい先生でしたが、道を誤って賭事に熱中しています。Kare
wa ii sensei deshita ga, michi o ayamatte kakegoto ni netchū shite imasu.
*He was a good teacher, but he took a wrong turn, and he's now
absorbed in gambling.*

michi o tsukeru — 道を付ける — *to pave the way*
[lit. to cut a path]
彼は、地震の研究に道を付けた人です。Kare wa, jishin no kenkyū ni
michi o tsuketa hito desu. *He's the one who paved the way for the
research on earthquakes.*

michikusa o kuu — 道草を食う — *to fool around on the way*
[lit. to eat grass on the roadside]
学校が終わったら、道草を食わないでまっすぐうちに帰ってきな
さい。Gakkō ga owattara, michikusa o kuwanaide massugu uchi ni
kaette kinasai. *Don't fool around after school, and come straight back
home.*

midokoro — 見所 — *merit*
midokoro no aru — 見所のある — *promising*
[lit. There's merit.]
彼は見所のある若者です。Kare wa midokoro no aru wakamono desu.
He's a promising young man.

---

migaki — 磨き — *polish*
migaki o kakeru — 磨きをかける — *to improve*
[lit. to polish something]
夏休みの間、テニスに磨きをかけました。Natsu yasumi no aida,
tenisu ni migaki o kakemashita. *During the summer recess, I improved
my tennis skills.*

---

migi — 右 — *right*
migi e narae — 右へ倣え — *to follow suit*
[lit. Right, dress!]
彼が賛成するとみんな右へ倣えで、その案はすぐ採用されました。
Kare ga sansei suru to minna migi e narae de, sono an wa sugu saiyō
saremashita. *The plan was quickly approved because everyone
followed suit when he favored it.*

migi kara hidari ni — 右から左に — *immediately (after receiving money
or something)*
[lit. from right to left]
彼女はお金をもらうと、右から左に使ってしまいます。Kanojo wa
okane o morau to, migi kara hidari ni tsukatte shimaimasu. *When she
gets money, she immediately spends it all.*

migi ni deru mono ga nai — 右に出る者がない — *the best*
[lit. There's nobody on the right side.]
冗談にかけては、彼の右にでる人はいません。Jōdan ni kakete wa, kare
no migi ni deru hito wa imasen. *When it comes to jokes, he's the best.*

migi to ieba hidari — 右と言えば左 — *to contradict everyone*
[lit. Someone says "left" when you say "right."]
彼女は右と言えば左というので、みんなが彼女を避けます。Kanojo
wa migi to ieba hidari to iu node, minna ga kanojo o sakemasu. *Since
she contradicts everyone, everyone avoids her.*

migiude — 右腕 — *right-hand man*
[lit. a right arm]

彼は有力な政治家の右腕として知られています。Kare wa, yūryoku
na seijika no migiude toshite shirarete imasu.　He's known as the
influential politician's right-hand man.

mikake — 見掛け — appearance
　mikakedaoshi — 見掛け倒し — deceptive image
　[lit. An appearance is upset.]
　彼女はインテリぶっていますが、実は見かけ倒しです。
　　Kanojo wa interi butte imasu ga, jitsu wa mikakedaoshi desu.
　　She's pretending to be an intellectual, but it's really a deceptive image.

mikka — 三日 — three days
　mikka ni agezu — 三日に上げず — frequently
　[lit. without a three-day interval]
　彼はホステスに会うため、三日に上げずバーに顔を出しています。
　　Kare wa hosutesu ni au tame, mikka ni agezu bā ni kao o dashite imasu.
　　He has been showing up at the bar frequently to see the hostess.

　mikkabōzu — 三日坊主 — to be unable to stick with anything
　[lit. a Buddhist priest for only three days]
　彼女は何をしても三日坊主です。Kanojo wa nani o shitemo mikkabōzu
　desu.　No matter what she does, she can't stick with anything.

mikoshi — 神輿 — portable shrine
　mikoshi o ageru — 神輿を上げる — to finally take action
　[lit. to raise a portable shrine]
　政府は、やっと政治改革の神輿を上げました。Seifu wa, yatto seiji
　kaikaku no mikoshi o agemashita.　The government finally took action
　for political reform.

　mikoshi o katsugu — 神輿を担ぐ — to cajole someone
　[lit. to carry a portable shrine]
　彼の神輿を担いで、宴会の準備の責任を引き受けさせました。
　　Kare no mikoshi o katsuide, enkai no junbi no sekinin o
　　hikiukesasemashita.　We cajoled him into taking charge of the
　　preparations for the party.

　mikoshi o sueru — 神輿を据える — to stay too long
　[lit. to lay a portable shrine down]
　彼がうちに来ると神輿を据えるので、妻が嫌がります。Kare ga uchi

ni kuru to mikoshi o sueru node, tsuma ga iyagarimasu.   *Because he always stays too long when he visits us, my wife isn't crazy about him.*

---

mimi — 耳 — *ear*

mimi ga hayai — 耳が早い — *to have big ears*
[lit. One's ears are fast.]
彼女は耳が早いので、近所の噂は全部知っています。
Kanojo wa mimi ga hayai node, kinjo no uwasa wa zenbu shitte imasu.
Because she has big ears, she knows all the neighborhood gossip.

mimi ga itai — 耳が痛い — *to make one's ears burn*
[lit. One's ears hurt.]
彼が私の間違いを指摘するのを聞いて、耳が痛かったです。
Kare ga watakushi no machigai o shiteki suru no o kiite, mimi ga itakatta desu.   *Listening to his pointing out my mistakes made my ears burn.*

mimi ga koeru — 耳が肥える — *to have an ear for something*
[lit. One's ears get enriched.]
彼女は親が音楽家なので、耳が肥えています。Kanojo wa oya ga ongakuka nanode, mimi ga koete imasu.   *Because her parents are musicians, she has an ear for music.*

mimi ni hairu — 耳に入る — *to learn*
[lit. Something enters into one's ear.]
彼女に赤ちゃんが生まれたというニュースが耳に入りました。Kanojo ni akachan ga umareta to iu nyūsu ga mimi ni hairimashita.   *I learned the news that she had a baby.*

mimi ni hasamu — 耳にはさむ — *to get wind of something*
[lit. to put something into one's ear]
彼が結婚したという噂を耳にはさみました。
Kare ga kekkon shita to iu uwasa o mimi ni hasamimashita.
I got wind of the rumor that he got married.

mimi ni ireru — 耳に入れる — *to tell someone something*
[lit. to put something into someone's ear]
耳に入れたいことがあるので、お目に掛かりたいのですが。Mimi ni iretai koto ga aru node, ome ni kakaritai no desu ga.   *I'd like to see you because I have something to tell you.*

mimi ni nokoru — 耳に残る — *to linger in one's ear*
[lit. Something remains in one's ear.]
彼女の言ったことが、今でも耳に残っています。Kanojo no itta koto

ga, ima demo mimi ni nokotte imasu. *What she said to me is still lingering in my ear.*

mimi ni suru — 耳にする — *to happen to hear something*
[lit. to reach one's ear]
彼が近いうちに社長になるという噂を耳にしました。Kare ga chikai uchi ni shachō ni naru to iu uwasa o mimi ni shimashita. *I happened to hear a rumor that he would become president soon.*

mimi ni tako ga dekiru — 耳にたこができる — *to be sick and tired of hearing something*
[lit. A callus grows in one's ear.]
彼女の苦情は、耳にたこができるほど聞きました。Kanojo no kujō wa, mimi ni tako ga dekiru hodo kikimashita. *I'm sick and tired of hearing her complaints.*

mimi ni tomaru — 耳に留まる — *to draw one's attention*
[lit. Something stays in one's ear.]
彼の意見が耳に留まりました。Kare no iken ga mimi ni tomarimashita. *His remarks drew my attention.*

mimi ni tsuku — 耳に付く — *to bother someone (noise)*
[lit. Noise sticks to one's ear.]
テレビの音が耳について、勉強に集中できません。Terebi no oto ga mimi ni tsuite, benkyō ni shūchū dekimasen. *With the noise of the TV bothering me, I can't concentrate on my studying.*

mimi o kasanai — 耳を貸さない — *to turn a deaf ear to something*
[lit. to not lend one's ear to something]
彼女は、両親の忠告に耳を貸しませんでした。Kanojo wa, ryōshin no chūkoku ni mimi o kashimasen deshita. *She turned a deaf ear to her parents' advice.*

mimi o katamukeru — 耳を傾ける — *to listen carefully*
[lit. to lean one's ear toward something]
父は、ラジオのニュース番組に耳を傾けていました。Chichi wa, rajio no nyūsu bangumi ni mimi o katamukete imashita. *My father was listening carefully to the news program on the radio.*

mimi o sobadateru — 耳をそばだてる — *to prick up one's ears*
[lit. to make one's ears stand up high]
同僚の内緒話に耳をそばだてました。Dōryō no naisho hanashi ni mimi o sobadatemashita. *I pricked up my ears at the whispering among my colleagues.*

mimi o soroete — 耳を揃えて — in full
[lit. by arranging the borders of bills neatly]
返済日の前に、借金を耳を揃えて返しました。Hensaibi no mae ni,
shakkin o mimi o soroete kaeshimashita.　I paid back the debt in full
before the due date.

mimi o sumasu — 耳を澄ます — to be all ears
[lit. to make one's ears clear]
社員は、社長の話に耳を澄ましました。Shain wa, shachō no hanashi
ni mimi o sumashimashita.　The employees were all ears during the
president's speech.

mimi o utagau — 耳を疑う — to be unable to believe one's ears
[lit. to doubt one's own ears]
彼が死んだと聞いたとき、耳を疑いました。Kare ga shinda to kiita
toki, mimi o utagaimashita.　When I heard that he had died, I couldn't
believe my ears.

mimiuchi suru — 耳打ちする — to whisper into someone's ear
[lit. to tap someone's ear]
お母さんが子供に何か耳打ちすると、子供は泣き止みました。Okāsan
ga kodomo ni nanika mimiuchi suru to, kodomo wa nakiyamimashita.
When the mother whispered something into her child's ear, he stopped
crying.

mimiyori na — 耳寄りな — worth listening to
[lit. coming nearer to one's ears]
それは会社にとって、耳寄りな情報です。Sore wa kaisha ni totte,
mimiyori na jōhō desu.　This information is worth listening to for the
company.

mimizawari — 耳障り — grating
[lit. to be offensive to one's ears]
彼女の声は、実に耳障りでした。Kanojo no koe wa, jitsu ni
mimizawari deshita.　Her voice was truly grating.

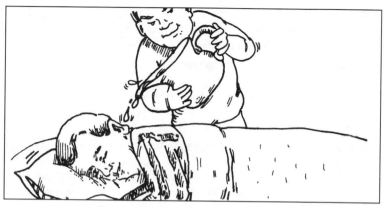

nemimi ni mizu — 寝耳に水 — *bolt out of the blue*
[lit. water into the ear of someone sleeping]
上司が突然会社を辞めたというニュースは、寝耳に水でした。
Jōshi ga totsuzen kaisha o yameta to iu nyūsu wa, nemimi ni mizu
deshita.   *The news that my boss suddenly quit the company was a bolt
out of the blue.*

---

miru — 見る — *to see, to look at*
　miru kage mo nai — 見る影もない — *down and out*
　[lit. There's no shadow to look at.]
　昔は大金持ちだった彼も、今は見る影もありません。Mukashi wa
　ōganemochi datta kare mo, ima wa miru kage mo arimasen.   *He was
　very rich before, but he's down and out now.*

　miru me ga aru — 見る目がある — *to have an eye for something*
　[lit. to have eyes to look at something]
　彼女には、個人の才能を見る目があります。Kanojo niwa, kojin no
　sainō o miru me ga arimasu.   *She has an eye for judging someone's
　talent.*

　miru me ga nai — 見る目がない — *to be a poor judge of something*
　[lit. to not have eyes to look at something]
　彼には、女性を見る目がありません。Kare niwa, josei o miru me ga
　arimasen.   *He's a poor judge of women.*

　miru ni mikaneru — 見るに見かねる — *to be unable to stand watching
　　something*
　[lit. to be unable to just look at something]

彼の料理の仕方を見るに見かねて、手伝いました。Kare no ryōri no
shikata o miru ni mikanete, tetsudaimashita.   *Because I couldn't stand
watching the way he was cooking, I helped him.*

mirukarani — 見るからに — *to just glance at something*
[lit. from a look]
あの子は、見るからに頭がいいのが分かります。Ano ko wa,
mirukarani atama ga ii no ga wakarimasu.   *Just glancing at that child, I
know that she's intelligent.*

mite minu furi o suru — 見て見ぬ振りをする — *to look the other way*
[lit. to pretend to not see anything]
友達がうそをつくのを、見て見ぬ振りをしました。Tomodachi ga
uso o tsuku no o, mite minu furi o shimashita.   *While my friend lied, I
looked the other way.*

---

mise — 店 — *shop*
mise o haru — 店を張る — *to open a store*
[lit. to spread a shop]
彼女は去年、銀座に店を張りました。Kanojo wa kyonen, Ginza ni
mise o harimashita.   *She opened a store in Ginza last year.*

mise o tatamu — 店を畳む — *to close a store*
[lit. to fold a shop]
彼は融資を受けられなくて、店を畳まねばなりませんでした。Kare wa
yūshi o ukerarenakute, mise o tatamaneba narimasen deshita.   *Because
he couldn't get a loan, he had to close his store.*

---

miso — 味噌 — *bean paste*
miso — 味噌 — *the beauty of something*
[lit. bean paste]
この製品は使いやすい。そこが味噌です。Kono seihin wa
tsukaiyasui. Soko ga miso desu.   *This product is easy to use. That's the
beauty of it.*

miso o tsukeru — 味噌をつける — *to make a mess of something*
[lit. to spread bean paste on something]
今度担当した事業計画では、味噌をつけてしまいました。Kondo
tantō shita jigyō keikaku dewa, miso o tsukete shimaimashita.   *I made a
mess of the recent business plan I was in charge of.*

---

mizu — 水 — *water*

mizu ga awanai — 水があわない — *to not agree with someone or something*
[lit. The water doesn't suit someone.]
彼には、大阪の水があいませんでした。Kare niwa, Ōsaka no mizu ga aimasen deshita. *Osaka didn't agree with him.*

mizu mo morasanu — 水も漏らさぬ — *airtight*
[lit. to not even leak water]
テロ行為を防ぐため、警察は水も漏らさぬ警戒をしています。Tero kōi o fusegu tame, keisatsu wa mizu mo morasanu keikai o shite imasu. *The police are keeping an airtight guard against terrorist acts.*

mizu ni nagasu — 水に流す — *to let bygones be bygones*
[lit. to flush something in water]
彼らは過去を水に流して、またつき合うことにしました。Karera wa kako o mizu ni nagashite, mata tsukiau koto ni shimashita. *They decided to resume their relationship and let bygones be bygones.*

mizu no awa ni naru — 水の泡になる — *to go down the drain*
[lit. to become a water bubble]
交渉が決裂して、これまでの努力が水の泡になりました。Kōshō ga ketsuretsu shite, kore made no doryoku ga mizu no awa ni narimashita. *With the negotiations breaking down, all our efforts until now have gone down the drain.*

mizu mo shitataru yō na — 水も滴るような — *breathtaking (person)*
[lit. as if water will drip]
彼は、水も滴るような美人と結婚しました。Kare wa, mizu mo shitataru yō na bijin to kekkon shimashita. *He married a woman of breathtaking beauty.*

mizu o akeru — 水をあける — *to open a lead*
[lit. to open water]
我が社は市場占有率で、競争相手に大きく水をあけています。Waga sha wa shijō sen-yū ritsu de, kyōsō aite ni ōkiku mizu o akete imasu. *Our company has opened a wide lead over our competitors for market share.*

mizu o mukeru — 水を向ける — *to entice someone*
[lit. to offer water]
彼女に水を向けて、秘密を話させました。Kanojo ni mizu o mukete, himitsu o hanasasemashita. *I enticed her into revealing her secret.*

mizu o sasu — 水を差す — *to throw cold water on something*
[lit. to pour water]
彼女は、夫の熱意に水を差しました。Kanojo wa, otto no netsui ni
mizu o sashimashita.   *She threw cold water on her husband's*
enthusiasm.

mizu o utta yō ni shizuka — 水を打つたように静か — *so quiet you*
could hear a pin drop
[lit. as quiet as if water were sprinkled]
彼女が話し始めると、会場は水を打つたように静かになりました。
Kanojo ga hanashihajimeru to, kaijō wa mizu o utta yō ni shizuka ni
narimashita.   *When she started talking, the room became so quiet you*
could hear a pin drop.

mizu to abura — 水と油 — *to never mix, to not get along*
[lit. water and oil]
彼と彼女は、水と油です。Kare to kanojo wa, nizu to abura desu.   *He*
and she don't get along with each other.

mizugiwadatta — 水際立つた — *brilliant, striking*
[lit. standing at the water's edge]
彼女の水際だつた演技に、観客は深く感動しました。Kanojo no
mizugiwadatta engi ni, kankyaku wa fukaku kandō shimashita.   *The*
audience was deeply impressed by her brilliant performance.

mizuirazu de — 水入らずで — *all by oneself*
[lit. without the interference of water]
妻と私は、週末を水入らずで過ごしました。Tsuma to watakushi wa
shūmatsu o mizuirazu de sugoshimashita.   *My wife and I spent the*
weekend all by ourselves.

mizukakeron — 水掛け論 — *endless dispute*
[lit. an argument like dumping water on each other]
彼らの議論は、水掛け論に発展しました。Karera no giron wa,
mizukakeron ni hatten shimashita.   *Their discussion developed into an
endless dispute.*

mizukusai — 水臭い — *distant, unfriendly, too formal*
[lit. to smell like water]
そんな水臭い話し方は止めよう。Sonna mizukusai hanashikata wa
yameyō.   *Let's stop speaking so formally.*

mizumashi suru — 水増しする — *to pad something*
[lit. to add water]
この請求書には、水増しした疑いがあります。Kono seikyūsho niwa,
mizumashi shita utagai ga arimasu.   *I have a suspicion that they padded
this bill.*

mizumono — 水物 — *an uncertain affair*
[lit. a watery thing]
選挙は水物だといわれています。Senkyo wa mizumono da to iwarete
imasu.   *They say that an election is an uncertain affair.*

mizushōbai — 水商売 — *the entertainment business (including
bartenders, bar hostesses, waiters, and so forth)*
[lit. the water business]
彼女は、水商売から足を洗って結婚しました。Kanojo wa,
mizushōbai kara ashi o aratte kekkon shimashita. *She quit the
entertainment business and got married.*

yobimizu — 呼び水 — *trigger*
[lit. priming water]

公共事業投資が呼び水になって、景気回復が始まりました。Kōkyō jigyō tōshi ga yobimizu ni natte, keiki kaifuku ga hajimarimashita. *With the investment in public works as a trigger, the ecomonic recovery has begun.*

---

moku — 黙 — *silence*

mokusatsu suru — 黙殺する — *to deliberately ignore something*
[lit. to kill something silently]

学校側は、学生の要請を黙殺しました。Gakkōgawa wa, gakusei no yōsei o mokusatsu shimashita. *The school administration ignored the students' requests.*

---

momu — 揉む — *to rub*

momikesu — 揉み消す — *to hush something up*
[lit. to rub and put out something]

政府は、汚職の噂を揉み消すのに必死です。Seifu wa oshoku no uwasa o momikesu no ni hisshi desu. *The government is making frantic efforts to hush up the rumor of corruption.*

---

mon — 門 — *gate*

mongen — 門限 — *curfew*
[lit. time restriction at a gate]

この寄宿舎の門限は午後十時です。Kono kishukusha no mongen wa gogo jūji desu. *The curfew for this dormitory is ten p.m.*

monzenbarai o kuu — 門前払いを食う — *to be turned away at a door*
[lit. to be gotten rid of in front of a gate]

有名な作家に会いに行きましたが、門前払いを食いました。Yūmei na sakka ni aini ikimashita ga, monzenbarai o kuimashita. *I went to see the famous novelist, but I was turned away at the door.*

---

mono — 物 — *thing, matter*

mono ga wakaru — 物が分かる — *to be sensible*
[lit. to understand things]

私の両親は、物がよく分かります。Watakushi no ryōshin wa, mono ga yoku wakarimasu. *My parents are very sensible.*

mono ni suru — 物にする — *to obtain*
[lit. to make something one's own]
やっと、興味のあった骨董の壷を物にしました。Yatto, kyōmi no atta
kottō no tsubo o mono ni shimashita.　*I finally obtained the antique jar
I was interested in.*

mono ni naru — 物になる — *to amount to something*
[lit. to become something]
彼は将来、物になるでしょう。Kare wa shōrai, mono ni naru deshō.
He may amount to something in the future.

mono no hazumi de — 物の弾みで — *propelled by the circumstances*
[lit. by the bounce of a thing]
物の弾みで、言ってはいけないことを言ってしまいました。
Mono no hazumi de, ittewa ikenai koto o itte shimaimashita.
Propelled by the circumstances, I said something I shouldn't have said.

mono no kazu dewa nai — 物の数ではない — *to be insignificant*
[lit. to count a number of things for nothing]
彼の脅かしなど、物の数ではありません。Kare no odokashi nado,
mono no kazu dewa arimasen.　*His threat is insignificant to me.*

mono o iu — 物を言う — *to matter, to count*
[lit. to say things]
最近の仕事環境で、物を言っているのがコンピュータの知識です。
Saikin no shigoto kankyō de, mono o itte iru no ga konpyūta no chishiki
desu.　*In the current work environment, it's the knowledge of computers
that counts.*

mono o iwasete — 物をいわせて — *by sheer force of something*
[lit. by resorting to something]
与党は、数に物を言わせて審議を打ち切りました。Yotō wa, kazu ni
mono o iwasete shingi o uchikirimashita.　*The majority party cut off the
deliberations by sheer force of numbers.*

mono tomo sezu ni — 物ともせずに — *refusing to give in to something*
[lit. by not making a big deal of something]
彼は病気を物ともせずに、仕事を続けました。Kare wa byōki o mono
tomo sezu ni, shigoto o tsuzukemashita.　*He kept working, refusing to
give in to his illness.*

mono tomo shinai — 物ともしない — *to defy something*
[lit. to not make something a concern]
彼女は、先生の警告を物ともしませんでした。Kanojo wa, sensei no

keikoku o mono tomo shimasen deshita.   She defied her teacher's warning.

mono wa iiyō — 物は言いよう — It's important how you say it.
[lit. The way of saying things matters.]
物は言いようだから、言葉に気をつけなさい。Mono wa ii yō dakara,
kotoba ni ki o tsukenasai.   Since it's important how you say it, you'd
better watch your mouth.

mono wa kangaeyō — 物は考えよう — Look on the bright side.
[lit. The way of thinking about things matters.]
物は考えようで、雨の週末は読書にいいです。Mono wa kangaeyō de,
ame no shūmatsu wa dokusho ni ii desu.   Look on the bright side: a
rainy weekend is good for reading.

mono wa sōdan — 物は相談 — It helps to talk things over.
[lit. Consultation is a thing of significance.]
物は相談なので、仕事について教授と話しました。
Mono wa sōdan nanode, shigoto ni tsuite kyōju to hanashimashita.
I spoke with the professor about my job because it helps to talk things
over.

mono wa tameshi — 物は試し — You won't know unless you try.
[lit. Trying has significance.]
物は試しだから、宝くじの券を買ってみました。Mono wa tameshi
dakara, takarakuji no ken o katte mimashita.   Since you won't know
unless you try, I bought lottery tickets.

monogusa — 物臭 — lazy
[lit. smelling of things]
彼は物臭だから、用事を頼んでも無駄ですよ。Kare wa monogusa
dakara, yōji o tanondemo muda desu yo.   Because he's lazy, asking him
to do an errand is a waste of time.

monoii o tsukeru — 物言いをつける — to object to something
[lit. to have a thing to say]
彼女は、彼の計画に物言いをつけました。Kanojo wa, kare no keikaku
ni monoii o tsukemashita.   She objected to his plan.

monomonoshii — 物々しい — elaborate
[lit. like something on top of something]
警察は首脳会談のため、物々しい警戒をしています。Keisatsu wa
shunō kaidan no tame, monomonoshii keikai o shite imasu.   The police
are on an elaborate alert for the leaders' conference.

monooji shinai — 物怖じしない — *to not flinch*
[lit. to not fear things]
彼は誰の前でも物怖じしません。Kare wa dare no mae demo monooji shimasen. *He doesn't flinch in front of anyone.*

monotarinai — 物足りない — *to be unsatisfactory*
[lit. to lack something]
彼女にとって、彼はボーイフレンドとして物足りませんでした。
Kanojo ni totte, kare wa bōifurendo toshite monotarimasen deshita. *For her, he was unsatisfactory as a boyfriend.*

monowakare ni naru — 物別れになる — *to end in failure*
[lit. to come to scatter things]
交渉は物別れになりました。Kōshō wa monowakare ni narimashita.
The negotiations ended in failure.

monowakari ga ii — 物わかりがいい — *considerate*
[lit. good at understanding things]
彼女に人気があるのは、とても物わかりがいいからです。Kanojo ni ninki ga aru no wa, totemo monowakari ga ii kara desu. *The reason for her popularity is that she's very considerate.*

monowarai — 物笑い — *laughingstock*
[lit. a laughing matter]
彼はいつも見当違いの質問をするので、物笑いになっています。
Kare wa itsumo kentōchigai no shitsumon o suru node, monowarai ni natte imasu. *Because he always asks irrelevant questions, he has become a laughingstock.*

monozuki — 物好き — *inquisitive*
[lit. liking things]
彼女は物好きで、何にでも手を付けようとします。Kanojo wa monozuki de, nani ni demo te o tsukeyō to shimasu. *Because she's inquisitive, she tries to get involved with everything.*

moto — 元 — *origin, source, principal*
moto mo ko mo nai — 元も子もない — *to lose everything*
[lit. There's neither the principal nor the interest.]
地震による被害のため、元も子もなくなってしまいました。Jishin ni yoru higai no tame, moto mo ko mo nakunatte shimaimashita. *I lost everything because of the earthquake damage.*

mōtō — 毛頭 — *bit*

mōtō nai — 毛頭無い — *not at all*
[lit. no hair or head]
彼女を疑う気持ちは毛頭ありません。Kanojo o utagau kimochi wa
mōtō arimasen.   *I have no intention at all of doubting her.*

---

motsu — 持つ — *to have, to carry*

mochiaji o ikasu — 持ち味を生かす — *to make the most of one's talents*
[lit. to make good use of one's taste]
会社は社員の持ち味を生かすため、人事再編成を行いました。Kaisha
wa shain no mochiaji o ikasu tame, jinji saihensei o okonaimashita.
*The company carried out a personnel reorganization to make the most of
the employees' talents.*

mochitsu motaretsu — 持ちつ持たれつ — *give and take*
[lit. to carry someone and to be carried by someone]
彼とは、持ちつ持たれつの仲です。Kare to wa, mochitsu motaretsu no
naka desu.   *I have a give-and-take relationship with him.*

moteamasu — 持て余す — *to not know what to do with something*
[lit. to have an excess of something]
彼女は子供が大きくなってから、時間を持て余しています。Kanojo
wa kodomo ga ōkiku natte kara, jikan o moteamashite imasu.   *Since her
children are grown, she doesn't know what to do with her time.*

mottekoi no — 持ってこいの — *just right*
[lit. by bringing someone or something in]
彼はその仕事には持ってこいです。Kare wa sono shigoto niwa
mottekoi desu.   *He's just the right person for that job.*

motte mawatta — 持って回った — *roundabout*
[lit. carrying something around]
彼女は持って回った言い方で、結婚の申し込みを断りました。
Kanojo wa motte mawatta iikata de, kekkon no mōshikomi o
kotowarimashita.   *She turned down the marriage proposal with a
roundabout way of speaking.*

---

mottomo — 尤も — *true*

mottomorashii — 尤もらしい — *plausible*
[lit. to seem to be true]
彼の言い訳は尤もらしいけれど、本当かどうかは分かりません。

Kare no iiwake wa mottomorashi keredo, hontō ka dō ka wa
wakarimasen. *Although his excuse sounds plausible, I don't know if
it's true or not.*

mu — 無 — *nothing*

mu ni kisuru — 無に帰する — *to be wasted*
[lit. to return to nothing]
雨で試合が中止になつたため、激しい練習が無に帰しました。Ame de
shiai ga chūshi ni natta tame, hageshii renshū ga mu ni kishimashita.
*Since the game was canceled because of rain, our rigorous practice was
wasted.*

mu ni suru — 無にする — *to waste something*
[lit. to make something nothing]
人の親切を無にするものではありません。Hito no shinsetsu o mu ni
suru mono dewa arimasen. *You should know better than to waste other
people's kindness.*

muda — 無駄 — *waste*

mudaashi o fumu — 無駄足を踏む — *to waste a trip*
[lit. to tread wasteful steps]
叔父に借金をしに行きましたが、断られて無駄足を踏みました。
Oji ni shakkin o shini ikimashita ga, kotowararete mudaashi o
fumimashita. *I wasted a trip to my uncle's when he turned down my
request for a loan.*

mudabone o oru — 無駄骨を折る — *to waste one's efforts*
[lit. to break one's bones wastefully]
彼女を説得しようとしましたが、無駄骨を折る結果に終わりました。
Kanojo o settoku shiyō to shimashita ga, mudabone o oru kekka ni
owarimashita. *I tried to persuade her but ended up wasting my efforts.*

mudaguchi o tataku — 無駄口を叩く — *to chatter aimlessly*
[lit. to sound a wasteful mouth]
無駄口を叩いているより勉強しなさい。Mudaguchi o tataite iru yori
benkyō shinasai. *You should study instead of chattering aimlessly.*

mukō — 向こう — *opposite side*

mukō ni mawasu — 向こうに回す — *to take someone on*
[lit. to send someone around to the opposite side]

彼は専門家を向こうに回して、対立的な見解を述べました。

Kare wa senmonka o mukō ni mawashite, tairitsuteki na kenkai o nobemashita.   *Taking on the specialist, he stated the opposing view.*

mukō o haru — 向こうを張る — *to compete*
[lit. to set against an opposite side]

地元の商店は新しいス−パ−の向こうを張って、バ−ゲンセ−ルを行っています。Jimoto no shōten wa atarashii sūpā no mukō o hatte, bāgensēru o okonatte imasu.   *The local stores are holding a bargain sale, competing with the new supermarket.*

mukōmizu na — 向こう見ずな — *reckless*
[lit. not looking at the opposite side]

彼の向こう見ずな言動を、お母さんはとても心配しています。

Kare no mukōmizu na gendō o, okāsan wa totemo shinpai shite imasu.

His mother is gravely concerned about his reckless speech and behavior.

---

muna — 胸 — *chest*

munasawagi ga suru — 胸騒ぎがする — *to feel uneasy*
[lit. One's chest becomes agitated.]

夫の帰宅がとても遅いので胸騒ぎがしましたが、無事でした。

Otto no kitaku ga totemo osoi node munasawagi ga shimashita ga, buji deshita.   *I felt uneasy when my husband was very late returning home, but he was okay.*

munazanyō suru — 胸算用する — *to figure on something*
[lit. to calculate something in one's own chest]

彼は、来年は課長になれると胸算用しています。Kare wa, rainen wa kachō ni nareru to munazanyō shite imasu.   *He figures on becoming a section chief next year.*

---

mune — 胸 — *chest*

mune ga hareru — 胸が晴れる — *to feel relieved*
[lit. One's chest is cleared.]

私に対する疑いが解けて、胸が晴れました。Watakushi ni taisuru utagai ga tokete, mune ga haremashita.   *I felt relieved because I was cleared of suspicion.*

mune ga harisakeru — 胸が張り裂ける — *to tear one apart*
[lit. One's chest bursts.]

深い悲しみで、胸が張り裂けました。Fukai kanashimi de, mune ga harisakemashita. *My grief tore me apart.*

mune ga hazumu — 胸が弾む — *to get excited*
[lit. One's chest bounces.]

この夏の旅行のことを考えると、いつも胸が弾みます。Kono natsu no ryokō no koto o kangaeru to, itsumo mune ga hazumimasu. *Whenever I think about our trip next summer, I get excited.*

mune ga ippai ni naru — 胸が一杯になる — *to get a lump in one's throat*
[lit. One's chest becomes full.]

彼女の悲しい話を聞いて、胸が一杯になりました。Kanojo no kanashii hanashi o kiite, mune ga ippai ni narimashita. *I got a lump in my throat hearing her sad story.*

mune ga suku — 胸がすく — *to be relieved*
[lit. One's chest becomes cleared.]

借金を返し終わって、胸がすきました。Shakkin o kaeshiowatte, mune ga sukimashita. *I'm relieved at having paid back the entire debt.*

mune ga tsumaru — 胸が詰まる — *to be choked up*
[lit. One's chest gets clogged.]

胸が詰まって、言葉がでませんでした。Mune ga tsumatte, kotoba ga demasen deshita. *Because I was choked up, I couldn't utter a word.*

mune ni himeru — 胸に秘める — *to keep something to oneself*
[lit. to conceal something in one's chest]

彼女は、いつか女優になる夢を胸に秘めていました。Kanojo wa, itsuka joyū ni naru yume o mune ni himete imashita. *She kept her dream of becoming an actress someday to herself.*

mune ni kotaeru — 胸に応える — *to hit one very hard*
[lit. Something responds to one's chest.]

父の訓戒が胸に応えました。Chichi no kunkai ga mune ni kotaemashita. *My father's admonition hit me very hard.*

mune ni osameru — 胸に納める — *to keep something to oneself*
[lit. to put something away in one's chest]

あなたの秘密は、私の胸だけに納めておきます。Anata no himitsu wa, watakushi no mune dake ni osamete okimasu. *I'll keep your secret just to myself.*

mune ni semaru — 胸に迫る — *to be filled with emotion*
[lit. Emotion compels one's chest.]

大学の卒業式で、喜びが胸に迫りました。Daigaku no sotsugyō shiki de, yorokobi ga mune ni semarimashita. *I was filled with joy at the college graduation ceremony.*

mune ni ukabu — 胸に浮かぶ — *to flash across one's mind*
[lit. Something floats in one's chest.]
素晴らしい考えが胸に浮かびました。Subarashii kangae ga mune ni ukabimashita. *A wonderful idea flashed across my mind.*

mune o fukuramaseru — 胸を膨らませる — *to have high hopes (about something)*
[lit. to expand one's chest]
彼は、成功の期待に胸を膨らませています。Kare wa, seikō no kitai ni mune o fukuramasete imasu. *He has high hopes that he'll be successful.*

mune o hatte — 胸を張って — *with one's head held high*
[lit. to throw out one's chest]
自分が正しいなら、胸を張ってそう言いなさい。Jibun ga tadashii nara, mune o hatte sō iinasai. *If you're right, say so with your head held high.*

mune o hazumasete — 胸を弾ませて — *excitedly*
[lit. by bouncing one's chest]
彼女は胸を弾ませて、プレゼントを開けました。Kanojo wa mune o hazumasete purezento o akemashita. *She opened the gift excitedly.*

mune o itameru — 胸を痛める — *to be worried about something*
[lit. to hurt one's own chest]
彼女は娘の将来について、胸を痛めています。Kanojo wa musume no shōrai ni tsuite, mune o itamete imasu. *She is worried about her daughter's future.*

mune o kogasu — 胸を焦がす — *to pine away with love for someone*
[lit. to scorch one's chest]
彼は、その女性に胸を焦がしています。Kare wa, sono josei ni mune o kogashite imasu. *He's pining away with love for that woman.*

mune o nadeorosu — 胸をなで下ろす — *to feel relieved*
[lit. to pat one's own chest down]
彼女は赤ちゃんの高熱が下がって、胸をなで下ろしました。Kanojo wa akachan no kōnetsu ga sagatte, mune o nadeoroshimashita. *When her baby's high fever went down, she felt relieved.*

mune o odoraseru — 胸を躍らせる — *to be excited*
[lit. to make one's chest jump]

彼はいい知らせを受けて、胸を躍らせました。Kare wa ii shirase o ukete, mune o odorasemashita.   *He was excited at receiving good news.*

mune o shimetsukeru — 胸を締め付ける — *to break one's heart*
[lit. to squeeze one's chest]
彼の悲しい話は、聞く人の胸を締め付けました。Kare no kanashii hanashi wa, kiku hito no mune o shimetsukemashita.   *His sad story broke the listeners' hearts.*

mune o sorasu — 胸を反らす — *to pride oneself on something*
[lit. to bend one's chest backward]
彼女は司法試験に受かって、胸を反らせました。Kanojo wa shihō shiken ni ukatte, mune o sorasemashita.   *She prides herself on having passed the bar exam.*

mune o tokimekasu — 胸をときめかす — *to get excited at something*
[lit. to make one's chest throb]
子供たちは、明日ディズニーランドへ行くので、胸をときめかしています。Kodomotachi wa, ashita Dizunīrando e iku node, mune o tokimekasete imasu.   *My children are getting excited at going to Disneyland tomorrow.*

mune o tsukareru — 胸を突かれる — *to be stunned*
[lit. to get stabbed in one's chest]
私に対する突然の批判に、胸を突かれました。Watakushi ni taisuru totsuzen no hihan ni, mune o tsukaremashita.   *I was stunned by the sudden criticism of me.*

mune o utsu — 胸を打つ — *to deeply move someone*
[lit. to hit someone's chest]
彼女の親切に胸を打たれました。Kanojo no shinsetsu ni mune o utaremashita.   *I was deeply moved by her kindness.*

---

mushi — 虫 — *insect, worm*
mushi ga ii — 虫がいい — *to take too much for granted*
[lit. One's worm is good.]
虫がいいことばかり言っていないで働きなさい。Mushi ga ii koto bakari itte inaide hatarakinasai.   *You should work instead of taking too much for granted.*

mushi ga sukanai — 虫が好かない — *to dislike someone*
[lit. An insect doesn't like someone.]
彼は虫が好かないけれど、才能があることは認めます。Kare wa

mushi ga sukanai keredo, sainō ga aru koto wa mitomemasu.   *Although I dislike him, I admit that he has talent.*

mushi ga tsuku — 虫が付く — *(a young woman) to have a no-good man as a lover*
[lit. An insect holds on to a young woman.]
娘に悪い虫が付いたようで心配です。Musume ni warui mushi ga tsuita yō de shinpai desu.   *I'm concerned that my daughter seems to have a no-good man as a lover.*

mushi mo korosanai — 虫も殺さない — *wouldn't hurt a fly*
[lit. wouldn't kill an insect]
彼女は虫も殺さないような顔をしていますが、実は手ごわい交渉相手です。Kanojo wa mushi mo korosanai yō na kao o shite imasu ga, jitsu wa tegowai kōshō aite desu.   *Although she looks as if she wouldn't hurt a fly, she's actually a tough counterpart in the negotiations.*

mushi no idokoro ga warui — 虫の居所が悪い — *to be in a bad mood*
[lit. The location of the worm is bad.]
父はこの週末、虫の居所が悪いです。Chichi wa kono shūmatsu, mushi no idokoro ga warui desu.   *My father has been in a bad mood this weekend.*

mushi no iki — 虫の息 — *to be at death's door*
[lit. an insect's breathing]
私が駆けつけたとき、祖父はすでに虫の息でした。Watakushi ga kaketsuketa toki, sofu wa sude ni mushi no iki deshita.   *When I rushed in, Grandfather was already at death's door.*

mushi no shirase — 虫の知らせ — premonition
[lit. the news brought by an insect]
彼が急死する直前に遺言を書いたのは、虫の知らせかも知れません。
Kare ga kyūshi suru chokuzen ni yuigon o kaita no wa, mushi no shirase
kamo shiremasen.　It could have been a premonition that made him
write a will just before his sudden death.

mushi no sukanai — 虫の好かない — disgusting, repulsive
[lit. disliked even by an inscct]
娘が、虫の好かない男とつき合っています。Musume ga, mushi no
sukanai otoko to tsukiatte imasu.　My daughter is dating a repulsive
guy.

mushizu ga hashiru — 虫酸が走る — to give someone the creeps
[lit. Insect acid runs through one's body.]
彼の名前を聞いただけで、虫酸が走ります。 Kare no namae o kiita
dake de, mushizu ga hashirimasu.　Just hearing his name gives me the
creeps.

nigamushi o kamitsubushita yō na — 苦虫を噛み潰したような — sour
[lit. like biting into a bitter worm]
彼女は失業して、苦虫を噛み潰したような顔をしています。Kanojo
wa shitsugyō shite, nigamushi o kamitsubushita yō na kao o shite imasu.
She's been looking sour since she lost her job.

musu — 蒸す — to steam
mushikaesu — 蒸し返す — to raise an issue again
[lit. to steam the same thing over again]
彼女は問題を蒸し返そうとしましたが、成功しませんでした。Kanojo
wa mondai o mushikaesō to shimashita ga, seikō shimasen deshita.
Although she tried to raise the issue again, she was unsuccessful.

muyō — 無用 — unworthiness
muyō no chōbutsu — 無用の長物 — white elephant
[lit. a long, unworthy item]
コンピュータを買って以来、古いタイプライターは無用の長物にな
りました。Konpyūta o katte irai, furui taipuraitā wa muyō no chōbutsu
ni narimashita.　Since we bought a computer, our old typewriter has
become a white elephant.

myaku — 脈 — *pulse*
myaku ga aru — 脈がある — *There's a ray of hope.*
[lit. There's a pulse.]
まだ脈がありそうなので、彼女をもう一度デートに誘ってみます。
Mada myaku ga arisō nanode, kanojo o mō ichido dēto ni sasotte
mimasu. *Because there still seems to be a ray of hope, I'll ask her
again for a date.*

---

na — 名 — *name*
na ga tōru — 名が通る — *well-known*
[lit. One's name passes through.]
彼は世界で名が通っているファッションデザイナーです。Kare wa
sekai de na ga tōtte iru fasshon dezainā desu. *He's a well-known
fashion designer worldwide.*

na ga ureru — 名が売れる — *to be famous*
[lit. One's name is selling.]
彼女は名が売れるようになるまで、ずいぶん苦労しました。Kanojo
wa na ga ureru yō ni naru made, zuibun kurō shimashita. *Until she
became famous, she went through real hardships.*

na mo nai — 名も無い — *unknown, obscure*
[lit. There's not even a name.]
名も無い歌手の歌が、突然はやり始めました。Na mo nai kashu no
uta ga, totsuzen hayarihajimemashita. *A song by an obscure singer has
suddenly become popular.*

na ni shi ou — 名にし負う —*famous*
[lit. carrying one's name on the back]
彼女は世界でも名にし負うピアニストで、素晴らしいコンサートで
した。Kanojo wa sekai demo na ni shi ou pianisuto de, subarashii
konsāto deshita. *She's a world-famous pianist, and her concert was
wonderful.*

na no tōtta — 名の通った — *well-known*
[lit. One's name passes through.]

夕べ、名の通った小説家と会う機会がありました。Yūbe, na no tōtta shōsetsuka to au kikai ga arimashita.　*Last night I had an opportunity to meet a well-known novelist.*

na o ageru — 名を挙げる — *to become famous*
[lit. to raise one's own name]
彼は、数学の天才として名を挙げています。Kare wa, sūgaku no tensai to shite na o agete imasu.　*He has become famous as a mathematical genius.*

na o haseru — 名を馳せる — *to be well-known*
[lit. to make one's name run]
彼は、偉大な実業家として名を馳せています。Kare wa, idai na jitsugyōka to shite na o hasete imasu.　*He is well-known as a great industrialist.*

na o karite — 名を借りて — *under the pretense of something*
[lit. by borrowing the name of something]
政府は赤字財政削減に名を借りて、増税しました。Seifu wa akaji zaisei sakugen ni na o karite, zōzei shimashita.　*The government raised taxes under the pretense of reducing the deficit.*

na o kegasu — 名を汚す — *to disgrace a reputation*
[lit. to soil one's name]
先生は万引で捕まって、学校の名を汚してしまいました。Sensei wa manbiki de tsukamatte, gakkō no na o kegashite shimaimashita.　*The teacher disgraced the school's reputation by being caught shoplifting.*

na o nasu — 名を成す — *to become famous*
[lit. to achieve one's name]
友達は、ゴルフのプロとして名を成しています。Tomodachi wa, gorufu no puro toshite na o nashite imasu.　*My friend has become famous as a professional golfer.*

na o nokosu — 名を残す — *to make one's name immortal*
[lit. to leave one's name]
彼女は、偉大なオペラ歌手として名を残しました。Kanojo wa, idai na opera kashu toshite na o nokoshimashita.　*She made her name immortal as a great opera singer.*

na o oshimu — 名を惜しむ — *to protect one's reputation*
[lit. to value one's name]
彼は教授としての名を惜しんで、非難に反論しました。Kare wa

kyōju toshite no na o oshinde, hinan ni hanron shimashita. *To protect his reputation as a professor, he refuted the accusations.*

nanori o ageru — 名乗りを上げる — *to announce something*
[lit. to give one's name to take part in something]
彼は、知事選挙の候補者として名乗りを上げました。Kare wa, chiji senkyo no kōhosha toshite nanori o agemashita. *He announced his candidacy for the gubernatorial election.*

---

nagai — 長い — *long*
nagai me de miru — 長い目で見る — *to take a long-range view*
[lit. to look at something with long eyes]
この株は、長い目で見ればいい投資になるでしょう。Kono kabu wa, nagai me de mireba ii tōshi ni naru deshō. *If you take the long-range view, these stocks will be a good investment.*

---

nagare — 流れ — *stream, flow*
nagare o kumu — 流れを汲む — *to belong to something*
[lit. to scoop up water from the stream]
彼女の花の生け方は、伝統的な流派の流れを汲んでいます。Kanojo no hana no ikekata wa, dentōteki na ryūha no nagare o kunde imasu.
Her style of flower arrangement belongs to a traditional school.

---

naka — 仲 — *relations*
naka ni hairu — 仲に入る — *to mediate*
[lit. to let oneself into relations]
友達と奥さんの仲に入って、口論を収めました。Tomodachi to okusan no naka ni haitte kōron o osamemashita. *By mediating for my friend and his wife, I settled their quarrel.*

naka o saku — 仲を裂く — *to drive a wedge between the two*
[lit. to split relations]
彼は、二人の仲を裂こうとたくらんでいます。Kare wa, futari no naka o sakō to takurande imasu. *He's plotting to drive a wedge between the two.*

---

naku — 泣く — *to cry*
naki o ireru — 泣きを入れる — *to beg for mercy*
[lit. to bring along one's crying]

学生は先生に泣きを入れて、試験を一週間延ばしてもらいました。
Gakusei wa sensei ni naki o irete, shiken o isshūkan nobashite
moraimashita. *The students begged the teacher for mercy and got the
exam postponed for a week.*

naki o miru — 泣きを見る — *to find oneself in a fix*
[lit. to see one's own crying]
彼女は投機に買った土地の値段が下がって、泣きを見ました。Kanojo
wa tōki ni katta tochi no nedan ga sagatte, naki o mimashita. *Because
the price of the land she bought for speculation went down, she found
herself in a fix.*

nakidokoro — 泣き所 — *Achilles' heel*
[lit. a spot for crying]
彼は仕事が出来ますが、英語が話せないのが泣き所です。Kare wa
shigoto ga dekimasu ga, eigo ga hanasenai no ga nakidokoro desu.
*He's an able worker, but his Achilles' heel is that he can't speak
English.*

nakigoto o naraberu — 泣き言を並べる — *to make idle complaints*
[lit. to display crying speech]
彼女はよく泣き言を並べるので、みんなが彼女を避けようとします。
Kanojo wa yoku nakigoto o naraberu node, minna ga kanojo o sakeyō to
shimasu. *Because she frequently makes idle complaints, everybody
tries to avoid her.*

nakineiri suru — 泣き寝入りする — *to have to accept something*
[lit. to cry oneself to sleep]
会社の決定は不当だったけれど、泣き寝入りするしかありませんで
した。Kaisha no kettei wa futō datta keredo, nakineiri suru shika
arimasen deshita. *Although the company's decision was unfair, I had
to accept it.*

nakiotosu — 泣き落とす — *to pull at someone's heartstrings*
[lit. to secure someone by crying]
妻を泣き落として、毎月の小遣いを増やしてもらいました。Tsuma
o nakiotoshite, maitsuki no kozukai o fuyashite moraimashita. *I got my
monthly allowance increased by pulling at my wife's heartstrings.*

---

naku 鳴く *to chirp*
nakazu tobazu — 鳴かず飛ばず — *to be inactive*
[lit. no chirping or flying]

私が好きな女優は、この三年間鳴かず飛ばずです。Watakushi ga
suki na joyū wa, kono san nen kan nakazu tobazu desu. *The actress I
like has been inactive for the last three years.*

---

nama — 生 — *raw, uncooked*
namakajiri no — 生かじりの — *superficial knowledge of something*
[lit. nibbling at something uncooked]
彼は生かじりの経済学しか知らないのに、専門家気取りです。Kare wa
namakajiri no keizaigaku shika shiranai noni, senmonka kidori desu.
*Although he has only a superficial knowledge of economics, he poses as
an expert.*

---

nameru — 嘗める — *to lick*
namete kakaru — 嘗めてかかる — *to take someone or something lightly*
[lit. to lick someone for something]
彼は彼女を嘗めてかかったので、討論では負けてしまいました。
Kare wa kanojo o namete kakatta node, tōron dewa makete
shimaimashita. *Because he took her lightly, he lost to her in a debate.*

---

nami — 波 — *wave*
nami ni noru — 波に乗る — *to ride the crest of something*
[lit. to ride on the waves]
彼女の商売は、時代の波に乗って繁盛しています。Kanojo no shōbai
wa, jidai no nami ni notte hanjō shite imasu. *Her business is
flourishing by riding the crest of the times.*

namikaze ga tatsu — 波風が立つ — *Troubles arise. (interpersonal)*
[lit. Waves and wind rise.]
結婚して一年後には、二人の間に波風が立ち始めました。Kekkon
shite ichi nen go niwa, futari no aida ni namikaze ga tachihajimemashita.
One year after the wedding, troubles began to arise between them.

---

namida — 涙 — *tear*
namida ni kureru — 涙に暮れる — *to cry one's eyes out*
[lit. It gets dark because of tears.]
彼は失恋した後一週間、涙に暮れていました。Kare wa shitsuren
shita ato isshūkan, namida ni kurete imashita. *After he lost his love, he
cried his eyes out for a week.*

namida ni shizumu — 涙に沈む — *to be dissolved in tears*
[lit. to submerge oneself in tears]
彼女は赤ちゃんを事故で亡くして、涙に沈んでいます。Kanojo wa
akachan o jiko de nakushite, namida ni shizunde imasu. *She is still
dissolved in tears at having lost her baby in an accident.*

namida o furutte — 涙を振るつて — *by repressing one's feelings*
[lit. by shaking one's tears off]
彼は涙を振るつて、同僚の横領を上司に告げました。Kare wa
namida o furutte, dōryō no ōryō o jōshi ni tsugemashita. *Repressing his
feelings, he reported his colleague's embezzlement to the boss.*

namida o moyōsu — 涙を催す — *to be moved to tears*
[lit. to feel the urge for tears]
彼女の年老いた親への献身に、涙を催しました。Kanojo no toshi oita
oya e no kenshin ni, namida o moyōshimashita. *I was moved to tears
by her total devotion to her elderly parents.*

namida o nomu — 涙を飲む — *to suppress one's chagrin*
[lit. to drink one's own tears]
彼はみんなの前で涙を飲んで、自らの失敗を認めました。Kare wa
minna no mae de namida o nonde, mizukara no shippai o mitomemashita.
He suppressed his chagrin and admitted his mistakes in front of everyone.

namida o sasou — 涙を誘う — *to move to tears*
[lit. to invite tears]
夕べ見た映画は、見る人の涙を誘いました。Yūbe mita eiga wa, miru
hito no namida o sasoimashita. *The movie we saw last night moved the
audience to tears.*

namidakin — 涙金 — *a small amount of consolation money*
[lit. tear money]
政府は地震の犠牲者に、取りあえず涙金を配りました。Seifu wa jishin
no giseisha ni, toriaezu namidakin o kubarimashita. *The government
hastily distributed a small amount of money to the earthquake victims.*

namidamoroi — 涙もろい — *to be easily moved to tears*
[lit. to be susceptible to tears]
母は涙もろくて、テレビ番組を見てはよく泣いています。Haha wa
namidamorokute, terebi bangumi o mite wa yoku naite imasu. *My
mother is easily moved to tears and often cries while watching TV
programs.*

nan — 難 — *difficulty, fault*

nankuse o tsukeru — 難癖をつける — *to find fault with someone or something*
[lit. to apply criticism to someone or something]
あの評論家は、彼女の素晴らしい演技に難癖をつけました。Ano hyōronka wa, kanojo no subarashii engi ni nankuse o tsukemashita. *That critic found fault with her wonderful acting.*

nanshoku o shimesu — 難色を示す — *to express disapproval*
[lit. to show a difficult color]
学校は、学生の要求に難色を示しました。Gakkō wa, gakusei no yōkyū ni nanshoku o shimeshimashita. *The school expressed its disapproval of the students' demands.*

---

nani — 何 — *what, something, anything, thing*

nani ga nandemo — 何が何でも — *no matter what*
[lit. even if something amounts to anything]
この仕事は、何が何でも今週中に終えるつもりです。Kono shigoto wa, nani ga nandemo konshū chū ni oeru tsumori desu. *No matter what, I intend to finish the work this week.*

nani ka ni tsukete — 何かにつけて — *one way or another*
[lit. by taking advantage of anything]
彼女は何かにつけて、人を批判します。Kanojo wa nanika ni tsukete, hito o hihan shimasu. *She criticizes others one way or another.*

nani kara nani made — 何から何まで — *everything*
[lit. anything from the beginning to the end]
アメリカに旅行して、何から何まで楽しみました。Amerika ni ryokō shite, nani kara nani made tanoshimimashita. *I made a trip to the United States and enjoyed everything.*

nani kuwanu kao — 何食わぬ顔 — *completely innocent look*
[lit. the face of someone who didn't eat anything]
彼は、何食わぬ顔でうそをつきます。Kare wa, nani kuwanu kao de uso o tsukimasu. *He lies with a completely innocent look.*

nani wa sate oki — 何はさておき — *first of all*
[lit. by putting things aside]
子供が生まれたとき、何はさておき両親に電話しました。Kodomo ga umareta toki, nani wa sate oki ryōshin ni denwa shimashita. *When the baby was born, first of all, I called my parents.*

nani wa tomo are — 何はともあれ — *anyway*
[lit. whatever a thing may be]
問題がたくさんありましたが、何はともあれ研究を終えました。Mondai
ga takusan arimashita ga, nani wa tomo are kenkyū o oemashita.
Although there were many problems, we finished the research anyway.

nani ya ka ya — 何やかや — *with one thing or another*
[lit. for this thing or for that thing]
彼は何やかやと言い訳を作つて、私によく会いに来ます。Kare wa
nani ya kaya to iiwake o tsukutte, watakushi ni yoku aini kimasu.   *He
comes to see me often with one excuse or another.*

---

narabu — 並ぶ — *to line up*
narabu mono ga inai — 並ぶ者がいない — *to be second to none*
[lit. There's nobody who can line up with someone.]
英語にかけては、社内で彼女に並ぶ者がいません。Eigo ni kakete
wa, shanai de kanojo ni narabu mono ga imasen.   *When it comes to
English, in the company, she's second to none.*

---

nareru — 慣れる — *to get familiar with someone or something*
nareai — 慣れ合い — *cozy relationship*
[lit. familiarity with each other]
この会社では、管理職と組合幹部の慣れ合いが目立ちます。
Kono kaisha dewa, kanrishoku to kumiai kanbu no nareai ga
medachimasu.   *In this company, the cozy relationship between
management and the senior labor union officials is conspicuous.*

naresome — 馴れ初め — *the beginning of love*
[lit. the start of getting familiar with each other]
彼らの馴れ初めは、去年の暮れのパーティーでした。
Karera no naresome wa, kyonen no kure no pātī deshita.
The beginning of their love was at a party at the end of last year.

---

nari — 鳴り — *ringing*
nari o hisomeru — 鳴りを潜める — *to keep a low profile*
[lit. to hide the ringing]
あの映画スターは交通事故を起こして以来、鳴りを潜めています。
Ano eiga sutā wa kōtsū jiko o okoshite irai, nari o hisomete imasu.
That movie star has kept a low profile since he caused a traffic accident.

nari o shizumete — 鳴りを静めて — *with hushed attention*
[lit. by making the ringing quiet]
社員は、鳴りを静めて社長の話を聞きました。Shain wa, nari o
shizumete shachō no hanashi o kikimashita.   *The company employees
listened to the president's speech with hushed attention.*

narimonoiri de — 鳴り物入りで — *with a lot of fanfare*
[lit. with gongs and drums]
政府は鳴り物入りで、新経済政策を促進しています。
Seifu wa narimonoiri de, shin keizai seisaku o sokushin shite imasu.
*The government is promoting the new economic policy with a lot of
fanfare.*

---

nariagaru — 成り上がる — *to rise to something suddenly*
narikin — 成金 — *nouveau riche*
[lit. rising suddenly to become rich]
彼は成金で、ロールスロイスを十台持っています。Kare wa narikin
de, Rōrusuroisu o jū dai motte imasu.   *He's nouveau riche and owns
ten Rolls Royces.*

---

nashi — 梨 — *pear, none*
nashi no tsubute — 梨の礫 — *to not have heard from someone*
[lit. no reaction to thrown stones]
色々な会社に履歴書を送ったけれど、梨の礫です。Iroiro na kaisha ni
rirekisho o okutta keredo, nashi no tsubute desu.   *Although I sent many
companies my résumé, I haven't heard from them.*

---

nawa — 縄 — *rope*
nawabari arasoi — 縄張り争い — *territorial dispute*
[lit. a quarrel over a roped-off place]
政党は選挙民をめぐって、縄張り争いを行っています。
Seitō wa senkyomin o megutte, nawabari arasoi o okonatte imasu.
*The political parties are engaging in territorial disputes over
constituents.*

---

ne — 根 — *root*
ne ga fukai — 根が深い — *to be deep-rooted*
[lit. The root is deep.]
米に対する国民の感情は、想像以上に根が深いです。Kome ni

taisuru kokumin no kanjō wa, sōzō ijō ni ne ga fukai desu. *Japanese feelings about rice are deep-rooted beyond imagination.*

ne mo ha mo nai — 根も葉もない — *to be completely groundless*
[lit. There are no leaves or roots.]
我が社が倒産するという噂には、根も葉もありません。
Waga sha ga tōsan suru to iu uwasa niwa, ne mo ha mo arimasen.
The rumor that our company will go under is completely groundless.

ne ni motsu — 根に持つ — *to hold a grudge against someone*
[lit. to have something at one's root]
彼女は私が言ったことを根に持って、口を聞きません。
Kanojo wa watakushi ga itta koto o ne ni motte, kuchi o kikimasen.
She holds a grudge against me for what I said and doesn't speak to me.

ne o orosu — 根を下ろす — *to take root in something*
[lit. to lower a root]
環境問題が、地域社会に根を下ろしました。Kankyō mondai ga, chiiki shakai ni ne o oroshimashita. *The environmental issues took root in the local community.*

ne wa — 根は — *deep down*
[lit. as for a root]
彼はぶっきらぼうだけれど、根は優しい人です。Kare wa bukkirabō dakeredo, ne wa yasashii hito desu. *Although he is abrupt, deep down he is gentle.*

nehori hahori — 根掘り葉掘り — *in great detail*
[lit. by digging roots and by digging leaves]
母は私の旅行計画について、根ほり葉ほり聞きました。Haha wa watakushi no ryokō keikaku ni tsuite, nehori hahori kikimashita. *My mother asked me about my travel plans in great detail.*

nemawashi o suru — 根回しをする — *to lay the groundwork*
[lit. to dig around the roots]
彼は、首相になるための根回しをしています。Karc wa, shushō ni naru tame no nemawashi o shite imasu. *He is laying the groundwork for becoming prime minister.*

---

ne — 音 — *sound*
ne o ageru — 音を上げる — *to whine*
[lit. to make sounds]
宿題の量が多いので、学生は音を上げています。Shukudai no ryō ga

ōi node, gakusei wa ne o agete imasu.   *The students are whining because of a lot of homework.*

---

ne — 値 — *price*
ne ga haru — 値が張る — *to be quite expensive*
[lit. A price stretches.]
このドレスは、デザイナ－物なので値が張りました。Kono doresu wa, dezainā mono nanode ne ga harimashita.   *Since it was a designer dress, it was quite expensive.*

---

negau — 願う — *to wish*
negattari kanattari — 願ったりかなつたり — *It's a wish come true.*
[lit. wishing something which then becomes reality]
この契約書にサインしていただければ、願ったりかなつたりです。
Kono keiyakusho ni sain shite itadakereba, negattari kanattari desu.   *If you'd sign this contract, it would be a wish come true.*

negattemonai — 願つてもない — *couldn't ask for something better*
[lit. Besides this, there won't be anything even if one wishes.]
先週の特売は、新しいス－ツを買うための願つてもない機会でした。
Senshū no tokubai wa, atarashii sūtsu o kau tame no negattemonai kikai deshita.   *I couldn't have asked for a better opportunity to buy a new suit than last week's sale.*

---

neji — ネジ — *screw*
neji o maku — ネジを巻く — *to rouse someone to do something*
[lit. to tighten a screw]
もっと一生懸命練習するように、監督は選手のネジを巻きました。
Motto isshōkenmei renshū suru yō ni, kantoku wa senshu no neji o *makimashita.*   *The manager roused the players to practice much harder.*

---

neko — 猫 — *cat*
neko mo shakushi mo — 猫も杓子も — *every Tom, Dick and Harry*
[lit. also a cat and a ladle]
最近は、猫も杓子もスキュ－バダイビングをしています。Saikin wa, neko mo shakushi mo sukyūbadaibingu o shite imasu.   *Nowadays, every Tom, Dick and Harry is doing scuba diving.*

neko ni katsuobushi — 猫に鰹節 — *like trusting a wolf to guard sheep*

[lit. trusting a cat to guard a dried bonito]

彼女にケーキ屋を任せるなんて、猫に鰹節というものです。 Kanojo ni kēki ya o makaseru nante, neko ni katsuobushi to iu mono desu. *Letting her manage a cake shop is like trusting a wolf to guard sheep.*

neko ni koban — 猫に小判 — *casting (one's) pearls before swine*
[lit. gold coins to a cat]
彼にクラシック音楽のコンサートの券を上げても、猫に小判です。 Kare ni kurashikku ongaku no konsāto no ken o agetemo, neko ni koban desu. *Giving him a ticket for a classical music concert is like casting pearls before swine.*

neko no hitai — 猫の額 — *a very small area*
[lit. a cat's forehead]
東京では、猫の額ほどの土地でも価値があります。 Tōkyō dewa, neko no hitai hodo no tochi demo kachi ga arimasu. *In Tokyo, even a very small piece of land is valuable.*

neko no me no yō ni kawaru — 猫の目のように変わる — *to change much too often*
[lit. to change like the eyes of a cat]
政府の経済政策は、猫の目のように変わります。 Seifu no keizai seisaku wa, neko no me no yō ni kawarimasu. *The government's economic policy changes much too often.*

neko no te mo karitai — 猫の手も借りたい — *to wish one could be two people*
[lit. to want to borrow a cat's paws]
昨日は引っ越しで、猫の手も借りたいほどの忙しさでした。 Kinō wa hikkoshi de, neko no te mo karitai hodo no isogashisa deshita. *When I moved yesterday, I was so busy that I wished I could be two people.*

neko o kaburu — 猫をかぶる — *to feign innocence*
[lit. to put a cat over oneself]

彼女はボーイフレンドの前では、猫をかぶっています。Kanojo wa
bōifurendo no mae de wa, neko o kabutte imasu.   *She's feigning
innocence in front of her boyfriend.*

nekobaba suru — 猫糞する — *to pocket something sneakily*
[lit. A cat defecates.]

彼は、地震の犠牲者のために集めた寄付金を猫糞していました。
Kare wa, jishin no giseisha no tame ni atsumeta kifukin o nekobaba shite
imashita.   *He was pocketing the donations he was collecting for the
earthquake victims.*

nekonadegoe — 猫撫で声 — *wheedling tone of voice*
[lit. one's voice when one pets a cat]

息子は猫撫で声で、マウンテンバイクをねだりました。Musuko wa
nekonadegoe de, maunten baiku o nedarimashita.   *In a wheedling tone
of voice, my son asked for a mountain bicycle.*

---

nen — 念 — *sense, idea, attention*

nen o ireru — 念を入れる — *to take special care with something*
[lit. to put one's attention to something]

お客を夕食に呼んだので、念を入れて料理しました。Okyaku o
yūshoku ni yonda node, nen o irete ryōri shimashita.   *Because we
invited guests for dinner, I took special care with the cooking.*

nen o osu — 念を押す — *to make sure of something*
[lit. to press someone's attention]

教授は学生が論文の提出を忘れないように、念を押しました。Kyōju wa gakusei ga ronbun no teishutsu o wasurenai yō ni, nen o oshimashita. *The professor made sure that the students wouldn't forget to submit their papers.*

nentō ni oku — 念頭に置く — *to keep something in mind*
[lit. to place something in one's idea]
安全を念頭に置いて、車を買うつもりです。Anzen o nentō ni oite, kuruma o kau tsumori desu. *We intend to buy a car keeping safety in mind.*

---

nen — 年 — *year*
nenki ga haitte iru — 年季が入っている — *veteran*
[lit. Years and seasons are put in.]
彼は政治で年季が入っているので、話がいつも面白いです。
Kare wa seiji de nenki ga haitte iru node, hanashi ga itsumo omoshiroi desu. *Because he's a veteran of politics, what he says is always interesting.*

---

nengu — 年貢 — *land-tax*
nengu no osamedoki — 年貢の納めどき — *The game is about over.*
[lit. It's about time to pay one's land-tax.]
そろそろ年貢の納め時で、首になるより引退するつもりです。
Sorosoro nengu no osamedoki de, kubi ni naru yori intai suru tsumori desu. *The game is about over, and I intend to retire rather than being fired.*

---

neru — 寝る — *to sleep*
negaeri o utsu — 寝返りを打つ — *to doublecross someone*
[lit. to roll over while sleeping]
彼は寝返りを打って、特許をライバル会社に売ってしまいました。
Kare wa negaeri o utte, tokkyo o raibaru gaisha ni utte shimaimashita. *He doublecrossed us and sold his patent to our rival company.*

netemo sametemo — 寝ても覚めても — *all the time*
[lit. asleep or awake]
夫は、寝ても覚めても仕事のことばかり考えています。Otto wa, netemo sametemo shigoto no koto bakari kangaete imasu. *My husband thinks only about his work all the time.*

nezame ga warui — 寝覚めが悪い — *to be conscience-stricken*

[lit. to be bad at waking from sleep]

彼女にしたことを思い返すと、寝覚めが悪いです。Kanojo ni shita
koto o omoikaesu to, nezame ga warui desu.   *I'm conscience-stricken
when I recall what I did to her.*

---

netsu — 熱 — *heat, temperature, fever*
netsu ga sameru — 熱が冷める — *One's enthusiasm fades.*
[lit. One's fever cools.]

彼の野球に対する熱が冷めたようです。Kare no yakyū ni taisuru netsu
ga sameta yō desu.   *His enthusiasm for baseball seems to have faded.*

netsu o ageru — 熱を上げる — *to be insane about someone or something*
[lit. to make one's temperature higher for someone or something]

彼女は彼に熱を上げています。Kanojo wa kare ni netsu o agete imasu.
She is insane about him.

---

ni — 二 — *two, second*
ni no ku ga tsugenai — 二の句が継げない — *to be dumbfounded*
[lit. to be unable to follow with the second word]

彼の恥知らずな行いには、二の句が継げませんでした。Kare no
hajishirazu na okonai niwa, ni no ku ga tsugemasen deshita.   *I was
dumfounded at his shameless behavior.*

ni no mai o enjiru — 二の舞を演じる — *to repeat someone's mistakes*
[lit. to perform the second dance]

株の投機で損して、父の二の舞を演じてしまいました。Kabu no tōki
de son shite, chichi no ni no mai o enjite shimaimashita.   *I repeated my
father's mistakes by losing money in stock speculation.*

ni no tsugi ni suru — 二の次にする — *to put something off*
[lit. to make something secondary]

バカンスは二の次にして、今は仕事に集中しています。Bakansu wa
ni no tsugi ni shite, ima wa shigoto ni shūchū shite imasu.   *By putting
my vacation off, I'm concentrating on my work now.*

nibansenji — 二番煎じ — *an imitation, a rehash*
[lit. brewing tea for the second time using the same tea leaves]

彼の意見は、新聞の社説の二番煎じに過ぎません。Kare no iken wa,
shinbun no shasetsu no nibansenji ni sugimasen.   *His opinion is just a
rehash of the newspaper editorial.*

ni — 荷 — *load*

ni ga kachisugiru — 荷が勝ちすぎる — *to be too heavy a load*
[lit. The load wins.]
その仕事は、私には荷が勝ちすぎます。 Sono shigoto wa, watakushi
niwa ni ga kachisugimasu.   *That job is too heavy a load for me.*

ni ga oriru — 荷が下りる — *A great weight has been lifted.*
[lit. A load comes off.]
報告書を書き終わって、荷が下りました。Hōkokusho o kaki owatte,
ni ga orimashita.   *A great weight has been lifted because I finished
writing the report.*

---

nieru — 煮える — *to boil*

niekiranai — 煮え切らない — *lukewarm*
[lit. to not reach the boiling point]
年末のボーナスについて、会社は煮えきらない返事を繰り返してい
ます。Nenmatsu no bōnasu ni tsuite, kaisha wa niekiranai henji o
kurikaeshite imasu.   *The company is repeating lukewarm responses
about the year-end bonus.*

nieyu o nomasareru — 煮え湯を飲まされる — *to be burned badly*
[lit. to be forced to drink boiling water]
彼が私の信用を裏切ったため、煮え湯を飲まされる思いでした。
Kare ga watakushi no shin-yō o uragitta tame, nieyu o nomasareru omoi
deshita.   *I was burned badly because he betrayed my trust.*

---

nigeru — 逃げる — *to run away, to flee*

nige o utsu — 逃げを打つ — *to dodge*
[lit. to set out to flee]
彼女は時間が無いからと、私の依頼に逃げを打ちました。Kanojo
wa jikan ga nai kara to, watakushi no irai ni nige o uchimashita.   *She
dodged my request by saying that she wouldn't have time.*

---

nirami — 睨み — *glare*

nirami o kikaseru — 睨みを利かせる — *to exert one's authority*
[lit. to make use of one's glare]
あの評論家は、文壇で睨みを利かせています。Ano hyōronka wa,
bundan de nirami o kikasete imasu.   *That critic is exerting his authority
over the literary world.*

niru — 似る — *to resemble*
nitari yottari — 似たり寄つたり — *to be much the same*
[lit. resembling and drawing near something]
みんなの意見が似たり寄つたりで、目立つものがありませんでした。
Minna no iken ga nitari yottari de, medatsu mono ga arimasen deshita.
Since everyone's opinion was much the same, there was nothing outstanding.

nitemo nitsukanu — 似ても似つかぬ — *to be not at all like someone*
[lit. to not resemble a bit]
息子は高校中退で、学者のお父さんとは似ても似ついていません。
Musuko wa kōkō chūtai de, gakusha no otōsan towa nitemo nitsuite
imasen. *The son is a high-school dropout and not at all like his father, who is a scholar.*

---

niru — 煮る — *to boil*
nitemo yaitemo kuenai — 煮ても焼いても食えない — *crafty*
[lit. to be unable to eat it even if you boil it or grill it]
彼は煮ても焼いても食えない男だと言う評判があります。Kare wa
nitemo yaitemo kuenai otoko da to iu hyōban ga arimasu. *He has a
reputation as a crafty fellow.*

---

nishi — 西 — *west*
nishi mo higashi mo wakaranai — 西も東も分からない — *to not know
what's what*
[lit. to not know east or west]
彼女は大学を卒業したのに、西も東も分かりません。Kanojo wa
daigaku o sotsugyō shita noni, nishi mo higashi mo wakarimasen.
*Although she graduated from a university, she doesn't know what's
what.*

---

nishiki — 錦 — *gorgeous (Japanese) brocade*
nishiki no mihata — 錦の御旗 — *just cause*
[lit. a brocaded banner]
会社はリストラを錦の御旗にして、早期退職を強要しています。
Kaisha wa risutora o nishiki no mihata ni shite, sōki taishoku o kyōyō
shite imasu. *Companies are forcing early retirement using
restructuring as just cause.*

nishiki o kazaru — 錦を飾る — *to return home in glory*
[lit. to decorate one's home with gorgeous brocade]
彼はプロ野球の選手になって、故郷に錦を飾りました。Kare wa
puro yakyū no senshu ni natte, kokyō ni nishiki o kazarimashita.   *He
became a professional baseball player and returned home in glory.*

niwaka — にわか — *sudden*
niwakajikomi — にわか仕込み — *cram*
[lit. suddenly trained]
外国に行くので、お茶とお花をにわか仕込みしています。Gaikoku
ni iku node, ocha to ohana o niwakajikomi shite imasu.   *Since I'm
going overseas, I'm cramming for tea ceremony and flower arrangement.*

nobetsu — のべつ — *always*
nobetsu makunashi ni — のべつ幕なしに — *incessantly*
[lit. always without dropping curtains]
パーティーのあいだ中、彼はのべつ幕なしに仕事の話を続けました。
Pātī no aida jū, kare wa nobetsu makunashi ni shigoto no hanashi o
tsuzukemashita.   *He talked incessantly about job-related things
throughout the party.*

nodo — 喉 — *throat*

nodo kara te ga deru hodo hoshii — 喉から手が出るほど ほしい —
to want something badly
[lit. like a hand coming out of one's throat]

彼女は、喉から手がでるほどピアノが欲しいです。Kanojo wa, nodo kara te ga deru hodo piano ga hoshii desu.   *She wants a piano so badly it hurts.*

nomu — 呑む — *to receive someone*
nonde kakaru — 呑んでかかる — *to make light of someone*
[lit. to set about receiving someone]
ベテランの政治家は、選挙運動で若い挑戦者を呑んでかかりました。Beteran no seijika wa, senkyo undō de wakai chōsensha o nonde kakarimashita.   *The veteran politician made light of the young challenger in the election campaign.*

noppiki — 退っ引き — *retreat*
noppiki naranai — 退っ引きならない — *unavoidable*
[lit. to be unable to retreat]
退っ引きならない事情があって、仕事にいけませんでした。Noppiki naranai jijō ga atte, shigoto ni ikemasen deshita.   *Because of unavoidable circumstances, I couldn't go to work.*

noren — 暖簾 — *curtain with a shop sign, room-dividing curtain*
noren o wakeru — 暖簾を分ける — *to let someone open a branch of one's shop*
[lit. to distribute a curtain displaying a shop sign]
近所の寿司屋は、息子に暖簾を分けました。Kinjo no sushiya wa, musuko ni noren o wakemashita.   *The sushi shop owner in our neighborhood let his son open a branch of the shop.*

noren ni udeoshi — 暖簾に腕押し — *like beating the air*
[lit. pushing a room-dividing curtain with one's arms]
彼女にデートを申し込みましたが、暖簾に腕押しでした。Kanojo ni dēto o mōshikomimashita ga, noren ni udeoshi deshita.   *I asked her for a date, but it was like beating the air.*

noru — 伸る — *to stretch*
noruka soruka — 伸るか反るか — *sink or swim*
[lit. stretch or bend]
伸るか反るか、とにかくやってみます。Noruka soruka, tonikaku yatte mimasu.   *Sink or swim, I'll try anyway.*

noshi — 熨斗 — *noshi (a gift ornament)*
noshi o tsukete — 熨斗を付けて — *gladly*
[lit. by attaching a gift ornament]
こんな古いテレビでよかったら、熨斗をつけてさしあげます。Konna
furui terebi de yokattara, noshi o tsukete sashiagemasu. *If you don't
mind that the TV is old, I'll give it to you gladly.*

nozomi — 望み — *hope*
nozomi o takusu — 望みを託す — *to pin one's hopes on someone or
something*
[lit. to leave one's hopes with someone or something]
コンピュータを買うため、大きなボーナスに望みを託しています。
Konpyūta o kau tame, ōkina bōnasu ni nozomi o takushite imasu. *I'm
pinning my hopes on a big bonus so I can buy a computer.*

nuka — 糠 — *rice bran*
nuka ni kugi — 糠に釘 — *to have no effect on someone*
[lit. to drive a nail into rice bran]
彼女への注意は全く糠に釘で、相変わらず浪費を続けています。
Kanojo e no chūi wa mattaku nuka ni kugi de, aikawarazu rōhi o
tsuzukete imasu. *My warnings had no effect on her, and she has been
wasting money as usual.*

nureru — 濡れる — *to get wet*
nureginu o kiserareru — 濡れ衣を着せられる — *to be falsely accused*
[lit. to be forced to put on wet clothes]
彼女は万引きの濡れ衣を着せられました。Kanojo wa manbiki no
nureginu o kiseraremashita. *She was falsely accused of shoplifting.*

nurete de awa — 濡れ手で粟 — *to make easy profits*
[lit. to grasp millet with a wet hand]
猛暑のために、ビール会社が濡れ手で粟の大儲けをしました。Mōsho
no tame ni, bīrugaisha ga nurete de awa no ōmōke o shimashita.
Because of the extremely hot summer, beer companies made easy profits.

o — 尾 — tail

ohire o tsukeru — 尾ひれを付ける — to exaggerate
[lit. to add a tail and fins]
彼は話しに尾ひれを付けるので、どこまで正確か分かりません。
Kare wa hanashi ni ohire o tsukeru node, doko made seikaku ka
wakarimasen.   Because he exaggerates, you don't know how accurate
his stories are.

oha uchikarasu — 尾羽打ち枯らす — to be down and out
[lit. One's tail feathers and wings wither.]
彼は賭事のために、尾羽打ち枯らしています。Kare wa kakegoto no
tame ni, oha uchikarashite imasu.   He's down and out because of gambling.

---

okado — お門 — gate

okado chigai — お門違い — barking up the wrong tree
[lit. the wrong gate]
彼を非難するのは、お門違いです。それは、彼のせいではないんで
すから。Kare o hinan suru no wa, okadochigai desu. Sore wa, kare no
sei dewa naindesu kara.   You're barking up the wrong tree by blaming
him. It isn't his fault.

---

oku — 奥 — depth, interior

oku no te — 奥の手 — ace in the hole
[lit. a deep hand]
弁護士は奥の手を使って、二者間の和解を達成しました。Bengoshi
wa oku no te o tsukatte, ni sha kan no wakai o tassei shimashita.   Using
his ace in the hole, the lawyer achieved an amicable settlement between
the two companies.

okuba ni mono ga hasamatta yō — 奥歯に物が挟まったよう —
mealy-mouthed
[lit. as if something were stuck between the back teeth]
奥歯に物が挟まったような言い方をしないで、はっきり言って下さい。
Okuba ni mono ga hasamatta yō na iikata o shinaide, hakkiri itte kudasai.
Don't be mealy-mouthed. Please tell me what you think.

---

okubi — おくび — *belch*

okubi nimo dasanai — おくびにも出さない — *to not give the slightest indication*
[lit. to not show something even in a belch]

彼女は社長の姪であることを、おくびにも出しませんでした。Kanojo wa shachō no mei de aru koto o, okubi nimo dashimasen deshita. *She never gave the slightest indication that she was the president's niece.*

---

omoi — 思い — *thought, feelings*

omoi o harasu — 思いを晴らす — *to pay off old scores*
[lit. to clear one's feelings]

去年負けたチ-ムに思いを晴らすため、今一生懸命練習しています。Kyonen maketa chīmu ni omoi o harasu tame, ima isshōkenmei renshū shite imasu. *We're practicing hard to pay off old scores with the team that beat us last year.*

omoi o haseru — 思いを馳せる — *to think of someone or something*
[lit. to make one's thoughts run]

彼は出張中も、家族のことに思いを馳せています。Kare wa shutchō chū mo, kazoku no koto ni omoi o hasete imasu. *He's thinking of his family even during a business trip.*

omoi o kakeru — 思いをかける — *to give one's heart to someone*
[lit. to set one's feelings on someone]

彼女は、友達のお兄さんに思いをかけました。Kanojo wa, tomodachi no oniisan ni omoi o kakemashita. *She gave her heart to her friend's older brother.*

omoi o yoseru — 思いを寄せる — *to take a fancy to someone*
[lit. to let one's feelings come closer to someone]

彼はよく行くバ-のホステスに、思いを寄せています。Kare wa yoku iku bā no hosutesu ni, omoi o yosete imasu. *He's taken a fancy to the hostess at a bar where he often goes.*

---

omoki — 重き — *weight*

omoki o nasu — 重きをなす — *to carry weight*
[lit. to achieve weight]

彼女は心理学の分野で、重きをなしています。Kanojo wa shinrigaku no bun-ya de, omoki o nashite imasu. *She carries weight in the field of psychology.*

omoki o oku — 重きを置く — *to emphasize something*
[lit. to place weight on something]
この会社は、先端技術の応用に重きを置いています。
Kono kaisha wa, sentan gijutsu no ōyō ni omoki o oite imasu.
This company is emphasizing the application of advanced technologies.

---

omote — 表 — *surface, outside, front*
 omote o kazaru — 表を飾る — *to keep up appearances*
 [lit. to decorate the exterior]
 あの会社は表を飾っているけれど、実は倒産寸前です。Ano kaisha
 wa omote o kazatte iru keredo, jitsu wa tōsan sunzen desu. *That
 company is keeping up appearances, but it's actually just about to go
 under.*

 omotekanban — 表看板 — *main occupation*
 [lit. a front signboard]
 彼女の表看板は医者ですが、詩人としても知られています。Kanojo
 no omotekanban wa isha desu ga, shijin toshite mo shirarete imasu.
 *Her main occupation is practicing medicine, but she's also known as a
 poet.*

---

on — 恩 — *kindness, favor, debt of gratitude*
 on ni kiseru — 恩に着せる — *to demand thanks*
 [lit. to make someone wear one's favor]
 彼に何かしてもらうと恩に着せるので、気軽に頼めません。Kare ni
 nanika shite morau to on ni kiseru node, kigaru ni tanomemasen.
 *Because he demands thanks for whatever he does, you can't ask him to
 do anything lightly.*

 on ni kiru — 恩に着る — *to be deeply grateful*
 [lit. to wear the favor given by someone]
 病気の時、彼女が一週間も世話してくれたので、恩に着ています。
 Byōki no toki, kanojo ga isshūkan mo sewa shite kureta node, on ni kite
 imasu. *Because she took care of me for a week when I was sick, I'm
 deeply grateful to her.*

 on o uru — 恩を売る — *to try to gain someone's gratitude*
 [lit. to sell gratitude to someone]
 彼は機会を見つけては、友達に恩を売ろうとします。Kare wa kikai

o mitsukete wa, tomodachi ni on o urō to shimasu. *He tries to gain his friends' gratitude at every opportunity.*

oni — 鬼 — *devil, demon*

oni no inu ma ni sentaku — 鬼の居ぬ間に洗濯 — *When the cat's away, the mice will play; to relax while someone of authority is away*
[lit. to do laundry while the demon is away]
お父さんが出張中だから、鬼の居ぬ間に洗濯しましょう。 Otōsan ga shutchō chū dakara, oni no inu ma ni sentaku shimashō. *Since Dad is away on a business trip, let's goof off.*

oni ni kanabō — 鬼に金棒 — *doubly powerful, effective, or productive*
[lit. to arm a demon with an iron rod]
彼はインテリだし、勉強さえすれば鬼に金棒です。Kare wa interi dashi, benkyō sae sureba oni ni kanabō desu. *Since he's intelligent, if he'd only study, he'd be doubly productive.*

oni no kubi demo totta yō ni — 鬼の首でも取ったように — *as if one were a conquering hero*
[lit. as if he had beheaded a demon]
彼はゴルフで私に勝っただけで、鬼の首でもとったように大喜びしています。Kare wa gorugu de watakushi ni katta dake de, oni no kubi demo totta yō ni ōyorokobi shite imasu. *He's as overjoyed as a conquering hero at having beaten me at golf.*

osae — 抑さえ — *weight*

osae ga kiku — 抑さえが効く — *to keep something in order*
[lit. One's weight is effective.]
人事部では、課長の抑えが効いています。Jinjibu dewa, kachō no osae ga kiite imasu. *The section chief is keeping the personnel department in order.*

oshi — 押し — *push*

oshi ga kiku — 押しが利く — *to carry weight*
[lit. One's push is effective.]
あの政治家は、国際貿易の舞台でも押しが利いています。Ano seijika wa, kokusai bōeki no butai demo oshi ga kiite imasu. *That politician carries weight in the arena of international trade.*

oshi ga tsuyoi — 押しが強い — *pushy*
[lit. One's push is strong.]
彼女は押しが強くて、何でも自分の思うことを通そうとします。

Kanojo wa oshi ga tsuyokute, nandemo jibun no omou koto o tōsō to
shimasu. *Because she's pushy, she tries to have everything her way.*

oshi mo osaremo senu — 押しも押されもせぬ — *recognized*
[lit. not pushing or being pushed]
彼は、世界で押しも押されもせぬ実業家です。Kare wa, sekai de oshi
mo osaremo senu jitsugyōka desu. *He's a globally recognized
industrialist.*

oshi no itte de — 押しの一手で — *doggedly*
[lit. nothing but purely pushing]
彼は押しの一手で、彼女に結婚を申し込みました。Kare wa oshi no
itte de, kanojo ni kekkon o mōshikomimashita. *He doggedly asked her
to marry him.*

osuna osuna — 押すな押すな — *to be jam-packed*
[lit. Don't push, don't push.]
祭日のため、デパートは押すな押すなのにぎわいでした。Saijitsu no
tame, depāto wa osuna osuna no nigiwai deshita. *Because of a holiday,
the department store was jam-packed.*

---

oto — 音 — *sound*
oto ni kiku — 音に聞く —*famous*
[lit. to hear someone or something's sounds]
昨日レストランで、音に聞く作家を見ました。 Kinō resutoran de, oto
ni kiku sakka o mimashita. *Yesterday, I saw a famous novelist at a
restaurant.*

---

otoko — 男 — *man, manliness*
otoko ga sutaru — 男が廃る — *to lose one's manly honor*
[lit. One's manliness diminishes.]
そんな卑怯な手段に訴えるなら、男が廃れますよ。Sonna hikyō na
shudan ni uttaeru nara, otoko ga sutaremasu yo. *If you resort to such
cowardly means, you'll lose your manly honor.*

otoko o ageru — 男を上げる — *to earn a reputation for manliness*
[lit. to raise one's manliness]
彼は子供を火事から救って、男を上げました。Kare wa kodomo o
kaji kara sukutte, otoko o agemashita. *He earned a reputation for
manliness by rescuing a child from a fire.*

pin — ピン — *one, the top, the beginning*

pin kara kiri made — ピンから切りまで — *to run the whole gamut*
[lit. from the top to the bottom]
候補者にはピンからキリまであるので、投票の際には気をつけるべきです。Kōhosha niwa pin kara kiri made aru node, tōhyō no sai niwa ki o tsukeru beki desu. *The candidates run the whole gamut, so you should be careful when you vote.*

pinhanesuru — ピンはねする — *to skim money*
[lit. set the top aside]
彼が契約金の三割をピンはねしていたのを、知りませんでした。Kare ga keiyakukin no san wari o pinhaneshite ita no o, shirimasen deshita. *I didn't know he was skimming 30 percent off my contract money.*

---

rachi — 埒 — *picket fence, bounds*

rachi ga akanai — 埒があかない — *to get nowhere*
[lit. A picket fence does not open.]
彼にいくら妥協の必要を説明しても、埒があきませんでした。Kare ni ikura dakyō no hitsuyō o setsumei shitemo, rachi ga akimasen deshita. *No matter how much I explained to him the need for a compromise, it got nowhere.*

rachi mo nai — 埒もない — *silly*
[lit. no bounds]
彼女は埒もない話を、長々と話し続けました。Kanojo wa rachi mo nai hanashi o, naganaga to hanashitsuzukemashita. *She kept talking her silly talk for a long time.*

rappa — ラッパ — *trumpet*

rappa o fuku — ラッパを吹く — *to blow one's own horn*

[lit. to blow a trumpet]

彼は自分の実績について、いつもラッパを吹いています。Kare wa jibun no jisseki ni tsuite, itsumo rappa o fuite imasu. *He is always blowing his own horn about his past performance.*

---

ri — 理 — *reason, principle, truth*

ri mo hi mo naku — 理も非もなく — *by any means*
[lit. with no principles or wrongs]

彼女は理も非も無く、金儲けに熱中しています。Kanojo wa ri mo hi mo naku, kanemōke ni netchū shite imasu. *She's engrossed in making money by any means.*

ri no tōzen — 理の当然 — *matter of course*
[lit. right on principle]

彼が怒ったのは、理の当然でした。Kare ga okotta no wa, ri no tōzen deshita. *His anger was a matter of course.*

---

rō — 労 — *labor, trouble, effort*

rō o ta to suru — 労を多とする — *to appreciate someone's efforts*
[lit. to find that someone's labor was extensive]

社長は、社員の労を多としました。Shachō wa, shain no rō o ta to shimashita. *The president appreciated his employees' efforts.*

rō o toru — 労を取る — *to take the trouble to do something*
[lit. to take up troubles]

教授は、私のために推薦状を書く労を取って下さいました。
Kyōju wa, watakushi no tame ni suisen jō o kaku rō o totte kudasaimashita. *The professor took the trouble to write a letter of recommendation for me.*

---

romei — 露命 — *life fragile like dew*

romei o tsunagu — 露命をつなぐ — *to live from hand to mouth*
[lit. to sustain a dew-like fragile life]

失業中は、持ち物を売って露命をつなぎました。Shitsugyō chū wa, mochimono o utte romei o tsunagimashita. *When I was unemployed, we lived from hand to mouth by selling our possessions.*

---

rotō — 路頭 — *roadside*

rotō ni mayou — 路頭に迷う — *to end up in the street, to become homeless*

[lit. to get lost at the roadside]

不景気が続いて、路頭に迷う人がでてきました。 Fukeiki ga tsuzuite, rotō ni mayou hito ga detekimashita. *Because of the lasting recession, people have begun to end up in the street.*

---

ron — 論 — *argument*

ron o matanai — 論を待たない — *to be beyond question*
[lit. to be needless to argue]

彼女が腕の立つ弁護士であることは、論を待ちません。Kanojo ga ude no tatsu bengoshi de aru koto wa, ron o machimasen. *That she's a capable lawyer is beyond question.*

---

ryū — 竜 — *dragon*

ryūtō dabi ni owaru — 竜頭蛇尾に終わる — *to peter out*
[lit. to start with a dragon's head and end with a snake's tail]

会社の拡張計画は、二年後には竜頭蛇尾に終わりました。Kaisha no kakuchō keikaku wa, ni nen go ni wa ryuto dabi ni owarimashita. *The company expansion plan petered out after two years.*

---

ryūin — 溜飲 — *gastric juices*

ryūin ga sagaru — 溜飲が下がる — *to feel great satisfaction*
[lit. Gastric juices go down.]

同僚に言いたいことを全部言って、溜飲が下がりました。Dōryō ni

iitai koto o zenbu itte, ryūin ga sagarimashita.   *When I said everything I wanted to say to my colleagues, I felt great satisfaction.*

---

ryūbi — 柳眉 — *beautiful eyebrows*
  ryūbi o sakadateru — 柳眉を逆立てる — *(for a beautiful woman) to glare angrily*
  [lit. to make one's beautiful eyebrows stand up]
  彼女は上司との仲を怪しまれて、柳眉を逆立てました。
  Kanojo wa jōshi to no naka o ayashimarete, ryūbi o sakadatemashita.
  When her relationship with her boss was called into question, she glared angrily.

---

saba — 鯖 — *mackerel*
  saba o yomu — 鯖を読む — *to cheat at counting*
  [lit. to count the number of mackerels]
  デモの主催者は、参加者の数の鯖を読みました。Demo no shusaisha wa, sankasha no kazu no saba o yomimashita.   *The organizer of the demonstration cheated at counting the number of participants.*

---

saihai — 采配 — *command baton*
  saihai o furu — 采配を振る — *to take charge of something*
  [lit. to swing a command baton]
  レストランの経営の采配を振っているのは、奥さんの方です。
  Resutoran no keiei no saihai o futte iru no wa, okusan no hō desu.   *She is the one who takes charge of the restaurant's business.*

---

saifu — 財布 — *wallet, purse*
  saifu no soko o hataku — 財布の底をはたく — *to spend all one's money*
  [lit. to tap the bottom of one's wallet]
  財布の底をはたいて、コンピュータを買いました。Saifu no soko o hataite, konpyūta o kaimashita.   *I spent all my money on a computer.*

  saifu no himo o nigiru — 財布の紐を握る — *to control a budget*
  [lit. to grip purse strings]

わが家では、妻が財布の紐を握っています。Wagaya dewa, tsuma ga saifu no himo o nigitte imasu.   *In my household, my wife controls the budget.*

---

saisaki — 幸先 — *future*
saisaki ga ii — 幸先が良い — *to be promising*
[The future is good.]
企画の提案で、部長の支持を得たのは幸先がいいです。Kikaku no teian de, buchō no shiji o eta no wa saisaki ga ii desu.   *It's promising that I got the department chief's support for my proposal for the project.*

---

saji — 匙 — *spoon*
saji o nageru — 匙を投げる — *to give up on something*
[lit. to throw away a spoon]
彼にそれをいくら説明しても分からないので、匙を投げました。
Kare ni sore o ikura setsumei shitemo wakaranai node, saji o nagemashita.   *Since he didn't get it, no matter how much I explained it, I gave up.*

sajikagen de — 匙加減で — *with discretion*
[lit. with the control of a spoonful of medicine]
交渉は、大使の匙加減でうまく行くと思います。Kōshō wa, taishi no sajikagen de umaku iku to omoimasu.   *I think that with the ambassador's discretion, the negotiations will turn out all right.*

---

saki — 先 — *future, first*
saki ga aru — 先がある — *promising*
[lit. There is a future.]
彼女にはハイテクの背景があるので、先があります。Kanojo niwa haiteku no haikei ga aru node, saki ga arimasu.   *Since she has a background in advanced technology, her future is promising.*

saki ga mieru — 先が見える — *The end is in sight.*
[lit. to be able to see the future]
やっと、この研究も先が見えてきました。Yatto, kono kenkyū mo saki ga miete kimashita.   *Finally, for this research the end is in sight.*

saki ni tatsu — 先に立つ — *to lead*
[lit. to stand in front of something]
今度の仕事は、私が先に立ってやりました。Kondo no shigoto wa,

watakushi ga saki ni tatte yarimashita.   *I was the one who led this work.*

saki o kosu — 先を越す — *to predict, to anticipate*
[lit. to go beyond the first]
妻の考えの先を越して、二人だけの旅行を提案しました。Tsuma no
kangae no saki o koshite, futari dake no ryokō o teian shimashita.
Anticipating my wife's wishes, I suggested a trip for just the two of us.

sakibō o katsugu — 先棒を担ぐ — *to pave the way*
[lit. to carry the front end of a stick]
彼は候補者のために、選挙運動の先棒を担いでいます。Kare wa
kōhosha no tame ni, senkyo undō no sakibō o katsuide imasu.   *He is
paving the way for the candidate in the election.*

sakibosori — 先細り — *decline, failing*
[lit. a skinny end]
彼は新しい事業を始めましたが、期待に反して先細りです。Kare
wa atarashii jigyō o hajimemashita ga, kitai ni hanshite sakibosori desu.
Although he started a new business, despite his hopes, it's failing.

---

saku — 策 — *plan*
saku o rōsuru — 策を弄する — *to scheme*
[lit. to resort to a plan]
彼女は策を弄して、その地位を得ようとしました。Kanojo wa saku o
rōshite, sono chii o eyō to shimashita.   *She schemed to gain that
position.*

---

sama — 様 — *appearance*
sama ni narranai — 様にならない — *to not have what it takes*
[lit. to be not up to appearance]
彼は先生として、様になりません。Kare wa sensei toshite, sama ni
narimasen.   *He doesn't have what it takes as a teacher.*

---

saya — 鞘 — *sheath*
moto no saya ni osamaru — 元の鞘に収まる — *to get back together*
[lit. to be put into an original sheath]
彼と彼女は一年の別居の後、元の鞘に収まりました。Kare to kanojo
wa ichi nen no bekkyo no ato, moto no saya ni osamarimashita.   *After a
one-year separation, he and she got back together.*

---

se — 背 — back

se ni hara wa kaerarenu — 背に腹は代えられぬ — *to have no choice*
[lit. to be unable to change one's belly for one's back]
急にお金が必要になり、背に腹は代えられないので質屋へ行きました。
Kyū ni okane ga hitsuyō ni nari, se ni hara wa kaerarenai node shichiya e
ikimashita.   *Suddenly I needed money, and because I had no other
choice, I went to a pawnshop.*

se o mukeru — 背を向ける — *to turn one's back on someone or
something*
[lit. to direct one's back to someone or something]
彼は、彼女の頼みに背を向けました。Kare wa, kanojo no tanomi ni se
o mukemashita.   *He turned his back on her request.*

sesuji ga samuku naru — 背筋が寒くなる — *A chill runs down one's
spine.*
[lit. One's back muscles get cold.]
ひどい交通事故を目撃して、背筋が寒くなりました。Hidoi kōtsū
jiko o mokugeki shite, sesuji ga samuku narimashita.   *Witnessing a
terrible traffic accident, a chill ran down my spine.*

sei — 精 — spirit

sei o dasu — 精を出す — *to exert oneself to do something, to work hard*
[lit. to put out one's spirit]
彼女は試験を控えて、勉強に精を出しています。Kanojo wa shiken o
hikaete, benkyō ni sei o dashite imasu.   *With the exam coming up soon,
she's exerting herself to study.*

seiippai — 精一杯 — *all one can do*
[lit. the maximum of one's spirit]
仕事で精一杯で、昼食を食べる時間がありませんでした。Shigoto de
seiippai de, chūshoku o taberu jikan ga arimasen deshita.   *All I could do
was work, and I didn't have time to eat lunch.*

seiippai yaru — 精一杯やる — *to do one's best*
[lit. to do something with the maximum of one's spirit]
企画を終わらせようと精一杯やりましたが、締め切りに間に合いま
せんでした。Kikaku o owaraseyō to seiippai yarimashita ga, shimekiri
ni maniaimasen deshita.   *I did my best to finish the project, but I
couldn't meet the deadline.*

seken — 世間 — *world, public, society*
  seken ga hiroi — 世間が広い — *to know many people*
  [lit. One's world is wide.]
  彼女は世間が広いので、選挙に出たら勝つでしょう。Kanojo wa
  seken ga hiroi node, senkyo ni detara katsu deshō. *Since she knows so*
  many people, she could win an election if she ran.

  seken ni deru — 世間に出る — *to enter the real world*
  [lit. to go out into the world]
  息子は大学を卒業し、仕事を見つけて、世間に出ました。Musuko wa
  daigaku o sotsugyō shi, shigoto o mitsukete, seken ni demashita. *My son*
  graduated from the university, found a job, and entered the real world.

  sekenbanashi — 世間話 — *small talk*
  [lit. a talk about society]
  彼に仕事の相談に行ったのですが、世間話になってしまいました。
  Kare ni shigoto no sōdan ni itta no desu ga, sekenbanashi ni natte
  shimaimashita. *I went to consult with him about my work, but it ended*
  up in small talk.

  sekenshirazu — 世間知らず — *naive*
  [lit. not knowing the world]
  彼女は世間知らずで、誰でもすぐ信用してしまいます。Kanojo wa
  sekenshirazu de, dare demo sugu shin-yō shite shimaimasu. *Since she's*
  naive, she immediately trusts anyone she meets.

  sekentei o tsukurou — 世間体を繕う — *to keep up appearances*
  [lit. to patch up one's appearances in society]
  彼は世間体を繕うために、娘を私立の学校に行かせています。 Kare
  wa sekentei o tsukurou tame ni, musume o shiritsu no gakkō ni ikasete
  imasu. *He's sending his daughter to a private school to keep up*
  appearances.

---

seki — 席 — *seat*
  seki no atatamaru hima mo nai — 席の暖まる暇もない — *to be very*
  busy
  [lit. There is no time for a seat to get warm.]
  彼はテレビニュースのレポーターになって以来、席の暖まる暇もあ
  りません。Kare wa terebi nyūsu no repōtā ni natte irai, seki no
  atatamaru hima mo arimasen. *Since he became a TV news reporter, he*
  has been very busy.

seki o aratamete — 席を改めて — *again on a different occasion*
[lit. by changing a seat]
それについては、席を改めて考えましょう。Sore ni tsuite wa, seki o
aratamete kangaemashō. *Let's consider it again on a different occasion.*

seki o hazusu — 席を外す — *to leave a room*
[lit. to get away from one's seat]
数分、席を外してもらえませんか。Sūfun, seki o hazushite
moraemasen ka. *Would you leave the room for a few minutes?*

seki o keru — 席を蹴る — *to storm out of the room*
[lit. to kick one's seat]
彼の案が否決されると、彼は席を蹴って会議室を出ていきました。
Kare no an ga hiketsu sareru to, kare wa seki o kette kaigishitsu o dete
ikimashita. *When his idea was voted down, he stormed out of the
conference room.*

seki o yuzuru — 席を譲る — *to give one's position to someone*
[lit. to give one's seat to someone]
彼は、社長の席を娘に譲って引退しました。Kare wa, shachō no seki
o musume ni yuzutte intai shimashita. *He gave his position as
president to his daughter and retired.*

---

sekimen — 赤面 — *red face*
　　sekimen no itari — 赤面の至り — *to be quite ashamed of oneself*
　　[lit. the height of a red face]

教授を彼女の秘書と間違えて、赤面の至りでした。Kyōju o kanojo no hisho to machigaete, sekimen no itari deshita. *I was quite ashamed of myself at assuming the professor was her secretary.*

---

sen — 線 — *line*

sen ga hosoi — 線が細い — *to project insecurity*
[lit. One's line is thin.]
彼には才能があっても線が細いから、この仕事には不向きです。
Kare niwa sainō ga attemo sen ga hosoi kara, kono shigoto niwa fumuki desu. *Because he projects insecurity despite his talent, he's not suitable for this job.*

sen o hiku — 線を引く — *to distinguish*
[lit. to draw a line]
政治家は、公私の別に線を引かねばなりません。Seijika wa, kōshi no betsu ni sen o hikaneba narimasen. *Politicians should distinguish the difference between public and private affairs.*

fukusen o haru — 伏線を張る — *to forestall*
[to put a line under something]
代替え策を作って、後の反対に伏線を張りました。Daigae saku o tsukutte, nochi no hantai ni fukusen o harimashita. *We forestalled later objections by making an alternate plan.*

heikōsen o tadoru — 平行線をたどる — *to not come to agreement*
[lit. to follow parallel lines]
長年の交渉にも関わらず、両者は平行線をたどっています。
Naganen no kōshō nimo kakawarazu, ryōsha wa heikōsen o tadotte imasu. *Despite years of negotiations, the two sides haven't come to agreement.*

yobōsen o haru — 予防線を張る — *to take preventive measures*
[lit. to outstretch a protective line]
批判される前に言い訳を言って、予防線を張りました。Hihan sareru mae ni iiwake o itte, yobōsen o harimashita. *I took preventive measures by giving my excuse before being criticized.*

---

sente — 先手 — *first move*

sente o utsu — 先手を打つ — *to forestall*
[lit. to take the first move]
競争相手に先手を打って、値引きで契約を申し込みました。Kyōsō

aite ni sente o utte, nebiki de keiyaku o mōshikomimashita. *By forestalling our competitor, we offered a contract at a cut-rate price.*

---

sentō — 先頭 — *lead, first*
sentō o kiru — 先頭を切る — *to take the lead*
[lit. to venture to be the first]
先頭を切って、週末の仕事を志願しました。Sentō o kitte, shūmatsu no shigoto o shigan shimashita. *I took the lead and volunteered to work on the weekend.*

---

setsu — 節 — *principles*
setsu o oru — 節を折る — *to yield to someone or something*
[lit. to break one's principles]
子供の願いに節を折って、子猫を飼うことを認めました。Kodomo no negai ni setsu o otte, koneko o kau koto o mitomemashita. *Yielding to my children's wishes, I approved of their keeping a kitten.*

---

sewa — 世話 — *care, trouble, help*
sewa ga nai — 世話がない — *astounding*
[lit. There is no care.]
あれほど言ったのにまだ分からないなんて、本当に世話がありません。Are hodo itta noni mada wakaranai nante, hontō ni sewa ga arimasen. *It's truly astounding that you haven't gotten it after I've told you so often.*

sewa ga yakeru — 世話が焼ける — *to require care*
[lit. One's help for others burns.]
子供はまだ小さいので、とても世話が焼けます。Kodomo wa mada chiisai node, totemo sewa ga yakemasu. *Since my children are still young, they require a lot of care.*

sewa ni naru — 世話になる — *to be under the care of someone*
[lit. to get someone's help]
年をとっても、子供の世話になるつもりはありません。Toshi o tottemo, kodomo no sewa ni naru tsumori wa arimasen. *I have no intention of being under the care of my children, even in my old age.*

sewa o yaku — 世話を焼く — *to take care of someone*
[lit. to heat the care of someone]
祖母は、孫の世話を焼くのが好きです。Sobo wa, mago no sewa o

yaku no ga suki desu.   *My grandmother loves to take care of her grandchildren.*

---

shakushi — 杓子 — *ladle*
　shakushijōgi — 杓子定規 — *to go by the book*
　[lit. a ladle and a ruler]
　彼はいつも杓子定規だから、柔軟性がありません。Kare wa itsumo
　shakushijōgi dakara, jūnansei ga arimasen.   *Because he always goes by*
　the book, he lacks flexibility.

---

shi — 四 — *four*
　shi no go no iu — 四の五の言う — *to find fault*
　[lit. to say four or to say five]
　彼女は何でも四の五の言うので、会議に呼びませんでした。Kanojo
　wa nandemo shi no go no iu node, kaigi ni yobimasen deshita.   *Since*
　she finds fault with everything, we didn't invite her to the meeting.

---

shi — 死 — *death*
　shinimizu o toru — 死に水を取る — *to be at someone's deathbed*
　[lit. to pour water on the mouth of someone who just died]
　家族が間に合わず、私が友達の死に水を取りました。Kazoku ga ma
　ni awazu, watakushi ga tomodachi no shinimizu o torimashita.   *Because*
　my friend's family couldn't make it on time, I was at his deathbed.

---

shian — 思案 — *thought*
　shian ni amaru — 思案に余る — *to be at one's wit's end*
　[lit. to exceed one's thought]
　彼女と結婚すべきか思案に余って、上司に相談しました。Kanojo to
　kekkon subeki ka shian ni amatte, jōshi ni sōdan shimashita.
　I conferred with my boss because I was at my wit's end about marrying
　my girlfriend or not.

　shian ni kureru — 思案に暮れる — *to be preoccupied*
　[lit. A day goes by while thinking.]
　彼女は離婚した後、どんな仕事を探せばいいのか思案に暮れました。
　Kanojo wa rikon shita ato, donna shigoto o sagaseba ii no ka shian ni
　kuremashita.   *After the divorce, she was preoccupied with the kind of*
　job she should look for.

---

shibai — 芝居 — *drama, theater*
  shibai o utsu — 芝居を打つ — *to put someone on*
  [lit. to run a play]
彼は芝居を打って同情を引いた後で、みんなからお金を借りました。
Kare wa shibai o utte dōjō o hiita ato de, minna kara okane o
karimashita.   *After putting us on to get our sympathy, he borrowed
money from everyone.*
  shibaigakaru — 芝居がかる — *histrionic*
  [lit. like a drama]
彼女の芝居がかった話し方が鼻につきます。Kanojo no shibaigakatta
hanashikata ga hana ni tsukimasu.   *Her histrionic way of talking stinks.*

---

shibire — 痺れ — *numbness*
  shibire o kirasu — 痺れを切らす — *to get antsy waiting for someone or
something*
  [lit. to have pins and needles]
三十分待っても注文した料理が来ないので、痺れを切らしました。
Sanjuppun mattemo chūmon shita ryōri ga konai node, shibire o
kirashimashita.   *We got antsy waiting 30 minutes for the food we ordered.*

---

shifuku — 私腹 — *one's own belly*
  shifuku o koyasu — 私腹を肥やす — *to line one's own pocket*
  [lit. to make one's own belly fat]
彼が帳簿をごまかして私腹を肥やしていたのを、知りませんでした。
Kare ga chōbo o gomakashite shifuku o koyashite ita no o, shirimasen
deshita.   *We didn't know that he was lining his own pocket by cooking
the accounts.*

---

shikii — 敷居 — *threshold (entrance)*
  shikii ga takai — 敷居が高い — *to be self-conscious about visiting someone*
  [lit. Someone's threshold is high.]
彼には借りがあるので、あのうちに行くのは敷居が高いです。Kare
ni wa kari ga aru node, ano uchi ni iku no wa shikii ga takai desu.
*Because I owe him some money, I feel self-conscious about visiting his
house.*

shimari — 締まり — *firmness*
shimari ga nai — 締まりがない — *lax*
[lit. There is no firmness.]
今週はボスが出張でいないので、オフィスには締まりがありません。
Konshū wa bosu ga shutchō de inai node, ofisu niwa shimari ga arimasen.
Because the boss is on a business trip this week, we've been lax in the office.

shimatsu — 始末 — *management*
shimatsu ni oenai — 始末に負えない — *unmanageable*
[lit. to be unable to assume management]
昨日友達の子供を預かりましたが、始末に負えませんでした。Kinō
tomodachi no kodomo o azukarimashita ga, shimatsu ni oemasen
deshita.　*I took care of my friend's children in my home yesterday, but
they were unmanageable.*

shin — 真 — *reality*
shin ni semaru — 真に迫る — *to be true to life*
[lit. to draw near reality]
彼女は真に迫るうそをつきました。Kanojo wa shin ni semaru uso o
tsukimashita.　*She told a lie that was true to life.*

shinkei — 神経 — *nerve*
shinkei ga futoi — 神経が太い — *to have nerves of steel*
[lit. One's nerves are thick.]
彼は神経が太いから、この仕事には最適です。Kare wa shikei ga futoi
kara, kono shigoto niwa saiteki desu.　*Because he has nerves of steel,
he's the best one for this work.*

shinkei ni sawaru — 神経にさわる — *to get on one's nerves*
[lit. to touch one's nerves]
彼の態度は神経にさわります。Kare no taido wa shinkei ni sawarimasu.
His behavior gets on my nerves.

shinkei o suriherasu — 神経をすり減らす — *to wear someone down*
[lit. to grind down someone's nerves]
会社の運命を左右する計画をまかされて、神経をすり減らしました。
Kaisha no unmei o sayū suru keikaku o makasarete, shinkei o
suriherashimashita.　*I was put in charge of a crucial project for the
company, and it wore me down.*

shinkei o togaraseru — 神経をとがらせる — *to become keenly aware of someone or something*
[lit. to sharpen one's nerves]
最近は、未成年の非行に警察が神経をとがらせています。Saikin wa, miseinen no hikō ni keisatsu ga shinkei o togarasete imasu. *Recently, the police have become keenly aware of juvenile delinquency.*

shinmi — 親身 — *kindness*
shinmi ni naru — 親身になる — *to devote oneself to someone*
[lit. to become kind to someone]
彼女が病気になったので、親身になって世話しました。Kanojo ga byōki ni natta node, shinmi ni natte sewa shimashita. *Because my girlfriend became ill, I devoted myself to taking care of her.*

shinogi — 鎬 — *the ridges on the sides of a sword blade*
shinogi o kezuru — 鎬を削る — *to compete furiously*
[lit. to scrape the ridges on the sides of a sword blade]
彼らは彼女の注意を引こうと、鎬を削っています。Karera wa kanojo no chūi o hikō to, shinogi o kezutte imasu. *They're competing furiously to get her attention.*

shinshō — 心証 — *impression*
shinshō o gaisuru — 心証を害する — *to make an unfavorable impression*
[lit. to harm one's impression]
仕事の面接で緊張しすぎて、心証を害してしまいました。Shigoto no mensetsu de kinchō shisugite, shinshō o gaishite shimaimashita. *Because I was too tense at the job interview, I made an unfavorable impression.*

shinshoku — 寝食 — *food and sleep*
shinshoku o wasurete   寝食を忘れて   *with intense devotion*
[lit. by forgoing food and sleep]
彼女は寝食を忘れて、子供を看病しました。Kanojo wa shinshoku o wasurete, kodomo o kanbyō shimashita. *With intense devotion, she took care of her sick child.*

shintai — 進退 — *one's course of action*
shintai kiwamaru — 進退窮まる — *to be baffled*

[lit. One's course of action comes to an end.]

彼は仕事の責任と妻の願いの間で、進退窮まっています。Kare wa shigoto no sekinin to tsuma no negai no aida de, shintai kiwamatte imasu. *He's baffled at how to reconcile his job responsibilities and his wife's wishes.*

shinzō — 心臓 — *heart*

shinzō ga tsuyoi — 心臓が強い — *to have the nerve/gall to do or say something*
[lit. One's heart is strong.]

彼女は心臓が強くて、言いたいことを誰にでも言います。Kanojo wa shizō ga tsuyokute, iitai koto o dare ni demo iimasu. *She has the nerve to say whatever she wants to say to anyone.*

shio — 潮 — *tide*

shiodoki o miru — 潮時を見る — *to wait for a good opportunity*
[lit. to watch for the time of the high or low tide]

彼は、会社を辞めて自分の事業を始める潮時を見ています。Kare wa, kaisha o yamete jibun no jigyō o hajimeru shiodoki o mite imasu. *He's waiting for a good opportunity to quit his job and start his own business.*

shippo — 尻尾 — *tail*

shippo o dasu — 尻尾を出す — *to reveal the truth*
[lit. to accidentally reveal one's tail]

彼は独身の振りをしていましたが、奥さんからの電話で尻尾を出してしまいました。Kare wa dokushin no furi o shite imashita ga, okusan kara no denwa de shippo o dashite shimaimashita. *Although he pretended to be single, the truth was revealed when a phone call came from his wife.*

shippo o furu — 尻尾を振る — *to ingratiate oneself with someone*
[lit. to wag one's tail]

あの俳優は、いつも評論家に尻尾を振っています。 Ano haiyū wa,
   itsumo hyōronka ni shippo o futte imasu.   *That actor is always
   ingratiating himself with critics.*

shippo o maite nigeru — 尻尾を巻いて逃げる — *to turn tail*
[lit. to curl one's tail and flee]

彼は仕事が厳しくなると、尻尾を巻いて逃げ出しました。 Kare wa
   shigoto ga kibishiku naru to, shippo o maite nigedashimashita.   *When
   the work got tough, he turned tail.*

shippo o tsukamu — 尻尾をつかむ — *to obtain evidence*
[lit. to grasp someone's tail]

その新聞記者は、官僚の汚職の尻尾をつかみました。 Sono shinbun
   kisha wa, kanryō no oshoku no shippo o tsukamimashita.   *That
   newspaper reporter obtained evidence of corruption by the bureaucrats.*

---

shira — 白 — *white*

shira o kiru — 白を切る — *to pretend not to know about something*
[lit. to stick with white]

彼は自分の間違いなのに、白を切っています。 Kare wa jibun no
   machigai nanoni, shira o kitte imasu.   *Although he made a mistake, he's
   pretending not to know about it.*

shiri — 尻 — *buttocks, bottom, hips*
   shiri ga karui — 尻が軽い — *rash*

[lit. One's buttocks are light.]

彼は尻が軽いたちなので、彼の判断は信用できません。Kare wa shiri ga karui tachi nanode, kare no handan wa shin-yō dekimasen. *He's so rash that you can't trust his judgment.*

shiri ga nagai — 尻が長い — *to stay too long*
[lit. One's bottom is stretching.]

彼は尻が長いので、彼が来るといつも食事を出さねばなりません。Kare wa shiri ga nagai node, kare ga kuru to itsumo shokuji o dasaneba narimasen. *Because he stays too long, whenever he visits us, we have to serve him a meal.*

shiri ga ochitsukanai — 尻が落ち着かない — *to not stay in one place long*
[lit. One's buttocks don't settle down.]

彼女はどんな仕事をしても、尻が落ち着きません。Kanojo wa donna shigoto o shitemo, shiri ga ochitsukimasen. *No matter what kind of job she has, she doesn't stay in one place long.*

shiri ga omoi — 尻が重い — *to be slow to act*
[lit. One's buttocks are heavy.]

彼女は尻が重いけれど、一度始めるといい仕事を速くします。Kanojo wa shiri ga omoi keredo, ichido hajimeru to ii shigoto o hayaku shimasu. *She's slow to act, but once she starts, she quickly does a good job.*

shiri ga wareru — 尻が割れる — *something bad to be brought to light*
[lit. One's buttocks split.]

彼の社長を失脚させる陰謀は、すぐ尻が割れてしまいました。Kare no shachō o shikkyaku saseru inbō wa, sugu shiri ga warete shimaimashita. *His plot to bring about the president's downfall was instantly brought to light.*

shiri ni hi ga tsuku — 尻に火がつく — *Time is fast running out.*
[lit. One's bottom catches fire.]
明日が結婚式ですが、準備のために尻に火がついています。Ashita
ga kekkonshiki desu ga, junbi no tame ni shiri ni hi ga tsuite imasu. *My
wedding is tomorrow, and the time for preparations is fast running out.*

shiri ni ho o kakeru — 尻に帆を掛ける — *to take to one's heels*
[lit. to set a sail to one's bottom]
彼が急に借りの返済を求めたので、尻に帆を掛けて逃げました。
Kare ga kyū ni kari no hensai o motometa node, shiri ni ho o kakete
nigemashita. *Because he suddenly asked for the repayment of the debt,
I took to my heels.*

shiri ni shikareru — 尻に敷かれる — *to be under one's wife's thumb*
[lit. A husband is put under a wife's buttocks.]
友達はみんな、私が妻の尻に敷かれていると思っています。
Tomodachi wa minna, watakushi ga tsuma no shiri ni shikarete iru to
omotte imasu. *All my friends think that I'm under my wife's thumb.*

shiri o atatameru — 尻を暖める — *to remain at the same place or
position*
[lit. to warm one's buttocks]
彼はもう二十年も、助教授として尻を暖めています。Kare wa mō
nijū nen mo, jokyōju toshite shiri o atatamete imasu. *He has remained
an assistant professor for 20 years already.*

shiri o hashoru — 尻をはしょる — *to cut something short*
[lit. to tuck up the bottom of one's kimono]
時間が無くなってきたので、講義の尻をはしょらなければなりませ

んでした。Jikan ga nakunatte kita node, kōgi no shiri o hashoranakereba narimasen deshita.　*Because time was running out, I had to cut short my lecture.*

shiri o makuru — 尻をまくる — *to assume a defiant attitude*
[lit. to pull up the bottom of one's kimono and reveal buttocks]
彼は彼の書いた報告書への批判に、尻をまくりました。
Kare wa kare no kaita hōkokusho e no hihan ni, shiri o makurimashita.
He assumed a defiant attitude toward criticism of the report he had written.

shiri o mochikomu — 尻を持ち込む — *to complain*
[lit. to bring one's bottom in]
彼女はステーキの品質について、肉屋へ尻を持ち込みました。
Kanojo wa sutēki no hinshitsu ni tsuite, nikuya e shiri o mochikomimashita.　*She complained to the butcher about the quality of the steak.*

shiri o nuguu — 尻を拭う — *to clean up someone's mess*
[lit. to wipe someone's bottom]
息子の尻を拭うため、先生に謝りに行きました。Musuko no shiri o nuguu tame, sensei ni ayamarini ikimashita.　*To clean up my son's mess, I went to see his teacher to apologize.*

shiri o sueru — 尻を据える — *to buckle down*
[lit. to set one's bottom firmly]
来週から、尻を据えてコンピュータの使い方を習います。Raishū kara, shiri o suete konpyūta no tsukaikata o naraimasu.　*Starting next week, I'll buckle down and learn how to use a computer.*

shiri o tataku — 尻を叩く — *to prod someone to do something*
[lit. to hit someone's buttocks]
娘の尻を叩いて、ピアノの稽古をさせました。Musume no shiri o tataite, piano no keiko o sasemashita.　*I prodded my daughter to practice the piano.*

shirōto — 素人 — *amateur*
shirōtobanare — 素人離れ — *to be far from amateurish*
[lit. leaving an amateur behind]
彼女の絵は、素人離れしています。Kanojo no e wa, shirōtobanare shite imasu.　*Her paintings are far from amateurish.*

shisen — 視線 — *one's eye*

shisen o abiru — 視線を浴びる — *to attract people's attention*
[lit. to be showered by people's eyes]

彼は会議で独創的な意見を述べて、出席者の視線を浴びました。

Kare wa kaigi de dokusōteki na iken o nobete, shussekisha no shisen o abimashita. *He attracted people's attention by stating some innovative opinions at the meeting.*

---

shisshō — 失笑 — *embarrassing laughter*

shisshō o kau — 失笑を買う — *to cause embarrassed laughter*
[lit. to buy embarrassing laughter]

問題を誤解して議論したので、失笑を買ってしまいました。Mondai o gokai shite giron shita node, shisshō o katte shimaimashita. *Because my arguments were based on a misconception, I caused embarrassed laughter.*

---

shita — 舌 — *tongue*

shita ga koeru — 舌が肥える — *to develop a taste for something*
[lit. One's tongue gets rich.]

沢山の美術館へ行って、現代芸術に対する舌が肥えました。Takusan no bijutsukan e itte, gendai geijutsu ni taisuru shita ga koemashita. *After visiting a lot of museums, I have developed a taste for contemporary art.*

shita ga mawaru — 舌が回る — *to be glib*
[lit. One's tongue spins.]

彼女は舌がよく回るので、言い訳が上手です。Kanojo wa shita ga
yoku mawaru node, iiwake ga jōzu desu. *Since she's really glib, she's
a master at excuses.*

shita no ne no kawakanu uchi ni — 舌の根の乾かぬ内に — *as soon as
one says something*
[lit. even before the bottom of one's tongue dries up]
彼は舌の根の乾かぬ内に、立場を翻しました。Kare wa shita no ne no
kawakanu uchi ni, tachiba o hirugaeshimashita. *As soon as he said it,
he flipped his position.*

shita no saki — 舌の先 — *only words*
[lit. the tip of a tongue]
彼女の約束は、舌の先だけです。Kanojo no yakusoku wa, shita no saki
dake desu. *Her promise is only words.*

shita o dasu — 舌を出す — *to laugh behind someone's back*
[lit. to stick one's tongue out]
彼は親の話を聞く振りをしていても、陰では舌を出しています。
Kare wa oya no hanashi o kiku furi o shite itemo, kage dewa shita o
dashite imasu. *He pretends to listen to what his parents say, but he's
laughing behind their backs.*

shita o maku — 舌を巻く — *to be astounded*
[lit. to curl one's tongue]
彼女の雄弁に舌を巻きました。Kanojo no yūben ni shita o
makimashita. *I was astounded by her eloquent speech.*

shitasaki sanzun — 舌先三寸 — *glib tongue, sweet talk*
[lit. three inches of a tongue]
彼は説明を求められて、舌先三寸でごまかしました。Kare wa
setsumei o motomerarete, shitasaki sanzun de gomakashimashita.
*When he was asked for an explanation, he got through it with his glib
tongue.*

shitatarazu — 舌足らず — *to not express oneself clearly*
[lit. not enough tongue]
私が舌足らずのため、混乱を引き起こして申し訳ありません。
Watakushi ga shitatarazu no tame, konran o hikiokoshite mōshiwake
arimasen. *I'm sorry for causing some confusion because I didn't
express myself clearly.*

shitatsuzumi o utsu — 舌鼓を打つ — *to eat something with gusto*
[lit. to click one's tongue like a drum]

この前の旅行では、その土地のご馳走に舌鼓を打ちました。Kono mae no ryokō dewa, sono tochi no gochisō ni shitatsuzumi o uchimashita. *On my last trip, I ate the local delicacies with gusto.*

nekojita — 猫舌 — *to be sensitive to anything hot (temperature)*
[lit. a cat's tongue]
彼女は猫舌で、熱いお茶は飲めません。Kanojo wa nekojita de, atsui ocha wa nomemasen. *Since she's sensitive to anything hot, she can't drink hot tea.*

nimaijita o tsukau — 二枚舌を使う — *to tell a lie*
[lit. to use two tongues]
彼女は二枚舌を使うので、信用できません。Kanojo wa nimaijita o tsukau node, shin-yō dekimasen. *Because she tells lies, you can't trust her.*

shitauchi suru — 舌打ちする — *to click one's tongue with displeasure*
[lit. to make one's tongue hit the palate]
彼は雑用を頼まれて、舌打ちしました。Kare wa zatsuyō o tanomarete, shitauchi shimashita. *He clicked his tongue with displeasure when he was asked to do errands.*

---

shita — 下 — *low, down*
   shita nimo okanai motenashi — 下にも置かないもてなし — *red carpet treatment*
   [lit. treatment so as not to lay someone down on the ground]
得意先の会社で、下にも置かないもてなしを受けました。Tokuisaki no kaisha de, shita nimo okanai motenashi o ukemashita. *We received the red carpet treatment at the client's company.*

---

shoku — 食 — *eating*
   shoku ga hosoi — 食が細い — *small eater*
   [lit. One's eating is narrow.]
彼女は食が細いけれど、いつも健康です。Kanojo wa shoku ga hosoi keredo, itsumo kenkō desu. *She's a small eater, but she stays healthy.*

   shoku ga susumu — 食が進む — *to have a big appetite*
   [lit. One's eating advances.]
夕べは母の手作りの料理で、食が進みました。Yūbe wa haha no tezukuri no ryōri de, shoku ga susumimashita. *I had a big appetite last night since it was my mother's cooking.*

shokushi ga ugoku — 食指が動く — *to have an itch for something*
[lit. An eating (index) finger moves.]
新しい車に、食指が動きます。Atarashii kuruma ni, shokushi ga ugokimasu. *I have an itch for a new car.*

shōmen — 正面 — *front*
shōmen kitte — 正面切って — *directly*
[lit. by cutting in the front]
正面切って彼を非難することが出来ませんでした。Shōmen kitte kare o hinan suru koto ga dekimasen deshita. *I couldn't blame him directly.*

shou — 背負う — *to carry something on the back*
shotte tatsu — 背負って立つ — *to shoulder the responsibility*
[lit. to carry something on the back and stand up]
社長の死後、奥さんが会社を背負って立っています。
Shachō no shigo, okusan ga kaisha o shotte tatte imasu. *Since the president's death, his wife has been shouldering the responsibility for the company.*

shu — 朱 — *vermilion*
shu o ireru — 朱を入れる — *to red-pencil (written material)*
[lit. to insert vermilion]
編集者は、有名な作家の原稿に朱を入れるのをためらいました。
Henshūsha wa, yūmei na sakka no genkō ni shu o ireru no o tameraimashita. *The editor hesitated to red-pencil the famous writer's manuscript.*

shūbi — 愁眉 — *knitted brows*
shūbi o hiraku — 愁眉を開く — *to breathe freely again*
[lit. to open knitted brows]
子供の高熱が下がって、愁眉を開きました。Kodomo no kōnetsu ga sagatte, shūbi o hirakimashita. *I breathed freely again when my child's high fever went down.*

shuchū — 手中 — *inside a palm*
shuchū ni osameru — 手中に収める — *to secure something*
[lit. put something inside one's palm]

彼は首相の座を手中に収めました。Kare wa shushō no za o shuchū ni osememashita. *He has secured the position of prime minister.*

---

shukō — 趣向 — *plan*
shukō o korasu — 趣向を凝らす — *to devise an elaborate plan*
[lit. to concentrate on a plan]
彼女は、両親の金婚式のために趣向を凝らしました。Kanojo wa, ryōshin no kinkonshiki no tame ni shukō o korashimashita. *She devised an elaborate plan for her parents' golden anniversary.*

---

shūshi — 宗旨 — *one's religion*
shūshi o kaeru — 宗旨を変える — *to switch one's belief, opinion, job, etc.*
[lit. to change one's religion]
彼は最近、革新から保守に政治信念の宗旨を変えました。Kare wa saikin, kakushin kara hoshu ni seiji shinnen no shūshi o kaemashita. *He recently switched his political beliefs from liberalism to conservatism.*

---

sode — 袖 — *sleeve*
sode ni sugaru — 袖にすがる — *to appeal to someone for mercy*
[lit. to cling to someone's sleeve]
兄の袖にすがって、宿題を助けてもらいました。Ani no sode ni sugatte, shukudai o tasukete moraimashita. *I appealed to my big brother for mercy and got him to help with my homework.*

sode ni suru — 袖にする — *to rebuff someone*
[lit. to put hands in sleeves and do nothing]
彼女は彼を袖にしました。Kanojo wa kare o sode ni shimashita. *She rebuffed him.*

sode no shita — 袖の下 — *money under the table, bribe*
[lit. under the sleeve]
彼は、袖の下を使って政府の契約をもらったそうです。Kare wa, sode no shita o tsukatte seifu no keiyaku o moratta sō desu. *He's said to have used money under the table to get the government contract.*

sode o hiku — 袖を引く — *to pluck someone's sleeve*
[lit. to pull someone's sleeve]
秘密の話しがあるので、彼女の袖を引きました。Himitsu no hanashi

ga aru node, kanojo no sode o hikimashita.   *I plucked her sleeve because I had something secret to tell her.*

sode o nurasu — 袖を濡らす — *to weep*
[lit. to wet one's sleeve]
お通夜では、全員が袖を濡らしました。Otsuya dewa, zen-in ga sode o nurashimashita.   *Everyone at the wake wept.*

sode o shiboru — 袖を絞る — *to be moved to tears*
[lit. to wring a tear-soaked sleeve]
とても悲しい映画だったので、袖を絞りました。Totemo kanashii eiga datta node, sode o shiborimashita.   *Because it was a very sad movie, I was moved to tears.*

sode o tsuranete — 袖を連ねて — *together*
[lit. by lining up sleeves together]
閣僚は、袖を連ねて辞職しました。Kakuryō wa, sode o tsuranete jishoku shimashita.   *The cabinet members resigned together.*

sode o wakatsu — 袖を分かつ — *to break off with someone*
[lit. to split a sleeve]
彼と彼女は二年の婚約の後、袖を分かちました。Kare to kanojo wa ni nen no kon-yaku no ato, sode o wakachimashita.   *He and she broke off with each other after a two-year engagement.*

---

sojō — 俎上 — *on the chopping block*
  sojō ni noseru — 俎上に載せる — *to bring up something for discussion*
  [lit. to put something on the chopping block]
  政府は、夏休みの延長を俎上に載せています。Seifu wa, natsuyasumi no enchō o sojō ni nosete imasu.   *The government has brought up for discussion the subject of longer summer vacations.*

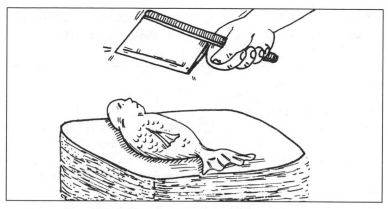

sojō no uo — 俎上の魚 — *to feel quite helpless*
[lit. fish on a chopping block]
病気で明日の試験の準備が出来ず、俎上の魚のような心境です。
Byōki de ashita no shiken no junbi ga dekizu, sojō no uo no yō na
shinkyō desu.　*I feel quite helpless because I'm sick and can't prepare
for tomorrow's exam.*

---

soko — 底 — *bottom*
soko ga asai — 底が浅い — *shallow*
[lit. The bottom is shallow.]
彼女の知識は広いけれど、底が浅いです。Kanojo no chishiki wa hiroi
keredo, soko ga asai desu.　*Her knowledge is vast but shallow.*

soko ga wareru — 底が割れる — *to fall apart*
[lit. The bottom breaks.]
彼の嘘は、すぐに底が割れてしまいました。Kare no uso wa, sugu ni
soko ga warete shimaimashita.　*His lie immediately fell apart.*

soko o tsuku — 底を突く — *to run out of something*
[lit. to hit the bottom]
夫が失業し、子供が入院し、貯金が底を突いてしまいました。Otto ga
shitsugyō shi, kodomo ga nyūin shi, chokin ga soko o tsuite
shimaimashita.　*Because my husband lost his job and our child was
hospitalized, our savings ran out.*

soko o watte hanasu — 底を割って話す — *to speak one's mind*
[lit. to speak by splitting one's bottom]

夕べは、父と底を割って話す機会がありました。Yūbe wa, chichi to soko o watte hanasu kikai ga arimashita.　*Last night I had an opportunity to speak my mind to my father.*

sōkō — 相好 — *face*
 sōkō o kuzusu — 相好を崩す — *to be all smiles*
 [lit. to soften one's face]
 彼女は、娘に子供が生まれて相好を崩しています。Kanojo wa, musume ni kodomo ga umarete sōkō o kuzushite imasu.　*She is all smiles because her daughter had a baby.*

son — 損 — *loss*
 sontokuzuku de — 損得ずくで — *for one's own gain*
 [lit. by purely calculating one's gains and losses]
 彼は損得ずくで人とつき合います。Kare wa sontokuzuku de hito to tsukiaimasu.　*He associates with others for his own gain.*

sora — 空 — *empty, feigned, sham*
 soradanomi ni suru — 空頼みにする — *to hope in vain*
 [lit. to rely on an empty hope]
 彼は昇給を受けることを、空頼みにしています。Kare wa shōkyū o ukeru koto o, soradanomi ni shite imasu.　*He's hoping in vain to get a raise.*

 soraibiki o kaku — 空いびきを搔く — *to feign sleep*
 [lit. to pretend to be snoring]
 父は母の苦情を聞きたくないので、空いびきを搔きました。Chichi wa haha no kujō o kikitakunai node, soraibiki o kakimashita.　*My father didn't want to hear my mother's complaints, so he feigned sleep.*

 soragoto — 空言 — *lie*
 [lit. empty words]
 彼は、言い訳に空言を言いました。Kare wa, iiwake ni soragoto o iimashita.　*He told a lie as his excuse.*

 soranamida — 空涙 — *crocodile tears*
 [lit. sham tears]
 彼は彼女に同情した振りをして、空涙を流しました。Kare wa kanojo ni dōjō shita furi o shite, soranamida o nagashimashita.　*He pretended that he sympathized with her and shed crocodile tears.*

sorazorashii — 空々しい — *insincere*
[lit. emptiness upon emptiness]
彼女は、上司に空々しいお世辞を言っています。Kanojo wa, jōshi ni
sorazorashii oseji o itte imasu.　*She's giving insincere compliments to
the boss.*

sori — 反り — *curve*
sori ga awanai — 反りが合わない — *to not see eye to eye*
[lit. Curves don't fit each other.]
彼と私は、反りが合いません。Kare to watakushi wa, sori ga aimasen.
He and I don't see eye to eye.

soroban — 算盤 — *abacus*
soroban ga awanai — 算盤が合わない — *It doesn't pay.*
[lit. An abacus doesn't fit.]
それをその値段で売っては、算盤が合いません。Sore o sono nedan de
uttewa, soroban ga aimasen.　*If you sell it at that price, it doesn't pay.*

soroban o hajiku — 算盤をはじく — *to calculate*
[lit. to use an abacus]
彼女は最初に算盤をはじかないと、何にもしません。Kanojo wa
saisho ni soroban o hajikanaito, nannimo shimasen.　*She won't do
anything unless she calculates beforehand.*

sorobandakai — 算盤高い — *to be calculating*
[lit. to be high in calculations]
彼は算盤高くて、得にならないことは決してしません。Kare wa
sorobandakakute, toku ni naranai koto wa kesshite shimasen.　*Being a
calculating person, he doesn't do a thing that won't benefit him.*

soto — 外 — *outside*
sotozura ga ii — 外面がいい — *to be affable in public*
[lit. An outside face is good.]
彼女は外面はいいけれど、うちではやかまし屋です。Kanojo wa
sotozura wa ii keredo, uchi dewa yakamashiya desu.　*She's affable in
public but a nitpicker at home.*

suberu — 滑る — *to slide, to slip*
suberikomi de — 滑り込みで — *barely*
[lit. by sliding into something]

彼は、滑り込みで選挙に当選しました。Kare wa, suberikomi de
senkyo ni tōsen shimashita. *He barely won the election.*

subettano korondano to iu — 滑つたの転んだのと言う — *to complain
of one thing or another*
[lit. to say that one slipped or fell down]
彼女は何をしても、滑つたの転んだのと言います。Kanojo wa nani o
shitemo, subettano korondano to iimasu. *She complains of one thing or
another no matter what she does.*

---

sui — 水 — *water*
suihō ni kisuru — 水泡に帰する — *to come to nothing*
[lit. to return to a water bubble]
雨で試合が中止になり、厳しい練習が水泡に帰してしまいました。
Ame de shiai ga chūshi ni nari, kibishii renshū ga suihō ni kishite
shimaimashita. *Because the game was canceled due to rain, our
rigorous practice came to nothing.*

suika mo jisezu — 水火も辞せず — *through it all*
[lit. without rejecting flood or fire]
彼は水火も辞せず、彼女を助けました。Kare wa suika mo jisezu,
kanojo o tasukemashita. *He helped her through it all.*

---

suji — 筋 — *line, logic*
suji ga chigau — 筋が違う — *to not stand to reason*
[lit. Logic is wrong.]
彼女が私を非難するのは、筋が違います。Kanojo ga watakushi o
hinan suru no wa, suji ga chigaimasu. *It doesn't stand to reason that
she blamed me.*

suji ga ii — 筋がいい — *to have an aptitude for something*
[lit. A line is good.]
息子は、野球の筋が良さそうです。Musuko wa, yakyū no suji ga
yosasō desu. *My son seems to have an aptitude for baseball.*

suji ga tatsu — 筋が立つ — *to be logical*
[lit. Logic stands up.]
彼の説明は、筋が立っています。Kare no setsumei wa, suji ga tatte
imasu. *There's logic in his explanation.*

suji o tōsu — 筋を通す — *to act according to one's principles*
[lit. to let logic go through something]

協議では、妥協するより筋を通すことを選びました。Kyōgi dewa, dakyō suru yori suji o tōsu koto o erabimashita. *In the talks, we chose to act according to our principles rather than compromise.*

suji o tōsu — 筋を通す — *to go through proper channels*
[lit. to put something through a line]
彼女は筋を通すより、社長に直接昇進を頼みに行きました。Kanojo wa suji o tōsu yori, shachō ni chokusetsu shōshin o tanomini ikimashita. *She went directly to the president to request a promotion rather than going through proper channels.*

---

sujigane — 筋金 — *steel reinforcement*
sujiganeiri no — 筋金入りの — *staunch*
[lit. steel-reinforced]
彼は、筋金入りの自由貿易主義者です。Kare wa, sujiganeiri no jiyū bōeki shugisha desu. *He's a staunch free-trader.*

---

sumi — 隅 — *corner*
sumi ni okenai — 隅に置けない — *There's more to one than meets the eye.*
[lit. to be unable to simply put someone in a corner]
彼女は、週末に小説を書いているそうです。彼女も隅に置けません。Kanojo wa, shūmatsu ni shōsetsu o kaite iru sō desu. Kanojo mo sumi ni okemasen. *I hear that she has been writing novels on the weekend. There's more to her than meets the eye.*

---

suna — 砂 — *sand*
suna o kamu yō na — 砂を噛むような — *dreary*
[lit. like chewing sand]
離婚してからは、砂を噛むような生活です。Rikon shite kara wa, suna o kamu yō na seikatsu desu. *Since my divorce, my life has been dreary.*

---

sune — すね — *shin*
sune ni kizu motsu — すねに傷持つ — *to have a shady past*
[lit. to have an old scar on one's shin]
彼はすねに傷持つ身なので、選挙には出られません。Kare wa sune ni kizu motsu mi nanode, senkyo niwa deraremasen. *Because he has a shady past, he can't run for election.*

sune o kajiru — すねをかじる — *to sponge off one's parent*
[lit. to gnaw one's parent's shin]
彼女は、いつまでも親のすねをかじるつもりです。Kanojo wa,
itsumademo oya no sune o kajiru tsumori desu. *She intends to sponge
off her parent forever.*

---

sushi — 鮨 — *sushi*
sushizume — 鮨詰め — *to be packed like sardines*
[lit. to be packed like *sushi*]
ディスコは、若い人で鮨詰めでした。Disuko wa, wakai hito de
sushizume deshita. *In the disco, young people were packed like
sardines.*

---

suteru — 捨てる — *to throw away*
sutemi de — 捨て身で — *in desperation*
[lit. by throwing one's body away]
彼は、捨て身でその問題に取り組みました。Kare wa, sutemi de sono
mondai ni torikumimashita. *He grappled with his problems in
desperation.*

suteta mono dewa nai — 捨てた物ではない — *to be not altogether
worthless*
[lit. It's not something to throw away.]
彼女のアイディアも、捨てた物ではありません。Kanojo no aidea mo,
suteta mono dewa arimasen. *Her idea is not altogether worthless.*

---

suzume — 雀 — *sparrow*
suzume no namida — 雀の涙 — *minuscule amount*
[lit. a sparrow's tear]
今度のボーナスは、雀の涙でした。Kondo no bōnasu wa, suzume no
namida deshita. *The bonus this time was minuscule.*

kitakiri suzume — 着た切り雀 — *to wear the same clothes*
[lit. a sparrow with the same clothes]
スーツケースを盗まれて、旅行中は着た切り雀でした。Sūtsukēsu o
nusumarete, ryokō chū wa kitakirisuzume deshita. *Because my luggage
was stolen, I wore the same clothes throughout the trip.*

T

taga — 箍 — *hoop*

taga ga yurumu — 箍が緩む — *to lose some of one's former vigor*
[lit. A hoop gets loose.]

父も七十を過ぎて、箍が緩んできました。Chichi mo nanajū o sugite, taga ga yurunde kimashita. *My father is now over seventy and has lost some of his former vigor.*

tai — 体 — *body*

tai o kawasu — 体をかわす — *to dodge something*
[lit. to avoid bodily crush]

彼は体をかわして、責任を逃れました。Kare wa tai o kawashite, sekinin o nogaremashita. *He dodged his responsibility.*

tai o nasu — 体を成す — *to be organized*
[lit. to achieve a body]

彼女の説明は、あまり体を成していません。Kanojo no setsumei wa, amari tai o nashite imasen. *Her explanation isn't well organized.*

taido — 態度 — *attitude*

taido ga ōkii — 態度が大きい — *to act big*
[lit. One's attitude is big.]

彼は新人なのに、態度が大きいです。Kare wa shinjin nanoni, taido ga ōkii desu. *Although he's a new face, he acts big.*

taifū — 台風 — *typhoon*

taifū no me — 台風の目 — *a leading figure*
[lit. the eye of a typhoon]

学園騒動では、彼らが台風の目になっています。Gakuen sōdō dewa, karera ga taifū no me ni natte imasu. *They're the leading figures in the campus revolt.*

taigai — 大概 — *general*

taigai ni suru — 大概にする — *to not carry something too far*
[lit. to remain in a general range]

人の批判も、大概にするべきです。Hito no hihan mo,
taigai ni suru beki desu. *You shouldn't carry your criticism of others
too far.*

---

taiko — 太鼓 — *drum*

taiko o motsu — 太鼓を持つ — *to flatter someone*
[lit. to hold a drum for someone]
彼女は上司の太鼓を持って、特別待遇を受けています。Kanojo wa
jōshi no taiko o motte, tokubetsu taigū o ukete imasu. *She's getting
special treatment by flattering the boss.*

taikoban o osu — 太鼓判を押す — *to give one's seal of approval*
[lit. to stamp with a large drum-like seal]
教授は、ピアニストとしての彼女の才能に太鼓判を押しました。
Kyōju wa, pianisuto to shite no kanojo no sainō ni taikoban o
oshimashita. *The professor gave his seal of approval to her talent as a
pianist.*

---

taisho — 大所 — *big standpoint*
taisho kōsho kara — 大所高所から — *from a broad perspective*
[lit. from a big and high standpoint]
その問題は、大所高所から接近すべきです。Sono mondai wa, taisho
kōsho kara sekkin subeki desu. *You must approach that issue from a
broad perspective.*

taisō — 大層 — *very much*

taisō mo nai — 大層もない — *much too much*
[lit. no less than very much]
その申し出は、私には大層もございません。Sono mōshide wa,
watakushi niwa taisō mo gozaimasen. *Your offer is much too much for
me.*

---

taka — 高 — *amount, high*

taka ga shireru — 高が知れる — *limited*
[lit. The amount is known.]
彼女の知識は、高が知れています。Kanojo no chishiki wa, taka ga
shirete imasu. *Her knowledge is limited.*

taka o kukuru — 高をくくる — *to take something lightly*
[lit. to put the amount together]
易しい試験だと、高をくくっていたのが大きな間違いでした。
Yasashii shiken da to, taka o kukutte ita no ga ōkina machigai deshita.
It was a big mistake for me to take the exam lightly.

takabisha ni deru — 高飛車に出る — *to act highhanded*
[lit. to advance a rook higher (deeper)]
私が女性のせいか、彼は高飛車に出てきました。Watakushi ga josei
no sei ka, kare wa takabisha ni dete kimashita. *He probably acted
highhanded because I was a woman.*

takami no kenbutsu — 高みの見物 — *to stand by idly*
[lit. to sightsee from a high point]
彼女は彼らが侮辱し合うのを、高みの見物していました。Kanojo
wa karera ga bujoku shiau no o, takami no kenbutsu shite imashita. *She
stood by idly while they were insulting each other.*

otakaku tomaru — お高くとまる — *to be stuck-up*
[lit. to perch high]
彼は有名かも知れないけれど、いつもお高くとまっています。Kare wa
yūmei kamoshirenai keredo, itsumo otakaku tomatte imasu. *He may be
famous, but he's always stuck-up.*

---

tama — 玉 — *jewel*

tama ni kizu — 玉に瑕 — *a fly in the ointment*
[lit. a scar on a jewel]
素晴らしいバカンスでしたが、一日豪雨が降ったのが玉に瑕でした。

Subarashii bakansu deshita ga, ichi nichi gōu ga futta no ga tama ni kizu deshita.   *We had a great vacation; but the fly in the ointment was one day of heavy rain.*

shōchū no tama — 掌中の玉 — *the apple of one's eye*
[lit. a jewel in one's palm]

あの家族では娘が掌中の玉であることを、みんな知っています。
Ano kazoku dewa musume ga shōchū no tama de aru koto o, minna shitte imasu.   *Everybody knows that the daughter is the apple of everyone's eye in that family.*

---

tamoto — 袂 — *kimono sleeve*

tamoto o tsuranete — 袂を連ねて — *acting together*
[lit. by lining up *kimono* sleeves together]

彼らは袂を連ねて、新政党に加わりました。Karera wa tamoto o tsuranete, shin seitō ni kuwawarimashita.   *Acting together, they joined a new political party.*

tamoto o wakatsu — 袂を分かつ — *to break off with someone*
[lit. to split a *kimono* sleeve]

二人の友達はつまらない議論の後、袂を分かちました。Futari no tomodachi wa tsumaranai giron no ato, tamoto o wakachimashita.   *My two friends broke off with each other after an argument over something trivial.*

---

tana — 棚 — *shelf*

tana ni ageru — 棚に上げる — *to ignore something self-indulgently*
[lit. to put something on a shelf]

彼は自分の欠点は棚に上げて、人の批判をします。
Kare wa jibun no ketten wa tana ni agete, hito no hihan o shimasu.
He criticizes other people while self-indulgently ignoring his own shortcomings.

tanaage suru — 棚上げする — *to shelve*
[lit. to put something on a shelf]

会社は、支店拡張計画を棚上げにしました。Kaisha wa, shiten kakuchō keikaku o tanaage ni shimashita.   *The company shelved the plan for expanding its branches.*

tanabota — 棚ぼた — *windfall*
[lit. a rice dumpling coated with sweet bean paste that fell from a shelf]

円高の棚ぼたで、輸入製品が安くなりました。Endaka no tanabota de, yunyū seihin ga yasuku narimashita.   *Because of the windfall from the yen appreciation, imported goods became cheaper.*

tanagokoro — 掌 — *palm*

tanagokoro o kaesu yō ni — 掌を返すように — *easily*
[lit. like flipping one's palm]
彼女は掌を返すように、質問に答えました。Kanojo wa tanagokoro o kaesu yō ni, shitsumon ni kotaemashita.   *She easily answered the question.*

tanagokoro o kaesu yō ni — 掌を返すように — *suddenly*
[lit. like flipping one's palm]
彼は電話の後、掌を返すように静かになりました。Kare wa denwa no ato, tanagokoro o kaesu yō ni shizuka ni narimashita.   *After the telephone call, he suddenly became quiet.*

tanagokoro o sasu yō ni akiraka — 掌を指すように明らか — *to be as clear as crystal*
[lit. to be clear like pointing one's own palm]
彼女が成功することは、掌を指すように明らかでした。Kanojo ga seikō suru koto wa, tanagokoro o sasu yō ni akiraka deshita.   *It was as clear as crystal that she would be successful.*

tate — 盾、楯 — *shield*

tate ni toru — 盾に取る — *to use something as an excuse*
[lit. to hold something as a shield]
彼は限られた予算を盾にとって、手抜き仕事を正当化しようとしました。Kare wa kagirareta yosan o tate ni totte, te-nuki shigoto o seitōka shiyō to shimashita.   *Using a limited budget as an excuse, he tried to justify his shoddy work.*

tate no hanmen — 盾の半面 — *just a part of something*
[lit. one side of a shield]
彼女は盾の半面だけ見て、彼の提案に賛成してしまいました。Kanojo wa tate no hanmen dake mite, kare no teian ni sansei shite shimaimashita.   *Seeing just a part of it, she agreed with his suggestion.*

tatetsuku — 楯突く — *to rebel against someone*
[lit. to thrust one's shield into the ground]
そのピッチャーは監督に楯突いて、チームを首になりました。Sono

pitchā wa kantoku ni tatetsuite, chīmu o kubi ni narimashita. *Having rebelled against the manager, the pitcher was let go from the team.*

---

tazei — 多勢 — *large number of people*
　tazei ni buzei — 多勢に無勢 — *to be outnumbered*
　[lit. a small number of people against a large number of people]
　会議では私たちは多勢に無勢で、私たちの提案は否決されました。
　Kaigi dewa watakushitachi wa tazei ni buzei de, watakushitachi no teian
　wa hiketsu saremashita. *We were outnumbered in the meeting, and our
　proposal was rejected.*

---

tazuna — 手綱 — *reins*
　tazuna o shimeru — 手綱を締める — *to rein someone in*
　[lit. to tighten the reins]
　事業実績を改善するため、社員の手綱を引き締めました。Jigyō
　jisseki o kaizen suru tame, shain no tazuna o hikishimemashita. *To
　improve our business performance, I reined in the employees.*

---

te — 手 — *hand, palm, arm*
　te ga aku — 手が空く — *to have a minute*
　[lit. One's hands get empty.]
　手が空いたら、この仕事をするのを手伝って下さい。Te ga aitara,
　kono shigoto o suru no o tetsudatte kudasai. *Please help me with this
　job when you have a minute.*

　te ga denai — 手が出ない — *to be beyond one's capability*
　[lit. One's hands can't come out and touch something.]
　試験はとても難しくて、手が出ませんでした。Shiken wa totemo
　muzukashikute, te ga demasen deshita. *The exam was so tough that the
　answers were beyond my capability.*

　te ga fusagaru — 手が塞がる — *to have one's hands full*
　[lit. One's hands are occupied.]
　今は手が塞がっているので、また後で来て下さい。Ima wa te ga
　fusagatte iru node, mata ato de kite kudasai. *Please come back later
　because I have my hands full now.*

　te ga hanareru — 手が離れる — *to have some free time*
　[lit. One's hands get off something.]
　子供が保育園に行くので、やっと手が放れます。Kodomo ga hoikuen

ni iku node, yátto te ga hanaremasu. *My child will start nursery school, so I'll finally have some free time.*

te ga hayai — 手が早い — *to be a womanizer*
[lit. One's hands are fast.]
彼は手が早いから、気をつけなさい。Kare wa te ga hayai kara, ki o tsukenasai. *Be careful, since he's a womanizer.*

te ga kakaru — 手が掛かる — *to be a handful*
[lit. One's hands are needed.]
二人の子供に、手が掛かります。Futari no kodomo ni, te ga kakarimasu. *My two children are a handful.*

te ga komu — 手が込む — *elaborate*
[lit. One's hands are put in.]
それは、非常に手が込んだ策略でした。Sore wa, hijō ni te ga konda sakuryaku deshita. *It was a very elaborate scheme.*

te ga mawaranai — 手が回らない — *no time for something*
[lit. One's hands can't make rounds.]
料理をしていたので、洗濯にまで手が回りませんでした。Ryōri o shite ita node, sentaku ni made te ga mawarimasen deshita. *Because I was cooking, there was no time for laundry.*

te ga nai — 手がない — *nothing one can do*
[lit. There are no hands.]
交渉では、相手側に譲歩するより手がありませんでした。Kōshō dewa, aitegawa ni jōho suru yori te ga arimasen deshita. *There was nothing we could do but make concessions to our counterpart in the negotiations.*

te ga suku — 手がすく — *to have a free moment*
[lit. One's hands get free.]
手がすいたら、休憩してお茶を飲みましょう。Te ga suitara, kyūkei shite ocha o nomimashō. *When you have a free moment, let's take a break and have some tea.*

te ga todoku — 手が届く — *to be thorough*
[lit. One's hands reach something.]
彼女の家は、庭の手入れまで実に手が届いていました。Kanojo no ie wa, niwa no teire made jitsu ni te ga todoite imashita. *At her house, even the gardening was very thorough.*

te ga tsukerarenai — 手が付けられない — *Nothing helps; to be out of control*
[lit. One can't touch something by hands.]

293

彼は一度怒り出すと、手が付けられません。Kare wa ichido okoridasu to, te ga tsukeraremasen. *Once he gets angry, nothing helps.*

te ga ushiro ni mawaru — 手が後ろに回る — *to be arrested*
[lit. One's hands go around one's back.]
彼女は横領の容疑で、手が後ろに回りました。Kanojo wa ōryō no yōgi de, te ga ushiro ni mawarimashita. *She was arrested on suspicion of embezzlement.*

te mo ashi mo denai — 手も足も出ない — *no match*
[lit. to be unable to put one's hands or legs out]
彼の論理に、手も足もでませんでした。Kare no ronri ni, te mo ashi mo demasen deshita. *I was no match for his logic.*

te ni amaru — 手に余る — *to be too much for one to handle*
[lit. to be excessive to one's hands]
その仕事は彼の専門外なので、手に余りました。Sono shigoto wa kare no senmon gai nanode, te ni amarimashita. *Because the work was outside his specialty, it was too much for him to handle.*

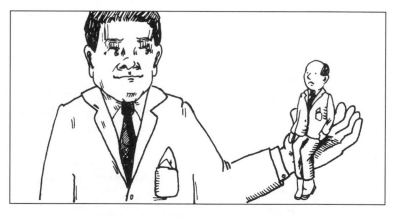

te ni noru — 手に乗る — *to fall for a scheme*
[lit. to ride in someone's hand]
彼の手に乗って、疑わしい事業に出資してしまいました。Kare no te ni notte, utagawashii jigyō ni shusshi shite shimaimashita. *Foolishly, I fell for his scheme to have me invest in his dubious business.*

te ni ochiru — 手に落ちる — *to fall into someone else's possession*
[lit. to fall into someone's hands]

ローンが返せずに、担保の土地は銀行の手に落ちてしまいました。
Rōn ga kaesezu ni, tanpo no tochi wa ginkō no te ni ochite shimaimashita.   *When I failed to repay the loan, the land I used as collateral fell into the bank's possession.*

te ni oenai — 手に負えない — *to be more than one can handle*
[lit. to be unable to carry someone or something in one's hand]
彼の説明は実に複雑で、私の手には負えませんでした。Kare no setsumei wa jitsu ni fukuzatsu de, watakushi no te niwa oemasen deshita.
Because his explanation was very complex, it was much more than I could handle.

te ni suru — 手にする — *to have, to gain*
[lit. to put something in one's hand]
彼女は突然大金を手にして、どうしようか迷っています。
Kanojo wa totsuzen taikin o te ni shite, dō shiyō ka mayotte imasu.
Suddenly having a big sum of money, she doesn't know what to do with it.

te ni te o totte — 手に手を取って — *hand-in-hand*
[lit. to take someone's hand with one's hand]
二社は手に手を取って、新技術の研究・開発を始めました。Nisha wa te ni te o totte, shin gijutsu no kenkyū・kaihatsu o hajimemashita.
Hand-in-hand the two companies began research and development on the new technology.

te ni toru yō ni — 手に取るように — *clearly*
[lit. as if picking up something with one's own hand]
彼女は何も言いませんでしたが、気持ちは手に取るように分かりました。Kanojo wa nani mo iimasen deshita ga, kimochi wa te ni toru yō ni wakarimashita.   *Although she said nothing, I understood her feelings clearly.*

te ni tsukanai — 手に付かない — *to be unable to bring oneself to do something*
[lit. Something doesn't come in contact with one's hand.]
素晴らしい天気なので、勉強が手に付きません。Subarashii tenki nanode, benkyō ga te ni tsukimasen.   *Because of the beautiful weather, I can't bring myself to study.*

te no uchi o miseru — 手の内を見せる — *to show one's hand*
[lit. to reveal what is inside one's hand]
交渉中は、こちら側の手の内をあまり見せないように気をつけました。

Kōshō chū wa, kochiragawa no te no uchi o amari misenai yō ni ki o tsukemashita. *During the negotiations, we were careful not to show our hand too much.*

te no ura o kaesu yō ni — 手の裏を返すように — *suddenly*
[lit. just like flipping the back of one's hand]
失業したら、ガールフレンドの態度が手の裏を返すように冷たくなりました。Shitsugyō shitara, gārufurendo no taido ga te no ura o kaesu yō ni tsumetaku narimashita. *Right after I lost my job, my girlfriend suddenly cooled off toward me.*

te o awaseru — 手を合わせる — *to beg someone*
[lit. to put one's open palms against each oher]
姉に手を合わせて、宿題を手伝ってもらいました。Ane ni te o awasete, shukudai o tetsudatte moraimashita. *I begged my big sister to help with my homework.*

te o dasu — 手を出す — *to get involved with someone or in something*
[lit. to thrust one's hand into something]
彼は株に手を出して、大儲けしました。Kare wa kabu ni te o dashite, ōmōke shimashita. *By getting involved in the stock market, he made big bucks.*

te o hiku — 手を引く — *to back out of something*
[lit. to draw one's hands away]
彼女は、土地の投機から手を引きました。Kanojo wa, tochi no tōki kara te o hikimashita. *She backed out of the land speculation deal.*

te o hirogeru — 手を広げる — *to extend a business*
[lit. to spread one's arms]
彼は短期間に手を広げすぎて、財政難に陥っています。Kare wa tan kikan ni te o hirogesugite, zaisei nan ni ochiitte imasu. *By extending his business too much too soon, he has fallen into financial difficulties.*

te o ireru — 手を入れる — *to go over something*
[lit. to put one's hand in something]
提出する前に、報告書にもう一度手を入れました。Teishutsu suru mae ni, hōkokusho ni mō ichido te o iremashita. *Before submitting the report, we went over it once more.*

te o kae shina o kae — 手を替え品を替え — *in many different ways*
[lit. by changing hands and changing goods]
手を替え品を替え彼女を説得しようとしましたが、無駄でした。Te

o kae shina o kae kanojo o settoku shiyō to shimashita ga, muda deshita. *I tried to persuade her in many different ways, but it didn't work.*

te o kakeru — 手をかける — *to do something with care and attention*
[lit. to put one's hand on something]
彼は手をかけて、蘭を育てています。Kare wa te o kakete, ran o sodatete imasu. *He's raising orchids with care and attention.*

te o kariru — 手を借りる — *to get help*
[lit. to borrow someone's hand]
引っ越ししたとき、友達の手を借りました。Hikkoshi shita toki, tomodachi no te o karimashita. *I got help from my friends when I moved.*

te o kasu — 手を貸す — *to help someone*
[lit. to lend one's hands to someone]
父が車を修理するのに手を貸しました。Chichi ga kuruma o shūri suru no ni te o kashimashita. *I helped my father repair his car.*

te o kiru — 手を切る — *to sever one's relations with someone*
[lit. to cut one's hand]
彼女は、ボーイフレンドと手を切る決心をしました。Kanojo wa, bōifurendo to te o kiru kesshin o shimashita. *She decided to sever her relations with her boyfriend.*

te o komaneku — 手をこまねく — *to look on helplessly*
[lit. to fold one's arms]
火事の現場で、人々は手をこまねくしかありませんでした。Kaji no genba de, hitobito wa te o komaneku shika arimasen deshita. *At the site of the fire, people could do nothing but look on helplessly.*

te o kudasu — 手を下す — *to directly involve oneself in something*
[lit. to lower one's hand onto something]
その問題は、社長が手を下して解決しました。Sono mondai wa, shachō ga te o kudashite kaiketsu shimashita. *The president directly involved himself in solving the problem.*

te o kumu — 手を組む — *to join hand-in-hand*
[lit. to lock each other's arm]
彼らは手を組んで、新しい事業を始めました。Karera wa te o kunde, atarashii jigyō o hajimemashita. *They joined hand-in-hand and started a new business.*

te o kuwaeru — 手を加える — *to refine something*
[lit. to add one's hand to something]

その企画は、もう一度手を加える必要があります。Sono kikaku wa, mō ichido te o kuwaeru hitsuyō ga arimasu. *You need to refine your planning once more.*

te o mawasu — 手を回す — *to take measures*
[lit. to go around with one's hand]
状況を改善するために、すでに手を回しておきました。Jōkyō o kaizen suru tame ni, sude ni te o mawashite okimashita. *I've already taken measures to improve the situation.*

te o musubu — 手を結ぶ — *to cooperate*
[lit. to join hands]
彼女と手を結んで、任務を達成しました。Kanojo to te o musunde, ninmu o tassei shimashita. *I accomplished the task by cooperating with her.*

te o nigiru — 手を握る — *to come to an agreement*
[lit. to grasp someone's hand]
議論を続けたけれど、最後には手を握りました。Giron o tsuzuketa keredo, saigo niwa te o nigirimashita. *We kept on arguing, but in the end we came to an agreement.*

te o nobasu — 手を伸ばす — *to expand*
[lit. to stretch one's arms]
最近あの会社は、映画産業にまで手を伸ばしています。Saikin ano kaisha wa, eiga sagyō ni made te o nobashite imasu. *Recently, that company has even expanded its business to the movie industry.*

te o nuku — 手を抜く — *to cut corners*
[lit. to withdraw one's hand]
地震で、建設会社が工事に手を抜いていたのが分かりました。Jishin de, kensetsugaisha ga kōji ni te o nuite ita no ga wakarimashita. *With the earthquake, it appeared that the construction companies had cut corners.*

te o nurasazu — 手を濡らさず — *without any effort*
[lit. by not wetting one's hands]
彼女は手を濡らさずに、金持ちになりました。Kanojo wa te o nurasazu ni, kanemochi ni narimashita. *She became rich without any effort.*

te o someru — 手を染める — *to undertake something*
[lit. to dip one's hand in dye]

彼が趣味として園芸に手を染めてから、十年になります。Kare ga shumi toshite engei ni te o somete kara, jū nen ni narimasu. *It's been ten years since he undertook gardening as his hobby.*

te o tsukaneru — 手をつかねる — *to be at a loss*
[lit. to hold one's arms]
彼女はその問題をどうしたらいいか、手をつかねています。Kanojo wa sono mondai o dō shitara ii ka, te o tsukanete imasu. *She's at a loss to know how to deal with the problem.*

te o tsukeru — 手を付ける — *to take on something*
[lit. to attach one's hand to something]
彼は、新しい研究の分野に手を付けました。Kare wa, atarashii kenkyū no bun-ya ni te o tsukemashita. *He took on a new field of research.*

te o tsukusu — 手を尽くす — *to do everything conceivable*
[lit. to exhaust one's hand]
顧客を満足させるために、手を尽くしました。Kokyaku o manzoku saseru tame ni, te o tsukushimashita. *We did everything conceivable to satisfy our clients.*

te o utsu — 手を打つ — *to shake hands on something*
[lit. to clap one's hands]
締め切り日については、今月末で手を打ちました。Shimekiribi ni tsuite wa, kongetsu matsu de te o uchimashita. *We shook hands on the end of this month as the date of the deadline.*

te o utsu — 手を打つ — *to take necessary measures*
[lit. to cast one's hands into something]
どの家庭も、大地震に備えて手を打っておくべきです。Dono katei mo, ōjishin ni sonaete te o utte oku beki desu. *Every home should take necessary measures for a big earthquake.*

te o wazurawasu — 手を煩わす — *to have help*
[lit. to cause someone's hands trouble]
友達の手を煩わせて、丸太小屋を作っています。Tomodachi no te o wazurawasete, marutagoya o tsukutte imasu. *I've been building a log cabin with help from my friends.*

te o yaku — 手を焼く — *to have a hard time*
[lit. to burn one's hand]
彼の頑固さには、手を焼いています。Kare no gankosa ni, te o yaite imasu. *We're having a hard time dealing with his stubbornness.*

akago no te o hineru yō — 赤子の手を捻るよう — to be like child's play
[lit. like twisting a baby's arm]
彼女にとって、テニスで彼を負かすのは赤子の手を捻るようなもの
でした。Kanojo ni totte, tenisu de kare o makasu no wa akago no te o
hineru yō na mono deshita.   It was like child's play for her to beat him
at tennis.

ōde o futte aruku — 大手を振って歩く — to swagger
[lit. to walk swinging one's extended arms]
彼はテニス大会で優勝してから、クラブの中を大手を振って歩いて
います。Kare wa tenisu taikai de yūshō shite kara, kurabu no naka o
ōde o futte aruite imasu.   Since he won the championship of the tennis
tournament, he has been swaggering around the club.

oku no te — 奥の手 — ace in the hole
[lit. a deep hand]
彼は奥の手を使って、契約を取り付けました。Kare wa oku no te o
tsukatte, keiyaku o toritsukemashita.   Using an ace in the hole, he won
the contract.

oteage — お手上げ — to be unable to do a thing
[lit. to raise one's hands]
資金不足で、研究はお手上げ状態です。Shikin busoku de, kenkyū wa
oteage jōtai desu.   Due to the lack of funds, we can't do a thing in our
research.

otenomono — お手の物 — one's forte
[lit. something in one's hand]
彼女は、市場分析ならお手の物です。Kanojo wa, shijō bunseki nara
otenomono desu.   Market analysis is her forte.

teashi o nobasu — 手足を伸ばす — to relax
[lit. to stretch one's arms and legs]
この週末に、やっと手足を伸ばすことが出来ました。Kono shūmatsu
ni, yatto teashi o nobasu koto ga dekimashita.   Finally, I was able to
relax last weekend.

teashi to natte — 手足となって — as a devoted helper
[lit. by becoming someone's hands and legs]
彼は彼女の手足となって、事業の成功のために働きました。Kare
wa kanojo no teashi to natte, jigyō no seikō no tame ni hatarakimashita.
He worked as a devoted helper for the success of her business.

tegusume hiite — 手ぐすねひいて — eagerly
[lit. by putting wax on an archery string with one's hand]
彼女は彼に仕返しする機会を、手ぐすねひいて待っています。Kanojo
wa kare ni shikaeshi suru kikai o, tegusune hiite matte imasu. She's
eagerly waiting for an opportunity to take revenge on him.

temawashi — 手回し — arrangement
[lit. putting one's hands around something]
手回しよく、会議の後で夕食が出ました。Temawashi yoku, kaigi no
ato de yūshoku ga demashita. With good arrangements, they served
dinner after the conference.

teochi — 手落ち — an oversight
[lit. dropping something from one's hand]
彼の名前をリストに入れなかったのは、私の手落ちです。Kare no
namae o risuto ni irenakatta no wa, watakushi no teochi desu. Not
including his name on the list was my oversight.

teshio ni kakeru — 手塩にかける — to raise someone with tender care
[lit. to handle something with salted hands]
彼女は、娘を手塩にかけて育てています。Kanojo wa, musume o
teshio ni kakete sodatete imasu. She's raising her daughter with tender
care.

tetori ashitori — 手取り足取り — with care and tenderness
[lit. by holding someone's arms and then legs with one's hands]
彼は手取り足取り、彼女にやり方を説明しました。Kare wa tetori
ashitori, kanojo ni yarikata o setsumei shimashita. With care and
tenderness, he explained the procedures to her.

yarite — やり手 — someone capable
[lit. one with a hand of action]
彼女はやり手だから、その仕事を任せても全く大丈夫です。Kanojo
wa yarite dakara, sono shigoto o makasetemo mattaku daijōbu desu.
Since she's capable, it's perfectly all right to put her in charge of that
work.

tedama — 手玉 — *small ball*

tedama ni toru — 手玉に取る — *to lead someone around by the nose*
[lit. to handle someone like a small ball]
彼女は、彼を手玉に取っています。Kanojo wa, kare o tedama ni totte
imasu. *She's leading him around by the nose.*

teko — 梃子 — *lever*

teko demo ugokanai — 梃子でも動かない — *to not budge an inch*
[lit. to not move even if a lever is applied]
彼らは譲歩を強要しましたが、彼は梃子でも動きませんでした。
Karera wa jōho o kyōyō shimashita ga, kare wa teko demo
ugokimasen deshita. *They tried to force concessions, but he didn't
budge an inch.*

tekoire suru — テコ入れする — *to shore something up*
[lit. to insert a lever]
財界は、政府が銀行部門にテコ入れするのを望んでいます。Zaikai
wa, seifu ga ginkō bumon ni tekoire suru no o nozonde imasu. *Big
business wants the government to shore up the banking sector.*

tetsu — 轍 — *track*

tetsu o fumu — 轍を踏む — *to fall into the same rut*
[lit. to step on the same track]
私は、サラリーマンとしての父の轍を踏みたくありません。
Watakushi wa, sararīman to shite no chichi no tetsu o fumitaku

arimasen. *I don't want to fall into the same rut my father did as an office worker.*

---

tettsui — 鉄槌 — *an iron hammer*
tettsui o kudasu — 鉄槌を下す — *to deal a severe blow*
[lit. to hammer down]
政府は、汚職官僚に鉄槌を下しました。Seifu wa, oshoku kanryō ni tettsui o kudashimashita. *The government dealt a severe blow to the corrupt bureaucrats.*

---

ten — 天 — *sky*
ten ni tsuba suru — 天に唾する — *to boomerang*
[lit. to spit skyward]
彼を批判したけれど、それは天に唾する結果になりました。Kare o hihan shita keredo, sore wa ten ni tsuba suru kekka ni narimashita. *I criticized him, but it boomeranged on me.*

ten o tsuku — 天を突く — *very tall*
[lit. hitting the sky]
故郷に帰って、天を突く ビルにびっくりしました。Kokyō ni kaette, ten o tsuku biru ni bikkuri shimashita. *Returning to my hometown, I was so surprised to see very tall buildings.*

---

tenbin — 天秤 — *beam*
tenbin ni kakeru — 天秤に掛ける — *to weigh the advantages of something*
[lit. to put something on a beam]
どの会社と契約を結ぶか、天秤に掛けました。Dono kaisha to keiyaku o musubu ka, tenbin ni kakemashita. *We weighed the advantages of concluding a contract with various companies.*

---

tenjō — 天井 — *ceiling*
tenjōshirazu — 天井知らず — *The sky is the limit.*
[lit. to not know the ceiling]
彼女は自尊心にかけては、天井知らずです。Kanojo wa jisonshin ni kakete wa, tenjōshirazu desu. *Talking about her ego, the sky is the limit.*

tenka — 天下 — *the whole world*

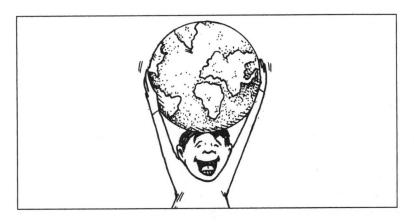

tenka o toru — 天下を取る — *to gain absolute control*
[lit. to pick up the whole world]

彼は家電の分野で、天下を取りたいと思っています。Kare wa kaden
no bun-ya de, tenka o toritai to omotte imasu.   *He wishes to gain
absolute control over the field of home appliances.*

tenkaharete — 天下晴れて — *officially*
[lit. with the sky cleared]

彼らは、天下晴れて夫婦になりました。Karera wa, tenkaharete fūfu-ni
narimashita.   *They officially became husband and wife.*

---

tensū — 点数 — *points*

tensūkasegi — 点数稼ぎ — *one's personal gain*
[lit. to earn points]

彼女は点数稼ぎのためなら、何でもします。Kanojo wa tensūkasegi
no tame nara, nandemo shimasu.   *She'll do anything for her personal
gain.*

---

tō — 当 — *right*

tō o eru — 当を得る — *to be just right*
[lit. to gain the right spot]

彼の言い分は、当を得ています。Kare no iibun wa, tō o ete imasu.
His claim is just right.

---

todo — とど — *mullet*

todo no tsumari — とどのつまり — *after all*
[lit. the end stage of a mullet's growth]

とどのつまり、彼女の意見が正しいことが分かりました。Todo no tsumari, kanojo no iken ga tadashii koto ga wakarimashita. *We learned that her opinion was correct after all.*

todome — 止め — *finishing blow*

todome o sasu — 止めを刺す — *to make certain of something*
[lit. to stab someone's throat with a finishing blow]

息子によく勉強するように、止めを刺しました。Musuko ni yoku benkyō suru yō ni, todome o sashimashita. *I made certain that my son would study hard.*

tōge — 峠 — *a mountain pass*

tōge o kosu — 峠を越す — *to turn the corner*
[lit. to go over a mountain pass]

日米二国間交渉が、やっと峠を越しました。Nichibei nikoku kan kōshō ga, yatto tōge o koshimashita. *The U.S.-Japan bilateral negotiations finally turned the corner.*

toguro — とぐろ — *coil*

toguro o maku — とぐろを巻く — *to hang around*
[lit. to coil oneself]

彼らは仕事中なのに、いつも喫茶店でとぐろを巻いています。Karera wa shigoto chū nanoni, itsumo kissaten de toguro o maite imasu. *Although it's business hours, they hang around the coffee shop all the time.*

tohō — 途方 — *direction*

tohō mo nai — 途方もない — *absurd*
[lit. without a direction]

彼女は、途方もない夢を追っています。Kanojo wa, tohō mo nai yume o otte imasu. *She's chasing an absurd dream.*

tohō ni kureru — 途方に暮れる — *to be at one's wit's end*
[lit. to spend time trying to find a direction]

突然首になって、途方に暮れています。Totsuzen kubi ni natte, tohō ni kurete imasu. *I'm at my wit's end at being fired suddenly.*

tōkaku — 頭角 — *top of a head*
tōkaku o arawasu — 頭角を現す — *to stand out*
[lit. to show the top of one's head]
彼はすでに子供の時に、数学の分野で頭角を現しました。Kare wa
sude ni kodomo no toki ni, sūgaku no bun-ya de tōkaku o
arawashimashita.   *Even when he was a child, he stood out in the field of*
mathematics.

toki — 時 — *time*
toki o kasegu — 時を稼ぐ — *to buy time, to get extra time*
[lit. to earn time]
病気を理由に、論文提出の時を稼ぎました。Byōki o riyū ni, ronbun
teishutsu no toki o kasegimashita.   *With my illness as an excuse, I got*
extra time for turning in my term paper.

toki o matsu — 時を待つ — *to bide one's time*
[lit. to wait for time]
彼女は声楽とピアノの稽古を受けながら、歌手になる時を待ってい
ます。Kanojo wa seigaku to piano no keiko o ukenagara, kashu ni naru
toki o matte imasu.   *While taking voice and piano lessons, she's biding*
her time to become a singer.

toki o ushinau — 時を失う — *to lose an opportunity*
[lit. to lose time]
不景気になって、転職の時を失ってしまいました。Fukeiki ni natte,
tenshoku no toki o ushinatte shimaimashita.   *With the downturn of the*
economy, I lost the opportunity to switch my job.

tokoro — 所 — *place*
tokoro o eru — 所を得る — *to find one's niche*
[lit. to gain a place]
彼はサラリーマンを辞めて、農業を始めて所を得ました。Kare wa
sararīman o yamete, nōgyō o hajimete tokoro o emashita.   *He found his*
niche in farming after quitting office work.

tokorokamawazu — 所構わず — *no matter where one is*
[lit. to not care about a place]
彼女は、所構わず娘の自慢をします。Kanojo wa, tokorokamawazu
musume no jiman o shimasu.   *She brags about her daughter no matter*
where she is.

tora — 虎 — *tiger*

tora no i o karite — 虎の威を借りて — *using someone else's authority*
[lit. by borrowing a tiger's authority]

彼は社長の虎の威を借りて、社員に超過勤務を強要します。Kare wa shachō no tora no i o karite, shain ni chōka kinmu o kyōyō shimasu. *Using the authority of the president, he forces the employees to work overtime.*

tora ni naru — 虎になる — *to get roaring drunk*
[lit. to become a tiger]

夕べバーを数軒回つた後、友達は虎になりました。Yūbe bā o sūken mawatta ato, tomodachi wa tora ni narimashita. *Last night my friend got roaring drunk after visiting several bars.*

tora no ko — 虎の子 — *one's treasure*
[lit. a tiger cub]

彼は、虎の子の骨董品の壷を割つてしまいました。Kare wa, tora no ko no kottōhin no tsubo o watte shimaimashita. *He broke the antique jar that was his treasure.*

tora no o o fumu omoi de — 虎の尾を踏む思いで — *gingerly*
[lit. feeling as if one were stepping on the tail of a tiger]

虎の尾を踏む思いで、社長に昇給を頼みました。Tora no o o fumu omoi de, shachō ni shōkyū o tanomimashita. *Gingerly, I asked the president for a raise.*

hariko no tora — 張り子の虎 — *paper tiger*
[lit. a papier-mache tiger]

彼は張り子の虎だから、恐れる必要はありません。Kare wa hariko no tora dakara, osoreru hitsuyō wa arimasen. *Since he's a paper tiger, you don't need to be afraid of him.*

---

toru — 取る — *to take*

toru ni tarinai — 取るに足りない — *for the birds*
[lit. not sufficient to take]
彼女の意見は取るに足りません。Kanojo no iken wa toru ni tarimasen. *Her opinions are for the birds.*

torumono mo toriaezu — 取る物も取りあえず — *without a moment's delay*
[lit. without taking things one should take]
子供が生まれたという知らせに、取る物も取りあえず病院に向かいました。Kodomo ga umareta to iu shirase ni, torumono mo toriaezu byōin ni mukaimashita. *Hearing that my baby had been born, I headed to the hospital without a moment's delay.*

---

toshi — 年 — *age*

toshi ni fusoku wa nai — 年に不足はない — *to be old enough*
[lit. There is no lack in someone's age.]
彼の年に不足はないけれど、考え方がまだ一面的です。Kare no toshi ni fusoku wa nai keredo, kangaekata ga mada ichimenteki desu. *He's old enough, but his way of thinking is still one-dimensional.*

ii toshi o shite — いい年をして — *too old to be doing something*
[lit. with good age]
彼はいい年をして、いつもお母さんのことを話しています。Kare wa ii toshi o shite, itsumo okāsan no koto o hanashite imasu. *He's too old to be talking about his mother all the time.*

---

tsubu — 粒 — *grain*

tsubu ga sorou — 粒が揃う — *to be the cream of the crop*
[lit. The grains are equally excellent.]
この作業班のメンバーは、粒が揃っています。Kono sagyō han no menbā wa, tsubu ga sorotte imasu. *The members of this task force are the cream of the crop.*

---

tsubushi — 潰し — *making scrap metal*

tsubushi ga kiku — 潰しが利く — *to have a marketable skill*
[lit. to be able to scrap something]

彼は色々潰しが利くから、今の仕事を辞めても大丈夫でしょう。

Kare wa iroiro tsubushi ga kiku kara, ima no shigoto o yametemo daijōbu deshō. *Because he has many marketable skills, he'll be all right if he quits his current job.*

---

tsubo — 壷 — *jar*

tsubo ni hamatta — 壷にはまった — *pertinent*
[lit. something fitting into a jar]

彼女は、いつも壷にはまった質問をします。Kanojo wa, itsumo tsubo ni hamatta shitsumon o shimasu. *She always asks pertinent questions.*

omou tsubo ni hamaru — 思う壷にはまる — *to play into someone's hands*
[lit. to fit into a jar as someone expects]

車を借りに行ったら母の思う壷にはまってしまい、一日中運転させられました。Kuruma o kari ni ittara haha no omou tsubo ni hamatte shimai, ichinichi jū unten saseraremashita. *Although I had gone to borrow my mother's car, I played into her hands and drove her around all day.*

---

tsue — 杖 — *cane*

tsue tomo hashira tomo tanomu — 杖とも柱とも頼む — *to rely on someone or something a lot*
[lit. to rely on someone or something like a cane or a pillar]

今度の計画では、彼女を杖とも柱とも頼んでいます。Kondo no kikaku dewa, kanojo o tsue tomo hashira tomo tanonde imasu. *We're relying on her a lot for the new project.*

---

tsuke — 付け — *bill*

tsuke ga mawatte kuru — 付けが回ってくる — *to come back to haunt one*
[lit. The bill comes to one later.]

この一年間、運動をせずにたくさん食べていた付けが回ってきました。Kono ichi nen kan, undō o sezu ni takusan tabete ita tsuke ga mawatte kimashita. *My eating a lot without any exercise for the past year has come back to haunt me.*

tsuki — 月 — *moon*

tsuki to suppon — 月とすっぽん — *as different as night and day*
[lit. the moon and a terrapin]

彼らは兄弟ですが、性格も趣味も月とすっぽんです。Karera wa
kyōdai desu ga, seikaku mo shumi mo tsuki to suppon desu. *Although
they're brothers, their characters and tastes are as different as night and
day.*

---

tsume — 爪 — *fingernail*

tsume ni hi o tomosu — 爪に灯をともす — *to lead a frugal life*
[lit. to light one's fingernail]

彼女はお金を貯めるため、爪に灯をともして暮らしました。Kanojo
wa okane o tameru tame, tsume ni hi o tomoshite kurashimashita. *To
save money, she led a frugal life.*

tsume no aka o senjite nomu — 爪の垢を煎じて呑む — *to learn a
lesson from someone*
[lit. to brew the dirt from someone's fingernails and drink it]

仕事熱心の彼の爪の垢を煎じて呑みなさい。Shigoto nesshin no kare
no tsume no aka o senjite nomimasai. *You should learn a lesson from
him for his devotion to his work.*

tsume o togu — 爪を研ぐ — *to prepare oneself to do something*
[lit. to sharpen one's fingernails]

彼女は離婚以来、前夫に仕返しするために爪を研いでいます。Kanojo
wa rikon irai, zenpu ni shikaeshi suru tame ni tsume o toide imasu.

Since the divorce, she's been preparing herself to take revenge against her former husband.

---

tsumi — 罪 — *guilt, sin, offense*
tsumi no nai — 罪のない — *innocent*
[lit. no offense intended]
彼は、彼女の罪のない冗談に腹を立てました。Kare wa, kanojo no tsumi no nai jōdan ni hara o tatemashita. *He got angry at her innocent joke.*

tsumi o kiseru — 罪を着せる — *to pin the blame on someone else*
[lit. to force someone to wear one's guilt]
従業員の不満に、彼女は私に罪を着せようとしました。Jūgyōin no fuman ni, kanojo wa watakushi ni tsumi o kiseyō to shimashita. *To respond to the employees' complaints, she tried to pin the blame on me.*

---

tsumuji — 旋毛 — *spiral of hair on the crown of the head*
tsumuji o mageru — 旋毛を曲げる — *to become nasty*
[lit. to bend the spiral of hair on the crown of one's head]
彼女は彼の言ったことに旋毛を曲げて、仕事を拒否しています。
Kanojo wa kare no itta koto ni tsumuji o magete, shigoto o kyohi shite imasu. *After what he said, she became nasty and is refusing to work.*

---

tsuna — 綱 — *rope*
tsunawatari o suru — 綱渡りをする — *to take a risk*
[lit. to try to walk across a tightrope]
彼は、先端技術投資で綱渡りしています。Kare wa, sentan gijutsu tōshi de tsunawatari o shite imasu. *He's taking a risk by investing in advanced technology.*

tanomi no tsuna — 頼みの綱 — *one's only hope*
[lit. the rope for one's hope]
この問題を解決するには、彼女が頼みの綱です。Kono mondai o kaiketsu suru niwa, kanojo ga tanomi no tsuna desu. *She's our only hope to solve this problem.*

---

tsuno — 角 — *horn*
tsuno o dasu — 角を出す — *to get one's back up*
[lit. to reveal one's horns]

妻が角を出さないように、早く帰らなければなりません。Tsuma ga tsuno o dasanai yō ni, hayaku kaeranakereba narimasen. *I should go back home early so that my wife won't get her back up.*

tsuno o hayasu — 角を生やす — *(for one's wife) to be jealous*
[lit. to grow horns]

妻は理由もなく、秘書と私の関係に角を生やしています。Tsuma wa riyū mo naku, hisho to watakushi no kankei ni tsuno o hayashite imasu. *For no reason, my wife is jealous of the relationship between my secretary and me.*

tsuno o oru — 角を折る — *to drop one's stubborn attitude*
[lit. to break one's horns]

彼女はやっと角を折って、パーティーに出席することに同意しました。Kanojo wa yatto tsuno o otte, pātī ni shusseki suru koto ni dōi shimashita. *Dropping her stubborn attitude, she finally agreed to attend the party.*

tsuno o tsukiawaseru — 角を突き合わせる — *to be at odds with each other*
[lit. to put horns against each other]

彼らは取るに足りない問題で、角を突き合わせています。Karera wa toru ni tarinai mondai de, tsuno o tsukiawasete imasu. *They're at odds with each other over minor things.*

---

tsura — 面 — *face*

tsura no kawa ga atsui — 面の皮が厚い — *thick-skinned, insensitive*
[lit. One's facial skin is thick.]

彼は面の皮が厚くて、遠慮を知りません。Kare wa tsura no kawa ga atsukute, enryo o shirimasen. *Since he's thick-skinned, he doesn't know what modesty is.*

tsurayogoshi — 面汚し — *disgrace*
[lit. dirtying someone's face]

彼女は、家族の面汚しです。Kanojo wa, kazoku no tsurayogoshi desu. *She's a disgrace to the family.*

ii tsura no kawa — いい面の皮 — *Serves (someone) right!*
[lit. good for someone's facial skin]

彼は、仕事怠慢で首を切られました。いい面の皮です。Kare wa, shigoto taiman de kubi o kiraremashita. Ii tsura no kawa desu. *He got fired for his negligence on the job. Serves him right!*

tsuraate ni — 面当てに — *out of spite*
[lit. to hit someone's face]
彼は彼女への面当てに、彼女の悪口を言っています。Kare wa kanojo e no tsuraate ni, kanojo no warukuchi o itte imasu. *He's badmouthing her out of spite.*

tsuru — 鶴 — *crane*
tsuru no hitokoe — 鶴の一声 — *voice of authority*
[lit. a crane's one voice]
父親の鶴の一声で、子供は喧嘩を止めました。Chichioya no tsuru no hitokoe de, kodomo wa kenka o yamemashita. *At the sound of their father's voice, the children stopped fighting.*

u — 鵜 — *cormorant*
u no me taka no me de — 鵜の目鷹の目で — *with sharp eyes*
[lit. with the eyes of a cormorant or a hawk]
彼女は、鵜の目鷹の目で投資の機会をうかがっています。Kanojo wa, u no me taka no me de tōshi no kikai o ukagatte imasu. *She's waiting with sharp eyes for an investment opportunity.*

unomi ni suru — 鵜呑みにする — *to swallow*
[lit. to swallow something as a cormorant does]
人の言うことをすぐ鵜呑みにしないで、最初にそれを確かめなさい。Hito no iu koto o sugu unomi ni shinai de, saisho ni sore o tashikamenasai. *You should examine what others say instead of swallowing it immediately.*

udatsu — うだつ — *short pillar supporting a ridgepole*
udatsu ga agaranai — うだつが上がらない — *to be unable to get ahead*
[lit. A short pillar supporting a ridgepole does not go up.]
彼はこの会社で十年になりますが、全然うだつが上がりません。Kare wa kono kaisha de jū nen ni narimasu ga, zenzen udatsu ga agarimasen. *He's been with this company for ten years but can't get ahead at all.*

ude — 腕 — *arm*

ude ga agaru — 腕が上がる — *One's skill improves.*
[lit. One's arms go up.]
最近、ゴルフの腕が上がりました。Saikin, gorufu no ude ga
agarimashita. *My golf has improved recently.*

ude ga kiku — 腕が利く — *to be capable*
[lit. One's arms are effective.]
この仕事には、腕が利く人が必要です。Kono shigoto niwa, ude ga
kiku hito ga hitsuyō desu. *We need someone capable for this job.*

ude ga naru — 腕が鳴る — *to be itching to do something*
[lit. One's arms are ringing.]
明日テニス大会に出るので、腕が鳴っています。Ashita tenisu taikai
ni deru node, ude ga natte imasu. *I'm itching to play tennis in the
competition tomorrow.*

ude ga tatsu — 腕が立つ — *skilled*
[lit. One's arms stand out.]
彼女は腕が立つ弁護士です。Kanojo wa ude ga tatsu bengoshi desu.
She's a skilled lawyer.

ude ni oboe ga aru — 腕に覚えがある — *to be confident of one's ability*
[lit. to remember something in one's arms]
水泳なら、腕に覚えがあります。Suiei nara, ude ni oboe ga arimasu.
I'm confident of my ability at swimming.

ude ni yori o kakeru — 腕によりをかける — *to outdo oneself*
[lit. to apply strands to one's arms]
妻は腕によりをかけて、子供の誕生日のためにケーキを焼きました。
Tsuma wa ude ni yori o kakete, kodomo no tanjōbi no tame ni kēki o
yakimashita. *My wife outdid herself baking a cake for our child's
birthday.*

ude o furuu — 腕を振るう — *to exercise one's skill*
[lit. to arouse one's arms]
夫は週末は、写真に腕を振るっています。Otto wa shūmatsu wa,
shashin ni ude o furutte imasu. *My husband is exercising his skill at
photography on the weekends.*

ude o kau — 腕を買う — *to value someone's skills*
[lit. to buy someone's arms]
会社は彼女の会計の腕を買って、経理部の責任者にしました。
Kaisha wa kanojo no kaikei no ude o katte, keiribu no sekininsha ni

shimashita. *Valuing her skills, the company put her in charge of the accounting office.*

ude o migaku — 腕を磨く — *to polish one's skill*
[lit. to polish one's arms]
彼はイタリア料理の腕を磨くために、ローマへ行きます。Kare wa Itaria ryōri no ude o migaku tame ni, Roma e ikimasu. *He'll go to Rome to polish his skill at Italian cooking.*

udezuku de — 腕ずくで — *by force*
[lit. thoroughly by means of one's arms]
彼女は腕ずくで、彼にその計画に同意させました。Kanojo wa udezuku de, kare ni sono keikaku ni dōi sasemashita. *She made him agree to the plan by force.*

---

udo — 独活 — *udo plant*
udo no taiboku — 独活の大木 — *big lout*
[lit. an *udo* plant grown to be a tree]
彼は独活の大木で、何の役にも立ちません。Kare wa udo no taiboku de, nan no yaku nimo tachimasen. *He's such a big lout that he isn't good at anything.*

---

ue — 上 — *top, high*
ue niwa ue ga aru — 上には上がある — *to go someone one better*
[lit. There is a top above a top.]
彼女は彼より金持ちだそうです。上には上があるものですね。Kanojo wa kare yori kanemochi da sō desu. Ue niwa ue ga aru mono desu ne. *I hear that she's richer than he. There's always someone to go you one better.*

ue o shita e no ōsawagi — 上を下への大騒ぎ — *chaos*
[lit. confusion in which things that should be kept high are put low and vice versa]
地震でビルの電気が切れ、上を下への大騒ぎになりました。Jishin de biru no denki ga kire, ue o shita e no ōsawagi ni narimashita. *The loss of electricity in the building during the earthquake caused chaos.*

---

ukime — 憂き目 — *misfortune*
ukime o miru — 憂き目を見る — *to go through hardship*
[lit. to see misfortune]
一年も失業するという憂き目を見ました。Ichi nen mo shitsugyō suru

to iu ukime o mimashita.   I went through the hardship of being
unemployed for a year.

---

uma — 馬 — horse
uma ga au — 馬が合う — to get along well with someone
[lit. A horse is just right.]
彼は、お父さんと馬が合いません。Kare wa, otōsan to uma ga
aimasen.   He doesn't get along well with his father.

shiriuma ni noru — 尻馬に乗る — to follow someone blindly
[lit. to ride the last horse in a pack]
彼女は人の尻馬に乗ってばかりいて、自分の意見がありません。
Kanojo wa hito no shiriuma ni notte bakari ite, jibun no iken ga
arimasen.   She always follows other people blindly and doesn't have
opinions of her own.

---

umai — 旨い — delicious
umai shiru o suu — 旨い汁を吸う — to get all the credit or profit
[lit. to sip delicious juice]
共同投資なのに、彼は自分だけうまい汁を吸おうとしています。
Kyōdō tōshi nanoni, kare wa jibun dake umai shiru o suō to shite imasu.
Although it's a joint investment, he's attempting to get all the profit for
himself.

---

umi — 生み — giving birth
umi no kurushimi — 生みの苦しみ — creative anxiety
[lit. labor pains]
彼女はその本を書くのに、生みの苦しみを味わいました。Kanojo
wa sono hon o kaku noni, umi no kurushimi o ajiwaimashita.   While
writing that book, she experienced creative anxiety.

---

umu — 有無 — existence or non-existence
umu o iwasazu — 有無を言わさず — willy-nilly
[lit. by not allowing someone to say existence or non-existence]
父は子供たちに有無を言わさず、お使いをさせました。Chichi wa
kodomotachi ni umu o iwasazu, otsukai o sasemashita.   Our father
made his children run errands willy-nilly.

---

un — 雲 — cloud

undei no sa — 雲泥の差 — world of difference
[lit. the difference between clouds and mud]
彼らの背景には、雲泥の差があります。Karera no haikei niwa,
   undei no sa ga arimasu.   There's a world of difference in their
   backgrounds.

unagi — 鰻 — eel

unagi no nedoko — 鰻の寝床 — long narrow place
[lit. an eel's bed]
彼の店は、鰻の寝床のような場所でした。Kare no mise wa, unagi no
   nedoko no yō na basho deshita.   His shop was a long narrow place.

unaginobori ni agaru — 鰻登りに上がる — to skyrocket
[lit. to go up high as an eel does]
最近の映画の大ヒットで、その俳優の人気は鰻登りに上がりました。
   Saishin no eiga no dai hitto de, sono haiyū no ninki wa unaginobori ni
   agarimashita.   With his latest movie a big hit, the actor's popularity has
   skyrocketed.

ura — 裏 — back, reverse side, lining

ura de ito o hiku — 裏で糸を引く — to maneuver behind the scenes
[lit. to pull a string from behind]
彼女が交渉を扱っていますが、裏で糸を引いているのは彼です。
   Kanojo ga kōshō o atsukatte imasu ga, ura de ito o hiite iru no wa kare

desu.   *She's handling the negotiations, but he's the one who is maneuvering behind the scenes.*

ura no ura o iku — 裏の裏を行く — *to outwit someone*
[lit. to go back and behind]
競争相手の裏の裏を行って、契約を取り付けました。Kyōsō aite no ura no ura o itte, keiyaku o toritsukemashita.   *We outwitted our competitors and won the contract.*

ura o kaku — 裏をかく — *to outsmart someone*
[lit. to scratch someone's back]
彼の裏をかいて、彼女との契約を取り付けました。Kare no ura o kaite, kanojo to no keiyaku o toritsukemashita.   *I outsmarted him and got her agreement on a contract.*

ura o toru — 裏を取る — *to make certain*
[lit. to check linings]
彼女の言っていることが本当かどうか、裏を取る必要があります。Kanojo no itte iru koto ga hontō ka dō ka, ura o toru hitsuyō ga arimasu. *We need to make certain if what she's saying is true or not.*

urabanashi — 裏話 — *inside story*
[lit. backtalk]
彼から彼女の過去について、裏話を聞きました。Kare kara kanojo no kako ni tsuite, urabanashi o kikimashita.   *I heard the inside story from him about her past.*

urahara — 裏腹 — *inconsistent*
[lit. a back and a belly]
彼の証言は裏腹です。Kare no shōgen wa urahara desu.   *His testimony is inconsistent.*

urakata — 裏方 — *one who remains behind the scenes*
[lit. a stagehand]
彼女は代議士の裏方として、政策を作っています。Kanojo wa daigishi no urakata to shite, seisaku o tsukutte imasu.   *She's formulating policies for the congressman while remaining behind the scenes.*

urame ni deru — 裏目に出る — *to backfire*
[lit. to come out inside out]
計画を批判したのが裏目に出て、仕事を任されてしまいました。Kcikaku o hihan shita no ga urame ni dete, shigoto o makasarete

shimaimashita. *My criticism of the plan backfired, and I was put in charge of carrying it out.*

uraomote — 裏表 — *two-faced*
[lit. back and surface]
彼の態度には裏表があるので、信用できません。Kare no taido niwa uraomote ga aru node, shin-yō dekimasen. *We can't trust him because he's two-faced.*

urazuke ga aru — 裏付けがある — *to have proof*
[lit. to have a lining]
私の議論には、裏付けがあります。Watakushi no giron niwa, urazuke ga arimasu. *I have proof for my argument.*

---

urami — 恨み — *grudge*
urami o kau — 恨みを買う — *to cause someone to hold a grudge*
[lit. to buy someone's grudge]
助言したつもりなのに、彼女の恨みを買ってしまいました。Jogen shita tsumori nanoni, kanojo no urami o katte shimaimashita. *I thought I was advising her, but it caused her to hold a grudge against me.*

---

ushiro — 後ろ — *back, rear*
ushiro o miseru — 後ろを見せる — *to reveal a weak point*
[lit. to show one's back]
彼女は彼と議論していて、つい後ろを見せてしまいました。Kanojo wa kare to giron shite ite, tsui ushiro o misete shimaimashita. *During the argument with him, she accidentally revealed her weak point.*

ushirogami o hikareru omoi de — 後ろ髪を引かれる思いで — *reluctantly*
[lit. with feelings as if the hair on the back of one's head is pulled back]
彼は後ろ髪を引かれる思いで、彼女に別れを告げました。Kare wa ushirogami o hikareru omoi de, kanojo ni wakare o tsugemashita. *He said good-by to her reluctantly.*

---

uso — 嘘 — *lie*
uso de katameru — 嘘で固める — *to pad one's story with lies*
[lit. to solidify one's story with lies]
彼女が自分の過去の話しを、嘘で固めていたことが分かりました。
Kanojo ga jibun no kako no hanashi o, uso de katamete ita koto ga

wakarimashita.   *We found out that she had padded the story about her past with lies.*

uso happyaku — 嘘八百 — *pack of lies*
[lit. eight hundred lies]
彼の言い訳は、嘘八百でした。Kare no iiwake wa, uso happyaku deshita.   *His excuse was a pack of lies.*

---

usugami — 薄紙 — *thin paper*
usugami o hagu yō ni — 薄紙をはぐように — *slowly but steadily (illness)*
[lit. as if peeling sheets of thin paper]
彼の病気は、薄紙をはぐようによくなっています。Kare no byōki wa, usugami o hagu yō ni yoku natte imasu.   *He's recovering from his illness slowly but steadily.*

---

utsu — 打つ — *to hit, to beat*
uteba hibiku — 打てば響く — *to be responsive*
[lit. to make sounds if one hits something]
彼に用事を頼むと、打てば響くようにしてくれます。Kare ni yōji o tanomu to, uteba hibiku yō ni shite kuremasu.   *When you ask him to do errands, he's very responsive.*

utte deru — 打って出る — *to actively enter something*
[lit. to go out beating a drum]
彼女は文学賞をもらって、文壇に打って出ました。Kanojo wa bungaku shō o moratte, bundan ni utte demashita.   *Winning a literary award, she actively entered the literary world.*

---

uwa — 上 — *upper, front*
uwamae o haneru — 上前をはねる — *to skim a percentage*
[lit. to flip the front part of a *kimono*]
彼は、労働者の賃金の上前をはねていました。Kare wa, rōdōsha no chingin no uwamae o hanete imashita.   *He was skimming a percentage of the laborers' wages.*

wa — 輪 — *wheel*

wa o kakeru — 輪をかける — *to stretch a fact*
[lit. to put wheels on a talk]
彼女は、話しに輪をかけました。Kanojo wa, hanashi ni wa o
kakemashita. *She stretched the facts in her talk.*

wa o kakete — 輪をかけて — *more*
[lit. by carrying someone or something on wheels]
お母さんは美人ですが、娘はお母さんに輪をかけてきれいです。
Okāsan wa bijin desu ga, musume wa okāsan ni wa o kakete kirei desu.
The mother is beautiful, but her daughter is more beautiful.

---

waga — 我が — *one's own*

waga i o eru — 我が意を得る — *to find something satisfying*
[lit. to get one's own wishes]
彼女の意見に我が意を得ました。Kanojo no iken ni waga i o emashita.
I found her opinion satisfying.

wagamonogao ni furumau — 我が物顔に振る舞う — *to lord it over
someone*
[lit. to act as if something is one's own]
あの会社では、社長の息子が我が物顔に振る舞っています。Ano
kaisha dewa, shachō no musuko ga wagamonogao ni furumatte imasu.
In that company, the president's son is lording it over the employees.

---

wakage — 若気 — *youthful vigor*

wakage no itari — 若気の至り — *youthful folly*
[lit. the result of youthful vigor]
彼は若気の至りで上司と口論して、仕事を辞めました。Kare wa wakage
no itari de jōshi to kōron shite, shigoto o yamemashita. *His youthful
folly caused him to have an argument with his boss and quit his job.*

---

waki — 脇 — *side, secondary*

waki ga amai — 脇が甘い — *to take things too lightly*
[lit. One's side is loose.]

彼女は何にでも脇が甘いから、すぐにだまされてしまいます。Kanojo
wa nani ni demo waki ga amai kara, sugu ni damasarete shimaimasu.
She's easily fooled because she takes everything too lightly.

wakime mo furazu — 脇目も振らず — *intently*
[lit. without casting one's eyes aside]
彼は、脇目も振らずに仕事しています。Kare wa, wakime mo furazu
ni shigoto shite imasu.　*He's working intently.*

wakiyaku ni mawaru — 脇役に回る — *to take a backseat*
[lit. to go around and take a secondary role]
彼は最近会社の経営を娘に任せて、脇役に回っています。Kare wa
saikin kaisha no keiei o musume ni makasete, wakiyaku ni mawatte
imasu.　*Recently, he's been taking a backseat by putting his daughter in
charge of managing the company.*

wakiyaku o hatasu — 脇役を果たす — *to play second fiddle to someone*
[lit. to fulfill a secondary role]
国際会議では、日本代表の脇役を果たしました。Kokusai kaigi dewa,
Nihon daihyō no wakiyaku o hatashimashita.　*I played second fiddle to
the chief Japanese delegate at the international conference.*

---

waku — 枠 — *frame*
waku ni hamaru — 枠にはまる — *to be the same old stuff*
[lit. Something fits in a frame.]
彼女の考えは枠にはまっていて、面白くありません。Kanojo no
kangae wa waku ni hamatte ite, omoshiroku arimasen.　*Her ideas are
the same old stuff and not interesting.*

---

wara — 藁 — *straw*
wara nimo sugaru — 藁にもすがる — *to be desperate (for help)*
[lit. to even cling to a straw]
財布を落として、藁にもすがる思いで道で知らない人にバス代を頼
みました。Saifu o otoshite, wara nimo sugaru omoi de michi de
shiranai hito ni basudai o tanomimashita.　*Because I lost my wallet, I
was desperate enough to ask a stranger in the street for bus fare.*

---

warai — 笑い — *laugh, smile*
warai ga tomaranai — 笑いが止まらない — *to exult*
[lit. One's laugh does not stop.]

彼は買った土地の値段が一年で倍になって、笑いが止まりません。
Kare wa katta tochi no nedan ga ichi nen de bai ni natte, warai ga
tomarimasen. *He's exulting because the price of the land doubled
within a year after his purchase.*

waraigoto dewa nai — 笑い事ではない — *It's no laughing matter.*
[lit. It's not something to laugh about.]
毎晩酔っぱらって帰ってくるなんて、笑い事ではありませんよ。
Maiban yopparatte kaette kuru nante, waraigoto dewa arimasen yo.
Every night you come back home drunk. It's no laughing matter.

waraimono ni naru — 笑い物になる — *to make a fool of oneself*
[lit. to become a target of laughter]
会議で全く見当違いの意見を述べて、笑い物になってしまいました。
Kaigi de mattaku kentō chigai no iken o nobete, waraimono ni natte
shimaimashita. *I made a fool of myself by stating a totally irrelevant
view at the meeting.*

---

ware — 我 — *oneself*

ware ni kaeru — 我に返る — *to come to one's senses*
[lit. to return to oneself]
彼女は買い物好きでしたが、去年我に返って投資を始めました。
Kanojo wa kaimonozuki deshita ga, kyonen ware ni kaette tōshi o
hajimemashita. *She loved shopping, but she came to her senses last
year and started investing money.*

ware o wasureru — 我を忘れる — *to be absorbed in something*
[lit. to forget oneself]
彼は素晴らしい景色に、全く我を忘れました。Kare wa subarashii
keshiki ni, mattaku ware o wasuremashita. *He was totally absorbed in
the beautiful scenery.*

waregachi ni — 我勝ちに — *everybody for himself or herself*
[lit. by trying to make oneself win]
ビュッフェ式パーティーでは、出席者は我勝ちに鮨を取り始めました。
Byuffe shiki pātī dewa, shussekisha wa waregachi ni sushi o
torihajimemashita. *It was everybody for himself at the buffet as people
started grabbing the sushi.*

warekansezu — 我関せず — *indifferent*
[lit. to not get oneself involved in something]
妹がお金に困っているのに、彼は我関せずで助けて上げません。

Imōto ga okane ni komatte iru noni, kare wa warekansezu de tasukete agemasen. *His young sister is in a financial mess, but he's indifferent to it and won't help her.*

waremo waremo to — 我も我もと — *by competing with one another*
[lit. Me too, me too!]
若者は、我も我もとロックコンサートの券を買おうとしています。
Wakamono wa, waremo waremo to rokku konsāto no ken o kaō to shite imasu. *The young people are competing with one another trying to buy rock concert tickets.*

wari — 割 — *rate*

wari ga warui — 割が悪い — *low-paying, unfavorable*
[lit. The rate is bad.]
今の仕事は割が悪いので、辞めようと思っています。Ima no shigoto wa wari ga warui node, yameyō to omotte imasu. *Because my current job is low paying, I'm thinking about quitting.*

wari ni awanai — 割に合わない — *to be not worth the trouble*
[lit. to not match with a rate]
その申し込みは、問題が多くて割に合いませんでした。Sono mōshikomi wa, mondai ga ōkute wari ni aimasen deshita. *The proposal had so many problems that it wasn't worth the trouble.*

wari o kuu — 割を食う — *to be a fall guy*
[lit. to eat an unfavorable rate]
共同作業の失敗で、私だけが割を食わねばなりませんでした。
Kyōdō sagyō no shippai de, watakushi dake ga wari o kuwaneba narimasen deshita. *When the joint project failed, I was the only fall guy.*

waru — 割る — *to split, to divide*

warikirenai — 割り切れない — *hard to swallow*
[lit. indivisible]
彼だけが昇進したのは、割り切れません。Kare dake ga shōshin shita nowa, warikiremasen. *It's hard to swallow the fact that only he got a promotion.*

warikiru — 割り切る — *to have a practical attitude*
[lit. to split something through]
彼は、会社の人員整理は必要と割り切っています。Kare wa, kaisha

no jin-in seiri wa hitsuyō to warikitte imasu.   *He has the practical attitude that the company's reduction in personnel is necessary.*

wattehairu — 割って入る — *to intervene*
[lit. to split and enter something]
彼らの口論に、割って入りました。Karera no kōron ni, watte hairimashita. *I intervened in their quarrel.*

---

waru — 悪 — *bad*

warufuzake — 悪ふざけ — *practical joke*
[lit. a bad joke]
彼は、悪ふざけが大好きです。Kare wa, warufuzake ga daisuki desu.
He likes to play practical jokes.

warunori suru — 悪乗りする — *to get carried away*
[lit. to take bad rides]
彼女はパーティーでのお世辞に悪乗りして、そこで直ぐ歌を歌い始めました。Kanojo wa pātī de no oseji ni warunori shite, soko de sugu uta o utaihajimemashita. *She got carried away with flattery at the party, and started to sing right there.*

---

wata — 綿 — *cotton*

wata no yō ni tsukareru — 綿のように疲れる — *to be dead tired*
[lit. to get tired like cotton]
妻は毎日小さい子供の世話で、綿のように疲れています。
Tsuma wa mainichi chiisai kodomo no sewa de, wata no yō ni tsukarete imasu. *Because my wife has to take care of our small children, she's dead tired.*

---

watari — 渡り — *ferry*

watari o tsukeru — 渡りを付ける — *to contact someone*
[lit. to make connections at a ferry]
交渉のために、その会社の代表者と渡りを付けました。Kōshō no tame ni, sono kaisha no daihyōsha to watari o tsukemashita. *For the negotiations, I contacted the representative of the company.*

ya — 矢 — *arrow*

ya mo tate mo tamarazu — 矢も楯もたまらず — *to have an uncontrollable urge*
[lit. to be unable to hold oneself back despite arrows or shields]
彼は俳優になりたくて、矢も楯もたまらず仕事を辞めました。Kare wa haiyū ni naritakute, ya mo tate mo tamarazu shigoto o yamemashita. *He had an uncontrollable urge to become an actor and quit his job.*

ya no saisoku o suru — 矢の催促をする — *to keep pressing someone for something*
[lit. to make an arrow-like demand]
高利貸しは元金と利子を揃えて返すように、矢の催促をしています。Kōrigashi wa gankin to rishi o soroete kaesu yō ni, ya no saisoku o shite imasu. *The loan shark keeps pressing me for full repayment of the principal with interest.*

shiraha no ya o tateru — 白羽の矢を立てる — *to single out*
[lit. to hit someone with a white-feathered arrow]
政府は諮問委員会の委員長として、彼女に白羽の矢を立てました。Seifu wa shimon iinkai no iinchō toshite, kanojo ni shiraha no ya o tatemashita. *The government singled her out to be the chair of an advisory committee.*

yaomote ni tatsu — 矢面に立つ — *to bear the thrust of something*
[lit. to stand in front of incoming arrows]
首相は、国民の政府批判の矢面に立っています。Shushō wa, kokumin no seifu hihan no yaomote ni tatte imasu. *The prime minister is bearing the thrust of the people's criticism of the government.*

---

ya — 野 — *field*

ya ni kudaru — 野に下る — *to leave a government job*
[lit. to go down to the field]
彼は去年野に下って、地方選挙に出馬しました。Kare wa kyonen ya ni kudatte, chihō senkyo ni shutsuba shimashita. *He left his government job last year and ran for a local election.*

---

yabu — 薮 — *bush*

yabu kara bō — 薮から棒 — *out of the blue*
[lit. a stick thrust out of a bush]

薮から棒の結婚の申し込みで、彼女は返事に困りました。Yabu kara bō no kekkon no mōshikomi de, kanojo wa henji ni komarimashita. *Because out of the blue he asked her to marry him, she didn't know what to say.*

yabuhebi ni naru — 薮蛇になる — *to backfire*
[lit. to poke at a bush and get a snake]

友達の議論の間に入ったら、薮蛇になって、彼らは私を非難し始めました。Tomodachi no giron no aida ni haittara, yabuhebi ni natte, karera wa watakushi o hinan shihajimemashita. *When I intervened in my friends' argument, it backfired and they started blaming me.*

---

yakebokkui — 焼けぼっくい — *charred stick*

yakebokkui ni hi ga tsuku — 焼けぼっくいに火がつく — *An old flame is rekindled.*
[lit. A charred stick caught fire.]

彼らは十年ぶりにあって、焼けぼっくいに火がつきました。Karera wa jū nen buri ni atte, yakebokkui ni hi ga tsukimashita. *They met for the first time in ten years, and the old flame was rekindled.*

---

yaki — 焼き — *tempering*

yaki ga mawaru — 焼きが回る — *to slow down in one's old age*
[lit. The tempering is complete.]

彼は焼きが回って、物忘れをよくします。Kare wa yaki ga mawatte, monowasure o yoku shimasu. *As he slows down in his old age, he often forgets things.*

yaki o ireru — 焼きを入れる — *to teach someone a lesson, to reprimand*
[lit. to temper someone]

彼女は最近遅刻が多いので、焼きを入れました。Kanojo wa saikin chikoku ga ōi node, yaki o iremashita. *Because she was often late to work recently, I taught her a lesson.*

yakimochi o yaku — 焼き餅を焼く — *to be jealous*
[lit. to burn grilled rice cakes]

彼は友達が映画女優と結婚したので、焼き餅を焼いています。Kare wa

tomodachi ga eiga joyū to kekkon shita node, yakimochi o yaite imasu. *He's jealous because his friend got married to a movie actress.*

---

yakusha — 役者 — *actor or actress, cast members*

yakusha ga ichimai ue — 役者が一枚上 — *to be a cut above someone*
[lit. The actor or the actress is one rank above someone.]
説得力にかけては、彼女は彼らより役者が上です。Settokuryoku ni kakete wa, kanojo wa karera yori yakusha ga ichimai ue desu. *In the art of persuasion, she's a cut above them.*

yakusha ga sorou — 役者が揃う — *Everyone is present.*
[lit. All the cast members are here.]
役者が揃ったから、会議を始めましょう。Yakusha ga sorotta kara, kaigi o hajimemashō. *Since everyone is present, let's start the meeting.*

yakushazoroi — 役者ぞろい — *to have real pros*
[lit. to have many actors and actresses]
あの弁護事務所は、役者ぞろいです。Ano bengo jimusho wa, yakushazoroi desu. *They have real pros in their law firm.*

---

yama — 山 — *mountain*

yama ga ataru — 山が当たる — *to guess right*
[lit. The mountain on which one speculated makes a profit.]
試験の問題は山が当たって、満点取りました。Shiken no mondai wa yama ga atatte, manten torimashita. *I guessed the exam questions correctly and got a perfect score.*

yama ga hazureru — 山が外れる — *to guess wrong*
[lit. The mountain on which one speculated takes a loss.]
食事が出ると期待していたのに、山が外れてお茶だけでました。Shokuji ga deru to kitai shite ita noni, yama ga hazurete ocha dake demashita. *Although I expected a meal, I guessed wrong and they served only tea.*

yama ga mieru — 山が見える — *to see the light at the end of the tunnel*
[lit. to be able to see a mountain]
長年の交渉も、やっと山が見え始めました。Naganen no kōshō mo, yatto yama ga miehajimemashita. *After many years of negotiations, we began to see the light at the end of the tunnel.*

yama o kakeru — 山をかける — *to speculate about something*
[lit. to bet a mountain on something]
彼は雨が降らないだろうと山をかけて、傘を持たずに出かけました。

Kare wa ame ga furanai darō to yama o kakere, kasa o motazu ni dekakemashita.   *He speculated that it wouldn't rain and left home without taking an umbrella.*

yama o kosu — 山を越す — *to be past the critical point*
[lit. to go over the mountain]
彼らの研究も、やっと山を越したようです。Karera no kenkyū mo, yatto yama o koeta yō desu.   *It seems that they're finally past the critical point in their research.*

yamaba o mukaeru — 山場を迎える — *to be at a crucial point*
[lit. to face a crucial moment]
成功するかどうか、彼女の事業は山場を迎えています。Seikō suru ka dō ka, kanojo no jigyō wa yamaba o mukaete imasu.   *Her business is at a crucial point in terms of whether it's going to succeed or not.*

yamakan — 山勘 — *hunch*
[lit. a calculation on mineral veins in mountains]
おじさんに会いに行ったら、小遣いをくれるという山勘が当たりました。Ojisan ni ai ni ittara, kozukai o kureru to iu yamakan ga atarimashita.   *My hunch, that when I went to see my uncle, he would give me some spending money, turned out to be right.*

yamai — 病 — *disease*
yamai kōkō ni iru — 病膏肓に入る — *Something is incurable.*
[lit. The disease is in a part too innermost to remedy.]
彼の釣りへの没頭ぶりは、今や病膏肓に入っています。Kare no tsuri e no bottōburi wa, imaya yamai kōkō ni itte imasu.   *His devotion to fishing is incurable by now.*

yamu — 止む — *to stop*
yamu ni yamarenu — 止むに止まれぬ — *unavoidable*
[lit. to be unable to stop if one tries to stop something]
彼は止むに止まれぬ事情から、学校を辞めなければなりませんでした。Kare wa yamu ni yamarenu jijō kara, gakkō o yamenakereba narimasen deshita.   *He had to quit school under unavoidable circumstances.*

yari — 槍 — *spear*
yaridama ni ageru — 槍玉にあげる — *to blame someone or something*
[lit. to stab someone with a spear]

犯罪の増加原因として、マスコミはテレビの暴力を槍玉に挙げました。
Hanzai no zōka gen-in toshite, masukomi wa terebi no bōryoku o
yaridama ni agemashita.   *The media blamed the violence on TV for the
increase in crime.*

yokoyari o ireru — 横槍を入れる — *to interfere with something*
[lit. to charge with a spear from the side]
彼女は、私たちの計画に横槍を入れようとしました。Kanojo wa,
watakushitachi no keikaku ni yokoyari o ireyō to shimashita.   *She tried
to interfere with our plan.*

---

yaseru — 痩せる — *to become thin*
yasetemo karetemo — 痩せても枯れても — *as poor as one is*
[lit. no matter how thin or withered one becomes]
痩せても枯れても、汚い仕事には関わりたくありません。
Yasetemo karetemo, kitanai shigoto niwa kakawaritaku arimasen.
As poor as I am, I won't get involved in dirty work.

yasegaman suru — やせ我慢する — *to put on a cool act*
[lit. to endure something with a thin disguise]
彼はパーティーに行きたいのに、やせ我慢していきませんでした。
Kare wa pātī ni ikitai noni, yasegaman shite ikimasen deshita.
Although he wanted to go to the party, he put on a cool act and didn't go.

---

yasui — 安い — *inexpensive*
yasukarō warukarō — 安かろう悪かろう — *You get what you pay for.*
[lit. If it's inexpensive, it will not be good.]
安かろう悪かろうと思っていましたが、この間の買い物では、安く
ていい物をたくさん見つけました。Yasukarō warukarō to omotte
imashita ga, kono aida no kaimono dewa, yasukute ii mono o takusan
mitsukemashita.   *Although I believe that you get what you pay for, I
found a lot of cheap but good-quality items while shopping the other day.*

---

yo — 世 — *society, world, era*
yo ga yo nara — 世が世なら — *in better times*
[lit. if an era was a good era for someone]
世が世なら、彼女は大政治家になっていたでしょう。Yo ga yo nara,
kanojo wa dai seijika ni natte ita deshō.   *In better times, she would have
become a great politician.*

yo ni deru — 世に出る — *to make it*
[lit. to come out in the world]
彼が芸術家として世に出てから、五年になりなす。Kare ga
geijutsuka toshite yo ni dete kara, go nen ni narimasu.   *It's been five
years since he made it as an artist.*

yo no kikoe — 世の聞こえ — *reputation*
[lit. hearing in public]
彼女は世の聞こえを気にして、人前ではタバコを吸いません。Kanojo
wa yo no kikoe o ki ni shite, hitomae dewa tabako o suimasen.   *Because
she's concerned about her reputation, she doesn't smoke in public.*

yo o saru — 世を去る — *to die*
[lit. to leave the world]
彼は、突然世を去りました。Kare wa, totsuzen yo o sarimashita.   *He
died suddenly.*

yo o shinobu — 世を忍ぶ — *to be in seclusion*
[lit. to hide oneself from society]
彼女は子供の死以来、世を忍んで暮らしています。Kanojo wa
kodomo no shi irai, yo o shinonde kurashite imasu.   *Since the death of
her child, she has been living in seclusion.*

yo o wataru — 世を渡る — *to make a living*
[lit. to walk across the world]
彼は小さなレストランのコックとして、世を渡っています。Kare
wa chiisana resutoran no kokku toshite, yo o watatte imasu.   *He makes
a living as the chef at a small restaurant.*

yowatari ga umai — 世渡りがうまい — *to know how to get ahead*
[lit. to be good at making a living]
彼女は世渡りがうまくて、各界の実力者とつき合っています。Kanojo
wa yowatari ga umakute, kakkai no jitsuryokusha to tsukiatte imasu.
*Because she knows how to get ahead, she's friendly with influential
people in many different walks of life.*

---

yo — 夜 — *night*

yo o hi ni tsuide — 夜を日に継いで — *night and day*
[lit. by connecting a night to a day]
鉄道の修復は、夜を日に継いで行われました。Tetsudō no shūfuku
wa, yo o hi ni tsuide okonawaremashita.   *They worked night and day on
the repair of the railway.*

yo o tessuru — 夜を徹する — to stay up all night
[lit. to go through an entire night]
締め切りに間に合わせるために、夜を徹して働きました。Shimekiri
ni maniawaseru tame ni, yo o tesshite hatarakimashita.   We stayed up
all night and worked to meet the deadline.

---

yobu — 呼ぶ — to call
  yobigoe ga takai — 呼び声が高い — to be prominently mentioned as
    something
[lit. Voices calling for someone are loud.]
彼は、将来首相になるという呼び声が高いです。Kare wa, shōrai
shushō ni naru to iu yobigoe ga takai desu.   He has been prominently
mentioned as a future prime minister.

  yobimizu ni naru — 呼び水になる — to trigger something
[lit. to become calling (priming) water]
価格競争の呼び水になったのは、安い輸入品の増加でした。Kakaku
kyōsō no yobimizu ni natta no wa, yasui yunyū hin no zōka deshita.
What triggered the price war was the increase of inexpensive imported
goods.

---

yodare — 涎 — saliva

yodare o tarasu — 涎を垂らす — to drool with envy
[lit. to drip one's saliva]

彼女は友達の婚約指輪を見て、涎を垂らしました。
Kanojo wa tomodachi no kon-yaku yubiwa o mite, yodare o
tarashimashita. *She drooled with envy when she saw her friend's*
engagement ring.

---

yoko — 横 — *side, sideways, lying sideways*

yoko kara mitemo tate kara mitemo — 横から見ても縦から見ても —
every inch
[lit. even looking at something sideways or vertically]
横から見ても縦から見ても、彼は本当の実業家です。Yoko kara
mitemo tate kara mitemo, kare wa hontō no jitsugyōka desu. *He's*
every inch an industrialist.

yoko no mono o tate nimo shinai — 横の物を縦にもしない — *won't*
lift a finger
[lit. to not stand up something that is lying on the floor]
他の人が忙しくても、彼女は横の物を縦にもしません。Hoka no hito
ga isogashikutemo, kanojo wa yoko no mono o tate nimo shimasen.
Even if other people are busy, she won't lift a finger.

yoko o muku — 横を向く — *to reject something*
[lit. to look sideways]
夫は、妻の頼みに横を向きました。Otto wa, tsuma no tanomi ni yoko
o mukimashita. *The husband rejected his wife's request.*

yokogamiyaburi — 横紙破り — *obstinate person*
[lit. to be difficult to tear Japanese paper sideways]
彼は横紙破りなので、一緒に仕事は出来ません。Kare wa
yokogamiyaburi nanode, issho ni shigoto wa dekimasen. *Because he's*
obstinate, we can't work with him.

yokoguruma o osu — 横車を押す — *to force one's will on someone*
[lit. to push a cart sideways]
みんなが彼女の提案に反対したけれど、彼女はそれでも横車を
押そうとしました。Minna ga kanojo no teian ni hantai shita keredo,
kanojo wa soredemo yokoguruma o osō to shimashita. *Although*
everyone opposed her proposal, she still tried to force her will on us.

yokomichi ni soreru — 横道にそれる — *to get sidetracked*
[lit. to stray into a side street]
演説が横道にそれて、彼が何をいいたかったのか分かりませんでした。
Enzetsu ga yokomichi ni sorete, kare ga nani o iitakatta no ka

wakarimasen deshita. *Because he got sidetracked during his speech, we didn't know what he wanted to say.*

---

yoku — 欲 — *greed, desire*
yoku mo toku mo nai — 欲も得もない — *to have no self-interest*
[lit. There is neither greed nor desire for gain.]
彼らの企画に、欲も得もなく助言しました。Karera no kikaku ni, yoku mo toku mo naku jogen shimashita. *With no self-interest I gave my advice on their project.*

yoku o ieba — 欲を言えば — *if one could suggest one thing*
[lit. if one can say one's desire]
この計画は素晴らしいですが、欲を言えば統計の裏付けがいります。
Kono keikaku wa subarashii desu ga, yoku o ieba tōkei no urazuke ga irimasu. *The plan is wonderful, but if I could suggest one thing, you need statistical backing.*

---

yomi — 読み — *reading*
yomi ga fukai — 読みが深い — *to be insightful*
[lit. One's reading is deep.]
彼女は景気の読みが深いので、投資の相談には最適です。Kanojo wa keiki no yomi ga fukai node, tōshi no sōdan niwa saiteki desu.
Because she is insightful about the economic climate, she's a perfect person to consult on investments.

---

yoru — 寄る — *to gather*
yoru to sawaru to — 寄ると触ると — *at every opportunity to gather*
[lit. whenever they gather or get in touch with each other]
彼らは、寄ると触ると新しい社長のうわさ話をしています。Karera wa, yoru to sawaru to atarashii shachō no uwasabanashi o shite imasu.
At every opportunity to gather, they gossip about the new president.

yotte takaru — 寄ってたかる — *to gang up on someone*
[lit. by gathering and swarming around someone]
外交問題で、野党は寄ってたかって政府を批判しています。
Gaikō mondai de, yatō wa yotte takatte seifu o hihan shite imasu.
The minority parties are ganging up on the government on diplomatic issues.

yōryō — 要領 — *point, knack*
yōryō ga ii — 要領がいい — *to be shrewd*
[lit. One's knack is good.]
彼女は要領が良くて、自分の得することには協力します。Kanojo wa yōryō ga yokute, jibun no toku suru koto niwa kyōryoku shimasu. *Since she's shrewd, she cooperates on things that are advantageous to her.*

yōryō o enai — 要領を得ない — *vague*
[lit. to not get someone's point]
彼の説明は、全然要領を得ませんでした。Kare no setsumei wa, zenzen yōryō o emasen deshita. *His explanation was very vague.*

---

yowai — 弱い — *weak*
yowane o haku — 弱音を吐く — *to whine*
[lit. to vomit the sound of weakness]
先週は仕事が厳しかったけれど、誰も弱音を吐きませんでした。
Senshū wa shigoto ga kibishikatta keredo, daremo yowane o hakimasen deshita. *Although the work was hard last week, nobody whined.*

---

yu — 湯 — *hot water*
yumizu no yō ni tsukau — 湯水のように使う — *to throw money around*
[lit. to spend money like water or hot water]
彼は大きい遺産を相続して以来、金を湯水のように使っています。
Kare wa ōkii isan o sōzoku shite irai, kane o yumizu no yō ni tsukatte imasu. *Ever since he inherited a large fortune, he's been throwing money around.*

---

yū — 勇 — *courage*
yū o kosu — 勇を鼓す — *to gather up one's courage*
[lit. to drum up one's courage]
彼女は勇を鼓して、上司に反対意見を述べました。Kanojo wa yū o koshite, jōshi ni hantai iken o nobemashita. *Gathering up her courage, she gave the opposing view to her boss.*

yūmei o haseru — 勇名を馳せる — *to win fame for one's bravery*
[lit. to make one's name run as a brave man]
彼は子供と年寄りを火事から救って、勇名を馳せました。Kare wa

kodomo to toshiyori o kaji kara sukutte, yūmei o hasemashita. *He won fame for his bravery by rescuing children and elderly people from a fire.*

yubi — 指 — *finger*

yubi o kuwaeru — 指をくわえる — *to look enviously at something*
[lit. to put a finger in one's mouth]
夫は、隣の家の新車に指をくわえています。Otto wa, tonari no ie no shinsha ni yubi o kuwaete imasu. *My husband is looking enviously at our next door neighbor's new car.*

yubi o sasu — 指を指す — *to backbite*
[lit. to point one's finger at someone]
彼女に指を指すより、言いたいことがあれば直接言いなさい。
Kanojo ni yubi o sasu yori, iitai koto ga areba chokusetsu iinasai.
If you have something to say, you should say it directly to her instead of backbiting.

yubi o someru — 指を染める — *to take something up*
[lit. to stain one's fingers]
母は五十歳の時に、絵画に指を染めました。Haha wa gojūssai no toki ni, kaiga ni yubi o somemashita. *My mother took up painting when she was fifty.*

yubiori kazoeru — 指折り数える — *to look forward to something*
[lit. to count something on one's fingers]
子供たちは、夏休みが来るのを指折り数えています。Kodomotachi wa, natsuyasumi ga kuru no o yubiori kazoete imasu. *My children are looking forward to summer recess, counting the days on their fingers.*

yubiori no — 指折りの — *prominent*
[lit. countable by bending one's fingers]
彼は、指折りの癌の専門家です。Kare wa, yubiori no gan no senmonka desu. *He is a prominent cancer researcher.*

ushiroyubi o sasareru — 後ろ指を差される — *to be talked about behind one's back*
[lit. a finger to be pointed at one's back]
後で後ろ指を指されないように、会議では非常に気を付けて話しました。Ato de ushiroyubi o sasarenai yō ni, kaigi dewa hijō ni ki o tsukete hanashimashita. *I spoke extremely carefully so that I wouldn't be talked about behind my back later.*

yume — 夢 — *dream*

yume o egaku — 夢を描く — *to picture something in one's mind*
[lit. to draw a dream]

彼女は、いつか医者になる夢を描いています。Kanojo wa, itsuka isha ni naru yume o egaite imasu. *She's picturing in her mind that she'll become a doctor some day.*

yume o idaku — 夢を抱く — *to have a dream*
[lit. to embrace a dream]

彼は、来年アメリカの大学に行く夢を抱いています。
Kare wa, rainen Amerika no daigaku ni iku yume o idaite imasu.
He has a dream of going to a university in the United States next year.

yume o miru — 夢を見る — *to dream*
[lit. to see a dream]

彼は、いつか金持ちになる夢を見ています。Kare wa, itsuka kanemochi ni naru yume o mite imasu. *He is dreaming of becoming rich someday.*

yume o takusu — 夢を託す — *to delegate one's hope to someone*
[lit. to entrust someone with one's dream]

彼は音楽家になる夢を、息子に託しました。Kare wa ongakuka ni naru yume o, musuko ni takushimashita. *He delegated his hope of becoming a musician to his son.*

yumeji o tadoru — 夢路をたどる — *to sleep, to fall asleep*
[lit. to follow a dream street]

子供たちは一日泳いでいたので、夕食後直ぐに夢路をたどりました。
Kodomotachi wa ichinichi oyoide ita node, yūshoku go sugu ni yumeji o tadorimashita. *Because the children were swimming all day, they fell asleep right after dinner.*

yumemonogatari — 夢物語 — *fantasy*
[lit. a dream story]

彼女は、彼の夢物語を信じています。Kanojo wa, kare no yumemonogatari o shinjite imasu. *She believes in his fantasy.*

masayume — 正夢 — *a dream that comes true*
[lit. a correct dream]

夕べ見た夢が、正夢になりました。Yube mita yume ga, masayume ni narimashita. *The dream I had last night came true.*

yūmei — 有名 — *famous*

yūmei mujitsu — 有名無実 — *in name only*
[lit. famous but no content]

あの歌手は有名無実で、歌の才能はありません。Ano kashu wa yūmei mujitsu de, uta no sainō wa arimasen.   *He's a singer in name only; he doesn't have any talent.*

yūmei zei — 有名税 — *price one has to pay for fame*
[lit. a tax on being famous]

嫌がらせ電話が、彼の有名税の一つです。Iyagarase denwa ga, kare no yūmei zei no hitotsu desu.   *Receiving harassing calls is part of the price he has to pay for fame.*

yumi — 弓 — *bow*

yumi o hiku — 弓を引く — *to rebel against someone*
[lit. to pull a bow]

その店員は店主に弓を引いて、競争相手の店で働き始めました。Sono ten-in wa tenshu ni yumi o hiite, kyōsō aite no mise de hatarakihajimemashita.   *The clerk rebelled against the shop owner and started working for a rival shop.*

yumi ore ya tsukiru made — 弓折れ矢尽きるまで — *to the end*
[lit. until a bow breaks and arrows are all gone]

一度事業を始めたからには、弓折れ矢尽きるまで頑張るつもりです。Ichido jigyō o hajimeta kara niwa, yumi ore ya tsukiru made ganbaru tsumori desu.   *Now that I've started my own business, I'll hold fast to the end.*

yūzū — 融通 — *adaptability*

yūzū ga kiku — 融通が利く — *to be flexible*
[lit. One's adaptability works.]

彼は融通が利くので、彼の意見はとても参考になります。Kare wa yūzū ga kiku node, kare no iken wa totemo sankō ni narimasu.   *Because he's flexible, his comments are quite instructive.*

Z

za — 座 — *seat, occasion*

za ga motenai — 座が持てない — *to not be able to carry on something*
[lit. to not be able to sustain an occasion]

彼女に紹介されましたが、その後、座が持てなくて困りました。
Kanojo ni shōkai saremashita ga, sono ato, za ga motenakute komarimashita. *I was introduced to her, but I had trouble carrying on a conversation afterward.*

za ga shirakeru — 座が白ける — *to spoil an occasion*
[lit. to make an occasion white]

素晴らしいパーティ－だったのに、彼が仕事の問題を述べ続けて、座が白けてしまいました。 Subarashii pātī datta noni, kare ga shigoto no mondai o nobetsuzukete, za ga shirakete shimaimashita. *Although it was a great party, he spoiled the occasion by carrying on about his problems at work.*

za ni tsuku — 座に着く — *to assume a position*
[lit. to arrive at a seat]

会社の再編成の後、私が社長の座に着きました。 Kaisha no saihensei no ato, watakushi ga shachō no za ni tsukimashita. *After the reorganization of the company, I assumed the position of president.*

za o hazusu — 座をはずす — *to leave a room*
[lit. to get out of a seat]

ちょっと内密の話しがあるので、座をはずしていただけませんか。
Chotto naimitsu no hanashi ga aru node, za o hazushite itadakemasen ka. *Since we're having a private talk, would you mind leaving the room?*

za o torimotsu — 座を取り持つ — *to act as a mediator*
[lit. to handle an occasion]

彼らの議論が終わりそうもないので、座を取り持つことにしました。
Karera no giron ga owarisō mo nai node, za o torimotsu koto ni shimashita. *I decided to act as a mediator because otherwise their argument would go on forever.*

chūza suru — 中座する — *to leave in the middle of something*
[lit. to get out of one's seat in the middle of something]

前からの面会の約束があつて、会議の途中で中座しました。Mae
kara no menkai no yakusoku ga atte, kaigi no tochū de chūza shimashita.
I left in the middle of the meeting because I had a previous engagement.

zehi — 是非 — *right or wrong*
zehi mo naku — 是非もなく — *without question*
[lit. without judging something to be right or wrong]
それは、是非もなくやらせていただきます。Sore wa, zehi mo naku
yarasete itadakimasu.   *Without question, I would love to do it.*

zen — 善 — *goodness*
zen wa isoge — 善は急げ — *better sooner than later*
[lit. to hurry up with something good]
善は急げで、ダイエットを始めました。Zen wa isoge de, daietto o
hajimemashita.   *I've started a diet; better sooner than later.*

zengo — 前後 — *front and rear*
zengo o wakimaezu — 前後をわきまえず — *recklessly*
[lit. to not know front or rear]
彼は前後をわきまえず、上司を批判しました。Kare wa zengo o
wakimaezu, jōshi o hihan shimashita.   *He criticized his supervisor
recklessly.*

zengo o wasureru — 前後を忘れる — *to be beside oneself*
[lit. to forget the front from the rear]
彼女は突然の悲しい知らせに、前後を忘れて泣きました。Kanojo
wa totsuzen no kanashii shirase ni, zengo o wasurete nakimashita. *She
was beside herself crying over the sudden sad news.*

zoku — 俗 — *common, banal*
zoku na — 俗な — *vulgar*
[lit. too much for common taste]
その雑誌は俗な記事が多いので、取るのを止めました。Sono zasshi
wa zoku na kiji ga ōi node, toru no o yamemashita.   *Because there are
many vulgar articles in that magazine, I stopped subscribing to it.*

zokuaku na — 俗悪な — *gross*
[lit. worldly bad]
最近は、テレビに俗悪な番組が増えています。Saikin wa, terebi ni

zokuaku na bangumi ga fuete imasu. *There are more and more gross programs on TV nowadays.*

zokubutsu — 俗物 — *a Philistine*
[lit. a banal person]
彼女は政治評論家を装っていますが、実は俗物です。 Kanojo wa seiji hyōronka o yosootte imasu ga, jitsu wa zokubutsu desu. *She pretends to be a commentator on politics, but in reality she's a Philistine.*

---

zu — 頭 — *head*

zu ga takai — 頭が高い — *arrogant*
[lit. One's head is high.]
彼は頭が高いので、渉外部には向きません。 Kare wa zu ga takai node, shōgai bu niwa mukimasen. *He's so arrogant that he isn't suitable for the public relations department.*

zutsū no tane — 頭痛の種 — *source of worry*
[lit. the seed of a headache]
あの会社では、労使関係が頭痛の種です。 Ano kaisha dewa, rōshi kankei ga zutsū no tane desu. *Labor-management relations are a source of worry in that company.*

---

zu — 図 — *chart, plan*

zu ni ataru — 図に当たる — *to be successful*
[lit. to get a plan right]
宣伝活動が図に当たって、我が社の売り上げが急増しました。 Senden katsudō ga zu ni atatte, waga sha no uriage ga kyūzō shimashita. *Because the advertising campaign was successful, our company's sales jumped up.*

zu ni noru — 図に乗る — *to have a swelled head*
[lit. to ride on a plan]
彼女は社長の秘書になって、図に乗っています。 Kanojo wa shachō no hisho ni natte, zu ni notte imasu. *She has had a swelled head since she became the president's secretary.*

zuboshi o sasu — 図星をさす — *to hit the nail on the head*
[lit. to point out a star on a chart]
彼は大きい地震を予言しましたが、まさに図星でした。 Kare wa ōkii jishin o yogen shimashita ga, masa ni zuboshi deshita. *He predicted a big earthquake, and he hit the nail on the head.*

ENGLISH-JAPANESE INDEX

The following is a selective index of useful words from the English translations of Japanese idioms. For example, if you wish to know a Japanese idiom associated with the word "alive," you should go to page 30 and locate "alive," which would be linked with the idiom "chi ga kayotte iru."

E
N
G
L
I
S
H
·
J
A
P
A
N
E
S
E

I
N
D
E
X

ENGLISH-JAPANESE INDEX

ENGLISH·JAPANESE INDEX

PART II
ENGLISH-JAPANESE

第２部
英語イディオム

Preface to Part II

Whether you are learning Japanese for personal, academic, or professional reasons, one of your main goals is to communicate with native speakers of the language. This means learning not only the grammar, pronunciation, and vocabulary, but also, as presented in Part I of this book, the idioms of Japanese. Now, in Part II, you will learn the other side of the coin, how to express the idioms of English to Japanese speakers.

In a conversation with a Japanese colleague, you may want to say that you're on pins and needles awaiting the results of contract negotiations. Or that something is on the tip of your tongue. How do you express these idioms in Japanese? Are there Japanese equivalents? You will find the answers here.

As you look through the English-Japanese idioms, you will see that in some cases an English idiom can be translated by a Japanese idiom; in most cases an English idiom is best translated by the meaning. Thus the English idiom "cast (one's) pearls before swine" is translated by the Japanese idiom *neko ni koban*, which means, literally, "give gold coins to a cat." But for "bury the hatchet," no such match exists, so the translation is *wakai suru*, for "get back on friendly terms."

Idioms are entered by key English words, listed alphabetically. To find an idiom, look under the key word. Each English idiom is followed by the Japanese meaning in both Japanese characters and Romaji, then an English sentence to illustrate the usage, and the Japanese translation.

As you use English-Japanese Idioms, not only will you be able to express your thoughts more confidently in Japanese, you'll gain new insights about the relationship between language and culture in both Japan and the English-speaking world.

日本人読者への序文

英語のイディオム

　第1篇の序文で、慣用句は単なる複合語ではなく、単語の組み合わせによって別の意味をもたらすものとして扱うと述べた。第2編でもそれは同様で、英語のイディオムも構成要素をつなぎ合わせただけでは分からない、独自の意味合いを持っているものという解釈に基づいている。

　イディオム、即ち慣用句は、文字通り人々が慣れ親しんで用いてきた語句。つまり、ネイティブスピーカーが好んで、或いは無意識によく使うことになる。生活と社会を反映しているゆえに、話し言葉ばかりでなく、かしこまらない書き言葉にもひんぱんに出てくる。しかし学校の教科書では学ぶ機会が少ないだけに、英語環境の中で戸惑うことがあるのもイディオムだ。

日本人としてのイディオムの用途

　ここで、改めて英語のイディオムの重要性を説く必要はないと思う。会話は当然のこと、新聞、雑誌、映画、テレビ番組などにもイディオムがあふれており、それの理解は欠かせないからだ。

　ここ第2編では、英語が自国語の人が英語のイディオムを日本語で表現できることばかりでなく、日本人がそれを学ぶことも目標としている。英語のイディオムの意味がつかめずにまごついたり、文字通りに受けとめて誤解してしまう。このようなことを避けたいなら、日頃からそれを知り、慣れておくことが大切になる。英語らしい英語の最たるもの。それがイディオムだといっても過言ではない。

　イディオムを知ることで、言葉ばかりか、文化や社会への理解度も深まるだろう。更に英語が上達すればするほど、言い回しの選択として、これが欠かせなくなる。またしゃれた言い方、気の利いた言い方などをして、ネイティブスピーカーを感銘させることが出来る利点もあるのがイディオムだろう。

　第2編では、ことわざも少々あるが、主として2000を越す英語のイディオムが選ばれている。イディオムの数に限りはないが、ここでの掲載分を知ることにより、英語の理解力が深まることは疑いない。

体裁と使い方

第2編は、次のようにアレンジされている。

　英語の見出し語、見出し語の下の英語のイディオムの双方とも、アルファベット順を追っている。
　各見出し語は、日本語、ローマ字を伴う。各見出し語の下には、それに関連するイディオムが続く。各イディオムとも、それに相当する日本語が、日本語、ローマ字の順に載せてあり、英語の用例、日本語訳、ローマ字訳が与えてある。
　知りたいイディオムの見つけ方だが、キーワード、つまり見出し語を利用する。すなわち、まず目的のイディオムの中から鍵になる言葉を選び、次にそれを見出し語として引けばいい。そこには関連のイディオムがアルファベット順に載せてあるから、容易に見つけることができるはずだ。

最後に

英語のイディオムには、まずそれに相当する日本語の慣用句があればそれを、無ければ、それに近い口語的表現を用いるようにしている。これによって、普段から親しみ深い日本語の表現との関連を知ることにより、そこから英語のイディオムにも親近感を持っていただければ幸いである。

account — 詳しい説明、帳簿 — *kuwashii setsumei, chōbo*
　blow-by-blow account/description — こまかい説明 — *komakai setsumei*
　The announcer gave a blow-by-blow account of the baseball game.
　アナウンサ‐は、野球の試合をこまかく伝えました。*Anaunsā wa, yakyū no shiai o komakaku tsutaemashita.*

　cook the accounts — 帳簿をごまかす — *chōbo o gomakasu*
　The bookkeeper was fired because he had been cooking the accounts.
　会計係は、帳簿をごまかしていたので首になりました。*Kaikeigakari wa, chōbo o gomakashite ita node kubi ni narimashita.*

---

ace — 切り札 — *kirifuda*
　ace in the hole — 最高の切り札 — *saikō no kirifuda*
　Although she's a college professor, her law degree is her ace in the hole.
　彼女は大学教授でも、最高の切り札は弁護士の資格です。*Kanojo wa daigaku kyōju demo, saikō no kirifuda wa bengoshi no shikaku desu.*

　hold all the aces — 切り札を全て握っている — *kirifuda o subete nigitte iru*
　He can't help but succeed; as the boss's son, he holds all the aces. 彼の
　出世は疑いなし。社長の息子で切り札を全て握っているのが、
　その理由です。*Kare no shusse wa utagai nashi. Shachō no musuko de kirifuda o subete nigitte iru no ga, sono riyū desu.*

---

act — 行為 — *kōi*
　act of God — 天災、不可抗力 — *tensai, fukukōryoku*
　The storm was devastating, but you can't blame anyone for an act of God.
　嵐は大被害をもたらしましたが、天災を人のせいにすることは
　出来ません。*Arashi wa dai higai o motarashimashita ga, tensai o hito no sei ni suru koto wa dekimasen.*

　caught in the act — 現場を目撃される — *genba o mokugeki sareru*
　While robbing a bank, the thief was caught in the act by the video monitor.
　強盗は銀行を襲っている最中、現場をビデオカメラで写されて

しまいました。*Gōtō wa ginkō o osotte iru saichū, genba o bideo kamera de utsusarete shimaimashita.*

get one's act together — まともになる — *matomo ni naru*

Unless you get your act together and start producing, you're going to be fired.　もっとまともになって仕事の成果を上げないと、首になりますよ。*Motto matomo ni natte shigoto no seika o agenai to, kubi ni narimasu yo.*

read someone the riot act — 厳しく叱りつける — *kibishiku shikaritsukeru*

When the outfielder dropped two successive fly balls, the manager read him the riot act.　外野の選手がフライを続けて二つ落したとき、監督は選手を厳しく叱りつけました。*Gaiya no senshu ga furai o tsuzukete futatsu otoshita toki, kantoku wa senshu o kibishiku shikaritsukemashita.*

tough act to follow — 抜群 — *batsugun*

Although the injured quarterback was a tough act to follow, his replacement did a great job.　負傷したクォーターバックは抜群だったけれど、代わりの選手も見事に役割を果たしました。*Fushō shita kuōtābakku wa batsugun datta keredo, kawari no senshu mo migoto ni yakuwari o hatashimashita.*

---

action — 行い — *okonai*

Actions speak louder than words. — 口より実践。 — *Kuchi yori jissen.*

I wish they'd follow through on their promises. Actions speak louder than words.　彼らが約束を果たすことを望んでいます。大切なのは、口より実践なんですから。*Karera ga yakusoku o hatasu koto o nozonde imasu. Taisetsu na no wa, kuchi yori jissen nan desu kara.*

Adam — アダム — *Adamu*

not know someone from Adam — 誰か全然知らない — *dareka zenzen shiranai*

Who's that guy with my daughter? I don't know him from Adam.　娘と一緒にいるあの男は誰ですか。私は誰か全然知りません。*Musume to issho ni iru ano otoko wa dare desu ka. Watakushi wa dareka zenzen shirimasen.*

---

ado — 騒ぎ — *sawagi*
　much ado about nothing — 空騒ぎ — *karasawagi*
　His plans to expand the business are always much ado about nothing.
　彼の事業拡張計画は、いつも空騒ぎです。*Kare no jigyō kakuchō*
　keikaku wa, itsumo karasawagi desu.

---

age — 年 — *toshi*
　act one's age — 年相応に振る舞う — *toshi sōō ni furumau*
　I wish he'd act his age and stop teasing his little brother.　あの子が年
　相応に振る舞って、弟をからかうのを止めてもらいたいものです。
　Ano ko ga toshi sōō ni furumatte, otōto o karakau no o yamete moraitai
　mono desu.

---

air — 空気 — *kūki*
　clear the air — 空気を一新する — *kūki o isshin suru*
　We've been angry with each other for too long. Let's talk it over and clear
　the air.　私達がお互いに怒りを持ってから、ずいぶん経っています。
　そこで話し合って、空気を一新しましょう。*Watakushitachi*
　ga otagai ni ikari o motte kara, zuibun tatte imasu. Soko de hanashiatte,
　kūki o isshin shimashō.

　full of hot air — 戯言 — *tawagoto*
　Don't believe anything he says—he's full of hot air.　彼は戯言ばかり
　言っているから、言うことは何も信じないように。*Kare wa*
　tawagoto bakari itte iru kara, iu koto wa nani mo shinjinai yō ni.

　out of thin air — 無から — *mu kara*
　Her excuse has no basis in fact. She made it up out of thin air.　彼女の言
　い訳には、事実の根拠は全くありません。彼女は、それを無から
　でっち上げたんですから。*Kanojo no iiwake niwa, jijitsu no konkyo*
　wa mattaku arimasen. Kanojo wa, sore o mu kara detchiagetandesu
　kara.

　up in the air — 宙に浮く — *chū ni uku*
　No decision has been made; everything is still up in the air.　まだ最終
　決定がありません。それで、全てが宙に浮いたままです。
　Mada saishū kettei ga arimasen. Sorede, subete ga chū ni uita mama
　desu.

　vanish into thin air — 蒸発する — *jōhatsu suru*

I haven't seen him in ages; he seems to have vanished into thin air.　彼に
は、ずいぶん長いこと会っていません。彼は、まるで蒸発して
しまったみたいです。*Kare niwa, zuibun nagai koto atte imasen. Kare
wa, marude jōhatsu shite shimatta mitai desu.*

walk on air — 足が地に着かない — *ashi ga chi ni tsukanai*

Ever since he got a raise, he's been walking on air.　彼は昇給を受けて
以来、足が地に着きません。*Kare wa shōkyū o ukete irai, ashi ga chi
ni tsukimasen.*

---

aisle — 通路 — *tsūro*

have them rolling in the aisles — 抱腹絶倒させる — *hōfuku zettō
saseru*

George is a great comedian. He always has the audience rolling in the
aisles.　ジョージは巧みな喜劇役者で、いつも聴衆を抱腹絶倒
させます。*Jōji wa takumi na kigeki yakusha de, itsumo chōshū o
hōfuku zettō sasemasu.*

---

alive — 生きて — *ikite iru*

alive and kicking — ぴんぴんしている — *pinpin shite iru*

Don't count him out; he's alive and kicking.　彼はぴんぴんしているん
ですから、のけ者にすべきではありません。*Kare wa pinpin shite
irundesu kara, nokemono ni subeki dewa arimasen.*

alive and well — 達者 — *tassha*

Tom? The last time I heard, he was alive and well in Nebraska.　トムですか。
彼ならこの前聞いたときには、ネブラスカで達者だとのことでした。
*Tomu desu ka. Kare nara kono mae kiita toki niwa, Neburasuka de
tassha da tono koto deshita.*

---

all — 全て — *subete*

after/when all is said and done — 最終的には — *saishūteki niwa*

After all was said and done, the meeting turned out well.　最終的には、
会議はいい結果に終わりました。*Saishūteki niwa, kaigi wa ii kekka
ni owarimashita.*

---

alley — 路地 — *roji*

right up/down someone's alley — お手の物／得意 — *otenomono/tokui*

Computers are right up his alley. コンピュータなら、彼のお手の物です。
Konpyūta nara, kare no otenomono desu.

up a blind alley — 行き詰まり — *ikizumari*
The police don't have any suspects in the murder; they're up a blind alley.
警察は殺人事件の容疑者が見つからずに、行き詰まっています。
Keisatsu wa satsujin jiken no yōgisha ga mitsukarazu ni, ikizumatte imasu.

alone — 一人で — *hitori de*
   go it alone — 一本立ちする — *ippondachi suru*
Now that his partner has pulled out, do you think he can go it alone?
共同出資者が辞めた後、彼は一本立ちしていけますか。*Kyōdō shusshisha ga yameta ato, kare wa ippondachi shite ikemasu ka.*

ants — 蟻 — *ari*
   get ants in one's pants — 手にものがつかない — *te ni mono ga tsukanai*
She's got ants in her pants waiting for the test results. 彼女は試験の結果を待って、手にものがつきません。*Kanojo wa shiken no kekka o matte, te ni mono ga tsukimasen.*

ape — 猿 — *saru*
   go ape (over someone or something) — 無我夢中になる — *mugamuchū ni naru*
They're going ape over the new actress in their favorite soap opera. 彼等は、気に入りの午後のメロドラマの新しい女優に無我夢中になっています。*Karera wa, kiniiri no gogo no merodorama no atarashii joyū ni mugamuchū ni natte imasu.*

appearance — 外見 — *gaiken*
   keep up appearances — 外見を繕う — *gaiken o tsukurou*
   I know you're all disappointed about losing the game, but let's try to smile and keep up appearances. 試合に負けてがっかりしているのは分かりますが、笑顔で外見を繕いましょう。*Shiai ni makete gakkari shite iru no wa wakarimasu ga, egao de gaiken o tsukuroimashō.*

put in an appearance — 顔を出す — *kao o dasu*

Although she could stay only briefly, she decided to put in an appearance at the reception. 彼女は少ししかいられませんが、それでもレセプションには顔を出すことにしました。 *Kanojo wa sukoshi shika iraremasen ga, soredemo resepushon niwa kao o dasu koto ni shimashita.*

appetite — 食欲 — *shokuyoku*

whet someone's appetite — 興味をそそる — *kyōmi o sosoru*

Seeing foreign films as a child whetted my appetite for travel. 子供の時に見た外国映画が、旅行への興味をそそりました。 *Kodomo no toki ni mita gaikoku eiga ga, ryokō e no kyōmi o sosorimashita.*

apple — 林檎 — *ringo*

apple of someone's eye — 目に入れても痛くない — *me ni iretemo itaku nai*

Her new baby son is the apple of her eye. 新しく産まれた男の子の赤ちゃんは、彼女の目に入れても痛くありません。*Atarashiku umareta otoko no ko no akachan wa, kanojo no me ni iretemo itaku arimasen.*

(like) apples and oranges — 別物 — *betsumono*

You can't compare college football and professional football; they're like apples and oranges. 大学とプロのアメフトを比べることは出来ません。それらは、全くの別物なんですから。 *Daigaku to puro no Amefuto o kuraberu koto wa dekimasen. Sorera wa, mattaku no betsumono nan desu kara.*

arm — 腕 — *ude*

cost an arm and a leg — 値が張る — *ne ga haru*

The new furniture is lovely, but it cost them an arm and a leg. 新しい家具は素晴らしいけれど、ずいぶん値が張りました。*Atarashii kagu wa subarashii keredo, zuibun ne ga harimashita.*

give one's right arm (for something) — 犠牲を いとわない — *gisei o itowanai*

I'd give my right arm for tickets to the Super Bowl. スーパーボールの券のためなら、犠牲をいといません。 *Sūpābōru no ken no tame nara, gisei o itoimasen.*

twist someone's arm — 無理強いする — *murijii suru*

I said "no," but the children twisted my arm, and I took them to the circus.
私はだめと言ったのですが、子供たちの無理強いで、サーカスに
連れて行かされました。*Watakushi wa dame to itta no desu ga,
kodomotachi no murijii de, sākasu ni tsurete ikasaremashita.*

up in arms — かんかんに怒る — *kankan ni okoru*

Everyone's up in arms about the new taxes.　新しい税金に、誰もが
かんかんに怒っています。*Atarashii zeikin ni, daremo ga kankan ni
okotte imasu.*

welcome someone with open arms — 大手を広げて大歓迎する —
ōte o hirogete dai kangei suru

When he returned from the army, his family welcomed him with open
arms.　彼が軍務を終えて帰還したとき、家族が大手を広げて
大歓迎しました。*Kare ga gunmu o oete kikan shita toki, kazoku ga ōte
o hirogete dai kangei shimashita.*

---

ax — 斧 — *ono*

get the ax — 首になる — *kubi ni naru*

After coming late to work every day for a month, he finally got the ax.
彼は一ヶ月毎日仕事に遅れてやってきて、首になりました。*Kare
wa ikkagetsu mainichi shigoto ni okurete yatte kite, kubi ni narimashita.*

have an ax to grind (with someone) — 腹に一物ある — *hara ni
ichimotsu aru*

Mary has an ax to grind with her supervisor.　メリーは、上司に対して
腹に一物あります。Merī wa, jōshi ni taishite hara ni ichimotsu
arimasu.

babe — 赤ん坊 — *akanbō*
　　babe in the woods — 素人 — *shirōto*
　　He was a good businessman, but as an ambassador, he's a babe in the
　　woods.　彼は有能なビジネスマンですが、大使としては素人です。
　　Kare wa yūnō na bijinesuman desu ga, taishi toshite wa shirōto desu.

baby — 赤ちゃん — *akachan*
　　(as) soft as a baby's bottom — 柔らかで滑らか — *yawaraka de
　　nameraka*
　　This cashmere feels as soft as a baby's bottom.　このカシミアは、
　　柔らかで滑らかです。*Kono kashimia wa, yawaraka de nameraka desu.*
　　throw the baby out with the bathwater — よくないことがあるからと、
　　全体を拒絶してしまう — *yoku nai koto ga aru kara to, zentai o
　　kyozetsu shite shimau*
　　The senator implored his colleagues to pass the bill and not to throw the
　　baby out with the bathwater.　よくないことがあるからと全体を拒絶
　　してしまわないように、上院議員は法案を可決することを同僚に
　　懇願しました。*Yokunai koto ga aru kara to zentai o kyozetsu shite
　　shimawanai yō ni, jōingiin wa hōan o kaketsu suru koto o dōryō ni
　　kongan shimashita.*

back — 後ろ／背中 — *ushiro/senaka*
　　behind someone's back — こっそりと — *kossori to*
　　Her father told her not to, but she went behind his back and attended the
　　party.　お父さんが駄目と言ったけれど、彼女はそれでもこっそりと
　　パーティーに出かけました。*Otōsan ga dame to itta keredo, kanojo
　　wa soredemo kossori to pātī ni dekakemashita.*

fall back on someone or something — 頼る — *tayoru*

If she loses her job, she can fall back on her trust fund. 　彼女はたとえ失業しても、信託財産に頼ることができます。*Kanojo wa tatoe shitsugyō shitemo, shintaku zaisan ni tayoru koto ga dekimasu.*

Get off (someone's) back! — 口出しするのを止めてもらいたい。— *Kuchidashi suru no o yamete moraitai.*

You always criticize my driving; I wish you'd get off my back! 　私の運転をいつも批判するけれど、口出しは止めて下さい。*Watakushi no unten o itsumo hihan suru keredo, kuchidashi wa yamete kudasai.*

get someone's back up — 腹を立てる — *hara o tateru*

She really got her back up when I asked her to stay away from my boyfriend. 　私のボーイフレンドに近寄らないように頼んだら、彼女は腹を立てました。*Watakushi no bōifurendo ni chikayoranai yō ni tanondara, kanojo wa hara o tatemashita.*

give someone a pat on the back — 賞賛する — *shōsan suru*

Sally deserves a pat on the back for her volunteer work with the elderly. サリーは、老人に対するボランティア活動で賞賛に値します。*Sarī wa, rōjin ni taisuru borantia katsudō de shōsan ni atai shimasu.*

give someone the shirt off one's back — 何でもあげる — *nandemo ageru*

Hank is so generous he'd give you the shirt off his back. 　ハンクはとても気前がよくて、人にすぐに何でもあげます。*Hanku wa totemo kimae ga yokute, hito ni sugu ni nandemo agemasu.*

have one's back to the wall — 進退窮まる — *shintai kiwamaru*

I have no more options; my back is to the wall. 　私は選択の余地がなくなって、進退窮まっています。*Watakushi wa sentaku no yochi ga nakunatte, shintai kiwamatte imasu.*

stab someone in the back — 裏切る — *uragiru*

I thought he was my friend, but he stabbed me in the back. 　彼は友達だと思っていましたが、私を裏切りました。*Kare wa tomodachi da to omotte imashita ga, watakushi o uragirimashita.*

turn one's back (on someone or something) — そっぽを向く — *soppo o muku*

Just when his friends needed help, John turned his back on them. 　友達が助けがいるときになったら、ジョンはそっぽを向きました。

Tomodachi ga tasuke ga iru toki ni nattara, Jon wa soppo o mukimashita.

You scratch my back and I'll scratch yours. — 持ちつ持たれつ — *mochitsu motaretsu*

You scratch my back and I'll scratch yours: If you teach me how to use a computer, I'll teach you how to play chess. 持ちつ持たれつでやりましょう。コンピュータの使い方を教えてくれたら、チェスのやり方を教えてあげます。*Mochitsu motaretsu de yarimashō. Konpyūta no tsukaikata o oshiete kuretara, chesu no yarikata o oshiete agemasu.*

---

backseat — 後ろの席 — *ushiro no seki*

take a backseat (to someone) — 脇役に甘んじる — *wakiyaku ni amanjiru*

As a coach, he takes a backseat to no one. コーチとして、彼が脇役に甘んじることは決してありません。*Kōchi toshite, kare ga wakiyaku ni amanjiru koto wa kesshite arimasen.*

---

backward — 後ろへ — *ushiro e*

backward(s) and forward(s) — 何から何まで — *nani kara nani made*

John knows the rules of football backwards and forwards. ジョンは、アメフトの規則は何から何まで知っています。*Jon wa, Amefuto no kisoku wa nani kara nani made shitte imasu.*

---

backyard — 裏庭 — *uraniwa*

in one's own backyard — 近所に — *kinjo ni*

He never thought he'd have such a wonderful elementary school practically in his own backyard. すぐ近所にそんなに素晴らしい小学校があろうとは、彼は思ってもいませんでした。*Sugu kinjo ni sonnani subarashii shōgakkō ga arō towa, kare wa omottemo imasen deshita.*

not in my backyard — 近所はご免だ — *kinjo wa gomen da*

They plan to build a football stadium here? Not in my backyard! ここにフットボールの球場を建てる計画があるんですか。私の近所はご免ですよ。*Koko ni futtobōru no kyūjō o tateru keikaku ga arundesu ka. Watakushi no kinjo wa gomen desu yo.*

---

bacon — ベ－コン — bēkon
bring home the bacon — 生活費を稼ぐ — seikatsu hi o kasegu
Now that Bill is the father of twins, he really has to bring home the bacon.
ビルは今や双子の父親なので、本当に生活費を稼がねばなりません。
Biru wa imaya futago no chichi oya nanode, hontō ni seikatsu hi o
kaseganeba narimasen.

bag — 袋 — fukuro
bag and baggage — 一切合切持って — issai gassai motte
Tom's wife got angry and walked out on him bag and baggage.　トムの
奥さんは怒って、ある物一切合切持って家を出ていきました。
Tomu no okusan wa okotte, aru mono issai gassai motte ie o dete
ikimashita.

bag of tricks — あらゆる手だて — arayuru tedate
Don't worry, he'll help us; he'll use his bag of tricks.　心配はいりませんよ。
彼があらゆる手だてを使って助けてくれるから。Shinpai wa
irimasen yo. Kare ga arayuru tedate o tsukatte tasukete kureru kara.

leave someone holding the bag — 責任を負わせる — sekinin o owaseru
Instead of facing the irate customers, the boss went home and left us
holding the bag.　怒っている顧客と対面する代わりに、上司は
帰宅してしまって、私達に責任を負わせました。Ikatte iru kokyaku
to taimen suru kawari ni, jōshi wa kitaku shite shimatte, watakushitachi
ni sekinin o owasemashita.

mixed bag — 善し悪しある — yoshi ashi aru
Our vacation was a mixed bag: the hotel was fabulous, but it rained every
day.　私達のバカンスは、善し悪しありました。ホテルは
素晴らしかったのですが、毎日雨が降ったのです。Watakushitachi
no bakansu wa, yoshi ashi arimashita. Hoteru wa subarashikatta no
desu ga, mainichi ame ga futta no desu.

bait — 釣りの餌 — tsuri no esa
fish or cut bait — やらないなら止める — yaranai nara yameru
Mr. Jones said he'd do the job, but he kept procrastinating. Finally we told
him to fish or cut bait.　ジョーンズさんはその仕事をやると
言いましたが、なかなか手を付けません。それでとうとう、
やらないなら止めるように彼に告げました。Jōnzu san wa sono

shigoto o yaru to iimashita ga, nakanaka te o tsukemasen. Sore de tōtō, yaranai nara yameru yō ni kare ni tsugemashita.

ball — 球 — *tama*

ball of fire — 猛烈な活躍ぶり — *mōretsu na katsuyaku buri*

That linebacker is in on every play; he's a real ball of fire. あのライ ンバッカ−はどのプレ−にもかかわって、猛烈な活躍ぶりをしています。 *Ano rainbakkā wa dono purē nimo kakawatte, mōretsu na katsuyaku buri o shite imasu.*

behind the eight ball — 絶体絶命 — *zettai zetsumei*

I borrowed his car and dented the fender. I'm behind the eight ball now. 彼の車を借りたのですがフェンダ−をへっこませて、絶体絶命です。 *Kare no kuruma o karita no desu ga fendā o hekkomasete, zettai zetsumei desu.*

carry the ball — 頼れる — *tayoreru*

Bill worked all night and finished the job. We depend on him to carry the ball. ビルは一晩中働いて、仕事を終えました。彼には、いつでも 頼ることが出来ます。*Biru wa hitoban jū hataraite, shigoto o oemashita. Kare niwa, itsu demo tayoru koto ga dekimasu.*

drop the ball — しくじる — *shikujiru*

We're counting on you to help us meet the deadline. Please don't drop the ball. 私達は締め切りに間に合うよう、あなたを頼りにして いるんです。それでどうぞ、しくじらないでください。 *Watakushitachi wa shimekiri ni ma ni au yō, anata o tayori ni shite irundesu. Sorede dōzo, shikujiranaide kudasai.*

get the ball rolling — 順調にスタ−トさせる — *junchō ni sutāto saseru*

We're counting on you to get the ball rolling on our next project. 次の 企画を順調にスタ−トさせるのに、あなたを頼りにしています。 *Tsugi no kikaku o junchō ni sutāto saseru noni, anata o tayori ni shite imasu.*

have a ball — とことんまで楽しむ — *tokoton made tanoshimu*

Sue's going on vacation; I hope she has a ball. ス−はバカンスに 行くので、彼女がそれをとことんまで楽しむことを願っています。 *Sū wa bakansu ni iku node, kanojo ga sore o tokoton made tanoshimu koto o negatte imasu.*

keep the ball rolling — このまま続ける — *kono mama tsuzukeru*
We're close to a solution now; let's keep the ball rolling.　解決間近
だから、このまま続けましょう。*Kaiketsu majika dakara, konomama
tsuzukemashō.*

on the ball — 的を得ている — *mato o ete iru*
Good thinking! You're really on the ball today.　なかなかいい考え
だね。今日はぴったり的を得ているよ。*Nakanaka ii kangae da ne.
Kyō wa pittari mato o ete iru yo.*

play ball (with someone) — 協調する — *kyōchō suru*
I wish they'd cooperate, but they refuse to play ball.　彼らが
協力してくれるといいんですが、協調するのを拒否しています。
*Karera ga kyōryoku shite kureru to iindesu ga, kyōchō suru no o kyohi
shite imasu.*

the ball is in one's court — 相手次第 — *aite shidai*
It's Ms. Jones's turn to respond. The ball is in her court.　今は全く相手
次第で、今度はジョーンズさんが応える番です。*Ima wa mattaku
aite shidai de, kondo wa Jōnzu san ga kotaeru ban desu.*

throw someone a curve ball — まごつかせる — *magotsukaseru*
I never expected that reaction. She really threw me a curve ball.　そんな
反応は全く予期もしていなかったのですが、彼女は私をまごつか
せたのです。*Sonna hannō wa mattaku yoki mo shite inakatta no desu
ga, kanojo wa watakushi o magotsukaseta no desu.*

whole ball of wax — 全てに — *subete ni*
I'm glad it's over. I'm fed up with this whole ball of wax.　全てにあき
あきしていたので、それが終わってほっとしました。*Subete ni
akiaki shite ita node, sore ga owatte hotto shimashita.*

---

balloon — 風船 — *fūsen*

go over like a lead balloon — 全然うけない — *zenzen ukenai*
That's a terrible idea. It'll go over like a lead balloon.　それはひどい
アイディアで、全然うけるはずがありません。*Sore wa hidoi aidia
de, zenzen ukeru hazu ga arimasen.*

send up a trial balloon — 探りを入れる — *saguri o ireru*
Let's send up a trial balloon to see how the new project will be received.
新企画がどの様に受け入れられるか知るため、探りを入れてみま

しょう。*Shin kikaku ga dono yō ni ukeirerareru ka shiru tame, saguri o irete mimashō.*

---

banana — バナナ — *banana*
  go bananas — 我を忘れる — *ware o wasureru*
  Hannah went bananas when she saw her new baby sister.　ハナは新しく
  生まれた妹を見たとき、我を忘れて興奮しました。*Hana wa atarashiku umareta imōto o mita toki, ware o wasurete kōfun shimashita.*

---

bandwagon — 楽隊が乗つた馬車 — *gakutai ga notta basha*
  climb on the bandwagon — 乗り遅れまいとする — *noriokuremai to suru*
  Now that the candidate looks like a winner, everyone's climbing on the
  bandwagon to support him.　あの候補者が勝つ見込みが強まったら、
  今や誰もが乗り遅れまいとして彼を支持しています。*Ano kōhosha ga katsu mikomi ga tsuyomattara, imaya daremo ga noriokuremai to shite kare o shiji shite imasu.*

---

bang — ずどん！ — *Zudon!*
  get a bang out of someone or something — わくわくする — *wakuwaku suru*
  He got a bang out of watching the home team win.　彼は地元チ－ムが
  勝つのを見て、わくわくしました。*Kare wa jimoto chīmu ga katsu no o mite, wakuwaku shimashita.*

---

baptism — 洗礼式 — *senrei shiki*
  baptism by fire — 砲火の洗礼 — *hōka no senrei*
  The rookie pitcher had a baptism by fire when his team lost 10 to nothing.
  新人投手は十対零で負けて、砲火の洗礼を受けました。*Shinjin tōshu wa juttai zero de makete, hōka no senrei o ukemashita.*

---

bark — 吠え声 — *hoegoe*
  one's bark is worse than one's bite — 口ほど悪くはない — *kuchi hodo waruku wa nai*
  He sounds fierce, but his bark is worse than his bite.　彼は荒々しく聞こ
  えますが、口ほど悪くはありません。*Kare wa araarashiku kikoemasu ga, kuchi hodo waruku wa arimasen.*

---

barrel — 樽 — *taru*

get someone over a barrel — 言いなりにする — *iinari ni suru*

John can't refuse us; we've got him over a barrel. ジョンは、私達を拒絶できません。それというのは、私達は彼を言いなりにしているからです。*Jon wa, watakushitachi o kyozetsu dekimasen. Sore to iu no wa, watakushitachi wa kare o iinari ni shite iru kara desu.*

---

base — 塁 — *rui*

(not) get to first base (with someone or something) — うまくいく／いかない — *umaku iku/ikanai*

Mr. Allen wants a lower price, but he can't get to first base with the sellers. アレン氏は低い値段を願っているけれど、売り手が拒否してうまくいきません。*Aren shi wa hikui nedan o negatte iru keredo, urite ga kyohi shite umaku ikimasen.*

off base — 事実にそぐわない — *jijitsu ni soguwanai*

No, I don't agree with you at all. You're way off base. あなたには、全く賛成できません。事実にそぐいませんよ。*Anata niwa, mattaku sansei dekimasen. Jijitsu ni soguimasen yo.*

touch base (with someone) — 連絡し合う — *renraku shiau*

Let's touch base again next week. また来週、連絡し合いましょう。*Mata raishū, renraku shiaimashō.*

---

bat — こうもり／打つ — *kōmori/utsu*

(as) blind as a bat — 目がかすむ — *me ga kasumu*

I can't read the small print anymore. I'm becoming as blind as a bat. 小さい文字は、もう読めません。目がかすんできているのです。*Chiisai moji wa, mō yomemasen. Me ga kasunde kite iru no desu.*

go to bat for someone — 代わりに一役買う — *kawari ni hitoyaku kau*

When they needed help, Ann went to bat for them. 彼らに助けが必要だったときに、アンが代わりに一役買いました。*Karera ni tasuke ga hitsuyō datta toki ni, An ga kawari ni hitoyaku kaimashita.*

have bats in the belfry — 狂っている — *kurutte iru*

He's acting so bizarre lately. I think he has bats in the belfry. 彼は最近、振る舞いがおかしいです。狂っているんじゃないですか。*Kare wa saikin, furumai ga okashii desu. Kurutte irunja nai desu ka.*

like a bat out of hell — 気違いじみた速さで — *kichigai jimita hayasa de*
Mary drives much too fast. She just rounded that corner like a bat out of
  hell. マリ－は、運転の仕方が速すぎます。ちょうど今も、かどを
  気違いじみた速さで回りました。*Marī wa, unten no shikata ga
  hayasugimasu. Chōdo ima mo, kado o kichigai jimita hayasa de
  mawarimashita.*

right off the bat — すぐさま — *sugu sama*
When he got his driver's license, he had an accident right off the bat.
  彼は運転面免許証を取って、すぐさま事故を起こしました。*Kare
  wa unten menkyoshō o totte, sugusama jiko o okoshimashita.*

---

bath — 風呂 — *furo*
take a bath (on something) — 大損する — *ōzon suru*
It seemed like a good investment, but I really took a bath on that one.
  いい投資だと思ったのですが、実際には大損してしまいました。
  *Ii tōshi da to omotta no desu ga, jissai niwa ōzon shite
  shimaimashita.*

---

bean — 豆 — *mame*
full of beans — 元気はつらつ — *genki hatsuratsu*
That child is full of beans today. その子供は、今日は元気はつらつ
  しています。*Sono kodomo wa, kyō wa genki hatsuratsu shite imasu.*

not know beans (about something) — 何にも知らない — *nani mo
  shiranai*
She claims to be an expert, but she doesn't know beans about real estate.
  彼女は専門家を装っていますが、不動産については何も知りません。
  *Kanojo wa senmonka o yosootte imasu ga, fudōsan ni tsuite wa nani mo
  shirimasen.*

spill the beans — 口を滑らす — *kuchi o suberasu*
It's a surprise party, so don't spill the beans. これは主客に秘密の
  パ－ティ－なんですから、口を滑らさないように。*Kore wa
  shukyaku ni himitsu no pātī nan desu kara, kuchi o suberasanai yō ni.*

---

bear — 熊 — *kuma*
(as) hungry as a bear — お腹がぺこぺこ — *onaka ga pekopeko*
He hasn't eaten since yesterday; he's hungry as a bear. 彼は昨日から

食べていないので、お腹がぺこぺこです。*Kare wa kinō kara tabete inai node, onaka ga pekopeko desu.*

loaded for bear — かんかんに怒る — *kankan ni okoru*
Henry's car was stolen today, and he's loaded for bear. 今日ヘンリーは車を盗まれて、かんかんに怒っています。*Kyō Henrī wa kuruma o nusumarete, kankan ni okotte imasu.*

---

beauty — 美しさ — *utsukushisa*
Beauty is only skin deep. — 容貌のみでは、人は分からない。— *Yōbō nomi dewa, hito wa wakaranai.*
That child is beautiful but unpleasant. Beauty is only skin deep.
あの子はきれいだけれど、性格がよくありません。
容貌のみでは、人は分からないものです。*Ano ko wa kirei dakeredo, seikaku ga yoku arimasen. Yōbō nomi dewa, hito wa wakaranai mono desu.*

---

beaver — ビーバー — *bībā*
(as) busy as a beaver — 猫の手も借りたいほど忙しい — *neko no te mo karitai hodo isogashii*
He can't go anywhere today. He's busy as a beaver painting his house.
彼は、今日はどこにも行けません。家にペンキを塗るので、猫の手も借りたいほど忙しいからです。*Kare wa, kyō wa doko nimo ikemasen. Ie ni penki o nuru node, neko no te mo karitai hodo isogashii kara desu.*

eager beaver — 張り切り屋 — *harikiriya*
Jack's a real eager beaver; he's always the first one in the office.
ジャックは張り切り屋で、オフィスにはいつも最初にやってきます。*Jakku wa harikiriya de, ofisu niwa itsumo saisho ni yatte kimasu.*

---

bed — ベッド — *beddo*
bed of roses — 安易なこと — *an-i na koto*
Working the late night shift is no bed of roses, but still she's always cheerful. 遅い夜勤は安易なことではありませんが、彼女はそれでもいつも朗らかです。*Osoi yakin wa an-i na koto dewa arimasen ga, kanojo wa soredemo itsumo hogaraka desu.*

---

bee — 蜂 — *hachi*

(as) busy as a bee — てんてこまいする — *tentekomai suru*
She's as busy as a bee preparing for her daughter's wedding.　彼女は娘の
結婚式の準備のために、てんてこまいしています。*Kanojo wa
musume no kekkon shiki no junbi no tame ni, tentekomai shite imasu.*

have/put a bee in one's/someone's bonnet — 思いつく／考えを植え
付ける — *omoitsuku/ kangae o uetsukeru*
We put a bee in his bonnet about sending the kids to summer camp.　子供
たちを夏のキャンプに行かせたらどうかと、彼に考えを植え付け
ました。*Kodomotachi o natsu no kyanpu ni ikasetara dō ka to, kare ni
kangae o uetsukemashita.*

beggar — 乞食 — *kojiki*

Beggars can't be choosers. — 贅沢は言えない。— *Zeitaku wa ienai.*
She doesn't like getting her cousin's hand-me-downs, but beggars can't be
choosers.　彼女はいとこのお古をもらうのは好きではありませんが、
贅沢は言えません。*Kanojo wa itoko no ofuru o morau no wa suki
dewa arimasen ga, zeitaku wa iemasen.*

bell — 鐘 — *kane*

ring a bell — ピンとくる — *pin to kuru*
He says we've met before, but it doesn't ring a bell with me.　彼は私達が
前に会ったことがあると言いますが、ぴんときません。Kare wa
watakushitachi ga mae ni atta koto ga aru to iimasu ga, pin to kimasen.

saved by the bell — 運よく救われる — *un yoku sukuwareru*
It just started to rain, and here comes our bus. Saved by the bell!　雨が
降りだしたときにちょうどバスが来て、運よく救われました。
Ame ga furidashita toki ni chōdo basu ga kite, un yoku sukuwaremashita.

with bells on — 大喜びで — *ōyorokobi de*

It sounds like a wonderful evening. I'll be there with bells on.　素晴らし
い夕べのようですね。大喜びで伺います。*Subarashii yūbe no yō
desu ne. Ōyorokobi de ukagaimasu.*

---

belt — バンド — *bando*

hit (someone) below the belt — 卑劣な手段を取る — *hiretsu na
shudan o toru*

That was hitting below the belt when you criticized him in front of his
colleagues.　あなたが彼を同僚の前で非難したのは、卑劣な手段
でした。*Anata ga kare o dōryō no mae de hinan shita no wa, hiretsu na
shudan deshita.*

tighten one's belt — 財布の紐を引き締める — *saifu no himo o
hikishimeru*

We'll have to tighten our belts for awhile until I find a new job.　新しく
仕事を見つけるまで、財布の紐を引き締めなければなりません。
*Atarashiku shigoto o mitsukeru made, saifu no himo o
hikishimenakereba narimasen.*

---

better — よりよい — *yoriyoi*

better late than never — 何もしないより遅れてでもした方がまし —
nani mo shinai yori okurete demo shita hō ga mashi

Her birthday was yesterday, but I'll send her flowers today. Better late than
never.　彼女の誕生日は昨日でしたが、私は今日、花を送ります。

何もしないより、遅れてでもした方がましですから。
*Kanojo no tanjōbi wa kinō deshita ga, watakushi wa kyō, hana o
okurimasu. Nani mo shinai yori, okurete demo shita hō ga mashi desu
kara.*

better off — まし — *mashi*
Mary would be better off working elsewhere. メリーは、どこかよそで
働いた方がましでしょう。*Merī wa, dokoka yoso de hataraita hō ga
mashi deshō.*

better safe than sorry — 後で後悔するより今のうちに安全を図って
置いた方がいい — *ato de kōkai suru yori ima no uchi ni anzen o
hakatte oita hō ga ii*
I'm going to get a flu shot. Better safe than sorry. 私は、流感の予防
注射をしてもらいます。後で後悔するより、今のうちに安全を
図っておいた方がいいですから。*Watakushi wa, ryūkan no yobō
chūsha o shite moraimasu. Ato de kōkai suru yori, ima no uchi ni anzen
o hakatte oita hō ga ii desu kara.*

---

bill — 勘定書 — *kanjōgaki*
  a clean bill of health — 健康そのものの証明書 — *kenkō sonomono no
  shōmeisho*
  Andrea has stopped worrying ever since her doctor gave her a clean bill of
  health. 医者が健康そのものの証明書をくれて以来、アンドレア
  は心配するのを止めました。*Isha ga kenkō sonomono no shōmeisho
  o kurete irai, Andorea wa shinpai suru no o yamemashita.*

  fill the bill — まさに完璧 — *masani kanpeki*
  A movie and dinner out would really fill the bill. 映画、そしてそれか
  らの食事は、まさに完璧です。*Eiga, soshite sorekara no shokuji wa,
  masa ni kanpeki desu.*

  foot the bill — 勘定を持つ — *kanjō o motsu*
  The boss is going to foot the bill for the company picnic this year.
  今年の会社のピクニックは、社長が勘定を持ってくれます。
  Kotoshi no kaisha no pikunikku wa, shachō ga kanjō o motte kuremasu.

  sell someone a bill of goods — うまく引っかける — *umaku hikkakeru*
  I didn't want a high-risk investment, but they sold me a bill of goods.
  私は危険な投資はしたくなかったのですが、彼らは私をうまく

引つかけました。*Watakushi wa kiken na tōshi wa shitaku nakatta no desu ga, karera wa watakushi o umaku hikkakemashita.*

---

bird — 鳥 — *tori*

A bird in the hand is worth two in the bush. — 明日の百より
今日の五十。— *Asu no hyaku yori kyō no gojū.*
I might find an apartment with a better view than this one,
   but a bird in the hand is worth two in the bush. これよりもいい
   眺めのアパートを見つけることが出来るかもしれませんが、
   明日の百より今日の五十です。*Kore yori mo ii nagame no apāto o
   mitsukeru koto ga dekiru kamo shiremasen ga, asu no hyaku yori kyō no
   gojū desu.*

A little bird told me. — 誰かさんから聞く。— *Dareka san kara kiku.*
How did I know today is your birthday? A little bird told me. 今日が
あなたの誕生日だっていうこと、私がどうやって知ったのか。
それは誰かさんから聞いたんですよ。*Kyō ga anata no tanjōbi datte
iu koto, watakushi ga dō yatte shitta no ka. Sore wa, dareka san kara
kiitandesu yo.*

(as) free as a bird — 全く自由の身 — *mattaku jiyū no mi*
I'd be glad to go shopping with you; I'm as free as a bird today. 買い物
には、喜んでお供します。私は、今日は全く自由の身なんですよ。
*Kaimono niwa, yorokonde otomo shimasu. Watakushi wa, kyō wa
mattaku jiyū no mi nandesu yo.*

birds and the bees — セックス — *sekkusu*
What's the best age for children to learn about the birds and the bees?
子供がセックスについて教わる最適の年は何歳でしょうか。
Kodomo ga sekkusu ni tsuite osowaru saiteki no toshi wa nansai deshō ka.

Birds of a feather flock together. — 類は友を呼ぶ。— *Rui wa tomo o
yobu.*
The quarterbacks usually pal around together in their free time. Birds of
   a feather flock together. クォーターバックは、普通は自由時間も
   一緒に付き合っています。類は友を呼ぶものです。*Kuōtābakku
   wa, futsū wa jiyū jikan mo issho ni tsukiatte imasu. Rui wa tomo o yobu
   mono desu.*

eat like a bird — 食が細い — *shoku ga hosoi*
Sally's so thin; she eats like a bird. サリーは、とても痩せています。

彼女は食が細いからです。*Sarī wa, totemo yasete imasu. Kanojo wa shoku ga hosoi kara desu.*

for the birds — くだらない — *kudaranai*
Many teenagers think doing chores is for the birds.　大勢の十代の
若者が、家事はくだらないと思っています。*Ōzei no jūdai no
wakamono ga, kaji wa kudaranai to omotte imasu.*

kill two birds with one stone — 一石二鳥 — *isseki nichō*
While I'm getting a haircut, I'll kill two birds with one stone and get a
manicure, too.　髪をカットしてもらっている間に、一石二鳥だから、
ついでにマニキュアもしてもらいます。*Kami o katto shite moratte
iru aida ni, isseki nichō dakara, tsuide ni manikyua mo shite moraimasu.*

The early bird catches the worm. — 早起きは三文の徳。— *Hayaoki
wa san mon no toku.*
Please be on time tomorrow. Remember, the early bird catches the worm.
明日は遅れないように。覚えているでしょ。早起きは三文の徳で
すよ。*Ashita wa okurenai yō ni. Oboete iru desho. Hayaoki wa san mon
no toku desu yo.*

---

bitter — 苦味 — *nigami*
　　take the bitter with the sweet — 苦楽ともに受け入れる — *kuraku
　　tomo ni ukeireru*
　　We won, but our quarterback was injured. We have to take the bitter with

the sweet.　私達が勝ちましたが、クォ - ターバックが怪我して、
苦楽ともに受け入れねばなりません。*Watakushitachi ga
kachimashita ga, kuōtābakku ga kega shite, kuraku tomo ni ukeireneba
narimasen.*

blanket — 毛布 — *mōfu*
wet blanket — 座を白けさせる人 — *za o shirakesaseru hito*
She's no fun at parties; she's a real wet blanket.　彼女は座を白けさせる
人だから、パ - ティ - では全然面白くありません。*Kanojo wa za o
shirakesaseru hito dakara, pātī dewa zenzen omoshiroku arimasen.*

blessing — 祝福 — *shukufuku*
blessing in disguise — 災い転じて福となる。 — *Wazawai tenjite fuku
to naru.*
The rain was a blessing in disguise. Our picnic was canceled, but a tree at
the picnic site was struck by lightning.　雨のために、災い転じて福
となりました。ピクニックは中止になりましたが、その場所の木
に雷が落ちたのです。*Ame no tame ni, wazawai tenjite fuku to
narimashita. Pikunikku wa chūshi ni narimashita ga, sono basho no ki ni
kaminari ga ochita no desu.*

blindfold — 目隠し — *mekakushi*
able to do something blindfolded — お茶の子さいさい — *ochanoko
saisai*
John can run the computer blindfolded.　ジョンは、コンピュ - タなど
お茶の子さいさいです。*Jon wa, konpyūta nado ochanoko saisai desu.*

blink — 瞬き — *mabataki*
on the blink — 故障している — *koshō shite iru*
My VCR is on the blink again. I have to take it to the repair shop.　ビデオ
がまた故障して、修理店に持って行かねばなりません。*Bideo ga
mata koshō shite, shūriten ni motte ikaneba narimasen.*

blood — 血 — *chi*
bad blood (between people) — 悪感情 — *aku kanjō*
Those brothers don't get along at all. There's bad blood between them.
あの兄弟は仲が良くなくて、実は二人の間には、悪感情が走って

います。*Ano kyōdai wa naka ga yoku nakute, jitsu wa futari no aida niwa, aku kanjō ga hashitte imasu.*

draw blood — いきり立つ — *ikiritatsu*

The negotiations were tough, but at least no blood was drawn.
交渉は厳しかったけれど、少なくとも誰もいきり立ちませんでした。
Kōshō wa kibishikatta keredo, sukunakutomo daremo ikiritachimasen deshita.

in cold blood — 残虐に — *zangyaku ni*

He killed several innocent victims in cold blood. 彼は、罪のない人を
数人残虐に殺しました。*Kare wa, tsumi no nai hito o sūnin zangyaku ni koroshimashita.*

in one's/the blood — 血統 — *kettō*

He's a great athlete. It's in his blood. 彼は優れた運動の選手ですが、
それは血統です。*Kare wa sugureta undō no senshu desu ga, sore wa kettō desu.*

make someone's blood boil — はらわたを煮えくり返す — *harawata o niekurikaesu*

The mayor's hypocrisy makes their blood boil. 市長の偽善に、彼らは
はらわたを煮えくり返しています。*Shichō no gizen ni, karera wa harawata o niekurikaeshite imasu.*

make someone's blood run cold — ぞっとさせる — *zotto saseru*

The ghost story made my blood run cold. 怪談を聞いて、ぞっとしま
した。*Kaidan o kiite, zotto shimashita.*

new blood — 新人 — *shinjin*

With the next election, the Senate should get some new blood. 次の選挙で、
上院には新人が何人か登場すべきです。*Tsugi no senkyo de, jōin niwa shinjin ga nannin ka tōjō subeki desu.*

sweat blood — ひどく心配する — *hidoku shinpai suru*

They were sweating blood until the escaped killer was caught. 彼らは
逃亡した殺人者が捕まるまで、ひどく心配していました。*Karera wa tōbō shita satsujinsha ga tsukamaru made, hidoku shinpai shite imashita.*

---

blow — 吹き飛ばす — *fukitobasu*

    blow someone away — びっくり仰天させる — *bikkuri gyōten saseru*

His winning the golf tournament just blows me away. 彼がゴルフの
トーナメントで勝ったのには、私はびっくり仰天しました。Kare
ga gorufu no tōnamento de katta no niwa, watakushi wa bikkuri gyōten
shimashita.

come to blows — 擦った揉んだの大騒ぎになる — sutta monda no
ōsawagi ni naru
They have a serious difference of opinion, but they probably won't come to
blows. 彼等には、深刻な意見の相違があります。けれども、
擦った揉んだの大騒ぎになることはないでしょう。Karera niwa,
shinkoku na iken no sōi ga arimasu. Keredomo, sutta monda no ōsawagi
ni naru koto wa nai deshō.

low blow — 卑劣なやり方 — hiretsu na yarikata
Firing him on his birthday was a low blow. 彼を誕生日に首にしたのは、
卑劣なやり方でした。Kare o tanjōbi ni kubi ni shita no wa, hiretsu na
yarikata deshita.

blue — 青 — ao
out of the blue — 突然 — totsuzen
Out of the blue, John asked Marcia to marry him. ジョンは突然、
マーシャに結婚を申し込みました。Jon wa totsuzen, Māsha ni
kekkon o mōshikomimashita.

bluff — 虚勢 — kyosei
call someone's bluff — 挑戦する — chōsen suru
John Smith says he's a great horseman. I'm going to call his bluff and
invite him to play polo with us. ジョン・スミスは、自分が馬術の
名手だと言っています。それで彼に挑戦して、私達のポロの試合
に招いてみるつもりです。Jon Sumisu wa, jibun ga bajutsu no meishu
da to itte imasu. Sorede kare ni chōsen shite, watakushitachi no poro no
shiai ni maneite miru tsumori desu.

board — 板 — ita
across the board — 一律に — ichiritsu ni
Because of budget constraints, they're eliminating jobs across the board.
予算緊縮のために、彼等は部署を一律に削減しています。Yosan
kinshuku no tame ni, karera wa busho o ichiritsu ni sakugen shite imasu.

back to the drawing board — 一から出直し — ichi kara denaoshi
They've rejected our proposal, so it's back to the drawing board. 彼等は
私達の提案を拒絶したので、一から出直しです。Karera wa
watakushitachi no teian o kyozetsu shita node, ichi kara denaoshi desu.

boat — 船 — fune
  in the same boat — 同じような困難な境遇にいる — onaji yō na
  konnan na kyōgū ni iru
  They've both been divorced recently, so they're in the same boat.
  彼等は二人とも最近離婚して、同じような困難な境遇にいます。
  Karera wa futari tomo saikin rikon shite, onaji yō na konnan na kyōgū ni
  imasu.

  rock the boat — 波風を立てる — namikaze o tateru
  Things are going well in the office now; don't rock the boat. 今オフィス
  では全てうまくいっているので、波風を立てないで下さい。Ima
  ofisu dewa subete umaku itte iru node, namikaze o tatenaide kudasai.

body — 体 — karada
  come/go in a body — そろって来る／行く — sorotte kuru/iku
  The teachers went in a body to see the principal to protest the new class
  schedule. 先生たちは新しい時間割に抗議するため、そろって
  校長に会いに行きました。Senseitachi wa, atarashii jikanwari ni kōgi
  suru tame, sorotte kōchō ni ai ni ikimashita.

  keep body and soul together — どうにか生計を立てる — dō ni ka
  seikei o tateru
  Many elderly people on fixed incomes have a hard time keeping body and
  soul together. 固定収入で暮らす年寄りの中には、どうにか生計
  を立てるのも難しい人が大勢います。Kotei shūnyū de kurasu
  toshiyori no naka niwa, dō ni ka seikei o tateru no mo muzukashii hito
  ga ōzei imasu.

  over my dead body — 死んでも反対 — shindemo hantai
  This company will sacrifice quality for profits over my dead body. この
  会社が品質を犠牲にして利益を得るのには、死んでも反対です。
  Kono kaisha ga hinshitsu o gisei ni shite rieki o eru no niwa, shindemo
  hantai desu.

bolt — 稲妻 — *inazuma*

bolt out of the blue — 青天の霹靂 — *seiten no hekireki*

The news of the disaster was a bolt out of the blue.　災害のニュースは、青天の霹靂でした。*Saigai no nyūsu wa, seiten no hekireki deshita.*

bombshell — 爆弾 — *bakudan*

drop a bombshell — 爆弾発言する — *bakudan hatsugen suru*

Mary dropped a bombshell with the news that she had married John. マリーは爆弾発言して、ジョンと結婚したというニュースを告げました。*Marī wa bakudan hatsugen shite, Jon to kekkon shita to iu nyūsu o tsugemashita.*

bone — 骨 — *hone*

bone of contention — 争いの種 — *arasoi no tane*

Whether or not to have children has been a bone of contention between them.　子供を作るかどうかが、二人の争いの種になっています。*Kodomo o tsukuru ka dō ka ga, futari no arasoi no tane ni natte imasu.*

bone up (on something) — 詰め込み勉強する — *tsumekomi benkyō suru*

Before he takes the exam, he has to bone up on his American history. 彼は試験を受ける前に、アメリカの歴史を詰め込み勉強しなければなりません。*Kare wa shiken o ukeru mae ni, Amerika no rekishi o tsumekomi benkyō shinakereba narimasen.*

chilled to the bone — 骨まで凍る — *hone made kōru*

After being out in the snowstorm, they were chilled to the bone.　彼等は吹雪の時に外にいた後、骨まで凍りました。*Karera wa fubuki no toki ni soto ni ita ato, hone made kōrimashita.*

cut something to the bone — 徹底的に切り詰める — *tetteiteki ni kiritsumeru*

With the new budget, we're cutting expenses to the bone.　新しい予算が理由で、私達は経費を徹底的に切り詰めています。*Atarashii yosan ga riyū de, watakushitachi wa keihi o tetteiteki ni kiritsumete imasu.*

feel/know something in one's bones — 直感で分かる — *chokkan de wakaru*

He's making promises he can't keep. I know it in my bones.　彼は果たせ

ない約束をしていますが、私にはそれが直感で分かります。*Kare wa hatasenai yakusoku o shite imasu ga, watakushi niwa sore ga chokkan de wakarimasu.*

have a bone to pick (with someone) — 話をつけたいことがある — *hanashi o tsuketai koto ga aru*

I have a bone to pick with you: why didn't you show up for the game yesterday? 君と話をつけたいことがある。昨日は、試合になぜ来なかったんだ。*Kimi to hanashi o tsuketai koto ga aru. Kinō wa, shiai ni naze konakattanda.*

no bones about it — 疑いの余地がない — *utagai no yochi ga nai*

No bones about it, he's going to win this election. 彼が選挙に勝つことに、疑いの余地がありません。*Kare ga senkyo ni katsu koto ni, utagai no yochi ga arimasen.*

---

book — 本 — *hon*

by the book — 規則に従って — *kisoku ni shitagatte*

He never bends the rules; he always goes by the book. 彼は決してずるいことはせず、いつも規則に従います。*Kare wa kesshite zurui koto wa sezu, itsumo kisoku ni shitagaimasu.*

crack a book — 本を開く — *hon o hiraku*

Although he never cracked a book in college, he got passing grades. 彼は大学では決して本を開きませんでしたが、それでも合格点を取りました。*Kare wa daigaku dewa kesshite hon o hirakimasen deshita ga, soredemo gōkaku ten o torimashita.*

read someone like an open book — 心を簡単に読み取る — *kokoro o kantan ni yomitoru*

Herb can't keep any secrets from his wife. She can read him like an open book. ハーブは、奥さんに隠し事が出来ません。なぜなら、彼女は彼の心を簡単に読み取ることが出来るからです。*Hābu wa, okusan ni kakushigoto ga dekimasen. Naze nara, kanojo wa kare no kokoro o kantan ni yomitoru koto ga dekiru kara desu.*

throw the book at someone — 厳しく罰する — *kibishiku bassuru*
Don't speed in that state. If you're caught, they'll throw the book at you.
あの州では、スピード違反はしないように。もし捕まると、厳し
く罰せられるからです。*Ano shū dewa, supīdo ihan wa shinai yō ni.*
Moshi tsukamaru to, kibishiku basserareru kara desu.

wrote the book on something — その道にかけては通だ — *sono michi*
ni kakete wa tsū da
John knows about buying used cars; he wrote the book on it.　ジョンは
中古車の買い方を知っていて、その道にかけては通です。*Jon wa*
chūkosha no kaikata o shitte ite, sono michi ni kakete wa tsū desu.

---

boot — ブーツ — *būtsu*
die with one's boots on — 死ぬまで働く — *shinu made hataraku*
He has no intention of retiring. He'll die with his boots on.　彼に、引退
する気はありません。死ぬまで働くつもりだからです。*Kare ni,*
intai suru ki wa arimasen. Shinu made hataraku tsumori dakara desu.

shake/quake in one's boots — 震え上がる — *furueagaru*
The idea of asking the boss for a raise had Mr. Smith shaking in his boots.
上司に昇給を頼もうと考えただけで、スミスさんは震え上がりま
した。*Jōshi ni shōkyū o tanomō to kangaeta dake de, Sumisu san wa*
furueagarimashita.

---

bootstraps — ブーツのつまみ皮 — *būtsu no tsumamigawa*
   pull oneself up by one's own bootstraps — 自力でうまくやってのける
   — *jiriki de umaku yatte nokeru*
   He's in trouble now, but he'll make it. He always pulls himself up by his
   own bootstraps. 彼は今は困難に陥っていても、きっと成功します。
   彼はいつも自力でうまくやってのけるからです。*Kare wa ima wa
   konnan ni ochiitte itemo, kitto seikō shimasu. Kare wa itsumo jiriki de
   umaku yatte nokeru kara desu.*

bottle — 瓶 — *bin*
   hit the bottle — 大酒を呑む — *ōzake o nomu*
   I know his divorce was devastating, but I hope he doesn't start
   hitting the bottle.   離婚がつらいのは分かりますが、
   それでも彼が大酒を飲み出さないといいのですが。*Rikon ga tsurai
   no wa wakarimasu ga, soredemo kare ga ōzake o nomidasanai to ii no
   desu ga.*

bottom — お尻／底 — *oshiri/soko*
   at the bottom of the ladder — 一番下から — *ichiban shita kara*
   Even the boss's daughter has to start out at the bottom of the ladder.
   たとえ社長のお嬢さんでも、一番下の地位から始めなければなり
   ません。*Tatoe shachō no ojōsan demo, ichiban shita no chii kara
   hajimenakereba narimasen.*

   from the bottom of one's heart — 心の底から — *kokoro no soko kara*
   I thank you from the bottom of my heart.   心の底からお礼を申し上げ
   ます。*Kokoro no soko kara orei o mōshiagemasu.*

   get to the bottom of something — 真相を突き止める — *shinsō o
   tsukitomeru*
   Who leaked the story to the press? We must get to the bottom of this.
   これをマスコミに漏らしたのは誰ですか。この件については、
   真相を突き止めなければなりません。*Kore o masukomi ni
   morashita no wa dare desu ka. Kono ken ni tsuite wa, shinsō o
   tsukitomenakereba narimasen.*

   hit (rock) bottom — どん底に陥る — *donzoko ni ochiiru*
   Often an alcoholic has to hit bottom before he or she can ask for help.
   アル中の人はしばしば、助けを求める前にどん底に陥らねばなり

ません。 *Aruchū no hito wa shibashiba, tasuke o motomeru mae ni donzoko ni ochiiraneba narimasen.*

scrape the bottom of the barrel — かすをかき集める — *kasu o kakiatsumeru*

The guy she's dating is a loser. She's really scraping the bottom of the barrel. 彼女がデートしている男は、人生の敗北者です。彼女は、本当にかすをかき集めているのです。 *Kanojo ga dēto shite iru otoko wa, jinsei no haibokusha desu. Kanojo wa, hontō ni kasu o kakiatsumete iru no desu.*

bow — お辞儀 — *ojigi*

bow out — 辞める — *yameru*

We had gotten a babysitter for Saturday night, but she had to bow out. 土曜日のために子守を雇いましたが、彼女は辞めなければなりませんでした。 *Doyōbi no tame ni komori o yatoimashita ga, kanojo wa yamenakereba narimasen deshita.*

take a bow — 賞賛を受ける — *shōsan o ukeru*

You deserve to take a bow for making this project a success. この企画を成功させたことで、あなたは賞賛を受ける資格があります。 *Kono kikaku o seikō saseta koto de, anata wa shōsan o ukeru shikaku ga arimasu.*

brain — 脳 — *nō*

beat one's brains out — 知恵を絞る — *chie o shiboru*

He's been beating his brains out to come up with a solution. 彼は解決策を見いだそうと、知恵を絞っています。 *Kare wa kaiketsu saku o miidasō to, chie o shibotte imasu.*

pick someone's brain(s) — 知恵を拝借する — *chie o haishaku suru*

She knows much more than I about this. I'll have to pick her brains. それについては彼女は私よりもっと知っているので、彼女の知恵を拝借しなければなりません。 *Sore ni tsuite wa kanojo wa watakushi yori motto shitte iru node, kanojo no chie o haishaku shinakereba narimasen.*

rack one's brain(s) — 頭を絞る — *atama o shiboru*

I've racked my brains, and I still can't remember where I met him. いくら頭を絞っても、彼と前にどこで会ったのか思い出せません。 *Ikura atama o shibottemo, kare to mae ni doko de atta no ka omoidasemasen.*

branch — 枝 — eda

offer an/the olive branch — 和平を申し出る — wahei o mōshideru

After their bitter disagreement, neither side wanted to offer the olive branch. 激しい論争の後、双方とも和平を申し出ようとしませんでした。Hageshii ronsō no ato, sōhō tomo wahei o mōshideyō to shimasen deshita.

bread — パン — pan

someone's bread and butter — 生活の糧 — seikatsu no kate

I hope he can continue working. That job is his bread and butter. その仕事はその人の生活の糧ですから、彼が仕事を続けられることを望んでいます。Sono shigoto wa kare no seikatsu no kate desu kara, kare ga shigoto o tsuzukerareru koto o nozonde imasu.

break — こわれる／機会 — kowareru/kikai

break down — こらえきれない — koraekirenai

When they heard the news of the assassination, they broke down and cried. 彼等は暗殺のニュースを聞いたとき、こらえきれずに泣きました。Karera wa ansatsu no nyūsu o kiita toki, koraekirezu ni nakimashita.

give someone a break — もう一度機会を与える — mō ichido kikai o ataeru

Although his payment was late, they gave him a break and didn't report it. 彼は支払いが遅れましたが、彼等はもう一度機会を与えて、それを報告しませんでした。Kare wa shiharai ga okuremashita ga, karera wa mō ichido kikai o ataete, sore o hōkoku shimasen deshita.

breast — 胸 — mune

make a clean breast of something — 洗いざらい述べる — araizarai noberu

The thief decided to make a clean breast of it and confess to all the robberies. 泥棒は、洗いざらい述べて全ての盗みを自白する決心をしました。Dorobō wa, araizarai nobete subete no nusumi o jihaku suru kesshin o shimashita.

breath — 息 — iki

breath of fresh air — すがすがしい空気 — sugasugashii kūki

What a pleasant attitude your secretary has! She's like a breath of fresh air. あなたの秘書の態度は、実に気持ちがいいです。彼女は、まるですがすがしい空気のようです。 *Anata no hisho no taido wa, jitsu ni kimochi ga ii desu. Kanojo wa, marude sugasugashii kūki no yō desu.*

Don't hold your breath. — 期待薄 — *kitai usu*

If you're expecting a raise, don't hold your breath. もしあなたが昇給を期待しているなら、それは期待薄ですよ。*Moshi anata ga shōkyū o kitai shite iru nara, sore wa kitai usu desu yo.*

save one's breath — 口をきいても無駄 — *kuchi o kiitemo muda*

If you think you can talk him out of it, you might as well save your breath. もし彼を説得して止めさせようと思っているなら、口をきいても無駄ですよ。*Moshi kare o settoku shite yamesaseyō to omotte iru nara, kuchi o kiitemo muda desu yo.*

take someone's breath away — 息を呑む — *iki o nomu*

The sunset was so magnificent it took my breath away. 夕焼けのあまりの美しさに、息を呑みました。*Yūyake no amari no utsukushisa ni, iki o nomimashita.*

waste one's breath — 話しても無駄 — *hanashitemo muda*

Mr. Green tried to talk some sense into his son, but he just wasted his breath. グリーンさんは息子に道理を言い含めようとしましたが、話しても無駄でした。*Gurīn san wa musuko ni dōri o iifukumeyō to shimashita ga, hanashitemo muda deshita.*

---

breeze — そよ風 — *soyokaze*

shoot the breeze — たわいない話しをして過ごす — *tawai nai hanashi o shite sugosu*

After dinner we just sat around shooting the breeze. 夕食の後くつろいで、たわいない話しをして時を過ごしました。*Yūshoku no ato kutsuroide, tawai nai hanashi o shite toki o sugoshimashita.*

---

bridge — 橋 — *hashi*

burn one's bridges (behind one) — 後戻りできない — *atomodori dekinai*

If you get angry and walk out, you may be burning your bridges behind you. 怒って行ってしまうなら、後戻りできないかもしれませんよ。 *Okotte itte shimau nara, atomodori dekinai kamo shiremasen yo.*

cross that bridge when one comes to it — その時になって対処する
— *sono toki ni natte taisho suru*
Why worry now about next week's meeting? We'll cross that bridge when
we come to it. 来週の会議を、今から心配する必要はありません。
その時になって対処すれば、それで十分です。*Raishū no kaigi o,*
ima kara shinpai suru hitsuyō wa arimasen. Sono toki ni natte, taisho
sureba sore de jūbun desu.

britches — ズボン — *zubon*
   too big for one's britches — 傲慢 — *gōman*
Since he became the starting quarterback, he's been too big for his britches.
彼はチーム第一のクォーターバックになって以来、傲慢になって
います。*Kare wa chīmu dai ichi no kuōtābakku ni natte irai, gōman ni*
natte imasu.

brother — 兄弟 — *kyōdai*
   be one's brother's keeper — 責任者 — *sekininsha*
I want him to take the job, but what can I do? I'm not my brother's keeper.
彼がその仕事を受け入れることを望んでいますが、私に何が出来
るでしょう。私は彼の責任者ではないんですから。*Kare ga sono*
shigoto o ukeireru koto o nozonde imasu ga, watakushi ni nani ga dekiru
deshō. Watakushi wa kare no sekininsha dewa naindesu kara.

brush — ブラシ — *burashi*
   give someone the brush-off — あっさりはねつける — *assari*
hanetsukeru
When he asked her for a date, she gave him the brush-off. 彼は彼女に
デートを申し込みましたが、彼女は彼をあっさりはねつけました。
Kare wa kanojo ni dēto o mōshikomimashita ga, kanojo wa kare o assari
hanetsukemashita.

bucket — バケツ — baketsu

kick the bucket — 死ぬ — shinu
The old farmer lived a good, long life, but he finally kicked the bucket.
あの年寄りのお百姓は長い実りある人生を送りましたが、とうと
う死にました。Ano toshiyori no ohyakushō wa nagai minori aru jinsei
o okurimashita ga, tōtō shinimashita.

bud — 芽 — me

nip something in the bud — 早めに手を打つ — hayame ni te o utsu
When she began arriving late to work, her supervisor decided to nip it in
the bud.　彼女が仕事に遅れてくるようになったので、彼女の
ボスはそれについて早めに手を打つことにしました。Kanojo ga
shigoto ni okurete kuru yō ni natta node, kanojo no bosu wa sore ni
tsuite hayame ni te o utsu koto ni shimashita.

bug — 虫 — mushi

(as) snug as a bug in a rug — 心地よい — kokochi yoi
Sitting by the fireplace covered with a shawl, she looked as snug as a bug
in a rug.　彼女はショールにくるまって暖炉のそばに座り、心地よ
さそうでした。Kanojo wa shōru ni kurumatte danro no soba ni
suwari, kokochi yosasō deshita.

bug someone — いらつかせる — iratsukaseru
I wish he'd leave me alone. He's been bugging me about this report all day.

彼が私を放っておいてくれるといいんですが。この報告書について、
私を一日中いらつかせているのです。*Kare ga watakushi o hootte
oite kureru to iindesu ga. Kono hōkokusho ni tsuite,watakushi o ichinichi
jū iratsukasete iru no desu.*

bull — 雄牛 — *oushi*

bull in a china shop — はらはらするほど不器用 — *harahara suru
hodo bukiyō*

Don't let him carry the glasses. He's as clumsy as a bull in a china shop.
彼にコップを運ばさせてはだめですよ。はらはらするほど不器用
なんですから。*Kare ni koppu o hakobasasete wa dame desu yo.
Harahara suru hodo bukiyō nandesu kara.*

full of bull — 嘘の固まり — *uso no katamari*
What a bunch of lies! He's full of bull.　嘘八百！彼は嘘の固まりです。
Uso happyaku! Kare wa uso no katamari desu.

hit the bull's-eye — 金的を射止める — *kinteki o itomeru*
Now we've got it exactly right. I think we've hit the bull's-eye!　今度
こそは、それを寸分違わず成し遂げました。私達は、金的を射止
めたと思います。*Kondo koso wa, sore o sunbun tagawazu
nashitogemashita. Watakushitachi wa, kinteki o itometa to omoimasu.*

shoot the bull — 大口を叩く — *ōguchi o tataku*
Last night John and Harry sat around for hours shooting the bull.　昨日の
晩、ジョンとハリーは何時間も大口を叩き合って過ごしました。
*Kinō no ban, Jon to Harī wa nan jikan mo ōguchi o tatakiatte
sugoshimashita.*

take/seize the bull by the horns — 自ら難局に取り組む — *mizukara
nankyoku ni torikumu*
Don't wait for others to make decisions for you. Take the bull by the horns.
人が決めてくれるのを待っていないで、自ら難局に取り組みなさい。
*Hito ga kimete kureru no o matte inaide, mizukara nankyoku ni
torikuminasai.*

bullet — 弾丸 — *dangan*

bite the bullet — 覚悟を決める — *kakugo o kimeru*
Mary had to bite the bullet and fire several incompetent employees.
マリーは覚悟を決めて、無能な従業員数人の首を切らねばなりま

せんでした。*Marī wa kakugo o kimete, munō na jūgyōin sūnin no kubi o kiraneba narimasen deshita.*

bump — 突き当たる／こぶ — *tsukiataru/kobu*

bump into someone — たまたま出くわす — *tamatama dekuwasu*

I hadn't seen Mr. Wagner in years, but yesterday I bumped into him on Main Street. 私はワグナーさんに長年会っていませんでしたが、昨日メインストリートで彼にたまたま出くわしました。*Watakushi wa Wagunā san ni naganen atte imasen deshita ga, kinō Mein sutorīto de kare ni tamatama dekuwashimashita.*

get/have goose bumps/pimples — 感動して／恐怖で鳥肌が立つ — *kandō shite/kyōfu de torihada ga tatsu*

Whenever I hear her sing, I get goose bumps. 彼女の歌を聴くと、いつも感動して鳥肌が立ちます。*Kanojo no uta o kiku to, itsumo kandō shite torihada ga tachimasu.*

like a bump on a log — 黙りこくって — *damarikokutte*

My son never says anything at parties; he just sits there like a bump on a log. 息子は、パーティーでは決してものを言いません。黙りこくって、そこに座っているだけです。*Musuko wa, pātī dewa kesshite mono o iimasen. Damarikokutte, soko ni suwatte iru dake desu.*

bundle — 束 — *taba*

bundle of nerves — 神経を高ぶらせる — *shinkei o takaburaseru*

He's a bundle of nerves waiting for the birth of his first child. 彼は最初の子供が生まれるのを待って、神経を高ぶらせています。*Kare wa saisho no kodomo ga umareru no o matte, shinkei o takaburasete imasu.*

make a bundle — 大儲けする — *ōmōke suru*

They made a bundle investing in that stock. 彼等はその株に投資して、大儲けしました。*Karera wa sono kabu ni tōshi shite, ōmōke shimashita.*

burner — バーナー — *bānā*

put something on the back burner — 延期する — *enki suru*

We can't make that decision. Let's put it on the back burner till the boss returns. 私達は、それを決めることが出来ません。それで、ボスが

393

帰ってくるまで延期しましょう。*Watakushitachi wa, sore o kimeru koto ga dekimasen. Sorede, bosu ga kaette kuru made enki shimashō.*

---

bush — 薮 — *yabu*

beat around the bush — 遠回しに言う — *tōmawashi ni iu*
Let's not beat around the bush. I want to get right to the point. 遠回しに言うのは止めましょう。私は、要点にズバリ触れたいです。*Tōmawashi ni iu no wa yamemashō. Watakushi wa, yōten ni zubari furetai desu.*

---

business — 仕事 — *shigoto*

drum up some business — 売り上げを伸ばす — *uriage o nobasu*
If they advertise more, they can drum up some business. 彼等はもっと宣伝すれば、売り上げを伸ばすことが出来ます。*Karera wa motto senden sureba, uriage o nobasu koto ga dekimasu.*

land-office business — 注文がたくさん舞い込んで 繁盛する — *chūmon ga takusan maikonde hanjō suru*
The company is doing a land-office business with their new software. その会社は、新しいソフトウェアの注文がたくさん舞い込んで繁盛しています。*Sono kaisha wa, atarashii sofutowea no chūmon ga takusan maikonde hanjō shite imasu.*

mean business — 本気だ — *honki da*
Do your homework, and this time I mean business! 宿題をやりなさい。今度は本気で言っているんですよ。*Shukudai o yarinasai. Kondo wa honki de itte irundesu yo.*

mind one's own business — お節介をしない — *osekkai o shinai*
He's always interfering with my work. I wish he'd mind his own business. 彼はいつも私の仕事に干渉していますが、お節介はしないでもらいたいと思います。*Kare wa itsumo watakushi no shigoto ni kanshō shite imasu ga, osekkai wa shinai de moraitai to omoimasu.*

monkey business — ごまかし — *gomakashi*
Let's keep our tax records straight—no monkey business! 税金の記録は正直につけて、ごまかしはしないようにしましょう。*Zeikin no kiroku wa shōjiki ni tsukete, gomakashi wa shinai yō ni shimashō.*

butter — バター — *batā*

butter someone up — 胡麻をする — *goma o suru*
He buttered his parents up for several weeks before he asked for a new
bicycle. 彼は新しい自転車をねだる前に、両親に数週間胡麻を
すりました。*Kare wa atarashii jitensha o nedaru mae ni, ryōshin ni
sūshūkan goma o surimashita.*

look as if butter wouldn't melt in one's mouth — 虫も殺さぬ顔をし
ている — *mushi mo korosanu kao o shite iru*
What a mean person! She looks as if butter wouldn't melt in her mouth.
彼女って、なんて意地の悪い人なんでしょう。虫も殺さぬ顔をし
ているくせに。*Kanojotte, nante iji no warui hito nandeshō. Mushi mo
korosanu kao o shite iru kuse ni.*

butterfly — 蝶々 — *chōchō*
get/have butterflies in one's stomach — 心臓がどきどきする —
shinzō ga dokidoki suru
Every time John has to make a speech, he gets butterflies in his stomach.
ジョンはスピーチをしなければならないときはいつも、心臓が
どきどきします。*Jon wa supīchi o shinakereba naranai toki wa
itsumo, shinzō ga dokidoki shimasu.*

button — ボタン — *botan*
press/push the panic button — 慌てふためく — *awatefutameku*

Please calm down. It's too soon to push the panic button. どうぞ気を
落ち着けて下さい。慌てふためくには、早すぎます。Dōzo ki o
ochitsukete kudasai. Awatefutameku niwa, hayasugimasu.

Cain — カイン — Kain
raise Cain — どんちゃん騒ぎを引き起こす — donchansawagi o
hikiokosu
The folks next door had a party and were raising Cain all night long.
隣の家の人はパーティーを開いて、一晩中どんちゃん騒ぎを引き
起こしていました。Tonari no ie no hito wa pātī o hiraite, hitoban jū
donchansawagi o hikiokoshite imashita.

call — 呼び出し — yobidashi
(above and) beyond the call of duty — 職務上の義務を越えて —
shokumu jō no gimu o koete
His working overtime all week was above and beyond the call of duty.
彼の一週間の超過勤務は、職務上の義務を越えていました。Kare
no isshūkan no chōka kinmu wa, shokumu jō no gimu o koete imashita.

a close call — 間一髪で免れる — kan ippatsu de manugareru
I had a close call this morning when a car almost crashed into mine. 今朝は
他の車が私のにぶつかりそうになりましたが、間一髪で免れました。
Kesa wa hoka no kuruma ga watakushi no ni butsukarisō ni narimashita
ga, kan ippatsu de manugaremashita.

can — 缶詰 — kanzume
open a can of worms — 厄介な事情があるのに気付く — yakkai na
jijō ga aru no ni kizuku
If they investigate the mayor's finances, they'll open a can of worms.
もし市長個人の金繰りを調べれば、彼には厄介な事情があるのに
気付くでしょう。Moshi shichō kojin no kaneguri o shirabereba, kare
niwa yakkai na jijō ga aru no ni kizuku deshō.

candle — ろうそく — *rōsoku*

burn the candle at both ends — 無理をしすぎる — *muri o shisugiru*

With a full-time job and classes too, you're burning the candle at both ends. あなたは正規の仕事と同時に授業で、無理をしすぎています よ。*Anata wa seiki no shigoto to dōji ni jugyō de, muri o shisugite imasu yo.*

can't hold a candle to someone — 格段の差がある — *kakudan no sa ga aru*

The coach is good, but he can't hold a candle to the one who just retired. 今のコーチは才能がありますが、最近引退した前任者とは格段の 差があります。*Ima no kōchi wa sainō ga arimasu ga, saikin intai shita zenninsha to wa kakudan no sa ga arimasu.*

---

cap — 帽子 — *bōshi*

put one's thinking cap on — じっくり考える — *jikkuri kangaeru*

We have to come up with a solution, so put your thinking cap on. 解決策を 見つけなければならないので、じっくり考えなさい。*Kaiketsu saku o mitsukenakereba naranai node, jikkuri kangaenasai.*

---

card — トランプ — *toranpu*

in the cards — 宿命 — *shukumei*

He wanted to study medicine, but it wasn't in the cards. 彼は医学を勉強 したかったのですが、そういう宿命にありませんでした。*Kare wa igaku o benkyō shitakatta no desu ga, sō iu shukumei ni arimasen deshita.*

lay/put one's cards on the table — 手の内を見せる — *te no uchi o miseru*

To avoid further delay, let's both lay our cards on the table. これ以上の 遅れを避けるために、お互いの手の内を見せましょう。*Kore ijō no okure o sakeru tame ni, otagai no te no uchi o misemashō.*

play one's cards close to one's chest/vest — 秘密主義 — *himitsu shugi*

We can't get any information from him. He plays his cards close to his vest. 彼は秘密主義なので、彼から情報を得るのは不可能です。 *Kare wa himitsu shugi nanode, kare kara jōhō o eru no wa fukanō desu*

play one's cards right/well — うまくやる — *umaku yaru*

If you play your cards right, you can be a branch manager by this time next

year. うまくやれば、来年の今頃までには支店長になれますよ。
Umaku yareba, rainen no imagoro made niwa shitenchō ni naremasu yo.

play one's trump card — 切り札を使う — *kirifuda o tsukau*

When the time was right, Mr. Jones played his trump card and closed the deal. ジョーンズさんはタイミングがいいときに切り札を使って、取引をまとめました。*Jōnzu san wa taimingu ga ii toki ni kirifuda o tsukatte, torihiki o matomemashita.*

the cards are stacked against one — 不利な立場に置かれる — *furi na tachiba ni okareru*

He keeps trying to succeed in business, but the cards are stacked against him. 彼はビジネスで成功しようと努力していますが、不利な立場に置かれています。*Kare wa bijinesu de seikō shiyō to doryoku shite imasu ga, furi na tachiba ni okarete imasu.*

---

care — 心配事 — *shinpaigoto*

not have a care in the world — 心配事が全くない — *shinpaigoto ga mattaku nai*

Sally is always so pleasant. She acts as if she doesn't have a care in the world. サリーはいつも陽気で、心配事が全くないかのように振る舞っています。*Sarī wa itsumo yōki de, shinpaigoto ga mattaku nai ka no yō ni furumatte imasu.*

---

carpet — カーペット — *kāpetto*

call someone on the carpet — 叱りつける — *shikaritsukeru*

When Tom took two hours for lunch, Hank called him on the carpet. トムがランチに二時間かけたときに、ハンクは彼を叱りつけました。*Tomu ga ranchi ni ni jikan kaketa toki ni, Hanku wa kare o shikaritsukemashita.*

roll out the red carpet for someone — 盛大にもてなす — *seidai ni motenasu*

He's an important person in his company. Let's roll out the red carpet for him. 彼はその会社の重要人物だから、盛大にもてなしましょう。*Kare wa sono kaisha no jūyō jinbutsu dakara, seidai ni motenashimashō.*

sweep something under the carpet/rug — 問題がない振りをする — *mondai ga nai furi o suru*

We'll have to deal with this. We can't just sweep it under the carpet.

私達はそれに対処しなければなりません。単に問題がない振りは
出来ません。*Watakushitachi wa sore ni taisho shinakereba narimasen.*
Tan ni mondai ga nai furi wa dekimasen.

---

cart — 荷馬車 — *nibasha*

put the cart before the horse — 順序を誤る — *junjo o ayamaru*
Don't put the cart before the horse. First paint the house, then put it up for
sale. 始めにペンキを塗ってから家を売りに出す、その順序を誤
らないようにしなさい。*Hajime ni penki o nutte kara ie o uri ni dasu,*
sono junjo o ayamaranai yō ni shinasai.

upset the apple cart — 計画を台無しにする — *keikaku o dainashi ni suru*
Don't tell him you're resigning yet; you don't want to upset the apple cart
now. 君が辞めることを、まだ彼に言わないように。計画を台無
しにしたくないだろ。*Kimi ga yameru koto o, mada kare ni iwanai yō*
ni. Keikaku o dainashi ni shitakunai daro.

---

case — 場合 — *baai*

make a federal case out of something — 大げさに騒ぎ立てる —
ōgesa ni sawagitateru
It was just a small accident, but he's making a federal case out of it.
それはほんの小さな事故でしたが、彼は大げさに騒ぎ立てています。
Sore wa honno chīsana jiko deshita ga, kare wa ōgesa ni sawagitatete
imasu.

---

cat — 猫 — *neko*

Cat got your tongue? — 口がきけなくなったのかな。 — *Kuchi ga kikenaku natta no kana.*

Why don't you speak up, Jim? Cat got your tongue? ジム、どうして話さないの。口がきけなくなったのかな。*Jimu, dōshite hanasanai no. Kuchi ga kikenaku natta no kana.*

let the cat out of the bag — 口を滑らす — *kuchi o suberasu*

It's supposed to be a secret for now, so don't let the cat out of the bag. これは今のところ秘密だから、口を滑らさないように。*Kore wa ima no tokoro himitsu dakara, kuchi o suberasanai yō ni.*

look like something the cat dragged in — どぶネズミのように見える — *dobu nezumi no yō ni mieru*

After walking home in the rain, Joe looked like something the cat dragged in. ジョ－は雨の中を歩いて家に帰ってきて、まるでどぶネズミのように見えました。*Jō wa ame no naka o aruite kaette kite, marude dobu nezumi no yō ni miemashita.*

look like the cat that swallowed the canary — 満足げな顔つきをする — *manzokuge na kaotsuki o suru*

What's Jill so happy about? She looks like the cat that swallowed the canary. ジルは満足げな顔つきをしているけれど、何がそんなに幸せなんですか。*Jiru wa manzokuge na kaotsuki o shite iru keredo, nani ga sonna ni shiawase nandesu ka.*

play cat and mouse (with someone) — 弄ぶ — *moteasobu*

If she'd stop playing cat and mouse with him, they might have a good relationship. 彼女が彼を弄ぶのを止めさえすれば、二人の間に好ましい関係が出来るかもしれないのですが。 *Kanojo ga kare o moteasobu no o yamesaesureba, futari no aida ni konomashii kankei ga dekiru kamo shirenai no desu ga.*

rain cats and dogs — 土砂降り — *doshaburi*
We can't go outside just yet; it's raining cats and dogs. 土砂降りなので、今は外に行けません。*Doshaburi nanode, ima wa soto ni ikemasen.*

When the cat's away, the mice will play. — 鬼の居ぬ間に洗濯 — *oni no inu ma ni sentaku*
As soon as his parents left for the evening, Hal invited several friends over. When the cat's away, the mice will play. 両親が夜に外出したとたん、ハルは友達を数人招きました。鬼の居ぬ間に洗濯というわけです。*Ryōshin ga yoru ni gaishutsu shita totan, Haru wa tomodachi o sūnin manekimashita. Oni no inu ma ni sentaku to iu wake desu.*

---

ceiling — 天井 — *tenjō*
hit the ceiling — 激怒する — *gekido suru*
When he saw the damage to his new car, he hit the ceiling. 彼は新しい車の損害を見て、激怒しました。*Kare wa atarashii kuruma no songai o mite, gekido shimashita.*

hit the glass ceiling — 女性ゆえに昇進を阻まれる — *josei yue ni shōshin o habamareru*
She was due for a promotion in her company, but she hit the glass ceiling. 彼女は会社で当然昇進を受けるべきでしたが、女性ゆえにそれを阻まれました。*Kanojo wa kaisha de tōzen shoshin o ukeru beki deshita ga, josei yue ni sore o habamaremashita.*

---

cent — セント — *sento*
not worth a red cent — 一文の価値もない — *ichi mon no kachi mo nai*
The camera keeps breaking down. It's not worth a red cent. このカメラは壊れてばかりいるので、一文の価値もありません。*Kono kamera wa kowarete bakari iru node, ichi mon no kachi mo arimasen.*

put one's two cents (worth) in — 些細ながら意見を付け加える — *sasai nagara iken o tsukekuwaeru*

I know you haven't asked my opinion, but I'd like to put my two cents in.
あなたは私の意見を聞いていませんが、些細ながら私のも付け
加えたいと思います。 *Anata wa watakushi no iken o kiite imasen ga,*
sasai nagara watakushi no mo tsukekuwaetai to omoimasu.

ceremony — 儀式 — *gishiki*
stand on ceremony — かしこまる — *kashikomaru*
Please relax and be comfortable. We don't need to stand on ceremony.
どうぞ気楽にして下さい。かしこまる必要はありません。*Dōzo*
kiraku ni shite kudasai. Kashikomaru hitsuyō wa arimasen.

chance — 機会 — *kikai*
fat chance — 全くの見込み薄 — *mattaku no mikomi usu*
You think she'll lend you her new car? Fat chance. 彼女が新車を
あなたに貸してくれると思っているんですか。全くの見込み薄
ですよ。*Kanojo ga shinsha o anata ni kashite kureru to omotte*
irundesu ka. Mattaku no mikomi usu desu yo.

change — 変化 — *henka*
have a change of heart — 気持ちを変える — *kimochi o kaeru*
At first he refused, but he's had a change of heart. 彼は最初は拒否しま
したが、気持ちを変えました。*Kare wa saisho wa kyohi shimashita*
ga, kimochi o kaemashita.

chapter — 章 — *shō*
chapter and verse — 細かく — *komakaku*
He expects his employees to follow the company rules chapter and verse.
彼は、従業員が会社の規則に細かく従うことを期待しています。
Kare wa, jūgyōin ga kaisha no kisoku ni komakaku shitagau koto o kitai
shite imasu.

chase — 追求 — *tsuikyū*
wild-goose chase — 当てのない追求 — *ate no nai tsuikyū*
Let's give up; we're on a wild-goose chase. もう諦めましょう。
私達は、当てのない追求をしているんですよ。*Mō akiramemashō.*
Watakushitachi wa ate no nai tsuikyū o shite irundesu yo.

check — 小切手 — *kogitte*

get/take a rain check — またこの次にさそってもらう — *mata kono tsugi ni sasotte morau*

I'm sorry I can't make it that night. Could I take a rain check? すみませんが、その晩は都合が悪いんです。またこの次に誘ってもらえますか。*Sumimasen ga, sono ban wa tsugō ga waruindesu. Mata kono tsugi ni sasotte moraemasu ka.*

give someone a blank check — 全権を与える — *zenken o ataeru*

They gave him a blank check to make any changes he wants in the organization. 彼等は彼が望む組織内の改革を何でも行うように、彼に全権を与えました。*Karera wa kare ga nozomu soshiki nai no kaikaku o nandemo okonau yō ni, kare ni zenken o ataemashita.*

cheek — 頬 — *hoo*

turn the other cheek — 無視する — *mushi suru*

He was extremely unpleasant to me, but I just turned the other cheek. 彼は私に対して極端に無愛想でしたが、私は単に彼を無視しました。*Kare wa watakushi ni taishite kyokutan ni buaisō deshita ga, watakushi wa tan ni kare o mushi shimashita.*

chest — 胸 — *mune*

get something off one's chest — 心につつかえている事を話して 胸をすっきりさせる — *kokoro ni tsukkaete iru koto o hanashite mune o sukkiri saseru*

I've been silent for a long time, but I have to get this off my chest. 私は長いこと黙っていましたが、この心につつかえている事を話して胸をすっきりさせねばなりません。*Watakushi wa nagai koto damatte imashita ga, kono kokoro ni tsukkaete iru koto o hanashite mune o sukkiri saseneba narimasen.*

chicken — チキン — *chikin*

chicken out (of something) — 臆病風を吹かして止める — *okubyō kaze o fukashite yameru*

He promised to go white-water rafting with us, but at the last minute he chickened out 彼は私達とゴムボートでの激流下りに行く約束をしていましたが、土壇場になって臆病風を吹かして止めました。

Kare wa watakushitachi to gomubōto de no gekiryū kudari ni iku yakusoku o shite imashita ga, dotanba ni natte okubyō kaze o fukashite yamemashita.

count one's chickens before they hatch — 捕らぬ狸の皮算用をする
— *toranu tanuki no kawazan-yō o suru*
It can be dangerous to count your chickens before they hatch. 捕らぬ狸の皮算用をするのは危ないです。*Toranu tanuki no kawazan-yō o suru no wa abunai desu.*

no spring chicken — そう若くはない — *sō wakaku wa nai*
Although he looks young, he's no spring chicken. 彼は若く見えるけれども、そう若くはありません。Kare wa wakaku mieru keredomo, sō wakaku wa arimasen.

run around like a chicken with its head cut off — やたらに走り回る
— *yatara ni hashirimawaru*
She's so excited she's running around like a chicken with its head cut off. 彼女はすっかり興奮して、やたらに走り回っています。*Kanojo wa sukkari kōfun shite, yatara ni hashirimawatte imasu.*

---

child — 子供 — *kodomo*
child's play — 朝飯前 — *asameshi mae*
Of course I can do the job. It's child's play. 勿論、私はその仕事が出来ます。それは私にとっては、朝飯前です。*Mochiron, watakushi wa sono shigoto ga dekimasu. Sore wa watakushi ni totte wa, asameshi mae desu.*

Children should be seen and not heard. — 人が話しているときに、口出ししないこと。— *Hito ga hanashite iru toki ni, kuchidashi shinai koto.*
Quiet down! Children should be seen and not heard. 静かにしなさい。人が話しているときに、口出ししないこと。*Shizuka ni shinasai. Hito ga hanashite iru toki ni, kuchidashi shinai koto.*

---

chin — 顎 — *ago*
keep one's chin up — 気落ちしないでいる — *kiochi shinaide iru*
Things may seem tough now, but keep your chin up and they'll improve. 今は何事も厳しいように見えるかもしれないけれど、気落ちしないでいればそのうちによくなりますよ。*Ima wa nanigoto mo*

kibishii yō ni mieru kamoshirenai keredo, kiochi shinaide ireba sono uchi ni yoku narimasu yo.

---

chink — 割れ目 — *wareme*

chink in one's armor — アキレス腱 — *akiresuken*

He seems tough, but I think we've found a chink in his armor. 彼は一見手ごわそうだけれど、私達は彼のアキレス腱を見つけたと思います。

Kare wa ikken tegowasō da keredo, watakushitachi wa kare no akiresuken o mitsuketa to omoimasu.

---

chip — 献金する／かけら — *kenkin/kakera*

chip in — 小金を寄付する — *kogane o kifu suru*

Tomorrow is Helen's birthday, and we're all chipping in for a present. 明日はヘレンの誕生日なので、プレゼントを買うためにみんなが小金を寄付しています。*Ashita wa Heren no tanjōbi nanode, purezento o kau tame ni minna ga kogane o kifu shite imasu.*

chip off the old block — 父親似の息子 — *chichioya ni no musuko*

Dr. Brown's son is in medical school. He's a chip off the old block. ブラウン医師の息子は、医大に行っています。彼は、父親似の息子です。*Buraun ishi no musuko wa, idai ni itte imasu. Kare wa, chichioya ni no musuko desu.*

have a chip on one's shoulder — けんか腰 — *kenkagoshi*

He's had a chip on his shoulder ever since he failed the exam. 彼は試験に落ちて以来、けんか腰です。*Kare wa shiken ni ochite irai, kenkagoshi desu.*

when the chips are down — いざというときには — *iza to iu toki niwa*

When the chips are down, I can always count on my sister. いざというときには、私はいつも姉を頼りに出来ます。*Iza to iu toki niwa, watakushi wa itsumo ane o tayori ni dekimasu.*

---

circle — 円 — *en*

come full circle — 以前の状態に戻る — *izen no jōtai ni modoru*

Now that the law has been repealed, things have come full circle. その法律が廃止された今は、事態は以前の状態に戻りました。*Sono hōritsu ga haishi sareta ima wa, jitai wa izen no jōtai ni modorimashita.*

go around in circles — 堂々巡りする — *dōdō meguri suru*

They kept going around in circles and couldn't decide on a course of action. 彼等は堂々巡りの議論を続けて、取るべき行動を決めることが出来ませんでした。Karera wa dōdō meguri no giron o tsuzukete, toru beki kōdō o kimeru koto ga dekimasen deshita.

in/into a vicious circle — 悪循環を繰り返して — aku junkan o kurikaeshite

The two countries are in a vicious circle of negotiations, threats, and reconciliations. 二国は、交渉、威嚇、和解の悪循環を繰り返しています。Ni koku wa, kōshō, ikaku, wakai no aku junkan o kurikaeshite imasu.

run circles around someone — 楽に勝てる — raku ni kateru

As a politician, he can run circles around his opponent. 政治家として、彼は競争相手に楽に勝つことが出来ます。Seijika toshite, kare wa kyōsō aite ni raku ni katsu koto ga dekimasu.

talk in circles — 堂々巡りの話しをする — dōdōmeguri no hanashi o suru

John thought he was making perfect sense, but actually he was talking in circles. ジョンは自分では完全に意味をなしていると思いましたが、実は堂々巡りの話しをしているのでした。Jon wa jibun dewa kanzen ni imi o nashite iru to omoimashita ga, jitsu wa dōdōmeguri no hanashi o shite iru no deshita.

cleaners — クリーニング屋 — kurīningu ya

take someone to the cleaners — すっからかんにする — sukkarakan ni suru

I thought their price would be fair, but they took me to the cleaners. 彼等の値段は公正だろうと思っていましたが、彼等は私をすっからかんにしました。Karera no nedan wa kōsei darō to omotte imashita ga, karera wa watakushi o sukkarakan ni shimashita.

clockwork — 時計仕掛け — tokeijikake

(as) regular as clockwork — 規則正しく — kisoku tadashiku

Our azaleas bloom every May, as regular as clockwork. わが家のつつじは、毎年規則正しく五月に咲きます。Wagaya no tsutsuji wa, maitoshi kisoku tadashiku gogatsu ni sakimasu.

go/run like clockwork — 完ぺきに進む — kanpeki ni susumu

The move to our new offices went like clockwork. 新しいオフィスへの

引っ越しは、完ぺきに進みました。*Atarashii ofisu e no hikkoshi wa,
kanpeki ni susumimashita.*

---

closet — 押入 — *oshiire*

come out of the closet — 自らの同性愛の傾向を公にする — *mizukara
no dōseiai no keikō o ōyake ni suru*

His friends were surprised when he came out of the closet.　友達たちは、
彼が自分の同性愛の傾向を公にしたときびっくりしました。
*Tomodachi wa, kare ga jibun no dōseiai no keikō o ōyake ni shita toki
bikkuri shimashita.*

---

cloud — 雲 — *kumo*

Every cloud has a silver lining. — 悪いことの反面にはよいこともある
— *warui koto no hanmen niwa yoi koto mo aru*

This may seem like a setback, but be positive. Every cloud has a silver
lining.　これは敗北に見えるかもしれないけれど、肯定的に考え
なさい。悪いことの反面には、よいこともありますよ。*Kore wa
haiboku ni mieru kamo shirenai keredo, kōteiteki ni kangaenasai. Warui
koto no hanmen niwa, yoi koto mo arimasu yo.*

on cloud nine — 天にも昇る心地 — *ten nimo noboru kokochi*

Ever since he met her, he's been on cloud nine.　彼は彼女に会って
以来、天にも昇る心地です。*Kare wa kanojo ni atte irai, ten nimo
noboru kokochi desu.*

under a cloud (of suspicion) — 疑いをかけられる — *utagai o kakerareru*

Until the thief is caught, everyone in the dormitory is under a cloud of
suspicion.　泥棒が捕まるまでは、寮にいる誰もが疑いをかけられ
ています。*Dorobō ga tsukamaru made wa, ryō ni iru daremo ga utagai
o kakerarete imasu.*

---

club — クラブ — *kurabu*

Join the club! — 私も同じ目にあっている。— *Watakushi mo onaji me
ni atte iru.*

Your car has been stolen? Join the club!　あなたの車が盗まれたんで
すって。私も同じ目にあっています。*Anata no kuruma ga
nusumaretandesutte? Watakushi mo onaji me ni atte imasu.*

coals — 石炭 — *sekitan*

(like) carrying coals to Newcastle — 必要ないことをする — *hitsuyō nai koto o suru*

Your garden is in full bloom, and I've just brought you flowers. This is like carrying coals to Newcastle. あなたの庭が花盛りなのに、花を持ってきてしまいました。これは、必要ないことでしたね。*Anata no niwa ga hanazakari nanoni, hana o motte kite shimaimashita. Kore wa, hitsuyō nai koto deshita ne.*

rake someone over the coals — 大目玉を食わす — *ōmedama o kuwasu*

I made a simple mistake, and the boss raked me over the coals. 単純な失敗をしただけなのに、ボスは私に大目玉を食わせました。*Tanjun na shippai o shita dake nanoni, bosu wa watakushi ni ōmedama o kuwasemashita.*

coast — 海岸 — *kaigan*

The coast is clear. — 気にすべき人は誰もいない。— *Ki ni subeki hito wa daremo inai.*

You can eat lunch at your desk now. The coast is clear. デスクでランチを食べてかまいませんよ。今、気にすべき人は誰もいませんから。*Desuku de ranchi o tabete kamaimasen yo. Ima, ki ni subeki hito wa daremo imasen kara.*

coattails — 燕尾服のすそ — *enbifuku no suso*

(ride) on someone's coattails — 人の人気にあやかって幸運を射止める — *hito no ninki ni ayakatte kōun o itomeru*

The senator rode to victory on the president's coattails. その上院議員は大統領の人気にあやかって、当選という幸運を射止めました。*Sono jōin giin wa daitōryō no ninki ni ayakatte, tōsen to iu kōun o itomemashita.*

cold — 外の寒いところ — *soto no samui tokoro*

keep someone out in the cold — 何も教えない — *nanimo oshienai*

Tell her what's going on. Don't keep her out in the cold. 彼女に、何が起こっているのか説明しなさい。彼女に何も教えないのはよくありません。*Kanojo ni, nani ga okotte iru no ka setsumei shinasai. Kanojo ni nanimo oshienai no wa yoku arimasen.*

collar — 襟 — *eri*

hot under the collar — かんかんに怒る — *kankan ni okoru*

The boss got hot under the collar when we missed our deadline.　私達が締め切りに間に合わなかったとき、ボスはかんかんに怒りました。*Watakushitachi ga shimekiri ni ma ni awanakatta toki, bosu wa kankan ni okorimashita.*

color — 色 — *iro*

(come through) with flying colors — 見事に — *migoto ni*

She passed the exams with flying colors.　彼女は、試験に見事に合格しました。*Kanojo wa, shiken ni migoto ni gōkaku shimashita.*

show one's true colors — 立場を明らかにする — *tachiba o akiraka ni suru*

Whose side is he on? I wish he'd show his true colors.　彼は、誰の側なんでしょうか。立場を明らかにしてもらいたいと思います。*Kare wa, dare no gawa nandeshō ka. Tachiba o akiraka ni shite moraitai to omoimasu.*

comb — 櫛 — *kushi*

go over something with a fine-tooth comb — 念入りに探す — *nen-iri ni sagasu*

We went over the area with a fine-tooth comb but couldn't find his contact lens.　私達はそこを念入りに探しましたが、彼のコンタクトレンズを見つけることが出来ませんでした。*Watakushitachi wa soko o nen-iri ni sagashimashita ga, kare no kontakuto renzu o mitsukeru koto ga dekimasen deshita.*

come — 来る — *kuru*

come around — 考えを変える — *kangae o kaeru*

John still refuses to face the truth, but he'll come around soon.　ジョンはまだ現実に直面するのを拒否していますが、近いうちに考えを変えるでしょう。*Jon wa mada genjitsu ni chokumen suru no o kyohi shite imasu ga, chikai uchi ni kangae o kaeru deshō.*

come clean — 正直に全てを話す — *shōjiki ni subete o hanasu*

If he doesn't come clean with me, I'll be forced to fire him.　もし彼が正直に全てを話さないなら、私は彼の首を切らねばなりません。

Moshi kare ga shōjiki ni subete o hanasanai nara, watakushi wa kare no kubi o kiraneba narimasen.

come down with something — 何かの病気になる — nanika no byōki ni naru

Our secretary has come down with the flu.　私達の秘書は、流感にかかっています。Watakushitachi no hisho wa, ryūkan ni kakatte imasu.

Come off it! — 馬鹿も休み休み言え。— Baka mo yasumiyasumi ie.

Come off it! You don't expect me to believe that nonsense, do you?
馬鹿も休み休み言いなさい。まさかそんな馬鹿らしい話しを私が信じるとは思っていないでしょ。Baka mo yasumiyasumi iinasai. Masaka sonna bakarashii hanashi o watakushi ga shinjiru to wa omotte inai desho.

come unglued — 感情を押さえ切れない — kanjō o osaekirenai

When they saw the hurricane damage, they came unglued.
彼等はハリケーンの被害を見たとき、感情を押さえ切れませんでした。Karera wa harikēn no higai o mita toki, kanjō o osaekiremasen deshita.

company — つき合い — tsukiai

part company — 絶縁する — zetsuen suru

They parted company because they couldn't agree on anything.　彼等は何事にも意見の相違があって、絶縁しました。Karera wa nanigoto nimo iken no sōi ga atte, zetsuen shimashita.

compliment — 誉め言葉 — *home kotoba*

fish for a compliment — 誉め言葉を聞きたがる — *homekotoba o kikitagaru*

Every time he does a good job, he's very obvious about fishing for compliments. 彼は何かいい仕事をする度に、誉め言葉を聞きたがるのは明らかです。*Kare wa nanika ii shigoto o suru tabi ni, homekotoba o kikitagaru no wa akiraka desu.*

(pay someone) a left-handed compliment — 侮辱を込めたお世辞を言う — *bujoku o kometa oseji o iu*

He said I look wonderful for someone my age. What a left-handed compliment! 彼は、私が年にしては若く見えると言いました。何という、侮辱を込めたお世辞なんでしょう。*Kare wa, watakushi ga toshi ni shite wa wakaku mieru to iimashita. Nan to iu, bujoku o kometa oseji nan deshō.*

---

condition — 条件 — *jōken*

in mint condition — 完ぺき — *kanpeki*

The car I want to buy is old, but it's in mint condition. 私が買いたい車は古いけれど、完ぺきです。*Watakushi ga kaitai kuruma wa furui keredo, kanpeki desu.*

---

convert — 改宗者 — *kaishūsha*

preach to the converted — 同好の士を説得する — *dōkō no shi o settoku suru*

He started asking her to vote for his candidate, but he was preaching to the converted. 彼は自分の推す候補者に投票するよう彼女に頼み始めましたが、それは同好の士を説得するようなものでした。*Kare wa jibun no osu kōhosha ni tōhyō suru yō kanojo ni tanomihajimemashita ga, sore wa dōkō no shi o settoku suru yō na mono deshita.*

---

cook — コック — *kokku*

Too many cooks spoil the broth. — 船頭多くして 船、山に登る。— *Sendō ōku shite fune, yama ni noboru.*

If we had fewer people here, we could make a decision. Too many cooks spoil the broth. もしここにいる人たちが少なければ、私達は結論に達することが出来るのですが。船頭多くして船、山に登るです。*Moshi koko ni iru hitotachi ga sukunakereba, watakushitachi wa ketsuron ni tassuru koto ga dekiru no desu ga. Sendō ōkushite fune, yama ni noboru desu.*

---

cool — 冷静さ／冷やす — *reiseisa/hiyasu*

blow/lose one's cool — 冷静さを失う — *reiseisa o ushinau*

No matter how much you disagree with him, try not to lose your cool. どんなに彼の意見に反対でも、冷静さを失わないようにしなさい。*Donna ni kare no iken ni hantai demo, reiseisa o ushinawanai yō ni shinasai.*

Cool it! — 頭を冷やせ。— *Atama o hiyase.*

Cool it, John. We'll get more done if you calm down. ジョン、頭を冷やしなさい。もしあなたが気を静めれば、私達は仕事をもっとはかどらせることが出来ます。*Jon, atama o hiyashinasai. Moshi anata ga ki o shizumereba, watakushitachi wa shigoto o motto hakadoraseru koto ga dekimasu.*

---

counsel — 意図 — *ito*

keep one's own counsel — 自分の考えを人に明かさない — *jibun no kangae o hito ni akasanai*

On this issue, it's best to keep your own counsel. この件に関しては、あなたは自分の考えを人に明かさないのが最善です。*Kono ken ni kanshite wa, anata wa jibun no kangae o hito ni akasanai no ga saizen desu.*

---

country — 国 — *kuni*

  another country heard from — 余計な口出し — *yokei na kuchidashi*

There goes Jim, interrupting. Another country heard from! ジムが人の
話に割って入って。余計な口出しです。*Jimu ga hito no hanashi ni
watte haitte. Yokei na kuchidashi desu.*

---

cow — 乳牛 — *nyūgyū*

  till/until the cows come home — 遅くまで — *osoku made*

Those students often stay out until the cows come home. この学生たちは、
よく遅くまで外出します。*Kono gakuseitachi wa, yoku osoku made
gaishutsu shimasu.*

---

crack — 砕く／割れ目 — *kudaku/wareme*

  crack (someone or something) up — 大笑いする — *ōwarai suru*

Every time he tells a joke, his colleagues crack up. 彼が冗談を言う度に、
同僚は大笑いします。*Kare ga jōdan o iu tabi ni, dōryō wa ōwarai
shimasu.*

  get cracking — 仕事に取りかかる — *shigoto ni torikakaru*

We have a lot of work to do. Let's get cracking. するべき仕事が山ほど
あります。さあ、取りかかりましょう。*Suru beki shigoto ga yama
hodo arimasu. Sā, torikakarimashō.*

  have/take a crack at something — 試しにやってみる — *tameshi ni
yatte miru*

You can't get the car started? Here, let me have a crack at it. 車のエンジン
がかからないんですか。では、私に試しにやらせて下さい。
*Kuruma no enjin ga kakaranaindesu ka. Dewa, watakushi ni tameshi ni
yarasete kudasai.*

  make cracks (about someone or something) — 冗談を飛ばす — *jōdan
o tobasu*

I wish he'd stop making cracks about our team. 彼が私達のチームに
ついて、冗談を飛ばすのを止めてもらいたいです。*Kare ga
wareware no chīmu ni tsuite, jōdan o tobasu no o yamete moraitai desu.*

  not all/what something is cracked up to be — 評判になっているほど

ではない — *hyoban ni natte iru hodo dewa nai*

This restaurant is good, but it's not what it's cracked up to be. この

レストランはいいですが、評判になっているほどではありません。
Kono resutoran wa ii desu ga, hyōban ni natte iru hodo dewa arimasen.

cradle — ゆりかご — *yurikago*

from the cradle to the grave — 一生 — *isshō*

Some people expect the government to take care of them from the cradle to the grave. 中には、政府が一生面倒を見てくれるのを期待している人がいます。*Naka niwa, seifu ga isshō mendō o mite kureru no o kitai shite iru hito ga imasu.*

rob the cradle — いい年をして相手が若すぎる — *ii toshi o shite aite ga wakasugiru*

John's new girlfriend is half his age; he's really robbing the cradle. ジョンの新しいガールフレンドの年は、彼の年の半分です。彼はいい年をして、相手が若すぎます。*Jon no atarashii gārufurendo no toshi wa, kare no toshi no hanbun desu. Kare wa ii toshi o shite, aite ga wakasugimasu.*

craw — 胃袋 — *ibukuro*

have something stick in one's craw — いらいらする — *iraira suru*

It really sticks in my craw that he's been late for work every day this week. 彼が今週は毎日仕事に遅れて来るのには、いらいらします。*Kare ga konshū wa mainichi shigoto ni okurete kuru no niwa, iraira shimasu.*

cream — クリーム — *kurīmu*

cream of the crop — 抜群 — *batsugun*

The new class of graduates is the cream of the crop. 今年度の卒業生は抜群です。*Kon nendo no sotsugyōsei wa batsugun desu.*

creek — 小川 — *ogawa*

up a/the creek (without a paddle) — 本当に困っている — *hontō ni komatte iru*

That was the last train! Now we're up the creek without a paddle. あれが終電車でした。私達は今、本当に困っています。*Are ga shū densha deshita. Watakushitachi wa ima, hontō ni komatte imasu.*

creep — ぞっとする感じ — *zotto suru kanji*

give someone the creeps — 気味が悪い — *kimi ga warui*

Let's get out of here; this place gives me the creeps. 急いでここを出ま
しょう。この場所は、気味が悪いです。*Isoide koko o demashō.
Kono basho wa, kimi ga warui desu.*

crow — からす — *karasu*

make someone eat crow — 過ちを認めさせる — *ayamachi o mitomesaseru*

He's going to pay for his mistake; they'll make him eat crow.
彼は、自分の失敗の代価を支払うことになります。なぜなら、
彼等は彼に過ちを認めさせるからです。*Kare wa, jibun no shippai
no daika o shiharau koto ni narimasu. Nazenara, karera wa kare ni
ayamachi o mitomesaseru kara desu.*

crystal — 水晶 — *suishō*

(as) clear as crystal — はっきりする — *hakkiri suru*

Thanks for the explanation; now it's as clear as crystal. 説明を有り難う。
これではっきりしました。*Setsumei o arigatō. Kore de hakkiri
shimashita.*

cucumber — キュウリ — *kyūri*

(as) cool as a cucumber — 落ち着き払って — *ochitsukiharatte*

In the midst of the earthquake, he stayed as cool as a cucumber. 地震の
最中に、彼は落ち着き払っていました。*Jishin no saichū ni, kare wa
ochitsukiharatte imashita.*

cuff — カフス — *kafusu*

off the cuff — 即席で — *sokuseki de*

She didn't prepare a speech; her remarks were off the cuff. 彼女は
スピーチの準備をしなかったので、彼女の話は即席でした。
*Kanojo wa supīchi no junbi o shinakatta node, kanojo no hanashi wa
sokuseki deshita.*

cup — 茶碗 — *chawan*

in one's cups — 酔っぱらって — *yopparatte*

He can't drive now; he's in his cups. 彼は今酔っぱらっているので、

車を運転できません。*Kare wa ima yopparatte iru node, kuruma o unten dekimasen.*

not one's cup of tea — 好みではない — *konomi dewa nai*
The paintings are good, but they're not my cup of tea. その絵は素晴らしいのですが、私の好みではありません。*Sono e wa subarashii no desu ga, watakushi no konomi dewa arimasen.*

curiosity — 好奇心 — *kōkishin*
    Curiosity killed the cat. — 詮索好きにもほどほどにすべきだ。 — *Sensakuzuki ni mo hodohodo ni subeki da.*
    Stop asking all those questions. Curiosity killed the cat. そのような質問をするのは止めなさい。詮索好きにもほどほどにすべきです。*Sono yō na shitsumon o suru no wa yamenasai. Sensakuzuki ni mo hodohodo ni subeki desu.*

curve — カーブ — *kābu*
    throw someone a curve (ball) — まごつかせる — *magotsukaseru*
    He threw me a curve asking me to work late; I had big plans for tonight. 今晩はすごい予定があったのに、彼は残業を求めて私をまごつかせました。*Konban wa sugoi yotei ga atta noni, kare wa zangyō o motomete watakushi o magotsukasemashita.*

cut — 切る — *kiru*
    cut above someone or something — 一段上 — *ichi dan ue*
    It's just a fast food restaurant, but it's a cut above the rest. それはファーストフードのレストランにすぎないけれど、他のよりは一段上です。*Sore wa fāsuto fūdo no resutoran ni suginai keredo, ta no yori wa ichi dan ue desu.*

    cut out to be something — 生まれつき向いている — *umaretsuki muite iru*
    Although he loves baseball, he's not cut out to be a player. 彼は野球が大好きだけれど、選手になるには生まれつき向いていません。*Kare wa yakyū ga daisuki da keredo, senshu ni naru niwa umaretsuki muite imasen.*

cylinder — シリンダー — *shirindā*
    firing/hitting on all cylinders — 全力を尽くす — *zenryoku o tsukusu*

With the new quarterback, our team is hitting on all cylinders.　新しい
クォーターバックの下で、チームは全力を尽くしています。
*Atarashii kuōtābakku no moto de, chīmu wa zenryoku o tsukushite
imasu.*

dagger — 短刀 — *tantō*

look daggers at someone — にらみつける — *niramitsukeru*
I must have made Jerry angry; he's looking daggers at me.　私は、
ジェリーを怒らせてしまったに違いありません。というのは、
彼は私をにらみつけているからです。*Watakushi wa, Jerī o
okorasete shimatta ni chigai arimasen. To iu no wa, kare wa watakushi o
niramitsukete iru kara desu.*

daisy — ひな菊 — *hinagiku*

(as) fresh as a daisy — 爽快／元気はつらつ — *sōkai/genki hatsuratsu*
I got a good night's sleep, and this morning I feel fresh as a daisy.　夕べは
ぐっすり寝て、今朝は気分爽快です。*Yūbe wa gussuri nete, kesa wa
kibun sōkai desu.*

pushing up daisies — 死んでいる — *shinde iru*
Is that fellow still alive? I thought he'd be pushing up daisies by now.
あの人は、まだ生きているんですか。彼はとっくに死んでいると
思っていました。*Ano hito wa, mada ikite irundesu ka. Kare wa
tokkuni shinde iru to omotte imashita.*

dark — 暗闇 — *kurayami*

in the dark (about someone or something) — つんぼ桟敷に置かれる
— *tsunbo sajiki ni okareru*
He hasn't told me anything about his plans. I'm in the dark.　彼は計画に
ついて、私に何も言っていません。私は、つんぼ桟敷に置かれて
いるのです。*Kare wa keikaku ni tsuite, watakushi ni nani mo itte
imasen. Watakushi wa, tsunbo sajiki ni okarete iru no desu.*

day — 昼間 — *hiruma*

(as) plain as day — 簡単明瞭 — *kantan meiryō*
Her directions were as plain as day.　彼女の道順の説明は、簡単明瞭
でした。*Kanojo no michijun no setsumei wa, kantan meiryō deshita.*

call it a day — これで切り上げる — *kore de kiriageru*
It's late; let's call it a day.　遅くなりました。今日はこれで切り
上げましょう。*Osoku narimashita. Kyō wa kore de kiriagemashō.*

day in and day out — 明けても暮れても — *akete mo kurete mo*
He works hard day in and day out.　彼は、明けても暮れても一生懸命
働いています。*Kare wa, akete mo kurete mo isshōkenmei hataraite
imasu.*

have a field day — 願ってもない機会を得る — *negatte mo nai kikai o
eru*
The media will have a field day with this scandal.　マスコミはこの
スキャンダルで、願ってもない機会を得るでしょう。*Masukomi
wa kono sukyandaru de, negatte mo nai kikai o eru deshō.*

have seen better days — おんぼろになる／盛りを過ぎる — *onboro ni
naru/sakari o sugiru*
This old car has seen better days.　この古い車は、すっかりおんぼろに
なってしまいました。*Kono furui kuruma wa, sukkari onboro ni natte
shimaimashita.*

in this day and age — 今時 — *imadoki*
I was surprised to hear such old-fashioned opinions in this day and age.
今時そんな古くさい意見を聞いて驚きました。*Imadoki sonna
furukusai iken o kiite odorokimashita.*

make a day of it — 一日を過ごす — *ichi nichi o sugosu*
Let's make a day of it tomorrow; we'll go shopping, have lunch, and see a
movie.　買い物をして、昼食を食べて、映画を見て、明日一日を
過ごしましょう。*Kaimono o shite, chūshoku o tabete, eiga o mite,
ashita ichi nichi o sugoshimashō.*

one's days are numbered — 先が長くない — *saki ga nagaku nai*
He thinks he'll be in charge forever, but his days are numbered.　彼は
自分が永久に責任者だと思っていますが、彼の先は長くありません。
*Kare wa jibun ga eikyū ni sekininsha da to omotte imasu ga, kare no
saki wa nagaku arimasen.*

save the day — 窮地を救う — *kyūchi o sukuu*

John just found the missing data and saved the day for the company.
ジョンは失われていたデータを今さっき見つけて、会社の窮地を
救いました。*Jon wa ushinawarete ita dēta o ima sakki mitsukete,
kaisha no kyūchi o sukuimashita.*

That'll be the day! — まさか。 — *Masaka!*

A big raise for everyone? That'll be the day! 　全員に大型昇給だつて。
まさか。*Zen-in ni ōgata shōkyū datte. Masaka!*

---

daylight — 日光 — *nikkō*

beat the living daylights out of someone — 打ちのめす — *uchinomesu*

The man said he'd beat the living daylights out of anyone who threatened
his son. 　その男は、息子を脅かす者は誰でも打ちのめしてやると
言いました。*Sono otoko wa, musuko o odokasu mono wa dare demo
uchinomeshite yaru to iimashita.*

frighten/scare the living daylights out of someone — すつかりおびえ

させる — *sukkari obiesaseru*

The auto accident scared the living daylights out of John. 　その交通事故は、
ジョンをすつかりおびえさせました。*Sono kōtsū jiko wa, Jon o
sukkari obiesasemashita.*

in broad daylight — 真つ昼間に — *mappiruma ni*

The robbery took place in broad daylight. 　真つ昼間に、強盗が
ありました。*Mappiruma ni gōtō ga arimashita.*

---

deadwood — 枯れ木 — *kareki*

cut out the deadwood — 役立たずを首にする — *yakutatazu o kubi ni suru*

If the company would cut out the deadwood, we'd be more productive.
会社が役立たずを首にすれば、もつと生産性が上がります。
Kaisha ga yakutatazu o kubi ni sureba, motto seisansei ga agarimasu.

---

death — 死 — *shi*

catch one's death (of cold) — ひどい風邪をひく — *hidoi kaze o hiku*

If you don't want to catch your death, you'd better change into some dry
clothes. 　ひどい風邪を ひきたく なかつたら、乾いた服に着替えた
方がいいですよ。*Hidoi kaze o hikitaku nakattara, kawaita fuku ni
kigaeta hō ga ii desu yo.*

look like death warmed over — 死人のように青ざめて見える — *shinin no yō ni aozamete mieru*
I haven't slept or bathed in 24 hours; I must look like death warmed over. 私はこの２４時間、寝ていないし風呂にも入っていません。それで、死人のように青ざめて見えるに違いありません。*Watakushi wa kono nijūyojikan, nete inai shi furo ni mo haitte imasen. Sorede, shinin no yō ni aozamete mieru ni chigai arimasen.*

thrilled to death — 嬉しくてたまらない — *ureshikute tamaranai*
When he received a promotion, he was thrilled to death. 彼は昇進を受けて、嬉しくてたまりませんでした。*Kare wa shōshin o ukete, ureshikute tamarimasen deshita.*

deck — 甲板 — *kanpan*
clear the decks — 場所を空ける — *basho o akeru*
The children cleared the decks when they heard the adults approach. 子供たちは大人が近付いてくるのを聞いて、場所を空けました。*Kodomotachi wa otona ga chikazuite kuru no o kiite, basho o akemashita.*

degree — 階級 — *kaikyū*
give someone the third degree — 厳しく問いただす — *kibishiku toitadasu*
If I'm late getting home, my parents will give me the third degree. 家に帰るのが遅くなると、両親は私を厳しく問いただします。*Ie ni kaeru no ga osoku naru to, ryōshin wa watakushi o kibishiku toitadashimasu.*

to the nth degree — 徹底的に／極度に — *tetteiteki ni/kyokudo ni*
She does her job to the nth degree. 彼女は、徹底的に仕事をします。*Kanojo wa, tetteiteki ni shigoto o shimasu.*

dent — へこみ — *hekomi*
make a dent in something — いくらか減らす — *ikura ka herasu*
I'd better work late today; I haven't made a dent in this stack of papers. この書類の山をいくらも減らしていないので、今日は残業すべきです。*Kono shorui no yuma o ikura mo herashite inai node, kyō wa zangyō subeki desu.*

desert — 相応の価値 — *sō-ō no kachi*

get one's just deserts — 当然の報いを受ける — *tōzen no mukui o ukeru*

When John was fired, most people thought he had gotten his just deserts. ジョンが首になったとき、大部分の人が、彼は当然の報いを 受けたと思いました。*Jon ga kubi ni natta toki, dai bubun no hito ga, kare wa tōzen no mukui o uketa to omoimashita.*

design — デザイン — *dezain*

have designs on someone or something — 下心がある — *shitagokoro ga aru*

Mary has designs on my new dress; I think she wants to borrow it for the party. メリーは、私の新しいドレスに対して下心があります。 彼女は、それをパーティーのために借りたいのです。*Merī wa, watakushi no atarashii doresu ni taishite shitagokoro ga arimasu. Kanojo wa, sore o pātī no tame ni karitai no desu.*

devil — 悪魔 — *akuma*

between the devil and the deep blue sea — 進退窮まって — *shintai kiwamatte*

He doesn't know what to decide; he's between the devil and the deep blue sea. 彼はどう決めたらいいか分からなくて、進退窮まっています。 *Kare wa dō kimetara ii ka wakaranakute, shintai kiwamatte imasu.*

catch the devil — 大目玉を食う — *ōmedama o kuu*

She's going to catch the devil for disobeying her parents. 彼女は両親の 言いつけにそむいて、大目玉を食うでしょう。*Kanojo wa ryōshin no iitsuke ni somuite, ōmedama o kuu deshō.*

give the devil his due — 例えひどい人でも、いいところは認めて あげる — *tatoe hidoi hito demo ii tokoro wa mitomete ageru*

He may be a tyrant, but his company makes a profit. Give the devil his due. 彼はワンマンかもしれませんが、彼の会社は利益を上げています。 例えひどい人でも、いいところは認めてあげるべきです。*Kare wa wanman kamo shiremasen ga, kare no kaisha wa rieki o agete imasu. Tatoe hidoi hito demo, ii tokoro wa mitomete ageru beki desu.*

play devil's advocate — あまのじゃくになる — *amanojaku ni naru*

Although I agree with you, let me play devil's advocate and argue for the other side. 私はあなたに賛成ですが、あまのじゃくになって相手側の立場から議論してみましょう。*Watakushi wa anata ni sansei desu ga, amanojaku ni natte aitegawa no tachiba kara giron shite mimashō.*

speak of the devil — 噂をすれば影とやら。 — *Uwasa o sureba kage to yara.*

Well, speak of the devil. We were just talking about you, Jane, and here you are. おや、噂をすれば影とやら。ジェーン、今あなたについて話しているところだったんですよ。ちょうどそこに、あなたが来たわけ。*Oya, uwasa o sureba kage to yara. Jēn, ima anata ni tsuite hanashite iru tokoro dattandesu yo. Chōdo soko ni, anata ga kita wake.*

---

diamond — ダイヤモンド — *daiyamondo*

diamond in the rough — 見かけによらぬ隠れた才能の持ち主／潜在的価値の ある物 — *mikake ni yoranu kakureta sainō no mochinushi/senzaiteki kachi no aru mono*

Jim hasn't had much schooling, but he's a diamond in the rough. ジムには大した学歴はありませんが、見かけによらぬ隠れた才能の持ち主です。*Jimu niwa taishita gakureki wa arimasen ga, mikake ni yoranu kakureta sainō no mochinushi desu.*

---

dime — 10セント硬貨 — *jussento kōka*

dime a dozen — そこらにごろごろしている — *sokora ni gorogoro shite iru*

People like him are a dime a dozen. 彼みたいな人は、そこらにごろごろしています。*Kare mitai na hito wa, sokora ni gorogoro shite imasu.*

not worth a dime — 一文の価値もない — *ichi mon no kachi mo nai*

This merchandise is inferior; it isn't worth a dime. この商品は品質が悪く、一文の価値もありません。*Kono shōhin wa hinshitsu ga waruku, ichi mon no kachi mo arimasen.*

turn on a dime — 小回りがきく — *komawari ga kiku*

What a great steering system! This car can turn on a dime. なんて素晴らしいハンドルなんだろう。この車は、小回りが実によくきく。*Nante subarashii handoru nandarō. Kono kuruma wa, komawari ga jitsu ni yoku kiku.*

dirt — 泥 — *doro*

dig up some dirt on someone — 汚点を暴き立てる — *oten o abakitateru*

They dug up some dirt on the mayor, and he was indicted for fraud.
彼等は市長の汚点を暴き立て、市長は詐欺で起訴されました。
Karera wa shichō no oten o abakitate, shichō wa sagi de kiso saremashita.

dirt cheap — ただも同然 — *tada mo dōzen*

They were lucky to find their apartment—the rent is dirt cheap. 家賃が ただも同然なので、彼等は今のマンションを見つけて運が よかつたです。*Yachin ga tada mo dōzen nanode, karera wa ima no manshon o mitsukete un ga yokatta desu.*

hit pay dirt — 求めていたものに行き当たる — *motomete ita mono ni ikiataru*

She hit pay dirt with her new book, a best seller. 彼女は最近出した本で、 求めていたものに行き当たりました。その本が、ベストセラ－に なったのです。*Kanojo wa saikin dashita hon de, motomete ita mono ni ikiatarimashita. Sono hon ga, besutoserā ni natta no desu.*

---

distance — 距離 — *kyori*

go the distance — やりぬく — *yarinuku*

The campaign is going to be tough. Do you think he can go the distance?
選挙運動が厳しくなるけれど、彼はやりぬくことが出来ると 思いますか。*Senkyo undō ga kibishiku naru keredo, kare wa yarinuku koto ga dekiru to omoimasu ka.*

keep one's distance (from someone or something) — 接触を避ける — *sesshoku o sakeru*

I haven't seen John recently. He's been keeping his distance since our misunderstanding. 最近、ジョンに会っていません。彼は意見の 食い違いがあって以来、接触を避けているのです。*Saikin, Jon ni atte imasen. Kare wa iken no kuichigai ga atte irai, sesshoku o sakete iru no desu.*

---

do — もたらす — *motarasu*

do someone proud — 得意がらせる — *tokuigaraseru*

John did his parents proud in the debate. ジョンは見事に討論して、

彼の両親を得意がらせました。Jon wa migoto ni tōron shite, kare no ryōshin o tokuigarasemashita.

doctor — 医者 — isha

just what the doctor ordered — 一番必要だったもの — ichiban hitsuyō datta mono

What a wonderful place to relax! This is just what the doctor ordered. なんて素晴らしい憩いの場所なんでしょう。これこそ、一番必要な ものだったんですよ。Nante subarashii ikoi no basho nandeshō. Kore koso, ichiban hitsuyō na mono dattandesu yo.

dog — 犬 — inu

(as) sick as a dog — ひどい病状 — hidoi byōjō

He had the flu last week and was sick as a dog. 彼は先週流感にかかって、ひどい病状でした。Kare wa senshū ryūkan ni kakatte, hidoi byōjō deshita.

dog and pony show — ありきたりの出し物 — arikitari no dashimono

I wish John would change his presentation. It's the same old dog and pony show. ジョンの発表は昔ながらのありきたりの出し物なので、彼がそれを変えることを願っています。Jon no happyō wa mukashi nagara no arikitari no dashimono nanode, kare ga sore o kaeru koto o negatte imasu.

dog-eat-dog — 我勝ちの — waregachi no

Do whatever you have to do to get the job; it's dog-eat-dog competition. その仕事を獲得するには、我勝ちの競争だし、しなければならないことは何でもしなさい。Sono shigoto o kakutoku suru niwa, waregachi no kyōsō dashi, shinakereba naranai koto wa nandemo shinasai.

Every dog has its day. — 誰にも、そのうち機会が巡ってくる — dare ni mo, sono uchi kikai ga megutte kuru

Don't be discouraged over one interview. Every dog has its day. 一度の面接で、がっかりすることはありません。誰にも、そのうち機会が巡ってくるものです。Ichido no mensetsu de, gakkari suru koto wa arimasen. Dare ni mo, sono uchi kikai ga megutte kuru mono desu.

go to the dogs — だめになる — dame ni naru

Our neighbors' garden has been going to the dogs while they're away on vacation. 近所の人の庭は、バカンスで留守の間にだめになって います。Kinjo no hito no niwa wa, bakansu de rusu no aida ni dame ni natte imasu.

let sleeping dogs lie — そのままにしておく — sono mama ni shite oku
If John doesn't remember the incident, don't bring it up; let sleeping dogs lie. ジョンがその出来事を覚えていないなら、その件を持ち出さ ないように。そのままにしておくのが一番です。Jon ga sono dekigoto o oboete inai nara, sono ken o mochidasanai yō ni. Sono mama ni shite oku no ga ichiban desu.

You can't teach an old dog new tricks. — 年寄りが、新しいことを学ぶ のは困難だ。 — Toshiyori ga, atarashii koto o manabu no wa konnan da.
We shouldn't expect Bill to adapt to the changes easily. You can't teach an old dog new tricks. 私達は、ビルが変化に簡単に順応するのを 期待すべきではありません。年寄りが、新しいことを学ぶのは 困難ですから。Watakushitachi wa, Biru ga henka ni kantan ni junnō suru no o kitai subeki dewa arimasen. Toshiyori ga, atarashii koto o manabu no wa konnan desu kara.

---

doghouse — 犬小屋 — inugoya
in the doghouse — 不興をこうむる — fukyō o kōmuru
I forgot to order the food for the party. I'm really in the doghouse now! パーティーの料理の注文を忘れてしまって、大変な不興を こうむっています。Pātī no ryōri no chūmon o wasurete shimatte, taihen na fukyō o kōmutte imasu.

---

dollar — ドル — doru
bet one's bottom dollar — 間違いなし — machigainashi
I'd bet my bottom dollar he's going to run for election again. 彼がまた 出馬することは間違いなしです。Kare ga mata shutsuba suru koto wa machigai nashi desu.

---

door — 戸／ドア — to/doa
at death's door — 危篤状態 — kitoku jōtai
He's at death's door after a bad fall from a ladder. 彼は梯子からの 落ち方がひどくて、危篤状態です。Kare wa hashigo kara no ochikata ga hidokute, kitoku jōtai desu.

behind closed doors — 密かに — *hisoka ni*
They're so secretive; every decision is made behind closed doors. 彼等は
非常に秘密主義で、何事も密かに決めています。*Karera wa hijō ni
himitsu shugi de, nanigoto mo hisoka ni kimete imasu.*

close the door (on someone or something) — 閉め出す — *shimedasu*
He turned down our idea for now, but he said he's not closing the door on
it. 彼は今のところ私達のアイディアを却下しましたが、それを
閉め出したわけではないと言いました。*Kare wa ima no tokoro
watakushitachi no aidia o kyakka shimashita ga, sore o shimedashita
wake dewa nai to iimashita.*

doornail — 鋲釘 — *byōkugi*
  (as) dead as a doornail — 間違いなく死んでいる — *machigai naku
  shinde iru*
Our car hit a raccoon; it's as dead as a doornail. 私達はアライグマを
ひいてしまい、それは間違いなく死んでいます。*Watakushitachi
wa araiguma o hiite shimai, sore wa machigai naku shinde imasu.*

dose — 服用量 — *fukuyō ryō*
  dose of one's own medicine — 同じ目 — *onaji me*
She's so nasty to everyone. Shall we give her a dose of her own medicine?
彼女は、誰に対しても意地悪です。私達も、彼女に同じ目に
あわせてやりましょうか。*Kanojo wa, dare ni taishite mo ijiwaru
desu. Watakushitachi mo, kanojo ni onaji me ni awasete yarimashō ka.*

dot — 点 — *ten*
  on the dot — きっかりに — *kikkari ni*
He always arrives at work at nine on the dot. 彼はいつも九時きっかりに
出勤します。*Kare wa itsumo ku ji kikkari ni shukkin shimasu.*

downhill — 下り坂 — *kudarizaka*
  downhill from here on — これから楽になる — *kore kara raku ni naru*
The difficult part is over; it's all downhill from here on. 難しい箇所は
終わりました。これからは、全て楽になります。*Muzukashii kasho
wa owarimashita. Kore kara wa, subete raku ni narimasu.*

  go downhill — 落ち目になる — *ochime ni naru*

He was a good lawyer, but lately his reputation has been going downhill. 彼は素晴らしい弁護士でしたが、最近、彼の評判は落ち目になっています。*Kare wa subarashii bengoshi deshita ga, saikin, kare no hyōban wa ochime ni natte imasu.*

draw — 抜き出し — *nukidashi*

beat someone to the draw — 出し抜く — *dashinuku*
I thought we had gotten our proposal in first, but another company beat us to the draw. 私達が最初に企画書を提出したと思いましたが、他の会社に出し抜かれてしまいました。*Watakushitachi ga saisho ni kikakusho o teishutsu shita to omoimashita ga, hoka no kaisha ni dashinukarete shimaimashita.*

quick on the draw/trigger — 何事にも反応が素早い — *nanigoto ni mo hannō ga subayai*
Mary's always first in line; she's quick on the draw. 彼女は何事にも反応が素早くて、行列ではいつも先頭に並びます。*Kanojo wa nanigoto ni mo hannō ga subayakute, gyōretsu de wa itsumo sentō ni narabimasu.*

dream — 夢 — *yume*

dream come true — 夢が実現する — *yume ga jitsugen suru*
Owning my own business is a dream come true. 夢が実現して、ビジネスオーナーになりました。*Yume ga jitsugen shite, bijinesu ōnā ni narimashita.*

pipe dream — 全くの空想 — *mattaku no kūsō*
His plan to win the lottery is a pipe dream. 彼の宝くじを当てるという計画は、全くの空想にすぎません。*Kare no takarakuji o ateru to iu keikaku wa, mattaku no kūsō ni sugimasen.*

dress — 服装 — *fukusō*

dressed to kill — 見事に決まった豪勢な身なりをする — *migoto ni kimatta gōsei na minari o suru*
Where is she going? She's dressed to kill. 彼女は、どこへ行くんでしょう。見事に決まった豪勢な身なりをしています。*Kanojo wa, doko e ikundeshō. Migoto ni kimatta gōsei na minari o shite imasu.*

give someone a (good) dressing down — 厳しく叱りつける — *kibishiku shikaritsukeru*

The boss was furious and gave me a good dressing down.　ボスはひどく
怒って、私を厳しく叱りつけました。*Bosu wa hidoku okotte,*
watakushi o kibishiku shikaritsukemashita.

drop — 落下／一滴 — *rakka/hitoshizuku*
　at the drop of a hat — すぐにでも — *sugu ni demo*
　He's ready to play golf at the drop of a hat.　彼はすぐにでも、ゴルフを
　する気が十分です。*Kare wa sugu ni demo, gorufu o suru ki ga jūbun*
　desu.

　drop in the bucket — 雀の涙 — *suzume no namida*
　We need a lot more than that for a down payment. That's just a drop in the
　bucket.　頭金としては、それよりもっと必要です。それだけでは、
　雀の涙にすぎません。*Atama kin toshite wa, sore yori motto hitsuyō*
　desu. Sore dake dewa, suzume no namida ni sugimasen.

drummer — 鼓手 — *koshu*
　march to a different drummer — 違った考え方を持つ — *chigatta*
　kangaekata o motsu
　Bill doesn't care what others think; he marches to a different drummer.
　ビルは、他人が何を考えようと気にしません。人とは違った
　考え方を持っているからです。*Biru wa, tanin ga nani o kangaeyō to*
　ki ni shimasen. Hito to wa chigatta kangaekata o motte iru kara desu.

druthers — 好み — *konomi*
　have one's druthers — 好みを選ぶ — *konomi o erabu*
　If I had my druthers, I'd live in a warm climate.　もし自分の好みを
　選べるなら、暖かい気候の所に住みます。*Moshi jibun no konomi o*
　eraberu nara, atatakai kikō no tokoro ni sumimasu.

duck — 鴨 — *kamo*
　as a duck takes to water — 楽々と — *rakuraku to*
　She learned to drive as a duck takes to water.　彼女は楽々と車の運転の
　仕方を覚えました。*Kanojo wa rakuraku to kuruma no unten no*
　shikata o oboemashita.

　be a sitting duck — 攻撃の格好の的 — *kōgeki no kakkō no mato*
　He became a sitting duck when he spoke his mind on the death penalty.

彼は死刑について思うことを述べたら、攻撃の格好の的に
なりました。*Kare wa shikei ni tsuite omoukoto o nobetara, kōgeki no
kakkō no mato ni narimashita.*

dead duck — 一巻の終わり — *ikkan no owari*
If I fail this exam, I'm a dead duck.　もしこの試験に落ちたら、私は
一巻の終わりです。*Moshi kono shiken ni ochitara, watakushi wa
ikkan no owari desu.*

get one's ducks in a row — 準備万端整える — *junbi bantan totonoeru*
We have all our ducks in a row for today's meeting.　私達は今日の
会議のために、準備万端整えてあります。*Watakushitachi wa kyo
no kaigi no tame ni, junbi bankan totonoete arimasu.*

dump — ごみ捨て場 — *gomi sute ba*
down in the dumps — 落ち込む — *ochikomu*
He's been down in the dumps all week.　彼は、今週ずっと落ち込んで
います。*Kare wa, konshū zutto ochikonde imasu.*

dust — 粉のような土 — *kona no yō na tsuchi*
bite the dust — 死ぬ — *shinu*
He was a good old soldier, but he finally bit the dust.　彼は優れた
ベテラン兵士でしたが、その彼もとうとう死にました。*Kare wa
sugureta beteran heishi deshita ga, sono kare mo tōtō shinimashita.*

Dutch — オランダの — *Oranda no*
Dutch treat — 自弁 — *jiben*
The brunch on Sunday is going to be Dutch treat.　日曜日のブランチは
自弁です。*Nichiyōbi no buranchi wa jiben desu.*

go Dutch — 自弁にする — *jiben ni suru*
Let's go Dutch at lunchtime today.　今日のランチは、自弁にしましょう。
Kyō no ranchi wa, jiben ni shimashō.

in Dutch (with someone) — まずいことになって — *mazui koto ni natte*
He's just wrecked his mother's new car; he's in Dutch with her now.
彼はお母さんの新車を壊してしまい、今は彼女とまずいことに
なっています。*Kare wa okāsan no shinsha o kowashite shimai, ima
wa kanojo to mazui koto ni natte imasu.*

ear — 耳 — *mimi*

be all ears — 耳を澄まして聞く — *mimi o sumashite kiku*
Go ahead and tell me your news. I'm all ears.　どうぞ伝えたいことが
あるなら言って下さい。耳を澄まして聞きますから。*Dōzo*
tsutaetai koto ga aru nara itte kudasai. Mimi o sumashite kikimasu kara.

bend someone's ear — 長話をする — *nagabanashi o suru*
I'm sorry I called: he bent my ear for an hour.　電話して後悔しています。
彼は一時間も長話をしたのです。*Denwa shite kōkai shite imasu.*
Kare wa ichi jikan mo nagabanashi o shita no desu.

fall on deaf ears — 無視される — *mushi sareru*
I tried to warn him about the problem, but it fell on deaf ears.　彼にその
問題について警告しようとしましたが、それは無視されました。
Kare ni sono mondai ni tsuite keikoku shiyō to shimashita ga, sore wa
mushi saremashita.

get/have someone's ear — 聞く気にさせる — *kiku ki ni saseru*
Now that you have his ear, maybe he'll listen to reason.　今あなたは彼を
聞く気にさせているから、多分あなたの言い分に耳を傾ける
でしょう。*Ima anata wa kare o kiku ki ni sasete iru kara, tabun anata*
no iibun ni mimi o katamukeru deshō.

go in one ear and out the other — 耳から耳へ抜けてしまう — *mimi kara mimi e nukete shimau*

When I scold my son, it goes in one ear and out the other.　息子を
しかっても、それは耳から耳へ抜けてしまいます。*Musuko o shikattemo, sore wa mimi kara mimi e nukete shimaimasu.*

have (keep) one's ear to the ground — 耳ざとい — *mimizatoi*

Tim has his ear to the ground; he always knows what the competition is planning.　ティムは耳ざとくて、競争相手が何を計画しているか
いつも知っています。*Timu wa mimizatokute, kyōsō aite ga nani o keikaku shite iru ka itsumo shitte imasu.*

lend an ear (to someone) — 耳を貸す — *mimi o kasu*

If you need someone to talk to, I'd be happy to lend an ear.　誰か話す
相手が必要なら、喜んで耳を貸します。*Dareka hanasu aite ga hitsuyō nara, yorokonde mimi o kashimasu.*

play something by ear — その場まかせでやる — *sono ba makase de yaru*

Let's not make plans for the weekend; we'll just play it by ear.　週末の
計画を立てるのは止めて、その場まかせでやりましょう。
Shūmatsu no keikaku o tateru no wa yamete, sono ba makase de yarimashō.

talk someone's ear off — うんざりするほど喋りまくる — *unzari suru hodo shaberimakuru*

When I saw him yesterday, he talked my ear off.　昨日彼に会ったら、
うんざりするほど喋りまくりました。*Kinō kare ni attara, unzari suru hodo shaberimakurimashita.*

turn a deaf ear (to someone or something) — 耳を貸さない — *mimi o kasanai*

When he asked his sister for a loan, she turned a deaf ear to him.　彼は
お姉さんに借金を申し込みましたが、彼女は耳を貸しませんでした。
Kare wa onēsan ni shakkin o mōshikomimashita ga, kanojo wa mimi o kashimasen deshita.

up to one's ears (in something) — 身動きがとれない — *miugoki ga torenai*

I'd love to play golf this afternoon, but I'm up to my ears in work.
今日の午後ゴルフをしたいけれど、仕事で身動きがとれません。

Kyō no gogo gorufu o shitai keredo, shigoto de miugoki ga toremasen.

wet behind the ears — 青二才 — *ao nisai*

He thinks he can handle the job, but he's still wet behind the ears. 　彼は
自分ではその仕事が扱えると思っていますが、まだ青二才に
すぎません。*Kare wa jibun de wa sono shigoto ga atsukaeru to omotte
imasu ga, mada ao nisai ni sugimasen.*

---

easier — もっと容易な — *motto yōi na*

  easier said than done — 言うは易く行うは難し — *iu wa yasuku
okonau wa katashi*

Finish this by Friday? That's easier said than done. 　これを金曜日までに
終わらせるんですか。それは、言うに易く行うに難しですよ。
*Kore o kin-yōbi made ni owaraserundesu ka. Sore wa, iu ni yasuku
okonau ni katashi desu yo.*

---

eel — 鰻 — *unagi*

  (as) slippery as an eel — 捕らえようがない — *toraeyō ga nai*

I can't get a straight answer out of him; he's as slippery as an eel. 　彼は
捕らえようがないので、彼から率直な答えを得ることは出来ません。
*Kare wa toraeyō ga nai node, kare kara sotchoku na kotae o eru koto wa
dekimasen.*

---

egg — 卵 — *tamago*

  have egg on one's face — 赤面する — *sekimen suru*

The weatherman had today's forecast all wrong; now he has egg on his
face. 　天気予報係は今日の予報を全く間違って、赤面しています。
*Tenki yohō gakari wa kyō no yohō o mattaku machigatte, sekimen shite
imasu.*

  put all one's eggs in one basket — 一つに全てを賭ける — *hitotsu ni
subete o kakeru*

You should diversify your investments. Don't put all your eggs in one
basket. 　投資は、多様化させるべきです。一つに全てを賭けない
ように。*Tōshi wa tayōka saseru beki desu. Hitotsu ni subete o
kakenaiyō ni.*

  walk on eggs/eggshells — 慎重に振る舞う — *shinchō ni furumau*

When the boss is in a bad mood, everyone has to walk on eggs around him.

上司の機嫌が悪いときには、誰もが慎重に振る舞わねばなりません。
Jōshi no kigen ga warui toki ni wa, daremo ga shinchō ni furumawaneba narimasen.

---

elbows — 肘 — *hiji*
rub elbows (with someone) — 付き合う — *tsukiau*
We work together, but we don't rub elbows outside the office.　私達は
一緒に仕事していますが、職場外での個人的な付き合いは
ありません。*Watakushitachi wa issho ni shigoto shite imasu ga, shokuba gai de no kojinteki na tsukiai wa arimasen.*

---

elephant — 象 — *zō*
white elephant — 無用の長物 — *muyō no chōbutsu*
My old computer is a white elephant.　私の古いコンピュータは、無用の
長物です。*Watakushi no furui konpyūta wa, muyō no chōbutsu desu.*

---

end — 終わり／端／先端 — *owari/hashi/sentan*
at the end of nowhere — 特にへんぴな所に — *tokuni henpi na tokoro ni*
She lives out in the country at the end of nowhere.　彼女は、田舎でも
特にへんぴな所に住んでいます。*Kanojo wa, inaka demo tokuni henpi na tokoro ni sunde imasu.*

at the end of one's rope — がまんの限界に来ている — *gaman no genkai ni kite iru*
Her kids are driving her crazy; she's at the end of her rope.　彼女の
子供たちは彼女を狂気に駆り立てて、彼女はもうがまんの限界に
来ています。*Kanojo no kodomotachi wa kanojo o kyōki ni karitatete, kanojo wa mō gaman no genkai ni kite imasu.*

can't see beyond the end of one's nose — 先のことが見えない — *saki no koto ga mienai*
Tom doesn't plan for the future. He can't see beyond the end of his nose.
トムは、将来の計画を立てません。先のことが見えないからです。
Tomu wa, shōrai no keikaku o tatemasen. Saki no koto ga mienai kara desu.

come to a dead end — 行き詰まる — *ikizumaru*
The police have no more clues in the case; they've come to a dead end.

警察はこの事件でそれ以上の手がかりがなく、行き詰まっています。
Keisatsu wa kono jiken de sore ijō no tegakari ga naku, ikizumatte imasu.

get the short end of the stick — 馬鹿を見る — *baka o miru*

He's been cheated again. He always seems to get the short end of the stick.
彼は、まただまされてしまいました。彼は、いつも馬鹿を見るみたいです。 *Kare wa, mata damasarete shimaimashita. Kare wa, itsumo baka o miru mitai desu.*

go off the deep end — 極端に走る／我を忘れる — *kyokutan ni hashiru/ware o wasureru*

Please consider what you're doing. Don't go off the deep end. 極端に走らずに、今していることを考慮に入れなさい。 *Kyokutan ni hashirazu ni, ima shite iru koto o kōryo ni irenasai.*

make both ends meet — 家計を何とかやり繰りする — *kakei o nantoka yarikuri suru*

With his small salary, he can't make both ends meet. 彼はサラリーが少なくて、家計のやり繰りが出来ません。 *Kare wa sararī ga sukunakute, kakei no yarikuri ga dekimasen.*

play both ends against the middle — 漁夫の利を得ようとする — *gyofu no ri o eyō to suru*

If you try to play both ends against the middle, you'll get into trouble.
漁夫の利を得ようともくろんだりすると、いざこざに巻き込まれますよ。 *Gyofu no ri o eyō to mokurondari suru to, izakoza ni makikomaremasu yo.*

---

enough — 十分 — *jūbun*

Enough is enough. — ものには限度がある。— *Mono ni wa gendo ga aru.*

Stop your arguing. Enough is enough. 言い争うのはやめなさい。 ものには限度があります。 *Iiarasou no wa yamenasai. Mono niwa gendo ga arimasu.*

leave/let well enough alone — するがまま／そのままにさせる — *suru ga mama/sono mama ni saseru*

It's not perfect, but I'm going to leave well enough alone. 完全ではありませんが、するがままにさせておきましょう。 *Kanzen dewa arimasen ga, suru ga mama ni sasete okimashō.*

not know enough to come in out of the rain — まともな判断が
できない — *matomo na handan ga dekinai*
She's so stupid she doesn't know enough to come in out of the rain.　彼女は
全くの愚か者で、まともな判断ができません。*Kanojo wa mattaku
no oroka mono de, matomo na handan ga dekimasen.*

---

envy — 嫉妬 — *shitto*
green with envy — 羨ましくてしょうがない — *urayamashikute shō ga nai*
When I saw his new car, I was green with envy.　彼の新車を見たとき、
羨ましくてしょうがありませんでした。*Kare no shinsha o mita toki,
urayamashikute shō ga arimasen deshita.*

---

everyone — 誰も — *daremo*
You can't please everyone. — 全員を満足させることは出来ない。
— *Zen-in o manzoku saseru koto wa dekinai.*
Some employees are unhappy with the new pension plan. You can't please
everyone.　従業員の中には、新しい年金計画に不満を抱いている
人がいます。全ての人を満足させることは出来ません。*Jūgyōin
no naka ni wa, atarashii nenkin keikaku ni fuman o idaite iru hito ga
imasu. Subete no hito o manzoku saseru koto wa dekimasen.*

---

everything — 全て — *subete*
everything but the kitchen sink — 何もかも — *nani mo ka mo*
When she goes on a trip, it seems as if she packs everything but the kitchen
sink.　彼女が旅行するときには、何もかも荷物に詰め込むみたい
です。*Kanojo ga ryokō suru toki ni wa, nani mo ka mo nimotsu ni
tsumekomu mitai desu.*

everything from soup to nuts — ありとあらゆる物 — *ari to arayuru mono*
What a feast we had last night! They served everything from soup to nuts.
夕べの大御馳走の素晴らしかったこと。ありとあらゆる物が、
でてきました。*Yūbe no ō gochisō no subarashikatta koto. Ari to
arayuru mono ga dete kimashita.*

---

expedition — 探検 — *tanken*
be/go on a fishing expedition — 情報を探り出そうとする　*jōhō o
saguridasō to suru*

What is he really trying to find out? I think he's on a fishing expedition.
彼は、一体何を見つけ出そうとしているのでしょうか。彼は、
何か情報を探り出そうとしていると思うのですが。*Kare wa, ittai*
nani o mitsukedasō to shite iru no deshō ka. Kare wa, nanika jōhō o
saguridasō to shite iru to omou no desu ga.

---

eye — 目 — *me*

bright-eyed and bushy-tailed — 朗らかで元気はつら つとして —
hogaraka de genki hatsuratsu to shite
You look bright-eyed and bushy-tailed this morning.　あなたは今朝、
朗らかで元気はつらつとしているようですね。*Anata wa kesa,*
hogaraka de genki hatsuratsu to shite iru yō desu ne.

eagle eye — 鋭い目 — *surudoi me*
With his eagle eye, he can spot a state trooper a mile away.　彼は鋭い目で、
一マイル先から州警察のパトカ－を突き止めることが出来ます。
Kare wa surudoi me de, ichi mairu saki kara shū keisatsu no patokā o
tsukitomeru koto ga dekimasu.

feast one's eyes (on someone or something) — 目の保養にする — *me*
no hoyō ni suru
Come feast your eyes on this sunset.　この夕焼けを見て、目の保養に
して下さい。*Kono yūyake o mite, me no hoyō ni shite kudasai.*

give someone or something a black eye — 面目を失なう — *menboku o*
ushinau
The recall of their product gave the company a black eye.　製品の回収で、
会社は面目を失いました。*Seihin no kaishū de, kaisha wa menboku o*
ushinaimashita.

have eyes in the back of one's head — 何でもお見通し — *nandemo omitōshi*

Nothing escapes the boss's attention; he has eyes in the back of his head.
ボスの目を逃れるものは、何もありません。彼は何でもお見通しです。 *Bosu no me o nogareru mono wa, nani mo arimasen. Kare wa nandemo omitōshi desu.*

more (to something) than meets the eye — 他にもっと何かある — *hoka ni motto nanika aru*

They haven't told us everything. There's more to this than meets the eye.
彼等は、私達に全てを告げていません。他にもっと何かあるのです。 *Karera wa, watakushitachi ni subete o tsugete imasen. Hoka ni motto nanika aru no desu.*

not believe one's eyes — 我が目を疑う — *waga me o utagau*

I can't believe my eyes: my daughter cleaned her room! 私は、我が目を疑いました。娘が自分の部屋を片づけたのです。 *Watakushi wa, waga me o utagaimashita. Musume ga jibun no heya o katazuketa no desu.*

one's eyes are bigger than one's stomach — 食べられないほど取りすぎる — *taberarenai hodo torisugiru*

I can't finish this second helping of pie. My eyes were bigger than my stomach. この二つ目のパイは食べ切れません。食べられないほど取りすぎてしまったのです。 *Kono futatsume no pai wa tabekiremasen. Taberarenai hodo torisugite shimatta no desu.*

face — 顔 — *kao*

fall flat on one's face — 失敗に終わってしまう — *shippai ni owatte shimau*

He tried to give a good presentation, but he fell flat on his face. 彼は素晴らしい発表をしようとしたのですが、失敗に終わってしまいました。*Kare wa subarashii happyō o shiyō to shita no desu ga, shippai ni owatte shimaimashita.*

keep a straight face — 真顔を保つ — *magao o tamotsu*

Although I tried not to laugh at his mistake, I couldn't keep a straight face. 彼の失敗を笑わないように心がけましたが、真顔を保つことが出来ませんでした。*Kare no shippai o warawanai yō ni kokorogakemashita ga, magao o tamotsu koto ga dekimasen deshita.*

lose face — 面子を失う — *mentsu o ushinau*

If we don't meet the deadline, we'll lose face. もし締め切りに間に合わなければ、私達は面子を失ってしまいます。*Moshi shimekiri ni maniawanakereba, watakushitachi wa mentsu o ushinatte shimaimasu.*

save face — 面目を保つ — *menboku o tamotsu*

Although she arrived late, she saved face by giving a great presentation. 彼女は遅刻して来ましたが、素晴らしい発表をして面目を保ちました。*Kanojo wa chikoku shite kimashita ga, subarashii happyō o shite menboku o tamochimashita.*

talk until one is blue in the face — 口を酸っぱくして話す — *kuchi o suppaku shite hanasu*

You can talk until you're blue in the face, but you'll never convince him he's wrong. いくら口を酸っぱくして話しても、彼が間違っていることを認めさせることは決して出来ないでしょう。*Ikura kuchi o suppaku shite hanashitemo, kare ga machigatte iru koto o mitomesaseru koto wa kesshite dekinai deshō.*

---

faith — 信念 — *shinnen*

in good faith — 誠意を込めて — *seii o komete*

He made the promise in good faith, but he couldn't keep it. 彼は誠意を込めて約束しましたが、それを果たすことが出来ませんでした。*Kare wa seii o komete yakusoku shimashita ga, sore o hatasu koto ga dekimasen deshita.*

pin one's faith/hopes on someone or something — 望みをかける — *nozomi o kakeru*

Don't pin your faith on this team; they can't win. どうせ勝つことが出来ないんですから、このチ-ムに望みをかけないように。*Dōse katsu koto ga dekinaindesu kara, kono chīmu ni nozomi o kakenai yō ni.*

take something on faith — 信用する — *shin-yō suru*

He took it on faith that his students wouldn't cheat on the exam. 彼は、学生が試験でカンニングをしないだろうと信用しました。*Kare wa, gakusei ga kanningu o shinai darō to shin-yō shimashita.*

---

fancy — 好み — *konomi*

strike one's fancy — 興味をそそる — *kyōmi o sosoru*

I'm giving my son cash for his birthday so he can buy whatever strikes his fancy. 私は息子が興味をそそるものを何でも買えるように、誕生日に現金をあげます。*Watakushi wa musuko ga kyōmi o sosoru mono o nandemo kaeru yō ni, tanjōbi ni genkin o agemasu.*

take a fancy to someone or something — 気に入る — *ki ni iru*

The boy took a fancy to the puppy and asked his parents if he could keep it. 男の子はその子犬が気に入って、両親に飼ってもいいか聞きました。*Otoko no ko wa sono koinu ga ki ni itte, ryōshin ni kattemo ii ka kikimashita.*

---

fashion — 様式 — *yōshiki*

after a fashion — どうにか — *dōnika*

She can cook after a fashion. 彼女は、どうにか料理が出来ます。*Kanojo wa, dōnika ryōri ga dekimasu.*

---

fat — 脂肪／太っている — *shibō/futotte iru*

chew the fat — おしゃべりする — *oshaberi suru*

Come sit down and let's chew the fat for awhile. ここに来て座って、ちょっとおしゃべりしましょう。*Koko ni kite suwatte, chotto oshaberi shimashō.*

fat and happy — すっかり満ち足りている — *sukkari michitarite iru*
Mary must have had a good vacation; she looks fat and happy.
メリーは素晴らしいバカンスを過ごしたに違いありません。
彼女は、すっかり満ち足りた様子です。*Merī wa subarashii*
bakansu o sugoshita ni chigai arimasen. Kanojo wa, sukkari michitarita
yōsu desu.

live off the fat of the land — ぜいたくな暮らしをする — *zeitaku na*
kurashi o suru
He won the lottery, and now he's living off the fat of the land.
彼は宝くじに当たって、今はぜいたくな暮らしをしています。
Kare wa takarakuji ni atatte, ima wa zeitaku na kurashi o shite imasu.

---

feast — ごちそう — *gochisō*
(either) feast or famine — 両極端 — *ryō kyokutan*
First they have too much work, then too little; it's either feast or famine.
彼等は仕事が多すぎたり、次には殆ど無かったり、全く両極端です。
Karera wa shigoto ga ōsugitari, tsugi ni wa hotondo nakattari, mattaku
ryō kyokutan desu.

---

feather — 羽根 — *hane*
knock someone over with a feather — 気が遠くなるほど驚く — *ki ga*
tōku naru hodo odoroku
When I saw my passing grade, you could have knocked me over with a
feather. 私は自分の合格の成績を見たとき、気が遠くなるほど
驚きました。*Watakushi wa jibun no gōkaku no seiseki o mita toki, ki*
ga tōku naru hodo odorokimashita.

ruffle someone's feathers — 機嫌を損じる — *kigen o sonjiru*
I know Mary's late, but if we start eating without her, we may ruffle her
feathers. マリーが遅いのは分かっていますが、彼女抜きで食べ
始めてしまうと、彼女の機嫌を損じかねません。*Marī ga osoi no*
wa wakatte imasu ga, kanojo nuki de tabehajimete shimau to, kanojo no
kigen o sonjikanemasen.

---

feed — 餌 — *esa*
chicken feed — はした金 — *hashitagane*
He'll do a good job for you, but he doesn't work for chicken feed. 彼は

いい仕事をしますが、はした金では働きません。*Kare wa ii shigoto o shimasu ga, hashitagane dewa hatarakimasen.*

feet — 足 — *ashi*

dead on one's feet — くたくた — *kutakuta*

I've been shopping all day, and I'm dead on my feet. 一日中買い物してくたくたです。*Ichi nichi jū kaimono shite kutakuta desu.*

drag one's feet — 足を引きずる — *ashi o hikizuru*

We need a decision from the boss on this, but he's dragging his feet. この件について上司の決定がいるのですが、彼は足を引きずっています。*Kono ken ni tsuite jōshi no kettei ga iru no desu ga, kare wa ashi o hikizutte imasu.*

(get) back on one's feet — 再起する — *saiki suru*

John lost his job recently, so his parents will help him until he gets back on his feet. 最近ジョンは失業したので、彼が再起するまで親が援助してくれます。*Saikin Jon wa shitsugyō shita node, kare ga saiki suru made oya ga enjo shite kuremasu.*

get/have cold feet — おじけづく — *ojikezuku*

I said I'd go parachuting with my friends, but now I have cold feet. 友達と一緒に落下傘降下をすると言ってはみたものの、今はおじけづいています。*Tomodachi to issho ni rakkasan kōka o suru to itte wa mita monono, ima wa ojikezuite imasu.*

get one's feet wet — 初の体験をする — *hatsu no taiken o suru*

John is just getting his feet wet at teaching. ジョンは、先生として初の体験をしているところです。*Jon wa, sensei toshite hatsu no taiken o shite iru tokoro desu.*

have feet of clay — 弱点がある — *jakuten ga aru*

The boss seems so strong, but we just learned he has feet of clay. 上司は自信満々に見えますが、弱点もあることを最近知りました。*Jōshi wa jishin manman ni miemasu ga, jakuten mo aru koto o saikin shirimashita.*

land on both/one's feet — 無事に切り抜ける — *buji ni kirinukeru*

She's in trouble now, but she'll land on her feet. 彼女は今困難に陥っていますが、無事に切り抜けるでしょう。*Kanojo wa ima konnan ni ochiitte imasu ga, buji ni kirinukeru deshō.*

stand on one's own two feet — 自力でやれる — *jiriki de yareru*
I don't want anyone's help with this. I can stand on my own two feet.
これに関しては、誰の援助も受けたくありません。私は、自力で
やっていけます。*Kore ni kanshite wa, dare no enjo mo uketaku
arimasen. Watakushi wa, jiriki de yatte ikemasu.*

sweep one off one's feet — 無我夢中にさせる — *mugamuchū ni saseru*
When Bill was courting Sally, he swept her off her feet.　ビルが
サリ－とデ－トしていたとき、彼は彼女を無我夢中にさせました。
*Biru ga Sarī to dēto shite ita toki, kare wa kanojo o mugamuchū ni
sasemashita.*

think on one's feet — 話しながら考える — *hanashinagara kangaeru*
If he wants to impress that audience, he'd better be able to think on his feet.
彼がこの聴衆を感銘させたいなら、話しながら考えられる余裕が
いります。*Kare ga kono chōshū o kanmei sasetai nara, hanashinagara
kangaerareru yoyū ga irimasu.*

fence — 垣根 — *kakine*
mend (one's) fences — 仲直りする — *nakanaori suru*
She had a fight with her brother, but she's going to call him up to mend her
fences.　彼女は弟と喧嘩しましたが、仲直りするために電話する
つもりです。*Kanojo wa otōto to kenka shimashita ga, nakanaori suru
tame ni denwa suru tsumori desu.*

on the fence — どっちつかずの態度をとる — *dotchi tsukazu no taido
o toru*
The candidate is on the fence about capital punishment.　候補者は、
死刑についてどっちつかずの態度をとっています。*Kōhosha wa,
shikei ni tsuite dotchi tsukazu no taido o totte imasu.*

fever — 熱 — *netsu*
cabin fever — 屋内に閉じこめられていらいらする — *okunai ni
tojikomerarete iraira suru*
Many people got cabin fever during the last snowstorm.　この前の
大吹雪の最中は、屋内に閉じこめられていらいらした人が大勢
いました。*Kono mae no ō fubuki no saichū wa, okunai ni
tojikomerarete iraira shita hito ga ōzei imashita.*

fiddle — バイオリン — *baiorin*

(as) fit as a fiddle — ぴんぴんして — *pinpin shite*
She's over 80 years old, and she's as fit as a fiddle.　彼女は八十歳を
越えていますが、ぴんぴんしています。*Kanojo wa hachijussai o
koete imasu ga, pinpin shite imasu.*

play second fiddle (to someone) — 脇役に回る — *wakiyaku ni mawaru*
He's leaving the family business because he's tired of playing second
fiddle to his brother.　彼はお兄さんの脇役に回るのに飽き飽きして、
家族が経営する事業から身を引こうとしています。*Kare wa
oniisan no wakiyaku ni mawaru no ni akiaki shite, kazoku ga keiei suru
jigyō kara mi o hikō to shite imasu.*

---

field — 外野／野原 — *gaiya/nohara*

out in left field — 変わっている — *kawatte iru*
You're way out in left field with that idea; it will never work.　あなたの
そのアイディアは変わりすぎているから、うまくいかないことは
確実です。*Anata no sono aidia wa kawarisugite iru kara, umaku ikanai
koto wa kakujitsu desu.*

play the field — 異性と手広く付き合う — *isei to tebiroku tsukiau*
John's not ready to settle down and get married. He wants to play the field
first.　ジョンは、まだ身を固めて結婚する気はありません。彼は、
その前に色々な女性と手広く付き合いたいのです。*Jon wa, mada
mi o katamete kekkon suru ki wa arimasen. Kare wa, sono mae ni iroiro
na josei to tebiroku tsukiaitai no desu.*

---

finger — 指 — *yubi*

get one's fingers burned — 苦い体験をする — *nigai taiken o suru*
I got my fingers burned the last time I tried to help him; once was enough.
この前彼を助けてあげようとして、苦い体験をしました。一度で
こりごりです。*Kono mae kare o tasukete ageyō to shite, nigai taiken o
shimashita. Ichido de korogori desu.*

have a finger in the pie — 首を突っ込む — *kubi o tsukkomu*
When I saw how well the deal was going, I knew John had a finger in the pie.
取引が実にうまくいっているのを見たとき、ジョンがこれに首を
突っ込んでいることが分かりました。*Torihiki ga jitsu ni umaku itte iru
no o mita toki, Jon ga kore ni kubi o tsukkonde iru koto ga wakarimashita.*

have something at one's fingertips — 何かを身近なところに
持っている — *nanika o mijika na tokoro ni motte iru*
She can get the job done fast; she has a lot of resources at her fingertips.
彼女は、素早く仕事を成し遂げることが出来ます。たくさんの
方策を、身近なところに持っているからです。*Kanojo wa,
subayaku shigoto o nashitogeru koto ga dekimasu. Takusan no hōsaku o,
mijika na tokoro ni motte iru kara desu.*

have sticky fingers — 手癖が悪い — *tekuse ga warui*
Be careful with your cash; that boy has sticky fingers. あの男の子は
手癖が悪いから、現金に気を付けなさい。*Ano otoko no ko wa
tekuse ga warui kara, genkin ni ki o tsukenasai.*

keep one's fingers crossed — 幸運を祈る — *kōun o inoru*
I hope you get the part in the play; I'm keeping my fingers crossed!
あなたが劇で役をもらうことを願って、幸運をお祈りします。
Anata ga geki de yaku o morau koto o negatte, kōun o oinori shimasu.

lay a finger on someone or something — 指一本でも触れる — *yubi
ippon demo fureru*
Even if he misbehaves, I don't want you to lay a finger on my child.
例えこの子の行儀が悪くても、私の子供には指一本でも触れないで
下さい。*Tatoe kono ko no gyōgi ga warukutemo, watakushi no kodomo
niwa yubi ippon demo furenaide kudasai.*

not lift a finger — 手伝おうとしない — *tetsudaō to shinai*
Although she likes to come for dinner, she never lifts a finger to help.
彼女はうちへ夕食に来るのは好きですが、決して手伝おうと
しません。*Kanojo wa uchi e yūshoku ni kuru no wa suki desu ga,
kesshite tetsudaō to shimasen.*

point the finger at someone — 非難する — *hinan suru*
If she hadn't pointed the finger at John, he would have gotten away with
the theft. もし彼女がジョンを非難しなかったら、彼は盗みに
成功していたでしょう。*Moshi kanojo ga Jon o hinan shinakattara,
kare wa nusumi ni seikō shite ita deshō.*

put one's finger on something — 指摘する — *shiteki suru*
I can't put my finger on the reason for the error just yet. 間違いの
理由については、まだ指摘できません。*Machigai no riyū ni tsuite
wa, mada shiteki dekimasen.*

slip through one's fingers — 消え失せる — *kieuseru*

John's broke again; money just seems to slip through his fingers.
ジョンは、また文無しです。お金はまるで消え失せて
しまったみたいです。*Jon wa, mata mon nashi desu. Okane wa
marude kieusete shimatta mitai desu.*

twist someone around one's little finger — 操る — *ayatsuru*

She gets anything she wants from her father; she can twist him around her
little finger.　彼女はお父さんから、欲しいものは何でも手に
入れることが出来ます。お父さんを操ることが出来るからです。
*Kanojo wa otōsan kara, hoshii mono wa nandemo te ni ireru koto ga
dekimasu. Otōsan o ayatsuru koto ga dekiru kara desu.*

work one's fingers to the bone — 身を粉にして働く — *mi o ko ni shite
hataraku*

He's working his fingers to the bone to pay for his children's college
tuition.　彼は子供の大学の学費を払うために、身を粉にして
働いています。*Kare wa kodomo no daigaku no gakuhi o harau tame
ni, mi o ko ni shite hataraite imasu.*

---

fire — 火 — *hi*

build a fire under someone — 発破をかける — *happa o kakeru*

She's late with her report. Can't you build a fire under her?　彼女は
報告書の提出が遅れています。彼女に発破をかけることは
出来ませんか。*Kanojo wa hōkokusho no teishutsu ga okurete imasu.
Kanojo ni happa o kakeru koto wa dekimasen ka.*

play with fire — 危険を冒す — *kiken o okasu*

You know that criticizing the boss is playing with fire.　あの上司を批判
するのは、危険を冒すことになるのは知っているでしょう。*Ano
jōshi o hihan suru no wa, kiken o okasu koto ni naru no wa shitte iru deshō.*

---

fish — 魚／釣りをする — *sakana/tsuri o suru*

be a cold fish — 冷淡な人 — *reitan na hito*

He never shows any emotion; he's a cold fish.　彼は決して感情を
示しません。冷淡な人なのです。*Kare wa kesshite kanjō o
shimeshimasen. Reitan na hito nanodesu.*

big fish/frog in a little/small pond — 狭い環境では抜き出た存在 —
semai kankyō dewa nukudeta sonzai

As the only Ph.D. on the high school faculty, he's a big fish in a little pond.
彼はその高校の教師の中でたった一人の博士号所有者なので、
狭い環境では抜き出た存在です。Kare wa sono kōkō no kyōshi no
naka de tatta hitori no hakase gō shoyūsha nanode, semai kankyō dewa
nukideta sonzai desu.

have other fish to fry — 他にするべきことがある — hoka ni suru beki
koto ga aru

I can't waste any more time here; I have other fish to fry. 私はここで、
これ以上時間を無駄に出来ません。他にするべきことがあるのです。
Watakushi wa koko de, kore ijō jikan o muda ni dekimasen. Hoka ni suru
beki koto ga aru no desu.

like a fish out of water — 場違い — ba chigai

At parties John feels like a fish out of water. パーティーでは、
ジョンは場違いの思いをします。Pātī dewa, Jon wa bachigai no
omoi o shimasu.

neither fish nor fowl — どっちなのか見分けがつかない — dotchi na
no ka miwake ga tsukanai

This book is neither fish nor fowl; I can't tell if it's a mystery or a love
story. この本はミステリーなのか恋愛小説なのか、見分けが
つきません。Kono hon wa misuterī na no ka ren-ai shōsetsu na no ka,
miwake ga tsukimasen.

There are other fish in the sea. — 他にもふさわしい人がたくさんいる。
— Hoka nimo fusawashii hito ga takusan iru.

Sally feels sad about losing her boyfriend, but she'll find out there are other fish in the sea. サリーはボーイフレンドを失って悲しんでいますが、他にもふさわしい人がたくさんいることに、そのうち気付くでしょう。*Sarī wa bōifurendo o ushinatte kanashinde imasu ga, hoka ni mo fusawashii hito ga takusan iru koto ni, sono uchi kizuku deshō.*

---

fit — 発作 — *hossa*

throw a fit — ものすごく怒る — *monosugoku okoru*
Mary threw a fit when her secretary arrived late. マリーは彼女の秘書が遅れてきたので、ものすごく怒りました。*Marī wa kanojo no hisho ga okurete kita node, monosugoku okorimashita.*

---

flash — ひらめき — *hirameki*

flash in the pan — 線香花火 — *senkō hanabi*
He seemed like a good pitcher, but he turned out to be a flash in the pan. 彼は好投手のように見受けられましたが、線香花火的に終わりました。*Kare wa kō tōshu no yō ni miukeraremashita ga, senkō hanabi teki ni owarimashita.*

in a flash — すぐに／あっと言う間に — *sugu ni/atto iu ma ni*
I have to leave now, but I'll be back in a flash. 私は行かなければなりませんが、すぐに戻ってきます。*Watakushi wa ikanakereba narimasen ga, sugu ni modotte kimasu.*

---

flesh — 肉体 — *nikutai*

flesh and blood — 親戚 — *shinseki*
She'll never turn her back on her cousin; he's her own flesh and blood. 彼女は、いとこを見捨てるようなことは決してしないでしょう。彼は彼女の親戚だからです。*Kanojo wa, itoko o misuteru yō na koto wa kesshite shinai deshō. Kare wa kanojo no shinseki dakara desu.*

flesh something out — 肉付けする — *nikuzuke suru*
This proposal is rather thin. We'll have to flesh it out before submitting it. この企画書は、内容がやや貧弱です。それで提出する前に、肉付けせねばならないでしょう。*Kono kikakusho wa, naiyō ga yaya hinjaku desu. Sorede teishutsu suru mae ni, nikuzuke seneba naranai deshō.*

in the flesh — 実際に — *jissai ni*

We didn't expect to see him at the party, but there he was in the flesh!
私達は、彼がパーティーに来ようとは思ってもいませんでした。
ところが本人が実際に来ているではありませんか。*Watakushitachi
wa, kare ga pātī ni koyō towa omottemo imasen deshita. Tokoroga,
honnin ga jissai ni kite iru dewa arimasen ka.*

floor — 床 — *yuka*

get in on the ground floor — 最初から加わる — *saisho kara kuwawaru*
This is a pretty good business deal; we were lucky to get in on the ground
floor. これは、なかなか素晴らしい商取引です。私達は、それに
最初から加われて運がよかったです。*Kore wa, nakanaka subarashii
shō torihiki desu. Watakushitachi wa, sore ni saisho kara kuwawarete un
ga yokatta desu.*

mop the floor up with someone — さんざんに打ち負かす — *sanzan
ni uchimakasu*
Our basketball team mopped the floor up with their biggest rival. 私達の
バスケのチームは、最大の宿敵をさんざんに打ち負かしました。
*Watakushitachi no basuke no chīmu wa, saidai no shukuteki o sanzan ni
uchimakashimashita.*

walk the floor — 落ち着きなく歩き回る — *ochitsuki naku
arukimawaru*
John walked the floor in the hospital until his baby was born. ジョンは
赤ちゃんが産まれるまで、病院の中を落ち着きなく歩き回りました。
*Jon wa akachan ga umareru made, byōin no naka o ochitsuki naku
arukimawarimashita.*

fly — 蝿／飛行 — *hae/hikō*

fly in the ointment — 玉に瑕 — *tama ni kizu*
The meeting went well; the only fly in the ointment was the late start.
会議はうまくいったのですが、開始時間の遅れが玉に瑕でした。
*Kaigi wa umaku itta no desu ga, kaishi jikan no okure ga tama ni kizu
deshita.*

fly on the wall — 盗み聞きする — *nusumigiki suru*

I'd like to be a fly on the wall when John introduces Sally to his family.
ジョンが家族にサリーを紹介するとき、それを盗み聞き
したいです。*Jon ga kazoku ni Sarī o shōkai suru toki, sore o
nusumigiki shitai desu.*

on the fly — 急いで — *isoide*

I don't have time to eat breakfast at home, so I usually grab something on
the fly. 私は、家で朝御飯を食べる時間がありません。それで
普通は急いで何か買って食べます。*Watakushi wa, ie de asagohan o
taberu jikan ga arimasen. Sorede futsū wa isoide nanika katte tabemasu.*

---

food — 食べ物 — *tabemono*

　food for thought — 確かに考えるべき事 — *tashika ni kangaeru beki
　koto*

　Thanks for telling me your idea; you've given me food for thought.
　あなたの考えを教えてくれてありがとう。それは、確かに私も
　考えるべき事です。*Anata no kangae o oshiete kurete arigatō. Sore
　wa, tashika ni watakushi mo kangaeru beki koto desu.*

---

fool — 馬鹿者 — *bakamono*

　fool's paradise — 幻 — *maboroshi*

　If you think you can get through college without studying, you're living in
　a fool's paradise. 勉強せずに大学を出られると思っているなら、
　それは幻を追っているようなものですよ。*Benkyō sezu ni daigaku o*

derareru to omotte iru nara, sore wa maboroshi o otte iru yō na mono desu yo.

make a fool of someone/oneself — 笑いものにする／物笑いになる — *waraimono ni suru/monowarai ni naru*

John got drunk at the office party and made a fool of himself.　ジョンは会社のパーティーで酔っぱらって、物笑いになりました。*Jon wa kaisha no pātī de yopparatte, monowarai ni narimashita.*

nobody's fool — あなどりがたい — *anadorigatai*

Don't underestimate Harry; he's nobody's fool.　彼を軽くあしらってはなりません。なかなかあなどりがたい人ですから。*Kare o karuku ashiratte wa narimasen. Nakanaka anadorigatai hito desu kara.*

on a fool's errand — 無駄足を踏む — *muda ashi o fumu*

She's gone on a fool's errand; the store is closed on Sunday.　彼女は無駄足を踏みに出かけました。その店は、日曜日には閉まっているのです。*Kanojo wa muda ashi o fumini dekakemashita. Sono mise wa, nichiyōbi niwa shimatte iru no desu.*

---

foot — 足 — *ashi*

get off on the wrong foot — 出だしでつまずく — *dedashi de tsumazuku*

I got off on the wrong foot with the teacher when I was late for class. 授業に遅れて、先生に対して出だしでつまずいてしまいました。*Jugyō ni okurete, sensei ni taishite dedashi de tsumazuite shimaimashita.*

get one's foot in the door — きっかけをつかむ — *kikkake o tsukamu*

She got her foot in the door by getting a job as a summer intern.　夏期研修生として、彼女は仕事を得るためのきっかけをつかみました。*Kaki kenshūsei toshite, kanojo wa shigoto o eru tame no kikkake o tsukamimashita.*

put one's best foot forward — 好印象を与えるようにする — *kō inshō o ataeru yō ni suru*

Try to put your best foot forward when you go on the interview tomorrow. 明日面接に行くときには、好印象を与えるように努力しなさい。*Ashita mensetsu ni iku toki niwa, kō inshō o ataeru yō ni doryoku shinasai.*

put one's foot down — 断固とした態度をとる — *danko to shita taido o toru*

Fred put his foot down and refused to lend his son any more money.
フレッドは断固とした態度をとって、息子にこれ以上のお金を
貸すことを拒否しました。 *Fureddo wa danko to shita taido o totte,*
musuko ni kore ijō no okane o kasu koto o kyohi shimashita.

put one's foot in one's mouth — ドジを踏む — *doji o fumu*
I didn't realize the man I insulted was the boss's husband. I really put my
foot in my mouth. 私が侮辱した人が、上司のご主人とは気が
つきませんでした。大変なドジを踏んでしまったのです。
Watakushi ga bujoku shita hito ga, jōshi no goshujin towa ki ga
tsukimasen deshita. Taihen na doji o funde shimatta no desu.

---

forest — 森林 — *shinrin*
　can't see the forest for the trees — 目先のことに気を取られて全体が
　　見えない — *mesaki no koto ni ki o torarete zentai ga mienai*
　She focuses on small problems and overlooks her blessings. She can't see
　　the forest for the trees. 彼女は小さい問題に焦点を当てて、自らの
　　幸運を見過ごしています。彼女は目先のことに気を取られて、
　　全体が見えないのです。 *Kanojo wa chiisai mondai ni shōten o atete,*
　　mizukara no kōun o misugoshite imasu. Kanojo wa mesaki no koto ni ki
　　o torarete, zentai ga mienai no desu.

---

fox 　狐 — *kitsune*
　(as) sly as a fox — ずるがしこい — *zurugashikoi*
　Don knows how to win any argument; he's as sly as a fox. 　ドンは

451

ずるがしこくて、どんな口論をしても勝ち方を知っています。
Don wa zurugashikokute, donna kōron o shitemo kachikata o shitte imasu.

freak — 変わった — *kawatta*
  (something) freak — ___狂 — ___*kyō*
  Bill has quite a collection of software. He's a real computer freak.
  ビルはソフトウェアをすごくたくさん持っていますが、それは
  彼がコンピュータ狂だからです。*Biru wa sofutowea o sugoku
  takusan motte imasu ga, sore wa kare ga konpyūta kyō dakara desu.*

friend — 友人 — *yūjin*
  fair-weather friend — 人が順調なときだけ調子がいい友人 — *hito ga
  junchō na toki dake chōshi ga ii yūjin*
  Tom's a fair-weather friend; he let me down when I needed help.   助けが
  いるときに私を落胆させたように、トムは人が順調なときだけ
  調子がいい友人です。*Tasuke ga iru toki ni watakushi o rakutan
  saseta yō ni, Tomu wa hito ga junchō na toki dake chōshi ga ii yūjin desu.*

fritz — 混乱状態 — *konran jōtai*
  on the fritz — 故障して — *koshō shite*
  I need a good repair shop; my VCR is on the fritz.   ビデオ装置が故障
  しているので、上手な修理店が必要です。*Bideo sōchi ga koshō
  shite iru node, jōzu na sūriten ga hitsuyō desu.*

frog — かえる — *kaeru*
  get/have a frog in one's throat — 声がしわがれる — *koe ga
  shiwagareru*
  Could I have a glass of water, please? I have a frog in my throat.   水を
  一杯いただけませんか。声がしわがれているので。*Mizu o ippai
  itadakemasen ka. Koe ga shiwagarete iru node.*

front — 前面 — *zenmen*
  put on a brave front — 平静を装う — *heisei o yosoou*
  He's really scared, but he's putting on a brave front.   彼は本当は恐いの
  ですが、平静を装っています。*Kare wa hontō wa kowai no desu ga,
  heisei o yosootte imasu.*

fruit — 果物 — *kudamono*

forbidden fruit — 禁じられているもの — *kinjirarete iru mono*

Children may try to sneak a sip of their parents' beer because they know it's forbidden fruit. 子供たちはそれが禁じられているものだけに、親のビールをこっそり一口試してみようとすることがあります。 *Kodomotachi wa sore ga kinjirarete iru mono dake ni, oya no bīru o kossori hitokuchi tameshite miyō to suru koto ga arimasu.*

fruitcake — フルーツケーキ — *furūtsu kēki*

(as) nutty as a fruitcake — 気違いじみた — *kichigai jimita*

At first she seemed quite lucid, but we soon realized she's as nutty as a fruitcake. 彼女は最初は全く正気に見えましたが、すぐに気違いじみていることに気がつきました。 *Kanojo wa saisho wa mattaku shōki ni miemashita ga, sugu ni kichigai jimite iru koto ni ki ga tsukimashita.*

fuel — 燃料 — *nenryō*

add fuel to the fire — 油を火に注ぐ — *abura o hi ni sosogu*

Bob is angry enough as it is; if you argue with him, it will only add fuel to the fire. ボブは今でさえ怒りにあふれています。それで彼と議論するなら、油を火に注ぐこと確実です。 *Bobu wa ima de sae ikari ni afurete imasu. Sore de kare to giron suru nara, abura o hi ni sosogu koto kakujitsu desu.*

fun — 楽しみ — *tanoshimi*

fun and games — 遊び — *asobi*

No more fun and games—it's time to get down to work. これで遊びは終わりで、今は仕事に取りかかる時です。 *Kore de asobi wa owari de, ima wa shigoto ni torikakaru toki desu.*

more fun than a barrel of monkeys — この上なく楽しい — *kono ue naku tanoshii*

The second grade soccer game was more fun than a barrel of monkeys. 小学校二年生のサッカーの試合は、この上なく楽しかったです。 *Shōgakkō ninensei no sakkā no shiai wa, kono ue naku tanoshikatta desu.*

fuse — ヒューズ — *hyūzu*

blow a fuse — 怒りを爆発させる — *ikari o bakuhatsu saseru*

The boss is going to blow a fuse when she sees the mess we've made of
this project.　ボスは私達がこの企画を台無しにしたのを知ったら、
怒りを爆発させるでしょう。*Bosu wa watakushitachi ga kono kikaku
o dainashi ni shita no o shittara, ikari o bakuhatsu saseru deshō.*

game — 試合 — *shiai*
　at this stage of the game — この段階で — *kono dankai de*
　You're so close to getting your college degree; don't give up at this stage
　of the game.　学士号がもうちょっとで取れそうなのに、この段階で
　諦めてはなりません。*Gakushi gō ga mō chotto de toresō nanoni,
　kono dankai de akiramete wa narimasen.*

　game that two can play — お互いさま — *otagaisama*
　If you're buying a car, remember that bargaining is a game that two can
　play.　車を買うなら、値段の駆け引きはお互いさまなことを
　覚えておくように。*Kuruma o kau nara, nedan no kakehiki wa
　otagaisama na koto o oboete oku yō ni.*

　(whole) new ball game — 新しい状況 — *atarashii jōkyō*
　With the change of administration in Washington, it's a whole new ball game.
　ワシントンで政権が変わって、全く新しい状況になりました。
　Washinton de seiken ga kawatte, mattaku atarashii jōkyō ni narimashita.

gangbusters — ギャング一掃が職務の警官 — *gyangu issō ga
shokumu no keikan*
　come on like gangbusters — 押しが強すぎる — *oshi ga tsuyosugiru*
　He's a good manager, but I wish he'd stop coming on like gangbusters.
　彼は管理職にある人としては有能だけど、押しが強すぎるのは
　困ったものです。*Kare wa kanri shoku ni aru hito to shite wa yūnō da
　keredo, oshi ga tsuyosugiru no wa komatta mono desu.*

gate — 門 — *mon*
　get/give (someone) the gate — 退散する／退散を命じる — *taisan*

suru/taisan o meijiru

When he asked for a raise, the boss gave him the gate. 彼が昇給を
求めたとき、上司は彼に退散を命じました。*Kare ga shōkyū o
motometa toki, jōshi wa kare ni taisan o meijimashita.*

---

gauntlet — 長手袋 — *naga tebukuro*

throw down the gauntlet — 戦いを挑む — *tatakai o idomu*

If you disobey your father, you'll be throwing down the gauntlet.
お父さんの言いつけにそむくなら、それは戦いを挑むような
ものですよ。*Otōsan no iitsuke ni somuku nara, sore wa tatakai o
idomu yō na mono desu yo.*

---

ghost — 幽霊 — *yūrei*

ghost of a chance — みじんの可能性も（ない）— *mijin no kanōsei mo
(nai)*

He doesn't have a ghost of a chance of winning the tennis match. 彼が
このテニスの試合に勝つ可能性は、みじんもありません。*Kare ga
kono tenisu no shiai ni katsu kanōsei wa, mijin mo arimasen.*

give up the ghost — 死ぬ — *shinu*

He's got a lot of living left to do; he's not ready to give up the ghost.
彼は生きているうちにしたいことがたくさんあるので、まだ死ぬ
気はありません。*Kare wa ikite iru uchi ni shitai koto ga takusan aru
node, mada shinu ki wa arimasen.*

---

gills — えら — *era*

green around the gills — 具合が悪い — *guai ga warui*

Whenever he's on a boat, he looks green around the gills. 彼は船に
乗ると、いつも具合が悪そうです。*Kare wa fune ni noru to, itsumo
guai ga warusō desu.*

---

glove — 手袋 — *tebukuro*

handle someone with kid gloves — 慎重に扱う — *shinchō ni atsukau*

He's quite temperamental; you have to handle him with kid gloves. 彼は
非常に気分屋なので、慎重に扱わねばなりません。*Kare wa hijō ni
kibun-ya nanode, shinchō ni atsukawaneba narimasen.*

glutton — 凝り屋 — *koriya*

glutton for punishment — 自虐的な傾向がある — *jigyakuteki na keikō ga aru*

He's playing tennis in 90 degree heat; he's a glutton for punishment.
彼は気温が華氏９０度の猛暑の中で、テニスをしています。
彼には、自虐的な傾向があるようです。 *Kare wa kion ga kashi kyūjū do no mōsho no naka de, tenisu o shite imasu. Kare niwa, jigyakuteki na keikō ga aru yō desu.*

goat — 山羊 — *yagi*

get someone's goat — 苛立たせる — *iradataseru*

He really gets Sally's goat when he teases her about her Southern accent
彼はサリ‐の南部のアクセントをからかって、彼女を本当に
苛立たせます。 *Kare wa Sarī no nanbu no akusento o karakatte, kanojo o hontō ni iradatasemasu.*

gold — 金 — *kin*

(as) good as gold — 信頼できる — *shinrai dekiru*

His word is as good as gold. 彼の言葉は信頼できます。 *Kare no kotoba wa shinrai dekimasu.*

goner — だめな人 — *dame na hito*

be a goner — 一巻の終わり — *ikkan no owari*

When Dad finds out I wrecked his car, I'm a goner. 私が父の車を
壊してしまったのを父が知ったら、私は一巻の終わりです。
Watakushi ga chichi no kuruma o kowashite shimatta no o chichi ga shittara, watakushi wa ikkan no owari desu.

good — いい／品 — *ii/shina*

all to the good — 幸い — *saiwai*

He left for work early, which was all to the good because he avoided a
traffic jam. 彼は早く仕事に出かけましたがそれが幸いで、交通
渋滞を避けることが出来たのです。 *Kare wa hayaku shigoto ni dekakemashita ga sore ga saiwai de, kōtsū jūtai o sakeru koto ga dekita no desu.*

get the goods on someone — 証拠をつかむ — *shōko o tsukamu*

I know he's cheating us; I'm going to get the goods on him. 彼が私達を
だましているのを、私は知っています。それで、私は彼について
証拠をつかむつもりです。 *Kare ga watakushitachi o damashite iru no
o, watakushi wa shitte imasu. Sorede, watakushi wa kare ni tsuite shōko
o tsukamu tsumori desu.*

never had it so good — これほどついたことはない — *kore hodo tsuita
koto wa nai*
Now that Mary's married to a millionaire, she's never had it so good.
メリーは大金持ちと結婚して、これほどついたことはありません
でした。 *Merī wa ōganemochi to kekkon shite, kore hodo tsuita koto wa
arimasen deshita.*

make good on something — 借りを返す — *kari o kaesu*
If you lend Bob the money, he'll make good on it. ボブにお金を
貸しても、彼は借りは必ず返します。 *Bobu ni okane o kashitemo,
kare wa kari wa kanarazu kaeshimasu.*

up to no good — 悪いことをたくらんでいる — *warui koto o
takurande iru*
I don't know why he's hanging around the cash register; he's up to no
good. 彼がなぜレジの回りをうろついているのか分かりませんが、
何か悪いことをたくらんでいるのです。 *Kare ga naze reji no
mawari o urotsuite iru no ka wakarimasen ga, nanika warui koto o
takurande iru no desu.*

goose — がちょう — *gachō*
cook one's goose — 破滅の身に落ち込ませる — *hametsu no mi ni
ochikomaseru*
I failed the bar exam; my goose is cooked now! 司法試験に落ちて、
私は今や破滅の身です。 *Shihō shiken ni ochite, watakushi wa
imaya hametsu no mi desu.*

grabs — わしづかみ — *washizukami*
up for grabs — 誰でも手に入れられる — *dare demo te ni irerareru*
Let's bid on the contract; it's up for grabs. この契約は誰でも手に
入れられそうだから、入札してみましょう。 *Kono keiyaku wa dare
demo te ni irerareso dakara, nyūsatsu shite mimashō.*

grain — 木目／粒 — *mokume/tsubu*
  go against the grain — 性分に合わない — *shōbun ni awanai*
  For most people, lying goes against the grain. 殆どの人は、うそを
  つくのが性分に合いません。*Hotondo no hito wa, uso o tsuku no ga
  shōbun ni aimasen.*

  take something with a grain/pinch of salt — 眉に唾をつけて聞く —
  mayu ni tsuba o tsukete kiku
  She says she'll arrive on time from now on, but I'm taking it with a grain
  of salt. 彼女はこれからは遅れずに来ると言いますが、
  私は眉に唾をつけて聞いています。*Kanojo wa kore kara wa
  okurezu ni kuru to iimasu ga, watakushi wa mayu ni tsuba o tsukete kiite
  imasu.*

---

grass — 草 — *kusa*
  let grass grow under one's feet — 何もせずにぐずぐずする — *nani
  mo sezu ni guzuguzu suru*
  Don't let any grass grow under your feet. Get the report done today!
  何もせずにぐずぐずしていないで、今日中にレポートを
  仕上げなさい。*Nani mo sezu ni guzuguzu shite inaide, kyō jū ni repōto
  o shiagenasai.*

---

grasshopper — ばった — *batta*
  knee-high to a grasshopper — 幼い子供の頃 — *osanai kodomo no koro*
  I've known that young man since he was knee-high to a grasshopper.
  私は、あの若者が幼い子供の頃から知っています。
  *Watakushi wa, ano wakamono ga osanai kodomo no koro kara shitte
  imasu.*

---

grave — 墓 — *haka*
  dig one's own grave — 自ら墓穴を掘る — *mizukara boketsu o horu*
  If you continue arguing with the boss, you'll be digging your own grave.
  上司と口論を続けるなら、自ら墓穴を掘ることになりますよ。
  *Jōshi to kōron o tsuzukeru nara, mizukara boketsu o horu koto ni
  narimasu yo.*

  turn over in one's grave — 草葉の陰で泣く — *kusaba no kage de naku*
  If Tom knew what his sons were doing now, he'd turn over in his grave.

息子たちが今何をしているかトムが知ったら、彼は草葉の陰で
泣くでしょう。*Musukotachi ga ima nani o shite iru ka Tomu ga
shittara, kare wa kusaba no kage de naku deshō.*

Greek — ギリシャ語 — *Girishago*
  (all) Greek to me — ちんぷんかんぷん — *chinpunkanpun*
  I can't understand this computer talk—it's all Greek to me. この
  コンピュータに関する話しはちんぷんかんぷんで、私には
  分かりません。*Kono konpyūta ni kansuru hanashi wa chinpunkanpun
  de, watakushi ni wa wakarimasen.*

---

grip — 把握 — *haaku*
  come to grips with something — 直面する — *chokumen suru*
  It's hard to come to grips with the death of a loved one. 愛する人の死に
  直面するのは容易ではありません。*Aisuru hito no shi ni chokumen
  suru no wa yōi dewa arimasen.*

  lose one's grip — 能力を失う — *nōryoku o ushinau*
  He used to be a good editor, but now he's losing his grip. 彼は以前は
  有能な編集者でしたが、今は能力を失いつつあります。*Kare wa
  izen wa yūnō na henshūsha deshita ga, ima wa nōryoku o ushinaitsutsu
  arimasu.*

---

gross — むかむかさせる — *mukamuka saseru*
  gross someone out — 吐き気を催させる — *hakike o moyōsaseru*
  His awful table manners gross me out. 彼のひどい食事の作法は、
  私に吐き気を催させます。*Kare no hidoi shokuji no sahō wa,
  watakushi ni hakike o moyōsasemasu.*

---

ground — 地面 — *jimen*
  break new ground — 新天地を開拓する — *shin tenchi o kaitaku suru*
  Our proposals are going to break new ground. 私達の提案は、新天地を
  開拓することになります。*Watakushitachi no teian wa, shin tenchi o
  kaitaku suru koto ni narimasu.*

  cover a lot of ground — 広い範囲をカバーする — *hiroi han-i o kabā
  suru*
  We covered a lot of ground in today's meeting. 今日の会議では、私達は

広い範囲をカバーしました。*Kyō no kaigi dewa, watakushitachi wa hiroi han-i o kabā shimashita.*

get something off the ground — スタートさせる — *sutāto saseru*
Let's get this project off the ground by next week.　来週までに、この企画をスタートさせましょう。*Raishū made ni, kono kikaku o sutāto sasemashō.*

lose ground — おくれをとる — *okure o toru*
The team lost ground while the quarterback recovered from his injuries last week.　そのチームは、先週クォーターバックが怪我から回復している間に、おくれをとってしまいました。*Sono chīmu wa, senshū kuōtābakku ga kega kara kaifuku shite iru aida ni, okure o totte shimaimashita.*

run something into the ground — やりすぎる — *yarisugiru*
You've already made your point; there's no need to run it into the ground. あなたはすでに言い分を通したんだから、それ以上やりすぎる必要はありません。*Anata wa sude ni iibun o tōshitandakara, sore ijō yarisugiru hitsuyō wa arimasen.*

stand one's ground — 一歩も譲らない — *ippo mo yuzuranai*
When you know you're right, you should stand your ground.
自分が正しいことが分かっているときには、一歩も譲るべきではありません。*Jibun ga tadashii koto ga wakatte iru toki niwa, ippo mo yuzuru beki dewa arimasen.*

gun — 鉄砲 — *teppō*
jump the gun — 先走りする — *sakibashiri suru*
Wait till his birthday to give him his present; don't jump the gun.　彼にプレゼントをあげるのは、先走りせずに彼の誕生日まで待ちなさい。*Kare ni purezento o ageru no wa, sakibashiri sezu ni kare no tanjōbi made machinasai.*

stick to one's guns — 一歩も引かない — *ippo mo hikanai*
Bob was glad he stuck to his guns and asked for a raise.　ボブは、一歩も引かずに昇給を求めてよかったと思いました。*Bobu wa, ippo mo hikazu ni shōkyū o motomete yokatta to omoimashita.*

habit — 習慣 — shūkan
  kick the habit — 悪習を絶つ — akushū o tatsu
  Once you start smoking, it can be hard to kick the habit.
  一度タバコを吸い出すと、その悪習を絶つのは容易では
  ありません。Ichido tabako o suidasu to, sono akushū o tatsu no wa yōi
  dewa arimasen.

---

hackles — うなじの毛 — unaji no ke
  get someone's hackles up — 頭に来る — atama ni kuru
  His rudeness really got my hackles up.　彼の無礼さには、本当に頭に
  来ました。Kare no bureisa niwa, hontō ni atama ni kimashita.

---

hair — 髪の毛 — kami no ke
  by a hair — 間一髪の差で — kan ippatsu no sa de
  That car missed hitting me by a hair!　私は、間一髪の差で車に
  はねられるのを免れました。Watakushi wa, kan ippatsu no sa de
  kuruma ni hanerareru no o manugaremashita.

  get in someone's hair — 苛立たせる — iradataseru
  This screaming child is getting in everyone's hair.　この泣き叫んでいる
  子は、みんなを苛立たせています。Kono nakisakende iru ko wa,
  minna o iradatasete imasu.

  give someone gray hair — 白髪になるほど心配をかける — shiraga ni
  naru hodo shinpai o kakeru
  My children's problems are giving me gray hair.　私の子供たちは
  色々な問題で、私が白髪になるほど心配をかけています。
  Watakushi no kodomotachi wa iroiro na mondai de, watakushi ga
  shiraga ni naru hodo shinpai o kakete imasu.

  let one's hair down — くつろぐ — kutsurogu
  John is too tense; he ought to let his hair down more.　ジョンは緊張の
  塊りだから、もっとくつろぐべきです。Jon wa kinchō no katamari
  dakara, motto kutsurogu beki desu.

make someone's hair curl — 身の毛をよだたせる — *mi no ke o yodataseru*

That ghost story will make your hair curl! あの怪談を聞くと、身の毛がよだつでしょう。*Ano kaidan o kiku to, mi no ke ga yodatsu deshō.*

make someone's hair stand on end — ぞっとさせる — *zotto saseru*

Seeing the auto accident made my hair stand on end. 交通事故を見て、ぞっとしました。*Kōtsū jiko o mite, zotto shimashita.*

split hairs — 細々したことを言う — *komagoma shita koto o iu*

No need to split hairs—I'll pay the check. 細々したことは言わないで。勘定は、私が払います。*Komagoma shita koto wa iwanaide. Kanjō wa, watakushi ga haraimasu.*

tear one's hair out — 髪の毛をかきむしる — *kami no ke o kakimushiru*

This traffic makes me want to tear my hair out. この交通状況には、髪の毛をかきむしりたくなります。*Kono kōtsū jōkyō ni wa, kami no ke o kakimushiritaku narimasu.*

---

hand — 手 — *te*

bite the hand that feeds one — 恩を仇で返す — *on o ada de kaesu*

Be kind to your father; don't bite the hand that feeds you. お父さんには親切にして、恩を仇で返すようなことはしないように。*Otōsan niwa shinsetsu ni shite, on o ada de kaesu yō na koto wa shinai yō ni.*

catch someone red-handed — 現場で捕まえる — *genba de tsukamaeru*

The police caught the thief red-handed. 警官は、泥棒を現場で捕まえました。*Keikan wa, dorobō o genba de tsukamaemashita.*

eat out of someone's hand(s) — 思いのままに従わせる — *omoi no mama ni shitagawaseru*

The new teacher has the students eating out of his hand. 新しい先生は、学生を彼の思いのままに従わせています。*Atarashii sensei wa, gakusei o kare no omoi no mama ni shitagawasete imasu.*

hand it to someone — (能力や功績を)それなりに評価する — *(nōryoku ya kōseki o) sorenari ni hyōka suru*

You have to hand it to him: he's a fine lawyer. 彼を、それなりに評価しなければなりません。彼は、すぐれた弁護士です。*Kare o, sorenari ni hyōka shinakereba narimasen. Kare wa, sugureta bengoshi desu.*

have one's hands tied — 何もできない — *nanimo dekinai*
Until the budget is approved, our hands are tied.　予算が認められる
までは、私達は何もできません。*Yosan ga mitomerareru made wa,
watakushitachi wa nanimo dekimasen.*

live from hand to mouth — その日暮らしをする — *sono hi gurashi o
suru*
Tom lost his job, and his family is living from hand to mouth.　トムが
失業して、彼の家族はその日暮らしをしています。*Tomu ga
shitsugyō shite, kare no kazoku wa sono hi gurashi o shite imasu.*

reveal/show one's hand — 手の内を明かす — *te no uchi o akasu*
He's not going to show his hand until the negotiations begin.　交渉が
始まるまでは、彼は手の内を明かしません。*Kōshō ga hajimaru
made wa, kare wa te no uchi o akashimasen.*

sit on one's hands — 手をこまねいている — *te o komaneite iru*
We need a decision right now. You can't just sit on your hands.　あなたは、
手をこまねいていることは出来ません。私達は、いますぐ決断が
いるのです。*Anata wa, te o komaneite iru koto wa dekimasen.
Watakushitachi wa, ima sugu ketsudan ga iru no desu.*

wait on someone hand and foot — 至れり尽くせりの世話をする —
itareri tsukuseri no sewa o suru
Mary's angry because her husband insists that she wait on him hand and
foot.　メリーは、夫が彼女に至れり尽くせりの世話を要求するので
怒っています。*Merī wa, otto ga kanojo ni itareri tsukuseri no sewa o
yōkyū suru node okotte imasu.*

wash one's hands of someone or something — 関係を絶つ — *kankei o
tatsu*
When his sister refused to get a job, he washed his hands of her.　妹が
仕事を見つけるのを拒否したとき、彼は妹との関係を絶ちました。
*Imoto ga shigoto o mitsukeru no o kyohi shita toki, kare wa imoto to no
kankei o tachimashita.*

with one hand tied behind one's back — いとも簡単に — *itomo
kantan ni*
I can beat him at tennis with one hand tied behind my back.　私はテニスで、
彼をいとも簡単に負かすことが出来ます。*Watakushi wa tenisu de,
kare o itomo kantan ni makasu koto ga dekimasu.*

handle — 柄／取っ手 — *e/totte*
  fly off the handle — かっとなる — *katto naru*
  Whenever we argue, he flies off the handle.　私達が議論するたびに、
  彼はかっとなります。*Watakushitachi ga giron suru tabi ni, kare wa*
  katto narimasu.

  get a handle on something — 理解する手がかりをつかむ — *rikai suru*
  tegakari o tsukamu
  He has to get a handle on the new software program soon.　彼はすぐに、
  このソフトウェアを理解する手がかりをつかまねばなりません。
  Kare wa sugu ni, kono sofutowea o rikai suru tegakari o tsukamaneba
  narimasen.

handwriting — 筆跡 — *hisseki*
  read/see the handwriting on the wall — 前兆が見て取れる — *zenchō*
  ga mite toreru
  We can see the handwriting on the wall: there's going to be a takeover.
  もうじき、会社の乗っ取りがあります。私達は、その前兆が見て
  取れます。*Mōjiki, kaisha no nottori ga arimasu. Watakushitachi wa,*
  sono zenchō ga mite toremasu.

hang — やり方／ぶら下がる — *yarikata/burasagaru*
  get/have the hang of something — こつをのみ込む — *kotsu o nomikomu*
  At first I didn't get the hang of desktop publishing, but now I have it.
  最初はデスクトップ出版のこつがのみ込めませんでしたが、今は
  分かります。*Saisho wa desuku toppu shuppan no kotsu ga*
  nomikomemasen deshita ga, ima wa wakarimasu.

  hang in there — 頑張り続ける — *ganbari tsuzukeru*
  Don't give up now—hang in there!　ここで諦めないで、頑張り
  続けなさい。*Koko de akiramenaide, ganbari tsuzukenasai.*

haste — あせり — *aseri*
  Haste makes waste. — 急いては事をし損じる。— *Seite wa, koto o*
  shisonjiru.
  Slow down. Haste makes waste.　もっと、ゆっくりやりなさい。
  急いては事をし損じますよ。*Motto, yukkuri yarinasai. Seite wa koto*
  o shisonjimasu yo.

hat — 帽子 — bōshi

be old hat — 目新しいものではない — meatarashii mono dewa nai
She thinks it's a new idea, but it's really old hat. 彼女はそれは新しい
考えだと思っていますが、別に目新しいものではありません。
Kanojo wa sore wa atarashii kangae da to omotte imasu ga, betsu ni
meatarashii mono dewa arimasen.

eat one's hat — 首をあげる — kubi o ageru
I know I'm right about this; if not, I'll eat my hat. これについては、
私が正しいことは分かっています。もし間違っていたら、首を
あげます。Kore ni tsuite wa, watakushi ga tadashii koto wa wakatte
imasu. Moshi machigatte itara, kubi o agemasu.

hat in hand — 頭を低くして — atama o hikuku shite
If Tom goes to the boss hat in hand, he'll get what he wants. トムは頭を
低くして社長に会いに行けば、欲しいものを手に入れることが出
来るでしょう。Tomu wa atama o hikuku shite shachō ni aini ikeba,
hoshii mono o te ni ireru koto ga dekiru deshō.

keep something under one's hat — 秘密を守る — himitsu o mamoru
I'll tell you our strategy if you promise to keep it under your hat. 秘密を
守ることを約束するなら、我々の戦略を教えてあげましょう。
Himitsu o mamoru koto o yakusoku suru nara, wareware no senryaku o
oshiete agemashō.

pass the hat — 寄付金を集める — kifukin o atsumeru
Let's pass the hat for a baby gift for our receptionist. 受付係にあげる
出産祝いのために、寄付金を集めましょう。Uketsukegakari ni
ageru shussan iwai no tame ni, kifukin o atsumemashō.

take off one's hat to someone — 敬意を表する — keii o hyōsuru
I take off my hat to you; you've built a fine company. 素晴らしい会社を
設立したあなたに、敬意を表します。Subarashii kaisha o setsuritsu
shita anata ni, keii o hyōshimasu.

toss one's hat into the ring — 出馬宣言する — shutsuba sengen suru
He's considering tossing his hat into the ring for the governorship. 彼は、
知事選への出馬宣言することを考えています。Kare wa, chiji sen e
no shutsuba sengen suru koto o kangaete imasu.

wear two hats — 二股かける — futamata kakeru
Bill wears two hats at the hotel: he's a desk clerk and a waiter. ホテルで、

ビルはフロント係とウェイターの二股かけています。*Hoteru de,*
Biru wa furonto gakari to ueitā no futamata kakete imasu.

hatchet — 手斧 — *te ono*
  bury the hatchet — 和解する — *wakai suru*
  They're tired of arguing, so they've decided to bury the hatchet.　彼等は
  口論に飽きて、和解することにしました。*Karera wa kōron ni*
  akite, wakai suru koto ni shimashita.

haul — たぐり — *taguri*
  over the long haul — 長い目で見て — *nagai me de mite*
  Over the long haul, stocks are the best investment.　長い目で見て、投資
  としては株が一番です。*Nagai me de mite, tōshi to shite wa kabu ga*
  ichiban desu.

have — 持つ — *motsu*
  have had it — 我慢の限界に達する — *gaman no genkai ni tassuru*
  I've had it with his incompetence. I'm going to fire him.　彼の無能さには、
  我慢の限界に達しました。私は、彼の首を切ります。*Kare no*
  munōsa ni wa, gaman no genkai ni tasshimashita. Watakushi wa, kare
  no kubi o kirimasu.

  have it made — 成功疑いなし — *seikō utagai nashi*
  Larry has it made now that he has his law degree.　ラリーは法律の学位を
  取って、今後の成功疑い無しです。*Rarī wa hōritsu no gakui o totte,*
  kongo no seikō utagai nashi desu.

  have it out (with someone) — 和解する — *wakai suru*
  John and Bob finally had it out yesterday, and now everything is fine.
  ジョンとボブは昨日とうとう和解して、今は全て順調です。*Jon*
  to Bobu wa kinō tōtō wakai shite, ima wa subete junchō desu.

havoc — 大被害 — *dai higai*
  wreak havoc — 大打撃をもたらす — *dai dageki o motarasu*
  The hurricane wreaked havoc along the Florida coast.　そのハリケーンは、
  フロリダ沿岸に大打撃をもたらしました。*Sono harikēn wa,*
  Furorida engan ni dai dageki o motarashimashita.

hawk — 鷹 — *taka*
  watch someone like a hawk — 注意深く見守る — *chūi bukaku mimamoru*
  If you think he's been stealing, just watch him like a hawk.　彼が盗みを働いていると思うなら、彼を注意深く見守りなさい。*Kare ga nusumi o hataraite iru to omou nara, kare o chūi bukaku mimamorinasai.*

---

hay — 干し草 — *hoshigusa*
  hit the hay — 寝る — *neru*
  It's past midnight—time to hit the hay.　真夜中を過ぎたから、寝る時間です。*Mayonaka o sugita kara, neru jikan desu.*

---

head — 頭 — *atama*
  bang/beat one's head against a (brick) wall — 時間の無駄 — *jikan no muda*
  Trying to reason with John is like banging my head against a brick wall.　ジョンに道理を説くのは、時間の無駄です。*Jon ni dōri o toku no wa, jikan no muda desu.*

  bite someone's head off — ものすごいけんまくで怒る — *monosugoi kenmaku de okoru*
  He's just trying to be helpful; there's no need to bite his head off.　彼は、手助けしようとしているだけです。だから、そんなものすごいけんまくで怒る必要はありません。*Kare wa, tedasuke shiyō to shite iru dake desu. Dakara, sonna monosugoi kenmaku de okoru hitsuyō wa arimasen.*

  bring something to a head — 決着の場に持ち出す — *ketchaku no ba ni mochidasu*
  I wish we could bring this situation to a head and resolve it.　私達がこの事態を決着の場に持ち出して、解決できたならと思います。*Watakushitachi ga, kono jitai o ketchaku no ba ni mochidashite, kaiketsu dekita nara to omoimasu.*

  bury one's head in the sand — 現実に目をつぶる — *genjitsu ni me o tsuburu*
  Bill prefers to bury his head in the sand rather than face his troubles.　ビルは問題に直面するより、現実に目をつぶる方を好みます。

Biru wa mondai ni chokumen suru yori, genjitsu ni me o tsuburu hō o konomimasu.

can't make heads or tails (out) of something — ちんぷんかんぷんだ — *chinpunkanpun da*

I can't make heads or tails out of this report.　この報告書は、ちんぷんかんぷんです。*Kono hōkokusho wa, chinpunkanpun desu.*

fall head over heels (in love) — 無我夢中になる — *muga muchū ni naru*

She's fallen head over heels for Bill.　彼女は、ビルに無我夢中になっています。*Kanojo wa, Biru ni muga muchū ni natte imasu.*

get one's head above water — 困難を切り抜ける — *konnan o kirinukeru*

I can lend you some money until you get your head above water.　あなたが困難を切り抜けるまで、お金をいくらか貸してあげてもいいです。*Anata ga konnan o kirinukeru made, okane o ikuraka kashite agetemo ii desu.*

give someone a swelled head — 自惚れさせる — *unubore saseru*

Stop praising Tom so much; you'll give him a swelled head.　トムをそんなに誉めるのは止めなさい。彼を自惚れさせることになりますよ。*Tomu o sonna ni homeru no wa yamenasai. Kare o unubore saseru koto ni narimasu yo.*

go to someone's head — 慢心する — *manshin suru*

Don't let your good grades go to your head; you have to continue studying.　成績がいいからといって慢心しないで、勉強を続けなければなりません。*Seiseki ga ii kara to itte manshin shinai de, benkyō o tsuzukenakereba narimasen.*

have something hanging over one's head — 頭から離れない — *atama kara hanarenai*

I can't relax with this deadline hanging over my head.　この締め切りが頭から離れなくて、くつろげません。*Kono shimekiri ga atama kara hanarenakute, kutsurogemasen.*

heads will roll — 首が飛ぶ — *kubi ga tobu*
If we don't meet the deadline, heads will roll.　私達がこの締め切りに
間に合わせないと、首がいくつも飛ぶでしょう。*Watakushitachi
ga kono shimekiri ni maniawasenai to, kubi ga ikutsumo tobu deshō.*

in over one's head — 手に負えない — *te ni oenai*
I don't know if Bob can handle the job; he's in over his head.　私は、
ボブがその仕事を扱えるかどうか疑問です。それは、彼の手に
負えないからです。*Watakushi wa, Bobu ga sono shigoto o atsukaeru
ka dō ka gimon desu. Sore wa, kare no te ni oenai kara desu.*

one's head is in the clouds — 回りのことに上の空 — *mawari no koto
ni uwanosora*
She could be a good student, but her head is usually in the clouds.　彼女は
優秀な学生になれるのですが、普通は回りのことに上の空です。
*Kanojo wa yūshū na gakusei ni nareru no desu ga, futsū wa mawari no
koto ni uwanosora desu.*

over someone's head — 難し過ぎる — *muzukashisugiru*
He's trying to understand computer programming, but it's over his head.
彼はコンピュータのプログラミングを理解しようとしていますが、
それは彼には難し過ぎます。*Kare wa konpyūta no puroguramingu o
rikai shiyō to shite imasu ga, sore wa kare ni wa muzukashisugimasu.*

---

heart　心臓／心　*shinzō／kokoro*
　eat one's heart out — 嘆き悲しむ — *nageki kanashimu*

She's eating her heart out over her daughter's illness. 彼女は、娘の病気を嘆き悲しんでいます。 *Kanojo wa, musume no byōki o nageki kanashinde imasu.*

have a heart — 情けを掛ける — *nasake o kakeru*
Have a heart; don't make us work late tonight. どうぞ情けを掛けて、今晩は私達に残業をさせないで下さい。 *Dōzo nasake o kakete, konban wa watakushitachi ni zangyō o sasenaide kudasai.*

have a heart of gold — 美しい心の持ち主 — *utsukushii kokoro no mochinushi*
That nurse is so kind to her patients; she has a heart of gold. あの看護婦は美しい心の持ち主で、患者にとてもやさしいです。 *Ano kangofu wa utsukushii kokoro no mochinushi de, kanja ni totemo yasashii desu.*

have one's heart set on something — 心に決める — *kokoro ni kimeru*
He has his heart set on a new sports car. 彼は新しいスポーツカーを手に入れることを心に決めています。 *Kare wa atarashii supōtsukā o te ni ireru koto o kokoro ni kimete imasu.*

know something by heart — 空で覚えている — *sora de oboete iru*
I know that poem by heart. 私は、その詩を空で覚えています。 *Watakushi wa, sono shi o sora de oboete imasu.*

one's heart is in one's mouth — 心臓がどきどきする — *shinzō ga dokidoki suru*
When the plane hit an air pocket, my heart was in my mouth. 飛行機が乱気流に遭遇したとき、心臓がどきどきしました。 *Hikōki ga rankiryū ni sōgū shita toki, shinzō ga dokidoki shimashita.*

pour one's heart out to someone — 心の内をぶちまける — *kokoro no uchi o buchimakeru*
Jane poured her heart out to me after her divorce. ジェーンは離婚の後、心の内を私にぶちまけました。 *Jēn wa rikon no ato, kokoro no uchi o watakushi ni buchimakemashita.*

take something to heart — 真剣に受けとめる — *shinken ni uketomeru*
She's just angry now; don't take her criticism to heart. 彼女は今は怒りに燃えているところなので、彼女の批判を真剣に受けとめるべきではありません。 *Kanojo wa ima wa ikari ni moete iru tokoro nanode, kanojo no hihan o shinken ni uketomeru beki dewa arimasen.*

to one's heart's content — 思う存分 — *omou zonbun*

She likes summer because she can eat peaches to her heart's content.
桃が思う存分食べられるので、彼女は夏が大好きです。*Momo ga omou zonbun taberareru node, kanojo wa natsu ga daisuki desu.*

wear one's heart on one's sleeve — 心の内をあらわに出している — *kokoro no uchi o arawa ni dashite iru*
It's easy to see how he feels about Helen: he's wearing his heart on his sleeve. 彼がヘレンをどう思っているか知るのは簡単です。彼は、心の内をあらわに出しているからです。*Kare ga Heren o dō omotte iru ka shiru no wa kantan desu. Kare wa, kokoro no uchi o arawa ni dashite iru kara desu.*

---

heaven — 天国 — *tengoku*
in seventh heaven — 有頂天 — *uchōten*
He's in seventh heaven when his team wins. 彼は自分のチ－ムが勝つと、有頂天になります。*Kare wa jibun no chīmu ga katsu to, uchōten ni narimasu.*

---

heel — 踵 — *kakato*
cool one's heels — 待たされる — *matasareru*
I arrived on time, but they left me cooling my heels in the waiting room. 私は時間通りについたのですが、待合い室で待たされました。*Watakushi wa jikan dōri ni tsuita no desu ga, machiaishitsu de matasaremashita.*

dig one's heels in — かたくなになる — *katakuna ni naru*
If you argue with him, he'll just dig his heels in. 彼と議論すると、彼はかたくなになるだけです。*Kare to giron suru to, kare wa katakuna ni naru dake desu.*

---

hell — 地獄 — *jigoku*
(as) mad as hell — かんかんに怒る — *kankan ni okoru*
He was mad as hell when his car was stolen. 彼は車を盗まれて、かんかんに怒りました。*Kare wa kuruma o nusumarete, kankan ni okorimashita.*

(be) hell to pay — 大変な目にあう — *taihen na me ni au*
If we don't clean up this mess, there will be hell to pay. 今このごたごたを片付けておかないと、私達は後で大変な目にあうでしょう。*Ima*

kono gotagota o katazukete okanai to, watakushitachi wa ato de taihen na me ni au deshō.

come hell or high water — 雨が降ろうが槍が降ろうが — *ame ga furō ga yari ga furō ga*
We'll get the job done come hell or high water. 雨が降ろうが槍が降ろうが、私達はこの仕事を必ずやり遂げます。*Ame ga furō ga yari ga furō ga, watakushitachi wa kono shigoto o kanarazu yaritogemasu.*

go to hell in a handbasket — ひどい状態になる — *hidoi jōtai ni naru*
With all the street crime, this city is going to hell in a handbasket. 街頭に犯罪が氾濫して、この都市はひどい状態になっています。*Gaitō ni hanzi ga hanran shite, kono toshi wa hidoi jōtai ni natte imasu.*

raise hell — 馬鹿騒ぎをする — *baka sawagi o suru*
Those kids have been raising hell every night since graduation. あの若者たちは、卒業してから毎晩のように馬鹿騒ぎをしています。*Ano wakamonotachi wa, sotsugyō shite kara maiban no yō ni baka sawagi o shite imasu.*

shot to hell — 完全にだめになる — *kanzen ni dame ni naru*
With the rain, our picnic plans were shot to hell. 雨で、私達のピクニックの計画は完全にだめになりました。*Ame de, watakushitachi no pikunikku no keikaku wa kanzen ni dame ni narimashita.*

---

hen — 雌鶏 — *mendori*
(as) mad as a wet hen — かんかんに怒る — *kankan ni okoru*
When his team lost, the coach was as mad as a wet hen. 彼のチームが負けたとき、監督はかんかんに怒りました。*Kare no chīmu ga maketa toki, kantoku wa kankan ni okorimashita.*

---

herring — 鰊 — *nishin*
red herring — 注意を脇にそらすもの — *chūi o waki ni sorasu mono*
Don't bring that subject up now; it's a red herring. その話題は、今は持ち出さないで下さい。注意を脇にそらすことになりますから。*Sono wadai wa, ima wa mochidasanaide kudasai. Chūi o waki ni sorasu koto ni narimasu kara.*

---

hide — 皮 — *kawa*
(neither) hide (n)or hair — 影も形もない — *kage mo katachi mo nai*

We haven't seen hide or hair of John for ages.　私達はずいぶん長いこと、ジョンの影も形も見ていません。Watakushitachi wa zuibun nagai koto, Jon no kage mo katachi mo mite imasen.

hill — 丘 — oka

as old as the hills — すごく古い — sugoku furui

Our car is as old as the hills.　私達の車は、すごく古いです。
Watakushitachi no kuruma wa, sugoku furui desu.

not amount to a hill of beans — たかが知れている — taka ga shirete iru

Don't be concerned about their little spat; it doesn't amount to a hill of beans.　彼等の口争いに、気を揉む必要はありません。どうせ、たかが知れているんですから。Karera no kuchi arasoi ni, ki o momu hitsuyō wa arimasen. Dōse, taka ga shirete irundesu kara.

not worth a hill of beans — 全く価値がない — mattaku kachi ga nai

This new plan isn't worth a hill of beans.　この新しい計画は、全く価値がありません。Kono atarashii keikaku wa, mattaku kachi ga arimasen.

over the hill — 峠を越して — tōge o koshite

The relief pitcher used to be good, but now he's over the hill.　あの救援の投手はかつては優秀でしたが、今は峠を越しています。Ano kyūen no tōshu wa katsute wa yūshū deshita ga, ima wa tōge o koshite imasu.

hip — 腰 — koshi

shoot from the hip — はっきりものを言う — hakkiri mono o iu

I don't like subterfuge; I wish he would shoot from the hip.　私は、逃げ口上は好きではありません。それで、彼にははっきりものを言ってもらいたいです。Watakushi wa nigekōjō wa suki dewa arimasen. Sorede, kare ni wa hakkiri mono o itte moraitai desu.

hog — 豚 — *buta*

eat high on the hog — 豪勢な食事をする — *gōsei na shokuji o suru*
This is quite a meal. We're eating high on the hog tonight.　これは大変な
御馳走で、私達は今晩は豪勢な食事をしています。*Kore wa taihen
na gochisō de, watakushitachi wa konban wa gōsei na shokuji o shite
imasu.*

go whole hog — とことんまでやる — *tokoton made yaru*
We might as well go whole hog: let's fly first class.　どうせとことんまで
やるからには、ファーストクラスで行きましょう。*Dōse tokoton
made yaru kara niwa, fāsutokurasu de ikimashō.*

live high on the hog — ぜいたくに暮らす — *zeitaku ni kurasu*
Since he won the lottery, John's been living high on the hog.　彼は
宝くじに当たって以来、ぜいたくに暮らしています。*Kare wa
takarakuji ni atatte irai, zeitaku ni kurashite imasu.*

---

hold — ホールド／保留 — *hōrudo/horyū*
no holds barred — ためらわずに — *tamerawazu ni*
Let's have an honest discussion, no holds barred.　ためらわずに、
正直な話し合いをしましょう。*Tamerawazu ni, shōjiki na hanashiai
o shimashō.*

on hold — 一時保留に — *ichiji horyū ni*
We don't have the funding, so that project is on hold for now.　資金不足の
ため、その企画は今のところ一時保留になっています。*Shikin*

busoku no tame, sono kikaku wa ima no tokoro ichiji horyū ni natte imasu.

hole — 穴 — *ana*

in the hole — 赤字で — *akaji de*

Since I overspent my budget this month, I'm $500 in the hole. 今月は予算以上使ってしまって、500ドルの赤字です。*Kongetsu wa yosan ijō tsukatte shimatte, go hyaku doru no akaji desu.*

pick holes in something — 弱点を突く — *jakuten o tsuku*

Any good defense lawyer could pick holes in the prosecution's case. 被告側の弁護士が優秀なら、検察側の論拠の弱点を突くことが出来ます。*Hikoku gawa no bengoshi ga yūshū nara, kensatsu gawa no ronkyo no jakuten o tsuku koto ga dekimasu.*

home — うち — *uchi*

come home to roost — 跳ね返りが来る — *hanekaeri ga kuru*

All his philandering is coming home to roost. 彼の今までの女漁りに、跳ね返りが来ています。*Kare no ima made no onna asari ni, hanekaeri ga kite imasu.*

hit one close to home — 深い影響をもたらす — *fukai eikyō o motarasu*

The rise of the yen hits them close to home. 円高は、彼等に深い影響をもたらします。*En daka wa, karera ni fukai eikyō o motarashimasu.*

honeymoon — 新婚旅行 — *shinkon ryokō*

The honeymoon is over. — 初期の親密な関係は終わり。— *Shoki no shinmitsu na kankei wa owari.*

The honeymoon is over; the fans are disappointed with the new coach. 初期の親密な関係は終わりました。ファンは今、新しいコーチに失望しています。*Shoki no shinmitsu na kankei wa owarimashita. Fan wa ima, atarashii kōchi ni shitsubō shite imasu.*

honor — 名誉 — *meiyo*

do the honors — 小穴 | 役む務めるる — *hosoto yaku o tsutomeru*

John, will you do the honors and propose a toast for the occasion?

ジョンさん、ホスト役を務めて、この機会のために乾杯を
申し出てもらえますか。*Jon san, hosuto yaku o tsutomete, kono kikai
no tame ni kanpai o mōshidete moraemasu ka.*

hook — かぎの手 — *kagi no te*

by hook or by crook — 何が何でも — *nani ga nan demo*
We'll meet the deadline by hook or by crook.   私達は、何が何でも
この締め切りに間に合わせます。*Watakushitachi wa, nani ga nan
demo kono shimekiri ni maniawasemasu.*

off the hook — 救われる — *sukuwareru*
He borrowed someone else's car, so I'm off the hook.
彼は誰か他の人から車を借りたので、私は救われました。
*Kare wa dareka hoka no hito kara kuruma o karita node, watakushi wa
sukuwaremashita.*

hook, line, and sinker — 完全にひっかかる — *kanzen ni hikkakaru*
She fell for his lie, hook, line, and sinker.   彼女は、彼の嘘に完全に
ひっかかりました。*Kanojo wa, kare no uso ni kanzen ni
hikkakarimashita.*

hoop — 輪 — *wa*

jump through hoops — 言いなりになる — *iinari ni naru*
They made him jump through hoops to get the job.   彼が仕事を
もらうのに、彼等は彼を言いなりにさせました。*Kare ga shigoto
o morau noni, karera wa kare o iinari ni sasemashita.*

hoot — やじる声 — *yajiru koe*

not give a hoot/two hoots about something — 全然気にかけない —
zenzen ki ni kakenai
She doesn't give two hoots about her grades.   彼女は、学校の成績を
全然気にかけません。*Kanojo wa, gakkō no seiseki o zenzen ki ni
kakemasen.*

horn — 角笛／角 — *tsunobue/tsuno*

blow one's own horn — 自画自賛する — *jiga jisan suru*
I hate to blow my own horn, but I think I did a pretty good job.   自画自賛
するのは好みませんが、なかなかいい仕事をしたと自分で思って

います。*Jiga jisan suru no wa konomimasen ga, nakanaka ii shigoto o shita to jibun de omotte imasu.*

on the horns of a dilemma — いずれを取つても救いようがない

ジレンマに陥つて — *izure o totte mo sukuiyō ga nai jirenma ni ochiitte*

She's on the horns of a dilemma: not to pay her tuition or not to pay her taxes. 　授業料を払わないか、税金を払わないか、彼女はいずれを取つても救いようがないジレンマに陥つています。*Jugyō ryō o harawanai ka, zeikin o harawanai ka, kanojo wa izure o tottemo sukuiyō ga nai jirenma ni ochiitte imasu.*

---

hornet — すずめ蜂 — *suzumebachi*

(as) mad as a hornet — かんかんに怒る — *kankan ni okoru*

He was as mad as a hornet when his car was stolen. 　彼は車が盗まれたとき、かんかんに怒りました。*Kare wa kuruma ga nusumareta toki, kankan ni okorimashita.*

stir up a hornet's nest — 面倒を引き起こす — *mendō o hikiokosu*

If you discuss politics with them, you'll stir up a hornet's nest. 　彼等と政治を議論すると、面倒を引き起こすことになりますよ。*Karera to seiji o giron suru to, mendō o hikiokosu koto ni narimasu yo.*

---

horse — 馬 — *uma*

back the wrong horse — 負け馬に賭ける — *make uma ni kakeru*

My candidate lost; I guess I backed the wrong horse. 　私の候補者が落選しました。私は、負け馬に賭けたんだと思います。*Watakushi no kōhosha ga rakusen shimashita. Watakushi wa, make uma ni kaketanda to omoimasu.*

beat a dead horse — 解決した問題を蒸し返す — *kaiketsu shita mondai o mushikaesu*

Why not just drop the subject? You're beating a dead horse. 　その件は取り下げたらどうですか。あなたは、解決した問題を蒸し返しているんですよ。*Sono ken wa, torisagetara dō desu ka. Anata wa, kaiketsu shita mondai o mushikaeshite irundesu yo.*

change horses in midstream — 進行中のことを途中で変える — *shinkō chū no koto o tochū de kaeru*

I'm voting for the incumbent mayor. We don't want to change horses in

midstream.　私は、現職の市長に投票します。進行中のことを
途中で変えたくありませんから。*Watakushi wa, genshoku no
shichō ni tōhyō shimasu. Shinkō chū no koto o tochū de kaetaku
arimasen kara.*

dark horse — 未知の実力者 — *michi no jitsuryokusha*
There may be a dark horse running for the presidency soon.　もうじき、
未知の実力者が大統領選に名乗りを上げてくるかもしれません。
*Mōjiki, michi no jitsuryokusha ga daitōryō sen ni nanori o agete kuru
kamo shiremasen.*

eat like a horse — 山のように食べる — *yama no yō ni taberu*
My teenage son eats like a horse.　私の十代の息子は、山のように
食べます。*Watakushi no jūdai no musuko wa, yama no yō ni
tabemasu.*

Hold your horses! — 頭を冷やせ。— *Atama o hiyase.*
Calm down! Hold your horses!　気を静めて。頭を冷やしなさい。*Ki o
shizumete. Atama o hiyashinasai.*

horse of a different color — 全く別の話 — *mattaku betsu no hanashi*
That suggestion is a horse of a different color.　その提案は、全く別の
話です。*Sono teian wa, mattaku betsu no hanashi desu.*

straight from the horse's mouth — 確かな筋から直接 — *tashika na
suji kara chokusetsu*
I got the news of the layoffs straight from the horse's mouth—the boss.
一時解雇の情報は、確かな筋、つまり社長から直接聞きました。
*Ichiji kaiko no jōhō wa, tashika na suji, tsumari shachō kara chokusetsu
kikimashita.*

Wild horses couldn't drag (someone). — 絶対にいやだ。— *Zettai ni
iya da.*
Wild horses couldn't drag me to that party.　私は、そのパーティーに
行くのは絶対にいやです。*Watakushi wa, sono pātī ni iku no wa
zettai ni iya desu.*

work like a horse — わき目もふらずに働く — *wakime mo furazu ni
hataraku*
That plumber works like a horse.　その水道屋は、わき目もふらずに
働きます。*Sono suidōya wa, wakime mo furazu ni hatarakimasu.*

hotcakes — ホットケーキ — *hottokēki*

sell like hotcakes — 飛ぶように売れる — *tobu yō ni ureru*
Her new novel is selling like hotcakes.　彼女の新しい小説は、
飛ぶように売れています。*Kanojo no atarashii shōsetsu wa, tobu yō
ni urete imasu.*

hour — 時間 — *jikan*

all hours (of the night) — 夜遅くまで — *yoru osoku made*
She's been studying until all hours of the night to pass the exam.　試験に
受かるように、彼女は夜遅くまで勉強しています。*Shiken ni ukaru
yō ni, kanojo wa yoru osoku made benkyō shite imasu.*

house — 聴衆／家 — *chōshū/ie*

bring down the house — 聴衆を沸かせる — *chōshū o wakaseru*
His speeches always bring down the house.　彼の演説は、いつも聴衆を
沸かせます。*Kare no enzetsu wa, itsumo chōshū o wakasemasu.*

eat someone out of house and home — 人を破産させるほどよく
食べる — *hito o hasan saseru hodo yoku taberu*
Their teenage sons are eating them out of house and home.　彼等の
十代の息子たちは、親を破産させるほどよく食べます。*Karera no
jūdai no musukotachi wa, oya o hasan saseru hodo yoku tabemasu.*

like a house on fire — 猛烈な勢いで — *mōretsu na ikioi de*
The team came back after halftime like a house on fire.　そのチームは
ハーフタイムの後、猛烈な勢いで反撃しました。*Sono chīmu wa,
hāfutaimu no ato, mōretsu na ikioi de hangeki shimashita.*

479

on the house — 店からの無料サービス — *mise kara no muryō sābisu*
The waiter said the dessert was on the house.　ウェイターは、デザートは
店からの無料サービスだと言いました。*Ueitā wa, dezāto wa mise
kara no muryō sābisu da to iimashita.*

put one's house in order — 身の回りを整理する — *mi no mawari o
seiri suru*
She wants to put her house in order before she dies.
彼女は、死ぬ前に身の回りを整理しておきたいと思っています。
*Kanojo wa, shinu mae ni mi no mawari o seiri shite okitai to omotte
imasu.*

ice — 氷 — *kōri*
 break the ice — 堅苦しさを破る — *katakurushisa o yaburu*
 Let's break the ice and introduce ourselves.　堅苦しさを破って、
 私達から自己紹介しましょう。*Katakurushisa o yabutte,
 watakushitachi kara jiko shōkai shimashō.*

 on thin ice — 危ない橋を渡る — *abunai hashi o wataru*
 He's on thin ice with that flimsy excuse.　彼は見え透いた言い訳を

使って、危ない橋を渡っています。*Kare wa miesuita iiwake o tsukatte, abunai hashi o watatte imasu.*

if — もし — *moshi*
  no ifs, ands, or buts — 議論の余地はない — *giron no yochi wa nai*
  I need it by five o'clock, no ifs, ands, or buts. それは五時までに絶対
  必要で、議論の余地はありません。*Sore wa go ji made ni zettai hitsuyō de, giron no yochi wa arimasen.*

image — イメージ — *iméji*
  spitting image — 生き写し — *ikiutsushi*
  She's the spitting image of her mother. 彼女は、お母さんに生き写し
  です。*Kanojo wa, okāsan ni ikiutsushi desu.*

inch — インチ — *inchi*
  come within an inch of doing something — もう少しでするところだ
  — *mō sukoshi de suru tokoro da*
  She came within an inch of marrying the wrong man. 彼女は、もう少しで
  ふさわしくない男と結婚してしまうところでした。*Kanojo wa, mō sukoshi de fusawashiku nai otoko to kekkon shite shimau tokoro deshita.*

  every inch a something — 百パーセント — *hyaku pāsento*
  Mary is every inch an artist. メリーは、百パーセント芸術家です。
  Merī wa, hyaku pāsento geijutsuka desu.

  Give someone an inch and he/she will take a mile. — 甘い顔をすると
  すぐに付け入る — *amai kao o suru to sugu ni tsukeiru*
  Don't extend her deadline; give her an inch and she'll take a mile. 彼女に
  甘い顔をするとすぐに付け入るから、締め切りは延ばさないように。
  Kanojo ni amai kao o suru to sugu ni tsukeiru kara, shimekiri wa nobasanai yō ni.

influence — 影響 — *eikyō*
  under the influence (of alcohol) — 酔っ払って — *yopparatte*
  If you're caught driving under the influence, you could lose your license.
  酔っぱらい運転で捕まると、免許証を失います。*Yopparai unten de tsukamaru to, menkyo shō o ushinaimasu.*

iron — 鉄 — *tetsu*

have too many irons in the fire — 一度にたくさんのことをし過ぎる
— *ichido ni takusan no koto o shisugiru*

If you have too many irons in the fire, you won't do anything well.　一度に
たくさんのことをし過ぎると、何もうまくできませんよ。*Ichido
ni takusan no koto o shisugiru to, nani mo umaku dekimasen yo.*

Strike while the iron is hot. — 好機を逃すな。— *Kōki o nogasuna.*

It's a good time to buy that stock; strike while the iron is hot.　その株を
買うのに、今がちょうどいいときです。好機を逃さないように。
Sono kabu o kau no ni, ima ga chōdo ii toki desu. Kōki o nogasanai yō ni.

jazz — ジャズ — *jazu*

jazz something up — 華やかにする — *hanayaka ni suru*

That outfit is too plain; you should jazz it up with some jewelry.　その
服装は地味すぎるから、装身具で華やかにするべきです。*Sono
fukusō wa jimisugiru kara, sōshingu de hanayaka ni suru beki desu.*

Jekyll — ジキル博士 — *Jikiru hakase*

Jekyll and Hyde — 二重人格者 — *nijū jinkaku sha*

He has two distinct personalities—a real Jekyll and Hyde.　彼は、二つの
全く別の個性を持っています。つまり、二重人格者なのです。
*Kare wa, futatsu no mattaku betsu no kosei o motte imasu. Tsumari, nijū
jinkaku sha na no desu.*

job — 仕事 — *shigoto*

do a snow job on someone — もっともらしい話しをする — *mottomo
rashii hanashi o suru*

He really did a snow job on her, lying about having a college degree.
彼は彼女にまことにもっともらしい話しをして、学士号があると
嘘をつきました。*Kare wa kanojo ni makoto ni mottomo rashii
hanashi o shite, gakushi gō ga aru to uso o tsukimashita.*

snow job — まやかしもの — *mayakashimono*
Their presentation sounded impressive, but it was really a snow job.
彼等の発表は印象的でしたが、それは実はまやかしものでした。
Karera no happyō wa inshōteki deshita ga, sore wa jitsu wa
mayakashimono deshita.

Johnny — ジョニ− — *Jonī*
Johnny-come-lately — 新入り — *shin-iri*
He's a Johnny-come-lately to the business, but he's doing well.   彼は
このビジネスでは新入りでも、よくやっています。*Kare wa kono*
bijinesu dewa shin-iri demo, yoku yatte imasu.

Johnny-on-the-spot — 頼りがいのある人 — *tayorigai no aru hito*
Bill is always there when you need him–a real Johnny-on-the-spot.
ビルは彼を必要とするときはいつもその場に来てくれる、本当に
頼りがいのある人です。*Biru wa kare o hitsuyō to suru toki wa itsumo*
sono ba ni kite kureru, hontō ni tayorigai no aru hito desu.

Jones — ジョ−ンズ — *jōnzu*
keep up with the Joneses — 隣近所と張り合う — *tonari kinjo to*
hariau
They bought a bigger house just to keep up with the Joneses.   彼等は
隣近所と張り合うために、今までのより大きな家を買いました。
Karera wa tonari kinjo to hariau tame ni, ima made no yori ōkina ie o
kaimashita.

judge — 裁判官 — *saibankan*
(as) sober as a judge — 全くしらふで — *mattaku shirafu de*
Jim likes to drink after work, but on the job he's as sober as a judge.
彼は仕事の後で飲むのが好きですが、仕事中は全くしらふです。
Kare wa shigoto no ato de nomu no ga suki desu ga, shigoto chū wa
mattaku shirafu desu.

juice — ジュ−ス — *jūsu*
stew in one's own juice — 勝手に怒る — *katte ni okoru*
Let him stew in his own juice a while, and he'll calm down.   彼には、
しばらくの間、勝手に怒らせておきなさい。そうすれば、やがて

落ち着きを取り戻します。*Kare niwa, shibaraku no aida, katte ni okorasete okinasai. Sō sureba, yagate ochitsuki o torimodoshimasu.*

jump — 跳躍 — *chōyaku*

get the jump on someone — 先んじる — *sakinjiru*

Mary's studying for the exam early so she can get the jump on her classmates. 彼女は級友に先んじることが出来るように、早くから試験のための勉強をしています。*Kanojo wa kyūyū ni sakinjiru koto ga dekiru yō ni, hayaku kara shiken no tame no benkyō o shite imasu.*

one jump ahead — 一歩先を進む — *ippo saki o susumu*

That company always stays one jump ahead of its competitors. あの会社は、いつも競争相手の会社の一歩先を進んでいます。*Ano kaisha wa, itsumo kyōsō aite no kaisha no ippo saki o susunde imasu.*

jury — 陪審 — *baishin*

the jury is still out — まだ一般的な評価が下っていない — *mada ippanteki na hyōka ga kudatte inai*

The jury is still out on the quality of that new computer software. その新しいコンピュータのソフトウェアの質に関しては、まだ一般的な評価が下っていません。*Sono atarashii konpyūta no sofutowea no shitsu ni kanshite wa, mada ippanteki na hyōka ga kudatte imasen.*

justice — 正義 — *seigi*

do justice to something — 大いに食べる／正しく表現する — *ōi ni taberu/tadashiku hyōgen suru*

I'd like a second helping of pie, but I couldn't do justice to it. パイのお代わりが欲しいのですが、食べても食べきれないと思います。*Pai no okawari ga hoshii no desu ga, tabetemo tabekirenai to omoimasu.*

He's more handsome than I expected; photos don't do him justice. 彼は思ったよりもハンサムです。写真は、彼を正しく表現していません。*Kare wa omotta yori mo hansamu desu. Shashin wa, kare o tadashiku hyōgen shite imasen.*

poetic justice — 因果応報 — *inga ōhō*

The thief was caught trying to rob an off-duty policeman; that's poetic justice. 強盗は、非番の警官を襲って捕まりました。これこそ、

因果応報です。*Gōtō wa, hiban no keikan o osotte tsukamarimashita. Kore koso, inga ōhō desu.*

keel — 竜骨 — *ryūkotsu*
  on an even keel — 平静に — *heisei ni*
  Whether we win the game or not, let's stay on an even keel.　試合に
  勝っても負けても、平静を保ちましょう。*Shiai ni kattemo
  maketemo, heisei o tamochimashō.*

keep — 生活の糧 — *seikatsu no kate*
  earn one's keep — 生活の糧に見合う雑用をする — *seikatsu no kate ni
  miau zatsuyō o suru*
  Bob can live at his parents' home as long as he earns his keep.　ボブは
  生活の糧に見合う雑用をする限りは、両親の家に住むことが
  出来ます。*Bobu wa seikatsu no kate ni miau zatsuyō o suru kagiri wa,
  ryōshin no ie ni sumu koto ga dekimasu.*

keg — 樽 — *taru*
  sitting on a powder keg — 一触即発の危機に瀕している — *isshoku
  sokuhatsu no kiki ni hinshite iru*
  With all the employee discontent, the company president is sitting on a
  powder keg.　社員の不満が高まって、社長は一触即発の危機に
  瀕しています。*Shain no fuman ga takamatte, shachō wa isshoku
  sokuhatsu no kiki ni hinshite imasu.*

kettle — やかん — *yakan*
  fine kettle of fish — お手上げの状態 — *oteage no jōtai*
  A water pipe just broke, and I can't find a plumber. This is a fine kettle of
  fish!　さっき水道管が破裂したけれど、水道屋は見つからない。
  全くお手上げの状態です。*Sakki suidō kan ga haretsu shita keredo,
  suidō ya wa mitsukaranai. Mattaku oteage no jōtai desu.*

---

kick — 興奮／蹴る — *kōfun/keru*

get a kick out of someone or something — とても楽しむ — *totemo tanoshimu*

I get a kick out of seeing my daughter play soccer. 娘がサッカーを するのを見るのは、とても楽しいです。*Musume ga sakkā o suru no o miru no wa, totemo tanoshii desu.*

kick oneself — 悔やむ — *kuyamu*

I could kick myself for forgetting her birthday. 彼女の誕生日を忘れて しまったことを、悔やんでいます。*Kanojo no tanjōbi o wasurete shimatta koto o, kuyande imasu.*

---

killing — 殺し — *koroshi*

make a killing — 大儲けする — *ōmōke suru*

John made a killing on the stock market last month. 先月ジョンは、 株式市場で大儲けしました。*Sengetsu Jon wa, kabushiki shijō de ōmōke shimashita.*

---

king — 国王 — *kokuō*

fit for a king — このうえない — *kono ue nai*

That was a meal fit for a king. それは、このうえない食事でした。 *Sore wa, kono ue nai shokuji deshita.*

a king's ransom — とてつもないお金 — *totetsu mo nai okane*

They pay a king's ransom to send their son to that private school. 彼等は 息子をあの私立の学校へ行かせるため、とてつもないお金を 払っています。*Karera wa musuko o ano shiritsu no gakkō e ikaseru tame, totetsu mo nai okane o haratte imasu.*

---

kiss — キス — *kisu*

kiss of death — 命取り — *inochi tori*

Missing the meeting was the kiss of death for the new employee. 会議を 見過ごしてしまったのは、新入社員にとっては命取りでした。 *Kaigi o misugoshite shimatta no wa, shinnyū shain ni totte wa inochi tori deshita.*

kiss something goodbye — 別れを告げる — *wakare o tsugeru*

If you don't lock your car at night, you can kiss it goodbye. 車を夜ロックしないのは、それに別れを告げるようなものです。

Kuruma o yoru rokku shinai no wa, sore ni wakare o tsugeru yō na mono desu.

kite — 凧 — tako
Go fly a kite! — あっちへ行け！ — Atchi e ike!
He told the panhandler to go fly a kite.
彼はものもらいに、あっちへ行けと言いました。
Kare wa monomorai ni, atchi e ike to iimashita.

kitten — 子猫 — koneko
(as) weak as a kitten — 弱々しい — yowayowashii
A week of the flu left her as weak as a kitten.　彼女は、一週間流感に
かかって弱々しいです。Kanojo wa, isshūkan ryūkan ni kakatte
yowayowashii desu.

knee — 膝 — hiza
on bended knee — 平身低頭して — heishin teitō shite
He went to the conference on bended knee to ask for a compromise.　彼は
妥協を乞うため、平身低頭して会議に出ました。Kare wa dakyō o
kou tame, heishin teitō shite kaigi ni demashita.

knife — ナイフ — naifu
go under the knife — 手術を受ける — shujutsu o ukeru
He trusts his surgeon; otherwise, he'd never go under the knife.　彼は
担当の外科医を信頼しています。そうでなければ、手術は絶対に
受けないでしょう。Kare wa tantō no gekai o shinrai shite imasu. Sō
de nakereba, shujutsu wa zettai ni ukenai deshō.

knock — 打つ — utsu
knock it off — いい加減にする — ii kagen ni suru
Knock it off, Joe. A temper tantrum won't help the situation.　ジョー、
いい加減にしなさい。かんしゃくを起こしても、この場の
役に立ちませんよ。Jō, ii kagen ni shinasai. Kanshaku o okoshitemo,
kono ba no yaku ni tachimasen yo.

knock oneself out — 一生懸命にする — isshokemmei ni suru
She knocked herself out cooking for the holidays.　彼女は祝日のために、

一生懸命に料理しました。*Kanojo wa shukujitsu no tame ni, isshōkenmei ni ryōri shimashita.*

knock someone dead — 素晴らしさでびっくりさせる — *subarashisa de bikkuri saseru*

Your proposal is going to knock them dead at the meeting.　会議では、あなたの提案はその素晴らしさでみんなをびっくりさせるでしょう。*Kaigi dewa, anata no teian wa sono subarashisa de minna o bikkuri saseru deshō.*

---

knot — 結び目 — *musubime*

tie (up) in knots — 気を転倒させる — *ki o tentō saseru*

The thought of going to the dentist has him tied up in knots.　歯医者に行くことを思って、彼は気が転倒しています。*Ha isha ni iku koto o omotte, kare wa ki ga tentō shite imasu.*

tie the knot — 結婚する — *kekkon suru*

John and Marsha finally tied the knot last month.　ジョンとマーシャは、先月とうとう結婚しました。*Jon to Māsha wa, sengetsu tōtō kekkon shimashita.*

---

knuckle — 拳で打つ／拳 — *kobushi de utsu/kobushi*

knuckle down — 真剣に取りかかる — *shinken ni torikakaru*

If you want to complete the project, you'd better knuckle down to work. この企画を完成させたいなら、真剣に取りかかるべきです。

Kono kikaku o kansei sasetai nara, shinken ni torikakaru beki desu.

knuckle under — 服従する — *fukujū suru*

You can't intimidate John; he doesn't knuckle under to anyone.　ジョンは
誰にも服従しないから、脅しをかけてもむだです。*Jon wa
dare nimo fukujū shinai kara, odoshi o kaketemo muda desu.*

rap someone's knuckles — 叱られる — *shikarareru*

Don't try his patience, or you'll get your knuckles rapped.　彼をいらいら
させると叱られるから、しないように。*Kare o iraira saseru to
shikarareru kara, shinai yō ni.*

L

labor — 仕事 — *shigoto*

    labor of love — 愛がゆえの労作 — *ai ga yue no rōsaku*

    Making her friend's wedding dress was a labor of love.　彼女が友達の
ウェディングドレスを仕立てたのは、愛がゆえの労作でした。
*Kanojo ga tomodachi no wedingudoresu o shitateta no wa, ai ga yue no
rōsaku deshita.*

---

language — 言葉 — *kotoba*

    speak the same language — 話が合う — *hanashi ga au*

    When it comes to business, John and I speak the same language.　ビジネスに
関しては、ジョンと私は話が合います。*Bijinesu ni kanshite wa, Jon
to watakushi wa hanashi ga aimasu.*

---

lap — 膝／なめる — *hiza/nameru*

    in the lap of luxury — 贅沢三昧に — *zeitaku zanmai ni*

    Since they inherited a fortune, they've been living in the lap of luxury.
彼等は巨大な資産を相続して以来、贅沢三昧に暮らしています。
*Karera wa kyodai na shisan o sōzoku shite irai, zeitaku zanmai ni
kurashite imasu.*

    lap up — 鵜呑みにする — *unomi ni suru*

    He laps up everything she says.　彼は、彼女の言うことを全て

鵜呑みにします。*Kare wa, kanojo no iu koto o subete unomi ni shimasu.*

lark — 雲雀 — *hibari*
(as) happy as a lark — 幸せで朗らか — *shiawase de hogaraka*
She's as happy as a lark working in her garden. 彼女は庭仕事を
している時には、幸せで朗らかです。*Kanojo wa niwa shigoto o
shite iru toki ni wa, shiawase de hogaraka desu.*

laugh — 笑い — *warai*
get/have the last laugh — 最後に笑う — *saigo ni warau*
They laughed when she ran for mayor, but she had the last laugh when she
won. 彼女が市長選に出馬したとき、彼等は笑いました。けれども
選挙に勝って最後に笑ったのは彼女でした。*Kanojo ga shichō sen
ni shutsuba shita toki, karera wa waraimashita. Keredomo senkyo ni
katte saigo ni waratta no wa kanojo deshita.*

laurels — 月桂冠 — *gekkeikan*
rest on one's laurels — 成功に甘んじる — *seikō ni amanjiru*
He ought to write another book. He's rested on his laurels too long. 彼は
成功に甘んじている期間が長すぎるから、次の本を書くべきです。
*Kare wa seikō ni amanjite iru kikan ga nagasugiru kara, tsugi no hon o
kaku beki desu.*

law — 法律 — *hōritsu*
law unto oneself — 思うままに振る舞う — *omou mama ni furumau*
The senator is a law unto himself; he parks anywhere he likes. あの上院
議員は、思うままに振る舞っています。例えば、どこでも自分の
好きなところに駐車してしまうのです。*Ano jōin giin wa, omou
mama ni furumatte imasu. Tatoeba, doko demo jibun no suki na tokoro
ni chūsha shite shimau no desu.*

lay down the law — 厳しく戒める — *kibishiku imashimeru*
The students are late to every class; the professor should lay down the law.
学生たちはいつもクラスに遅れて来るので、教授は彼等を厳しく
戒めるべきです。*Gakuseitachi wa kurasu ni itsumo okurete kuru
node, kyōju wa karera o kibishiku imashimeru beki desu.*

take the law into one's own hands — 自らの手で裁きをつける —
mizukara no te de sabaki o tsukeru
After he was robbed, he decided to take the law into his own hands and buy
a gun. 彼は強盗にあった後、自らの手で裁きをつけること、
そしてそのためにピストルを買うことに決めました。*Kare wa
gōtō ni atta ato, mizukara no te de sabaki o tsukeru koto, soshite sono
tame ni pisutoru o kau koto ni kimemashita.*

leaf — 葉 — *ha*
　turn over a new leaf — 心を入れ替える — *kokoro o irekaeru*
　They're going to turn over a new leaf and accept foreign imports.
　彼等は心を入れ替えて、輸入品を受け入れることにします。
　Karera wa kokoro o irekaete, yu-nyū hin o ukeireru koto ni shimasu.

league — 連盟 — *renmei*
　not in the same league with someone or something — 格が違う —
　kaku ga chigau
　He's a good candidate, but he's not in the same league with the incumbent.
　彼はいい候補者ですが、現職者とは格が違います。
　*Kare wa ii kōhosha desu ga, genshoku sha to wa kaku ga
　chigaimasu.*

leap — 跳躍 — *chōyaku*
　by leaps and bounds — トントン拍子に — *tonton byōshi ni*
　Their profits are growing by leaps and bounds. 彼等の利益は、トントン
　拍子に増えています。*Karera no rieki wa, tonton byōshi ni fuete
　imasu.*

lease — 賃借り — *chingari*
　new lease on life — 寿命が延びる — *jumyō ga nobiru*
　His heart transplant gave him a new lease on life. 彼は心臓移植手術に
　よって、寿命が延びました。*Kare wa shinzō ishoku shujutsu ni yotte,
　jumyō ga nobimashita.*

leather — 皮 — *kawa*
　hell-bent for leather — 猛烈な勢いで — *mōretsu na ikioi de*
　She drove down the street hell-bent for leather. 彼女は町中を、猛烈な

勢いで運転しました。*Kanojo wa machinaka o, mōretsu na ikioi de unten shimashita.*

---

left — 左 — *hidari*

hang a left — 左に曲がる — *hidari ni magaru*

When you get to the stop sign, hang a left. 一時停止の標識に来たら、左に曲がりなさい。*Ichiji teishi no hyōshiki ni kitara, hidari ni magarinasai.*

---

leg — 足 — *ashi*

not have a leg to stand on — 論理の拠り所がない — *ronri no yoridokoro ga nai*

Don't try to make excuses; you don't have a leg to stand on. あなたには論理の拠り所がないから、言い訳はしないようにしなさい。*Anata ni wa ronri no yoridokoro ga nai kara, iiwake wa shinai yō ni shinasai.*

on someone's or something's last legs — 寿命間近 — *jumyō majika*

I need a new car; this one is on its last legs. この車は寿命間近で、新しいのが必要です。*Kono kuruma wa jumyō majika de, atarashii no ga hitsuyō desu.*

pull someone's leg — 担ぐ — *katsugu*

You can't play golf this Saturday? You must be pulling my leg. 土曜日にゴルフが出来ないんだって。僕を担いでいるんだろう。*Doyōbi ni gorufu ga dekinaindatte. Boku o katsuide irundarō.*

---

length — 長さ — *nagasa*

go to any length — ありとあらゆる手を尽くす — *ari to arayuru te o tsukusu*

We'll go to any length to resolve the trade issue. この貿易の懸案を解決するためには、ありとあらゆる手を尽くすつもりです。*Kono bōeki no ken-an o kaiketsu suru tame niwa, ari to arayuru te o tsukusu tsumori desu.*

---

lesson — 授業 — *jugyō*

teach someone a lesson — 戒める — *imashimeru*

I was bragging about my tennis, but he taught me a lesson by beating me.

私はテニスがうまいのを自慢していましたが、彼に負けていい
戒めになりました。*Watakushi wa tenisu ga umai no o jiman shite
imashita ga, kare ni makete ii imashime ni narimashita.*

---

let — させる — *saseru*

let someone down — 期待に背く — *kitai ni somuku*
I'm counting on your help; don't let me down.　あなたの助けを頼りに
しているんですから、私の期待に背かないで下さい。*Anata no
tasuke o tayori ni shite irundesu kara, watakushi no kitai ni somukanaide
kudasai.*

let someone have it — 厳しく叱りつける — *kibishiku shikaritsukeru*
When she showed up late, the boss let her have it.　彼女が遅れてきたので、
上司は彼女を厳しく叱りつけました。*Kanojo ga okurete kita node,
jōshi wa kanojo o kibishiku shikaritsukemashita.*

let someone in on something — 内緒のことを教える — *naisho no
koto o oshieru*
I'll let you in on a secret, but please don't tell anyone.　秘密を教えて
あげるけど、人には言わないで下さい。*Himitsu o oshiete ageru
kedo, hito ni wa iwanaide kudasai.*

let something ride — そのままで続行させる — *sono mama de zokkō
saseru*
Although the plan isn't perfect, we've decided to let it ride.　その計画は
完全ではありませんが、私達はそれをそのままで続行させることに
決めました。*Sono keikaku wa kanzen dewa arimasen ga,
watakushitachi wa sore o sonomama de zokkō saseru koto ni
kimemashita.*

let something slide — おろそかにする — *orosoka ni suru*
Jim got into trouble when he let his studies slide.　ジムは勉強を
おろそかにして、厄介なことになっています。*Jimu wa benkyō o
orosoka ni shite, yakkai na koto ni natte imasu.*

let something slip (out) — うっかり漏らす — *ukkari morasu*
Bob let it slip that he's quitting his job.　ボブは会社を辞めることを、
うっかり漏らしてしまいました。*Bobu wa kaisha o yameru koto o,
ukkari morashite shimaimashita.*

let up — 勢いを弱める — *ikioi o yowameru*

The rain hasn't let up for days.　雨はこの数日間、勢いを弱めていません。
Ame wa kono sūjitsu kan, ikioi o yowamete imasen.

letter — 手紙 — *tegami*
  bread-and-butter letter — 家庭でのもてなしへのお礼状 — *katei de
  no motenashi e no orei jō*
  After her weekend at the Smiths, Jane wrote them a bread-and-butter letter.
  ジェーンはスミス家で週末を過ごした後、家庭でのもてなしへの
  お礼状を書きました。*Jēn wa Sumisu ke de shūmatsu o sugoshita ato,
  katei de no motenashi e no orei jō o kakimashita.*

  to the letter — その通りに — *sono tōri ni*
  The chairman expects us to follow his instructions to the letter.　会長は、
  彼の指令に私達がその通りに従うことを期待しています。*Kaichō
  wa, kare no shirei ni watakushitachi ga sono tōri ni shitagau koto o kitai
  shite imasu.*

level — 水平 — *suihei*
  on the level — 正直に — *shōjiki ni*
  I don't know if I can trust John. Do you think he's on the level?
  私は、ジョンが信用出来るかどうか分かりません。
  あなたは、彼が正直だと思いますか。
  *Watakushi wa, Jon ga shin-yō dekiru ka dō ka wakarimasen. Anata wa,
  kare ga shōjiki da to omoimasu ka.*

liberty — 自由 — *jiyū*
  take liberties — 勝手気ままにする — *katte kimama ni suru*
  If he continues to take liberties with my car, I'm going to get angry.　彼が
  これ以上私の車を勝手気ままに使うなら、私の我慢にも限度が
  あります。*Kare ga kore ijō watakushi no kuruma o katte kimama ni
  tsukau nara, watakushi no gaman ni mo gendo ga arimasu.*

lid — 蓋 — *futa*
  flip one's lid — かっとなる — *katto naru*
  If the opposition party wins, he's going to flip his lid.　もし野党が勝てば、
  彼はかっとなるでしょう。*Moshi yatō ga kateba, kare wa katto naru
  deshō.*

keep a lid on something — 内密にしておく — *naimitsu ni shite oku*
I'll tell you who won, but please keep a lid on it for now. 誰が勝ったか
教えてあげるけれど、それは今のところ内密にしておいてください。
*Dare ga katta ka oshiete ageru keredo, sore wa ima no tokoro naimitsu
ni shite oite kudasai.*

life — 人生／生活 — *jinsei/seikatsu*

(as) big as life — 当の本人 — *tō no honnin*
We didn't expect him to show up, but there he was, as big as life. 私達は、
彼がやってくるとは思っていませんでした。けれども、当の本人が
そこに来ていたではありませんか。*Watakushitachi wa, kare ga
yatte kuru to wa omotte imasen deshita. Keredomo, tō no honnin ga soko
ni kite ita dewa arimasen ka.*

Get a life! — しっかりしろ！ — *Shikkari shiro!*
Why are you always hanging around doing nothing? Get a life!
なぜ、いつも何もしないでぶらぶらしているんだ。
しっかりしろ！*Naze, itsumo nanimo shinai de burabura shite irunda.
Shikkari shiro!*

life of the party — パーティーの花 — *pātī no hana*
Jane is always the life of the party. ジェーンは、いつもパーティーの
花です。*Jēn wa, itsumo pātī no hana desu.*

not on your life — 何が何でもだめ — *nani ga nan demo dame*
I won't give up—not on your life! 私は、絶対に諦めません。何が
何でもだめです。*Watakushi wa, zettai ni akiramemasen. Nani ga nan
demo dame desu.*

take one's life in one's hands — 自らの命を危険にさらす — *mizukara
no inochi o kiken ni sarasu*
If you let him drive, you're taking your life in your hands. もし彼に運転
させるなら、自らの命を危険にさらすことになりますよ。*Moshi
kare ni unten saseru nara, mizukara no inochi o kiken ni sarasu koto ni
narimasu yo.*

light — 明かり／光 — *akari/hikari*

get/give the green light 許可を得る／許可を与える *kyoka o
eru/kyoka o ataeru*
He got the green light to make some concessions. 彼は、いくらか譲歩

してもいいという許可を得ました。*Kare wa, ikuraka jōho shitemo ii to iu kyoka o emashita.*

see the light — やがて分かる — *yagate wakaru*
At first I didn't agree with them, but then I saw the light.　最初は彼等に賛成しませんでしたが、やがて彼等の言い分が分かりました。*Saisho wa karera ni sansei shimasen deshita ga, yagate karera no iibun ga wakarimashita.*

see the light at the end of the tunnel — 見通しがつく — *mitōshi ga tsuku*
This project seemed endless, but now I can see the light at the end of the tunnel.　この企画は果てしなく続くように思われましたが、今は見通しがつきました。*Kono kikaku wa hateshinaku tsuzuku yō ni omowaremashita ga, ima wa mitōshi ga tsukimashita.*

lightning — 稲妻 — *inazuma*
Lightning never strikes twice (in the same place). — 同じ不運がくり返されることはまれ。— *Onaji fuun ga kurikaesareru koto wa mare.*
Your car won't get stolen again; lightning never strikes twice.　あなたの車がまた盗まれることはないでしょう。同じ不運がくり返されることはまれです。*Anata no kuruma ga mata nusumareru koto wa nai deshō. Onaji fuun ga kurikaesareru koto wa mare desu.*

like greased lightning — 電光石火のごとく — *denkō sekka no gotoku*
That horse runs like greased lightning.　あの馬は、電光石火のごとく走ります。*Ano uma wa, denkō sekka no gotoku hashirimasu.*

lily — 百合の花 — *yuri no hana*
gild the lily — すでに完ぺきなものに余計な手を加える — *sude ni kanpeki na mono ni yokei na te o kuwaeru*
She doesn't need makeup; that would be gilding the lily.　彼女にお化粧はいりません。それは、すでに完ぺきなものに余計な手を加えるようなものです。*Kanojo ni okeshō wa irimasen. Sore wa, sude ni kanpeki na mono ni yokei na te o kuwaeru yō na mono desu.*

limb — 手足 — *teashi*
out on a limb — 自らを危険にさらして — *mizukara o kiken ni sarashite*

He went out on a limb and predicted a recession.　彼は自らを危険に
さらして、景気後退を予言しました。*Kare wa mizukara o kiken ni
sarashite, keiki kōtai o yogen shimashita.*

line — 線／行 — *sen/gyō*

draw a/the line — 一線を画する — *issen o kakusuru*

Don't lend them any more money. You have to draw the line somewhere.
彼等にこれ以上お金を貸さないように。あなたは、どこかで一線を
画さなければなりません。*Karera ni kore ijō okane o kasanai yō ni.
Anata wa, dokoka de issen o kakusanakereba narimasen.*

drop a line — 便りを書く — *tayori o kaku*

Don't forget to drop me a line while you're gone.　旅行中は、忘れずに
便りを下さい。*Ryokō chū wa, wasurezu ni tayori o kudasai.*

end of the line — お別れ／終わり — *owakare/owari*

It's been fun working together, but I guess this is the end of the line.
これまで楽しんで一緒に働いてきましたが、これでお別れだと
思います。*Kore made tanoshinde issho ni hataraite kimashita ga, kore
de owakare da to omoimasu.*

fall in(to) line — 一致団結する — *itchi danketsu suru*

For their party to stay in power, they'd better fall into line behind their
leader.　彼等の政党が権力の座を守るためには、指導者の下で
一致団結するべきです。*Karera no seitō ga kenryoku no za o mamoru
tame ni wa, shidōsha no moto de itchi danketsu suru beki desu.*

feed someone a line — 取り入ろうとしておべっかを使う — *toriirō to
shite obekka o tsukau*

What he said is nonsense; he's feeding you a line.　彼が言ったことは、
全くのたわごとです。彼はあなたに取り入ろうとして、おべっかを
使っているのです。*Kare ga itta koto wa, mattaku no tawagoto desu.
Kare wa anata ni toriirō to shite, obekka o tsukatte iru no desu.*

keep someone in line — コントロールする — *kontorōru suru*

If she can't keep her own kids in line, how can she teach kindergarten?
彼女が自分の子供をコントロール出来ないのに、どうして幼稚園で
教えることが出来るんでしょう。*Kanojo ga jibun no kodomo o
kontorōru o dekinai noni, dō shite yōchien de oshieru koto ga
dekirundeshō.*

lay something on the line — はっきり言う — *hakkiri iu*

The boss laid it on the line: shape up or hand in your resignation. 　上司は、はっきり言いました。 もっとしっかり仕事をするか、辞表を提出するか、そのどちらかだと。*Jōshi wa, hakkiri iimashita. Motto shikkari shigoto o suru ka, jihyō o teishutsu suru ka, sono dochiraka da to.*

out of line — 不適切 — *futekisetsu*

John's remarks were way out of line. 　ジョンの言葉は、全く不適切でした。*Jon no kotoba wa, mattaku futekisetsu deshita.*

read between the lines — 言外の意味を読み取る — *gengai no imi o yomitoru*

When you read between the lines, the prognosis for his recovery isn't good. 言外の意味を読み取ると、彼の回復に対する予後診断はよくありません。*Gengai no imi o yomitoru to, kare no kaifuku ni taisuru yogo shindan wa yoku arimasen.*

sign on the dotted line — 正式に署名する — *seishiki ni shomei suru*

He never signs on the dotted line without checking with his lawyer. 　彼は自分の弁護士と相談せずには、正式な署名は絶対にしません。*Kare wa jibun no bengoshi to sōdan sezu ni wa, seishiki na shomei wa zettai ni shimasen.*

the bottom line — 肝心かなめのところ — *kanjin kaname no tokoro*

We don't have much time; let's just get to the bottom line. 　時間があまりないから、肝心かなめのところに取りかかりましょう。*Jikan ga amari nai kara, kanjin kaname no tokoro ni torikakarimashō.*

---

linen — 敷布 — *shikifu*

  air/wash one's dirty linen in public — 内輪の恥をさらけ出す — *uchiwa no haji o sarakedasu*

  I hate hearing about his marital problems. He shouldn't air his dirty linen in public. 　私は、彼の結婚問題を聞くのが嫌です。彼は、内輪の恥をさらけ出すべきではありません。*Watakushi wa, kare no kekkon mondai o kiku no ga iya desu. Kare wa, uchiwa no haji o sarakedasu beki dewa arimasen.*

---

lion — ライオン — *raion*

  the lion's share — 一番大きな分け前 — *ichiban ōkina wakemae*

She inherited the lion's share of her mother's estate.　彼女は、お母さんの
遺産の一番大きな分け前を相続しました。*Kanojo wa, okāsan no
isan no ichiban ōkina wakemae o sōzoku shimashita.*

---

lip — 唇 — *kuchibiru*

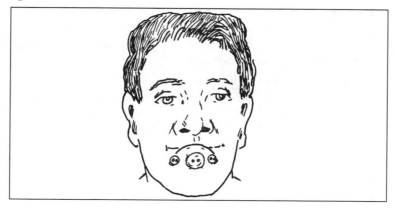

button one's lip — 口をつぐむ — *kuchi o tsugumu*
No more questions; just button your lip!　質問はこれで打ち切りだから、
口をつぐみなさい。*Shitsumon wa kore de uchikiri dakara, kuchi o
tsuguminasai.*

keep a stiff upper lip — 逆境にも毅然と対処する — *gyakkyō nimo
kizen to taisho suru*
Things are tough right now, but try to keep a stiff upper lip.　今は色々と
つらいかも知れませんが、逆境にも毅然と対処するようにしなさい。
*Ima wa iroiro to tsurai kamoshiremasen ga, gyakkyō ni mo kizen to
taisho suru yō ni shinasai.*

---

live — 生きる — *ikiru*
live and learn — また一つ勉強になった — *mata hitotsu benkyō ni natta*
They invested too heavily in one stock. Live and learn.　彼等の投資は、
一つの株に集中しすぎました。彼等にとっては、また一つ勉強に
なりました。*Karera no tōshi wa, hitotsu no kabu ni shūchū
shisugimashita. Karera ni totte wa, mata hitotsu benkyō ni narimashita.*

live and let live — 口出ししない — *kuchidashi shinai*

Their daughter never cleans her room; but they just live and let live.　彼等の娘は、自分の部屋を決して掃除しません。けれども、彼等は娘のことに口出ししないことにしています。*Karera no musume wa, jibun no heya o kesshite sōji shimasen. Keredomo, karera wa musume no koto ni kuchidashi shinai koto ni shite imasu.*

live it up — 愉快に過ごす — *yukai ni sugosu*
Jim works too hard; he should live it up a little.　ジムは働き過ぎなので、もうちょっと愉快に過ごすべきです。*Jimu wa hatarakisugi nanode, mō chotto yukai ni sugosu beki desu.*

live (something) down — 恥を克服する — *haji o kokufuku suru*
He'll never live down being late to his own wedding.　彼は、自分の結婚式に遅れた恥を決して克服することが出来ないでしょう。*Kare wa, jibun no kekkon shiki ni okureta haji o kesshite kokufuku suru koto ga dekinai deshō.*

load — 荷 — *ni*

get a load of someone or something — 見る — *miru*
Get a load of that driver! He's going much too fast.　あのドライバーを見てみなさい。運転速度が、あまりにも速すぎます。*Ano doraibā o mite minasai. Unten sokudo ga amari ni mo hayasugimasu.*

a load off one's mind — 心の重荷が下りる — *kokoro no omoni ga oriru*
I'm glad the job is done; that's a load off my mind.　その仕事が終わって、ほっとしています。これで、心の重荷が下りました。*Sono shigoto ga owatte, hotto shite imasu. Kore de, kokoro no omoni ga orimashita.*

take a load off one's feet — 楽にする — *raku ni suru*
You look tired; sit down and take a load off your feet.　疲れているみたいですねえ。座って、楽にして下さい。*Tsukarete iru mitai desu nē. Suwatte, raku ni shite kudasai.*

lock — 錠 — *jō*

lock, stock, and barrel — ありとあらゆる物 — *ari to arayuru mono*
The thieves cleaned us out—lock, stock, and barrel.　泥棒はありとあらゆる物を持っていき、わが家を一掃しました。*Dorobō wa ari to arayuru mono o motte iki, waga ya o issō shimashita.*

log — 丸太 — *maruta*

(as) easy as falling off a log — 簡単至極 — *kantan shigoku*

Barbara said that passing the bar exam was as easy as falling off a log. バーバラは、司法試験に合格するのは簡単至極だったと言いました。 *Bābara wa, shihō shiken ni gōkaku suru no wa kantan shigoku datta to iimashita.*

sleep like a log — ぐっすり眠る — *gussuri nemuru*

Despite the noise downstairs, I slept like a log last night. 階下の騒音にも かかわらず、昨日の晩はぐっすり眠りました。 *Kaika no sōon nimo kakawarazu, kinō no ban wa gussuri nemurimashita.*

loggerheads — 鉄球棒 — *tekkyū bō*

at loggerheads (with someone) — 対立して — *tairitsu shite*

The two countries are at loggerheads over trade issues again. その両国は、 貿易問題でまた対立しています。 *Sono ryōkoku wa, bōeki mondai de mata tairitsu shite imasu.*

long — 長い — *nagai*

long and (the) short of it — 言ってしまえば そういうこと — *itte shimaeba sō iu koto*

You can't have a new bike, and that's the long and the short of it. 新しい 自転車はだめ。言ってしまえば、そういうことだよ。 *Atarashii jitensha wa dame. Itte shimaeba, sō iu koto da yo.*

look — 目つき — *metsuki*

dirty look — 険しい表情 — *kewashii hyōjō*

When he cut in line ahead of her, she gave him a dirty look. 彼が彼女の 前に割り込んだので、彼女は険しい表情で彼を見ました。 *Kare ga kanojo no mae ni warikonda node, kanojo wa kewashii hyōjo de kare o mimashita.*

loon — アビ（鳥の名前） — *abi(tori no namae)*

(as) crazy as a loon — 頭が完全にいかれている — *atama ga kanzen ni ikarete iru*

Don't take anything he says seriously. He's as crazy as a loon. 彼は頭が 完全にいかれているから、彼の言うことを深刻に受け取らない

ように。 *Kare wa atama ga kanzen ni ikarete iru kara, kare no iu koto wa shinkoku ni uketoranai yō ni.*

---

loop — 輪 — *wa*

in the loop — 内輪に — *uchiwa ni*
Fred's opinions are valuable; let's keep him in the loop. フレッドの意見は価値があるから、彼を内輪に入れておきましょう。
Fureddo no iken wa kachi ga aru kara, kare o uchiwa ni irete okimashō.

out of the loop — 内輪漏れして — *uchiwa more shite*
No one listens to John anymore; he's out of the loop. ジョンが内輪漏れしてからは、もう誰も彼の言うことを聞きません。*Jon ga uchiwa more shite kara wa, mō daremo kare no iu koto o kikimasen.*

knock/throw someone for a loop — 愕然とさせる — *gakuzen to saseru*
The news of the layoffs threw him for a loop. 一時解雇のニュースは、彼を愕然とさせました。*Ichiji kaiko no nyūsu wa, kare o gakuzen to sasemashita.*

---

loss — 損失／喪失 — *sonshitsu/sōshitsu*

cut one's losses — 損失を食い止める — *sonshitsu o kuitomeru*
That car needs too many repairs. I'm going to sell it now and cut my losses. この車は、修理の必要があり過ぎます。それで今これを売って、将来の損失を食い止めるつもりです。*Kono kuruma wa, shūri no hitsuyō ga arisugimasu. Sorede ima kore o utte, shōrai no sonshitsu o kuitomeru tsumori desu.*

throw someone for a loss — 呆然とさせる — *bōzen to saseru*
The news that my son failed the exam threw me for a loss. 息子が試験に落ちたという知らせに、呆然としてしまいました。*Musuko ga shiken ni ochita to iu shirase ni, bōzen to shite shimaimashita.*

---

lost — 失った — *ushinatta*

lost on someone — 通じない — *tsūjinai*
The humor of the situation was lost on Susan; she didn't understand it. その場のユーモアは、スーザンには通じませんでした。彼女には、分からなかったのです。*Sono ba no yūmoa wa, Sūzan ni wa tsūjimasen deshita. Kanojo niwa, wakaranakatta no desu.*

lot — 運命 — *unmei*

cast/throw in one's lot with someone or something — 運命を共にする — *unmei o tomo ni suru*

He decided to cast in his lot with his brother's new business. 彼は、お兄さんの新しい事業と運命を共にすることにしました。*Kare wa, oniisan no atarashii jigyō to unmei o tomo ni suru koto ni shimashita.*

love — 愛 — *ai*

for love or money — 絶対に — *zettai ni*

I wouldn't deceive him for love or money. 彼を裏切るようなことは、絶対にしません。*Kare o uragiru yō na koto wa, zettai ni shimasen.*

no love lost — なんらの親愛の情もない — *nanra no shin-ai no jō mo nai*

There's no love lost between the two brothers. 二人の兄弟の間には、なんらの親愛の情もありません。*Futari no kyōdai no aida niwa, nanra no shin-ai no jō mo arimasen.*

luck — 幸運／幸運を得る — *kōun/kōun o eru*

down on one's luck — 運に見放されている — *un ni mihanasarete iru*

Jim just lost his job, and he's down on his luck. ジムは失業して、運に見放されています。*Jimu wa shitsugyō shite, un ni mihanasarete imasu.*

luck out — つきが回る — *tsuki ga mawaru*

Bob lucked out today: he won the jackpot. ボブは今日はつきが回って、宝くじで大当たりしました。*Bobu wa kyō wa tsuki ga mawatte, takarakuji de ōatari shimashita.*

press/push one's luck — いつまでもつきを期待する — *itsumademo tsuki o kitai suru*

Now that you're ahead, quit gambling; don't press your luck. 勝っているときに、賭けるのを止めなさい。いつまでもつきを期待せぬことです。*Katte iru toki ni, kakeru no o yamenasai. Itsumademo tsuki o kitai senu koto desu.*

lump — 塊 — *katamari*

get/have a lump in one's throat — 胸にあついものがこみ上げる — *mune ni atsui mono ga komiageru*

She had a lump in her throat at her son's graduation. 息子の卒業式で、
彼女の胸にあついものがこみ上げました。*Musuko no sotsugyō
shiki de, kanojo no mune ni atsui mono ga komiagemashita.*

---

lunch — 昼食 — *chūshoku*
out to lunch — ぼけっとしている — *boketto shite iru*
What's the matter with Bob? He seems out to lunch lately. ボブは、
どうかしたんですか。最近、ぼけっとしているみたいですけれど。
Bobu wa, dō ka shitandesu ka. Saikin, boketto shite iru mitai desu keredo.

---

lurch — 窮地 — *kyūchi*
leave someone in the lurch — すっぽかす — *suppokasu*
He promised me a ride, but he left me in the lurch. 彼は車に乗せてくれる
約束をしたのに、それをすっぽかしました。*Kare wa kuruma ni
nosete kureru yakusoku o shita noni, sore o suppokashimashita.*

---

make — 作る — *tsukuru*
make believe — 振りをする — *furi o suru*
I'm going to make believe I didn't hear you say that. あなたがそんな
ことを言ったのを、聞かなかった振りをしてあげます。*Anata ga
sonna koto o itta no o, kikanakatta furi o shite agemasu.*

make do — 間に合わせる — *maniawaseru*
We can't afford a new computer now; we'll have to make do with this one.
新しいコンピュータを買う余裕がないので、今ので間に合わせねば
なりません。*Atarashii konpyūta o kau yoyū ga nai node, ima no de
maniawaseneba narimasen.*

make good — 果たす — *hatasu*
Bill always makes good on his promises. ビルは、いつも約束を
果たします。*Biru wa, itsumo yakusoku o hatashimasu.*

make oneself scarce — こっそり立ち去る — *kossori tachisaru*
When the children began yelling, he made himself scarce. 子供たちが

わめき始めると、彼はこっそり立ち去りました。Kodomotachi ga wameki hajimeru to, kare wa kossori tachisarimashita.

make or break someone — 大成功させるか大失敗させるか二つに一つ — dai seikō saseru ka dai shippai saseru ka futatsu ni hitotsu

This new venture will make or break us. この新しい投機で、私達は大成功するか大失敗するか、二つに一つです。Kono atarashii tōki de, watakushitachi wa dai seikō suru ka dai shippai suru ka, futatsu ni hitotsu desu.

---

man — 人／男／男性 — hito/otoko/dansei

low man on the totem pole — 地位が最も低い人 — chii ga mottomo hikui hito

Bill has no say around here; he's low man on the totem pole. ビルには、発言権がありません。彼は、ここでは地位が最も低い人だからです。Biru ni wa, hatsugen ken ga arimasen. Kare wa, koko dewa chii ga mottomo hikui hito dakara desu.

man-about-town — 粋人 — suijin

Jim knows all the best nightspots here; he's a real man-about-town. ジムは本当の粋人で、この土地の最高級のナイトクラブはみんな知っています。Jimu wa hontō no suijin de, kono tochi no saikōkyū no naitokurabu wa minna shitte imasu.

man in the street — 一般の人 — ippan no hito

The mayor needs to know what the man in the street is thinking. 一般の人が何を考えているか、市長はそれを知る必要があります。Ippan no hito ga nani o kangaete iru ka, shichō wa sore o shiru hitsuyō ga arimasu.

man to man — 率直に — sotchoku ni

I need your honest opinion. Can we talk man to man? 私は、あなたの正直な意見が必要です。率直な話し合いが出来ますか。Watakushi wa, anata no shōjiki na iken ga hitsuyō desu. Sotchoku na hanashiai ga dekimasu ka.

new man — 生まれ変わった人 — umare kawatta hito

After his vacation, John felt like a new man. バカンスの後、ジョンは生まれ変わったように感じました。Bakansu no ato, Jon wa umare kawatta yō ni kanjimashita.

odd man out — 異分子 — *ibunshi*
If you don't follow football in this town, you're the odd man out.
この町に住みながらアメフトに興味がないなら、異分子です。
Kono machi ni suminagara Amefuto ni kyōmi ga nai nara, ibunshi desu.

One man's meat is another man's poison. — たで食う虫も好き好き
— *tade kuu mushi mo sukizuki*
He loves boxing, and I hate it. One man's meat is another man's poison.
彼はボクシングが大好きですが、私は大嫌い。たで食う虫も好き
好きです。*Kare wa bokushingu ga daisuki desu ga, watakushi wa
daikirai. Tade kuu mushi mo sukizuki desu.*

separate the men from the boys — 能力の違いがものをいう —
nōryoku no chigai ga mono o iu
We need your best negotiating skills now; this will separate the men from
the boys. あなたのあらん限りの交渉の巧みさを必要としています。
今こそ、能力の違いがものをいうときだからです。*Anata no aran
kagiri no kōshō no takumisa o hitsuyō to shite imasu. Ima koso, nōryoku
no chigai ga mono o iu toki dakara desu.*

the man — お偉方 — *oeragata*
Don't get in trouble, or you'll have to deal with the man. お偉方と対処
することにならないように、面倒は引き起こさないこと。*Oeragata
to taisho suru koto ni naranai yō ni, mendō wa hikiokosanai koto.*

marbles — おはじき — *ohajiki*
lose one's marbles — 気がふれる — *ki ga fureru*
I must have lost my marbles—driving the wrong way down a one-way
street! 一方通行の道を逆に運転するなんて、私は気がふれたに
違いありません。*Ippō tsūkō no michi o gyaku ni unten suru nante,
watakushi wa ki ga fureta ni chigai arimasen.*

not have all one's marbles — まともではない — *matomo dewa nai*
Mary's been acting strange lately, as if she doesn't have all her marbles.
メリーの最近の振る舞いは奇妙で、ちょっとまともではない
みたいです。*Merī no saikin no furumai wa kimyō de, chotto matomo
dewa nai mitai desu.*

marines — 海兵隊 — *kaiheitai*
tell it to the marines — 嘘つけ — *uso tsuke*

You'll arrive on time? Tell it to the marines.　時間通りに着くって。
嘘つけ。*Jikan dōri ni tsukutte. Uso tsuke.*

---

mark — 出発点／的 — *shuppatsu ten/mato*
　toe the mark — 規則を守る — *kisoku o mamoru*
　If you toe the mark, you'll do well in this company.　規則を守りさえ
　すれば、この会社でうまくやれるでしょう。Kisoku o mamorisae
　sureba, kono kaisha de umaku yarcru dcshō.

　wide of the mark — 的外れ — *mato hazure*
　They tried to negotiate, but their best efforts were wide of the mark.　彼等は
　交渉しようとしましたが、最善の努力も的外れでした。*Karera wa*
　kōshō shiyō to shimashita ga, saizen no doryoku mo mato hazure deshita.

---

master — 主君 — *shukun*
　be a past master at something — その道の大家 — *sono michi no taika*
　That author is a past master at producing best sellers.　あの著者は、
　ベストセラ－を生み出すことにかけてはその道の大家です。*Ano*
　chosha wa, besutoserā o umidasu koto ni kakete wa sono michi no taika
　desu.

---

match — 競争相手 — *kyōsō aite*
　meet one's match — 好敵手に出くわす — *kōtekishu ni dekuwasu*
　John is a fine defense lawyer, but he's met his match in this prosecutor.
　ジョンは優秀な被告側の弁護士ですが、この検察官は彼が
　出くわした好敵手です。*Jon wa yūshū na bengoshi desu ga, kono*
　kensatsukan wa kare ga dekuwashita kōtekishu desu.

---

meal — 食事 — *shokuji*
　square meal — まともな食事 — *matomo na shokuji*
　Let's go to a restaurant. I haven't had a square meal in days.　レストランへ
　行きましょう。私はこの数日、まともな食事をしていないんですよ。
　Resutoran e ikimashō. Watakushi wa, kono sūjitsu matomo na shokuji o
　shite inaindesu yo.

---

measure 分量 *bunryō*
　for good measure — おまけに — *omake ni*

When I bought a car, the dealer threw in the floor mats for good measure.
車を買つたとき、ディ－ラ－はおまけに床マットをくれました。
Kuruma o katta toki, dīrā wa omake ni yuka matto o kuremashita.

meat — 肉 — *niku*
meat-and-potatoes — 単純な舌の — *tanjun na shita no*
Don't give him any fancy food; he's a meat-and-potatoes guy.
彼は単純な舌の人だから、凝つた料理を出す必要はありません。
Kare wa tanjun na shita no hito dakara, kotta ryōri o dasu hitsuyō wa arimasen.

medicine — 薬 — *kusuri*
take one's medicine — 罰を受け入れる — *batsu o ukeireru*
He misbehaved, and he has to take his medicine: no TV for a week. 彼は
よくない振る舞いをしたため、一週間テレビ禁止という罰を受け
入れなければなりません。*Kare wa yoku nai furumai o shita tame,
isshūkan terebi kinshi to iu batsu o ukeirenakereba narimasen.*

medium — 中間 — *chūkan*
strike a happy medium — 間を取る — *aida o toru*
I want Chinese food, you want Indian. Let's strike a happy medium and get
Thai. 私は中華料理が食べたいけれど、あなたはインド料理が
食べたい。それで間を取つて、タイ料理にしましょう。*Watakushi
wa chūka ryōri ga tabetai keredo, anata wa Indo ryōri ga tabetai.
Sorede aida o totte, Tai ryōri ni shimashō.*

meet — 会う — *au*
meet halfway — 歩み寄る — *ayumiyoru*
I know we disagree on this issue, but couldn't we meet halfway?
この問題について私達が賛成できないのは分かつていますが、
歩み寄ることは出来ませんか。*Kono mondai ni tsuite
watakushitachi ga sansei dekinai no wa wakatte imasu ga, ayumiyoru
koto wa dekimasen ka.*

mend — 改良 — *kairyō*
on the mend — 快方に向かつている — *kaihō ni mukatte iru*
He was sick all last week, but he's on the mend now. 彼は先週はずつと

病気でしたが、今は快方に向かっています。*Kare wa senshū wa
zutto byōki deshita ga, ima wa kaihō ni mukatte imasu.*

---

method — 方法 — *hōhō*

method in/to one's madness — 一見おかしな考えも筋道が立っている
— *ikken okashina kangae mo sujimichi ga tatte iru*
I thought he was making a mistake, but now I see there's method
in his madness. 初めは彼が間違っていると思いましたが、
今は一見おかしな考えも筋道が立っているのが分かりました。
*Hajime wa kare ga machigatte iru to omoimashita ga,
ima wa ikken okashina kangae mo sujimichi ga tatte iru no ga
wakarimashita.*

---

midair — 中空 — *chūkū*

leave someone hanging in midair — 満たされない気持ちを募らせる
— *mitasarenai kimochi o tsunoraseru*
When the battery went dead during the game, we were left hanging in
midair. ゲームの途中でラジオの電池が切れてしまい、私達は
満たされない気持ちを募らせました。*Gēmu no tochū de rajio no
denchi ga kirete shimai, watakushitachi wa mitasarenai kimochi o
tsunorasemashita.*

leave something hanging in midair — 宙に浮いたままにする — *chū
ni uita mama ni suru*
Let's not leave the decision hanging in midair. 決定は、宙に浮いた
ままにしないようにしましょう。*Kettei wa, chū ni uita mama ni
shinai yō ni shimashō.*

---

middle — 中央 — *chūō*

middle-of-the-road — 中道派の — *chūdō ha no*
He usually votes for the middle-of-the-road candidate. 彼は普通は、
中道派の候補者に投票します。*Kare wa futsū wa, chūdō ha no
kōhosha ni tōhyō shimasu.*

---

might — 力 — *chikara*

(with) might and main — 全力をあげて — *zenryoku o agete*
With all their might and main, the defense prevented a touchdown.

防御側のチ−ムは、全力をあげてタッチダウンを妨げました。

Bōgyogawa no chīmu wa, zenryoku o agete tatchidaun o samatagemashita.

mile — マイル — *mairu*

  miss by a mile — 的外れもいいところ — *mato hazure mo ii tokoro*

  I thought I could guess the winner, but I missed by a mile.   私は勝者を
当てられると思いましたが、的外れもいいところでした。

  *Watakushi wa shōsha o aterareru to omoimashita ga, mato hazure mo ii
tokoro deshita.*

milk — 牛乳 — *gyūnyū*

  cry over spilled milk — やり直しのきかないことを悔やむ —

  yarinaoshi no kikanai koto o kuyamu

  So you forgot the appointment. Don't cry over spilled milk.   あなたは
面会の約束を忘れてしまった。それはそうとして、やり直しの
きかないことを悔やんでもしょうがありませんよ。*Anata wa
menkai no yakusoku o wasurete shimatta. Sore wa sō to shite, yarinaoshi
no kikanai koto o kuyandemo shō ga arimasen yo.*

mill — 製粉機 — *seifunki*

  through the mill — くたくたになって／ひどい経験をして —

  kutakuta ni natte/hidoi keiken o shite

  John had his taxes audited today; he's really been through the mill.
今日ジョンは税金を調べられて、本当にくたくたになって
しまいました。*Kyō Jon wa zeikin o shiraberarete, hontō ni kutakuta ni
natte shimaimashita.*

mincemeat — 小間切れの肉 — *komagire no niku*

  make mincemeat out of someone or something — 痛い目にあわせる

  — *itai me ni awaseru*

  He's going to make mincemeat out of his opponent in the debate.   彼は
討論で、相手を痛い目にあわせるつもりです。*Kare wa tōron de,
aite o itai me ni awaseru tsumori desu.*

mind — 心 — *kokoro*

  blow one's mind — 腰を抜かす — *koshi o nukasu*

  When she saw the new shopping mall, it blew her mind.   彼女は新しい

ショッピングモールを見て、腰を抜かしました。*Kanojo wa atarashii shoppingu mōru o mite, koshi o nukashimashita.*

boggle one's/the mind — びっくりせざるをえない — *bikkuri sezaru o enai*

The field of genetic engineering boggles the mind.　遺伝子工学の分野には、びっくりせざるをえません。*Idenshi kōgaku no bun-ya ni wa, bikkuri sezaru o emasen.*

have a good mind to do something — 心積もりがある — *kokoro zumori ga aru*

The newpaper is late again. I have a good mind to cancel my subscription. 新聞の配達が、また遅れました。それで、定期購読を止める心積もりがあります。*Shinbun no haitatsu ga, mata okuremashita. Sorede, teiki kōdoku o yameru kokoro zumori ga arimasu.*

have a mind like a steel trap — 頭が切れる — *atama ga kireru*

He's a formidable negotiator; he has a mind like a steel trap.　彼は頭が切れるので、手ごわい交渉担当者です。*Kare wa atama ga kireru node, tegowai kōshō tantōsha desu.*

have half a mind to do something — 殆どその気になる — *hotondo sono ki ni naru*

This meeting is so boring. I have half a mind to leave.　この会議はあまりにも退屈なので、殆ど席を立つ気になっています。*Kono kaigi wa amarinimo taikutsu nanode, hotondo seki o tatsu ki ni natte imasu.*

in one's mind's eye — 心の中で — *kokoro no naka de*

In my mind's eye I can see her in her garden.　心の中で、私は庭にいる彼女の姿を思い浮かべることが出来ます。*Kokoro no naka de, watakushi wa niwa ni iru kanojo no sugata o omoiukaberu koto ga dekimasu.*

in one's right mind — まともで — *matomo de*

Jim isn't in his right mind today; that was a bad decision.　誤つた判断を下したことから分かるように、ジムは今日はまともではありません。*Ayamatta handan o kudashita koto kara wakaru yō ni, Jimu wa kyō wa matomo dewa arimasen.*

lose one's mind — 気が狂う — *ki ga kuruu*

What a stupid thing to do! Has he lost his mind?　なんて馬鹿なことを

したんでしょう。彼は気でも狂ったんですか。*Nante baka na koto*
o shitandeshō. Kare wa ki demo kuruttandesu ka.

one-track mind — 一つのことしか頭にない — *hitotsu no koto shika*
atama ni nai
He has a one-track mind: all he thinks of is food.　彼は、一つのこと
しか頭にありません。彼が考えることといえば、それは食べ物の
ことだけです。*Kare wa, hitotsu no koto shika atama ni arimasen.*
Kare ga kangaeru koto to ieba, sore wa tabemono no koto dake desu.

read someone's mind — 心を察する — *kokoro o sassuru*
I know he'd like to go home now; I can read his mind.　私は彼の心が
察せるので、彼が今うちに帰りたがっているのが分かります。
Watakushi wa kare no kokoro ga sasseru node, kare ga ima uchi ni
kaeritagatte iru no ga wakarimasu.

slip one's mind — うっかり忘れる — *ukkari wasureru*
I was supposed to call him today, but it slipped my mind.　私は今日彼に
電話することになっていたのですが、うっかり忘れてしまいました。
Watakushi wa kyō kare ni denwa suru koto ni natte ita no desu ga,
ukkari wasurete shimaimashita.

speak one's mind — 思っていることを率直に話す — *omotte iru koto*
o sotchoku ni hanasu
Please feel free to speak your mind on this issue.　この件については、
遠慮無く思っていることを率直に話して下さい。*Kono ken ni*
tsuite wa, enryo naku omotte iru koto o sotchoku ni hanashite kudasai.

weigh on one's mind — 心にひっかかる — *kokoro ni hikkakaru*
He can't relax with the deadline weighing on his mind.　彼は締め切りが
心にひっかかって、くつろぐことが出来ません。*Kare wa*
shimekiri ga kokoro ni hikkakatte, kutsurogu koto ga dekimasen.

---

mine — 鉱山 — *kōzan*
　back to the salt mines — 仕事に戻る時間 — *shigoto ni modoru jikan*
　Our break is over. Back to the salt mines!　休憩時間は終わり。さあ、
　仕事に戻る時間です。*Kyūkei jikan wa owari. Sā, shigoto ni modoru*
　jikan desu.

　gold mine of information — 又とない情報源 — *mata to nai jōhō gen*
　The foreign minister is a gold mine of information on trade issues.　外務

大臣は、貿易問題に関しては又とない情報源です。*Gaimu daijin wa, bōeki mondai ni kanshite wa mata to nai jōhō gen desu.*

---

miss — やりそこない — *yarisokonai*
A miss is as good as a mile. — だめだったことには違いない — *dame datta koto ni wa chigai nai*
I know the score was close, but a miss is as good as a mile. 得点が近かったのは分かっていますが、だめだったことには違いありません。*Tokuten ga chikakatta no wa wakatte imasu ga, dame datta koto ni wa chigai arimasen.*

near miss — 間一髪で免れる — *kan ippatsu de manugareru*
That was a near miss—he almost hit us! 彼は私達の車に衝突しそうになりましたが、間一髪で免れました。*Kare wa watakushitachi no kuruma ni shōtotsu shisō ni narimashita ga, kan ippatsu de manugaremashita.*

Missouri — ミズーリ — *Mizūri*
be from Missouri — 証拠を見るまで信じない — *shōko o miru made shinjinai*
I suspect his motives; I'm from Missouri. 私は彼の動機に疑いがあるので、証拠を見るまで信じません。*Watakushi wa kare no dōki ni utagai ga aru node, shōko o miru made shinjimasen.*

---

mold — 鋳型 — *igata*
cast in the same mold — まるで同じ — *marude onaji*
The brothers are cast in the same mold: they're both poets. あの兄弟はまるで同じで、二人とも詩人です。*Ano kyōdai wa marude onaji de, futari tomo shijin desu.*

---

moment — 瞬間 — *shunkan*
live for the moment — その場限りの生き方をする — *sono ba kagiri no ikikata o suru*
She lives for the moment and never plans for her future. 彼女はその場限りの生き方をしていて、将来の計画など決して立てません。*Kanojo wa sono ba kagiri no ikikata o shite ite, shōrai no keikaku nado kesshite tatemasen.*

moment of truth — 現実に直面するとき — *genjitsu ni chokumen suru toki*

Now for the moment of truth: the exam results.　現実に直面するときが来ました。試験の結果の発表です。*Genjitsu ni chokumen suru toki ga kimashita. Shiken no kekka no happyō desu.*

money — お金 — *okane*

easy money — 楽に稼げるお金 — *raku ni kasegeru okane*

Take the job. It's easy money.　その仕事をやりなさい。そうすれば、楽にお金が稼げますよ。*Sono shigoto o yarinasai. Sō sureba, raku ni okane ga kasegemasu yo.*

have money to burn — お金が有り余るほどある — *okane ga ariamaru hodo aru*

Look at her spend! She acts as if she has money to burn.　彼女のお金の使い方を見てご覧なさい。彼女は、お金が有り余るほどあるかのように振る舞っています。*Kanojo no okane no tsukaikata o mite goran nasai. Kanojo wa, okane ga ariamaru hodo aru ka no yō ni furumatte imasu.*

hush money — 口止め料 — *kuchidome ryō*

They got caught trying to pay hush money to a witness.　彼等は、目撃者に口止め料を払おうとして捕まりました。*Karera wa, mokugekisha ni kuchidome ryō o haraō to shite tsukamarimashita.*

in the money — 金持ち — *kanemochi*

His horse just came in first. He's in the money now.　彼の馬が一等になって、彼は今や金持ちです。*Kare no uma ga ittō ni natte, kare wa ima ya kanemochi desu.*

made of money — 金のなる木 — *kane no naru ki*

She thinks her mother is made of money.　彼女は、お母さんが金のなる木だと思っています。*Kanojo wa, okāsan ga kane no naru ki da to omotte imasu.*

make good money — いいお金を稼ぐ — *ii okane o kasegu*

Although he makes good money, he can't afford a new house.　彼はいいお金を稼いでいますが、新しい家は買えません。*Kare wa ii okane o kaseide imasu ga, atarashii ie wa kaemasen.*

marry money — 金持ちと結婚する — *kanemochi to kekkon suru*
She plans to marry money so she won't have to work.　彼女は将来
働かなくてもいいように、金持ちと結婚する計画を立てています。
*Kanojo wa shōrai hatarakanakutemo ii yō ni, kanemochi to kekkon suru
keikaku o tatete imasu.*

Money burns a hole in one's pocket. — 金遣いが激しい — *kane zukai
ga hageshii*
Money burns a hole in his pocket—he spends it all.　彼は金遣いが
激しくて、入ったお金は全て使ってしまいます。*Kare wa kane
zukai ga hageshikute, haitta okane wa subete tsukatte shimaimasu.*

money is no object — 値段はどうでもいい — *nedan wa dō demo ii*
She ordered new furniture as if money were no object.　彼女は値段は
どうでもいいかのごとく、新しい家具を注文しました。*Kanojo
wa nedan wa dō demo ii ka no gotoku, atarashii kagu o chūmon
shimashita.*

Money is the root of all evil. — お金は諸悪の根元 — *okane wa shoaku
no kongen*
As they fought over the inheritance, they realized that money is the root of
all evil.　彼等は遺産相続で争っているときに、お金は諸悪の
根元であることに気付きました。*Karera wa isan sōzoku de
arasotte iru toki ni, okane wa shoaku no kongen de aru koto ni
kizukimashita.*

money talks — お金がものを言う — okane ga mono o iu
He can get anything he wants. Money talks. 彼は、欲しい物は何でも
手に入れることが出来ます。お金がものを言うからです。Kare
wa, hoshii mono wa nandemo te ni ireru koto ga dekimasu. Okane ga
mono o iu kara desu.

on the money — ぴったり — pittari
His estimate of our taxes was right on the money. 私達の税金についての
彼の見積りは、正にぴったりでした。Watakushitachi no zeikin ni
tsuite no kare no mitsumori wa, masa ni pittari deshita.

pour money down the drain — 無駄遣いする — mudazukai suru
Instead of pouring more money down the drain, let's get a new car.
無駄遣いを続ける代わりに、新車を買いましょう。Mudazukai o
tsuzukeru kawari ni, shinsha o kaimashō.

Put your money where your mouth is. — 現金を賭ける — genkin o
kakeru
If you think you can beat me at tennis, put your money where your mouth
is. テニスで私を負かすことが出来ると思うなら、現金を賭けて
やってみましょう。Tenisu de watakushi o makasu koto ga dekiru to
omou nara, genkin o kakete yatte mimashō.

throw good money after bad — 無駄金をつぎ込む — mudagane o
tsugikomu
Instead of throwing good money after bad, let's buy a new TV. 無駄金を
つぎ込むより、新しいテレビを買いましょう。Mudagane o
tsugikomu yori, atarashii terebi o kaimashō.

---

monkey — 猿 — saru
make a monkey (out) of someone — 笑いものにする — waraimono ni
suru
He just made a monkey out of himself by getting drunk at the party. 彼は
パーティーで酔っ払って、自らを笑いものにしてしまいました。
Kare wa pātī de yopparatte, mizukara o waraimono ni shite
shimaimashita.

monkey around — いじくりまわす — ijikurimawasu
I wish he'd stop monkeying around with the VCR. 彼が録画装置を
いじくりまわすのを、止めてもらいたいです。Kare ga rokuga

sōchi o ijikurimawasu no o yamete moraitai desu.

month — 月 — *tsuki*
for/in a month of Sundays — 長い間 — *nagai aida*
He hasn't had a drink in a month of Sundays.　彼は、長い間お酒を
飲んでいません。*Kare wa, nagai aida osake o nonde imasen.*

moon — 月 — *tsuki*
ask for the moon — 法外な要求をする — *hōgai na yōkyū o suru*
He's not asking for the moon, just a little of your time.　彼は法外な
要求をしているのではなく、単にあなたの時間を多少さいて
もらいたいと願っているだけです。*Kare wa hōgai na yōkyū o shite
iru no dewa naku, tan ni anata no jikan o tashō saite moraitai to negatte
iru dake desu.*

once in a blue moon — まれに — *mare ni*
They splurge on an expensive dinner once in a blue moon.　彼等はまれに
ぜいたくなディナーを楽しみます。*Karera wa mare ni zeitaku na
dinā o tanoshimimasu.*

promise the moon — 途方もない約束をする — *tohō mo nai yakusoku
o suru*
He promised her the moon, but it was all lies.　彼は彼女に途方もない
約束をしましたが、それは全て嘘でした。*Kare wa kanojo ni tohō
mo nai yakusoku o shimashita ga, sore wa subete uso deshita.*

more — もっと — *motto*
more than someone bargained for — 思ったよりも大変 — *omotta
yori mo taihen*
She offered to help, but the work was more than she bargained for.
彼女はその仕事を手伝うことを申し出ましたが、それは
思ったよりも大変でした。*Kanojo wa sono shigoto o
tetsudau koto o mōshidemashita ga, sore wa omotta yori mo taihen
deshita.*

the more the merrier — 人数は多ければ多いほど楽しい — *ninzū wa
ōkereba ōi hodo tanoshii*
Your friends are welcome at our party—the more the merrier.　あなたの
友達も、パーティーに来れば歓迎します。人数は、多ければ多い

ほど楽しいですから。*Anata no tomodachi mo, pātī ni kureba kangei shimasu. Ninzū wa, ōkereba ōi hodo tanoshii desu kara.*

---

morning — 朝 — *asa*
  morning after — 二日酔い — *futsuka yoi*
  The party was fun, but the morning after isn't. パーティーは楽しかった けれど、二日酔いは別の話です。*Pātī wa tanoshikatta keredo, futsuka yoi wa betsu no hanashi desu.*

---

most — 最高 — *saikō*
  make the most of something — 最大限に活用する — *saidaigen ni katsuyō suru*
  Let's make the most of this good weather. この素晴らしい天気を、 最大限に活用しましょう。*Kono subarashii tenki o, saidaigen ni katsuyō shimashō.*

---

mothballs — 防虫剤 — *bōchūzai*
  put something in mothballs — しまい込む — *shimaikomu*
  We put our old TV in mothballs until we can give it away. 古いテレビは、 誰かにあげるまでしまい込んでおきましょう。*Furui terebi wa, dareka ni ageru made shimaikonde okimashō.*

---

mother — 母親 — *hahaoya*

  tied to one's mother's apron strings — 母親べったり — *hahaoya bettari*

He's a grown man, and he's still tied to his mother's apron strings.　彼は
大人なのに、未だに母親べったりです。*Kare wa otona nanoni,*
imada ni hahaoya bettari desu.

---

motion — 動作 — *dōsa*
　go through the motions — している振りをする — *shite iru furi o suru*
　He doesn't want to work today; he's just going through the motions.　彼は
　今日は仕事をしたくないので、単にしている振りをしています。
　Kare wa kyō wa shigoto o shitakunai node, tan ni shite iru furi o shite
　imasu.

---

mountain — 山 — *yama*
　make a mountain out of a molehill — 大げさに言う — *ōgesa ni iu*
　This isn't a big deal; you're making a mountain out of a molehill.　あなたは
　大げさに言っているけれど、それは大したことではありません。
　Anata wa ōgesa ni itte iru keredo, sore wa taishita koto dewa arimasen.

---

mouse — ねずみ — *nezumi*
　(as) poor as a church mouse — とても貧乏 — *totemo binbō*
　His sister is as poor as a church mouse.　彼の妹は、とても貧乏です。
　Kare no imōto wa, totemo binbō desu.

　(as) quiet as a mouse — とても静か — *totemo shizuka*
　If you let me attend the meeting, I'll be quiet as a mouse.　もし私を会議に
　出席させてくれるなら、とても静かにしています。*Moshi*
　watakushi o kaigi ni shusseki sasete kureru nara, totemo shizuka ni shite
　imasu.

---

mouth — 口 — *kuchi*
　bad-mouth someone or something — 悪口を言う — *warukuchi o iu*
　She's bad-mouthing her colleague behind his back.　彼女は同僚について、
　彼の陰で悪口を言っています。*Kanojo wa dōryō ni tsuite, kare no*
　kage de warukuchi o itte imasu.

　down in the mouth — しょげている — *shogete iru*
　He looks down in the mouth over the economic situation.　彼は景気に
　ついてしょげている様子です。*Kare wa keiki ni tsuite shogete iru*
　yōsu desu.

foam at the mouth — 口から泡を吹くほど — *kuchi kara awa o fuku hodo*
He was so angry he was foaming at the mouth.　彼は、口から泡を吹く
ほど怒っていました。*Kare wa, kuchi kara awa o fuku hodo okotte
imashita.*

have a big mouth — おしゃべり — *oshaberi*
Don't trust her to be discreet; she has a big mouth.　彼女はおしゃべり
だから、口を控えると思わないこと。*Kanojo wa oshaberi dakara,
kuchi o hikaeru to omowanai koto.*

make someone's mouth water — 食欲を誘う — *shokuyoku o sasou*
The aroma of bread baking makes my mouth water.　パンを焼く
おいしそうな匂いが食欲を誘います。*Pan o yaku oishisō na nioi ga
shokuyoku o sasoimasu.*

run off at the mouth — 長々と喋りまくる — *naganaga to
shaberimakuru*
John is quite opinionated; he's running off at the mouth again.　ジョンは
頑固に自分の意見を主張するたちで、また長々と喋りまくって
います。*Jon wa ganko ni jibun no iken o shuchō suru tachi de, mata
naganaga to shaberimakutte imasu.*

say a mouthful — 正に核心を突く — *masa ni kakushin o tsuku*
You said a mouthful when you predicted the mayor would be a disaster.
あなたがこの市長は災いの元だと予言したとき、正に核心を
突いていたのです。*Anata ga kono shichō wa wazawai no moto da to
yogen shita toki, masa ni kakushin o tsuite ita no desu.*

shoot one's mouth off — ぺらぺら喋りまくる — *perapera
shaberimakuru*
He's no expert, but he's always shooting his mouth off about investments.
彼は大した知識もないのに、投資についていつもぺらぺら
喋りまくっています。*Kare wa taishita chishiki mo nai noni, tōshi ni
tsuite itsumo perapera shaberimakutte imasu.*

---

move — 動き — *ugoki*

get a move on — 急ぐ — *isogu*
Let's get a move on; we're late for the party.　急ぎましょう。さもないと、
パーティーに遅れてしまいます。*Isogimashō. Samonaito, pātī ni
okurete shimaimasu.*

---

make moves on someone — 手を出す — *te o dasu*
He tries to make moves on every woman he meets.　彼は会った女性には
全て、手を出そうとします。*Kare wa atta josei ni wa subete, te o
dasō to shimasu.*

mover — 引っ越し屋 — *hikkoshi ya*
movers and shakers — 実力者 — *jitsuryokusha*
Bill is one of the movers and shakers of the industry.　ビルはその産業の
実力者の一人です。*Biru wa sono sangyō no jitsuryokusha no hitori
desu.*

prime mover — 原動力 — *gendōryoku*
She was a prime mover in the renovation project.　彼女は、その改築
計画の原動力の役目を果たしました。*Kanojo wa, sono kaichiku
keikaku no gendōryoku no yakume o hatashimashita.*

much — たくさん — *takusan*
so much for someone or something — これでおしまい — *kore de
oshimai*
He broke all his promises to me—so much for trust!　彼は私にした約束を
全部破ったので、彼に対する信用もこれでおしまいです。*Kare
wa watakushi ni shita yakusoku o zenbu yabutta node, kare ni taisuru
shin-yō mo kore de oshimai desu.*

mud — 泥 — *doro*
(as) clear as mud — 意味がさっぱり分からない — *imi ga sappari
wakaranai*
These instructions are as clear as mud.　これらの指図は、意味が
さっぱり分かりません。*Korera no sashizu wa, imi ga sappari
wakarimasen.*

mule — 騾馬 — *raba*
(as) stubborn as a mule — 頑固一徹 — *ganko ittetsu*
He won't follow his doctor's advice; he's stubborn as a mule.　彼は頑固
一徹で、医者の助言に全く従いません。*Kare wa ganko ittetsu de,
isha no jogen ni mattaku shitagaimasen.*

mum — 無言の — *mugon no*

mum's the word — 誰にも漏らさない — *darenimo morasanai*
Mum's the word about our plans to restructure. 我々の再構築計画に
ついては、誰にも漏らさないで下さい。*Wareware no sai kōchiku
keikaku ni tsuite wa, darenimo morasanai de kudasai.*

murder — 殺人 — *satsujin*

cry/scream bloody murder — 怒りの叫びをあげる — *ikari no sakebi o
ageru*
They screamed bloody murder when their taxes were raised. 増税が
あったとき、彼等は怒りの叫びをあげました。*Zōzei ga atta toki,
karera wa ikari no sakebi o agemashita.*

muscle — 筋肉 — *kinniku*

muscle in (on something) — 力ずくで押し入る — *chikarazuku de
oshiiru*
Another company is trying to muscle in on our territory. 他の会社が、
私達の領域に力ずくで押し入ろうとしています。*Hoka no kaisha
ga, watakushitachi no ryōiki ni chikarazuku de oshiirō to shite imasu.*

not move a muscle — 身動き一つしない — *miugoki hitotsu shinai*
The new recruits didn't move a muscle as the officer spoke. 将校が
話しているとき、新兵は身動き一つしませんでした。*Shōkō ga
hanashite iru toki, shinpei wa miugoki hitotsu shimasen deshita.*

music — 音楽 — *ongaku*

face the music — 自らの欠陥に甘んじる — *mizukara no kekkan ni
amanjiru*
We didn't meet our sales quota; now we have to face the music. 私達は
ノルマを満たせず、自らの欠陥に甘んじなければなりません。
*Watakushitachi wa noruma o mitasezu, mizukara no kekkan ni
amanjinakereba narimasen.*

music to one's ears — このうえない知らせ — *kono ue nai shirase*
When my son said he passed the exams, it was music to my ears. 息子が
試験に受かったと告げたとき、それはこのうえない知らせでした。
*Musuko ga shiken ni ukatta to tsugeta toki, sore wa kono ue nai shirase
deshita.*

must — 絶対必要な — zettai hitsuyō na

be a must — 絶対必要条件 — zettai hitsuyō jōken

If you want to work for that company, a Ph.D. is a must.　その会社で働きたいなら、博士号が絶対必要条件です。Sono kaisha de hatarakitai nara, hakasegō ga zettai hitsuyō jōken desu.

mustard — からし — karashi

cut the mustard — すべき事をする — subeki koto o suru

John was fired; he couldn't cut the mustard in that job.　ジョンはすべき事が出来なくて、首になりました。Jon wa subeki koto ga dekinakute, kubi ni narimashita.

muster — 検閲 — ken-etsu

pass muster — お許しを得る — oyurushi o eru

Do you think this outfit will pass muster with Mom and Dad?　この服装で、父と母のお許しを得ることが出来ると思いますか。Kono fukusō de, chichi to haha no oyurushi o eru koto ga dekiru to omoimasu ka.

nail — 爪 — tsume

(another) nail in someone or something's coffin — 命取り — inochi tori

Every customer they lost was another nail in the company's coffin.　失った顧客のどれもが、会社の命取りになりました。Ushinatta kokyaku no doremo ga, kaisha no inochi tori ni narimashita.

(as) hard as nails — 堅くて融通性がない — katakute yūzūsei ga nai

Their head negotiator is as hard as nails.　交渉相手の責任者は、堅くて融通性がありません。Kōshō aite no sekininsha wa, katakute yūzūsei ga arimasen.

hit the nail on the head — 図星をつく — zuboshi o tsuku

His analysis of the issues hit the nail on the head.　彼の問題の分析は、図星をついていました。Kare no mondai no bunseki wa, zuboshi o tsuite imashita.

nail someone or something down — はっきりさせる — hakkiri saseru
I'm trying to get an answer, but I can't nail him down. 彼から答えを
得ようとしているのですが、はっきりさせることが出来ません。
Kare kara kotae o eyō to shite iru no desu ga, hakkiri saseru koto ga
dekimasen.

---

name — 名前 — namae
  call someone names — 悪口を言う — warukuchi o iu
  If we stop calling each other names, maybe we can resolve the dispute.
  私達がお互いに悪口を言い合うのをよせば、論争の決着が付くで
    しょう。Watakushitachi ga otagai ni warukuchi o iiau no o yoseba,
    ronsō no ketchaku ga tsuku deshō.

  clear one's name — 汚名をそそぐ — omei o sosogu
  He was unfairly accused of wrongdoing, and he's trying to clear his name.
  彼は不当に悪事を非難されて、汚名をそそごうとしています。
  Kare wa futō ni akuji o hinan sarete, omei o sosogō to shite imasu.

  in name only — 名目だけ — meimoku dake
  He's senile now; he's the boss in name only. 彼は今はぼけてしまって、
  社長というのは名目だけです。Kare wa ima wa bokete shimatte,
  shachō to iu no wa meimoku dake desu.

  make a name (for oneself) — 名声を馳せる — meisei o haseru
  He has made a name for himself as a surgeon. 彼は外科医として、
  名声を馳せています。Kare wa gekai to shite, meisei o hasete imasu.

  name of the game — 肝心な点 — kanjin na ten
  In this company, quality is the name of the game. この会社では、品質が
  肝心な点です。Kono kaisha dewa, hinshitsu ga kanjin na ten desu.

  one's name is mud — 顔が潰れる — kao ga tsubureru
  If I don't meet this deadline, my name is mud. この締め切りに間に
  合わなければ、私は顔が潰れてしまいます。Kono shimekiri ni
  maniawanakereba, watakushi wa kao ga tsuburete shimaimasu.

throw someone's name around — 人の名を知り合いのごとく使う — *hito no na o shiriai no gotoku tsukau*

John thinks he can get favors by throwing his boss's name around. ジョンは社長の名を知り合いのごとく使えば、好意を受けられると思っています。*Jon wa shachō no na o shiriai no gotoku tsukaeba, kōi o ukerareru to omotte imasu.*

to one's name — 持つて — *motte*

These days, he doesn't have a penny to his name. 最近、彼は一銭も持っていません。*Saikin, kare wa issen mo motte imasen.*

worthy of the name — 名に値する — *na ni atai suru*

No mayor worthy of the name would try to raise taxes now. 市長の名に値する人は、誰も今、増税をしようとはしないでしょう。*Shichō no na ni atai suru hito wa, dare mo ima, zōzei o shiyō to wa shinai deshō.*

---

nature — 性質 — *seishitsu*

second nature — 第二の天性 — *dai ni no tensei*

Working hard is second nature to Bill. 仕事に励むことは、ビルの第二の天性です。*Shigoto ni hagemu koto wa, Biru no dai ni no tensei desu.*

---

neck — 首 — *kubi*

break one's neck (to do something) — 骨を折る — *hone o oru*

I broke my neck to get the report in on time. 報告書の提出が締め切りに

間に合うように、骨を折りました。*Hōkokusho no teishutsu ga shimekiri ni maniau yō ni, hone o orimashita.*

breathe down one's neck — こまごまと監視する — *komagoma to kanshi suru*

It's hard to work with him breathing down my neck. 彼は私をこまごまと監視するので、一緒に働くのは容易ではありません。*Kare wa watakushi o komagoma to kanshi suru node, issho ni hataraku no wa yōi dewa arimasen.*

catch/get it in the neck — 大目玉を食う — *ōmedama o kuu*

If we miss the meeting, we're going to catch it in the neck. もし会議に出ないと、私達は大目玉を食います。*Moshi kaigi ni denai to, watakushitachi wa ōmedama o kuimasu.*

neck and neck — 大接戦を繰り広げる — *dai sessen o kurihirogeru*

These two applicants are neck and neck for the job. 二人の志願者は、この仕事を得ようと大接戦を繰り広げています。*Futari no shigansha wa, kono shigoto o eyō to dai sessen o kurihirogete imasu.*

neck of the woods — 近く — *chikaku*

Come see me if you're ever in my neck of the woods. 近くまで来たら、私の所にも寄ってください。*Chikaku made kitara, watakushi no tokoro ni mo yotte kudasai.*

risk one's neck — 身を危険にさらす — *mi o kiken ni sarasu*

He's not going to risk his neck doing something foolish. 彼は、馬鹿なことをして身を危険にさらすようなことはしません。*Kare wa, baka na koto o shite mi o kiken ni sarasu yō na koto wa shimasen.*

save one's neck — 危機から救う — *kiki kara sukuu*

He saved my neck by lending me the rent money. 彼は家賃を貸してくれることによって、私を危機から救ってくれました。*Kare wa yachin o kashite kureru koto ni yotte, watakushi o kiki kara sukutte kuremashita.*

stick one's neck out — あえて危険を冒す — *aete kiken o okasu*

I'm going to stick my neck out and predict an early victory. 私はあえて危険を冒して、早期の勝利を予言します。*Watakushi wa aete kiken o okashite, sōki no shōri o yogen shimasu.*

up to one's neck — 身動きがとれない — *miugoki ga torenai*

I can't join you for dinner; I'm up to my neck in work. 私は仕事で

身動きがとれないので、ディナーには行けません。*Watakushi wa shigoto de miugoki ga torenai node, dinā niwa ikemasen.*

need — 必要 — *hitsuyō*
  crying need for someone or something — 絶対に必要 — *zettai ni hitsuyō*
  The school has a crying need for new computers.　学校は、新しいコンピュータが絶対に必要です。*Gakkō wa, atarashii konpyūta ga zettai ni hitsuyō desu.*

needle — 針 — *hari*
  needle in a haystack — 無駄骨を折る — *mudabone o oru*
  Trying to find my contact lens is like looking for a needle in a haystack. 私のコンタクトレンズを見つけようとするのは、無駄骨を折るようなものです。*Watakushi no kontakuto renzu o mitsukeyō to suru no wa, mudabone o oru yō na mono desu.*

nerve — 神経 — *shinkei*
  get on one's nerves — いらいらさせる — *iraira saseru*
  This loud music is getting on everyone's nerves.　このやかましい音楽は、みんなをいらいらさせています。*Kono yakamashii ongaku wa, minna o iraira sasete imasu.*

  get up the/enough nerve — 勇気を奮い起こす — *yūki o furuiokosu*
  He can't get up the nerve to ask her for a date.　彼は、彼女にデートを申し込むための勇気を奮い起こすことが出来ません。*Kare wa, kanojo ni dēto o mōshikomu tame no yūki o furuiokosu koto ga dekimasen.*

  of all the nerve — けしからん — *keshikaran*
  He's kept us waiting for an hour. Of all the nerve!　私達を一時間も待たせるなんて、彼はけしからん。*Watakushitachi o ichi jikan mo mataseru nante, kare wa keshikaran.*

nest — 巣 — *su*
  feather one's (own) nest — 私腹を肥やす — *shifuku o koyasu*
  They discovered that the city council chairman was feathering his own nest.　彼等は、市議会議長が私腹を肥やしていたことを発見

しました。Karera wa, shi gikai gichō ga shifuku o koyashite ita koto o hakken shimashita.

---

news — ニュース — nyūsu

No news is good news. — 便りがないのはよい便り。 — Tayori ga nai no wa yoi tayori.

He hasn't received his test results yet. No news is good news. 彼は、まだ検査の結果をもらっていません。便りがないのはよい便りです。 Kare wa, mada kensa no kekka o moratte imasen. Tayori ga nai no wa yoi tayori desu.

---

nick — 刻み目 — kizamime

in the nick of time — きわどい所で — kiwadoi tokoro de

They got to the hospital in the nick of time for the baby's delivery. 彼等は出産のために、きわどい所で病院に着きました。Karera wa shussan no tame ni, kiwadoi tokoro de byōin ni tsukimashita.

---

nickel — 五セント硬貨 — go sento kōka

nickel and dime someone — こまごまとお金を搾り取る — komagoma to okane o shiboritoru

The club nickels and dimes us to death with all these extra fees. クラブは色々な特別料金をかけて、私達からこまごまとお金を搾り取ります。 Kurabu wa iroiro na tokubetsu ryōkin o kakete, watakushitachi kara komagoma to okane o shiboritorimasu.

---

night — 夜 — yoru

(as) different as night and day — 全く違う — mattaku chigau

The two brothers are as different as night and day. あの二人は兄弟でも、全く違います。Ano futari wa kyōdai demo, mattaku chigaimasu.

call it a night — 今晩はこれでひきあげる — konban wa kore de hikiageru

I'm going to call it a night; I have to get up early tomorrow. 今晩は、これでひきあげます。明日は早起きしなければなりませんから。 Konban wa, kore de hikiagemasu. Ashita wa hayaoki shinakereba narimasen kara.

make a night of it — 徹夜してそれをする — tetsuya shite sore o suru

They made a night of it and partied till dawn. 彼等は徹夜して、明け方 までパーティーをしました。*Karera wa tetsuya shite, akegata made pātī o shimashita.*

nine — 九 — *kyū*

dressed to the nines — 盛装して — *seisō shite*
They're dressed to the nines for church today. 彼等は今日、盛装して 教会に行きます。*Karera wa kyō, seisō shite kyōkai ni ikimasu.*

nip — 一つねり — *hitotsuneri*

nip and tuck — 互角 — *gokaku*
We were nip and tuck in the bidding on the contract. 私達は、契約の 入札では互角でした。*Watakushitachi wa, keiyaku no nyūsatsu dewa gokaku deshita.*

nitty — シラミの卵が多い — *shirami no tamago ga ōi*

get down to the nitty-gritty — 要点に本腰を入れる — *yōten ni hongoshi o ireru*
Once the preliminaries were over, we got down to the nitty-gritty. 準備が 終わって、要点に本腰を入れました。*Junbi ga owatte, yōten ni hongoshi o iremashita.*

no — いいえ — *iie*

no sooner said than done — 言うやいなやそれができて — *iu ya ina ya sore ga dekite*
We just asked for coffee, and here it is; no sooner said than done. 私達がコーヒーを頼んだばかりなのに、言うやいなやそれが できてきました。*Watakushitashi ga kōhī o tanonda bakari nanoni, iu ya ina ya sore ga dekite kimashita.*

not take no for an answer — 嫌とは言わせない — *iya to wa iwasenai*
Let's go to dinner. I won't take no for an answer. ディナーに 行きましょう。嫌とは言わせませんよ。*Dīnā ni ikimashō. Iya to wa iwasemasen yo.*

nod — つなずき — *unazuki*

get the nod — 選ばれる — *erabareru*

When the boss retires, his son will get the nod. 社長が引退すると、息子が後継者として選ばれるでしょう。*Shachō ga intai suru to, musuko ga erabareru deshō.*

nod off — 居眠りする — *inemuri suru*
I nodded off for a while during class today. 今日は授業中に、ちょっと居眠りをしてしまいました。*Kyō wa jugyō chū ni, chotto inemuri o shite shimaimashita.*

noggin — 小型ジョッキ — *kogata jokki*
  use one's noggin — 頭を使う — *atama o tsukau*
  Use your noggin and you'll come up with a solution. 頭を使えば、解決策が浮かぶでしょう。*Atama o tsukaeba, kaiketsu saku ga ukabu deshō.*

none — 何もない — *nani mo nai*
  have none of something — 受け付けない — *uketsukenai*
  John tried to explain his lateness, but the boss was having none of it. ジョンが遅れたわけを説明しようとしても、上司はそれを受け付けませんでした。*Jon ga okureta wake o setsumei shiyō to shitemo, jōshi wa sore o uketsukemasen deshita.*

  none the wiser — 気がつかない — *ki ga tsukanai*
  If you don't tell them about it, they'll be none the wiser. もしあなたが教えないなら、彼等はそれについて気がつかないでしょう。*Moshi anata ga oshienai nara, karera wa sore ni tsuite ki ga tsukanai deshō.*

  second to none — 抜群 — *batsugun*
  That restaurant is second to none in the city. あのレストランは、この市では抜群です。*Ano resutoran wa, kono shi dewa batsugun desu.*

noodle — うどん — *udon*
  use one's noodle — 頭を使う — *atama o tsukau*
  If you use your noodle, you'll pass the course easily. 頭を使えば、その科目は簡単に合格できます。*Atama o tsukaeba, sono kamoku wa kantan ni gōkaku dekimasu.*

nook — すみ — *sumi*
  nook and cranny — すみからすみまで — *sumi kara sumi made*

The child looked for her lost doll in every nook and cranny.　その子は、なくした人形をすみからすみまで探しました。*Sono ko wa, nakushita ningyō o sumi kara sumi made sagashimashita.*

---

nose — 鼻 — *hana*

(as) plain as the nose on one's face — 極めて明らか — *kiwamete akiraka*

The answer is as plain as the nose on your face.　答えは、極めて明らかです。*Kotae wa, kiwamete akiraka desu.*

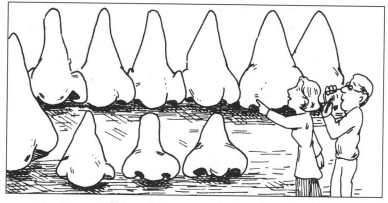

count noses — 頭数を数える — *atama kazu o kazoeru*

Let's count noses and see who's here.　頭数を数えて、ここに誰が来ているか調べましょう。*Atama kazu o kazoete, koko ni dare ga kite iru ka shirabemashō.*

cut off one's nose to spite one's face — かえって自分を損させてしまう — *kaette jibun o son sasete shimau*

If you quit your job in anger, you'll be cutting off your nose to spite your face.　怒って仕事を辞めてしまうと、かえって自分を損させてしまいますよ。*Okotte shigoto o yamete shimau to, kaette jibun o son sasete shimaimasu yo.*

follow one's nose — まっすぐ行く — *massugu iku*

Just follow your nose down this street, and you'll see the bank.　銀行は、この道をまっすぐ行けばわかりますよ。*Ginkō wa, kono michi o massugu ikeba wakarimasu yo.*

get/keep one's nose out of someone's business — 人のことに首を
突っ込まない — hito no koto ni kubi o tsukkomanai
I wish he'd keep his nose out of my family's business. 彼には、私の家族
のことに首を突っ込まないでもらいたいです。Kare niwa,
watakushi no kazoku no koto ni kubi o tsukkomanai de moraitai desu.

have one's nose in a book — いつも本を読んでいる — itsumo hon o
yonde iru
My sister loves to read; she always has her nose in a book. 私の姉は
読書が好きで、いつも本を読んでいます。Watakushi no ane wa
dokusho ga suki de, itsumo hon o yonde imasu.

keep one's nose clean — 悪事から身を遠ざける — akuji kara mi o
tōzakeru
Please keep your nose clean and stay away from drugs. 悪事から身を
遠ざけて、麻薬には手を出さないように。Akuji kara mi o tōzakete,
mayaku niwa te o dasanai yō ni.

keep/put one's nose to the grindstone — せっせと働く — sesse to
hataraku
If you keep your nose to the grindstone, you can save enough for
retirement. せっせと働けば、引退のために十分お金を貯める
ことが出来ます。Sesse to hatarakeba, intai no tame ni jūbun okane o
tameru koto ga dekimasu.

lead someone (around) by the nose — 人の思い通りにさせる — hito
no omoidōri ni saseru
No one can lead John around by the nose; he makes his own decisions.
誰も、ジョンを人の思い通りにさせることが出来ません。彼は、
自分のことは自分で決めるからです。Dare mo, Jon o hito no
omoidōri ni saseru koto ga dekimasen. Kare wa, jibun no koto wa jibun
de kimeru kara desu.

look down one's nose at someone or something — 軽蔑の眼差しで
眺める — keibetsu no manazashi de nagameru
They looked down their noses at his lack of style. 彼等は彼に品の良さが
ないのを、軽蔑の眼差しで眺めました。Karera wa kare ni hin no
yosa ga nai no o, keibetsu no manazashi de nagamemashita.

nose about/around — 嗅ぎ回る — kagimawaru
Barbara is nosing around for information on the reorganization.

バーバラは、会社再編成の情報を嗅ぎ回っています。 *Bābara wa, kaisha saihensei no jōhō o kagimawatte imasu.*

on the nose — 正にその通り — *masa ni sono tōri*

His prediction about the election results was right on the nose. 彼の選挙の結果の予測は、正にその通りでした。 *Kare no senkyo no kekka no yosoku wa, masa ni sono tōri deshita.*

one's nose is in the air — お高くとまる — *otakaku tomaru*

He's a real snob; his nose is always in the air. 彼は本当の気取り屋で、いつもお高くとまっています。 *Kare wa hontō no kidoriya de, itsumo otakaku tomatte imasu.*

one's nose is out of joint — 気分を損ねる — *kibun o sokoneru*

Mary's nose is out of joint because she wasn't invited to the party. メリーはそのパーティーに招待されなかったので、気分を損ねています。 *Merī wa sono pātī ni shōtai sarenakatta node, kibun o sokonete imasu.*

pay through the nose — とてつもない金を払う — *totetsu mo nai kane o harau*

If you borrow money from them, you'll pay through the nose. あの人達から金を借りると、とてつもない金を払わなければなりませんよ。 *Ano hitotachi kara kane o kariru to, totetsu mo nai kane o harawanakereba narimasen yo.*

poke/stick one's nose into something — 余計な口出しをする — *yokei na kuchidashi o suru*

He's always poking his nose into our financial affairs. 彼は、いつも私達の家計のやりくりに余計な口出しをしています。 *Kare wa, itsumo watakushitachi no kakei no yurikuri ni yokei na kuchidashi o shite imasu.*

put someone's nose out of joint — 気を悪くする — *ki o waruku suru*

When he didn't get a promotion, it put his nose out of joint. 彼は昇進を受けなかったので、気を悪くしました。 *Kare wa shōshin o ukenakatta node, ki o waruku shimashita.*

(right) under one's nose — 目の前 — *me no mae*

The answer was right under his nose. 答えは、目の前にあったのです。 *Kotae wa, me no mae ni atta no desu.*

rub someone's nose in it — しつこく追求する — *shitsukoku tsuikyū suru*

He's sorry for his mistake; don't rub his nose in it. 彼は犯した失敗を
すまなく思っているから、これ以上しつこく追求しないように。
Kare wa okashita shippai o sumanaku omotte iru kara, kore ijō shitsukoku tsuikyū shinai yō ni.

thumb one's nose at someone or something — 鼻であしらう — *hana de ashirau*

She'll get in trouble if she continues thumbing her nose at the rules.
彼女が規則を鼻であしらうなら、そのうちに面倒に巻き込まれる
でしょう。*Kanojo ga kisoku o hana de ashirau nara, sono uchi ni mendō ni makikomareru deshō.*

turn up one's nose at something — 小馬鹿にする — *kobaka ni suru*

He can be helpful. Don't turn up your nose at his advice. 彼の助言は、
役立ちます。だから、それを小馬鹿にしてはなりません。*Kare no jogen wa, yakudachimasu. Dakara, sore o kobaka ni shite wa narimasen.*

win by a nose — 鼻の差で勝つ — *hana no sa de katsu*

He won the race by a nose. 彼は、競争に鼻の差で勝ちました。*Kare wa, kyōsō ni hana no sa de kachimashita.*

---

nosedive — 急降下 — *kyūkōka*

go into a nosedive/take a nosedive — 暴落する — *bōraku suru*

The stock market took a nosedive after the election. 株式市場は、
選挙の後、暴落しました。*Kabushiki shijō wa, senkyo no ato, bōraku shimashita.*

---

notch — 刻み目 — *kizamime*

take someone down a notch — 鼻っ柱をへし折る — *hanappashira o heshioru*

He's so arrogant; someone should take him down a notch. 彼は実に傲慢
なので、誰かが彼の鼻っ柱をへし折るべきです。*Kare wa jitsu ni gōman nanode, dareka ga kare no hanappashira o heshioru beki desu.*

---

note — 覚え書き／音符 — *oboegaki/onpu*

compare notes — 意見や情報を交換する — *iken ya jōhō o kōkan suru*

Let's compare notes on the product and come up with a marketing strategy.

この製品について意見を交換して、販売戦略を練り上げましょう。
Kono seihin ni tsuite iken o kōkan shite, hanbai senryaku o neriagemashō.

hit/strike a sour note — 気まずい雰囲気になる — *kimazui fun-iki ni naru*

The negotiations hit a sour note when John walked out. ジョンが突然席を立つて、交渉は気まずい雰囲気になりました。*Jon ga totsuzen seki o tatte, kōshō wa kimazui fun-iki ni narimashita.*

strike the right note — 期待通りの効果を上げる — *kitai dōri no kōka o ageru*

His anniversary gift struck just the right note with his wife. 彼の奥さんへの結婚記念日のプレゼントは、期待通りの効果を上げました。*Kare no okusan e no kekkon kinenbi no purezento wa, kitai dōri no kōka o agemashita.*

take note of (something) — 注意を払う — *chūi o harau*

Take note of his technique and you'll improve your own golf game. 彼のテクニックに注意を払えば、あなたはゴルフが上達するでしょう。*Kare no tekunikku ni chūi o haraeba, anata wa gorufu ga jōtatsu suru deshō.*

---

nothing — 何もない — *nani mo nai*

come to nothing — 水の泡になる — *mizu no awa ni naru*

With the budget cuts, our plans to expand came to nothing. 予算削減で、私達の拡張計画は水の泡になりました。*Yosan sakugen de, watakushitachi no kakuchō keikaku wa mizu no awa ni narimashita.*

have nothing on someone — 証拠がない — *shōko ga nai*

The police can't hold the suspect; they have nothing on him. 警察は証拠がないので、容疑者を留置することが出来ませんでした。*Keisatsu wa shōko ga nai node, yōgisha o ryūchi suru koto ga dekimasen deshita.*

have nothing to do with someone or something — 関わりを持たない — *kakawari o motanai*

She has nothing to do with liars. 彼女は、嘘つきとは関わりを持ちません。*Kanojo wa, usotsuki to wa kakawari o mochimasen.*

Here goes nothing. — だめかもしれないけれど、やってみよう。—

Dame kamo shirenai keredo, yatte miyō.
It's time for my speech. Here goes nothing! 私が演説する番がきました。
だめかも知れないけれど、やってみましょう。Watakushi ga
enzetsu suru ban ga kimashita. Dame kamo shirenai keredo, yatte
mimashō.

in nothing flat — 瞬く間に — matataku ma ni
I'll have this work done in nothing flat. 私は、この仕事を瞬く間に
終わらせます。Watakushi wa, kono shigoto o matataku ma ni
owarasemasu.

next to nothing — 無いに等しい — nai ni hitoshii
He can't help us; he knows next to nothing about this subject. その件に
ついては彼の知識は無いに等しいので、私達の助けになりません。
Sono ken ni tsuite wa kare no chishiki wa nai ni hitoshii node,
watakushitachi no tasuke ni narimasen.

not know from nothing — 頭が鈍い — atama ga nibui
Don't expect answers from them; they don't know from nothing. 彼らは
頭が鈍いから、答えは期待しないこと。Karera wa atama ga nibui
kara, kotae wa kitai shinai koto.

nothing doing — 絶対にだめ — zettai ni dame
You want to stay home from school today? Nothing doing. 今日は学校を
休みたいって。絶対にだめです。Kyō wa gakkō o yasumitaitte.
Zettai ni dame desu.

nothing short of something — ほとんどそれに近い — hotondo sore ni
chikai
His recovery was nothing short of a miracle. 彼の病気からの回復は、
ほとんど奇跡に近いものでした。Kare no byōki kara no kaifuku wa,
hotondo kiseki ni chikai mono deshita.

nothing to it — 別になんということもない — betsu ni nan to iu koto
mo nai
I can fix your car. There's nothing to it. あなたの車なら、直せますよ。
それは、別になんということもありません。Anata no kuruma nara,
naosemasu yo. Sore wa, betsu ni nan to iu koto mo arimasen.

nothing to sneeze at — 馬鹿にしたものではない — baka ni shita
mono dewa nai
His experience is nothing to sneeze at. 彼の経験は、馬鹿にしたもの

ではありません。*Kare no keiken wa, baka ni shita mono dewa arimasen.*

nothing to write home about — 別になんということもない — *betsu ni nan to iu koto mo nai*

That movie was nothing to write home about. その映画は、別になんということもありませんでした。*Sono eiga wa, betsu ni nan to iu koto mo arimasen deshita.*

Nothing ventured, nothing gained. — 虎穴に入らずんば虎児を得ず。 — *Koketsu ni irazunba koji o ezu.*

Let's invest in that stock. Nothing ventured, nothing gained. あの株に、投資しましょう。虎穴に入らずんば虎児を得ずですよ。*Ano kabu ni, tōshi shimashō. Koketsu ni irazunba, koji o ezu desu yo.*

stop at nothing — 手段を選ばない — *shudan o erabanai*

He'll stop at nothing to get what he wants. 彼は欲しいものを手に入れるためには、手段を選びません。*Kare wa hoshii mono o te ni ireru tame niwa, shudan o erabimasen.*

sweet nothings — 愛のささやき — *ai no sasayaki*

Those two are always whispering sweet nothings to each other. あの二人は、いつも愛のささやきを交わし合っています。*Ano futari wa, itsumo ai no sasayaki o kawashiatte imasu.*

to say nothing of someone or something — それは勿論の事 — *sore wa mochiron no koto*

He still has errands to do, to say nothing of homework. 彼は宿題は勿論の事、まだしなければならない用事がいくつかあります。*Kare wa shukudai wa mochiron no koto, mada shinakereba naranai yōji ga ikutsuka arimasu.*

want for nothing — 何でも持っている — *nandemo motte iru*

Jill spends all her money on her daughter, who wants for nothing. ジルは娘のために持ち金は全て使うので、娘は何でも持っています。*Jiru wa musume no tame ni mochigane wa subete tsukau node, musume wa nandemo motte imasu.*

---

notice — 注意 — *chūi*

sit up and take notice 注目する *chūmoku suru*

The new congressman's speech made everyone sit up and take notice.

新人議員の演説に、誰もが注目しました。*Shinjin giin no enzetsu ni, daremo ga chūmoku shimashita.*

---

notion — 意向 — *ikō*

have half a notion/mind to do something — ほぼ決心する — *hobo kesshin suru*

I have half a notion to get tickets for the concert.　私はコンサートの券を手に入れようと、ほぼ決心しました。*Watakushi wa konsāto no ken o te ni ireyō to, hobo kesshin shimashita.*

---

now — 今 — *ima*

(every) now and then — 時々 — *tokidoki*

They play tennis every now and then.　彼等は、時々テニスをします。*Karera wa, tokidoki tenisu o shimasu.*

now or never — これ限りの機会 — *kore kagiri no kikai*

Bob's going to ask for a raise. It's now or never.　ボブは、昇給を求めることに決めました。今こそ、これ限りの機会だからです。*Bobu wa, shōkyū o motomeru koto ni kimemashita. Ima koso, kore kagiri no kikai dakara desu.*

---

nowhere — どこにもない — *doko nimo nai*

out of nowhere — 突然 — *totsuzen*

When I got a flat tire, Joe appeared out of nowhere to help fix it.　私のタイヤがパンクしたとき、ジョーが突然現れて直すのを手伝ってくれました。*Watakushi no taiya ga panku shita toki, Jō ga totsuzen arawarete naosu no o tetsudatte kuremashita.*

get nowhere fast — 行き詰まる — *ikizumaru*

The negotiations are getting nowhere fast; let's take a break.　交渉が行き詰まっているので、ちょっと休憩しましょう。*Kōshō ga ikizumatte iru node, chotto kyūkei shimashō.*

in the middle of nowhere — 人里離れたところに — *hitozato hanareta tokoro ni*

He built a new house in the middle of nowhere.　彼は、人里離れたところに新しい家を建てました。*Kare wa, hitozato hanareta tokoro ni atarashii ie o tatemashita.*

---

number — 数字 — *sūji*

by the numbers — 規則通りに — *kisoku dōri ni*

If we do it by the numbers, we can't go wrong. 規則通りにやれば、私達が失敗することはありません。 *Kisoku dōri ni yareba, watakushitachi ga shippai suru koto wa arimasen.*

do a number on someone or something — 面食らわせる — *menkurawaseru*

She really did a number on Bob when she broke their date. 彼女はデートの約束を破って、ボブを本当に面食らわせました。 *Kanojo wa dēto no yakusoku o yabutte, Bobu o hontō ni menkurawasemashita.*

get/have someone's number — 正体をつかむ — *shōtai o tsukamu*

They won't get away with this deception. We have their number. 彼等に、このごまかしを成功させることは許しません。私達は、彼等の正体をつかんでいるんですから。 *Karera ni, kono gomakashi o seikō saseru koto wa yurushimasen. Watakushitachi wa, karera no shōtai o tsukande irundesu kara.*

hot number — 近頃大受けだ — *chikagoro ōuke da*

His new novel is a hot number in all the bookstores. 彼の新しい小説は、近頃どの本屋でも大受けです。 *Kare no atarashii shōsetsu wa, chikagoro dono hon-ya demo ōuke desu.*

number one — 自らの利益を大切にする — *mizukara no rieki o taisetsu ni suru*

Use your head and look out for number one. 頭を活用して、自らの利益を大切にしなさい。 *Atama o katsuyō shite, mizukara no rieki o taisetsu ni shinasai.*

one's number is up — 最早これまで — *mohaya kore made*

Most voters agree the mayor's number is up. 市長の運も最早これまでという事には、大部分の有権者が賛成しています。 *Shichō no un mo mohaya kore made to iu koto niwa, daibubun no yūkensha ga sansei shite imasu.*

---

nut — 木の実 — *kinomi*

nuts about someone or something — 無我夢中 — *mugamuchū*

John is nuts about his new computer. ジョンは、新しいコンピュータに無我夢中です。 *Jon wa, atarashii konpyūta ni mugamuchū desu.*

nuts and bolts — 根本 — *konpon*
If you learn the nuts and bolts of your job, you'll move up fast. あなたは
仕事の根本を学びさえすれば、急速に昇進できるでしょう。
*Anata wa shigoto no konpon o manabi sae sureba, kyūsoku ni shōshin
dekiru deshō.*

nut case — 愚か者 — *oroka mono*
Ever since he met Jane, he's been acting like a nut case. 彼はジェーンに
会って以来、愚か者のような振る舞い方をしています。*Kare wa
Jēn ni atte irai, orokamono no yō na furumaikata o shite imasu.*

tough nut to crack — 難物 — *nanbutsu*
I can't figure out what Hank wants; he's a tough nut to crack.ハンクは
難物で、彼は何がいるのか見当がつきません。*Hanku wa nanbutsu
de, kare wa nani ga iru no ka kentō ga tsukimasen.*

nutshell — 木の実の殻 — *kinomi no kara*
   in a nutshell — かいつまんで — *kaitsumande*
Please give us your main points in a nutshell. あなたの要点を、
かいつまんで言って下さい。*Anata no yōten o, kaitsumande itte
kudasai.*

oat — オート麦 — *ōto mugi*
   feel one's oats — 興奮して飛び回る — *kōfun shite tobimawaru*
The children were feeling their oats the week before Halloween.
子供たちはハロウィーンの一週間前、興奮して飛び回っていました。
*Kodomotachi wa Harowīn no isshūkan mae, kōfun shite tobimawatte
imashita.*

occasion — 場合 — *baai*
   rise to the occasion — 挑戦を受けて立つ — *chōsen o ukete tatsu*
The negotiators rose to the occasion and concluded a trade agreement.
交渉の当事者は挑戦を受けて立ち、貿易協定を合意させました。

Kōshō no tōjisha wa chōsen o ukete tachi, bōeki kyōtei o gōi sasemashita.

odds — 勝ち目 — kachime

odds and ends — 雑用 — zatsuyō

I have some odds and ends to take care of before I leave the office.
オフィスを出る前に、雑用を片付けなければなりません。Ofisu o deru mae ni, zatsuyō o katazukenakereba narimasen.

oil — オイル — oiru

burn the midnight oil — 深夜まで働く — shin-ya made hataraku

John is burning the midnight oil to complete the project. ジョンはその プロジェクトを終わらせるために、深夜まで働いています。Jon wa sono purojekuto o owaraseru tame ni, shin-ya made hataraite imasu.

pour oil on troubled waters — 問題を鎮める — mondai o shizumeru

Let's call John to help settle this; he's good at pouring oil on troubled waters. これを解決するために、ジョンに助けを求めましょう。彼は、問題を鎮めるのが上手です。Kore o kaiketsu suru tame ni, Jon ni tasuke o motomemashō. Kare wa, mondai o shizumeru no ga jōzu desu.

once — 一度 — ichido

give someone the once-over — ちらっと見て品定めする — chiratto mite shinasadame suru

When the new employee arrived, everyone gave him the once-over. 新入 社員が着いたとき、誰もが彼を素ちらっと見て品定めしました。 Shinnyū shain ga tsuita toki, daremo ga kare o chiratto mite shinasadame shimashita.

once over lightly — いい加減に — ii kagen ni

He did his homework once over lightly. 彼は、宿題をいい加減に しました。Kare wa, shukudai o iikagen ni shimashita.

one — 一 — ichi

back to square one — 振り出しに戻る — furidashi ni modoru

When the job offer fell through, his job search was back to square one.
申し出のあった仕事がだめになったとき、彼の就職活動は

振り出しに戻りました。*Mōshide no atta shigoto ga dame ni natta toki, kare no shūshoku katsudō wa furidashi ni modorimashita.*

like one of the family — 家族の一員のように — *kazoku no ichiin no yō ni*
They treat their daughter's friend like one of the family.　彼等は、娘の友達を家族の一員のように扱っています。*Karera wa, musume no tomodachi o kazoku no ichiin no yō ni atsukatte imasu.*

new one on someone — 信じ難いニュース — *shinjigatai nyūsu*
The mayor was arrested? That's a new one on me.　市長が逮捕されたんですか。それは、信じ難いニュースです。*Shichō ga taiho saretandesu ka. Sore wa, shinjigatai nyūsu desu.*

one and all — 一人一人に — *hitori hitori ni*
The notice went out to one and all.　一人一人に通知がいきました。*Hitori hitori ni tsūchi ga ikimashita.*

one and only — 有名で才能にあふれた — *yūmei de sainō ni afureta*
The pitcher—the one and only John Doe—was introduced.　有名で才能にあふれた投手のジョン・ドーが紹介されました。*Yūmei de sainō ni afureta tōshu no Jon Dō ga shōkai saremashita.*

one and the same — 同一人物 — *dōitsu jinbutsu*
The famous poet and the governor are one and the same.　あの有名な詩人と州知事は、同一人物です。*Ano yūmei na shijin to shū chiji wa, dōitsu jinbutsu desu.*

one in a million — ユニーク — *yunīku*
Her mother-in-law is so talented. She's one in a million.　彼女の義理のお母さんはとても才能に富んでいて、ユニークです。*Kanojo no giri no okāsan wa totemo sainō ni tonde ite, yunīku desu.*

one up (on someone) — 差を付ける — *sa o tsukeru*
With this new technology, we're one up on our competitors.　この新しい技術で、私達は競争相手に差を付けています。*Kono atarashii gijutsu de, watakushitachi wa kyōsō aite ni sa o tsukete imasu.*

pull a fast one — ごまかす — *gomakasu*
Watch him closely; he may try to pull a fast one.　彼はごまかそうとするかもしれないので、彼から目を離さないように。*Kare wa gomakasō to suru kamo shirenai node, kare kara me o hanasanai yō ni.*

onion — タマネギ — *tamanegi*

know one's onions — 知るべき事に精通している — *shiru beki koto ni seitsū shite iru*

He'll solve the problem; he knows his onions.　彼は知るべき事に精通しているので、その問題を解決するでしょう。*Kare wa shiru beki koto ni seitsū shite iru node, sono mondai o kaiketsu suru deshō.*

---

onto — 上へ — *ue e*

onto something — 何か真実を探り当てる — *nanika shinjitsu o saguriateru*

That's an interesting theory. You may be onto something.　それは興味のある説です。あなたは、何か真実を探り当てるかもしれません。*Sore wa kyōmi no aru setsu desu. Anata wa, nanika shinjitsu o saguriateru kamo shiremasen.*

---

open — 開けた場所／開いた — *hiraketa basho/hiraita*

get something out in the open — 目をつぶるのを止す — *me o tsuburu no o yosu*

If we get our disagreements out in the open, we can resolve them.　賛成できない点があることに私達が目をつぶるのを止せば、それを解決できます。*Sansei dekinai ten ga aru koto ni watakushitachi ga me o tsuburu no o yoseba, sore o kaiketsu dekimasu.*

leave oneself wide open to something — 自らをそれにさらす — *mizukara o sore ni sarasu*

By arriving late, John left himself wide open to criticism.　ジョンは遅刻して、自らを批判にさらすことになりました。*Jon wa chikoku shite, mizukara o hihan ni sarasu koto ni narimashita.*

---

openers — 最初 — *saisho*

for openers — 初めに — *hajime ni*

For openers, they played the national anthem.　初めに、国歌演奏がありました。*Hajime ni, kokka ensō ga arimashita.*

---

orbit — 軌道 — *kidō*

go into orbit — 有頂天になる — *uchōten ni naru*

When their candidate won, they went into orbit.　支持する候補者が

勝ったとき、彼等は有頂天になりました。 *Shiji suru kōhosha ga katta toki, karera wa uchōten ni narimashita.*

order — 注文／順序 — *chūmon/junjo*

in apple-pie order — きちんと整えて — *kichin to totonoete*
Her office is always in apple-pie order. 彼女のオフィスは、いつも きちんと整えてあります。 *Kanojo no ofisu wa, itsumo kichin to totonoete arimasu.*

order of the day — 必需品 — *hitsuju hin*
Umbrellas are the order of the day in April. 傘は、四月には必需品です。 *Kasa wa, shigatsu niwa hitsuju hin desu.*

order in — 出前を頼む — *demae o tanomu*
I don't feel like cooking tonight; let's order in. 今夜は料理する気に なれないので、出前を頼みましょう。 *Kon-ya wa ryōri suru ki ni narenai node, demae o tanomimashō.*

ordinary — 普通の — *futsū no*
out of the ordinary — ずば抜けて — *zubanukete*
That restaurant is good but nothing out of the ordinary. あれはいい レストランですが、特にずば抜けているわけではありません。 *Are wa ii resutoran desu ga, toku ni zubanukete iru wake dewa arimasen.*

other — 他の — *hoka no*

made for each other — お似合いのカップル — *oniai no kappuru*
Marsha and John seem made for each other.　マーシャとジョンは、
お似合いのカップルみたいです。*Māsha to Jon wa, oniai no kappuru
mitai desu.*

none other than someone — 他ならぬ本人 — *hoka naranu honnin*
The vocalist was none other than the boss.　歌手は、他ならぬ社長本人
でした。*Kashu wa, hoka naranu shachō honnin deshita.*

---

ounce — オンス — *onsu*

An ounce of prevention is worth a pound of cure. — 治療よりも
予防が肝心。— *Chiryō yori mo yobō ga kanjin.*
I just got a flu shot. An ounce of prevention is worth a pound of cure.
私は流感の予防注射をしてもらいましたが、治療よりも予防が
肝心だからです。*Watakushi wa ryūkan no yobō chūsha o shite
moraimashita ga, chiryō yori mo yobō ga kanjin dakara desu.*

---

outdoors — 屋外 — *okugai*

as big as all outdoors — ものすごく広い — *monosugoku hiroi*
His new office is as big as all outdoors.　彼の新しいオフィスは、もの
すごく広いです。*Kare no atarashii ofisu wa, monosugoku hiroi desu.*

---

overboard — 船外に — *sengai ni*

go overboard — 度を過ごす — *do o sugosu*
Let's get them a nice gift, but try not to go overboard.　彼等に素晴らしい
ギフトはあげるけれど、度を過ごさないようにしましょう。
*Karera ni subarashii gifuto wa ageru keredo, do o sugosanai yō ni
shimashō.*

---

owl — ふくろう — *fukurō*

(as) wise as an owl — 何でもものをよく知っている — *nandemo mono
o yoku shitte iru*
My grandfather is as wise as an owl.　祖父は、何でもものをよく
知っています。*Sofu wa, nandemo mono o yoku shitte imasu.*

night owl — 宵っ張り — *yoippari*
She's a real night owl; she always reads until 3 A.M.　彼女は

宵っ張りで、いつも午前三時まで本を読みます。*Kanojo wa yoippari de, itsumo gozen san ji made hon o yomimasu.*

own — 自分自身 — *jibun jishin*

come into one's own — 正当な評価を受ける — *seitō na hyōka o ukeru*
With her wonderful new job, she has finally come into her own. 彼女は
やりがいのある新しい仕事を始めて、やっと正当な評価を
受けました。*Kanojo wa yarigai no aru atarashii shigoto o hajimete, yatto seitō na hyōka o ukemashita.*

hold one's own — 誰にも引けを取らない — *dare ni mo hike o toranai*
When it comes to computers, Jack can hold his own. コンピュータに
かけては、ジャックは誰にも引けを取りません。*Konpyūta ni kakete wa, Jakku wa dare nimo hike o torimasen.*

on one's own — 自分で — *jibun de*
I don't need help; I can do it on my own. 誰の助けもいりません。
それは、自分で出来ますから。*Dare no tasuke mo irimasen. Sore wa, jibun de dekimasu kara.*

own up (to something) — 告白する — *kokuhaku suru*
If you don't own up to your mistakes, they won't trust you again. 犯した
間違いを告白しないなら、彼等はあなたを二度と信用しませんよ。
Okashita machigai o kokuhaku shinai nara, karera wa anata o ni do to shin-yō shimasen yo.

ox — 雄牛 — *oushi*

(as) strong as an ox — すごい力持ち — *sugoi chikaramochi*
That sumo wrestler is as strong as an ox. あの力士は、すごい力持ちです。
Ano rikishi wa, sugoi chikaramochi desu.

pace — 歩調 — *hochō*

put one through one's paces — 能力を試す — *nōryoku o tamesu*
They put the new secretary through her paces before hiring her. 彼等は

新しい秘書を雇う前に、彼女の能力を試しました。*Karera wa atarashii hisho o yatou mae ni, kanojo no nōryoku o tameshimashita.*

---

pain — 苦痛 — *kutsū*

feel no pain — 酔っ払う — *yopparau*
Tom's been drinking for hours; he's feeling no pain.　トムは数時間も飲み続けて、酔っ払っています。*Tomu wa sūjikan mo nomitsuzukete, yopparatte imasu.*

give someone a pain — いらいらさせる — *iraira saseru*
She gives me a pain with her constant complaining.　彼女は絶え間なく苦情を述べて、私をいらいらさせます。*Kanojo wa taema naku kujō o nobete, watakushi o iraira sasemasu.*

have growing pains — 成長の悩み — *seichō no nayami*
Tom's new company misplaced some orders. They're having growing pains.　トムの新しい会社は、注文の品を幾つか送り間違えてしまいました。彼等は、成長の悩みを味わっているのです。*Tomu no atarashii kaisha wa, chūmon no shina o ikutsuka okurimachigaete shimaimashita. Karera wa, seichō no nayami o ajiwatte iru no desu.*

pain in the neck — 厄介者／厄介物 — *yakkaimono/yakkaimono*
This homework is a real pain in the neck.　この宿題は、本当に厄介物です。*Kono shukudai wa, hontō ni yakkaimono desu.*

take (great) pains — 努力を惜しまない — *doryoku o oshimanai*
They took great pains with the renovation of their home.　彼等は自宅の大改築のために、努力を惜しみませんでした。*Karera wa jitaku no dai kaichiku no tame ni, doryoku o oshimimasen deshita.*

---

pale — 青ざめた — *aozameta*

beyond the pale — 容認の限度を遥かに超える — *yōnin no gendo o haruka ni koeru*
Her lies are beyond the pale.　彼女の嘘は、容認の限度を遥かに超えています。*Kanojo no uso wa, yōnin no gendo o haruka ni koete imasu.*

---

palm — 掌 — *tenohira*

grease/oil someone's palm — 袖の下を使う — *sode no shita o tsukau*
He'll do you a favor if you grease his palm first.　彼に袖の下を使えば、

あなたに都合のいいことをやってくれます。*Kare ni sode no shita o tsukaeba, anata ni tsugō no ii koto o yatte kuremasu.*

have an itchy/itching palm — チップを欲しがる — *chippu o hoshigaru*
Our waiter obviously has an itchy palm.　私達の係りのウェイターは、明らかにチップを欲しがっています。*Watakushitachi no kakari no ueitā wa, akiraka ni chippu o hoshigatte imasu.*

know someone or something like the palm of one's hand — 知り尽くしている — *shiritsukushite iru*
He knows this city like the palm of his hand.　彼はこの都市のことを、知り尽くしています。*Kare wa kono toshi no koto o, shiritsukushite imasu.*

---

pan — 平鍋 — *hiranabe*
out of the frying pan into the fire — 事態がますます悪化して — *jitai ga masumasu akka shite*
He lost his wallet, then his job; he went out of the frying pan into the fire.
彼は財布を無くした後失業し、事態がますます悪化しました。*Kare wa saifu o nakushita ato shitsugyō shi, jitai ga masumasu akka shimashita.*

pan out — うまくいく — *umaku iku*
We had high hopes for the negotiations, but things didn't pan out.　私達は交渉に大きな望みをかけていましたが、何事も、うまくいきませんでした。*Watakushitachi wa kōshō ni ōkina nozomi o kakete imashita ga, nanigoto mo umaku ikimasen deshita.*

Pandora — パンドラ — *Pandora*
open Pandora's box — 思いも寄らない難儀を招く — *omoi mo yoranai nangi o maneku*
When Tim asked her why she was upset, without realizing it, he opened Pandora's box.　ティムが彼女になぜ気分を損ねているのか聞いたとき、それとは気付かず、思いも寄らない難儀を招くことになったのです。*Timu ga kanojo ni naze kibun o sokonete iru ka kiita toki, sore to wa kizukazu, omoi mo yoranai nangi o maneku koto ni natta no desu.*

---

pants — ズボン — *zubon*
beat the pants off someone — 負かす — *makasu*

Our team beat the pants off our opponents last week.　我がチ－ムは、
先週、相手チ－ムを負かしました。*Waga chīmu wa, senshū, aite
chīmu o makashimashita.*

catch one with one's pants down — 現場を押さえる — *genba o osaeru*
They caught him with his pants down when he tried to sell the stolen
goods.　彼等は、彼が盗品を売ろうとしている現場を押さえました。
Karera wa, kare ga tōhin o urō to shite iru genba o osaemashita.

wear the pants — 家庭内の権力を握っている — *katei nai no kenryoku
o nigitte iru*
Mary wears the pants in her family.　メリ－は、彼女の家庭内の権力を
握っています。*Merī wa, kanojo no katei nai no kenryoku o nigitte
imasu.*

---

paper — 紙 — *kami*
walking papers — 解雇通知 — *kaiko tsūchi*
John just got his walking papers from the boss.　ジョンはたった今、
上司から解雇通知を受け取りました。*Jon wa tatta ima, jōshi kara
kaiko tsūchi o uketorimashita.*

---

par — 平均の — *heikin no*
par for the course — それが普通 — *sore ga futsū*
The service was bad? That's par for the course in this restaurant.
サ－ビスが悪かったって。そのレストランでは、それが普通ですよ。
Sābisu ga warukattatte. Sono resutoran dewa, sore ga futsū desu yo.

up to par — 並 — *nami*
Her work hasn't been up to par lately.　彼女の仕事は、最近は並以下です。
Kanojo no shigoto wa, saikin wa nami ika desu.

---

part — 部分 — *bubun*
do one's part — 仕事の分担を果たす — *shigoto no buntan o hatasu*
If we each do our part, we can succeed.　私達は銘々が仕事の分担を
果たせば、成功を遂げることが出来ます。*Watakushitachi wa
meimei ga shigoto no buntan o hataseba, seikō o togeru koto ga
dekimasu.*

part and parcel (of something) — 重要な部分 — *jūyō na bubun*
A graduate degree is part and parcel of the qualifications for the job.

大学院の学位は、この仕事の資格として重要な部分です。
Daigakuin no gakui wa, kono shigoto no shikaku to shite jūyō na bubun desu.

parting of the ways — 縁を切る — *en o kiru*
Bill and his sister came to a parting of the ways.
ビルと妹は、縁を切りました。
Biru to imōto wa, en o kirimashita.

---

party — パーティー — *pātī*
The party's over. — 楽しんでいるときが終わる。 — *Tanoshinde iru toki ga owaru.*
We have to get to work now. The party's over. 私達は、仕事に戻らねばなりません。楽しんでいるときは、終わったのです。
Watakushitachi wa, shigoto ni modoraneba narimasen. Tanoshinde iru toki wa owatta no desu.

throw a party — パーティーを催す — *pātī o moyōsu*
Bob's friends threw a party for his graduation. 友達はボブの卒業を祝って、パーティーを催しました。*Tomodachi wa Bobu no sotsugyō o iwatte, pātī o moyōshimashita.*

---

pass — 形勢／通過 — *keisei/tsūka*
come to a pretty pass — 困難な状況を迎える — *konnan na jōkyō o mukaeru*
Things have come to a pretty pass when no one is safe from crime.
誰もが犯罪に脅かされて、困難な状況を迎えています。
Daremo ga hanzai ni obiyakasarete, konnan na jōkyō o mukaete imasu.

make a pass at someone — モーションをかける — *mōshon o kakeru*
He shouldn't have made a pass at his secretary. 彼は、彼の秘書にモーションをかけるべきではありませんでした。*Kare wa, kare no hisho ni mōshon o kakeru beki dewa arimasen deshita.*

---

pasture — 牧場 — *bokujō*
put someone or something out to pasture — 引退させる — *intai saseru*
He can still do good work; it's not time to put him to pasture. 彼はまだいい仕事が出来ます。それで、今は彼を引退させるときでは

ありません。*Kare wa mada ii shigoto ga dekimasu. Sorede, ima wa kare o intai saseru toki dewa arimasen.*

---

pat — 軽くたたくこと — *karuku tataku koto*
  pat on the back — 賞賛 — *shōsan*
  Tom deserves a pat on the back for his good work.　トムは素晴らしい仕事をしたので、賞賛に値します。*Tomu wa subarashii shigoto o shita node, shōsan ni atai shimasu.*

---

path — 道 — *michi*
  beat a path to someone's door — 会いに来る人の絶え間がない — *aini kuru hito no taema ga nai*
  Once he won the election, everyone beat a path to his door.　選挙に勝ってからは、彼に会いに来る人の絶え間がありません。*Senkyo ni katte kara wa, kare ni aini kuru hito no taema ga arimasen.*

  lead someone down the garden path — だます — *damasu*
  It was sad to see her lead her friends down the garden path.　彼女が友達をだますのを見るのは、悲しいことでした。*Kanojo ga tomodachi o damasu no o miru no wa, kanashii koto deshita.*

  path of least resistance — 安易な道 — *an-i na michi*
  She took the path of least resistance and gave in to her daughter's demands.　彼女は安易な道をとって、娘の要求を聞き入れました。*Kanojo wa an-i na michi o totte, musume no yōkyū o kikiiremashita.*

---

patience — 忍耐 — *nintai*
  try someone's patience — 苛立たせる — *iradataseru*
  His uncooperative attitude is trying our patience.　彼の非協力的な態度は、私達を苛立たせています。*Kare no hi kyōryokuteki na taido wa, watakushitachi o iradatasete imasu.*

---

pause — 休止 — *kyūshi*
  give someone pause — ためらわせる — *tamerawaseru*
  The forecast for rain has given us pause about planning a picnic.　雨の天気予報で、ピクニックの計画をためらっています。*Ame no tenki yohō de, pikunikku no keikaku o tameratte imasu.*

---

pavement — 舗道 — *hodō*

pound the pavement — 歩き回る — *arukimawaru*
To find a job these days, you may have to pound the pavement for months.
仕事を見つけるには、近頃はせっせと歩き回らねばならないかも
しれません。*Shigoto o mitsukeru niwa, chikagoro wa sesse to
arukimawaraneba naranai kamo shiremasen.*

peace — 平和 — *heiwa*
　hold one's peace — 口を閉じる — *kuchi o tojiru*
When you're angry, it's sometimes best to hold your peace.
怒っているときには、口を閉じるのが場合によっては最上の
策です。*Okotte iru toki ni wa, kuchi o tojiru no ga baai ni yotte wa
saijō no saku desu.*

peanut — 南京豆 — *nankinmame*
　for peanuts — はした金のために — *hashitagane no tame ni*
Even if he's desperate, he won't work for peanuts.　彼はたとえ困りに
困っていても、はした金のためには働きません。*Kare wa tatoe
komarini komatte itemo, hashitagane no tame ni wa hatarakimasen.*

pearl — 真珠 — *shinju*
　cast (one's) pearls before swine — 猫に小判 — *neko ni koban*
Serving them fine wine is like casting pearls before swine.　あの人達に
素晴らしいワインを出すのは、猫に小判のようなものです。*Ano*

hitotachi ni subarashii wain o dasu no wa, neko ni koban no yō na mono desu.

pearls of wisdom — ごもっともな説 — *gomottomo na setsu*
I wonder what pearls of wisdom the speaker will share with us tonight.
今晩は、あの講演者がどんなごもっともな説を披露するか
いぶかっています。 *Konban wa, ano kōensha ga donna gomottomo na setsu o hirō suru ka ibukatte imasu.*

pebble — 小石 — *koishi*
not the only pebble on the beach — 単なる一人に過ぎない — *tan naru hitori ni suginai*
Don't worry about what he thinks; he's not the only pebble on the beach.
彼が何を考えているか、気にする必要はありません。彼は、単なる
一人に過ぎないんですから。 *Kare ga nani o kangaete iru ka, ki ni suru hitsuyō wa arimasen. Kare wa, tan naru hitori ni suginaindesu kara.*

pedestal — 台座 — *daiza*
put someone on a pedestal — あがめる — *agameru*
She put her son on a pedestal and ignored all his shortcomings. 彼女は
息子をあがめて、彼の欠点を全て無視しました。 *Kanojo wa musuko o agamete, kare no ketten o mushi shimashita.*

peep — ぴーぴーいう鳴き声 — *pīpī iu nakigoe*
hear a peep out of someone — ささやきを聞く — *sasayaki o kiku*
After the children went to bed, we didn't hear a peep out of them.
子供たちが寝た後、私達はささやきさえ聞きませんでした。
Kodomotachi ga neta ato, watakushitachi wa sasayaki sae kikimasen deshita.

peg — 木栓 — *mokusen*
square peg in a round hole — そりが合わない — *sori ga awanai*
Among his colleagues, he's a square peg in a round hole. 彼は、同僚と
そりが合いません。 *Kare wa, dōryō to sori ga aimasen.*

take someone down a peg — 鼻をへし折る — *hana o heshioru*
That pitcher is so arrogant, but our team took him down a peg. あの投手は
実に高慢ですが、私達のチームは彼の鼻をへし折ってやりました。

Ano tōshu wa jitsu ni kōman desu ga, watakushitachi no chīmu wa kare no hana o heshiotte yarimashita.

penny — 一セント硬貨 — *issento kōka*
A penny for your thoughts. — 何をぼんやり考えているのか。 — *Nani o bon-yari kangaete iru no ka.*
You've been so quiet. A penny for your thoughts. あなたはさっきから とても静かですが、何をぼんやり考えているのですか。*Anata wa sakki kara totemo shizuka desu ga, nani o bon-yari kangaete iru no desu ka.*
A penny saved is a penny earned. — 節約したお金は、稼いだお金と 同じ。 — *Setsuyaku shita okane wa, kaseida okane to onaji.*
She likes bargain sales. A penny saved is a penny earned.
彼女は、バーゲンセールが好きです。節約したお金は、稼いだお金と 同じと思っているからです。*Kanojo wa, bāgen sēru ga suki desu. Setsuyaku shita okane wa, kaseida okane to onaji to omotte iru kara desu.*

cost someone a pretty penny — そうとうする — *sōtō suru*
I'm sure that outfit cost her a pretty penny. 彼女の服装がそうとうした のは確実です。*Kanojo no fukusō ga sōtō shita no wa kakujitsu desu.*

cut someone off without a penny/cent — 小遣いをあげるのを止める — *kozukai o ageru no o yameru*
Mary was forced to work when her mother cut her off without a penny.
お母さんはメリーにお小遣いをあげるのを止めたので、彼女は 働かなければなりませんでした。*Okāsan wa Merī ni okozukai o ageru no o yameta node, kanojo wa hatarakanakereba narimasen deshita.*

penny wise and pound foolish — 一文惜しんで大金を失う — *ichi mon oshinde taikin o ushinau*
To save money, he avoids dental checkups. He's penny wise and pound foolish. 彼はお金を節約するために、歯の定期検査を避けています。 彼は一文惜しんで、大金を失うことになるでしょう。*Kare wa okane o setsuyaku suru tame ni, ha no teiki kensa o sakete imasu. Kare wa ichi mon oshinde, taikin o ushinau koto ni naru deshō.*

pinch pennies — 大節約をする — *dai setsuyaku o suru*

He's pinching pennies to save money for his college tuition. 彼は大学の
学費をためるために、大節約をしています。 *Kare wa daigaku no
gakuhi o tameru tame ni, dai setsuyaku o shite imasu.*

---

perish — 消え去る — *kiesaru*
  Perish the thought. — そんなことは、思ってもみたくない。 —
  Sonna koto wa, omottemo mitaku nai.
  He's running for election? Perish the thought. 彼が選挙に出馬
  するんだって。そんなことは、思ってもみたくありません。
  *Kare ga senkyo ni shutsuba surundatte. Sonna koto wa, omottemo
  mitaku arimasen.*

---

person — 人 — *hito*
  feel like a new person — 生き返ったような気がする — *ikikaetta yō na
  ki ga suru*
  After a good night's sleep, you'll feel like a new person. 一晩ぐっすり
  寝た後は、生き返ったような気がするでしょう。*Hitoban gussuri
  neta ato wa, ikikaetta yō na ki ga suru deshō.*

Peter — ピーター — *pītā*
  rob Peter to pay Paul — 借金を借金で穴埋めする — *shakkin o
  shakkin de anaume suru*
  If you borrow money to pay your bills, you're robbing Peter to pay Paul.
  請求書の支払いにお金を借りるのは、借金を借金で穴埋めして
  いることですよ。*Seikyūsho no shiharai ni okane o kariru no wa,
  shakkin o shakkin de anaume shite iru koto desu yo.*

---

pick — 突く／選ぶ — *tsuku/erabu*
  pick on someone — あら探しをする — *arasagashi o suru*
  Whenever he's in a bad mood, he starts picking on his sister. 彼は機嫌が
  悪いときはいつも、妹のあら探しを始めます。*Kare wa kigen ga
  warui toki wa itsumo, imōto no arasagashi o hajimemasu.*

  picked over — 売り切れて — *urikirete*
  If we're late to the sale, everything will be picked over. 特売に
  行き遅れると、残らず売り切れているでしょう。*Tokubai ni
  ikiokureru to, nokorazu urikirete iru deshō.*

pickle — 漬け物 — *tsukemono*

in a pickle — 困って — *komatte*
John is in a pickle; he's lost his keys. ジョンは、かぎを無くして
困っています。*Jon wa, kagi o nakushite komatte imasu.*

---

pie — パイ — *pai*
  (as) easy as (apple) pie — 朝飯前 — *asameshi mae*
  Passing the test was easy as pie.
  試験に合格するのは、朝飯前でした。
  Shiken ni gōkaku suru no wa, asameshi mae deshita.

  eat humble pie — 屈辱に甘んじる — *kutsujoku ni amanjiru*
  When we beat the top-rated team, they had to eat humble pie. 私達が
  最強チームを破って、相手は屈辱に甘んじなければなりません
  でした。*Watakushitachi ga saikyō chīmu o yabutte, aite wa kutsujoku
  ni amanjinakereba narimasen deshita.*

  pie in the sky — 絵空事 — *esoragoto*
  Their plan to build a swimming pool is just pie in the sky. 彼等のプールを
  作ろうとする計画は、絵空事に過ぎません。*Karera no pūru o
  tsukurō to suru keikaku wa, esoragoto ni sugimasen.*

---

piece — 一部分 — *ichi bubun*
  conversation piece — 話の種 — *hanashi no tane*
  His antique Japanese sword is a real conversation piece. 彼の骨董品の

日本刀は、話の種として正に格好です。Kare no kottōhin no
Nihontō wa, hanashi no tane toshite masa ni kakkō desu.

give someone a piece of one's mind — 大目玉を食わせる — ōmedama
o kuwaseru

If he's late again today, I'm going to give him a piece of my mind.　今日も
また彼が遅刻するなら、大目玉を食わせるつもりです。Kyō mo
mata kare ga chikoku suru nara, ōmedama o kuwaseru tsumori desu.

go to pieces — 我を忘れる — ware o wasureru

They went to pieces at the news of their friend's sudden death.　友達の
突然の死の知らせに、彼等は我を忘れました。Tomodachi no
totsuzen no shi no shirase ni, karera wa ware o wasuremashita.

piece of cake — 朝飯前 — asameshi mae

I'll finish this report for you soon; it's a piece of cake.　この報告書は、
すぐに終わらせます。そんなこと、朝飯前ですから。Kono
hōkokusho wa, sugu ni owarasemasu. Sonna koto, asameshi mae desu
kara.

piece of the action — 関わり — kakawari

He just bought a new restaurant, and he's giving his son a piece of the
action.　彼は最近レストランを買って、息子にも関わりを持たせる
つもりです。Kare wa saikin resutoran o katte, musuko nimo kakawari
o motaseru tsumori desu.

thrilled to pieces — 足が地に着かない — ashi ga chi ni tsukanai

They were thrilled to pieces at the results of the election.　彼等は選挙の
結果を知って、地に足が着きませんでした。Karera wa senkyo no
kekka o shitte, chi ni ashi ga tsukimasen deshita.

say/speak one's piece — 心の内をさらけ出す — kokoro no uchi o
sarakedasu

John felt better after he had said his piece during the meeting.　会議で
心の内をさらけ出して、ジョンはすっきりした思いをしました。
Kaigi de kokoro no uchi o sarakedashite, Jon wa sukkiri shita omoi o
shimashita.

pig — 豚 — buta

buy a pig in a poke — 実物を見もせずに買う — jitsubutsu o mi mo
sezu ni kau

Before you make an offer, go see the car; don't buy a pig in a poke.　払う
用意がある値段を言ってしまう前に、車を見に行きなさい。
実物を見もせずに買うべきではありません。*Harau yōi ga aru
nedan o itte shimau mae ni, kuruma o mi ni ikinasai. Jitsubutsu o mi mo
sezu ni, kau beki dewa arimasen.*

pig out — たらふく食べる — *tarafuku taberu*
As usual, everyone pigged out at Thanksgiving dinner.　いつもながら、
感謝祭には誰もがたらふく食べました。*Itsumo nagara, kanshasai
niwa daremo ga tarafuku tabemashita.*

---

pill — 丸薬 — *gan-yaku*
bitter pill to swallow — 受け入れがたい — *ukeiregatai*
The cutbacks in government funding are a bitter pill to swallow.　政府の
基金削減は、受け入れがたいです。*Seifu no kikin sakugen wa,
ukeiregatai desu.*

---

pillar — 柱 — *hashira*
from pillar to post — 転々と — *tenten to*
Rather than move his children from pillar to post, he sent them to boarding
school.　彼は子供たちを転々と移動させる代わりに、寄宿舎の
ある学校に入れました。*Kare wa kodomotachi o tenten to idō saseru
kawari ni, kishukusha no aru gakkō ni iremashita.*

---

pin — 針 — *hari*
on pins and needles — 気を揉んで — *ki o monde*
Everyone was on pins and needles waiting for the verdict.　誰もが判決を
待ちながら、気を揉んでいました。*Daremo ga hanketsu o
machinagara, ki o monde imashita.*

pin someone down — はっきりさせる — *hakkiri saseru*
We need a decision from him, but we can't pin him down.　私達は彼の
決断がいるのですが、彼をはっきりさせることが出来ません。
*Watakushitachi wa kare no ketsudan ga iru no desu ga, kare o hakkiri
saseru koto ga dekimasen.*

pin something on someone — 濡れ衣を着せる — *nureginu o kiseru*
Don't try to pin the blame on others.　他人に非難の濡れ衣を着せない
ようにしなさい。*Tanin ni hinan no nureginu o kisenai yō ni shinasai.*

so quiet you could hear a pin drop — 水を打ったように静か — mizu
o utta yō ni shizuka

Before the verdict was announced, it was so quiet you could hear a pin
drop.　判決の宣告がある前は、水を打ったように静かでした。
Hanketsu no senkoku ga aru mae wa, mizu o utta yō ni shizuka deshita.

pinch — 困難 — konnan

in a pinch — 差し迫った場合には — sashisematta baai niwa

I don't like this kind of paper, but it will do in a pinch.　この種の紙は好き
ではありませんが、差し迫った場合にはこれでも間に合います。
Kono shu no kami wa suki dewa arimasen ga, sashisematta baai ni wa
kore demo maniaimasu.

pinch-hit (for someone) — 代役を務める — daiyaku o tsutomeru

Can you pinch-hit for John Doe today? He's out sick.　今日は、ジョン・
ドウの代役を務めてくれますか。彼は、病気で休んでいます。
Kyō wa, Jon Dō no daiyaku o tsutomete kuremasen ka. Kare wa, byōki
de yasunde imasu.

pink — ピンク — pinku

in the pink — 元気があふれて — genki ga afurete

After his workout, he felt in the pink.　彼は体を鍛える体操をした後、
元気があふれるのを感じました。Kare wa karada o kitaeru taisō o
shita ato, genki ga afureru no o kanjimashita.

pipe — 歌う／パイプ — utau/paipu

pipe down — 静かにする — shizuka ni suru

Please pipe down in there! We can't concentrate.　そこの人、静かにして。
こっちは集中できないから。Soko no hito, shizuka ni shite. Kotchi
wa shūchū dekinai kara.

pipe up — はっきり述べる — hakkiri noberu

She amazed them by piping up with a suggestion during the meeting.
彼女が会議ではっきり提案して、彼等の目を見張らせました。
Kanojo ga kaigi de hakkiri teian shite, karera no me o miharasemashita.

Put that in your pipe and smoke it! — そのつもりでいなさい。 —
Sono tsumori de inasai.

I don't agree, and you can put that in your pipe and smoke it!　私は賛成

できないから、そのつもりでいなさい。Watakushi wa sansei
dekinai kara, sono tsumori de inasai.

---

piper — 笛吹き — fue fuki
　pay the piper — 報いが来る — mukui ga kuru
　If you don't invest wisely, you'll have to pay the piper some day.　賢明に
　投資しないと、いつかその報いが来るでしょう。Kenmei ni tōshi
　shinai to, itsuka sono mukui ga kuru deshō.

---

pit — 穴 — ana
　the pits — 最低 — saitei
　John says his job is the pits.
　ジョンは、彼の仕事は最低だと言っています。
　Jon wa, kare no shigoto wa saitei da to itte imasu.

---

pitch — 調子／投げる — chōshi/nageru
　make a pitch for someone or something — 売り込む — urikomu
　The company is making a big pitch for its new product.　その会社は、
　新製品をしきりに売り込んでいます。Sono kaisha wa, shin seihin o
　shikiri ni urikonde imasu.

　pitch in — 目的達成のために貢献する — mokuteki tassei no tame ni
　kōken suru
　To meet the deadline, everyone must pitch in and help.　締め切りに
　間に合わせるためには、誰もが貢献して手助けすべきです。
　Shimekiri ni maniawaseru tame ni wa, daremo ga kōken shite tedasuke
　subeki desu.

---

place — 場所 — basho
　fall in/into place — 型をなす — kata o nasu
　The pieces of the plan are all falling into place.
　その計画は、いずこも型をなしてきています。
　Sono keikaku wa, izuko mo kata o nashite kite imasu.

　feel out of place — 場違いな気がする — bachigai na ki ga suru
　He usually feels out of place at large parties.　彼は大きなパーティーでは、
　いつも場違いな気がします。Kare wa ōkina pātī dewa, itsumo
　bachigai na ki ga shimasu.

in the wrong place at the wrong time — 巻き添えを食つて — *makizoe o kutte*

The innocent victim was in the wrong place at the wrong time. 無実の被害者は、巻き添えを食つたのです。*Mujitsu no higaisha wa, makizoe o kutta no desu.*

know one's place — 身の程をわきまえる — *minohodo o wakimaeru*

As a new employee, Joe should be more reserved. He doesn't know his place. ジョーは新入社員として、もっと控え目にするべきです。彼は、身の程をわきまえません。*Jō wa shinnyū shain toshite, motto hikaeme ni suru beki desu. Kare wa, minohodo o wakimaemasen.*

put one in one's place — 身の程を思い知らせる — *minohodo o omoishiraseru*

If you boast too much, the coach will put you in your place. あまり自慢しすぎると、コーチはあなたに身の程を思い知らせるでしょう。*Amari jiman shisugiru to, kōchi wa anata ni minohodo o omoishiraseru deshō.*

put oneself in someone else's place/shoes — 人の立場に立ってみる — *hito no tachiba ni tatte miru*

Put yourself in John's place, and you'll stop criticizing him. あなたもジョーの立場に立ってみれば、彼を批判するのを止めるでしょう。*Anata mo Jō no tachiba ni tatte mireba, kare o hihan suru no o yameru deshō.*

---

plague — 伝染病 — *densenbyō*

avoid someone or something like the plague — バイ菌のように避ける — *baikin no yō ni sakeru*

Since his illness, he avoids alcohol like the plague. 彼は病気以来、酒類をバイ菌のように避けています。*Kare wa byōki irai, sakerui o baikin no yō ni sakete imasu.*

---

plan — 計画 — *keikaku*

best-laid plans/schemes of mice and men — 練りに練った計画 — *nerini netta keikaku*

When his business failed, he knew the best laid plans of mice and men can go astray. 彼は事業が失敗したとき、練りに練った計画でさえうまくいかないことがあるのを学びました。*Kare wa jigyō ga*

*shippai shita toki, nerini netta keikaku de sae umaku ikanai koto ga aru
no o manabimashita.*

play — 遊び／遊ぶ／演じる — *asobi/asobu/enjiru*

make a play (for someone) — 口説こうとする — *kudokō to suru*
Although he made a play for her, he wasn't successful.　彼は彼女を
口説こうとしましたが、うまくいきませんでした。*Kare wa
kanojo o kudokō to shimashita ga, umaku ikimasen deshita.*

play fast and loose with someone or something — いい加減にする —
iikagen ni suru
John was fired for playing fast and loose with the truth.　ジョンは事実を
いい加減にして当てにならないので、首になりました。*Jon wa
jijitsu o iikagen ni shite ate ni naranai node, kubi ni narimashita.*

play for keeps — いつまでも続ける — *itsu made mo tsuzukeru*
When he gets married, he'll play for keeps.　彼は一度結婚したら、
いつまでも続けるつもりです。*Kare wa ichido kekkon shitara, itsu
made mo tsuzukeru tsumori desu.*

play hard to get — 気のなさそうな振りをする — *ki no nasasō na furi
o suru*
When Jane pursued Jim, he played hard to get.　ジェーンが彼に
付き合いを求めたとき、彼は気のなさそうな振りをしました。
*Jēn ga kare ni tsukiai o motometa toki, kare wa ki no nasasō na furi o
shimashita.*

play (it) safe — 大事をとる — *daiji o toru*
Let's play it safe and get flu shots this year.　大事をとって、今年は
流感の予防注射を受けましょう。*Daiji o totte, kotoshi wa ryūkan no
yobō chūsha o ukemashō.*

play out — 結末をもたらす — *ketsumatsu o motarasu*
They don't know how the negotiations will play out.　彼等は、交渉が
どの様な結末をもたらすか分かりません。*Karera wa, kōshō ga
dono yō na ketsumatsu o motarasu ka wakarimasen.*

play up to someone — おべっかを使う — *obekka o tsukau*
She's always playing up to the teacher.　彼女はいつも、先生に
おべっかを使っています。*Kanojo wa itsumo, sensei ni obekka o
tsukatte imasu.*

plea — 嘆願 — *tangan*
  cop a plea — 罪を認める — *tsumi o mitomeru*
  If he cops a plea, he'll get a lighter sentence.   もし彼が罪を認めるなら、刑が軽くなるでしょう。 *Moshi kare ga tsumi o mitomeru nara, kei ga karuku naru deshō.*

---

please — 喜ばせる — *yorokobaseru*
  You can't please everyone. — 誰もかも満足させるのは無理。 — *Dare mo ka mo manzoku saseru no wa muri.*
  She doesn't like our new computers? You can't please everyone.   彼女は、私達の新しいコンピュ－タが気に入らないんですか。誰もかも満足させるのは無理ですね。 *Kanojo wa, watakushitachi no atarashii konpyūta ga ki ni iranaindesu ka. Dare mo ka mo manzoku saseru no wa muri desu ne.*

---

plot — 筋 — *suji*
  The plot thickens. — 事が面白くなりそうだ。 — *Koto ga omoshiroku narisō da.*
  John and his wife are taking separate vacations? The plot thickens. ジョンと奥さんのバカンスは、別々なんですか。事が面白くなりそうですね。 *Jon to okusan no bakansu wa, betsubetsu nan desu ka. Koto ga omoshiroku narisō desu ne.*

---

pocket — ポケット — *poketto*
  have someone in one's pocket — 言いなりにする — *iinari ni suru*
  She'll do anything he says; he has her in his pocket.   彼女は、彼の言うことは何でもします。彼は、彼女を言いなりにしているのです。 *Kanojo wa, kare no iu koto wa nandemo shimasu. Kare wa, kanojo o iinari ni shite iru no desu.*

  line one's own pockets — 私腹を肥やす — *shifuku o koyasu*
  The city treasurer is lining his own pockets with our tax money.   市の出納局長は、我々の納税金で私腹を肥やしています。 *Shi no suitō kyokuchō wa, wareware no zeikin de shifuku o koyashite imasu.*

---

point 点 *ten*
  have a low boiling point — 気が短い — *ki ga mijikai*

John gets furious at every little thing; he has a low boiling point.　ジョンは
気が短くて、ちょっとしたことでもすぐに怒りだします。*Jon wa
ki ga mijikakute, chotto shita koto demo sugu ni okoridashimasu.*

jumping-off point — 出発点 — *shuppatsu ten*
Working as a law clerk is a good jumping-off point for a law student.
法廷の書記として働くのは、法律を勉強している学生にはいい
出発点です。*Hōtei no shoki toshite hataraku no wa, hōritsu o benkyō
shite iru gakusei ni wa ii shuppatsu ten desu.*

make points — 気に入られる — *ki ni irareru*
Jim always stays after school trying to make points with the teacher.
ジムは先生に気に入られようとして、授業の後いつも残っています。
Jimu wa sensei ni ki ni irareyō to shite, jugyō no ato itsumo nokotte imasu.

sore point — 苦い点 — *nigai ten*
The trade imbalance is a sore point between the two countries.　貿易の
不均衡が、二国間の苦い点です。*Bōeki no fukinkō ga, ni koku kan no
nigai ten desu.*

the point of no return — 引くに引かれぬ所 — *hiku ni hikarenu tokoro*
They can't stop now; the negotiations are at the point of no return.　交渉は
引くに引かれぬ所に来ているので、彼等は今さら止められません。
*Kōshō wa hiku ni hikarenu tokoro ni kite iru node, karera wa imasara
yameraremasen.*

---

pole — 極／棒 — *kyoku/bō*

poles apart — 極端に違って — *kyokutan ni chigatte*
The two sides in the negotiations are still poles apart.　交渉で、双方の
立場はいまだに極端に違っています。*Kōshō de, sōhō no tachiba wa
imada ni kyokutan ni chigatte imasu.*

wouldn't touch something with a ten-foot pole — 絶対に触れない —
zettai ni furenai
I wouldn't touch that issue with a ten-foot pole.　私は、その問題に
ついては絶対に触れません。*Watakushi wa, sono mondai ni tsuite wa
zettai ni furemasen.*

---

polish — 磨く — *migaku*

polish something off — さっさと平らげる — *sassa to tairageru*

After dinner, he polished off the leftovers.　夕食が済んでから、彼は残り物をさっさと平らげました。 *Yūshoku ga sunde kara, kare wa nokorimono o sassa to tairagemashita.*

---

port — 港 — *minato*
any port in a storm — 窮余の一策 — *kyūyo no issaku*
She doesn't like her job, but any port in a storm.
彼女は今の仕事が好きではありませんが、それも窮余の一策です。
Kanojo wa ima no shigoto ga suki dewa arimasen ga, sore mo kyūyo no issaku desu.

---

position — 地位 — *chii*
jockey for position — 昇進のために人を出し抜こうとする — *shōshin no tame ni hito o dashinukō to suru*
The employees are all jockeying for position.　社員はみんな、昇進のために人を出し抜こうとしています。 *Shain wa minna, shōshin no tame ni hito o dashimukō to shite imasu.*

---

possum — 袋ネズミ — *fukuronezumi*
play possum — 目立たないようにじっとする／眠っている振りをする — *medatanai yō ni jitto suru/nemutte iru furi o suru*
Bob knows the answer, but he's playing possum.　ボブは答えを知っているのですが、目立たないようにじっとしています。 *Bobu wa kotae o shitte iru no desu ga, medatanai yō ni jitto shite imasu.*

---

pot — 鍋 — *nabe*
go to pot — だめになる — *dame ni naru*
Since he won't work outdoors in the heat, his garden is going to pot.
彼は暑いときには外で働こうとしないので、庭は駄目になってきています。 *Kare wa atsui toki niwa soto de hatarakō to shinai node, niwa wa dame ni natte kite imasu.*

the pot calling the kettle black — 目糞、鼻糞を笑う — *mekuso hanakuso o warau*
The mayor said his opponent was dishonest; that's the pot calling the kettle black.　市長は彼の敵が不正直だと言っていますが、それは目糞が鼻糞を笑うようなものです。 *Shichō wa kare no seiteki ga*

*fushōjiki da to itte imasu ga, sore wa mekuso ga hanakuso o warau yō
na mono desu.*

potato — じゃがいも — *jagaimo*
  hot potato — 取り扱いが難しい課題 — *toriatsukai ga muzukashii
  kadai*
  The tax issue is a hot potato in our city.　税金問題は、この市では
  取り扱いが難しい課題です。*Zeikin mondai wa, kono shi dewa
  toriatsukai ga muzukashii kadai desu.*

pour — 注ぐ — *sosogu*
  pour/lay it on thick — おべっかを使う — *obekka o tsukau*
  He really poured it on thick when he called the boss a genius.　彼は
  上役が天才だと言って、おべっかを使いました。*Kare wa uwayaku
  ga tensai da to itte, obekka o tsukaimashita.*

powder — 粉 — *kona*
  take a powder — ずらかる — *zurakaru*
  When it was time for the exam, Bill took a powder.　いざ試験を受ける
  ときになったら、ビルはずらかってしまいました。*Iza shiken o
  ukeru toki ni nattara, Biru wa zurakatte shimaimashita.*

power — 権力 — *kenryoku*
  power behind the throne — 黒幕 — *kuromaku*
  The company chairman's wife is the power behind the throne.　その会社
  では、会長の奥さんが黒幕です。*Sono kaisha dewa, kaichō no
  okusan ga kuromaku desu.*

  powers that be — お偉方 — *oeragata*
  The powers that be have decided on longer work hours for our employees.
  お偉方は、社員の勤務時間を増やすことに決めました。*Oeragata
  wa, shain no kinmu jikan o fuyasu koto ni kimemashita.*

practice — 実行 — *jikkō*
  practice what one preaches — 自らの言葉を守る — *mizukara no
  kotoba o mamoru*
  Although he smokes, he tells others not to; he should practice what he

preaches. 彼はタバコを吸いながら、人には吸わないように言っています。彼は、自らの言葉を守るべきです。*Kare wa tabako o suinagara, hito ni wa suwanai yō ni itte imasu. Kare wa, mizukara no kotoba o mamoru beki desu.*

praise — 賞賛 — *shōsan*

damn someone or something with faint praise — 心にもない誉め言葉でけなす — *kokoro nimo nai homekotoba de kenasu*
John damned the applicant with faint praise, calling him "very nice."
ジョンは志願者にとてもいいと言って、心にもない誉め言葉でけなしました。*Jon wa shigansha ni totemo ii to itte, kokoro nimo nai homekotoba de kenashimashita.*

sing someone's praises — ほめちぎる — *homechigiru*
She sang the praises of the new secretary.
彼女は、新しい秘書をほめちぎりました。
Kanojo wa, atarashii hisho o homechigirimashita.

pride — 誇り — *hokori*

burst with pride — 誇りに満ちあふれる — *hokori ni michiafureru*
His wife was bursting with pride when Jim graduated from medical school.
ジムが医大を卒業したとき、彼の奥さんは誇りに満ちあふれました。
Jimu ga idai o sotsugyō shita toki, kare no okusan wa hokori ni michiafuremashita.

pride and joy — 誇りの種 — *hokori no tane*
Their son is their pride and joy. 息子は、彼等の誇りの種です。
Musuko wa, karera no hokori no tane desu.

Pride goes before a fall. — 驕れる者久しからず。 — *Ogoreru mono hisashikarazu.*
He bragged of his success, then he went bankrupt. Pride goes before a fall.
彼は自分の成功に鼻高々でしたが、その後、破産してしまいました。驕れる者久しからず。*Kare wa jibun no seikō ni hana takadaka deshita ga, sono go, hasan shite shimaimashita. Ogoreru mono hisashikarazu.*

swallow one's pride — 恥を忍ぶ — *haji o shinobu*
I swallowed my pride and apologized for my outburst of anger. 私は恥を忍んで、怒りを爆発させてしまったことを謝りました。*Watakushi*

wa haji o shinonde, ikari o bakuhatsu sasete shimatta koto o
ayamarimashita.

---

prime — 全盛 — *zensei*

in the prime of life — 人生の盛り — *jinsei no sakari*
When he won the election, he was in the prime of life.　選挙に勝つとき、
彼は人生の盛りにいました。*Senkyo ni katta toki, kare wa jinsei no*
sakari ni imashita.

past someone's or something's prime — 盛りを過ぎる — *sakari o*
sugiru
He's a fine actor, but he's past his prime.　彼は素晴らしい俳優でしたが、
今は盛りを過ぎました。*Kare wa subarashii haiyū deshita ga, ima wa*
sakari o sugimashita.

---

promise — 約束 — *yakusoku*
empty promise — 果たせもせぬ約束 — *hatasemo senu yakusoku*
Don't be misled by someone who makes empty promises.　果たせもせぬ
約束をする人に惑わされないように。*Hatasemo senu yakusoku o*
suru hito ni madowasarenai yō ni.

---

proof — 証拠 — *shōko*
proof of the pudding is in the eating — 試してみないと分からない —
tameshite minai to wakaranai
Test drive the car before you buy it; the proof of the pudding is in the
eating.　車は、買う前に試運転しなさい。試してみないと
分からないものですからね。*Kuruma wa, kau mae ni shiunten*
shinasai. Tameshite minai to wakaranai mono desu kara ne.

---

prop — 支柱 — *shichū*
knock the props out from under someone — 人の自信／心の
よりどころ／財源を破滅させる — *hito no jishin/kokoro no*
yoridokoro/zaigen o hametsu saseru
The layoffs knocked the props out from under the factory workers.
一時解雇は、工場の従業員の財源を破滅させました。
Ichiji kaiko wa, kōjō no jūgyōin no zaigen o hametsu sasemashita.

proportion — 割合 — *wariai*
  blow something out of all proportion — 大げさに騒ぎ立てる — *ōgesa ni sawagitateru*
  The media blew the issue out of all proportion.　マスコミは、その問題を大げさに騒ぎ立てました。*Masukomi wa, sono mondai o ōgesa ni sawagitatemashita.*

---

psych — 心を動揺させる — *kokoro o dōyō saseru*
  psych someone out — 腹を探る — *hara o saguru*
  He tried to psych his counterpart out before the negotiations.　彼は交渉の前に、相手の腹を探ろうとしました。*Kare wa kōshō no mae ni, aite no hara o sagurō to shimashita.*

  psych someone up — 心を奮い立たせる — *kokoro o furuitataseru*
  I had to psych myself up before the exam.　私は試験の前に、自らの心を奮い立たさなければなりませんでした。*Watakushi wa shiken no mae ni, mizukara no kokoro o furuitatasanakereba narimasen deshita.*

  psyched up (for something) — 奮い立って — *furuitatte*
  The team is psyched up for the game.　チームは試合の前に奮い立っています。*Chīmu wa shiai no mae ni furuitatte imasu.*

---

pull — 引っ張る力 — *hipparu chikara*
  have pull — 顔がきく — *kao ga kiku*
  Bill always gets a good table; he has a lot of pull in this restaurant.　ビルはこのレストランでは顔がきくので、いつもいいテーブルをもらいます。*Biru wa kono resutoran dewa kao ga kiku node, itsumo ii tēburu o moraimasu.*

  pull oneself together — 気を取り直す — *ki o torinaosu*
  After the funeral we had to pull ourselves together and go back to work. 葬式の後、私達は気を取り直して仕事に戻らなければなりませんでした。*Sōshiki no ato, watakushitachi wa ki o torinaoshite shigoto ni modoranakereba narimasen deshita.*

  pull something off — 成し遂げる — *nashitogeru*
  We met the deadline! I'm glad we could pull it off.　私達は、締め切りに間に合いました。それを成し遂げることが出来て嬉しいです。*Watakushitachi wa, shimekiri ni maniaimashita. Sore o nashitogeru koto ga dekite, ureshii desu.*

pull something on someone — だます — *damasu*
If you're trying to pull something on me, it won't work.　私をだまそうと
しても、うまくいきませんよ。*Watakushi o damasō to shitemo,*
umaku ikimasen yo.

pull something together — うまくまとめる — *umaku matomeru*
Let's have a party soon; I'll see if I can pull something together.　近い
うちに、パーティ-を開きましょう。私がうまくまとめられるか
どうか、やってみます。*Chikai uchi ni, pātī o hirakimashō.*
Watakushi ga umaku matomerareru ka dō ka yatte mimasu.

pull through — 回復する — *kaifuku suru*
He's quite sick now, but he is expected to pull through.　彼は今は重病
ですが、回復する見込みです。*Kare wa ima wa jūbyō desu ga,*
kaifuku suru mikomi desu.

pull together — 協力し合う — *kyōryoku shiau*
If we all pull together, we can get the job done.　もしみんなが協力
し合えば、私達はこの仕事を成し遂げることが出来ます。*Moshi*
minna ga kyōryoku shiaeba, watakushitachi wa kono shigoto o
nashitogeru koto ga dekimasu.

---

punch — パンチ — *panchi*
(as) pleased as punch — 大喜びする — *ōyorokobi suru*
He was as pleased as punch when he was promoted.　彼は昇進を受けて、
大喜びしました。*Kare wa shōshin o ukete, ōyorokobi shimashita.*

beat someone to the punch — 出し抜く — *dashinuku*
He wanted to announce the merger, but the media beat him to the punch.
彼は会社の合併を自分で発表したかったのですが、マスコミに
出し抜かれてしまいました。*Kare wa kaisha no gappei o jibun de*
happyō shitakatta no desu ga, masukomi ni dashinukarete
shimaimashita.

pull any/one's punches — 手加減する — *tekagen suru*
Give me your frank opinion; don't pull any punches.　手加減しないで、
率直な意見を述べてください。*Tekagen shinai de, sotchoku na iken o*
nobete kudasai.

take/throw a punch at someone — 殴りかかる — *nagurikakaru*
The candidate almost took a punch at his opponent during the debate.

候補者は討論中、相手にほとんど殴りかかるところでした。
Kōhosha wa tōron chū, aite ni hotondo nagurikakaru tokoro deshita.

purse — ハンドバッグ — *handobaggu*

make a silk purse out of a sow's ear — もとが悪いのにいいものを
作る — *moto ga warui noni ii mono o tsukuru*
Remodeling that house is useless; you can't make a silk purse out of a
sow's ear. もとが悪いのにいいものを作るのは無理だから、その
家の改築はする価値がありません。*Moto ga warui noni ii mono o
tsukuru no wa muri dakara, sono ie no kaichiku wa suru kachi ga
arimasen.*

push — 押し — *oshi*

if push comes to shove — 事が悪化すれば — *koto ga akka sureba*
If push comes to shove, we can count on Mike. 事が悪化すれば、
私達はマイクを頼りに出来ます。*Koto ga akka sureba,
watakushitachi wa Maiku o tayori ni dekimasu.*

put — 置く — *oku*

put off by someone or something — 胸がむかつく — *mune ga
mukatsuku*
They're put off by his constant bragging. 彼の果てしない自慢に、
彼等は胸がむかついています。*Kare no hateshinai jiman ni, karera
wa mune ga mukatsuite imasu.*

put someone or something down — 見くびる — *mikubiru*
Although she works hard, Mary's boss is always putting her down.
メリーは一生懸命働きますが、上司は彼女を見くびっています。
*Merī wa isshōkenmei hatarakimasu ga, jōshi wa kanojo o mikubitte
imasu.*

put someone on — かつぐ — *katsugu*
You can't mean that; you must be putting me on. 本気じゃないでしょ。
私をかついでいるに違いありません。*Honki ja nai desho. Watakushi
o katsuide iru ni chigai arimasen.*

put something over on someone — 一杯食わす — *ippai kuwasu*
Bob is so gullible; it's easy to put something over on him. ボブはすぐ
真に受けるので、彼に一杯食わすのは簡単です。*Bobu wa sugu ma*

ni ukeru node, kare ni ippai kuwasu no wa kantan desu.

put/set something right — 事を正す — *koto o tadasu*
After their argument, John tried to put things right.　彼等が口論した後、
ジョンは気まずさを正そうとしました。*Karera ga kōron shita ato,*
Jon wa kimazusa o tadasō to shimashita.

put up or shut up — 実行するかこれからは口をつぐむ — *jikkō suru*
ka kore kara wa kuchi o tsugumu
He promised her an engagement ring; he should put up or shut up.　彼は
彼女に婚約指輪を約束したのだから、実行するか、これからは
口をつぐむべきです。*Kare wa kanojo ni kon-yaku yubiwa o*
yakusoku shita no dakara, jikkō suru ka kore kara wa kuchi o tsugumu
beki desu.

put upon — うまく使われる — *umaku tsukawareru*
With all the demands on his time, he's feeling put upon by his coworkers.
彼は時間のかかる頼み事をたくさんされて、同僚にうまく使われて
いるような気がしています。*Kare wa jikan no kakaru tanomigoto o*
takusan sarete, dōryō ni umaku tsukawarete iru yō na ki ga shite imasu.

put up with someone or something — 我慢する — *gaman suru*
The voters are not going to put up with a tax increase.　有権者は、
増税に我慢するつもりはありません。*Yūkensha wa, zōzei ni gaman*
suru tsumori wa arimasen.

---

putty — パテ — *pate*
putty in someone's hands — 言いなりになる — *iinari ni naru*
John is putty in his wife's hands; he does anything she says.　ジョンは
奥さんの言いなりになって、言われることは何でもします。
Jon wa okusan no iinari ni natte, iwareru koto wa nandemo shimasu.

QT — 静か — *shizuka*
on the QT — 秘密に — *himitsu ni*
He agreed to meet with the opposition leaders on the QT.　彼は、野党の

指導者たちと秘密に会うことに同意しました。Kare wa, yatō no shidōshatachi to himitsu ni au koto ni dōi shimashita.

---

quantity — 量 — ryō
unknown quantity — 未知数の人物 — michisū no jinbutsu
The new prime minister is an unknown quantity. 新しい首相は、
未知数の人物です。Atarashii shushō wa, michisū no jinbutsu desu.

---

question — 質問／問題 — shitsumon/mondai
beg the question — まだはっきりせぬものを確かだと見なす —
mada hakkiri senu mono o tashika da to minasu
Stop making plans before you receive approval; you're begging the
question. 許可を受ける前に、計画をたてるのは止めなさい。
あなたは、まだはっきりせぬものを確かだと見なしているのです。
Kyoka o ukeru mae ni, keikaku o tateru no wa yamenasai. Anata wa,
mada hakkiri senu mono o tashika da to minashite iru no desu.

beside the question/point — 問題外 — mondai gai
The issue of funding is beside the point. 資金融資の件は、問題外です。
Shikin yūshi no ken wa, mondai gai desu.

beyond question — 疑いない — utagainai
Our mayor's integrity is beyond question. 我が市の市長の誠実さは、
疑いありません。Waga shi no shichō no seijitsusa wa, utagai
arimasen.

bring/call something into question — 疑いをもたらす — utagai o
motarasu
The scandal brought their judgment into question. スキャンダルは、
彼等の判断力に疑いをもたらしました。Sukyandaru wa, karera no
handanryoku ni utagai o motarashimashita.

out of the question — 不可能 — fukanō
We're so busy that a vacation is out of the question this year. 私達は
とても忙しいので、今年はバカンスは不可能です。Watakushitachi
wa totemo isogashii node, kotoshi wa bakansu wa fukanō desu.

pop the question — 結婚を申し込む — kekkon o mōshikomu
John decided to pop the question to Mary tonight. ジョンは、今晩
メリーに結婚を申し込むことにしました。Jon wa, konban Merī ni

kekkon o mōshikomu koto ni shimashita.

without question — 疑いなく — *utagai naku*
Mother will help us without question.　母は、疑いなく私達を助けて
くれるでしょう。*Haha wa, utagai naku watakushitachi o tasukete
kureru deshō.*

---

quick — 傷口の肉／速い — *kizuguchi no niku/hayai*
cut someone to the quick — 人の感情をひどく傷つける — *hito no
kanjō o hidoku kizutsukeru*
Her sarcastic remarks cut him to the quick.　彼女の皮肉な言葉は、彼を
ひどく傷つけました。*Kanojo no hiniku na kotoba wa, kare o hidoku
kizutsukemashita.*

quick and dirty — 速くていい加減な — *hayakute iikagen na*
Please do the job right; we don't want a quick and dirty solution.　私達は
速くていい加減な解決は望まないので、仕事はしっかりやって
下さい。*Watakushitachi wa hayakute iikagen na kaiketsu wa
nozomanai node, shigoto wa shikkari yatte kudasai.*

---

quit — やめる — *yameru*
call it quits — 終わりにする — *owari ni suru*
It's 6 o'clock, time to call it quits for today.　六時だから、今日は
これで終わりにする時間です。*Roku ji dakara, kyō wa kore de owari
ni suru jikan desu.*

race — 競争 — *kyōsō*

rat race — 神経をすり減らす仕事上の競争 — *shinkei o suriherasu shigoto jō no kyōsō*

He's ready to retire and leave the rat race.　彼は、引退して神経を
すり減らす仕事上の競争を止める心積もりです。*Kare wa, intai
shite shinkei o suriherasu shigoto jō no kyōsō o yameru kokorozumori desu.*

run the good race — 最善を尽くす — *saizen o tsukusu*

I admire Peter; he's always run the good race.　ピーターはいつも最善を
尽くすので、彼を敬服しています。*Pītā wa itsumo saizen o tsukusu
node, kare o keifuku shite imasu.*

Slow and steady wins the race. — 急がば回れ。 — *Isogaba maware.*

After years of hard work, he's successful. Slow and steady wins the race.
彼は何年も一生懸命働いた後で成功しました。急がば回れは本当
です。*Kare wa nannen mo isshōkenmei hataraita ato de seikō
shimashita. Isogaba maware wa hontō desu.*

rack 破壊 *hakai*

go to rack and ruin — 荒れ果てる — *arehateru*

Their summer cabin is going to rack and ruin.　彼等の避暑用の山小屋は、

荒れ果てようとしています。*Karera no hisho yō no yamagoya wa, arehateyō to shite imasu.*

rag — ぼろ切れ — *borogire*
chew the rag — だべる — *daberu*
We should have been working instead of sitting around chewing the rag.
私達は腰を下ろしてだべっているよりも、働いているべきでした。
Watakushitachi wa koshi o oroshite dabette iru yori mo, hataraite iru beki deshita.

from rags to riches — 貧乏人から金持ちに — *binbōnin kara kanemochi ni*
The winner of the lottery went from rags to riches in minutes. 宝くじの当選者は、あっと言う間に貧乏人から金持ちになりました。
Takarakuji no tōsensha wa, atto iu ma ni binbōnin kara kanemochi ni narimashita.

in rags — ぼろを着て — *boro o kite*
Now that she has a job, she can't walk around in rags anymore. 彼女は今は職があるので、最早ぼろを着て歩き回るわけにはいきません。
Kanojo wa ima wa shoku ga aru node, mohaya boro o kite arukimawaru wake ni wa ikimasen.

rag trade — ファッション業界 — *fasshon gyōkai*
Tom enjoys his work as a designer in the rag trade. トムは、ファッション業界でデザイナーとしての仕事を楽しんでいます。*Tomu wa, fasshon gyōkai de dezainā toshite no shigoto o tanoshinde imasu.*

rage — 熱望 — *netsubō*
all the rage — 大人気 — *dai ninki*
Japanese food is all the rage in the United States now. 日本料理は、今アメリカで大流行です。*Nihon ryōri wa, ima Amerika de dai ryūkō desu.*

rain — 雨 — *ame*
be rained out — 雨天中止 — *uten chūshi*
The picnic was rained out yesterday. 昨日、ピクニックは雨天中止になりました。*Kinō, pikunikku wa uten chūshi ni narimashita.*
(as) right as rain — 正にその通り — *masa ni sono tōri*

Her argument was as right as rain.　彼女の議論は、正にその通り
でした。*Kanojo no giron wa, masa ni sono tōri deshita.*

It never rains but it pours. — 泣きっ面に蜂 — *nakittsura ni hachi*
I've lost my wallet, and now the car won't start. It never rains but it pours.
財布を無くした後、今度は車のエンジンがかかりません。全く、
泣きっ面に蜂です。*Saifu o nakushita ato, kondo wa kuruma no enjin
ga kakarimasen. Mattaku, nakittsura ni hachi desu.*

rain or shine — 降っても照っても — *futtemo tettemo*
The party will take place rain or shine.　パーティーは、降っても
照っても行われます。*Pātī wa, futtemo tettemo okonawaremasu.*

---

rally — 集中する — *shūchū suru*
  rally (a)round someone or something — 助けに駆けつける — *tasuke
ni kaketsukeru*
When John became seriously ill, his friends all rallied round to help.
ジョンが重病になったとき、友達が助けに駆けつけました。
Jon ga jūbyō ni natta toki, tomodachi ga tasuke ni kaketsukemashita.

---

ramble — ぶらつく — *buratsuku*
ramble on about someone or something — とりとめもなく話す —
toritome mo naku hanasu
The speaker rambled on about politics much too long.　講演者は、政治に
ついてとりとめもなく長々と話し過ぎました。*Kōensha wa, seiji ni
tsuite toritome mo naku naganaga to hanashisugimashita.*

---

rank — 地位 — *chii*
  close ranks behind someone or something — 支持して一致団結する
— *shiji shite itchi danketsu suru*
This is the time to close ranks behind our chairman.　会長を支持して
一致団結するときです。*Kaichō o shiji shite, itchi danketsu suru toki
desu.*

  pull rank (on someone) — 地位を笠に着て命令する — *chii o kasa ni
kite meirei suru*
If you try to pull rank on him, you'll get nowhere.　地位を笠に着て
命令するなら、どうにもならないでしょう。*Chii o kasa ni kite kare
ni meirei suru nara, dō nimo naranai deshō.*

rank and file — 大衆 — *taishū*

The advertising campaign was aimed at the rank and file.　宣伝活動は、大衆を目当てにしました。*Senden katsudō wa, taishū o meate ni shimashita.*

rant — わめく — *wameku*

rant and rave — わめき散らす — *wamekichirasu*

He can rant and rave all day, but I won't change my decision.　彼が一日中わめき散らしても、私は決定を変えるつもりはありません。*Kare ga ichinichi jū wamekichirashitemo, watakushi wa kettei o kaeru tsumori wa arimasen.*

rap — 非難 — *hinan*

beat the rap — 刑罰を逃れる — *keibatsu o nogareru*

A good lawyer can help a defendant beat the rap.
有能な弁護士は、被告が刑罰を逃れるのを助けることが出来ます。*Yūnō na bengoshi wa, hikoku ga keibatsu o nogareru no o tasukeru koto ga dekimasu.*

take the rap (for someone or something) — 罪を着る — *tsumi o kiru*

She was innocent, but she took the rap for her daughter.　彼女は潔白ですが、娘のために罪を着ました。*Kanojo wa keppaku desu ga, musume no tame ni tsumi o kimashita.*

raring — すてきな — *suteki na*

raring to go — うずうずする — *uzuuzu suru*

Kirsten can't wait for school to start; she's raring to go.　キアスティンは学校が始まるのが待ち遠しくて、うずうずしています。*Kiasutin wa gakkō ga hajimaru no ga machidōshikute, uzuuzu shite imasu.*

rat — ねずみ — *nezumi*

rat on someone — 告げ口する — *tsugeguchi suru*

A good friend won't rat on you.　親友は、友達の告げ口は決してしないものです。*Shin-yū wa, tomodachi no tsugeguchi wa kesshite shinai mono desu.*

smell a rat — 臭いと思う — *kusai to omou*

His story sounds phony; I smell a rat.　彼の話は怪しげで、私は臭いと

思います。*Kare no hanashi wa ayashige de, watakushi wa kusai to omoimasu.*

rate — 評価する — *hyōka suru*
rate with someone — お気に入り — *okiniiri*
Emma really rates with her boss.　エマは、彼女のボスのお気に入りです。*Ema wa, kanojo no bosu no okiniiri desu.*

rattle — がたがた走る — *gatagata hashiru*
rattle off — すらすら言える — *surasura ieru*
My daughter can rattle off the names of all 50 states.　私の娘は、五十州の名前を全部すらすらと言えます。*Watakushi no musume wa, gojusshū no namae o zenbu surasura to iemasu.*

raw — 生の — *nama no*
in the raw — 素っ裸で — *suppadaka de*
The youngsters sometimes go swimming in the raw.　小さい子供たちは、ときどき素っ裸で泳ぎにいきます。*Chiisai kodomotachi wa, tokidoki suppadaka de oyogi ni ikimasu.*

reach — 手を伸ばす — *te o nobasu*
out of reach — 手の届かない — *te no todokanai*
Her goals always seem to be just out of reach.　彼女の目標は、いつもほんのちょっと手の届かないところにあるみたいです。*Kanojo no mokuhyō wa, itsumo honno chotto te no todokanai tokoro ni aru mitai desu.*

within one's reach — 手の届く範囲内に — *te no todoku han-i nai ni*
Victory is within our reach.　勝利は、手の届く範囲内にあります。*Shōri wa, te no todoku han-i nai ni arimasu.*

read — 読む — *yomu*
mind reader — 人の心を読みとれる人 — *hito no kokoro o yomitoreru hito*
Yoko knows exactly what I want; she's a mind reader.　洋子さんは人の心が読みとれる人で、私が本当に何が欲しいか分かります。*Yōko san wa hito no kokoro ga yomitoreru hito de, watakushi ga hontō ni nani*

ga hoshii ka wakarimasu.

read something into something — 他の意味を勘ぐる — *hoka no imi o kanguru*
Don't read too much into his expression. 彼の表情や声の調子から、あんまり他の意味を勘ぐらないように。*Kare no hyōjō ya koe no chōshi kara, anmari hoka no imi o kanguranai yō ni.*

read up on someone or something — 調べて知っておく — *shirabete shitte oku*
Before the meeting, you should read up on the agenda topics. 会議前に、議事項目の話題について調べて知っておくべきです。*Kaigi mae ni, giji kōmoku no wadai ni tsuite shirabete shitte oku beki desu.*

ready — 準備できた — *junbi dekita*
ready, willing, and able — いつでも喜んで — *itsu demo yorokonde*
If you need anyone to help, I'm ready, willing, and able. 誰かの助けがいるなら、私がいつでも喜んでします。*Dareka no tasuke ga iru nara, watakushi ga itsu demo yorokonde shimasu.*

real — 本当の — *hontō no*
for real — 本当に — *hontō ni*
We've heard everyone is getting a bonus. Is this for real? 全員がボーナスをもらうと聞いたんですが、本当ですか。*Zen-in ga bōnasu o morau to kiitandesu ga, hontō desu ka.*

get real — 目を覚ませ — *me o samase*
An honest politician? Get real. 正直な政治家ですって。目を覚ましなさい。*Shōjiki na seijika desutte. Me o samashinasai.*

rear — 後ろ — *ushiro*
bring up the rear — どん尻 — *donjiri*
It seems as if our group is always bringing up the rear. 私達のグループは、いつもどん尻にいるみたいです。*Watakushitachi no gurūpu wa, itsumo donjiri ni iru mitai desu.*

reason — 理由 — *riyū*
listen to reason — 道理に従う — *dōri ni shitagau*
If he would listen to reason, he'd make the right decision. もし彼が道理に

従えば、正しい決定を下すことが出来ます。*Moshi kare ga dōri ni shitagaeba, tadashii kettei o kudasu koto ga dekimasu.*

stand to reason — もちろんの事だ — *mochiron no koto da*
It stands to reason that this plan will succeed. この計画が成功するのは、もちろんの事です。*Kono keikaku ga seikō suru no wa, mochiron no koto desu.*

---

record — 記録 — *kiroku*
off the record — 表沙汰にしない条件付きで — *omotezata ni shinai jōken tsuki de*
He spoke to the reporter off the record. 彼は、表沙汰にしない条件付きで記者に話しました。*Kare wa, omotezata ni shinai jōken tsuki de kisha ni hanashimashita.*

---

reckon — 計算する — *keisan suru*
reckon with someone or something — 対処する — *taisho suru*
If you don't treat them well, you'll have to reckon with me. もし彼等を丁寧に待遇しないなら、この先、私と対処せねばなりませんよ。*Moshi karera o teinei ni taigū shinai nara, kono saki, watakushi to taisho seneba narimasen yo.*

---

red — 赤 — *aka*
in the red — 赤字で — *akaji de*
We can't afford to be in the red for much longer. 私達は、この先いつまでも赤字でいることは出来ません。*Watakushitachi wa, kono saki itsu made mo akaji de iru koto wa dekimasen.*

out of the red — 赤字を免れて — *akaji o manugarete*
They predict our company will be out of the red after next month. 我が社は来月を過ぎると赤字を免れると、彼等は予言しています。*Waga sha wa raigetsu o sugiru to akaji o manugareru to, karera wa yogen shite imasu.*

see red — 激怒する — *gekido suru*
The mayor's behavior made his constituents see red. 市長の振る舞いは、有権者を激怒させました。*Shichō no furumai wa, yūkensha o gekido sasemashita.*

---

rein — 手綱 — *tazuna*
　free rein — 一任する — *ichinin suru*
　His company has given him free rein to update all computer equipment.
　会社は、コンピュータのあらゆる装置を最新のものに入れ替える
　のを、彼に一任しました。*Kaisha wa, konpyūta no arayuru sōchi o*
　saishin no mono ni irekaeru no o, kare ni ichinin shimashita.

---

religion — 宗教 — *shūkyō*
　get religion — 心を入れ替える — *kokoro o irekaeru*
　After his heart attack, he got religion. Now he's exercising and eating
　carefully.　心臓麻痺の発作の後、彼は心を入れ替えました。今は
　運動をし、食べ物に気をつけています。*Shinzō mahi no hossa no*
　ato, kare wa kokoro o irekaemashita. Ima wa undō o shi, tabemono ni ki
　o tsukete imasu.

---

resistance — 抵抗 — *teikō*
　path of least resistance — 一番楽な方法 — *ichiban raku na hōhō*
　They took the path of least resistance and compromised.　彼等は一番
　楽な方法を採って、妥協しました。*Karera wa ichiban raku na hōhō*
　o totte, dakyō shimashita.

---

resort — 頼み — *tanomi*
　as a last resort — 最後の手段として — *saigo no shudan toshite*
　She'll agree to surgery only as a last resort.　彼女は最後の手段として
　のみ、手術を受けるのに同意するでしょう。*Kanojo wa saigo no*
　shudan toshite nomi, shujutsu o ukeru no ni dōi suru deshō.

---

rest — 休息 — *kyūsoku*
　be laid to rest — 埋葬される — *maisō sareru*
　He was laid to rest in a small cemetery near his home.　彼は、家の
　近くの墓地に埋葬されました。*Kare wa, ie no chikaku no bochi ni*
　maisō saremashita.

　give it a rest — くどくど話すのを止める — *kudokudo hanasu no o*
　yameru
　We've heard your opinion, Mary; now give it a rest.　メリーさん、
　あなたの意見はもう聞きました。これ以上、くどくど話すのは

止めて下さい。Merī san, anata no iken wa mō kikimashita. Kore ijō, kudokudo hanasu no wa yamete kudasai.

lay/put something to rest — 忘れ去る — wasuresaru

Now that you know our plans, you can put your concerns to rest. 今は私達の計画が分かったのだから、心配を忘れ去ることが出来るでしょ。Ima wa watakushitachi no keikaku ga wakatta no dakara, shinpai o wasuresaru koto ga dekiru desho.

rest assured — 安心する — anshin suru

You can rest assured that they'll do a good job for you. 彼等はいい仕事をしますから安心してください。Karera wa ii shigoto o shimasu kara anshin shite kudasi.

---

retreat — 退却 — taikyaku

beat a (hasty) retreat — 急いで逃げ出す — isoide nigedasu

The thieves beat a hasty retreat when they heard the police siren. 泥棒はパトカーのサイレンを聞いて、急いで逃げ出しました。Dorobō wa patokā no sairen o kiite, isoide nigedashimashita.

---

rhyme — 韻 — in

no/without rhyme or reason — 筋道が通っていない — sujimichi ga tōtte inai

His suggestion had no rhyme or reason.
彼の提案は、筋道が通っていませんでした。
Kare no teian wa, sujimichi ga tōtte imasen deshita.

---

rib — 肋骨 — abarabone

stick to one's ribs — 満腹感がある — manpuku kan ga aru

A salad isn't enough; for lunch he needs something that'll stick to his ribs.
サラダだけでは十分ではありません。昼食には、彼は何か満腹感があるものが必要です。Sarada dake dewa jūbun dewa arimasen. Chūshoku ni wa, kare wa nanika manpuku kan ga aru mono ga hitsuyō desu.

---

rich — 金持ち — kanemochi

strike it rich — 大儲けする — ōmōke suru

John struck it rich investing in the technology industry. ジョンは技術

関連産業に投資して、大儲けしました。*Jon wa gijutsu kanren
sangyō ni tōshi shite, ōmōke shimashita.*

---

riddance — 排除 — *haijo*
  good riddance (to bad rubbish) — いい厄介払い — *ii yakkaibarai*
Our incompetent secretary is quitting—good riddance!　私達の無能な
秘書が仕事を辞めるので、いい厄介払いになります。
*Watakushitachi no munō na hisho ga shigoto o yameru node, ii
yakkaibarai ni narimasu.*

---

ride — 乗車／乗る — *jōsha/noru*
  come/go along for the ride — ドライブを楽しみにしてついてくる —
doraibu o tanoshimi ni shite tsuite kuru
When I drove my husband to work, our son came along for the ride.　私が
運転して夫を仕事に送っていったとき、息子がドライブを楽しみに
してついてきました。*Watakushi ga unten shite otto o shigoto ni
okutte itta toki, musuko ga doraibu o tanoshimi ni shite tsuite kimashita.*

  hitch a ride — 車に便乗する — *kuruma ni binjō suru*
When my car broke down, I hitched a ride with my neighbor.　私の車が
故障したとき、近所の人の車に便乗させてもらいました。
*Watakushi no kuruma ga koshō shita toki, kinjo no hito no kuruma ni
binjō sasete moraimashita.*

  ride roughshod over someone or something — 手荒く扱う — *tearaku
atsukau*
The chairman rides roughshod over his staff during meetings.　会長は、
会議中に彼の部下を手荒く扱います。*Kaichō wa, kaigi chū ni kare
no buka o tearaku atsukaimasu.*

  ride something out — 何とか乗り越える — *nantoka norikoeru*
The downsizing was unpleasant, but they rode it out. 会社の規模縮小は
愉快なことではありませんでしたが、彼等はそれを何とか
乗り越えました。*Kaisha no kibo shukushō wa yukai na koto dewa
arimasen deshita ga, karera wa sore o nantoka norikoemashita.*

  riding high — 意気揚々 — *iki yōyō*
With his new novel a success, the author is riding high. 新しい小説が
当たって、その作家は意気揚々としています。*Atarashii shōsetsu
ga atatte, sono sakka wa iki yōyō to shite imasu.*

take someone for a ride — だます — *damasu*

The unscrupulous stockbroker took his customers for a ride. はじ知らずの 株のブ－ロ－カ－は、彼の顧客をだましました。*Hajishirazu no kabu no burōkā wa, kare no kokyaku o damashimashita.*

thumb a ride — ヒッチハイクする — *hitchihaiku suru*

Thumbing a ride can be dangerous. ヒッチハイクは、危険の可能性が あります。*Hitchihaiku wa, kiken no kanōsei ga arimasu.*

---

right — 右／正当／権利 — *migi/seitō/kenri*

hang a right — 右折する — *usetsu suru*

When you get to the next traffic light, hang a right. 次の信号に来たら、 右折します。*Tsugi no shingō ni kitara, usetsu shimasu.*

in the right — 正しい — *tadashii*

Even though I was in the right, I got a parking ticket. 私が正しいにもか かわらず、駐車違反の券を渡されてしまいました。*Watakushi ga tadashii nimo kakawarazu, chūsha ihan no ken o watasarete shimaimashita.*

right away — 直ぐ — *sugu*

Please bring us our check right away. お勘定を直ぐお願いします。 *Okanjō o sugu onegai shimasu.*

right on — やった／そうだ／いいぞ／すごい — *yatta/sō da/ii zo/sugoi*

You passed the test? Right on! 試験に受かったって。やったね！ *Shiken ni ukattatte. Yatta ne!*

yield the right-of-way — 先行権を譲る — *senkō ken o yuzuru*

You must always yield the right-of-way at that intersection. あの交差点 では、常に先行権を譲らねばなりません。*Ano kōsaten dewa, tsune ni senkō ken o yuzuraneba narimasen.*

---

ring — ベルの音／響き／鳴る — *beru no oto/hibiki/naru*

give someone a ring — 電話する — *denwa suru*

I'll give you a ring later, and we'll make plans for dinner. 後で電話する から、その時にディナ－の計画を立てましょう。*Ato de denwa suru kara, sono toki ni dinā no keikaku o tatemashō*

have a familiar ring — 聞き覚えがある — *kikioboe ga aru*

This sales pitch has a familiar ring; I think I've heard it before. この

売り込み方に覚えがあるのは、前にそれを聞いたことがある
からだと思います。*Kono urikomikata ni oboe ga aru no wa, mae ni
sore o kiita koto ga aru kara da to omoimasu.*

ring true — 正しく響く — *tadashiku hibiku*
We want to believe him, but his explanation doesn't ring true.　私達は
彼を信じたいのですが、彼の説明には正しい響きがありません。
*Watakushitachi wa kare o shinjitai no desu ga, kare no setsumei ni wa
tadashii hibiki ga arimasen.*

run rings around someone — 楽に勝てる — *raku ni kateru*
That tennis player can run rings around any opponent.　あのテニスの
選手は、どんな相手でも楽に勝てます。*Ano tenisu no senshu wa,
donna aite demo raku ni katemasu.*

---

rip — 裂く — *saku*

rip into someone or something — 激しく攻撃する — *hageshiku kōgeki
suru*
The party leader ripped into the opposition.　その党の指導者は、対立
政党を激しく攻撃しました。*Sono tō no shidōsha wa, tairitsu seitō o
hageshiku kōgeki shimashita.*

rip someone or something off — ペテンにかける — *peten ni kakeru*
When they saw the hotel, they knew their travel agent had ripped them off.
彼等はそのホテルを見たとき、旅行代理店の業者が彼等をペテンに
かけたことが分かりました。*Karera wa sono hoteru o mita toki,
ryokō dairiten no gyōsha ga karera o peten ni kaketa koto ga
wakarimashita.*

---

rise — 上昇／起きる — *jōshō/okiru*

get a rise out of someone — 怒らせる — *okoraseru*
Henry's teasing always gets a rise out of Sally.　ヘンリーのからかいは、
いつもサリーを怒らせます。*Henrī no karakai wa, itsumo Sarī o
okorasemasu.*

give rise to something — もたらす — *motarasu*
This agreement should give rise to improved trade relations.　この合意は、
貿易関係に改善をもたらすべきです。*Kono gōi wa, bōeki kankei ni
kaizen o motarasu beki desu.*

Rise and shine! — 元気よく起きる時間だ！ — *Genki yoku okiru jikan da!*

It's 7 o'clock, John. Rise and shine! ジョン、七時だから、元気よく起きる時間ですよ！ *Jon, shichiji dakara, genki yoku okiru jikan desu yo!*

rise up — 蜂起する — *hōki suru*

If the rulers get too repressive, the people may rise up against them. もし支配者があまりにも抑圧的だと、国民は蜂起するかもしれません。 *Moshi shihaisha ga amari nimo yokuatsuteki da to, kokumin wa hōki suru kamo shiremasen.*

---

risk — 危険 — *kiken*

calculated risk — あらかじめ考慮された危険 — *arakajime kōryo sareta kiken*

Having the surgery is a calculated risk. 手術を受けることには、あらかじめ考慮された危険が含まれています。 *Shujutsu o ukeru koto niwa, arakajime kōryo sareta kiken ga fukumarete imasu.*

run the risk (of something) — 危険を冒す — *kiken o okasu*

If you make the boss angry, you run the risk of being fired. もし上司を怒らせると、首になる危険を冒しますよ。 *Moshi jōshi o okoraseru to, kubi ni naru kiken o okashimasu yo.*

---

river — 川 — *kawa*

sell someone down the river — 裏切る — *uragiru*

John's testimony sold Tom down the river. ジョンは、証言でトムを裏切りました。 *Jon wa shōgen de Tomu o uragirimashita.*

send someone up the river — 刑務所に送り込む — *keimusho ni okurikomu*

The judge sent the embezzler up the river for 10 years. 裁判官は、横領の犯人を刑務所に十年間送り込みました。 *Saibankan wa, ōryō no hannin o keimusho ni jū nen kan okurikomimashita.*

---

road — 道 — *michi*

hit the road — 道に就く — *michi ni tsuku*

It's midnight—time to hit the road. 午前０時だから、帰宅の道に就く時間です。 *Gozen reiji dakara, kitaku no michi ni tsuku jikan desu.*

---

robbery — 強盗 — *gōtō*

highway robbery — べらぼうな値段 — *berabō na nedan*

To foreigners, prices in Tokyo often seem like highway robbery.　外国人に
とっては、東京の値段はべらぼうな値段のように思われます。
*Gaikokujin ni totte wa, Tōkyō no nedan wa berabō na nedan no yō ni
omowaremasu.*

Robin Hood — ロビン・フッド — *Robin Huddo*

all around Robin Hood's barn — 回り道をして行く — *mawarimichi o
shite iku*

We had to go all around Robin Hood's barn to find the location of the
company picnic.　会社のピクニックの場所を見つけるために、
私達は回り道をして行かねばなりませんでした。*Kaisha no
pikunikku no basho o mitsukeru tame ni, watakushitachi wa
mawarimichi o shite ikaneba narimasen deshita.*

---

rock — 岩 — *iwa*

(as) steady as a rock — 着実な — *chakujitsu na*

We can always depend on Bill; he's as steady as a rock.　ビルは着実
なので、私達はいつも彼を頼りに出来ます。*Biru wa chakujitsu
nanode, watakushitachi wa itsumo kare o tayori ni dekimasu.*

between a rock and a hard place — 進退窮まって — *shintai kiwamatte*

Will he side with his wife or his mother? He's between a rock and a
hard place.　奥さんかお母さん。彼はどちらの側につくか、進退
窮まっています。*Okusan ka okāsan. Kare wa dochira no gawa ni
tsuku ka, shintai kiwamatte imasu.*

have rocks in one's head — 頭がおかしい — *atama ga okashii*

She must have had rocks in her head to quit that fantastic job.　あの
素晴らしい仕事を辞めるとは、彼女は頭がおかしいに違い
ありません。*Ano subarashii shigoto o yameru towa, kanojo wa atama
ga okashii ni chigai arimasen.*

rock-bottom — 最低の — *saitei no*

The salesman said this was their rock-bottom price for the car.
セールスマンは、これがこの車の最低の値段だと言いました。
Sērusuman wa, kore ga kono kuruma no saitei no nedan da to iimashita.

on the rocks — 暗礁に乗り上げて — *anshō ni noriagete*

I hear Bill's marriage is on the rocks. ビルの結婚は暗礁に乗り上げて いると聞いています。 *Biru no kekkon wa anshō ni noriagete iru to kiite imasu.*

---

rocker — 揺り椅子 — *yuriisu*

off one's rocker — 頭がどうかしている — *atama ga dōka shite iru*

If you expect me to go hang gliding with you, you're off your rocker. もし私があなたとハンググライダーに乗りに行くと思っている なら、あなたは頭がどうかしています。 *Moshi watakushi ga anata to hanguguraidā ni norini iku to omotte iru nara, anata wa atama ga dōka shite imasu.*

---

roll — 回転 — *kaiten*

on a roll — 調子の波に乗って — *chōshi no nami ni notte*

Nothing can stop us now; we're on a roll. 私達は調子の波に乗って いるので、今は何事も私達を阻むことが出来ません。 *Watakushitachi wa chōshi no nami ni notte iru node, ima wa nanigoto mo watakushitachi o habamu koto ga dekimasen.*

Rome — ローマ — *Rōma*

fiddle while Rome burns — 大事をよそに小事をもてあそぶ — *daiji o yoso ni shōji o moteasobu*

Where was the mayor during the crisis? He always fiddles while Rome burns. 危機の最中、市長は一体どこにいたのでしょうか。彼は いつも、大事をよそに小事をもてあそぶ癖があるのです。 *Kiki no saichū, shichō wa ittai doko ni ita no deshō ka. Kare wa itsumo, daiji o yoso ni shōji o moteasobu kuse ga aru no desu.*

Rome wasn't built in a day. — ローマは一日にしてならず。 — *Rōma wa ichi nichi ni shite narazu.*

Don't expect results immediately. Remember, Rome wasn't built in a day. 結果を直ぐに期待しないように。ローマは一日にしてならずと いう言葉を、覚えているでしょう。 *Kekka o sugu ni kitai shinai yō ni. Rōma wa ichi nichi ni shite narazu to iu kotoba o, oboete iru deshō.*

When in Rome, do as the Romans do — 郷に入っては郷に従え。 *Gō ni itte wa gō ni shitagae.*

In Japan I use chopsticks often. When in Rome, do as the Romans do.

日本にいるときには、私はよく箸を使います。郷に入っては郷に
従えですから。*Nihon ni iru toki ni wa, watakushi wa yoku hashi o
tsukaimasu. Gō ni itte wa gō ni shitagae desu kara.*

roof — 屋根 — *yane*
   hit the roof — 激怒する — *gekido suru*
   Her father hit the roof when he caught her smoking.　彼女のお父さんは、
   娘がタバコを吸っている現場を見つけて激怒しました。*Kanojo no
   otōsan wa, musume ga tabako o sutte iru genba o mitsukete gekido
   shimashita.*

   raise the roof — 大騒ぎする — *ōsawagi suru*
   Everyone raised the roof at the party last night.　夕べはパーティーで、
   誰もが大騒ぎしました。*Yūbe wa pātī de, daremo ga ōsawagi
   shimashita.*

rope — 縄 — *nawa*
   give one enough rope and one will hang oneself — 放って置けばやり
   すぎて自滅すること請け合いだ — *hootte okeba yarisugite jimetsu
   suru koto ukeai da*
   She's such a liar, but give her enough rope and she'll hang herself.　彼女は
   大嘘つきだけど、放って置けば嘘をつきすぎて自滅すること
   請け合いで す。*Kanojo wa ō usotsuki dakedo, hootte okeba uso o
   tsukisugite jimetsu suru koto ukeai desu.*

   know the ropes — 事情に通じている — *jijō ni tsūjite iru*

If you have questions, ask Tom; he knows the ropes around here.　質問が
あれば、トムに聞きなさい。彼は、ここでの事情に通じているから。
*Shitsumon ga areba, Tomu ni kikinasai. Kare wa, koko de no jijō ni
tsūjite iru kara.*

on the ropes — 危機に瀕して — *kiki ni hinshite*
Without a tax break soon, many small businesses will be on the ropes.
近いうちに税金の救済がないと、たくさんの小企業が危機に
瀕するでしょう。*Chikai uchi ni zeikin no kyūsai ga nai to, takusan no
shō kigyō ga kiki ni hinsuru deshō.*

rope into — 口車に乗せる — *kuchiguruma ni noseru*
Rob was sorry he got roped into helping plan the party.　ロブは口車に
乗せられてパーティーの計画を助けることになったのを後悔
しました。*Robu wa kuchiguruma ni noserarete pātī no keikaku o
tasukeru koto ni natta no o kōkai shimashita.*

show someone the ropes — ここでのやり方を教える — *koko de no
yarikata o oshieru*
Mary's a new employee; can you show her the ropes?　メリーは新しい
従業員だから、彼女にここでのやり方を教えてくれますか。
*Merī wa atarashii jūgyōin dakara, kanojo ni koko de no yarikata o
oshiete kuremasu ka.*

---

rose — バラ — *bara*
come out/up smelling like a rose — 面目を保つ — *menboku o tamotsu*
After the scandal the senator came out smelling like a rose.　スキャンダルの
後、その上院議員は面目を保つことができました。*Sukyandaru no
ato, sono jōin giin wa menboku o tamotsu koto ga dekimashita.*

come up roses — うまくいく — *umaku iku*
Our problems are over; everything is coming up roses.　問題が片づいて、
全てがうまくいっています。*Mondai ga katazuite, subete ga umaku
itte imasu.*

---

rough — 荒い／手荒くする — *arai/tearaku suru*
rough-and-tumble — 荒々しい — *araarashii*
The city council had a rough-and-tumble session today.　今日の市議会の
審議は、荒々しくなりました。*Kyō no shigikai no shingi wa,
araarashiku narimashita.*

---

rough someone up — 痛めつける — *itametsukeru*
The muggers roughed him up badly.　辻強盗は、彼をひどく
痛めつけました。*Tsuji gōtō wa, kare o hidoku itametsukemashita.*

---

row — 畝 — *une*

tough/hard row to hoe — 並大抵の努力ではない — *namitaitei no
doryoku dewa nai*
Working all day and taking classes at night is a tough row to hoe.　一日中
働いて夜に授業を受けるのは、並大抵の努力ではありません。
*Ichi nichi jū hataraite yoru ni jugyō o ukeru no wa, namitaitei no
doryoku dewa arimasen.*

---

rub — こする — *kosuru*

rub off (on someone) — 乗り移る — *noriutsuru*
I wish some of John's good luck would rub off on me.　ジョンの幸運が、
いくらかでも私に乗り移ったらと願っています。*Jon no kōun ga,
ikuraka demo watakushi ni noriutsuttara to negatte imasu.*

rub something in — しつこく責める — *shitsukoku semeru*
Mary knows she messed up. You don't have to rub it in.　メリーは失敗を
しでかしたのを知っているから、しつこく責めることはないです。
*Merī wa shippai o shidekashita no o shitte iru kara, shitsukoku semeru
koto wa nai desu.*

---

rug — 絨毯 — *jūtan*

pull the rug out (from under someone) — 足をすくう — *ashi o sukuu*
When they cut his budget, they pulled the rug out from under him.　彼の
予算を削減して、彼等は彼の足をすくいました。*Kare no yosan o
sakugen shite, karera wa kare no ashi o sukuimashita.*

sweep something under the rug — 目をつぶる — *me o tsuburu*
We have to deal with the allegations. We can't sweep them under the rug.
私達は、その容疑に対処しなければなりません。それに目をつぶる
ことは出来ないのです。*Watakushitachi wa sono yōgi ni taisho
shinakereba narimasen. Sore ni me o tsuburu koto wa dekinai no desu.*

---

rule — 規則 — *kisoku*

rule of thumb — 一般原則 — *ippan gensoku*

It's a good rule of thumb to proofread everything you write.　一般原則
として、自分の書いたものに目を通して間違いを直すのは
いいことです。Ippan gensoku toshite, jibun no kaita mono ni me o
tōshite machigai o naosu no wa ii koto desu.

rule something out — 除外する — jogai suru

It looks like suicide, but the police haven't ruled anything out.　それが
自殺に見えても、警察は他の可能性も除外していません。Sore ga
jisatsu ni mietemo, keisatsu wa ta no kanōsei mo jogai shite imasen.

---

run — 走る — hashiru

do something on the run — あわただしい合間を縫って —
awatadashii aima o nutte

I don't have much time for lunch today, so I have to eat on the run.
今日は昼食のための時間があまりないので、あわただしい
合間を縫って食べなければなりません。Kyō wa chūshoku no tame
no jikan ga amari nai node, awatadashii aima o nutte tabenakereba
narimasen.

dry run — 予行演習 — yokō enshū

We're going to have a dry run for the dedication ceremony.　私達は、
開所式のための予行演習を行います。Watakushitachi wa, kaisho
shiki no tame no yokō enshū o okonaimasu.

give one a run for one's money — 善戦しててこずらせる — zensen
shite tekozuraseru

They may win, but we'll give them a run for their money in the campaign.
彼等が勝つでしょうが、私達は選挙運動では善戦して、彼等を
てこずらせるつもりです。Karera ga katsu deshō ga, watakushitachi
wa senkyo undō dewa zensen shite, karera o tekozuraseru tsumori desu.

have a run of bad luck — 一連の不運に見舞われる — ichiren no fuun
ni mimawareru

John's had a run of bad luck with his investments.　ジョンは、投資で
一連の不運に見舞われました。Jon wa, tōshi de ichiren no fuun ni
mimawaremashita.

in the long run — 長期的に — chōkiteki ni

Things may be difficult now, but they'll work out in the long run.　今は
事が困難かもしれませんが、長期的にはうまくいくでしょう。

Ima wa koto ga konnan kamo shiremasen ga, chōkiteki ni wa umaku iku deshō.

in the running — 競争して — kyōsō shite

Is that candidate still in the running?　あの候補者は、いまだに競争しているのですか。Ano kōhosha wa, imada ni kyōsō shite iru no desu ka.

in the short run — 短期的に — tankiteki ni

In the short run, renting an apartment is a good idea.　短期的には、マンションを借りるのはいいアイディアです。Tankiteki niwa, manshon o kariru no wa ii aidia desu.

out of the running — もはや考慮から外されて — mohaya kōryo kara hazusarete

Our team is out of the running for the Super Bowl this year.　私達のチームは、今年はもはやスーパーボール出場への考慮から外されています。Watakushitachi no chīmu wa, kotoshi wa mohaya sūpābōru shutsujō e no kōryo kara hazusarete imasu.

run-of-the-mill — ありきたりの — arikitari no

Nothing special happened; it was a run-of-the-mill meeting.　特に何も起こらず、会議はありきたりのものでした。Toku ni nani mo okorazu, kaigi wa arikitari no mono deshita.

run someone ragged — てんてこまいさせる — tentekomai saseru

Susan's children ran her ragged today.　スーザンの子供たちは、彼女を今日てんてこまいさせました。Sūzan no kodomotachi wa, kanojo o kyō tentekomai sasemashita.

run riot — 騒ぎ回る — sawagimawaru

Parents should never let their children run riot in a restaurant.　親は、レストランで子供たちが騒ぎ回らないようにさせなければなりません。Oya wa, resutoran de kodomotachi ga sawagimawaranai yō ni sasenakereba narimasen.

run scared — びくびくする — bikubiku suru

Toward the end of the campaign, the mayor was running scared.　選挙戦が終わりに近付いて、市長はびくびくしていました。Senkyo sen ga owari ni chikazuite, shichō wa bikubiku shite imashita.

run short (of something) — 足りなくなる — tarinaku naru

She always runs short of money before payday.　彼女はいつも、給料日の

前にお金が足りなくなります。*Kanojo wa itsumo, kyūryōbi no mae ni okane ga tarinaku narimasu.*

run that/it by someone (again) — もう一度言う — *mō ichido iu*
I don't understand what you said. Could you run that by me again, please?
あなたの言ったことが分かりません。もう一度言って
もらえませんか。*Anata no itta koto ga wakarimasen. Mō ichido itte moraemasen ka.*

run wild — したい放題のことをする — *shitai hōdai no koto o suru*
Our neighbors usually let their children run wild. 近所の人は、いつも
子供たちにしたい放題のことをさせています。*Kinjo no hito wa, itsumo kodomotachi ni shitai hōdai no koto o sasete imasu.*

---

runaround — 回避 — *kaihi*
  get the runaround — 言い逃れの返事をされる — *iinogare no henji o sareru*
When he tried to get an appointment with the boss, he got the runaround.
彼は上司との面談の約束を取り付けようとしましたが、言い逃れの
返事をされました。*Kare wa jōshi to no mendan no yakusoku o toritsukeyō to shimashita ga, iinogare no henji o saremashita.*

  give someone the runaround — 言い逃れをする — *iinogare o suru*
When she tried to get a decision, they gave her the runaround. 彼女が
決断を取り付けようとしたら、彼等は言い逃れをしました。
Kanojo ga ketsudan o toritsukeyō to shitara, karera wa iinogare o shimashita.

---

rustle — さっさと動く — *sassa to ugoku*
  rustle something up — 有り合わせのもので素早く料理する —
ariawase no mono de subayaku ryōri suru
If you're hungry, I can rustle something up. お腹が空いているなら、
有り合わせのもので素早く料理してあげましょう。*Onaka ga suite iru nara, ariawase no mono de subayaku ryōri shite agemashō.*

---

sack — 袋 — fukuro

　get the sack — 首になる — kubi ni naru

　As he expected, John got the sack yesterday. 　ジョンは思っていた
　とおり、昨日、首になりました。Jon wa omotte ita tōri, kinō, kubi ni
　narimashita.

　hit the sack — 寝る — neru

　I'm sleepy; I think I'll hit the sack. 　眠たいので、寝ようと思います。
　Nemutai node, neyō to omoimasu.

　sack out — 眠り込む — nemurikomu

　Jim sacked out on our couch last night. 　ジムは昨日の晩、私達の家の
　ソファーで眠り込んでしまいました。Jimu wa kinō no ban,
　watakushitachi no ie no sofā de nemurikonde shimaimashita.

sad — 悲しい — kanashii

　sadder but wiser — 悲しい経験で賢明になる — kanashii keiken de
　　kenmei ni naru

　After we learned the truth, we were sadder but wiser.
　真実を学んだ後、私達は悲しい経験で賢明になりました。
　Shinjitsu o mananda ato, watakushitachi wa kanashii keiken de kenmei
　ni narimashita.

saddle — 鞍 — kura

　saddle someone with something — 縛る — shibaru

　He doesn't want to be saddled with a house now, but his wife wants one.
　彼は今は家で財政的に縛られたくないけれど、奥さんは
　それを欲しがっています。Kare wa ima wa ie de zaiseiteki ni
　shibararetakunai keredo, okusan wa sore o hoshigatte imasu.

safe — 安全な — anzen na

　safe and sound — 無事に — buji ni

　They were relieved when their son returned from skiing safe and sound.
　彼等は、息子がスキーから無事に帰ってきたのでほっとしました。

Karera wa, musuko ga sukī kara buji ni kaette kita node hotto
shimashita.

safety in numbers — 身の安全には数が頼みになる — mi no anzen
niwa kazu ga tanomi ni naru

After dinner, we all walked to the garage together; there's safety in
numbers. ディナーの後、私達はみんな一緒に駐車場まで
歩きました。身の安全には、数が頼みになるからです。Dinā no
ato, watakushitachi wa minna issho ni chūshajō made arukimashita. Mi
no anzen niwa, kazu ga tanomi ni naru kara desu.

---

sail — 帆／帆走する — ho/hansō suru

clear sailing — 順風満帆 — junpū manpan

Once we finish the report, it's clear sailing for our project. この報告書を
終わらせれば、その後この企画は順風満帆です。Kono hōkokusho
o owasareba, sono ato kono kikaku wa junpū manpan desu.

sail through something — 楽々やってのける — rakuraku yatte nokeru

Don't worry about the exam; you'll sail right through it. あなたはその
試験を楽々やってのけるだろうから、心配はいりません。

Anata wa sono shiken o rakuraku yatte nokeru darō kara, shinpai wa
irimasen.

---

salt — 塩 — shio

rub salt in/into the wound — わざとそれ以上嫌な思いをさせる —
wazato sore ijō iya na omoi o saseru

He just broke his leg; don't rub salt in the wound by inviting him to a
dance.　彼は最近、足を折ってしまいました。それで彼をダンスに
招いたりして、わざとそれ以上嫌な思いをさせないように。*Kare
wa saikin, ashi o otte shimaimashita. Sorede kare o dansu ni maneitari
shite, wazato sore ijō iya na omoi o sasenai yō ni.*

salt of the earth — このうえない善良な人 — *kono ue nai zenryō na
hito*
Mary's the salt of the earth. She'll do anything for a friend.　メリーは
このうえない善良な人で、友達のためなら何でもします。*Merī
wa kono ue nai zenryō na hito de, tomodachi no tame nara nandemo
shimasu.*

salt something away — 蓄える — *takuwaeru*
She tries to salt something away every month.　彼女は、毎月お金を
いくらか蓄えようと努めています。*Kanojo wa, maitsuki okane o
ikuraka takuwaeyō to tsutomete imasu.*

worth one's salt — 給料分の値打ちが十分ある — *kyūryō bun no
neuchi ga jūbun aru*
The new quarterback is really worth his salt.　新しいクォーターバックは、
給料分の値打ちが十分あります。*Atarashii kuōtābakku wa, kyūryō
bun no neuchi ga jūbun arimasu.*

same — 同じ — *onaji*

all the same (to someone) — 構わなければ — *kamawanakereba*
If it's all the same to you, I'm leaving early today.　もし構わなければ、
今日は早く出ます。*Moshi kamawanakereba, kyō wa hayaku demasu.*

same here — 私も同じ — *watakushi mo onaji*
You like sushi? Same here!　あなたは鮨が好きなんですか。私も同じ
です。*Anata wa sushi ga suki nan desu ka. Watakushi mo onaji desu.*

the same to you — あなたも御同様に — *anata mo godōyō ni*
Bill: Have a nice evening. Tom: The same to you.
ビル：「楽しい夕べを」。トム：「ビルさんも御同様に」。
Biru: "Tanoshii yūbe o." Tomu: "Biru san mo godōyō ni."

sardine — 鰯 — iwashi

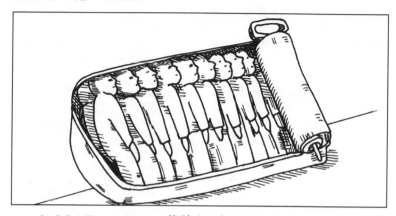

packed (in) like sardines — 鮨詰めになつて — sushizume ni natte

The disco was so crowded we were packed in like sardines. ディスコは
すごく込んでいたので、私達は鮨詰めになつてしまいました。
Disuko wa sugoku konde ita node, watakushitachi wa sushizume ni natte
shimaimashita.

---

say — 言う — iu

get/have a/one's say — 言い分を述べる — iibun o noberu

Tom deserves to have his say before we make a final decision. 私達が
最終決定を下す前に、トムには彼の言い分を述べる権利があります。
Watakushitachi ga saishū kettei o kudasu mae ni, Tomu niwa kare no
iibun o noberu kenri ga arimasu.

on someone's say-so — その人の権限に基づいて — sono hito no
kengen ni motozuite

We signed the agreement on the president's say-so. 私達は、社長の
権限に基づいて合意書に署名しました。Watakushitachi wa, shachō
no kengen ni motozuite gōisho ni shomei shimashita.

---

scare — 恐怖 — kyōfu

scared stiff — 恐れおののいて — osore ononoite

She was scared stiff when her car went out of control. 彼女は運転中の
車がコントロールを失ったとき、恐れおののいてしまいました。

Kanojo wa unten chū no kuruma ga kontorōru o ushinatta toki, osore ononoite shimaimashita.

scene — 場面 — *bamen*

create/make a scene — 騒ぎ立てて人目を引く — *sawagitatete hitome o hiku*

He always creates a scene if a waiter brings him lukewarm coffee.
ウエイターの持ってきたコーヒーが生温いと、彼はいつも
騒ぎ立てて人目を引きます。*Ueitā no mottekita kōhī ga namanurui to, kare wa itsumo sawagitatete hitome o hikimasu.*

make the scene — 行く — *iku*

You must make the scene tonight; we'll all be there. 今晩は、君も
行かなきゃだめだよ。僕たちも、みんな行っているから。*Konban wa, kimi mo ikanakya dame da yo. Bokutachi mo, minna itte iru kara.*

school — 学校 — *gakkō*

school of hard knocks — 厳しい実社会 — *kibishii jisshakai*

He learned his trade in the school of hard knocks. 彼は、厳しい実社会で
職を身につけました。*Kare wa, kibishii jisshakai de shoku o mi ni tsukemashita.*

score — 得点 — *tokuten*

have a score to settle — 片をつけるべきことがある — *kata o tsukeru beki koto ga aru*

I have a score to settle with John before we can be friends again. 私達が
また友達になるためには、私はジョンと片をつけるべきことが
あります。*Watakushitachi ga mata tomodachi ni naru tame niwa, watakushi wa Jon to kata o tsukeru beki koto ga arimasu.*

know the score — 事実をつかんでいる — *jijitsu o tsukande iru*

Unless you know the score, don't offer your opinion. 事実をつかんで
いない限り、自分の意見を述べない方が賢明です。*Jijitsu o tsukande inai kagiri, jibun no iken o nobenai hō ga kenmei desu.*

scratch — 零点 — *reiten*

from scratch — 零から — *zero kara*

When the negotiations failed, we had to start over from scratch. 交渉が

失敗して、私達は零からやり直さなければなりませんでした。
Kōshō ga shippai shite, watakushitachi wa zero kara yarinaosanakereba narimasen deshita.

---

screw — ネジ／ネジを締める — *neji/neji o shimeru*

have a screw loose — 正気ではない — *shōki dewa nai*

These days John seems to have a screw loose. ジョンは最近、正気ではないみたいです。*Jon wa saikin, shōki dewa nai mitai desu.*

screw something up — へまをして台無しにする — *hema o shite dainashi ni suru*

This job is important; let's not do anything to screw things up. この仕事は大切だから、へまをして事を台無しにしないようにしましょう。*Kono shigoto wa taisetsu dakara, hema o shite koto o dainashi ni shinai yō ni shimashō.*

put the screws (on someone) — 締め上げる — *shimeageru*

The police put the screws on him, and he confessed. 警察が締め上げて、彼は白状しました。*Keisatsu ga shimeagete, kare wa hakujō shimashita.*

---

sea — 海 — *umi*

(all) at sea about something — どうしていいか分からない — *dō shite ii ka wakaranai*

When it comes to computers, he's all at sea. コンピュータのことになると、彼はどうしていいか分かりません。*Konpyūta no koto ni naru to, kare wa dō shite ii ka wakarimasen.*

---

seam — 縫い目 — *nuime*

burst at the seams — はちきれる — *hachikireru*

This attache case is so full it's bursting at the seams. このアタッシュケースは一杯で、はちきれそうです。*Kono atasshukēsu wa ippai de, hachikiresō desu.*

come/fall apart at the seams — 自制心を失う — *jiseishin o ushinau*

With all the stress today, he's coming apart at the seams. 今日はストレス続きで、彼は自制心を失いつつあります。*Kyō wa sutoresu tsuzuki de, kare wa jiseishin o ushinaitsutsu arimasu.*

---

search — 探す — *sagasu*
 search high and low — くまなく探す — *kumanaku sagasu*
 I've searched high and low for my keys, but I can't find them.　鍵を
 くまなく探したのですが、見つかりません。*Kagi o kumanaku
 sagashita no desu ga, mitsukarimasen.*

---

season — 季節 — *kisetsu*
 open season — 寄ってたかって批判する — *yotte takatte hihan suru*
 Since the scandal, it's been open season on the congressman.
 スキャンダル以来、誰もがあの議員を寄ってたかって批判して
 います。*Sukyandaru irai, daremo ga yotte takatte ano giin o hihan
 shite imasu.*

---

seat — 臀部／席 — *denbu/seki*
 by the seat of one's pants — 勘に頼って — *kan ni tayotte*
 He set up the equipment by the seat of his pants.　彼は、勘に頼って
 装置を設定しました。*Kare wa, kan ni tayotte sōchi o settei
 shimashita.*

 hot seat — 難しい立場 — *muzukashii tachiba*
 Since his indictment, the mayor has been on the hot seat.　市長は起訴
 されて以来、難しい立場に立っています。*Shichō wa kiso sarete
 irai, muzukashii tachiba ni tatte imasu.*

---

see — 見る — *miru*
 see/think fit — 必要を認める — *hitsuyō o mitomeru*
 Because he didn't see fit to ask for directions, they got lost.　彼が道順を
 聞く必要を認めなかったので、彼等は道に迷ってしまいました。
 *Kare ga michijun o kiku hitsuyō o mitomenakatta node, karera wa michi
 ni mayotte shimaimashita.*

 see someone through — 面倒を見尽くす — *mendō o mitsukusu*
 We saw John through his illness before we left on our trip.　私達は
 病気のジョンの面倒を見尽くしてから、旅行に出ました。
 *Watakushitachi wa byōki no Jon no mendō o mitsukushite kara, ryokō ni
 demashita.*

 see something through — 完了させる — *kanryō saseru*
 They want to see the project through before they take their vacation.

彼等はバカンスに行く前に、この企画を完了させたいです。*Karera wa bakansu ni iku mae ni, kono kikaku o kanryō sasetai desu.*

see through someone or something — 見通す — *mitōsu*
When Mary told a lie, her mother saw right through it. メリーが嘘を ついたとき、彼女のお母さんはそれをすっかり見通しました。 *Merī ga uso o tsuita toki, kanojo no okāsan wa sore o sukkari mitōshimashita.*

see to someone or something — 気を配る — *ki o kubaru*
Please see to the lights before you lock up. 閉める前に、明かりにも 気を配って下さい。*Shimeru mae ni, akari nimo ki o kubatte kudasai.*

seeing is believing — 百聞は一見に如かず — *hyakubun wa ikken ni shikazu*
I never thought he would stop smoking, but seeing is believing. 彼が タバコを止めるとは思ってもいませんでしたが、百聞は一見に しかずです。*Kare ga tabako o yameru towa omotte mo imasen deshita ga, hyakubun wa ikken ni shikazu desu.*

---

seed — 種 — *tane*
go to seed — ひどくなる — *hidoku naru*
Peeling paint, leaky pipes, broken windowpanes—his place is going to seed! はげたペンキ、水漏れするパイプ、破れた窓ガラス。 ここは、ひどくなります。*Hageta penki, mizumore suru paipu, yabureta mado garasu. Koko wa, hidoku narimasu.*

---

sell — 売る — *uru*
sell out — 寝返りを打つ — *negaeri o utsu*
Don't worry about Bill; he'd never sell out to our competitors. ビルに ついては心配いりません。彼は、競争相手の会社に寝返りを 打ったりしませんから。*Biru ni tsuite wa shinpai irimasen. Kare wa, kyōsō aite no kaisha ni negaeri o uttari shimasen kara.*

sell someone on something — 納得させる — *nattoku saseru*
We'll have to sell the boss on this plan before we can proceed. 私達は この計画に取りかかる前に、社長を納得させねばなりません。 *Watakushitachi wa kono keikaku ni torikakaru mae ni, shachō o nattoku saseneba narimasen.*

sell someone or something short — 見くびる — *mikubiru*
Mary knows her job; don't sell her short.　メリーは自らの仕事をよく
知っているから、彼女を見くびってはいけません。*Merī wa mizukara
no shigoto o yoku shitte iru kara, kanojo o mikubitte wa ikemasen.*

---

send — 送る — *okuru*
get/give a big send-off — 送別会を開く — *sōbetsu kai o hiraku*
When Jim joined the army, we gave him a big send-off.　ジムが陸軍に
入隊したとき、私達は彼のために大送別会を開きました。*Jimu ga
rikugun ni nyūtai shita toki, watakushitachi wa kare no tame ni dai
sōbetsu kai o hirakimashita.*

send someone packing — お払い箱にする — *oharaibako ni suru*
When they saw how incompetent he was, they sent him packing.　彼が
どんなに無能か分かったとき、彼等は彼をお払い箱にしました。
*Kare ga donna ni munō ka wakatta toki, karera wa kare o oharaibako ni
shimashita.*

---

senses — 正気／判断力 — *shōki/handan ryoku*
come to one's senses — 正気に戻る — *shōki ni modoru*
Mary was being unreasonable, but she finally came to her senses.　メリーは
理屈にかないませんでしたが、やっと正気に戻りました。*Merī
wa rikutsu ni kanaimasen deshita ga, yatto shōki ni modorimashita.*

horse sense — 実用的な知識 — *jitsuyōteki na chishiki*
John doesn't have a college degree, but he does have horse sense.　ジョンは
学士号は持っていませんが、実用的な知識があります。*Jon wa
gakushi gō wa motte imasen ga, jitsuyōteki na chishiki ga arimasu.*

out of one's senses — 気が触れる — *ki ga fureru*
Mary quit her job? Is she out of her senses?　メリーが仕事を辞めたって。
彼女は気が触れたのではないですか。*Merī ga shigoto o yametatte!
Kanojo wa, ki ga fureta no dewa nai desu ka.*

take leave of one's senses — 正気を失う — *shōki o ushinau*
What a foolish thing to do! He must have taken leave of his senses.
なんて馬鹿なことをしたんでしょう。彼は正気を失ったに違い
ありません。*Nante baka na koto o shitandeshō. Kare wa, shōki o
ushinatta ni chigai arimasen.*

serve — 仕える — *tsukaeru*

serve someone right — 当然の報い — *tōzen no mukui*

He failed the exam. It serves him right; he never studies.　彼は試験に
落ちてしまいましたが、当然の報いです。彼は、全然勉強
しないんですから。*Kare wa shiken ni ochite shimaimashita ga, tōzen
no mukui desu. Kare wa, zenzen benkyō shinaindesu kara.*

service — 奉仕 — *hōshi*

pay lip service (to something) — 口では調子のいいことを言う —
kuchi dewa chōshi no ii koto o iu

John pays lip service to better education, but he won't join the PTA.
ジョンは教育の改善について口では調子のいいことを言っても、
ＰＴＡには加わろうとしません。*Jon wa kyōiku no kaizen ni tsuite
kuchi dewa chōshi no ii koto o itte mo, pītīē ni wa kuwawarō to
shimasen.*

set — 据え付ける — *suetsukeru*

set someone back something — お金がかかる — *okane ga kakaru*

Last night's dinner set me back $200.　昨夜のディナーは、２００ドル
かかりました。*Sakuya no dīnā wa, ni hyaku doru kakarimashita.*

set someone or something straight — はっきりさせる — *hakkiri
saseru*

They were confused about what happened, so John set them straight.
彼等は何が起こったか混乱していたので、ジョンがはっきり
させました。*Karera wa nani ga okotta ka konran shite ita node, Jon
ga hakkiri sasemashita.*

set someone up — 罠にかける — *wana ni kakeru*

When he was caught selling drugs, he said that someone had set him up.
彼は麻薬を売っていて捕まったとき、誰かが彼を罠にかけたんだ
と言いました。*Kare wa mayaku o utte ite tsukamatta toki, dareka ga
kare o wana ni kaketanda to iimashita.*

settle — 据える — *sueru*

settle for something — 受け入れる — *ukeireru*

They want a three-bedroom house, and they won't settle for anything less.
彼等は寝室が三部屋ある家が欲しいので、それ以下のものは

受け入れません。*Karera wa shinshitsu ga mi heya aru ie ga hoshii node, sore ika no mono wa ukeiremasen.*

settle up — 清算する — *seisan suru*
John paid the bill last night; I want to settle up with him today.　昨日の晩はジョンが勘定を払ったので、私は今日それを清算したいです。*Kinō no ban wa Jon ga kanjō o haratta node, watakushi wa kyō sore o seisan shitai desu.*

---

shadow — 影 — *kage*
afraid of one's own shadow — ちょっとしたことにもびくびくする — *chotto shita koto ni mo bikubiku suru*
That child is so timid he's afraid of his own shadow.　その子はとても臆病なので、ちょっとしたことにもびくびくします。*Sono ko wa totemo okubyō nanode, chotto shita koto ni mo bikubiku shimasu.*

beyond the shadow of a doubt — 疑いなく — *utagai naku*
They proved his guilt beyond the shadow of a doubt.　彼等は彼の有罪を、疑いなく証明しました。*Karera wa kare no yūzai o, utagai naku shōmei shimashita.*

---

shake — 揺さぶり — *yusaburi*
give someone a fair shake — 公平な扱いをする — *kōhei na atsukai o suru*
Every employee gets a fair shake around here.　ここでは、従業員一人一人が公平な扱いを受けています。*Koko dewa, jūgyōin hitori hitori ga kōhei na atsukai o ukete imasu.*

no great shakes — 大したことはない — *taishita koto wa nai*
He's no great shakes at computers.　彼は、コンピュータにかけては大したことありません。*Kare wa, konpyūta ni kakete wa taishita koto arimasen.*

shake someone or something down — 金をゆすり取る — *kane o yusuritoru*
The gangsters tried to shake the merchants down for protection money.　ギャングは商店主たちから、用心棒料として金をゆすり取ろうとしました。*Gyangu wa shōten shu tachi kara, yōjinbō ryō toshite kane o yusuritorō to shimashita.*

---

shame — 恥 — haji

crying shame — 恥の極み — haji no kiwami

It's a crying shame that our city streets are so dangerous. この市の
街頭がひどく危険なのは、恥の極みです。Kono shi no gaitō ga
hidoku kiken na no wa, haji no kiwami desu.

put someone to shame — 恥ずかしい思いをさせる — hazukashii omoi
o saseru

John's report put us to shame. ジョンの素晴らしい報告書は、私達に
恥ずかしい思いをさせました。Jon no subarashii hōkokusho wa,
watakushitachi ni hazukashii omoi o sasemashita.

Shame on someone. — 恥を知れ — haji o shire

You made your sister cry, Billy? Shame on you! ビリー、妹を泣かせた
でしょ。恥を知りなさい。Birī, imōto o nakaseta desho. Haji o
shirinasai.

---

shape — 作る — tsukuru

shape up — もっとしっかり仕事する — motto shikkari shigoto suru

Mary should shape up if she wants to keep her job. メリーは今の
仕事を続けたいなら、もっとしっかり仕事すべきです。Merī wa
ima no shigoto o tsuzuketai nara, motto shikkari shigoto subeki desu.

Shape up or ship out. — もっとしっかり仕事するか止めるかの
どちらかだ。— Motto shikkari shigoto suru ka yameru ka no
dochiraka da.

Stop making excuses for your poor performance. Shape up or ship out!
貧弱な仕事実績への言い訳は止めなさい。もっとしっかり
仕事するか、止めるか、そのどちらかです。Hinjaku na shigoto
jisseki e no iiwake wa yamenasai. Motto shikkari shigoto suru ka,
yameru ka, sono dochiraka desu.

---

shave — ひげそり — higesori

close shave — 危機一髪 — kiki ippatsu

The truck nearly hit us! That was a close shave. トラックが、私達を
もう少しではねそうになりました。それは、実に危機一髪の
ところでした。Torakku ga, watakushitachi o mō sukoshi de haneso ni
narimashita. Sore wa, jitsu ni kiki ippatsu no tokoro deshita.

---

sheep — 羊 — *hitsuji*
black sheep of the family — 一家の厄介者 — *ikka no yakkai mono*
His behavior is outrageous; he's the black sheep of the family.　彼の
振る舞いは、まともではありません。それで、彼は一家の厄介者
です。*Kare no furumai wa, matomo dewa arimasen. Sorede, kare wa
ikka no yakkai mono desu.*

sheet — シーツ — *shītsu*
(as) white as a sheet — 顔面蒼白 — *ganmen sōhaku*
He was as white as a sheet when he heard the sad news.　彼はその悲しい
ニュースを聞いて、顔面蒼白になりました。*Kare wa sono kanashii
nyūsu o kiite, ganmen sōhaku ni narimashita.*

shell — 貝殻 — *kaigara*
come out of one's shell — 自分の殻から抜け出す — *jibun no kara
kara nukedasu*
He should come out of his shell and socialize more.　彼は自分の殻から
抜け出して、もっと社交的になるべきです。*Kare wa jibun no kara
kara nukedashite, motto shakōteki ni naru beki desu.*

shellacking — 殴打 — *ōda*
get/take/give a shellacking — 完敗する — *kanpai suru*
Our team took a shellacking in the championship game.　私達のチームは、
選手権をかけた試合で完敗しました。*Watakushitachi no chīmu wa,
senshuken o kaketa shiai de kanpai shimashita.*

shine — 輝き — *kagayaki*
take a shine to someone or something — 一目で好きになる — *hitome
de suki ni naru*
He's really taken a shine to his new grandson.　彼は、新しく生まれた
孫息子が一目で好きになりました。*Kare wa, atarashiku umareta
magomusuko ga hitome de suki ni narimashita.*

ship — 船 — *fune*
desert/leave a sinking ship — 困難に陥っているものを見捨てる —
konnan ni ochiitte iru mono o misuteru
The company isn't doing well, and many employees are leaving the sinking

ship.　経営状態が良くなく、大勢の社員が困難に陥っている
会社を見捨てています。*Keiei jōtai ga yoku naku, ōzei no shain ga
konnan ni ochiitte iru kaisha o misutete imasu.*

one's ship comes in — お金を儲ける — *okane o mōkeru*
When my ship comes in, I'll build my dream house.　お金を儲けたら、
夢に描いていた家を建てるつもりです。*Okane o mōketara, yume ni
egaite ita ie o tateru tsumori desu.*

run a tight ship — 完全に掌握する — *kanzen ni shōaku suru*
Mr. Jones is a good manager; he runs a tight ship.　ジョーンズ氏は
有能な経営者で、部下を完全に掌握しています。*Jōnzu shi wa
yūnō na keieisha de, buka o kanzen ni shōaku shite imasu.*

ships that pass in the night — 出くわす機会がまたとない —
dekuwasu kikai ga mata to nai
Although we work for the same company, we're like ships that pass in the
night.　私達は同じ会社で働いていますが、出くわす機会がまたと
ありません。*Watakushitachi wa onaji kaisha de hataraite imasu ga,
dekuwasu kikai ga mata to arimasen.*

---

shirt — シャツ — *shatsu*

give someone the shirt off one's back — 何でもあげる — *nandemo
ageru*
John is so good-natured he'd give you the shirt off his back.　ジョンは
親切で、何でも人にあげるでしょう。*Jon wa shinsetsu de, nandemo
hito ni ageru deshō.*

Keep your shirt on! — いらいらしないで！ — *Iraira shinai de!*
Keep your shirt on! I'll be there in a minute.　いらいらしないで。
直ぐに行くから。*Iraira shinai de! Sugu ni iku kara.*

lose one's shirt — すっからかんになる — *sukkarakan ni naru*
John lost his shirt playing poker last night.　ジョンは、昨日の晩
ポーカーですっからかんになってしまいました。
Jon wa, kinō no ban pōkā de sukkarakan ni natte shimaimashita.

---

shoe — 靴 — *kutsu*

(as) comfortable as an old shoe — とても心地がいい — *totemo
kokochi ga ii*

Their house is as comfortable as an old shoe.　彼等の家は、とても
居心地がいいです。Karera no ie wa, totemo igokochi ga ii desu.

drop the other shoe — 残りをすませる — nokori o sumaseru
The doctor said that he had found a tumor. Then he dropped the other shoe:
it was malignant.　医者は腫瘍の存在を知らせ、それから残りを
告げました。腫瘍は、悪性だったのです。Isha wa shuyō no sonzai
o shirase, sorekara nokori o tsugemashita. Shuyō wa akusei datta no
desu.

fill someone's shoes — 代わりを務める — kawari o tsutomeru
Paul was an excellent lawyer, but Tom can fill his shoes.　ポールは
優れた弁護士でしたが、トムはポールの代わりを務めることが
出来ます。Pōru wa sugureta bengoshi deshita ga, Tomu wa Pōru no
kawari o tsutomeru koto ga dekimasu.

If the shoe fits, wear it. — 思い当たる人は、気をつけろ。—
Omoiataru hito wa, ki o tsukero.
Some of you are neglecting your work. If the shoe fits, wear it.　ここは、
仕事をおろそかにしている人がいます。思い当たる人は、気を
つけなさい。Koko niwa, shigoto o orosoka ni shite iru hito ga imasu.
Omoiataru hito wa, ki o tsukenasai.

put oneself in someone else's shoes — 相手の立場になってみる —
aite no tachiba ni natte miru
If you put yourself in his shoes, you'll understand why he's so strict.
彼の立場になってみれば、なぜ彼がそんなに厳しいか分かる
でしょう。Kare no tachiba ni natte mireba, naze kare ga sonna ni
kibishii ka wakaru deshō.

step into someone's shoes — 跡を継ぐ — ato o tsugu
When Mr. Smith leaves, Mr. Jones is prepared to step into his shoes.
スミス氏が去ると、ジョーンズ氏が跡を継ぐ準備が出来ています。
Sumisu shi ga saru to, Jōnzu shi ga ato o tsugu junbi ga dekite imasu.

The shoe is on the other foot. — 立場が逆になる — tachiba ga gyaku
ni naru
Now that the news anchor is being interviewed, the shoe is on the other
foot.　ニュース番組の総合司会者がインタビューされて、今は
立場が逆になっています。Nyūsu bangumi no sōgō shikaisha ga
intabyū sarete, ima wa tachiba ga gyaku ni natte imasu.

shoestring — 靴紐 — *kutsuhimo*

get along on a shoestring — 爪に灯をともして暮らす — *tsume ni hi o tomoshite kurasu*

With little income, they're used to getting along on a shoestring. 彼等は収入が殆ど無いので、爪に灯をともして暮らすのに慣れています。 *Karera wa shūnyū ga hotondo nai node, tsume ni hi o tomoshite kurasu no ni narete imasu.*

shop — 店 — *mise*

talk shop — 仕事の話しをする — *shigoto no hanashi o suru*

This is a social occasion, but there they are, talking shop. 社交の場だというのに、またあの人達、仕事の話しをしています。 *Shakō no ba da to iu noni, mata ano hitotachi, shigoto no hanashi o shite imasu.*

short — 短い — *mijikai*

short and sweet — 短くて要を得ている — *mijikakute yō o ete iru*

It's been a long day, so I hope he'll keep his presentation short and sweet. 忙し尽くめの日だったので、彼の発表が短くて要を得ているといいんですけれど。 *Isogashizukume no hi datta node, kare no happyō ga mijikakute yō o ete iru to iindesu keredo.*

shot — 発射／狙い／試み — *hassha/nerai/kokoromi*

call the shots/tune — 采配を振るう — *saihai o furuu*

In our company, Ms. Doe calls the shots. 我が社では、ドーさんが采配を振るっています。 *Waga sha dewa, Dō san ga saihai o furutte imasu.*

give something one's best shot — 最善を尽くす — *saizen o tsukusu*

This project is difficult, but I'm going to give it my best shot. この企画は容易ではありませんが、私は最善を尽くすつもりです。 *Kono kikaku wa yōi dewa arimasen ga, watakushi wa saizen o tsukusu tsumori desu.*

have/take a shot at something — 挑戦する — *chōsen suru*

I failed the course, but I'm going to take another shot at it. 私はその科目に落ちましたが、もう一度挑戦してみるつもりです。 *Watakushi wa sono kamoku ni ochimashita ga, mō ichido chōsen shite miru tsumori desu.*

(not) by a long shot — とんでもない — *tondemonai*
Are we giving up? Not by a long shot.　私達が諦めるかつて。
とんでもない。*Watakushitachi ga akirameru katte. Tondemonai.*

off like a shot — 鉄砲玉のように飛び出す — *teppōdama no yō ni
tobidasu*
When the teacher dismissed the class, Johnny was off like a shot.　授業が
終わるや、ジョニ－は鉄砲玉のようにクラスを飛び出しました。
*Jugyō ga owaru ya, Jonī wa teppōdama no yō ni kurasu o
tobidashimashita.*

shot in the arm — 励ましの即効薬 — *hagemashi no sokkō yaku*
The phone call from his son gave Ted a shot in the arm.　息子からの
電話が、テッドを励ます即効薬になりました。*Musuko kara no
denwa ga, Teddo o hagemasu sokkō yaku ni narimashita.*

shot in the dark — 全くの当てずっぽう — *mattaku no atezuppō*
This strategy was a shot in the dark, but it worked.　この戦略は全くの
当てずっぽうでしたが、うまくいきました。*Kono senryaku wa
mattaku no atezuppō deshita ga, umaku ikimashita.*

---

shoulder — 肩 — *kata*

get/give someone the cold shoulder — よそよそしくする —
yosoyososhiku suru
I guess she's still angry, because she gave me the cold shoulder today.
彼女は、まだ怒っているようです。なぜなら、今日、私に
よそよそしくしたからです。*Kanojo wa, mada okotte iru yō desu.
Nazenara, kyō, watakushi ni yosoyososhiku shita kara sesu.*

on someone's shoulders — 自らの双肩に — *mizukara no sōken ni*
The committee chairman has a lot of responsibility on his shoulders.
委員長は、自らの双肩に多大な責任を担っています。*Iinchō wa,
mizukara no sōken ni tadai na sekinin o ninatte imasu.*

put one's shoulder to the wheel — 本腰を入れる — *hongoshi o ireru*
If you put your shoulder to the wheel, you can finish the job soon.
本腰を入れるなら、あなたはこの仕事を直に終わらせることが
出来ます。*Hongoshi o ireru nara, anata wa kono shigoto o jiki ni
owaraseru koto ga dekimasu.*

shoulder to shoulder — 一致団結して — *itchi danketsu shite*

The union members stood shoulder to shoulder to present their demands.
組合員は一致団結して立ち並び、彼等の要求を提出しました。
*Kumiaiin wa itchi danketsu shite tachinarabi, karera no yōkyū o
teishutsu shimashita.*

straight from the shoulder — あるがままに — *aru ga mama ni*
Bill gave us the news straight from the shoulder; he didn't hold anything
back.　ビルはその知らせをあるがままに私達に伝え、何も
隠しだてしませんでした。*Biru wa sono shirase o aru ga mama ni
watakushitachi ni tsutae, nani mo kakushidate shimasen deshita.*

---

shout — 叫ぶ — *sakebu*
all over but the shouting — 片が付く — *kata ga tsuku*
The merger is complete; it's all over but the shouting.　会社の合併は
完了して、これで片が付きました。*Kaisha no gappei wa kanryō
shite, kore de kata ga tsukimashita.*

---

show — ショー — *shō*

dog and pony show — ありきたりの実演や展示 — *arikitari no jitsuen
ya tenji*
His dog and pony show is interesting, but no one's buying anything.　彼の
実演や展示は面白いけれどありきたりで、買う人は誰もいません。
*Kare no jitsuen ya tenji wa omoshiroi keredo arikitari de, kau hito wa
daremo imasen.*

get the show on the road — 事に取りかかる — *koto ni torikakaru*
Enough talk; let's get the show on the road! 話しはこれ位にして、実際に事に取りかかりましょう。*Hanashi wa kore gurai ni shite, jissai ni koto ni torikakarimashō.*

steal the show/spotlight — 人気をさらう — *ninki o sarau*
Whenever she performs, she steals the show. 彼女が演技するときはいつでも、人気をさらいます。*Kanojo ga engi suru toki wa itsu demo, ninki o saraimasu.*

sick — 病気の — *byōki no*
    sick and tired of someone or something — うんざりして — *unzari shite*
    Everyone is sick and tired of their complaining. 彼等の不平不満には、誰もがうんざりしています。*Karera no fuhei fuman niwa, daremo ga unzari shite imasu.*

side — 側／方 — *kawa/hō*
    get on one's good side — 気に入られる — *ki ni irareru*
    If you want Robert to approve this, you'd better get on his good side. ロバートにこれを認めてもらいたかったら、彼に気に入られるようにするべきです。*Robāto ni kore o mitomete moraitakattara, kare ni ki ni irareru yō ni suru beki desu.*

    get up on the wrong side of the bed — 寝起きが悪い — *neoki ga warui*
    I'm in such a bad mood; I must have gotten up on the wrong side of the bed. 私の機嫌がよくないのは、今朝、寝起きが悪かったからに違いありません。*Watakushi no kigen ga yokunai no wa, kesa, neoki ga warukatta kara ni chigai arimasen.*

    know which side one's bread is buttered on — 何が自分の得になるか知っている — *nani ga jibun no toku ni naru ka shitte iru*
    He always obeys the boss; he knows which side his bread is buttered on. 彼がいつも上司の言うことに従うのは、何が自分の得になるか知っているからです。*Kare ga itsumo jōshi no iu koto ni shitagau no wa, nani ga jibun no toku ni naru ka shitte iru kara desu.*

    laugh out of the other side of one's mouth — 得意満面だったのが急にしょげる — *tokui manmen datta no ga kyū ni shogeru*
    He boasted he'd win, but he lost; now he's laughing out of the other side of

his mouth. 彼は勝つのだと自慢していましたが、負けて
しまいました。それで今は、得意満面だったのが急にしょげて
います。Kare wa katsu no da to jiman shite imashita ga, makete
shimaimashita. Sorede ima wa, tokui manmen datta no ga kyū ni shogete
imasu.

split one's sides laughing — 腹を抱えて笑う — hara o kakaete warau
The movie was so funny we split our sides laughing. その映画はすごく
おかしかったので、私達は腹を抱えて笑ってしまいました。Sono
eiga wa sugoku okashikatta node, watakushitachi wa hara o kakaete
waratte shimaimashita.

take sides — 一方の肩を持つ — ippō no kata o motsu
Bill and Pete were arguing, but I didn't want to take sides. ビルとピートが
議論していましたが、私は一方の肩を持つことはしたくありません
でした。Biru to Pīto ga giron shite imashita ga, watakushi wa ippō no
kata o motsu koto wa shitaku arimasen deshita.

the wrong side of the tracks — 貧困住宅街 — hinkon jūtaku gai
She came from the wrong side of the tracks, but now she's quite successful.
彼女は貧困住宅街の生まれですが、今はとても成功しています。
Kanojo wa hinkon jūtaku gai no umare desu ga, ima wa totemo seikō
shite imasu.

---

sight — 視力／光景 — shiryoku/kōkei

lower one's sights — 目標を低くする — mokuhyō o hikuku suru
He wanted to attend a top university, but he's had to lower his sights.
彼は一流大学に行きたかったけれど、目標を低くしなければ
なりませんでした。Kare wa ichiryū daigaku ni ikitakatta keredo,
mokuhyō o hikuku shinakereba narimasen deshita.

Out of sight, out of mind. — 見なければ気にせずに済む —
minakereba ki ni sezu ni sumu
Better hide the candy. Out of sight, out of mind. キャンディーは、隠して
しまった方がいいです。見なければ、気にせずに済みますから。
Kyandī wa, kakushite shimatta hō ga ii desu. Minakereba, ki ni sezu ni
sumimasu kara.

raise one's sights — 目標を高める — mokuhyō o takameru
Why don't you raise your sights and become a doctor? 目標を高めて、

医者になったらどうですか。*Mokuhyō o takamete, isha ni nattara dō desu ka.*

sight for sore eyes — 会えて嬉しい — *aete ureshii*

Dad is back from his trip; he's a sight for sore eyes. 父が旅行から帰ってきて、会えて嬉しいです。*Chichi ga ryokō kara kaette kite, aete ureshii desu.*

---

sign — 署名する — *shomei suru*

sign on — 加わる — *kuwawaru*

Paul signed on with our company last week. ポールは先週、私達の会社に加わりました。*Pōru wa senshū, watakushitachi no kaisha ni kuwawarimashita.*

sign over — 正式に譲り渡す — *seishiki ni yuzuriwatasu*

He signed over his shares of stock to his son. 彼は株の持ち分を、息子に正式に譲り渡しました。*Kare wa kabu no mochibun o, musuko ni seishiki ni yuzuriwatashimashita.*

sign up — 合意の署名をする — *gōi no shomei o suru*

He signed up to join a health club recently. 彼は最近ヘルスクラブの会員になるため、合意の署名をしました。
Kare wa saikin herusukurabu no kaiin ni naru tame, gōi no shomei o shimashita.

signed, sealed, and delivered — 正式手続きを終えて — *seishiki tetsuzuki o oete*

When the contract is signed, sealed, and delivered, the work can begin. この契約の正式手続きを終えると、仕事が始まります。*Kono keiyaku no seishiki tetsuzuki o oeru to, shigoto ga hajimarimasu.*

---

sin — 罪 — *tsumi*

(as) ugly as sin — みにくい限り — *minikui kagiri*

The opossum they caught was as ugly as sin. 彼等が捕まえた袋ネズミは、みにくい限りでした。*Karera ga tsukamaeta fukuronezumi wa, minikui kagiri deshita.*

---

sink — 沈む — *shizumu*

sink or swim — 運命が決まる — *unmei ga kimaru*

The company will sink or swim with this new technology. この新技術

次第で、会社の今後の運命が決まるでしょう。*Kono shin gijutsu shidai de, kongo no kaisha no unmei ga kimaru deshō.*

---

sit — 座る — *suwaru*

sit tight — 辛抱して待つ — *shinbō shite matsu*
If you can sit tight, we'll have an answer for you in an hour. 辛抱して待てるなら、一時間で回答できるでしょう。*Shinbō shite materu nara, ichi jikan de kaitō dekiru deshō.*

sitting pretty — 豪華な暮らしをして — *gōka na kurashi o shite*
Now that he has written a best selling novel, John is sitting pretty. ジョンは書いた小説がベストセラーになってから、豪華な暮らしをしています。*Jon wa kaita shōsetsu ga besutoserā ni natte kara, gōka na kurashi o shite imasu.*

---

situation — 状況 — *jōkyō*

no-win situation — どうしようもない状態 — *dō shiyō mo nai jōtai*
If he works late, his wife is angry; if he doesn't, his boss is. It's a no-win situation. 遅くまで働けば奥さんが怒るし、そうしなければ上司が怒るし、彼はどうしようもない状態に陥っています。
Osoku made hatarakeba okusan ga okoru shi, sō shinakereba jōshi ga okoru shi, kare wa dō shiyō mo nai jōtai ni ochiitte imasu.

---

six — 六 — *roku*

at sixes and sevens — 何をしていいか分からずに — *nani o shite ii ka wakarazu ni*
Jill has been at sixes and sevens since her children left for college.
子供たちが大学に進学して家を出てから、ジルは何をしていいか分からずにいます。*Kodomotachi ga daigaku ni shingaku shite ie o dete kara, Jiru wa nani o shite ii ka wakarazu ni imasu.*

six of one and half dozen of the other — いずれにしても似たり寄ったり — *izure ni shitemo nitari yottari*
This restaurant or that one? It's six of one and half dozen of the other. このレストランにするか、それともあのレストランにするか。いずれにしても、似たり寄ったりです。*Kono resutoran ni suru ka soretomo ano resutoran ni suru ka. Izure ni shitemo, nitari yottari desu.*

size — 寸法／計る — sunpō/hakaru

beat/cut/take someone down to size — 鼻をへし折る — hana o heshioru

We tried to argue our point, but their negotiators cut us down to size. 私達はこちら側の主眼点を主張しようとしたけれど、交渉相手に鼻をへし折られてしまいました。Watakushitachi wa kochira gawa no shugan ten o shuchō shiyō to shita keredo, kōshō aite ni hana o heshiorarete shimaimashita.

size someone or something up — 品定めをする — shinasadame o suru

When the negotiators met, they tried to size each other up. 交渉担当者が会ったとき、彼等はお互いの品定めをしようとしました。Kōshō tantōsha ga atta toki, karera wa otagai no shinasadame o shiyō to shimashita.

That's about the size of it. — そういうことだ。 — Sō iu koto da.

Is the information accurate? Yes, that's about the size of it. この情報は正確かつて。もちろん、そういうことです。Kono jōhō wa seikaku katte. Mochiron, sō iu koto desu.

skeleton — 骸骨 — gaikotsu

skeleton in the closet — 内輪の秘め事 — uchiwa no himegoto

He has too many skeletons in his closet to run for public office. 彼には内輪の秘め事が多すぎるで、公職には立候補できません。Kare niwa uchiwa no himegoto ga ōsugiru node, kōshoku niwa rikkōho dekimasen.

skin — 皮膚 — hifu

skin and bones — やせ細って — yasehosotte

Since she began her diet, she's become nothing but skin and bones. ダイエットを始めて以来、彼女はすっかりやせ細ってしまいました。Daietto o hajimete irai, kanojo wa sukkari yasehosotte shimaimashita.

by the skin of one's teeth — 間一髪で — kan ippatsu de

He made the train by the skin of his teeth. 彼は、間一髪で汽車に間に合いました。Kare wa kan ippatsu de, kisha ni maniaimashita.

get under someone's skin — いらいらさせる — iraira saseru

She's so annoying; she gets under everyone's skin. 彼女は本当に神経にさわるたちで、人をいらいらさせます。Kanojo wa hontō ni *shinkei ni sawaru tachi de, hito o iraira sasemasu.*

jump out of one's skin — 驚いて飛び上がる — *odoroite tobiagaru*
When I heard the sudden noise, I nearly jumped out of my skin. 突然の
物音を聞いて、驚いて飛び上がりそうになりました。*Totsuzen no
monooto o kiite, odoroite tobiagarisō ni narimashita.*

no skin off one's nose/teeth — 知ったことではない — *shitta koto
dewa nai*
If she quits her job, it's no skin off my nose. 彼女が仕事を辞めても、
私の知ったことではありません。*Kanojo ga shigoto o yametemo,
watakushi no shitta koto dewa arimasen.*

save one's skin — 面目を失わずにすむ — *menboku o ushinawazu ni sumu*
John saved his skin by signing the new clients yesterday. ジョンは昨日、
何人か新しい顧客の署名にこぎ着けて、面目を失わずにすみました。
*Jon wa kinō, nannin ka atarashii kokyaku no shomei ni kogitsukete,
menboku o ushinawazu ni sumimashita.*

soaked to the skin — ずぶ濡れになって — *zubunure ni natte*
The children were out in the rain and got soaked to the skin. 子供たちは
雨の中を外にいて、ずぶ濡れになりました。*Kodomotachi wa ame
no naka o soto ni ite, zubunure ni narimashita.*

skip — 飛び越す — *tobikosu*
skip out on someone or something — 置き去りにする — *okizari ni
suru*
Bill skipped out on his family and is being sued for child support. ビルは
家族を置き去りにして、子供の養育費の件で訴えられています。
*Biru wa kazoku o okizari ni shite, kodomo no yōikuhi no ken de
uttaerarete imasu.*

skull — 頭蓋骨 — *zugaikotsu*
get something through someone's (thick) skull — 頭に入れる —
atama ni ireru
He should get it through his thick skull that we start work at 9 A.M.
私達は午前九時に働き始めることを、彼は頭に入れるべきです。
*Watakushitachi wa gozen ku ji ni hatarahi hajimeru koto o, kara wa
atama ni ireru beki desu.*

sky — 空 — *sora*

be/seem sky-high — とてつもなく高い — *totetsu mo naku takai*

To Westerners, prices in Japan seem sky-high. 欧米人にとって、日本
での値段はとてつもなく高く感じられます。 *Ōbei jin ni totte,
Nihon de no nedan wa totetsu mo naku takaku kanjiraremasu.*

out of a clear blue sky — 突然 — *totsuzen*

Out of a clear blue sky, Mary asked John for a divorce. 突然、メリーは
ジョンに離婚を求めました。*Totsuzen, Merī wa Jon ni rikon o
motomemashita.*

praise someone or something to the skies — 褒めちぎる —
homechigiru

When the senator came to town, he praised the mayor to the skies. その
上院議員が町にやってきたとき、彼は市長を褒めちぎりました。
*Sono jōin giin ga machi ni yatte kita toki, kare wa shichō o
homechigirimashita.*

reach for the sky — 目標を高く掲げる — *mokuhyō o takaku kakageru*

Why not reach for the sky? You have a good chance of succeeding.
目標を高く掲げたらどうですか。あなたには、成功する機会が
十分ありますよ。*Mokuhyō o takaku kakagetara dō desu ka. Anata
niwa, seikō suru kikai ga jūbun arimasu yo.*

The sky's the limit. — 金に糸目を付けなくていい。— *Kane ni itome
o tsukenakute ii.*

Don't hold back on expenses for this project. The sky's the limit. この
企画には、経費を押さえる必要はありません。金に糸目を
付けなくていいのです。*Kono kikaku niwa, keihi o osaeru hitsuyō
wa arimasen. Kane ni itome o tsukenakute ii no desu.*

slap — ぴしゃっと打つ — *pishatto utsu*

slap on the wrist — 軽いいましめ — *karui imashime*

Although she was caught cheating, she only got a slap on the wrist.
彼女はカンニングしていて捕まったけれど、軽いいましめを
受けただけでした。*Kanojo wa kanningu shite ite tsukamatta keredo,
karui imashime o uketa dake deshita.*

slap in the face — 打撃 — *dageki*

Losing the election was a slap in the face for the ruling party. 選挙に

負けたことは、与党にとっては打撃でした。*Senkyo ni maketa koto wa, yotō ni totte wa dageki deshita.*

slap/throw together — 急いで支度をする — *isoide shitaku o suru*
On short notice, Sally slapped together a meal for the group. 急に知らせがあって、サリ−はグル−プのために急いで食事の支度をしました。*Kyū ni shirase ga atte, Sarī wa gurūpu no tame ni isoide shokuji no shitaku o shimashita.*

slate — スレ−ト — *surēto*
start off/over with a clean slate — 新規まき直しする — *shinki makinaoshi suru*
Let's forget our past failures and start over with a clean slate. 過去の失敗を忘れて、新規まき直ししましょう。*Kako no shippai o wasurete, shinki makinaoshi shimashō.*

sleep — 睡眠／眠る — *suimin/nemuru*
lose sleep (over someone or something) — 心配する — *shinpai suru*
I know you're concerned about this, but don't lose any sleep over it. あなたがそれについて気にしているのは分かりますが、心配しないように。*Anata ga sore ni tsuite ki ni shite iru no wa wakarimasu ga, shinpai shinai yō ni.*

sleep on something — 一晩考えてみる — *hitoban kangaete miru*
The chairman said he wanted to sleep on it before making a decision. 会長は、決断を下す前に一晩考えてみたいと言いました。*Kaichō wa, ketsudan o kudasu mae ni hitoban kangaete mitai to iimashita.*

sleep something off — 効いて眠る — *kiite nemuru*
John's upstairs sleeping off the effects of the medication. ジョンは二階で、薬が効いて眠っています。*Jon wa nikai de, kusuri ga kiite nemutte imasu.*

sleeve — 袖 — *sode*
have something up one's sleeve — 何か計画がある — *nanika keikaku ga aru*
Mr. Doe says he can help us; I think he has something up his sleeve. ド−氏が私達を助けてくれると言うからには、彼には何か計画が

あると思います。*Dō shi ga watakushitachi o tasukete kureru to iu
kara niwa, kare ni wa nanika keikaku ga aru to omoimasu.*

roll one's sleeves up — 腕まくりする — *udemakuri suru*
It's time to roll up our sleeves and get back to work. 腕まくりして、
仕事に戻るときです。*Udemakuri shite, shigoto ni modoru toki desu.*

---

slip — 滑る — *suberu*
slip of the tongue — 単なる失言 — *tannaru shitsugen*
He didn't mean to say what he did; it was a slip of the tongue. 彼の
言ったことに、意図はありませんでした。それは単なる失言
だったのです。*Kare no itta koto ni, ito wa arimasen deshita. Sore wa
tannaru shitsugen datta no desu.*

let something slip — うっかり喋ってしまう — *ukkari shabette shimau*
The party is supposed to be a surprise, so don't let it slip. この
パーティーは主客には隠してあるら、うっかり喋ってしまわない
ように。*Kono pātī wa shukyaku niwa kakushite aru kara, ukkari
shabette shimawanai yō ni.*

---

sly — ずるい — *zurui*
do something on the sly — こっそりとする — *kossori to suru*
The children were watching a forbidden TV program on the sly.
子供たちは、禁じられているテレビ番組をこっそりと見ていました。
Kodomotachi wa, kinjirarete iru terebi bangumi o kossori to mite imashita.

---

smile — 微笑み — *hohoemi*
crack a smile — 笑顔を見せる — *egao o miseru*
No matter what, Joe never cracks a smile. どんなことがあっても、
ジョーは決して笑顔を見せません。*Donna koto ga attemo, Jō wa
kesshite egao o misemasen.*

---

smoke — 煙 — *kemuri*
go up in smoke — 消え去る — *kiesaru*
When the quarterback was injured, the team's hopes went up in smoke.
クォーターバックが負傷して、チームの望みが消え去って
しまいました。*Kuōtābakku ga fushō shite, chīmu no nozomi ga
kiesatte shimaimashita.*

smoke and mirrors — ぎまん — *giman*
The mayor's plans are all smoke and mirrors.　市長の計画は、ぎまんに
満ちています。*Shichō no keikaku wa, giman ni michite imasu.*

Where there's smoke, there's fire. — 火の無い所に煙は立たない。—
Hi no nai tokoro ni kemuri wa tatanai.
He denies stealing, but each week, more money is missing. Where there's
smoke, there's fire.　彼は盗みを否定しますが、それでも毎週、
お金が無くなっています。彼が何と言おうと、火の無い所に煙は
立ちません。*Kare wa nusumi o hitei shimasu ga, sore demo maishū
okane ga nakunatte imasu. Kare ga nan to iō to, hi no nai tokoro ni
kemuri wa tachimasen.*

---

smooth — 滑らかにする — *nameraka ni suru*
smooth something over — 事を和らげる — *koto o yawarageru*
After the argument, they both tried to smooth things over.　口論の後、
彼等は双方とも事を和らげようとしました。*Kōron no ato, karera
wa sōhō tomo koto o yawarageyō to shimashita.*

---

snake — 蛇 — *hebi*
snake in the grass — 卑劣な人間 — *hiretsu na ningen*
What a terrible person! She's a real snake in the grass.　何てひどい人
なんでしょう。彼女は、実に卑劣な人間です。*Nante hidoi hito nan
deshō. Kanojo wa, jitsu ni hiretsu na ningen desu.*

---

snap — ぷっつり切る — *puttsuri kiru*
snap out of something — 振り切る — *furikiru*
I hope she'll snap out of her bad mood and get down to work.　彼女が
機嫌の悪さを振り切って仕事に取りかかるのを、望んでいます。
*Kanojo ga kigen no warusa o furikitte shigoto ni torikakaru no o,
nozonde imasu.*

---

snowball — 雪玉 — *yukidama*
(not) have a snowball's chance in hell — 見込みが全くない — *mikomi
ga mattaku nai*
We don't have a snowball's chance in hell of winning the game this week.
私達が今週の試合に勝つ見込みは、全くありません。

Watakushitachi ga konshū no shiai ni katsu mikomi wa, mattaku arimasen.

---

snuff — 嗅ぎタバコ — *kagi tabako*
  (not) up to snuff — (不)適切 — *(fu)tekisetsu*
  Joe's performance hasn't been up to snuff lately. ジョーの最近の
  仕事ぶりは、適切ではありません。*Jō no saikin no shigotoburi wa, tekisetsu dewa arimasen.*

---

son — 息子 — *musuko*
  son of a bitch — 畜生 — *chikushō*
  That son of a bitch just stole the lady's purse! あの畜生がたった今、
  女性のハンドバッグを盗んだんだ！ *Ano chikushō ga tatta ima, josei no handobaggu o nusundanda!*

  son of a gun — こん畜生 — *konchikushō*
  Son of a gun! I lost my wallet! こん畜生！財布をなくしてしまった！
  Konchikushō! Saifu o nakushite shimatta!

---

song — 歌 — *uta*
  for a song — ただ同然で — *tada dōzen de*
  They bought their furniture for a song. 彼等は家具を、ただ同然で
  買いました。*Karera wa kagu o, tada dōzen de kaimashita.*

  go into one's song and dance — 御託を並べる — *gotaku o naraberu*
  Whenever he's late, Eugene goes into his song and dance about traffic.

ユージーンは遅くなるといつも、道路の混雑について御託を
並べます。 *Yūjīn wa osoku naru to itsumo, dōro no konzatsu ni tsuite gotaku o narabemasu.*

swan song — 最後の置き土産 — *saigo no okimiyage*
Last month's performance was the actor's swan song.　先月の公演が、
あの俳優の最後の置き土産になりました。*Sengetsu no kōen ga, ano haiyū no saigo no okimiyage ni narimashita.*

---

sorrow — 悲しみ — *kanashimi*

drown one's sorrows/troubles — 酔って悲しみ／悩みを忘れようと
する — *yotte kanashimi/nayami o wasureyō to suru*
After his divorce, Jim went to a bar to drown his sorrows.　ジムは離婚の
後、酔って悲しみを忘れようとバーに行きました。*Jimu wa rikon no ato, yotte kanashimi o wasureyō to bā ni ikimashita.*

---

sort — 種類 — *shurui*

out of sorts — 気分がすぐれれない — *kibun ga sugurenai*
He's out of sorts today. Maybe he's coming down with the flu.　彼は、今日は
気分がすぐれれません。多分、流感にかかっているのです。*Kare wa, kyō wa kibun ga suguremasen. Tabun, ryūkan ni kakatte iru no desu.*

---

soul — 魂 — *tamashii*

not tell a living soul — 人には言わない — *hito ni wa iwanai*
You can trust me with your secret; I won't tell a living soul.　あなたの
秘密については、私を信じて大丈夫です。人には絶対に言いません
から。*Anata no himitsu ni tsuite wa, watakushi o shinjite daijōbu desu. Hito ni wa zettai ni iimasen kara.*

---

sound — 叩いて調べる — *tataite shiraberu*

sound someone out — 打診する — *dashin suru*
Let's sound them out to see what they think of the proposal.　この提案に
ついて彼等がどう思うか、打診してみましょう。*Kono teian ni tsuite karera ga dō omou ka, dashin shite mimashō.*

---

soup — スープ — *supu*

(as easy as) duck soup — お茶の子さいさい — *ochanoko saisai*

Passing this course is as easy as duck soup. この科目に通るのは、お茶の子さいさいです。*Kono kamoku ni tōru no wa, ochanoko saisai desu.*

---

spade — 鋤 — *suki*
call a spade a spade — ズバリと言う — *zubari to iu*
Let's call a spade a spade: this cease-fire is doomed to failure. ズバリと言いましょう。この停戦は失敗する宿命です。*Zubari to iimashō. Kono teisen wa, shippai suru shukumei desu.*

---

spell — 綴る — *tsuzuru*
spell something out — 詳しく説明する — *kuwashiku setsumei suru*
John doesn't understand his role; we'll have to spell it out for him. ジョンは、彼の役割が分かりません。それで私達は、彼に詳しく説明しなければならないでしょう。*Jon wa, kare no yakuwari ga wakarimasen. Sorede watakushitachi wa, kare ni kuwashiku setsumei shinakereba naranai deshō.*

---

spit — 唾 — *tsuba*
be the spit and image of someone — 瓜二つ — *uri futatsu*
Suzy is the spit and image of her mother. スージーは、お母さんと瓜二つです。*Sūjī wa, okāsan to uri futatsu desu.*

---

sponge — スポンジ — *suponji*
throw in the sponge/towel — さじを投げる — *saji o nageru*
He's sick of this project; he's ready to throw in the sponge. 彼はこの企画にあきあきして、さじを投げる覚悟です。*Kare wa kono kikaku ni akiaki shite, saji o nageru kakugo desu.*

---

spoon — さじ — *saji*
born with a silver spoon in one's mouth — 裕福な家に生まれる — *yūfuku na ie ni umareru*
Tom never worries about money; he was born with a silver spoon in his mouth. トムは、お金については決して心配しません。裕福な家に生まれたからです。*Tomu wa, okane ni tsuite wa kesshite shinpai shimasen. Yūfuku na ie ni umareta kara desu.*

spoon-feed someone — 懇切丁寧に教えすぎる — *konsetsu teinei ni oshiesugiru*

Bob spoon-feeds his students; they never work out problems for themselves.　ボブは懇切丁寧に教えすぎるので、学生たちは自分で問題を解くことが決してありません。*Bobu wa konsetsu teinei ni oshiesugiru node, gakuseitachi wa jibun de mondai o toku koto ga kesshite arimasen.*

spot — 点 — *ten*

have a soft spot in one's heart for someone or something — 好きだ — *suki da*

Sarah has a soft spot in her heart for her youngest grandson.　サラは、一番小さい孫息子が好きです。*Sara wa, ichiban chiisai magomusuko ga suki desu.*

hit the spot — 正にこの上ない — *masa ni kono ue nai*

I get so thirsty after gardening; this iced tea really hits the spot.　庭仕事をして喉がとても乾いたので、このアイスティーは正にこの上ありません。*Niwa shigoto o shite nodo ga totemo kawaita node, kono aisutī wa masa ni kono ue arimasen.*

in a spot — 困って — *komatte*

I'm in a spot: I have no cash, and the restaurant doesn't take credit cards.　現金はないし、レストランはクレジットカードを受け入れないし、困っています。*Genkin wa nai shi, resutoran wa kurejittokādo o ukeirenai shi, komatte imasu.*

put someone on the spot — 苦境に立たせる — *kukyō ni tataseru*

They put John on the spot by asking him for the finished report.　彼等は完了した報告書を要求して、ジョンを苦境に立たせました。*Karera wa kanryō shita hōkokusho o yōkyū shite, Jon o kukyō ni tatasemashita.*

sore spot — 苦い点 — *nigai ten*

Don't ask about her grades; that's a sore spot with her.　彼女に成績を聞かないように。それが、彼女の苦い点ですから。*Kanojo ni seiseki o kikanai yō ni. Sore ga, kanojo no nigai ten desu kara.*

spotlight — 脚光 — *kyakkō*

in the spotlight — 脚光を浴びる — *kyakkō o abiru*

The senator enjoys being in the spotlight.　あの上院議員は、脚光を
浴びるのが好きです。*Ano jōin giin wa, kyakkō o abiru no ga suki
desu.*

steal the spotlight — 一身に注目を集める — *isshin ni chūmoku o
atsumeru*
Whenever we give a presentation, John tries to steal the spotlight.　私達が
発表するときはいつも、ジョンが一身に注目を集めようとします。
*Watakushitachi ga happyō suru toki wa itsumo, Jon ga isshin ni
chūmoku o atsumeyō to shimasu.*

---

spread — 広げる — *hirogeru*
　spread it on thick — 大げさな言い方をする — *ōgesa na iikata o suru*
Listen to Mary praising the boss. She's really spreading it on thick.
メリ - が上司をほめるのを聞いてご覧なさい。彼女は本当に
大げさな言い方をしているから。*Merī ga jōshi o homeru no o kiite
goran nasai. Kanojo wa hontō ni ōgesa na iikata o shite iru kara.*

　spread oneself too thin — 手を広げすぎる — *te o hirogesugiru*
Jim has taken on too many responsibilities; he's spreading himself too thin.
ジムはあまりにも多くの責任を引き受けて、手を広げすぎています。
Jimu wa amari ni mo ōku no sekinin o hikiukete, te o hirogesugite imasu.

---

spring — 跳ねる — *haneru*
　spring for something — 何かしてくれる — *nanika shite kureru*
Do you think we can get Dad to spring for a new TV?　新しいテレビを
買ってくれるよう、お父さんを同意させることができると
思いますか。*Atarashii terebi o katte kureru yō, otōsan o dōi saseru
koto ga dekiru to omoimasu ka.*

---

spur — 拍車 — *hakusha*
on the spur of the moment — 突然 — *totsuzen*
On the spur of the moment they decided to get married.　突然、彼等は
結婚することに決めました。*Totsuzen, karera wa kekkon suru koto ni
kimemashita.*

---

square — 四角に区切る — *shikaku ni kugiru*
　squared away — 準備が出来て — *junbi ga dekite*

Are we all squared away for tomorrow's meeting? 明日の会議のための
準備がすっかり出来ていますか。Ashita no kaigi no tame no junbi ga
sukkari dekite imasu ka.

squeak — きしむ — kishimu
  squeak by/through — どうにかやってのける — dōnika yatte nokeru
  We barely squeaked by with a last-minute win. 私達は、土壇場で
  どうにか勝つことが出来ました。Watakushitachi wa, dotanba de
  dōnika katsu koto ga dekimashita.

squirrel — リス — risu
  squirrel something away — 貯める — tameru
  Every week he manages to squirrel away part of his allowance. 彼は毎週、
  なんとかお小遣いの一部を貯めています。Kare wa maishū, nantoka
  okozukai no ichibu o tamete imasu.

stab — 刺す — sasu
  take a stab at something — やってみる — yatte miru
  I don't know if I can answer all your questions, but I'll take a stab at it.
  あなたの質問の全てに答えられるかどうか分かりませんが、
  やってみます。Anata no shitsumon no subete ni kotaerareru ka dō ka
  wakarimasen ga, yatte mimasu.

stack — 煙突 — entotsu
  blow one's stack — ものすごく怒る — monosugoku okoru
  When she came home after her curfew, her father blew his stack. 彼女が
  門限過ぎて帰宅すると、お父さんがものすごく怒りました。Kanojo
  ga mongen sugite kitaku suru to, otōsan ga monosugoku okorimashita.

stake — 杭 — kui
  pull up stakes — 場所を変える — basho o kaeru
  Tom has decided to pull up stakes and move to Montana. トムは場所を
  変え、モンタナに引っ越すことに決めました。Tomu wa basho o
  kae, Montana ni hikkosu koto ni kimemashita.

stand — 立つ — tatsu
  stand behind someone or something — 保証する — hoshō suru

This company always stands behind its products.　この会社は、常に
自社の製品を保証します。*Kono kaisha wa, tsune ni jisha no seihin o
hoshō shimasu.*

stand by someone — 助ける — *tasukeru*
Whenever she gets in trouble, her mother stands by her.　彼女が面倒に
巻き込まれるといつでも、お母さんが助けてくれます。*Kanojo ga
mendō ni makikomareru to itsu demo, okāsan ga tasukete kuremasu.*

stand corrected — 自らの間違いを認める — *mizukara no machigai o
mitomeru*
I know I made a mistake, and I stand corrected.　私が間違いをしたのは
分かっているし、それを認めます。*Watakushi ga machigai o shita
no wa wakatte iru shi, sore o mitomemasu.*

stand someone up — すっぽかす — *suppokasu*
They had a date last night, but Peter stood her up.　彼等には夕べ
デートの約束がありましたが、ピーターは彼女をすっぽかしました。
*Karera niwa yūbe dēto no yakusoku ga arimashita ga, Pītā wa kanojo o
suppokashimashita.*

take a stand — 立場をとる — *tachiba o toru*
The congressman has taken a stand against raising taxes.　その下院議員は、
増税に反対の立場をとっています。*Sono kain giin wa, zōzei ni
hantai no tachiba o totte imasu.*

---

star — 星 — *hoshi*
see stars — 目から火が出る — *me kara hi ga deru*
When he was hit on the head by a baseball, he saw stars.　彼は野球の
球が頭に当たって、目から火が出ました。*Kare wa yakyū no tama
ga atama ni atatte, me kara hi ga demashita.*

stars in one's eyes — 目を輝かせる — *me o kagayakaseru*
Mary gets stars in her eyes when she makes plans for her wedding.
メリーは自分の結婚式の計画を立てるときは、目を輝かせます。
*Merī wa jibun no kekkon shiki no keikaku o tateru toki wa, me o
kagayakasemasu.*

thank one's lucky stars — 幸運に感謝する — *kōun ni kansha suru*
After the collision, they thanked their lucky stars they were wearing
seatbelts.　車の衝突の後、彼等はシートベルトを着用していた

幸運に感謝しました。Kuruma no shōtotsu no ato, karera wa
shītoberuto o chakuyō shite ita kōun ni kansha shimashita.

---

starch — 洗濯糊 — sentaku nori

take the starch out of someone — げんなりさせる — gennari saseru
The heat and humidity took the starch out of me. 高温と湿気で、
げんなりしてしまいました。Kōon to shikke de, gennari shite
shimaimashita.

---

start — 開始／始める — kaishi/hajimeru

for starters — まず初めに — mazu hajime ni
For starters, let's select a chairperson. まず初めに、議長を
選びましょう。Mazu hajime ni, gichō o erabimashō.

get a head start (on someone or something) — 先手を取る — sente o
toru
By working on Sunday, I got a head start on Monday's meeting.
日曜日に仕事して、月曜日の会議の先手を取りました。
Nichiyōbi ni shigoto shite, getsuyōbi no kaigi no sente o torimashita.

get off to a flying start — 幸先のいいスタートを切る — saisaki no ii
sutāto o kiru
When we all agreed on the agenda, the meeting got off to a flying start.
私達は全員が議題に賛成して、幸先のいいスタートを切りました。
Watakushitachi wa zen-in ga gidai ni sansei shite, saisaki no ii sutāto o
kirimashita.

start something — ごたごたを起こす — gotagota o okosu
Johnny, be a good boy and don't start anything at school! ジョニー、
いい子にして、学校ではごたごたを起こすんじゃありませんよ。
Jonī, ii ko ni shite, gakkō dewa gotagota o okosunja arimasen yo.

---

state — 状態 — jōtai

fine state of affairs — ひどい状態 — hidoi jōtai
This is a fine state of affairs—now we're hopelessly lost! これは、
ひどい状態です。私達は、どうしようもないほど道に迷って
しまいました。Kore wa hidoi jōtai desu. Watakushitachi wa, dō shiyō
mo nai hodo michi ni mayotte shimaimashita.

lie in state — 遺体が安置される — itai ga anchi sareru

The deceased president will lie in state in the Capitol rotunda on Friday. 大統領の遺体は、金曜日に議事堂の円形大広間に安置されます。 Daitōryō no itai wa, kin-yōbi ni gijidō no enkei ōhiroma ni anchi saremasu.

---

stead — 利益 — rieki

stand someone in good stead — 大いに役立つ — ōi ni yakudatsu
A good education will stand you in good stead all your life. いい教育は、 あなたの人生を通じて大いに役立つでしょう。Ii kyōiku wa, anata no jinsei o tsūjite ōini yakudatsu deshō.

---

steam — 蒸気 — jōki

blow/let off steam — 怒りを発散させる — ikari o hassan saseru
Leave him alone; he needs to blow off steam for awhile. 彼はしばらく 怒りを発散させる必要があるので、一人にしておきなさい。 Kare wa shibaraku ikari o hassan saseru hitsuyō ga aru node, hitori ni shite okinasai.

under one's own steam — 自力で — jiriki de
We were skeptical, but Joan finished the project under her own steam. 私達は疑っていましたが、ジョーンは自力でその企画を 終わらせました。Watakushitachi wa utagatte imashita ga, Jōn wa jiriki de sono kikaku o owarasemashita.

---

steer — 舵／舵を取る — kaji/kaji o toru

give someone a bum steer — ろくでもない助言をする — roku de mo nai jogen o suru
He gave me a bum steer when he recommended this investment. 彼は この投資を推薦して、私にろくでもない助言をしました。Kare wa kono tōshi o suisen shite, watakushi ni roku de mo nai jogen o shimashita.

steer clear (of someone or something) — 避ける — sakeru
Better steer clear of the boss today! He's in a bad mood. 今日はボスを 避けた方がいいですよ。機嫌が悪いですから。Kyō wa bosu o saketa hō ga ii desu yo. Kigen ga warui desu kara.

---

step — 歩調 — hochō

in step (with someone or something) — 先端をいく — sentan o iku

This store keeps in step with the latest fashions.　この店は、最新の
ファッションの先端をいっています。 *Kono mise wa, saishin no
fasshon no sentan o itte imasu.*

out of step (with someone or something) — 遅れて — *okurete*
The board of directors is out of step with the times.　重役会は、時代
遅れです。 *Jūyaku kai wa, jidai okure desu.*

watch one's step — 言動に気を付ける — *gendō ni ki o tsukeru*
John had better watch his step or he's going to offend the client.　顧客を
怒らせないように、ジョンは言動に気を付けるべきです。
Kokyaku o okorasenai yō ni, Jon wa gendō ni ki o tsukeru beki desu.

---

stew — シチュー — *shichū*

in/into a stew — やきもきする — *yakimoki suru*
Don't get into a stew about the deadline.　締め切りについて、やきもき
しないように。 *Shimekiri ni tsuite, yakimoki shinai yō ni.*

---

stick　棒きれ／くっつく — *bōkire/kuttsuku*
more than one can shake a stick at — 数え切れないほどの —
kazoekirenai hodo no
There were more people at the market than you could shake a stick at.
市場には、数え切れないほどの大勢の人がいました。 *Ichiba niwa,
kazoekirenai hodo no ōzei no hito ga imashita.*

stick around — しばらくいる — *shibaraku iru*

633

If you can stick around after work, we can talk.　仕事の後しばらく
いられるなら、話すことが出来ます。*Shigoto no ato shibaraku
irareru nara, hanasu koto ga dekimasu.*

stick by/with someone or something — 信頼を寄せる — *shinrai o
yoseru*

No matter what she does, her mother always sticks by her.　彼女が何を
しても、お母さんは彼女に信頼を寄せています。*Kanojo ga nani o
shite mo, okāsan wa kanojo ni shinrai o yosete imasu.*

stick-in-the-mud — 昔気質 — *mukashi katagi*

Nick is no stick-in-the-mud; he's always ready for a good time.　ニックは
昔気質どころか、いつでも楽しもうとする気が十分です。*Nikku wa
mukashi katagi dokoro ka, itsu demo tanoshimō to suru ki ga jūbun desu.*

---

stink — 嫌な臭い — *iya na nioi*

create/make/raise a stink — 騒ぎ立てる — *sawagitateru*

The media created a stink over the candidate's remarks.　マスコミは、
その候補者の発言に関して騒ぎ立てました。*Masukomi wa, sono
kōhosha no hatsugen ni kanshite sawagitatemashita.*

---

stir — 動き／かき回す — *ugoki/kakimawasu*

cause a stir — 動揺をもたらす — *dōyō o motarasu*

The sudden loud noise caused a stir in the conference room.　突然の
大音響が、会議室に動揺をもたらしました。*Totsuzen no dai onkyō
ga, kaigi shitsu ni dōyō o motarashimashita.*

stir up — 引き起こす — *hikiokosu*

Please keep quiet; don't stir up trouble.　どうぞ口をつぐんで、問題を
引き起こさないでください。*Dōzo kuchi o tsugunde, mondai o
hikiokosanai de kudasai.*

---

stitch — 縫い目 — *nuime*

in stitches — 腹の皮が痛くなるほど笑わせる — *hara no kawa ga itaku
naru hodo warawaseru*

Ira is so funny; he had everyone in stitches last night.　アイラは本当に
滑稽で、夕べはみんなを腹の皮が痛くなるほど笑わせました。
*Aira wa hontō ni kokkei de, yūbe wa minna o hara no kawa ga itaku
naru hodo warawasemashita.*

stock — 信用 — *shin-yō*

take no stock in something — 信じない — *shinjinai*

You shouldn't take any stock in what he says. 彼の言うことを、信じるべきではありません。*Kare no iu koto o, shinjiru beki dewa arimasen.*

take stock of something — 評価する — *hyōka suru*

As soon as he took stock of the situation, Ken knew what to do. 状況を評価するや否や、ケンは何をすべきか分かりました。*Jōkyō o hyōka suru ya ina ya, Ken wa nani o subeki ka wakarimashita.*

---

stomach — 食べる／胃 — *taberu/i*

can't stomach someone or something — 我慢できない — *gaman dekinai*

We can't stomach his constant complaining any more. 彼の絶え間ない苦情には、私達はもはや我慢できません。*Kare no taema nai kujō niwa, watakushitachi wa mohaya gaman dekimasen.*

turn one's stomach — 胸がむかつく — *mune ga mukatsuku*

Listening to that candidate turns my stomach. あの候補者が話すのを聞くと、胸がむかつきます。*Ano kōhosha ga hanasu no o kiku to, mune ga mukatsukimasu.*

---

stone — 石 — *ishi*

A rolling stone gathers no moss. — 転石、苔をむさず。 — *Tenseki, koke o musazu.*

Jane keeps changing jobs and has nothing to show for her work. A rolling stone gathers no moss. ジェーンは仕事を変え続けるので、職が身に付きません。正に、「転石、苔をむさず」です。*Jēn wa shigoto o kaetsuzukeru node, shoku ga mi ni tsukimasen. Masa ni, "tenseki, koke o musazu" desu.*

cast the first stone — 非難の口火を切る — *hinan no kuchibi o kiru*

I don't want to cast the first stone, but that presentation was inadequate. 非難の口火を切りたくありませんが、その報告は不十分でした。*Hinan no kuchibi o kiritaku arimasen ga, sono hōkoku wa fujūbun deshita.*

(just/within) a stone's throw — ほんの目と鼻の先 — *honno me to hana no saki*

The post office is just a stone's throw from here.   郵便局は、ここから ほんの目と鼻の先にあります。*Yūbinkyoku wa, koko kara honno me to hana no saki ni arimasu.*

leave no stone unturned — あらゆる手段を尽くす — *arayuru shudan o tsukusu*

They promised to leave no stone unturned to find the source of the problem.   彼等は問題の源を突き止めるために、あらゆる手段を 尽くすことを約束しました。*Karera wa mondai no minamoto o tsukitomeru tame ni, arayuru shudan o tsukusu koto o yakusoku shimashita.*

---

stop — 休止 — *kyūshi*

pull out all the stops — 全力を尽くす — *zenryoku o tsukusu*

They're pulling out all the stops to make the campaign a success.   彼等は 選挙運動を成功させるために、全力を尽くしています。*Karera wa senkyo undō o seikō saseru tame ni, zenryoku o tsukushite imasu.*

---

store — 店 — *mise*

mind the store — 面倒を見る — *mendō o miru*

When John travels, we have to stay in the office and mind the store. ジョンが旅行するときには、私達はオフィスに残って仕事の面倒を 見なければなりません。*Jon ga ryokō suru toki ni wa, watakushitachi wa ofisu ni nokotte shigoto no mendō o minakereba narimasen.*

set great store in someone or something — 大いに期待を寄せる — *ōi ni kitai o yoseru*

He sets great store in investing for the future.   将来のために、彼は 投資に期待を寄せています。*Shōrai no tame ni, kare wa tōshi ni kitai o yosete imasu.*

---

storm — 嵐 — *arashi*

take someone or something by storm — 人気をさらう — *ninki o sarau*

His new novel is taking the country by storm.   彼の新しい小説は、 全国で人気をさらっています。*Kare no atarashii shōsetsu wa, zenkoku de ninki o saratte imasu.*

---

story — 話し — *hanashi*

cock-and-bull story — 馬鹿げた作り話 — *bakageta tsukuribanashi*

When we asked why he was late, he gave us a cock-and-bull story.   彼に

遅れたわけを聞くと、私達に馬鹿げた作り話をしました。Kare ni okureta wake o kiku to, watakushitachi ni bakageta tsukuribanashi o shimashita.

make a long story short — かいつまんで言えば — kaitsumande ieba
To make a long story short, we can't come to the party tonight.
かいつまんで言えば、私達は今晩のパーティーには行かれないということです。Kaitsumande ieba, watakushitachi wa konban no pātī niwa ikarenai to iu koto desu.

straight — まっすぐ — massugu
   straight and narrow — まじめ一方の生活 — majime ippō no seikatsu
   Since his election, he's been following the straight and narrow.
   当選以来、彼はまじめ一方の生活を送っています。
   Tōsen irai, kare wa majime ippō no seikatsu o okutte imasu.

straw — わら — wara
   clutch/grasp at straws — わらにもすがる思いをする — wara ni mo sugaru omoi o suru
   He's grasping at straws if he still thinks we can work out a compromise.
   私達が妥協する用意があると今でも考えているなら、彼はわらにもすがる思いをしているのです。Watakushitachi ga dakyō suru yōi ga aru to ima demo kangaete iru nara, kare wa wara ni mo sugaru omoi o shite iru no desu.

   last straw — 堪忍袋の緒が切れる — kanninbukuro no o ga kireru
   He's late again? This is the last straw; I'm firing him. 彼がまた遅刻したって。もう堪忍袋の緒が切れたから、彼の首を切ります。
   Kare ga mata chikoku shitatte. Mō kanninbukuro no o ga kireta kara, kare no kubi o kirimasu.

   straw that broke the camel's back — 我慢の限界を越えて — gaman no genkai o koete
   Joe's lying was the straw that broke the camel's back. Sue is divorcing him.
   ジョーの嘘は、スーの我慢の限界を越えました。彼女は、彼と離婚します。Jō no uso wa, Sū no gaman no genkai o koemashita. Kanojo wa, kare to rikon shimasu.

streak — 光線 — *kōsen*
  talk a blue streak — 早口で喋りまくる — *hayakuchi de shaberimakuru*
There's no peace and quiet during Linda's visits; she talks a blue streak.
  リンダが来ると早口で喋りまくるので、静かで落ち着いた一時は
  全然ありません。 *Rinda ga kuru to hayakuchi de shaberimakuru node,
shizuka de ochitsuita hitotoki wa zenzen arimasen.

---

street — 道 — *michi*

  (live) on easy street — ぜいたくに暮らす — *zeitaku ni kurasu*
Ever since his investment paid off, he's been living on easy street.
  投資が成果をもたらして以来、彼はぜいたくに暮らしています。
Tōshi ga seika o motarashite irai, kare wa zeitaku ni kurashite imasu.

---

strike — ストライク／見つける — *sutoraiku/mitsukeru*
  get/have two strikes against one — 不利な立場に立つ — *furi na
tachiba ni tatsu*
People who don't learn to read have two strikes against them.　読み方を
習わない人は、不利な立場に立っています。*Yomikata o narawanai
hito wa, furi na tachiba ni tatte imasu.*

  strike it rich — 急に金持ちになる — *kyū ni kanemochi ni naru*
Bill hopes to strike it rich by winning the lottery.　ビルは、宝くじに
当たって急に金持ちになりたいと思っています。*Biru wa,
takarakuji ni atatte kyū ni kanemochi ni naritai to omotte imasu.*

---

string — 紐／だます — himo/damasu

no strings attached — 何の条件もなしに — nan no jōken mo nashi ni
He offered to give me his old car with no strings attached. 彼の古い車を
何の条件もなしにくれると、彼が申し出てくれました。Kare no
furui kuruma o nan no jōken mo nashi ni kureru to, kare ga mōshidete
kuremashita.

pull strings — コネを使う — kone o tsukau
If he has to, he'll pull strings to get what he wants. 必要とあれば彼は
コネを使って、欲しいものを手に入れます。Hitsuyō to areba kare
wa kone o tsukatte, hoshii mono o te ni iremasu.

string someone along — 気を持たせる — ki o motaseru
He promised to marry her, but now she thinks he's just stringing her along.
彼は結婚を約束したけれど、彼女は今は、彼は彼女に気を
持たせているだけだと思っています。Kare wa kekkon o yakusoku
shita keredo, kanojo wa ima wa, kare wa kanojo ni ki o motasete iru
dake da to omotte imasu.

stuff — 材料 — zairyō

know one's stuff — 知るべき事を知っている — shiru beki koto o shitte iru
When it comes to computers, Bob really knows his stuff. コンピュータに
関しては、ボブは知るべき事を実によく知っています。Konpyūta
ni kanshite wa, Bobu wa shiru beki koto o jitsu ni yoku shitte imasu.

stuff and nonsense — 馬鹿げたこと — bakageta koto
He's too tired to do his chores? Stuff and nonsense! 彼は疲れすぎて
用事が出来無いって。そんな馬鹿げた言葉は通用しない！
Kare wa tsukaresugite yōji ga dekinaitte. Sonna bakageta kotoba wa
tsūyō shinai!

style — 様式 — yōshiki

cramp someone's style — 束縛感を味わわせる — sokubaku kan o
ajiwawaseru
When the company reduced his expense account, it really cramped his
style. 会社が彼の接待費を減らしたとき、彼は本当に束縛感を
味わいました。Kaisha ga kare no settai hi o herashita toki, kare wa
hontō ni sokubaku kan o ajiwaimashita.

suit — 同じ組の持ち札／スーツ — *onaji kumi no mochifuda/sūtsu*

follow suit — 後に続く — *ato ni tsuzuku*

When John volunteered his services, several friends followed suit.
ジョンが奉仕の仕事に志願すると、数人の友達が後に続きました。
Jon ga hōshi no shigoto ni shigan suru to, sūnin no tomodachi ga ato ni tsuzukimashita.

birthday suit — 真っ裸で — *mappadaka de*

Young children enjoy swimming in their birthday suits. 小さい
子供たちは、真っ裸で水泳を楽しみます。*Chiisai kodomotachi wa, mappadaka de suiei o tanoshimimasu.*

sun — 太陽 — *taiyō*

under the sun — 世界中至る所で — *sekai jū itaru tokoro de*

Everyone under the sun admires that singer. 世界中至る所で、誰もが
あの歌手を賞賛しています。*Sekai jū itaru tokoro de, daremo ga ano kashu o shōsan shite imasu.*

sweat — 汗 — *ase*

by the sweat of one's brow — 額に汗して — *hitai ni ase shite*

He built his house by the sweat of his brow. 彼は、額に汗して家を
建てました。*Kare wa, hitai ni ase shite ie o tatemashita.*

no sweat — お安いご用 — *oyasui goyō*

You want me to do this again? No sweat. 私がもう一度それをするのを、
お望みですか。お安いご用です。*Watakushi ga mō ichido sore o suru no o, onozomi desu ka. Oyasui goyō desu.*

sweat something out — 待ちわびる — *machiwabiru*

This election is close; everyone is sweating out the results. この選挙は
大接戦で、誰もが結果を待ちわびています。*Kono senkyo wa dai sessen de, daremo ga kekka o machiwabite imasu.*

sweet — 甘い — *amai*

all sweetness and light — 優しさのかたまり — *yasashisa no katamari*

Minutes ago he was yelling at everyone, but now he's all sweetness and light. 彼は数分前はみんなを怒鳴り散らしていたのに、今は
優しさのかたまりです。*Kare wa sūfun mae wa minna o donarichirashite ita noni, ima wa yasashisa no katamari desu.*

sweet on someone — 熱を上げる — *netsu o ageru*
My son is sweet on the girl who lives next door. 私の息子は、隣の家の
女の子に熱を上げています。 *Watakushi no musuko wa, tonari no ie
no onna no ko ni netsu o agete imasu.*

swim — 水泳 — *suiei*
in/into the swim of things — 日頃の活動 — *higoro no katsudō*
He's been away, but now he's eager to get back into the swim of things.
彼はしばらく旅行で不在でしたが、今は日頃の活動に戻るべく
張り切っています。 *Kare wa shibaraku ryokō de fuzai deshita ga, ima
wa higoro no katsudō ni modoru beku harikitte imasu.*

swing — 振動 — *shindō*
in full swing — たけなわになって — *takenawa ni natte*
By early next fall, the presidential campaign will be in full swing. 次の
初秋までには、大統領選はたけなわになっているでしょう。*Tsugi
no shoshū made ni wa, daitōryō sen wa takenawa ni natte iru deshō.*

switch — 転轍機 — *tentetsuki*
asleep at the switch — うっかりして — *ukkari shite*
Our waiter is asleep at the switch; he hasn't taken our orders yet. 私達の
ウェイターはうっかりしていて、注文をまだ取っていません。
Watakushitachi no weitā wa ukkari shite ite, chūmon o mada totte imasen.

swoop — 急降下 — *kyū kōka*
at/in one fell swoop — 一挙に — *ikkyo ni*
She did all her Christmas shopping in one fell swoop. 彼女は、全ての
クリスマスショッピングを一挙に済ませてしまいました。*Kanojo
wa, subete no kurisumasu shoppingu o ikkyo ni sumasete shimaimashita.*

sword — 刀 — *katana*
cross swords — 渡り合う — *watariau*
Although they disagree, they don't want to cross swords with the CEO.
彼等は社長の意見に反対ですが、彼と渡り合いたくありません。
*Karera wa shachō no iken ni hantai desu ga, kare to watariaitaku
arimasen.*

T

T — ティ － — *tī*

done to a T — 完ぺきに料理されて — *kanpeki ni ryōri sarete*
He likes his steak done to a T.　彼は、注文通りに完ぺきに料理された
ステーキを好みます。*Kare wa, chūmon dōri ni kanpeki ni ryōri
sareta sutēki o konomimasu.*

suit someone to a T — ぴったりだ — *pittari da*
This condo suits me to a T.　このマンションは、私にぴったりです。
Kono manshon wa, watakushi ni pittari desu.

table — テーブル — *tēburu*

on the table — 検討されている最中 — *kentō sarete iru saichū*
My suggestion is on the table now.　私の提案は、今、検討されている
最中です。*Watakushi no teian wa, ima, kentō sarete iru saichū desu.*

turn the tables — 形勢を一変させる — *keisei o ippen saseru*
We've turned the tables on our opponent; now we have the upper hand.
私達は競争相手に対して形勢を一変させて、今は有利な立場に
あります。*Watakushitachi wa kyōsō aite ni taishite keisei o ippen
sasete, ima wa yūri na tachiba ni arimasu.*

under the table — 袖の下 — *sode no shita*
They insist on being paid under the table to approve the license.　彼等は
免許を認める代わりに、袖の下を受けることを主張しています。
*Karera wa menkyo o mitomeru kawari ni, sode no shita o ukeru koto o
shuchō shite imasu.*

tack — 鋲 — *byō*

get down to brass tacks — 核心に触れる — *kakushin ni fureru*
Enough of the preliminaries; it's time to get down to brass tacks.　準備は
もう十分で、核心に触れるときが来ました。*Junbi wa mō jūbun de,
kakushin ni fureru toki ga kimashita.*

tail — しっぽ — *shippo*

tail wagging the dog — 本末転倒 — *honmatsu tentō*

This child is making all the family decisions; it's the tail wagging the dog.
この子どもが、その家族に関する事柄の全ての決定を下しています。
それは、本末転倒です。*Kono kodomo ga, sono kazoku ni kansuru
kotogara no subete no kettei o kudashite imasu. Sore wa, honmatsu tentō
desu.*

---

take — 取る — *toru*

take after someone — 似ている — *nite iru*
Their son takes after his paternal grandfather.　彼等の息子は、父方の
お爺さんに似ています。*Karera no musuko wa, chichigata no ojīsan
ni nite imasu.*

take something back — 取り消す — *torikesu*
I'm sorry for what I just said; I take it back.　言つたことを済まなく
思っているので、取り消します。*Itta koto o sumanaku omotte iru
node, torikeshimasu.*

take something in — 見に行く — *mi ni iku*
We decided to take in a movie tonight.　私達は、今晩、映画を見に
行くことにしました。*Watakushitachi wa, konban, eiga o mi ni iku
koto ni shimashita.*

take it — 我慢する — *gaman suru*
I'm annoyed at his rudeness, and I'm not going to take it anymore.　彼の
無礼さは実に不愉快で、もうこれ以上我慢する気はありません。
*Kare no bureisa wa jitsu ni fuyukai de, mō kore ijō gaman suru ki wa
arimasen.*

take off — 売り上げが急増し始める — *uriage ga kyūzō shihajimeru*
Our new product has really taken off this month.
我が社の新製品は、今月、本格的に売り上げが急増し始めました。
*Waga sha no shin seihin wa, kongetsu, honkakuteki ni uriage ga kyūzō
shihajimemashita.*

take something on — 受け入れる — *ukeireru*
We can't take on any new responsibilities now.　私達は、今は新しい
任務を受け入れられません。*Watakushitachi wa, ima wa atarashii
ninmu o ukeireraremasen.*

take something over — 引き継ぐ — *hikitsugu*
When he retires, his daughter will take over the business.　彼が引退すると、

娘が事業を引き継ぎます。Kare ga intai suru to, musume ga jigyō o hikitsugimasu.

take someone or something wrong — 悪く取る — waruku toru
Don't take this wrong, but you have to be more productive. 悪く取らないでもらいたいのですが、あなたはもっと仕事の効率を上げなければなりません。Waruku toranaide moraitai no desu ga, anata wa motto shigoto no kōritsu o agenakereba narimasen.

take something out on someone — 八つ当たりする — yatsuatari suru
If you're angry about something, you mustn't take it out on your family. 何かについて怒っていても、家族に八つ当たりしてはなりません。Nanika ni tsuite okotte itemo, kazoku ni yatsuatari shite wa narimasen.

take something lying down — じっと我慢する — jitto gaman suru
He insulted me, and I'm not going to take it lying down. 彼が私を侮辱したので、じっと我慢しているつもりはありません。Kare ga watakushi o bujoku shita node, jitto gaman shite iru tsumori wa arimasen.

take to something — 好きになる — suki ni naru
He tried to learn golf, but he didn't take to it. 彼はゴルフを習おうとしましたが、好きになれませんでした。Kare wa gorufu o naraō to shimashita ga, suki ni naremasen deshita.

take something up — 始める — hajimeru
She took up tennis at age 65 and plays quite well. 彼女は六十五歳の時にテニスを始め、なかなか上手です。Kanojo wa rokujū go sai no toki ni tenisu o hajime, nakanaka jōzu desu.

take up with someone — 交わる — majiwaru
My son has taken up with a bad crowd of kids. 私の息子は、不良少年の仲間と交わっています。Watakushi no musuko wa, furyō shōnen no nakama to majiwatte imasu.

taken aback — 呆気にとられる — akke ni torareru
We were taken aback to hear that Tom had retired. トムが引退したと聞いて、私達は呆気にとられました。Tomu ga intai shita to kiite, watakushitachi wa akke ni toraremashita.

taken in by someone or something — まんまとだまされる — manma to damasareru
They were taken in by his promises, none of which he kept. 彼等は彼の

約束にまんまとだまされ、彼の方は約束を一つも守りませんでした。
Karera wa kare no yakusoku ni manma to damasare, kare no hō wa yakusoku o hitotsu mo mamorimasen deshita.

---

tale — 話し — *hanashi*
tell tales out of school — 秘密を漏らす — *himitsu o morasu*
Telling tales out of school will make you unpopular. 秘密を漏らすと、人に嫌われますよ。*Himitsu o morasu to, hito ni kirawaremasu yo.*

---

talk — 話し／話す — *hanashi/hanasu*
all talk (and no action) — 口先ばかり — *kuchisaki bakari*
Don't believe Tom's promises; he's all talk. トムの約束を信じない方がいいです。彼は、口先ばかりですから。*Tomu no yakusoku o shinjinai hō ga ii desu. Kare wa, kuchisaki bakari desu kara.*

have a heart-to-heart talk — 腹を割って話す — *hara o watte hanasu*
Before you accept his proposal, we should have a heart-to-heart talk. あなたが彼の申し出を受け入れる前に、私達は腹を割って話すべきです。*Anata ga kare no mōshide o ukeireru mae ni, watakushitachi wa hara o watte hanasu beki desu.*

talk back — 口答えする — *kuchigotae suru*
Don't talk back to the teacher. 先生に、口答えしてはいけません。*Sensei ni, kuchigotae shite wa ikemasen.*

talk down to someone — 人を見下した口調で話す — *hito o mikudashita kuchō de hanasu*
Bob always talks down to his employees. ボブはいつも従業員に、人を見下した口調で話します。*Bobu wa itsumo jūgyōin ni, hito o mikudashita kuchō de hanashimasu.*

talk of the town — みんなの話の種 — *minna no hanashi no tane*
The new rock group is the talk of the town. この新しいロックグループは、みんなの話の種になっています。*Kono atarashii rokku gurūpu wa, minna no hanashi no tane ni natte imasu.*

talk someone out of doing something — しないように説得するのに成功する — *shinai yō ni settoku suru no ni seikō suru*
Her friends talked her out of quitting school. 友達は、彼女が学校を辞めないように説得するのに成功しました。*Tomodachi wa, kanojo*

ga gakkō o yamenai yō ni settoku suru no ni seikō shimashita.

talked out — 言いたいことは言い尽くす — iitai koto wa iitsukusu
I can't say one more thing on this subject. I'm all talked out. 　この件に
ついては、私はもう一言も言えません。言いたいことは言い
尽くしましたから。Kono ken ni tsuite wa, watakushi wa mō hitokoto
mo iemasen. Iitai koto wa iitsukushimashita kara.

---

taste — 味 — aji
    get/give (someone) a taste of one's own medicine — 同じ目を味わう
　／味わわせる — onaji me o ajiwau/ajiwawaseru
Let's keep him waiting, and give him a taste of his own medicine.
彼を待たせて、彼にも同じ目を味わわせましょう。Kare o
matasete, kare nimo onaji me o ajiwawasemashō.

    leave a bad taste in one's mouth — 後味の悪い思いをさせる —
atoaji no warui omoi o saseru
The misunderstanding left a bad taste in my mouth. 　その誤解は、私に
後味の悪い思いをさせました。Sono gokai wa, watakushi ni atoaji no
warui omoi o sasemashita.

---

teacher — 先生 — sensei
    be the teacher's pet — 先生のお気に入り — sensei no okiniiri
She never gets scolded because she's the teacher's pet. 　彼女は先生の
お気に入りなので、叱られたことがありません。Kanojo wa sensei
no okiniiri nanode, shikarareta koto ga arimasen.

---

tear — 涙／引き裂く — namida/hikisaku
    cry/shed crocodile tears — 空涙を流す — sora namida o nagasu
Whenever this toddler wants attention, she sheds crocodile tears. 　その
小さい子は構ってもらいたいときにはいつも、空涙を流します。
Sono chiisai ko wa kamatte moraitai toki ni wa itsumo, sora namida o
nagashimasu.

    tear into someone or something — 叱りつける — shikaritsukeru
When Joe arrived home late, his father really tore into him. 　ジョーが
遅く家に帰ったので、お父さんが彼を厳しく叱りつけました。
Jō ga osoku ie ni kaetta node, otōsan ga kare o kibishiku
shikaritsukemashita.

teeth — 歯 — *ha*

  armed to the teeth — 武器で重装備して — *buki de jūsōbi shite*

The bank robbers were armed to the teeth. 銀行強盗は、武器で重装備していました。*Ginkō gōtō wa, buki de jūsōbi shite imashita.*

  fed up to one's teeth — 愛想を尽かして — *aiso o tsukashite*

The voters are fed up to the teeth with corrupt politicians. 有権者は、汚職政治家に愛想を尽かしています。*Yūkensha wa, oshoku seijika ni aiso o tsukashite imasu.*

  fight tooth and nail — あらゆる手段を尽くして戦う — *arayuru shudan o tsukushite tatakau*

The mayor promised to fight a tax increase tooth and nail. 市長は、増税に反対してあらゆる手段を尽くして戦うと約束しました。*Shichō wa, zōzei ni hantai shite arayuru shudan o tsukushite tatakau to yakusoku shimashita.*

  lie through one's teeth — ぬけぬけと嘘をつく — *nukenuke to uso o tsuku*

The defendant is obviously lying through his teeth. 被告は、明らかにぬけぬけと嘘をついています。*Hikoku wa, akiraka ni nukenuke to uso o tsuite imasu.*

  set someone's teeth on edge — 神経に障る — *shinkei ni sawaru*

If she's there, I'm leaving; she always sets my teeth on edge. もし彼女がそこに来ているなら、私は行ってもそのまま帰ります。彼女は、いつも私の神経に障りますから。*Moshi kanojo ga soko ni kite iru nara, watakushi wa ittemo sonomama kaerimasu. Kanojo wa, itsumo watakushi no shinkei ni sawarimasu kara.*

  sink one's teeth into something — 身を打ち込む — *mi o uchikomu*

Bob can't wait to sink his teeth into his new assignment. ボブは、新しい仕事に身を打ち込むのが待ち遠しくてたまりません。*Bobu wa, atarashii shigoto ni mi o uchikomu no ga machidōshikute tamarimasen.*

  sweet tooth — 甘いものに目がない — *amai mono ni me ga nai*

John really has a sweet tooth; dessert is his favorite course. ジョンは本当に甘いものに目がなくて、デザートが彼の一番好きなコースです。*Jon wa hontō ni amai mono ni me ga nakute, dezāto ga kare no ichiban suki na kōsu desu.*

tell — 話す — *hanasu*

  tell someone off — 叱りつける — *shikaritsukeru*

  Next time he's late, I'm going to tell him off. このつぎ彼が遅刻した時には、叱りつけるつもりです。*Kono tsugi kare ga chikoku shita toki niwa, shikaritsukeru tsumori desu.*

tempest — 大嵐 — *ōarashi*

  tempest in a teapot — 空騒ぎ — *kara sawagi*

  This isn't a serious crisis; it's a tempest in a teapot. これは深刻な危機ではなくて、ほんの空騒ぎにすぎません。*Kore wa shinkoku na kiki dewa nakute, honno kara sawagi ni sugimasen.*

term — 合意／言葉／関係 — *gōi/kotoba/kankei*

  come to terms (with someone or something) — 受け入れる — *ukeireru*

  Betty hasn't yet come to terms with her mother's death. ベティーは、まだお母さんの死を受け入れることが出来ません。*Betī wa, mada okāsan no shi o ukeireru koto ga dekimasen.*

  in no uncertain terms — あからさまに — *akarasama ni*

  In no uncertain terms, he told the new employees what he expects of them. 彼は、従業員に何を期待しているかを、あからさまに伝えました。*Kare wa, jūgyōin ni nani o kitai shite iru ka o, akarasama ni tsutaemashita.*

  on speaking terms — 口をきく仲 — *kuchi o kiku naka*

  They haven't been on speaking terms since their disagreement. 彼等は意見の相違があって以来、口をきいていません。*Karera wa iken no sōi ga atte irai, kuchi o kiite imasen.*

test — 試験 — *shiken*

  acid test — 厳しい試練 — *kibishii shiren*

  For Betty, the acid test will be meeting her prospective in-laws. ベティーにとって厳しい試練は、将来の義父母になるかもしれない人に会うことでしょう。*Betī ni totte kibishii shiren wa, shōrai no gifubo ni naru kamo shirenai hito ni au koto deshō.*

thick — 藪 — *yabu*

  through thick and thin — 苦楽を共にしてきた — *ku raku o tomo ni shite kita*

John and Bill have been friends through thick and thin. ジョンとビルは、
苦楽を共にしてきた友達です。*Jon to Biru wa, ku raku o tomo ni
shite kita tomodachi desu.*

---

thieves — 泥棒 — *dorobō*
   (as) thick as thieves — とても仲がいい — *totemo naka ga ii*
   The three brothers are as thick as thieves. あの三人兄弟は、とても
   仲がいいです。*Ano sannin kyōdai wa, totemo naka ga ii desu.*

---

thing — もの — *mono*
   be all things to all men — あらゆる人を満足させる — *arayuru hito o
   manzoku saseru*
   If you try to be all things to all men, you'll fail. あらゆる人を満足
   させようとすると、失敗するでしょう。*Arayuru hito o manzoku
   saseyō to suru to, shippai suru deshō.*

   first things first — 肝心なことを最初にする — *kanjin na koto o
   saisho ni suru*
   First things first: I'd like to propose a toast. 肝心なことを最初に
   しましょう。それで、乾杯を申し出たいと思います。*Kanjin na
   koto o saisho ni shimashō. Sorede, kanpai o mōshidetai to omoimasu.*

   greatest thing since sliced bread — 今までに最高のもの — *ima made
   ni saikō no mono*
   This new software is the greatest thing since sliced bread. この
   ソフトウェアは、今までに最高のものです。*Kono sofutowea wa,
   ima made ni saikō no mono desu.*

   have a thing going — いい仲になっている — *ii naka ni natte iru*
   Look at Betty and Joe together; I think they have a thing going.
   ベティーとジョーが一緒にいるのを見てご覧。あの二人は、いい
   仲になっていると思うよ。*Betī to Jō ga issho ni iru no o mite
   goran. Ano futari wa, ii naka ni natte iru to omou yo.*

   know a thing or two — よく知っている — *yoku shitte iru*
   Ask Bill to help you; he knows a thing or two about computers. ビルに
   助けを求めなさい。彼は、コンピュータについてはよく知って
   いるから。*Biru ni tasuke o motomenasai. Kare wa, konpyuta ni tsuite
   wa yoku shitte iru kara.*

tell someone a thing or two — 責めたてる — *semetateru*

When I kept Mary waiting, she told me a thing or two.　メリーを待たせ
続けたので、彼女は私を責めたてました。*Merī o matasetsuzuketa
node, kanojo wa watakushi o semetatemashita.*

Things are looking up. — 状況が好転している。— *Jōkyō ga kōten
shite iru.*

I've been sick for a week, but today things are looking up.　私はこの
一週間病気ですが、今日は状況が好転しています。*Watakushi wa
kono isshūkan byōki desu ga, kyō wa jōkyō ga kōen shite imasu.*

too much of a good thing — 過ぎたるは、及ばざるがごとし —
sugitaru wa, oyobazaru ga gotoshi

More than one dessert is too much of a good thing.　デザートも一つ
以上は、「過ぎたるは、及ばざるがごとし」になります。
*Dezāto mo hitotsu ijō wa, "sugitaru wa, oyobazaru ga gotoshi" ni
narimasu.*

think — 考える — *kangaeru*

got another think coming — 考え直すべきだ — *kangaenaosu beki da*

If he thinks he can get away with this, he's got another think coming.
もし彼がこれでごまかせると思っているなら、考え直すべきです。
*Moshi kare ga kore de gomakaseru to omotte iru nara, kangaenaosu
beki desu.*

think twice — もう一度よく考える — *mō ichido yoku kangaeru*

If I were you, I'd think twice about taking leave tomorrow.　私があなた
だったら、明日休みを取ることについては、もう一度よく
考えますね。*Watakushi ga anata dattara, ashita yasumi o toru koto ni
tsuite wa, mō ichido yoku kangaemasu ne.*

wishful thinking — 叶わぬ願い — *kanawanu negai*

I'm hoping for a raise, but I know it's wishful thinking.　私は昇給を
望んでいますが、それが叶わぬ願いであることは知っています。
*Watakushi wa shōkyū o nozonde imasu ga, sore ga kanawanu negai de
aru koto wa shitte imasu.*

thorn — 刺 — *toge*

thorn in someone's side — 苦痛の種 — *kutsū no tane*

Her lazy daughter has always been a thorn in her side.　怠け者の娘は、

彼女にとっていつも苦痛の種になっています。*Namakemono no musume wa, kanojo ni totte itsumo kutsū no tane ni natte imasu.*

thought — 考え — *kangae*

get/have second thoughts — 考え直す — *kangaenaosu*

Are you having second thoughts about taking the job? あなたはこの職に就くことについて、考え直しているのですか。*Anata wa kono shoku ni tsuku koto ni tsuite, kangaenaoshite iru no desu ka.*

on second thought — 思い直して — *omoinaoshite*

On second thought, let's have dinner at home tonight. 思い直したんだけれど、今晩は家で食事しましょう。*Omoinaoshitanda keredo, konban wa ie de shokuji shimashō.*

throat — 喉 — *nodo*

cut one's own throat — 自分で自分の首を絞める — *jibun de jibun no kubi o shimeru*

If you complain to the boss about his son, you'll be cutting your own throat. 社長に彼の息子について苦情を述べるなら、あなたは自分で自分の首を絞めることになりますよ。*Shachō ni kare no musuko ni tsuite kujō o noberu nara, anata wa jibun de jibun no kubi o shimeru koto ni narimasu yo.*

force/ram/shove someone or something down one's throat — 無理強いする — *muri jii suru*

We should go slowly and not force the changes down people's throats. 私達は慎重に事を運んで、人々に変化を無理強いしないようにするべきです。*Watakushitachi wa shinchō ni koto o hakonde, hitobito ni henka o muri jii shinai yō ni suru beki desu.*

jump down someone's throat — 大目玉を食らわす — *ōmedama o kuruwasu*

When Linda asked Dad for a loan, he jumped down her throat. リンダが借金を申し込むと、お父さんは彼女に大目玉を食らわせました。*Rinda ga shakkin o mōshikomu to, otōsan wa kanojo ni ōmedama o kurawasemashita.*

thumb — 親指 — *oyayubi*

all thumbs — 不器用で — *bukiyō de*

I can't sew very well because I'm all thumbs. 私は不器用なので、
裁縫がよくできません。*Watakushi wa bukiyō nanode, saihō ga yoku
dekimasen.*

green thumb — 園芸の才能 — *engei no sainō*
Mary's garden is beautiful; she has a green thumb.　メリーの庭が美しい
のは、彼女に園芸の才能があるからです。*Merī no niwa ga
utsukushii no wa, kanojo ni engei no sainō ga aru kara desu.*

stick out like a sore thumb — 人目に付く — *hitome ni tsuku*
If you wear that outfit to the party, you'll stick out like a sore thumb.
その服をパーティーに着ていくと、人目に付きますよ。*Sono fuku
o pātī ni kite iku to, hitome ni tsukimasu yo.*

thumbs up/down — 認めて／反対して — *mitomete/hantai shite*
The boss gave thumbs up to our proposal.　上司は、私達の提案を
認めました。*Jōshi wa, watakushitachi no teian o mitomemashita.*

twiddle one's thumbs — 手持ちぶさたでいる — *temochibusata de iru*
We're sitting around twiddling our thumbs until our project gets funded.
私達は企画が資金を得るまで、手持ちぶさたに座っています。
*Watakushitachi wa kikaku ga shikin o eru made, temochibusata ni
suwatte imasu.*

under one's thumb — 思うままに — *omou mama ni*
His wife has him under her thumb.　彼の奥さんは、彼を思うままに
しています。*Kare no okusan wa, kare o omou mama ni shite imasu.*

thunder — 雷 — *kaminari*

steal someone's thunder — 出し抜く — *dashinuku*

When the governor made the announcement, he stole the mayor's thunder.
州知事はその発表を行って、市長を出し抜きました。*Shū chiji wa sono happyō o okonatte, shichō o dashinukimashita.*

ticket — 券 — *ken*

vote a straight ticket — 同じ党の候補者に投票する — *onaji tō no kōhosha ni tōhyō suru*

Bob's a good Republican; he always votes a straight ticket. ボブは忠実な共和党の支持者で、いつも同じ党の候補者に投票します。*Bobu wa chūjitsu na kyōwatō no shijisha de, itsumo onaji tō no kōhosha ni tōhyō shimasu.*

tickle — くすぐる — *kusuguru*

tickled pink — とても喜んで — *totemo yorokonde*

They were tickled pink to receive your letter. 彼等はあなたから手紙をもらって、とても喜びました。*Karera wa anata kara tegami o moratte, totemo yorokobimashita.*

tide — 潮に乗る — *shio ni noru*

tide someone over — ピンチをしのぐ — *pinchi o shinogu*

May I borrow twenty dollars to tide me over till tomorrow? ピンチをしのぐのに、明日まで二十ドル貸してもらえますか。*Pinchi o shinogu noni, ashita made ni jū doru kashite moraemasu ka.*

time — 時間／時代／時 — *jikan/jidai/toki*

about time — どうにかこうにか — *dōnika kōnika*

It's about time for dinner. どうにかこうにか、晩御飯ができました。*Dōnika kōnika, ban gohan ga dekimashita.*

ahead of one's time — 時代に先んじて — *jidai ni sakinjite*

This architect has always been ahead of his time. この建築家は、常に時代に先んじています。*Kono kenchikuka wa, tsune ni jidai ni sakinjite imasu*

behind the times — 時代遅れで — *jidai okure de*

Our city government is behind the times: they don't use computers.

私達の市政府は時代遅れで、コンピュータを使っていません。
Watakushitachi no shi seifu wa jidai okure de, konpyūta o tsukatte imasen.

bide one's time — 好機をじっと待つ — *kōki o jitto matsu*
He's biding his time before asking for a raise.　彼は、昇給を頼む好機を
じっと待っています。*Kare wa, shōkyū o tanomu kōki o jitto matte
imasu.*

give someone a hard time — さんざんな目にあわせる — *sanzan na
me ni awaseru*
When I asked to borrow the car, Dad gave me a hard time.　車を貸してと
頼むと、父は私をさんざんな目にあわせました。*Kuruma o kashite
to tanomu to, chichi wa watakushi o sanzan na me ni awasemashita.*

have the time of one's life — この上なく素晴らしい時を過ごす —
kono ue naku subarashii toki o sugosu
When they visited Japan, they had the time of their lives.　彼等は日本を
訪問したとき、この上なく素晴らしい時を過ごしました。*Karera
wa Nihon o hōmon shita toki, kono ue naku subarashii toki o
sugoshimashita.*

keep up with the times — 時勢に従う — *jisei ni shitagau*
Peter should keep up with the times and buy a computer.　ピーターは
時勢に従って、コンピュータを買うべきです。*Pītā wa jisei ni
shitagatte, konpyūta o kau beki desu.*

kill time — 暇を潰す — *hima o tsubusu*
We have to kill some time downtown until the movie starts.　私達は
映画が始まるまで、繁華街で暇を潰さなければなりません。
*Watakushitachi wa eiga ga hajimaru made, hankagai de hima o
tsubusanakereba narimasen.*

live on borrowed time — どうにか命をつなぐ — *dōnika inochi o
tsunagu*
With the restructuring pending, our department is living on borrowed time.
会社のリストラがまだ未定なので、私達の部はどうにか命を
つないでいます。*Kaisha no risutora ga mada mitei nanode,
watakushitachi no bu wa dōnika inochi o tsunaide imasu.*

Long time no see. — 久しぶり — *hisashiburi*
Hi, Jerry. Long time no see.　やあ、ジェリー。久しぶりだね。
Yā, Jerī. Hisashiburi da ne.

make good time — すらすら行く — *surasura iku*
Traffic was light, so we made good time getting to work this morning.
道が込んでいなかったので、今朝は出勤するのにすらすら
行きました。*Michi ga konde inakatta node, kesa wa shukkin suru noni surasura ikimashita.*

not give one the time of day — 見向きもしない — *mimuki mo shinai*
Helen is angry with me; she won't give me the time of day. ヘレンは
私のことを怒っていて、見向きもしません。*Heren wa watakushi no koto o okotte ite, mimuki mo shimasen.*

---

tip — 先端 — *sentan*
on the tip of one's tongue — 口先まで出かかって — *kuchisaki made dekakatte*
I'll remember his name in a minute; it's on the tip of my tongue. 彼の
名前は、直に思い出します。それは、口先まで出かかって
いるんですから。*Kare no namae wa, jiki ni omoidashimasu. Sore wa, kuchi saki made dekakatte irundesu kara.*

---

toast — トースト — *tōsuto*
(as) warm as toast — ぽかぽかと暖かい — *pokapoka to atatakai*
With the sun streaming in, it's as warm as toast in here. 日光が
差し込んで、ここはぽかぽかと暖かいです。*Nikkō ga sashikonde, koko wa pokapoka to atatakai desu.*

---

toe — 爪先 — *tsumasaki*
on one's toes — 息つく暇もなく — *iki tsuku hima mo naku*
My children keep me on my toes. 子供たちは、私に息つく暇も
与えません。*Kodomotachi wa, watakushi ni iki tsuku hima mo ataemasen.*

Tom — トム — *Tomu*
(every) Tom, Dick, and Harry — 猫も杓子も — *neko mo shakushi mo*
That club is private; they don't want every Tom, Dick, and Harry joining.
あのクラブは会員制で、猫も杓子も会員になるのは望んでいません。
Ano kurabu wa kaiin sei de, neko mo shakushi mo kaiin ni naru no wa nozonde imasen.

---

ton — トン — *ton*

hit someone like a ton of bricks — 衝撃を与える — *shōgeki o ataeru*
The news of the invasion hit us like a ton of bricks.　侵略のニュースが、
私達に衝撃を与えました。*Shinryaku no nyūsu ga, watakushitachi ni
shōgeki o ataemashita.*

---

tongue — 舌 — *shita*

bite one's tongue — 口を閉ざす — *kuchi o tozasu*
I had to bite my tongue to keep from insulting him.　彼を侮辱しない
ように、口を閉ざさなければなりませんでした。*Kare o bujoku
shinai yō ni, kuchi o tozasanakereba narimasen deshita.*

cause tongues to wag — 噂の種になる — *uwasa no tane ni naru*
Their indiscreet behavior is causing tongues to wag.　二人のおおっぴらな
振る舞いは、噂の種になっています。*Futari no ooppira na furumai
wa, uwasa no tane ni natte imasu.*

hold one's tongue — 口をつぐむ — *kuchi o tsugumu*
You should hold your tongue when the teacher is talking.　先生が話して
いるときには、口をつぐむべきです。*Sensei ga hanashite iru toki ni
wa, kuchi o tsugumu beki desu.*

---

top — てっぺん — *teppen*

blow one's top — かんかんに怒る — *kankan ni okoru*
Dad is going to blow his top when he learns Bobby took the car.　ボビーが
父の車を運転して行ってしまったのを知ったら、父はかんかんに
怒るでしょう。*Bobī ga chichi no kuruma o unten shite itte shimatta no
o shittara, chichi wa kankan ni okoru deshō.*

on top of the world — 有頂天になって — *uchōten ni natte*
She's on top of the world since she was promoted.　彼女は昇進を受けて
以来、有頂天になっています。*Kanojo wa shōshin o ukete irai,
uchōten ni natte imasu.*

off the top of one's head — 直ぐに — *sugu ni*
I can't answer that question off the top of my head.　その質問は、直ぐ
には答えられません。*Sono shitsumon wa, sugu ni wa kotaeraremasen.*

on top of something — 最新の情報を手に入れて — *saishin no jōhō o
te ni irete*

The TV reporters are staying on top of the hostage situation.　テレビの
レポーターは、人質事件の最新の情報を手に入れています。
*Terebi no repōtā wa, hitojichi jiken no saishin no jōhō o te ni irete
imasu.*

---

torch — たいまつ — *taimatsu*

carry a/the torch for someone — 片思いする — *kataomoi suru*

Although Mary is happily married, Bill is still carrying the torch for her.
メリーは幸せな結婚をしていますが、ビルはまだ彼女に片思い
しています。*Merī wa shiawase na kekkon o shite imasu ga, Biru wa
mada kanojo ni kataomoi shite imasu.*

---

touch — 接触／能力 — *sesshoku/nōryoku*

lose one's touch — 腕が鈍る — *ude ga niburu*

Tom's still a good tennis player; he hasn't lost his touch.　トムは今でも
テニスが上手で、腕が鈍っていません。*Tomu wa ima demo tenisu
ga jōzu de, ude ga nibutte imasen.*

lose touch — 付き合いが途絶える — *tsukiai ga todaeru*

We've lost touch with the Smiths recently.　私達は、最近、スミス夫妻
との付き合いが途絶えています。*Watakushitachi wa, saikin, Sumisu
fusai to no tsukiai ga todaete imasu.*

out of touch — ご無沙汰して — *gobusata shite*

I don't think I could teach math anymore; I'm out of touch.　私は数学には
ご無沙汰していたので、もはや、教えることができないと思います。
*Watakushi wa sūgaku ni wa gobusata shite ita node, mohaya, oshieru
koto ga dekinai to omoimasu.*

---

tough — 耐える — *taeru*

tough it out — 頑張る — *ganbaru*

Although he doesn't feel well, he decided to tough it out and go to the
office.　彼は気分がすぐれませんが、頑張って出勤することに
しました。*Kare wa kibun ga suguremasen ga, ganbatte shukkin suru
koto ni shimashita.*

---

towel — タオル — *taoru*

throw in the towel — 負けを認める — *make o mitomeru*

Let's keep working; I'm not ready to throw in the towel yet. 　働き
続けましょう。私はまだ、負けを認める気はありません。
*Hataraki tsuzukemashō. Watakushi wa mada, make o mitomeru ki wa
arimasen.*

---

tower — 塔 — *tō*
  ivory tower — 象牙の塔 — *zōge no tō*
  John is unrealistic about investing; he lives in an ivory tower. 　ジョンは
  象牙の塔にこもっているので、投資については非現実的です。
  *Jon wa zōge no tō ni komotte iru node, tōshi ni tsuite wa hi genjitsuteki
  desu.*

  tower of strength — 頼みの綱 — *tanomi no tsuna*
  His family has been a tower of strength to him during his ordeal. 　彼が
  困難を味わっているときには、家族が頼みの綱です。*Kare ga
  konnan o ajiwatte iru toki ni wa, kazoku ga tanomi no tsuna desu.*

---

town — 町 — *machi*
  go to town — 精を出す — *sei o dasu*
  She really went to town cooking for Thanksgiving this year. 　サリーは
  今年、感謝祭の料理に精を出しました。*Sarī wa kotoshi, kansha sai
  no ryōri ni sei o dashimashita.*

  (out) on the town — 外で飲んで食べて大いに楽しむ — *soto de
  nonde tabete ōi ni tanoshimu*
  Let's go out on the town tonight. 　今晩は外で飲んで食べて、大いに
  楽しみましょう。*Konban wa soto de nonde tabete, ōi ni
  tanoshimimashō.*

  paint the town red — 盛り場に出て飲み騒ぐ — *sakariba ni dete
  nomisawagu*
  We need to celebrate; we intend to paint the town red tonight. 　私達は
  お祝いの必要があるので、今晩は盛り場に出て飲み騒ぐつもりです。
  *Watakushitachi wa oiwai no hitsuyō ga aru node, konban wa sakariba ni
  dete nomi sawagu tsumori desu.*

---

toy — もてあそぶ — *moteasobu*
  toy with (the idea of) something — 心に浮かべる — *kokoro ni
  ukaberu*

Jack is toying with the idea of buying a sailboat.　ジャックは、ヨットを
買う考えを心に浮かべています。*Jakku wa, yotto o kau kangae o
kokoro ni ukabete imasu.*

---

track — 軌道 — *kidō*

cover one's tracks — 証拠を隠す — *shōko o kakusu*

The embezzler didn't cover his tracks well.　横領の犯人は、証拠を
うまく隠しませんでした。*Ōryō no hannin wa, shōko o umaku
kakushimasen deshita.*

get/have the inside track — 有利な立場を得る／に立つ — *yūri na
tachiba o eru/ni tatsu*

Joe has the inside track on becoming company chairman.　ジョーは
会長になるのに、有利な立場に立っています。*Jō wa kaichō ni
naru noni, yūri na tachiba ni tatte imasu.*

keep/lose track of someone or something — 見失わない／見失う —
miushinawanai/miushinau

It's easy to lose track of time when you're enjoying yourself.　大いに
楽しんでいるときには、時間を見失うのは簡単です。*Ōi ni
tanoshinde iru toki ni wa, jikan o miushinau no wa kantan desu.*

---

train — 汽車 — *kisha*

gravy train — ぼろ儲けの仕事 — *boromōke no shigoto*

With his new job, Bill is on the gravy train.　ビルは新しい仕事で、
ぼろ儲けしています。*Biru wa atarashii shigoto de, boromōke shite
imasu.*

train of thought — まとまった考え — *matomatta kangae*

When the phone call interrupted me, I lost my train of thought.　突然の
電話に邪魔されて、まとまった考えを失ってしまいました。
*Totsuzen no denwa ni jama sarete, matomatta kangae o ushinatte
shimaimashita.*

---

treat — 御馳走 — *gochisō*

Dutch treat — 自弁 — *jiben*

The brunch on Sunday is going to be Dutch treat.　日曜日のブランチは
自弁です。*Nichiyōbi no buranchi wa jiben desu.*

---

treatment — 待遇 — *taigū*

give someone the red-carpet treatment — 貴賓待遇する — *kihin taigū suru*

When he went to Japan on a business trip, his hosts gave him the red-carpet treatment. 彼が仕事で日本に行つたとき、招待側は彼を貴賓待遇しました。*Kare ga shigoto de Nihon ni itta toki, shōtai gawa wa kare o kihin taigū shimashita.*

tree — 木 — *ki*

bark up the wrong tree — 見当違いのことをする — *kentō chigai no koto o suru*

If you blame the players, you're barking up the wrong tree. It's the coach's fault. 選手を非難するのは見当違いで、それはコーチの責任です。*Senshu o hinan suru no wa kentō chigai de, sore wa kōchi no sekinin desu.*

trick — 策略 — *sakuryaku*

do the trick — 効き目がある — *kikime ga aru*

Take these pills every four hours; that should do the trick. この錠剤を四時間ごとに飲みなさい。そうすれば、効き目があるはずです。*Kono jōzai o yo jikan goto ni nominasai. Sō sureba, kikime ga aru hazu desu.*

know/try/use every trick in the book — あらゆる手段を知っている／尽くす — *arayuru shudan o shitte iru/tsukusu*

She tries every trick in the book to get money from her mother. 彼女はお母さんからお金をもらうためには、あらゆる手段を尽くします。*Kanojo wa okāsan kara okane o morau tame niwa, arayuru shudan o tsukushimasu.*

tricks of the trade — 仕事の上で必要なこと — *shigoto no ue de hitsuyō na koto*

Jill is a good teacher; she knows all the tricks of the trade. ジルは有能な先生で、仕事の上で必要なことは全て知っています。*Jiru wa yūnō na sensei de, shigoto no ue de hitsuyō na koto wa subete shitte imasu.*

trolley — トロリーカー — *tororīkā*

off one's trolley — 気が狂つて — *ki ga kurutte*

Sam wants to run for mayor; he must be off his trolley.　サムが市長選に
出馬を望んでいるのは、気が狂っているからに違いありません。
Samu ga shichō sen ni shutsuba o nozonde iru no wa, ki ga kurutte iru
kara ni chigaiarimasen.

trouble — 心配／面倒 — *shinpai/mendō*

borrow trouble — 取り越し苦労する — *torikoshigurō suru*

You're not going to fail the exam; don't borrow trouble.　試験には
落ちないだろうから、取り越し苦労することはありません。
Shiken niwa ochinai darō kara, torikoshigurō suru koto wa arimasen.

spell trouble — 困ったことがあるのを意味する — *komatta koto ga*
aru no o imi suru

This note from Johnny's teacher spells trouble.　ジョニーの先生からの
手紙は、困ったことがあるのを意味します。*Jonī no sensei kara no*
tegami wa, komatta koto ga aru no o imi shimasu.

tube — 管 — *kuda*

down the tubes — だめになって — *dame ni natte*

With the recession, their business is going down the tubes.　不景気で、
彼等の事業はだめになっています。*Fukeiki de, karera no jigyō wa*
dame ni natte imasu.

tune — 曲／調子 — *kyoku/chōshi*

change one's tune — 態度を改める — *taido o aratameru*

When the rude boy learned I was his new teacher, he changed his tune.
あの礼儀をわきまえない男の子は、私が彼の新しい先生だと知ると、
態度を改めました。*Ano reigi o wakimaenai otoko no ko wa,*
watakushi ga kare no atarashii sensei da to shiru to, taido o
aratamemashita.

sing a different tune — 態度を一変させる — *taido o ippen saseru*

Now that I may become her mother-in-law, she's singing a different tune.
私が義母になるかもしれないと気付いて、彼女は今、態度を一変
させています。*Watakushi ga gibo ni naru kamo shirenai to kizuite,*
kanojo wa ima, taido o ippen sasete imasu.

to the tune of — 大枚 — *taimai*

The restaurant was good, but I paid to the tune of a hundred dollars apiece.

レストランはよかつたけれど、私は一人当たり大枚百ドルの割で
勘定を払いました。*Resutoran wa yokatta keredo, watakushi wa hitori
atari taimai hyaku doru no wari de kanjō o haraimashita.*

tune out — 注意を払わない — *chūi o harawanai*
When her parents scold her, she usually tunes out.　両親が叱つても、
彼女は大抵、注意を払いません。*Ryōshin ga shikattemo, kanojo wa
taitei, chūi o haraimasen.*

---

turkey — 七面鳥 — *shichimenchō*
cold turkey — 自力でぴたつと止める — *jiriki de pitatto yameru*
When Ken quit smoking, he did it cold turkey.　ケンが禁煙したときは、
自力でぴたつと止めました。*Ken ga kin-en shita toki wa, jiriki de
pitatto yamemashita.*

talk turkey — 真剣に話す — *shinken ni hanasu*
We're serious about these proposals. Are you ready to talk turkey?
私達は、この提案については本気です。これについて、真剣に
話す用意がありますか。*Watakushitachi wa, kono teian ni tsuite wa
honki desu. Kore ni tsuite, shinken ni hanasu yōi ga arimasu ka.*

---

turn — 回転／曲がる／曲げる — *kaiten/magaru/mageru*
at every turn — 事あるごとに — *koto aru goto ni*
We came to negotiate, but we've been frustrated at every turn.　私達は
交渉しに来たのですが、事あるごとにいらだたしさを味わつて
います。*Watakushitachi wa kōshō shi ni kita no desu ga, koto aru goto
ni iradatashisa o ajiwatte imasu.*

One good turn deserves another. — 親切に親切で報いるのは当然だ。
— *Shinsetsu ni shinsetsu de mukuiru no wa tōzen da.*
He helped me before, so I'm helping him now. One good turn deserves
another.　彼は前に私を助けてくれたので、今度は私が彼を助けます。
親切に親切で報いるのは当然です。*Kare wa mae ni watakushi o
tasukete kureta node, kondo wa watakushi ga kare o tasukemasu.
Shinsetsu ni shinsetsu de mukuiru no wa tōzen desu.*

take a turn for the better/worse — 好転する／悪化する — *kōten
suru/akka suru*
His illness is serious, and he has taken a turn for the worse.　彼は重病で、
病状は悪化しています。*Kare wa jūbyō de, byōjō wa akka shite imasu.*

turn in — 寝る — *neru*

Our neighbors always turn in by 9 o'clock. 隣の人は、いつも九時まで には寝ます。*Tonari no hito wa, itsumo ku ji made ni wa nemasu.*

turn someone off — うんざりさせる — *unzari saseru*

Her political extremism has turned off all her friends. 彼女の極端な 政治の信念は、友達みんなをうんざりさせています。*Kanojo no kyokutan na seiji no shinnen wa, tomodachi minna o unzari sasete imasu.*

turn someone on — 熱中させる — *netchū saseru*

The concert turned the children on to the beauty of classical music. そのコンサートは、子供たちをクラシック音楽の美しさに熱中 させました。*Sono konsāto wa, kodomotachi o kurashikku ongaku no utsukushisa ni netchū sasemashita.*

---

turtle — 亀 — *kame*

turn turtle — ひっくり返る — *hikkurikaeru*

The car spun out of control and turned turtle in the ravine. その車は コントロールを失って、小さな谷の中でひっくり返りました。 *Sono kuruma wa kontorōru o ushinatte, chiisana tani no naka de hikkurikaerimashita.*

---

two — 二 — *ni*

put two and two together — 筋道立てて考える — **s**ujimichi tatete *kangaeru*

When I put two and two together, I realized what had happened. 筋道 立てて考えて、何が起こったのかを悟りました。*Sujimichi tatete kangaete, nani ga okotta no ka o satorimashita.*

two's company, three's a crowd — 三人目は邪魔になる — *san nin me wa jama ni naru*

I don't want to tag along with you and your date. Two's company, three's a crowd. あなたのデートについて行く気はありません。三人目は 邪魔になりますから。*Anata no dēto ni tsuite iku ki wa arimasen. San nin me wa jama ni narimasu kara.*

uncle — 叔父さん — *ojisan*
  say uncle — 参つたと言う — *maitta to iu*
  Kathy never stops arguing until I say uncle.　キャシ－は、私が参つたと
  言うまで議論を止めません。*Kyashī wa, watakushi ga maitta to iu*
  made giron o yamemasen.

up — 上に — *ue ni*
  up and around — 起きあがつて動き回れる — *okiagatte ugoki*
  mawareru
  Jenny was sick last week, but she's up and around now.　先週ジェニ－は
  病気でしたが、今は起きあがつて動き回れます。*Senshū Jenī wa*
  byōki deshita ga, ima wa okiagatte ugokimawaremasu.

  ups and downs — 浮き沈み — *ukishizumi*
  They've had their ups and downs, but they're still happily married.
  彼等には彼等なりの浮き沈みがありましたが、それでも幸せな
  結婚生活を送つています。*Karera ni wa karera nari no ukishizumi ga*
  arimashita ga, soredemo shiawase na kekkon seikatsu o okutte imasu.

upshot — 最後の一矢 — *saigo no ichi ya*
  the upshot of something — 結果 — *kekka*
  What was the upshot of your meeting with the ambassador?　大使との
  会見の結果はどうですか。*Taishi to no kaiken no kekka wa dō desu*
  ka.

uptake — 理解 — *rikai*
  slow/quick on the uptake — 頭の回転が遅い／早い — *atama no*
  kaiten ga osoi/hayai
  You may have to explain it twice; he's slow on the uptake.　彼は頭の
  回転が遅いから、二度説明しなければならないかもしれません。
  Kare wa atama no kaiten ga osoi kara, nido setsumei shinakereba
  naranai kamoshiremasen.

use — 使用 — *shiyō*
  put something to good use — 活用する — *katsuyō suru*
  You can be sure we'll put this gift to good use. このギフトは、確かに
  活用させてもらいます。*Kono gifuto wa, tashika ni katsuyō sasete*
  moraimasu.

value — 価値 — *kachi*
  take something at face value — そのまま受け入れる — *sono mama*
  ukeireru
  Don't try to analyze his decision; just take it at face value. 彼の決定を
  分析しようとしないで、そのまま受け入れるべきです。*Kare no*
  kettei o bunseki shiyō to shinai de, sono mama ukeireru beki desu.

variety — 変化 — *henka*
  Variety is the spice of life. — 多様性が、人生に興味を添える。—
  Tayōsei ga, jinsei ni kyōmi o soeru.
  He enjoys meeting people from other countries. Variety is the spice of life.
  彼は、外国から来た人達に会うのを楽しみにしています。多様性が、
  人生に興味を添えるからです。*Kare wa, gaikoku kara kita hitotachi*
  ni au no o tanoshimi ni shite imasu. Tayōsei ga, jinsei ni kyōmi o soeru
  kara desu.

vengeance — 復讐 — *fukushū*
  do something with a vengeance — 勢いよくする — *ikioi yoku suru*
  Ken is pruning his hedges with a vengeance. ケンは、生け垣を勢い
  よく刈り込んでいます。*Ken wa, ikegaki o ikioi yoku karikonde imasu.*

view — 眺め — *nagame*
  bird's-eye view — 概略 — *gairyaku*
  The tour gave us a bird's-eye view of the museum's Japanese art
  collection. 見学して、その美術館の日本美術品収集の概略を知る
  ことができました。*Kengaku shite, sono bijutsukan no Nihon*

bijutsuhin shūshū no gairyaku o shiru koto ga dekimashita.

take a dim view of something — 疑わしく思っている — *utagawashiku omotte iru*

Our director takes a dim view of his excuses.　重役は、彼の言い訳を疑わしく思っています。*Jūyaku wa, kare no iiwake o utagawashiku omotte imasu.*

---

villain — 悪者 — *warumono*

villain of the piece — 悪の源 — *aku no minamoto*

Who forgot to bring the sandwiches? I think John is the villain of the piece. 誰が、サンドイッチを持ってくるのを忘れたんですか。悪の源はジョンだと思います。*Dare ga, sandoitchi o motte kuru no o wasuretandesu ka. Aku no minamoto wa Jon da to omoimasu.*

---

wagon — 荷馬車 — *ni basha*

fix someone's wagon — 仕返しする — *shikaeshi suru*

Bill stole my dictionary, but I fixed his wagon. I reported him to the teacher.　ビルは私の辞書を盗みましたが、私は仕返しをしてやりました。彼のことを先生に言いつけたのです。*Biru wa watakushi no jisho o nusumimashita ga, watakushi wa shikaeshi o shite yarimashita. Kare no koto o sensei ni iitsuketa no desu.*

on the wagon — 酒類を止めて — *sake rui o yamete*

Serve Jane iced tea instead of beer; she's on the wagon.　ジェーンには、ビールの代わりにアイスティーをあげなさい。彼女は、酒類を断っています。*Jēn niwa, bīru no kawari ni aisutī o agenasai. Kanojo wa, sake rui o tatte imasu.*

---

walk — 歩み／歩く — *ayumi/aruku*

all walks of life — ありとあらゆる階層の人々 — *ari to arayuru kaisō no hitobito*

People from all walks of life are attending this performance.　ありと

あらゆる階層の人々が、この公演を見に来ています。*Ari to arayuru kaisō no hitobito ga, kono kōen o mi ni kite imasu.*

walk all over someone — ひどく扱う — *hidoku atsukau*
He's so rude; he walks all over his subordinates. 彼は実に無礼で、部下をひどく扱っています。*Kare wa jitsu ni burei de, buka o hidoku atsukatte imasu.*

---

wall — 壁 — *kabe*
climb the wall(s) — 神経を苛立たせる — *shinkei o iradataseru*
When he first stopped smoking, he was climbing the walls. 彼がタバコを止めた当初は、神経を苛立たせていました。*Kare ga tabako o yameta tōsho wa, shinkei o iradatasete imashita.*

off the wall — まともではない — *matomo dewa nai*
His questions are so bizarre, really off the wall. 彼の質問は実に奇妙で、本当にまともではありません。*Kare no shitsumon wa jitsu ni kimyō de, hontō ni matomo dewa arimasen.*

to the wall — 窮地に — *kyūchi ni*
The last recession drove them to the wall. この前の景気後退は、彼等を窮地に追いつめました。*Kono mae no keiki kōtai wa, karera o kyūchi ni oitsumemashita.*

---

wallop — 強打 — *kyōda*
pack a wallop — すごく効き目がある — *sugoku kikime ga aru*
This hot pepper sauce really packs a wallop! この唐辛子のソースは、すごく効き目があります。*Kono tōgarashi no sōsu wa, sugoku kikime ga arimasu.*

---

warpath — 敵対行為 — *tekitai kōi*
on the warpath — けんか腰で — *kenkagoshi de*
Be careful around Jim today; he's on the warpath. 今日ジムはけんか腰だから、彼には気を付けた方がいいですよ。*Kyō Jimu wa kenkagoshi dakara, kare ni wa ki o tsuketa hō ga ii desu yo.*

---

warrant — 令状 — *reijō*
sign one's own death warrant — 自らの破滅を招く — *mizukara no hametsu o maneku*

If she starts drinking again, she'll be signing her own death warrant.
彼女がまた酒類を飲み出すと、自らの破滅を招くことになる
でしょう。 *Kanojo ga mata sake rui o nomidasu to, mizukara no
hametsu o maneku koto ni naru deshō.*

---

wart — いぼ — *ibo*
warts and all — あばたもえくぼで — *abata mo ekubo de*
Her husband is a peculiar man, but she loves him warts and all.   彼女の
夫は変わり者ですが、彼女は彼をあばたもえくぼの愛しようです。
*Kanojo no otto wa kawarimono desu ga, kanojo wa kare o abata mo
ekubo no aishiyō desu.*

---

wash — 洗濯物／洗う — *sentakumono/arau*
come out in the wash — 結局はうまくいく — *kekkyoku wa umaku
iku*
We've encountered a minor problem, but it will all come out in the wash.
私達は今ちょっとした問題に当面していますが、結局は全て
うまくいくでしょう。*Watakushitachi wa ima chotto shita mondai ni
tōmen shite imasu ga, kekkyoku wa subete umaku iku deshō.*

washed up — おしまいになって — *oshimai ni natte*
With this serious injury, his football career is washed up.   このひどい
怪我で、彼のフットボールの経歴は、おしまいになって
しまいました。*Kono hidoi kega de, kare no futtobōru no keireki wa
oshimai ni natte shimaimashita.*

---

water — 水 — *mizu*
get into hot water — 面倒を引き起こす — *mendō o hikiokosu*
This boy is always getting into hot water.   この男の子は、いつも面倒を
引き起こしています。*Kono otoko no ko wa, itsumo mendō o
hikiokoshite imasu.*

hold water — 理屈に合う — *rikutsu ni au*
His alibi doesn't hold water.　彼のアリバイは、理屈に合いません。
Kare no aribai wa, rikutsu ni aimasen.

like water off a duck's back — 蛙の面に水 — *kaeru no tsura ni mizu*
Criticism rolls off him like water off a duck's back.　彼は批判されても、
蛙の面に水です。*Kare wa hihan saretemo, kaeru no tsura ni mizu desu.*

pour/throw cold water on something — 水を差す — *mizu o sasu*
Mary's dad poured cold water on her vacation plans when he refused to
　pay.　メリーのお父さんはお金を出すのを拒否して、彼女の
　バカンスの計画に水を差しました。*Merī no otōsan wa okane o dasu
no o kyohi shite, kanojo no bakansu no keikaku ni mizu o sashimashita.*

water down — 弱める — *yowameru*
With the budget cuts, our plans for expansion have been watered down.
　予算削減で、私達の拡張計画は弱められてしまいました。*Yosan
sakugen de, watakushitachi no kakuchō keikaku wa yowamerarete
shimaimashita.*

water over the dam — 今さらどうしようもない過去のこと —
imasara dō shiyō mo nai kako no koto
Now that the plan has been adopted, our objections are water over the dam.
　今はこの計画の採用が決まって、私達の反対は今さらどうしよう
も ない過去のことになってしまいました。*Ima wa kono keikaku no
saiyō ga kimatte, watakushitachi no hantai wa imasara dō shiyō mo nai
kako no koto ni natte shimaimashita.*

water under the bridge — 昔のこと — *mukashi no koto*
Please forget our past differences; that's all water under the bridge. 前に
私達に意見の相違があったことは、忘れてください。それはみんな、
昔のことですから。*Mae ni watakushitachi ni iken no sōi ga atta koto
wa, wasurete kudasai. Sore wa minna, mukashi no koto desu kara.*

---

wave — 波 — *nami*
  make waves — 波風を立てる — *namikaze o tateru*
Peter will go along with the majority; he doesn't like to make waves.
ピーターは波風を立てたくないので、多数派に同調するでしょう。
Pītā wa namikaze o tatetaku nai node, tasū ha ni dōchō suru deshō.

---

way — 道／方法／距離／方向 — *michi/hōhō/kyori/hōkō*
  all the way — 徹頭徹尾 — *tettō tetsubi*
Those fans support their team all the way. これらのファンは、彼等の
チームを徹頭徹尾、支持しています。*Korera no fan wa, karera no
chīmu o tettō tetsubi, shiji shite imasu.*

  by way of somewhere — 経由で — *keiyu de*
He drove to Washington by way of Philadelphia. 彼はフィラデルフィア
経由で、ワシントンまで運転しました。*Kare wa Firaderufia keiyu
de, Washinton made unten shimashita.*

  come a long way — 随分進歩をとげる — *zuibun shinpo o togeru*
John has come a long way since graduating from college. ジョンは大学を
卒業して以来、随分進歩をとげました。*Jon wa daigaku o sotsugyō
shite irai, zuibun shinpo o togemashita.*

  get/have one's way — 自らの考えを通す — *mizukara no kangae o
tōsu*
Jim is so convincing; he always manages to get his way. ジムはとても
説得力があるので、いつもうまく自らの考えを通します。*Jimu
wa totemo settokuryoku ga aru node, itsumo umaku mizukara no kangae
o tōshimasu.*

  go out of one's way — わざわざする — *wazawaza suru*
Mary went out of her way to help us today. メリーは今日、私達を
わざわざ助けてくれました。*Merī wa kyō, watakushitachi o
wazawaza tasukete kuremashita.*

have a way with something — 扱いが上手 — *atsukai ga jōzu*

Helen is a good speaker; she has a way with words. ヘレンは言葉の
扱いが上手なので、演説の名手です。*Heren wa kotoba no atsukai
ga jōzu nanode, enzetsu no meishu desu.*

have it both/two ways — 二股をかける — *futamata o kakeru*

She wants equal opportunity and special treatment; you can't have it both
ways. 彼女は機会均等と特別待遇の両方を望んでいますが、
二股をかけることはできません。*Kanojo wa kikai kintō to tokubetsu
taigū no ryōhō o nozonde imasu ga, futamata o kakeru koto wa
dekimasen.*

in a bad way — 危機に瀕する — *kiki ni hinsuru*

Tomorrow is the test, and I haven't studied yet. I'm in a bad way. 明日は
試験だけれどまだ勉強していないので、危機に瀕しています。
*Ashita wa shiken da keredo mada benkyō shite inai node, kiki ni hinshite
imasu.*

know one's way around — 事情に明るい — *jijō ni akarui*

Henry can help with the license; he knows his way around city hall.
免許の件は、ヘンリーが助けてくれます。彼は、市役所の事情に
明るいですから。*Menkyo no ken wa, Henrī ga tasukete kuremasu.
Kare wa, shi yakusho no jijō ni akarui desu kara.*

look the other way — 見て見ない振りをする — *mite minai furi o
suru*

I can't look the other way while you deliberately deceive them. あなたが
彼等を故意に騙しているのに、見て見ない振りをすることは
できません。*Anata ga karera o koi ni damashite iru no ni, mite minai
furi o suru koto wa dekimasen.*

parting of the ways — 袂を分かつ — *tamoto o wakatsu*

Tom and Helen have reached a parting of the ways. トムとヘレンは、
袂を分かつことになりました。*Tomu to Heren wa, tamoto o wakatsu
koto ni narimashita.*

rub someone the wrong way — 神経を逆撫でする — *shinkei o
sakanade suru*

Her question rubbed me the wrong way. 彼女の質問は、私の神経を
逆撫でしました。*Kanojo no shitsumon wa, watakushi no shinkei o
sakanade shimashita.*

take something the wrong way — 悪く取る — *waruku toru*
Please don't take this the wrong way, but this color isn't appropriate.
どうぞ悪く取らないで下さい。でも、その色はふさわしく
ありません。*Dōzo waruku toranaide kudasai. Demo, sono iro wa
fusawashiku arimasen.*

That's the way the ball bounces. — とかくこの世はままならぬ。—
Tokaku kono yo wa mama naranu.
He canceled our appointment? That's the way the ball bounces. 彼は、
私達との面会の約束を取り消したんですか。とかくこの世は
ままになりません。*Kare wa, watakushitachi to no menkai no
yakusoku o torikeshitandesu ka. Tokaku kono yo wa mama ni narimasen.*

work one's way up — 出世する — *shusse suru*
He worked his way up from mail clerk to vice president. 彼は、会社の
郵便係から副社長に出世しました。*Kare wa, kaisha no yūbingakari
kara fuku shachō ni shusse shimashita.*

worm one's way out of something — 何とか逃げ切る — *nantoka
nigekiru*
We know he's guilty, but he'll probably worm his way out of it. 私達は
彼が有罪であることが分かっていますが、彼は多分それから
何とか逃げ切ってしまうでしょう。*Watakushitachi wa kare ga yūzai
de aru koto ga wakatte imasu ga, kare wa tabun sore kara nantoka
nigekitte shimau deshō.*

---

weakness — 弱み — *yowami*
have a weakness for something — 目がない — *me ga nai*
He has a weakness for sweets. 彼は、甘いものに目がありません。
Kare wa, amai mono ni me ga arimasen.

---

wear — 着る — *kiru*
wear someone down — 神経を消耗させる — *shinkei o shōmō saseru*
The pressure of this job is wearing me down. この仕事の圧力が、私の
神経を消耗させています。*Kono shigoto no atsuryoku ga, watakushi
no shinkei o shōmō sasete imasu.*

wear someone out — くたくたにさせる — *kutakuta ni saseru*
Spending all day with his young children wears him out. 小さい
子供たちと一日過ごすと、彼はくたくたになってしまいます。

Chiisai kodomotachi to ichinichi sugosu to, kare wa kutakuta ni natte shimaimasu.

---

weasel — いたち — *itachi*

weasel out of something — 言い逃れする — *iinogare suru*
You promised to do the dishes; don't try to weasel out of it.　皿洗いを
すると約束したんだから、今さら言い逃れをしようとしないで
下さい。*Sara arai o suru to yakusoku shitanda kara, imasara iinogare
o shiyō to shinai de kudasai.*

---

weather — 天気 — *tenki*

lovely weather for ducks — 雨が降っている — *ame ga futte iru*
We can't have our picnic today, but it's lovely weather for ducks!　今日は
雨が降っているから、ピクニックはできません。*Kyō wa ame ga
futte iru kara, pikunikku wa dekimasen.*

under the weather — 気分がすぐれない — *kibun ga sugurenai*
I'll have to cancel today's appointments; I'm feeling under the weather.
気分がすぐれないので、今日の面会の約束は取り消さなければ
なりません。*Kibun ga sugurenai node, kyō no menkai no yakusoku wa
torikesanakereba narimasen.*

---

weight — 重み／体重 — *omomi/taijū*

carry a lot of weight — 絶大な影響を及ぼす — *zetsudai na eikyō o
oyobosu*
The mayor's opinions carry a lot of weight with our delegation.　市長の
意見は、我が代表団に絶大な影響を及ぼしています。*Shichō no
iken wa, waga daihyōdan ni zetsudai na eikyō o oyoboshite imasu.*

carry the weight of the world on one's shoulders — この世の悩みを
一手に背負い込む — *kono yo no nayami o itte ni shoikomu*
Cheer up! You look as if you're carrying the weight of the world on your
shoulders.　元気を出しなさい。この世の悩みを一手に背負い込んで
いるみたいに見えますよ。*Genki o dashinasai. Kono yo no nayami o
itte ni shoikonde iru mitai ni miemasu yo.*

pull one's (own) weight — 自分の役割を果たす — *jibun no yakuwari
o hatasu*
In this office, we each have to pull our own weight.このオフィスでは、

一人一人が自分の役割を果たさなければなりません。*Kono ofisu dewa, hitori hitori ga jibun no yakuwari o hatasanakereba narimasen.*

throw one's weight around — 権力を振り回す — *kenryoku o furimawasu*

If he tries to throw his weight around here, he's going to be very unpopular. 彼がここで権力を振り回そうとすれば、すごく嫌われるでしょう。 *Kare ga koko de kenryoku o furimawasō to sureba, sugoku kirawareru deshō.*

worth its weight in gold — 非常に価値がある — *hijō ni kachi ga aru*

Mary's advice is worth its weight in gold. メリーの助言は、非常に価値があります。*Merī no jogen wa, hijō ni kachi ga arimasu.*

---

welcome — 歓迎 — *kangei*

wear out one's welcome — 愛想尽かしをされる — *aisozukashi o sareru*

It's time to leave now; we don't want to wear out our welcome. 愛想尽かしをされないように、そろそろ失礼する時間です。 *Aisozukashi o sarenai yō ni, sorosoro shitsurei suru jikan desu.*

---

well — よく — *yoku*

well-off — 裕福な — *yūfuku na*

Peter is well-off; he can easily afford to send all his children to college. ピーターは裕福なので、子供たちをみんな大学に行かせることができます。*Pītā wa yūfuku nanode, kodomotachi o minna daigaku ni ikaseru koto ga dekimasu.*

well-to-do — 裕福で社会的地位のある — *yūfuku de shakaiteki chii no aru*

She comes from a well-to-do family; they own several large companies. 彼女の家族は裕福で社会的地位があり、大会社をいくつか持っています。*Kanojo no kazoku wa yūfuku de shakaiteki chii ga ari, daigaisha o ikutsu ka motte imasu.*

---

wet — 濡れた — *nureta*

all wet — 間違って — *machigatte*

If you think they're going to lower taxes, you're all wet. もし彼等が税金を下げると考えているなら、あなたは間違っています。

Moshi karera ga zeikin o sageru to kangaete iru nara, anata wa machigatte imasu.

whack — 強打 — *kyōda*
out of whack — 調子がおかしい — *chōshi ga okashii*
The air conditioning is out of whack; please call the service company.
エアコンの調子がおかしいので、修理会社を呼んでください。
Eakon no chōshi ga okashii node, shūri gaisha o yonde kudasai.

take a whack at something — やってみる — *yatte miru*
I've never done any gardening, but I'd like to take a whack at it.　園芸の経験はありませんが、やってみたいと思います。*Engei no keiken wa arimasen ga, yatte mitai to omoimasu.*

whale — 鯨 — *kujira*
have a whale of a time — 素晴らしい時 — *subarashii toki*
Everyone had a whale of a time at the class reunion.　同窓会で、誰もが素晴らしい時を過ごしました。*Dōsōkai de, daremo ga subarashii toki o sugoshimashita.*

wheel — 車輪／車で運ぶ — *sharin/kuruma de hakobu*

big wheel — 有力者 — *yūryokusha*
Cathy Doe is a big wheel in the publishing industry.　キャシー・ドーは、出版業界の有力者です。*Kyashī Dō wa, shuppan gyōkai no yūryokusha desu.*

spin one's wheels — 無駄骨を折る — *mudabone o oru*
We need to take a break. We've been spinning our wheels all morning.
私達は午前中ずっと無駄骨を折っているので、一息入れる必要が
あります。*Watakushitachi wa gozen chū zutto mudabone o otte iru
node, hitoiki ireru hitsuyō ga arimasu.*

wheel and deal — 腕を振るう — *ude o furuu*
He enjoys the wheeling and dealing of a political campaign. 彼は、政治
運動で腕を振るうのを楽しんでいます。*Kare wa, seiji undō de ude
o furuu no o tanoshinde imasu.*

---

while — 時 — *toki*
worth one's while — 労力の価値がある — *rōryoku no kachi ga aru*
It's not worth our while to argue about this; let's just forget it. それに
ついて議論しても労力の無駄だから、忘れましょう。*Sore ni tsuite
giron shite mo rōryoku no muda dakara, wasuremashō.*

---

whip — かき回す — *kaimawasu*
whip something up — 急いで作る — *isoide tsukuru*
If you're hungry, I can whip up something to eat. お腹が空いているなら、
何か食べるものを急いで作れますよ。*Onaka ga suite iru nara,
nanika taberu mono o isoide tsukuremasu yo.*

---

whistle — 風の音／笛／のど — *kaze no oto/fue/nodo*
(as) clean as a whistle — とてもきれい — *totemo kirei*
Sarah's room was a mess, but now it's clean as a whistle. サラの部屋は
ひどく汚かったけれど、今はとてもきれいです。*Sara no heya wa
hidoku kitanakatta keredo, ima wa totemo kirei desu.*

blow the whistle (on someone or something) — 悪事を暴く — *akuji o
abaku*
When the police blew the whistle on the mayor, many citizens were
shocked. 警察が市長の悪事を暴いたとき、市民はショックを
受けました。*Keisatsu ga shichō no akuji o abaita toki, shimin wa
shokku o ukemashita.*

wet one's whistle — のどをうるおす — *nodo o uruosu*
You look thirsty; you can wet your whistle with this iced tea. のどが
渇いているみたいですね。このアイスティーでのどをうるおして

ください。Nodo ga kawaite iru mitai desu ne. Kono aisutī de nodo o uruoshite kudasai.

---

why — なぜ — naze
  whys and wherefores — いわれ因縁 — iware innen
  I don't know all the whys and wherefores of the agreement, but I know it works. 私は、合意のいわれ因縁の全ては知りません。けれども、それが効き目を現しているのは知っています。Watakushi wa, gōi no iware innen no subete wa shirimasen. Keredomo, sore ga kikime o arawashite iru no wa shitte imasu.

---

wig — かつら — katsura
  flip one's wig — 怒り出す／興奮する — okoridasu/kōfun suru
  Mother's going to flip her wig when she sees the mess we've made. 母は私達がどんなに散らかしたか見たら、怒り出すでしょう。Haha wa watakushitachi ga donna ni chirakashita ka mitara, okoridasu deshō.

---

wild — 野生の — yasei no
  wild about someone or something — 熱を上げて — netsu o agete
  The critics are wild about the film that opened last night. 評論家たちは、昨日の晩封切りになった映画に熱を上げています。Hyōronkatachi wa, kinō no ban fūkiri ni natta eiga ni netsu o agete imasu.

---

wildfire — 野火 — nobi
  spread like wildfire — すごい勢いで広まる — sugoi ikioi de hiromaru
  The news about the takeover has spread like wildfire. 会社乗っ取りのニュースが、すごい勢いで広まりました。Kaisha nottori no nyūsu ga, sugoi ikioi de hiromarimashita.

---

will — 意思 — ishi
  of one's own free will — 自由意思で — jiyū ishi de
  Whatever you decide, it should be of your own free will. 何を決めようとも、それは自らの自由意思に基づくべきです。Nani o kimeyō tomo, sore wa mizukara no jiyū ishi ni motozuku beki desu.
  Where there's a will, there's a way. — 意思あるところに、

道は通ずる。— *Ishi aru tokoro ni, michi wa tsūzuru.*

There's not much time, but we can do it. Where there's a will, there's a way. 時間はあんまりありませんが、私達はできますよ。「意思あるところに、道は通ずる」ですから。 *Jikan wa amari arimasen ga, watakushitachi wa dekimasu yo. "Ishi aru tokoro ni, michi wa tsūzuru" desu kara.*

---

willies — 怖じ気 — *ojike*

give someone the willies — 不安感を掻き立てる — *fuan kan o kakitateru*

He's so odd; he gives me the willies. 彼は実に奇妙で、私の不安感を掻き立てます。 *Kare wa jitsu ni kimyō de, watakushi no fuan kan o kakitatemasu.*

---

wind — 風 — *kaze*

get wind of something — 嗅ぎつける — *kagitsukeru*

Mary got wind of the party, so it won't be a surprise. メリーはパーティーのことを嗅ぎつけてしまったので、当日、驚きの要素はありません。 *Merī wa pātī no koto o kagitsukete shimatta node, tōjitsu, odoroki no yōso wa arimasen.*

in the wind — 起ころうとして — *okorō to shite*

I think a merger is in the wind. 私は、会社の合併が起ころうとしていると思います。 *Watakushi wa, kaisha no gappei ga okorō to shite iru to omoimasu.*

see which way the wind is blowing — まず成り行きを見定める — *mazu nariyuki o misadameru*

Before proposing any changes, let's see which way the wind is blowing. 変更を申し出る前に、まず成り行きを見定めましょう。 *Henkō o mōshideru mae ni, mazu nariyuki o misadamemashō.*

take the wind out of someone's sails — 鼻をへし折る — *hana o heshioru*

It took the wind out of John's sails when Bill scored higher on the test than he did. ビルはテストでジョンより高い点数をとって、ジョンの鼻をへし折りました。 *Biru wa tesuto de Jon yori takai tensū o totte, Jon no hana o heshiorimashita.*

wing — 翼 — *tsubasa*

clip one's wings — 活動を制限する — *katsudō o seigen suru*

Meg's Dad clipped her wings by cutting her allowance.　メグのお父さんは小遣いを減らして、彼女の活動を制限しました。*Megu no otōsan wa kozukai o herashite, kanojo no katsudō o seigen shimashita.*

take someone under one's wing — かばう — *kabau*

When I was new in the office, Mary took me under her wing.　私がこのオフィスに来たばかりの頃、メリーは私をかばってくれました。*Watakushi ga kono ofisu ni kita bakari no koro, Merī wa watakushi o kabatte kuremashita.*

---

wink — ウィンク — *winku*

(catch) forty winks — 昼寝する — *hirune suru*

I need to catch forty winks before tonight's party.　今晩のパーティーの前に、昼寝する必要があります。*Konban no pātī no mae ni, hirune suru hitsuyō ga arimasu.*

not sleep a wink — 一睡もしない — *issui mo shinai*

He didn't sleep a wink last night because he was worried about his business.　彼は事業のことが心配で、昨晩は一睡もしませんでした。*Kare wa jigyō no koto ga shinpai de, sakuban wa issui mo shimasen deshita.*

---

wire — 針金 — *harigane*

down to the wire — 最後の最後に — *saigo no saigo ni*

As the campaign gets down to the wire, the rhetoric is getting more heated. 選挙運動が最後の最後になって、誇張された言い回しに熱が帯びてきています。*Senkyo undō ga saigo no saigo ni natte, kochō sareta iimawashi ni netsu ga obite kite imasu.*

get someone's wires crossed — 話しがもつれる — *hanashi ga motsureru*

We must have gotten our wires crossed. I thought our appointment was tomorrow.　私達の話しがもつれてしまったようです。私は、面会の約束は明日だと思っていました。*Watakushitachi no, hanashi ga motsurete shimatta yō desu. Watakushi wa menkai no yakusoku wa ashita da to omotte imashita.*

wise — 賢い — *kashikoi*

wise up — 賢明になる — *kenmei ni naru*

I wish he'd wise up and realize that she can't be trusted. 彼が賢明に
なって、彼女は信用できないことに気付いてもらいたいと思います。
*Kare ga kenmei ni natte, kanojo wa shin-yō dekinai koto ni kizuite
moraitai to omoimasu.*

---

wit — 知恵 — *chie*

at one's wit's end — 頭を抱えて — *atama o kakaete*

I'm at my wit's end trying to deal with this lazy, incompetent person.
私はこの怠け者で無能な人間を扱うのに、頭を抱えています。
*Watakushi wa kono namakemono de munō na ningen o atsukau no ni,
atama o kakaete imasu.*

frighten/scare the wits out of someone — 恐くて縮みあがる —
kowakute chijimiagaru

The movie scared the wits out of us. その映画は恐くて、私達は
縮みあがってしまいました。*Sono eiga wa kowakute, watakushitachi
wa chijimiagatte shimaimashita.*

keep one's wits about one — 冷静さを保つ — *reiseisa o tamotsu*

If you keep your wits about you, you can solve the problem. 冷静さを
保つなら、あなたは問題を解決できます。*Reiseisa o tamotsu nara,
anata wa mondai o kaiketsu dekimasu.*

wolf — 狼 — *ōkami*

cry wolf — デマを飛ばす — *dema o tobasu*

The mayor says the city is out of funds, but, as usual, he's crying wolf.
市長は市の予算が尽き果てたと言っていますが、いつもの通り、
デマを飛ばしているのです。*Shichō wa shi no yosan ga tsukihateta to itte imasu ga, itsumo no tōri, dema o tobashite iru no desu.*

keep the wolf from the door — やっとの暮らしを立てる — *yatto no kurashi o tateru*

She works hard, but she's having trouble keeping the wolf from the door.
彼女は一生懸命働いていますが、やっとの暮らしを立てるのにも
苦労しています。*Kanojo wa isshōkenmei hataraite imasu ga, yatto no kurashi o tateru no ni mo kurō shite imasu.*

throw someone to the wolves — 犠牲にする — *gisei ni suru*

The senator needed someone to take the blame, so he threw Bob to the wolves. その上院議員は誰かに責任を取らせる必要があったので、ボブを犠牲にしました。*Sono jōin giin wa dareka ni sekinin o toraseru hitsuyō ga atta node, Bobu o gisei ni shimashita.*

wolf in sheep's clothing — 羊の皮を着た狼 — *hitsuji no kawa o kita ōkami*

You shouldn't trust him; he's a wolf in sheep's clothing. 彼は羊の皮を
着た狼ですから、信用してはいけません。*Kare wa hitsuji no kawa o kita ōkami desu kara, shin-yō shite wa ikemasen.*

wood — 材木 — *zaimoku*

knock on wood — うまくいきますように — *umaku ikimasu yō ni*
We hope to move into our new home next month—knock on wood!
私達は、来月新しい家に移り住むことを望んでいます。うまく
いきますように。*Watakushitachi wa, raigetsu atarashii ie ni
utsurisumu koto o nozonde imasu. Umaku ikimasu yō ni.*

out of the woods — 危機を脱して — *kiki o dasshite*
The medication seems to be working, but he's not out of the woods yet.
薬が効き目を現しているようですが、彼はまだ危機を脱して
いません。*Kusuri ga kikime o arawashite iru yō desu ga, kare wa
mada kiki o dasshite imasen.*

wool — 羊毛 — *yōmō*

pull the wool over someone's eyes — たぶらかす — *taburakasu*
Our teacher is smart; don't try to pull the wool over her eyes. 私達の
先生は頭が切れるから、彼女をたぶらかそうとしないように。
*Watakushitachi no sensei wa atama ga kireru kara, kanojo o taburakasō
to shinai yō ni.*

word — 言葉 — *kotoba*

(as) good as one's word — した約束は守る — *shita yakusoku wa mamoru*
If Jim says he'll be there, you can count on him. He's as good as his word.
ジムがそこにいると言ったら、彼を当てにできます。彼はした
約束は守りますから。*Jimu ga soko ni iru to ittara, kare o ate ni
dekimasu. Kare wa shita yakusoku wa mamorimasu kara.*

break one's word — 約束を破る — *yakusoku o yaburu*
I've never known Mary to break her word. 私は、メリーが約束を
破ったという例を知りません。*Watakushi wa, Merī ga yakusoku o
yabutta to iu rei o shirimasen.*

by word of mouth — 口コミで — *kuchikomi de*
They rarely advertise; customers learned about the sale by word of mouth.
彼等は殆ど宣伝しないので、消費者は特売を口コミで知りました。
*Karera wa hotondo senden shinai node, shōhisha wa tokubai o
kuchikomi de shirimashita.*

eat one's words — 前言の誤りを認める — *zengen no ayamari o
mitomeru*

Their team said they'd beat us badly, but we made them eat their words. 彼等のチームは私達をこてんこてんに負かすと言っていましたが、私達はその言葉の誤りを認めさせました。 *Karera no chīmu wa watakushitachi o kotenkoten ni makasu to itte imashita ga, watakushitachi wa sono kotoba no ayamari o mitomesasemashita.*

get a word in edgeways/edgewise — 口を挟む — *kuchi o hasamu*
He talks so much it's hard to get a word in edgewise. 彼はものすごくよく話すので、口を挟むことは困難です。 *Kare wa monosugoku yoku hanasu node, kuchi o hasamu koto wa konnan desu.*

get/have the final/last word — 最終決定権を握る／持つ — *saishū kettei ken o niguru/motsu*
Mother gets the last word on whether we can have a dog. 私達が犬を飼えるかどうかについて、母が最終決定権を握っています。 *Watakushitachi ga inu o kaeru ka dō ka ni tsuite, haha ga saishū kettei ken o nigitte imasu.*

hang on someone's every word — 一言一句に耳を傾ける — *ichigen ikku ni mimi o katamukeru*
When the lawyer spoke, the jurors were hanging on his every word. 弁護士が話すと、陪審員は彼の一言一句に耳を傾けました。 *Bengoshi ga hanasu to, baishin-in wa kare no ichigen ikku ni mimi o katamukemashita.*

have a word (with someone) — 個人的に話す — *kojinteki ni hanasu*
Could you come to my office, please? I'd like to have a word with you.

私のオフィスに来てくれますか。個人的に話したいことが
あります。*Watakushi no ofisu ni kite kuremasu ka. Kojinteki ni
hanashitai koto ga arimasu.*

have words (with someone) — 言い争いする — *iiarasoi suru*
Bill had words with Tom last week, and they haven't spoken since.　先週
ビルはトムと言い争いをして、それ以来二人は口を利いていません。
*Senshū Biru wa Tomu to iiarasoi o shite, sore irai futari wa kuchi o kiite
imasen.*

keep one's word — 約束を守る — *yakusoku o mamoru*
We can count on the prime minister to keep his word.　首相が約束を
守ることは、期待できます。*Shushō ga yakusoku o mamoru koto wa,
kitai dekimasu.*

leave word — 伝言を残す — *dengon o nokosu*
Please leave word with Mr. Doe's secretary about the meeting.　会議に
ついて、ド－氏の秘書に伝言を残してください。*Kaigi ni tsuite,
Dō shi no hisho ni dengon o nokoshite kudasai.*

mark my word(s) — 私の言葉をしっかり覚えておく — *watakushi no
kotoba o shikkari oboete oku*
Mark my words—if you don't study, you'll fail the course.　私の言葉を、
しっかり覚えておきない。勉強しないと、この科目に落第しますよ。
*Watakushi no kotoba o, shikkari oboete okinasai. Benkyō shinai to, kono
kamoku ni rakudai shimasu yo.*

not breathe a word — 口外しない — *kōgai shinai*
Don't breathe a word to anyone, but we're going to have a baby.　私達に
赤ちゃんが産まれることは、口外しないように。*Watakushitachi ni
akachan ga umareru koto wa, kōgai shinai yō ni.*

put in a good word — 推薦する — *suisen suru*
If you're having an interview with the boss, I'll put in a good word for you.
あなたが社長と面接するなら、私はあなたを推薦しましょう。
*Anata ga shachō to mensetsu suru nara, watakushi wa anata o suisen
shimashō.*

take the words out of one's mouth — 人の言おうとしたことを先に
言う — *hito no iō to shita koto o saki ni iu*
We certainly should break for dinner! You took the words right out of my
mouth.　確かに、ディナ－のために休憩するべきです。私も

言おうとしたことを、あなたが先に言ったんですよ。 *Tashika ni, dīnā no tame ni kyūkei suru beki desu. Watakushi mo iō to shita koto o, anata ga saki ni ittandesu yo.*

Them's fighting words! — 争いを誘う言葉だ。 — *Arasoi o sasou kotoba da.*

Re-elect the mayor? Them's fighting words! 市長の再選ですって。それは争いを誘う言葉ですよ。 *Shichō no saisen desutte. Sore wa arasoi o sasou kotoba desu yo.*

weigh one's words — 言葉を吟味する — *kotoba o ginmi suru*

Before you speak, you'd better weigh your words. 話す前に、言葉を吟味するべきです。 *Hanasu mae ni, kotoba o ginmi suru beki desu.*

word to the wise — 忠告 — *chūkoku*

Here's a word to the wise: don't be late to work tomorrow. これは忠告です。明日は、仕事に遅れて来ないように。 *Kore wa chūkoku desu. Ashita wa, shigoto ni okurete konai yō ni.*

---

work — 仕事／働く — *shigoto/hataraku*

All work and no play makes Jack a dull boy. — よく学び、よく遊べ。 — *Yoku manabi, yoku asobe.*

You should take a vacation: all work and no play makes Jack a dull boy. あなたは、バカンスを取るべきです。「よく学び、よく遊べ」ですよ。 *Anata wa, bakansu o toru beki desu. "Yoku manabi, yoku asobe" desu yo.*

dirty work — 下働き — *shitabataraki*

Joe gets all the recognition while Mary does the dirty work. メリーが下働きをしている間に、ジョーがあらゆる功績を認められています。 *Merī ga shitabataraki o shite iru aida ni, Jō ga arayuru kōseki o mitomerarete imasu.*

have one's work cut out for one — 難題がひかえている — *nandai ga hikaete iru*

If you want to get this proposal approved, you have your work cut out for you. その提案を認めてもらいたいと思っているなら、あなたには難題がひかえていますよ。 *Sono teian o mitomete moraitai to omotte iru nara, anata niwa nandai ga hikaete imasu yo.*

in the works — 企画されている最中 — *kikaku sarete iru saichū*

A merger between the two companies is in the works. その二社間の
合併が、企画されている最中です。*Sono ni sha kan no gappei ga,
kikaku sarete iru saichū desu.*

knock off work — 仕事を切り上げる — *shigoto o kiriageru*
I'm going to knock off work early today and play some golf. 今日は
仕事を早めに切り上げて、少しゴルフをするつもりです。*Kyō wa
shigoto o hayame ni kiriagete, sukoshi gorufu o suru tsumori desu.*

shoot the works — 有り金をつぎ込む — *arigane o tsugikoku*
We decided to shoot the works on our vacation this year. 私達は、今年
のバカンスに有り金をつぎ込むことに決めました。*Watakushitachi
wa, kotoshi no bakansu ni arigane o tsugikomu koto ni shimashita.*

the works — 何から何まで — *nani kara nani made*
I want an entire new wardrobe—the works! 私は全く新しい衣装を、
しかもそれを何から何まで欲しいです。*Watakushi wa mattaku
atarashii ishō o, shikamo sore o nani kara nani made hoshii desu.*

work on someone or something — 働きかける — *hatarakikakeru*
He worked on his parents to get them to buy him a new car. 彼は新しい
車を買ってくれるように、両親に働きかけました。*Kare wa
atarashii kuruma o katte kureru yō ni, ryōshin ni hatarakikakemashita.*

work something out — 問題を解決する — *mondai o kaiketsu suru*
They've had some problems in their marriage, but they're working them
out. 彼等には結婚生活上の問題がいくらかありますが、問題を
解決すべく努力しています。*Karera ni wa kekkon seikatsu jō no
mondai ga ikuraka arimasu ga, mondai o kaiketsu subeku doryoku shite
imasu.*

work someone in — 飛び入りで組み込む — *tobiiri de kumikomu*
The doctor's schedule is full today, but if you come around noon, we'll
work you in. 今日は医者の予定が詰まっていますが、お昼頃
来れば、飛び入りで予定に組み込んであげます。*Kyō wa isha no
yotei ga tsumatte imasu ga, ohiru goro kureba, tobiiri de yotei ni
kumikonde agemasu.*

world — 社会／世界 — *shakai/sekai*
  come/move down/up in the world — 落ちぶれる／出世する —
  ochibureru/shusse suru

Jim is a doctor now; he has really come up in the world. ジムは今や医者です。彼は本当に出世しました。*Jimu wa ima ya isha desu. Kare wa hontō ni shusse shimashita.*

dead to the world — ぐっすり眠って — *gussuri nemutte*
Dad got home late last night, and he's still dead to the world. 父は昨日の晩遅く帰ってきて、まだぐっすり眠っています。*Chichi wa kinō no ban osoku kaette kite, mada gussuri nemutte imasu.*

in a world of one's own — 自分だけの世界に閉じこもって — *jibun dake no sekai ni tojikomotte*
Don't expect any friendly chitchat from Jill; she's in a world of her own. ジルからは、親しげな軽い会話は期待しないように。彼女は、自分だけの世界に閉じこもっているからです。*Jiru kara wa, shitashige na karui kaiwa o kitai shinai yō ni. Kanojo wa, jibun dake no sekai ni tojikomotte iru kara desu.*

look at the world through rose-colored glasses — 何もかも素晴らしいと見なす — *nani mo ka mo subarashii to minasu*
Bill's always optimistic; he looks at the world through rose-colored glasses. ビルは常に楽天的で、この世の何もかも素晴らしいと見なしています。*Biru wa tsune ni rakutenteki de, kono yo no nani mo ka mo subarashii to minashite imasu.*

out of this world — 最高 — *saikō*
Mom's apple pie is out of this world. 母の作るアップルパイは最高です。*Haha no tsukuru appuru pai wa saikō desu.*

set the world on fire — 功成り名遂げる — *kō nari na togeru*
Our son may not set the world on fire, but he should have a satisfying career. 息子は功成り名遂げることはないでしょうが、満足のいく経歴を持つことは間違いありません。*Musuko wa kō nari na togeru koto wa nai deshō ga, manzoku no iku keireki o motsu koto wa machigai arimasen.*

think the world of someone or something — 素晴らしいと思う — *subarashii to omou*
Everyone thinks the world of our governor. 誰もが、私達の知事は素晴らしいと思っています。*Daremo ga, watakushitachi no chiji wa subarashii to omotte imasu.*

worlds apart — 全くかけ離れている — *mattaku kakehanarete iru*

The two sides in the negotiations sometimes seem worlds apart.
交渉中の両者は、時に立場が全くかけ離れているみたいです。
Koshō chū no ryōsha wa, toki ni tachiba ga mattaku kakehanarete iru mitai desu.

---

worm — 虫 — *mushi*
The worm has turned. — 普段はおとなしい人が豹変する。 — *Fudan wa otonashii hito ga hyōhen suru.*
Kevin is suddenly standing up for his own rights. The worm has turned.
ケビンは、突然、自分の権利を守ろうとしています。普段は
おとなしい彼が、豹変したのです。*Kebin wa, totsuzen, jibun no kenri o mamorō to shite imasu. Fudan wa otonashii kare ga, hyōhen shita no desu.*

worm something out of someone — 何とか聞き出す — *nantoka kikidasu*
The boys didn't want to admit anything, but Mother wormed the truth out of them. 男の子たちは何も認めたくありませんでしたが、
お母さんは子供たちから何とか真実を聞き出しました。*Otoko no ko tachi wa nani mo mitometaku arimasen deshita ga, okāsan wa kodomotachi kara nantoka shinjitsu o kikidashimashita.*

---

worst — 最悪の — *saiaku no*
if worst comes to worst — これ以上ない最悪の状態になったら — *kore ijō nai saiaku no jōtai ni nattara*
If worst comes to worst and it rains, the graduation ceremonies will be moved indoors. 雨が降るというこれ以上ない最悪の状態に
なったら、卒業式は屋内に移ります。*Ame ga furu to iu kore ijō nai saiaku no jōtai ni nattara, sotsugyō shiki wa okunai ni utsurimasu.*

---

wrap — 包み — *tsutsumi*
keep something under wraps — 隠しておく — *kakushite oku*
They kept their new computer line under wraps until the press conference.
彼等は記者会見の時まで、新しいシリーズのコンピュータを
隠しておきました。*Karera wa kisha kaiken no toki made, atarashii shirīzu no konpyūta o kakushite okimashita.*

wrench — スパナ — *supana*
throw a monkey wrench into something — ぶちこわしにする —
buchikowashi ni suru
Jay's resignation threw a monkey wrench into our plans.　ジェイの
辞任は、私達の計画をぶちこわしにしました。*Jei no jinin wa,*
watakushitachi no keikaku o buchikowashi ni shimashita.

wringer — 絞り機 — *shibori ki*
put someone through the wringer — さんざんな思いをさせる —
sanzan na omoi o saseru
The boss put me through the wringer over my request for sick leave.
病欠を要請したのに対して、上司は私にさんざんな思いを
させました。*Byōketsu o yōsei shita no ni taishite, jōshi wa watakushi*
ni sanzan na omoi o sasemashita.

wrist — 手首 — *tekubi*
slap someone's wrist — 戒める — *imashimeru*
Although she had stolen a bicycle, the judge slapped her wrist and released
her.　彼女は自転車を盗みましたが、判事は戒めただけで彼女を
放免しました。*Kanojo wa jitensha o nusumimashita ga, hanji wa*
imashimeta dake de kanojo o hōmen shimashita.

write — 書く — *kaku*
write someone off — 見捨てる — *misuteru*
Although our team has lost several games, don't write us off yet.　私達の
チームはいくつか試合に負けましたが、まだ見捨てるべきでは
ありません。*Watakushitachi no chīmu wa ikutsuka shiai ni*
makemashita ga, mada misuteru beki dewa arimasen.

write something off — 見切りをつける — *mikiri o tsukeru*
We'll have to write off that computer monitor and get a new one.　私達は
そのコンピュータモニターに見切りをつけて、新しいのを
買わなければなりません。*Watakushitachi wa sono konpyūta monitā*
ni mikiri o tsukete, atarashii no o kawanakereba narimasen.

X — エックス — *ekkusu*

X marks the spot. — ×印があるのがその場所だ。 — *Batsu jirushi ga aru no ga, sono basho da.*

I've made this map so you can find our house tonight. X marks the spot. 今晩あなたが私達の家を見つけられるように、地図を書きました。×印のあるのが家の場所です。*Konban anata ga watakushitachi no ie o mitsukerareru yō ni, chizu o kakimashita. Batsu jirushi no aru no ga, ie no basho desu.*

year — 年 — *toshi*

along/on/up in years — 年をとって — *toshi o totte*

He's up in years, but he's in excellent health. 彼は年をとってはいても、素晴らしく健康です。*Kare wa toshi o totte wa itemo, subarashiku kenkō desu.*

year in, year out — 年がら年中 — *nengara nenjū*

I'm tired of the same old routine year in, year out; I need a long vacation. 私は、年がら年中、相変わらず決まり切ったことをするのにあきあきしています。それで、長いバカンスが必要です。*Watakushi wa, nengara nenjū, aikawarazu kimarikitta koto o suru no ni akiaki shite imasu. Sorede, nagai bakansu ga hitsuyō desu.*

yesterday — 昨日 — *kinō*

(not) born yesterday — 世間知らず（ではない） — *seken shirazu (dewa nai)*

You can't fool Mary; she wasn't born yesterday. メリーを騙すことはできません。彼女は、世間知らずではないんだから。*Merī o damasu koto wa dekimasen. Kanojo wa, seken shirazu dewa naindakara.*

Z

Z — ゼット — *zetto*

catch some Zs — 寝ておく — *nete oku*

I'd better catch some Zs; I have a long drive tomorrow morning. 　私は、今晩は寝ておいた方がいいでしょう。明日の朝は、長距離の運転をしますから。*Watakushi wa, konban wa nete oita hō ga ii deshō. Ashita no asa wa, chōkyori no unten o shimasu kara.*

zero — 零 — *zero*

zero in on something — 焦点を合わせる — *shōten o awaseru*

Let's try to zero in on the problem here. 　さてここでは、問題に焦点を合わせましょう。*Sate koko dewa, mondai ni shōten o awasemashō.*

zonk — 意識を失う — *ishiki o ushinau*

zonk out — 眠る — *nemuru*

I'm exhausted; I have to zonk out on the couch for a few hours. 　私は疲労困ぱいしているので、数時間ソファ‐で眠らなければなりません。*Watakushi wa hirō konpai shite iru node, sū jikan sofā de nemuranakereba narimasen.*

JAPANESE-ENGLISH INDEX

The following is a selective index of useful expressions from the Japanese translations of English idioms. For example, if you wish to know an English idiom associated with the expression "ao nisai," you should go to page 432 and locate "ao nisai," which would be linked with the idiom "wet behind the ears."

JAPANESE·ENGLISH INDEX

J
A
P
A
N
E
S
E
·
E
N
G
L
I
S
H

I
N
D
E
X

Break the Foreign Language Barrier with Barron's Language Series!